PHYSICAL DISTRIBUTION CASE STUDIES

PHYSICAL DISTRIBUTION CASE STUDIES

BY JACK W. FARRELL

CAHNERS PHYSICAL DISTRIBUTION SERIES

Cahners Books

Boston, Massachusetts

International Standard Book Number: 0-8436-1404-8
Library of Congress Catalog Card Number: 72-91987
Second Printing
New material Copyright © 1973 by Cahners Publishing Company, Inc.
© 1972, 1971, 1970, 1969, 1968, 1967 by Cahners Publishing Co., Inc.
Printed in the United States of America.
Halliday Lithograph Corporation, West Hanover, Massachusetts, U.S.A.

Table of Contents

Foreword

When a management concept is introduced, the evolutionary process involving its acceptance and implementation is often a long one. The physical distribution or business logistics concept has been no exception. The regrouping of functions that is necessitated by its implementation is difficult of achievement for many companies. Internal managements have viewed with caution the total system approach to distribution, and some still do. While recognizing that the goal is highly desirable, the possible ramifications of its adoption through organizational restructuring requires a thorough understanding of the problems that may be encountered. During the 1960's, the acceptance of this concept was broadened to include many business firms, and during the present decade further significant expansion is expected. The increased use of the computer, providing as it does greater data accessibility and heightened control, has given impetus to the adoption of the physical distribution concept.

The utilization of a new concept can be accelerated through the use of a method or system that promotes understanding of the concept in its innovative aspects and in its application to business. If the effectiveness of physical distribution is to be fully realized, we need to have a broader exposure of management applications of the concept throughout all sectors of business and, insofar as possible, to particularize its application to individual business firms. One of the best methods of promoting an understanding of the potentialities of physical distribution or logistics is through the use of actual case studies as is accomplished in this book. The valuable experiences of forty-two leading companies in their internal management exploration of the advantages of physical distribution to their total management picture and the problems encountered in its implementation, both policy and operational, are provided in thorough "on-site" reports.

Each of the cases is prefaced by specific comments concerning the company, its general organization, factors that led to its adoption of physical distribution, the benefits that have been realized from the regrouping of functions, and other significant factors. A detailed description of the manner in which physical distribution has been adapted to the individual needs of the firm is then provided. The diversity of applications that have been structured to satisfy varying management requirements is noted, as well as the underlying factors that contributed to the varied implementation.

The book is logically divided into chapters that group cases that illustrate similarities or contrasts in concepts and trends. Some illustrate the boldness of some managements in the adoption of the physical distribution concept. Other cases depict a gradual adoptive process. Each case is of value in demonstrating the manner in which particular problems have been approached and solutions sought.

Chapter I, "Gearing the Organization for Physical Distribution," contains the reorganization experiences of a number of large firms. The adoption of physical distribution occurred in the Noxell Corporation at the time of a total management reorganization. In Blue Bell, the profit center concept is applied to the firm's physical distribution department which operates in competition with commercial companies for its firm's physical distribution. Scovill Manufacturing Company's logistics program is carried on by a traffic department which embraces the transportation-distribution activities and utilizes many innovative approaches. Liggett & Myers brought together separate company sectors and controls cost relationships carefully, as in Noxell. The Carter Co. has modern distribution centers that are centered around product rather than geographical factors.

"Logistics in the Giant Companies" covers the experiences of Eastman Kodak, Western Electric, Phillips Petroleum, and Honeywell. All place heavy reliance on the computer, employ operations research techniques, use advanced personnel techniques, and operate some of the largest distribution departments.

Chapter III, "Where Management Science Plays a Major Part," emphasizes the utilization of operations research techniques in such companies as Carrier Air Conditioning, Martin-Brower Company, Stop & Shop, the Hormel Company, Canadian Canners, and the Steelcase Company. The application of linear programming, cathode ray tube communication units tied to computers, and the use of PERT charts are some of the programs described in this chapter.

Companies, such as Abbott Laboratories, Warner-Chilcott division of Warner-Lambert, Recognition Equipment Company, and Consolidated Edison Company, place greater emphasis on manufacturing, as contrasted to marketing, and tend in their managements toward materials management. That is the subject of the cases in Chapter IV.

The food industries, with their critical interest in careful control of distribution costs, are the subject of Chapter V. Their diversified approaches include specialized handling techniques, pool and bulk shipping, simulation techniques, and extensive use of the computer. Leading food companies provide the case studies for this section.

The application of physical distribution management to the area of bulk shipments is studied in Chapter VI. Transport costs are critical in moving raw material that is low in value, and in-house mechanization and handling systems and efficient warehouse facilities are imperative to effective cost control. American Smelting and Refining Company and Hiram Walker Limited provide examples of companies that transport heavy volumes of raw materials to and between plants, as well as distributing internationally.

"Surmounting Small Shipment Problems" is an area of great concern to many companies, particularly those which do not have a high proportion of larger movements with which to combine smaller shipments. The manner in which Macklanburg-Duncan Co., CBS Records, and Avon Products use multi-phase consolidations is discussed. Break-bulk points from which movements can go to several regions, effective order processing, good field communications and other factors are thoroughly covered.

Another element of physical distribution is modern packaging, which is the subject of the cases in Chapter VIII. The protective packaging for fragile shipments, and innovative methods of packaging for greater distribution reliability and cost savings as practiced by the subject companies, provide valuable insight into solutions to problems in this area.

Logistics as applied to foreign trade adds dimensions to physical distribution not encountered in domestic logistics. Customs requirements, paperwork essentials, diverse trade areas, and different monetary systems are only some of the activities requiring a specialized knowledge. Chapter IX deals with specific problems in international trade, and the methods employed by a number of companies in their handling of this function. With the influx of companies entering international trade, these case studies should be of particular value.

Unique distribution operations are examined in the final chapter. These cases are exemplary of firms whose operations do not fit a general pattern, perhaps because of the nature of the business, or due to unusual service requirements, or the type of market.

This book provides an excellent collection of carefully selected and relevant case studies. Recognizing the fact that companies adapt the physical distribution concept to their individual requirements, the studies offer a broad mix of management applications. The author's academic and business experience are evident in the depth of understanding and insight provided in these cases. I have used many of the studies in the classroom where they have had an excellent reception. The book would be a noteworthy addition to any physical distribution department's reference library and of unusual value to students in their physical distribution and logistics courses.

Charles A. Taff
Professor and Chairman
Department of Business Administration
University of Maryland

PHYSICAL DISTRIBUTION CASE STUDIES

CHAPTER I

Gearing the Organization for Physical Distribution

The emergence of physical distribution management, or business logistics, directly parallels other significant changes in the courses of American management practices. The era of its emergence has also witnessed vast expansion and substantial diversification of numerous enterprises. It has seen as well a revolution in accountability and control brought on largely by electronic data processing. All of these things create an organizational ferment within American industry. On the one hand, sophisticated data communications systems point toward more effective central control than was previously possible. On the other, expansion for many has been so great that numerous companies, despite progress in management controls, find some form of polycentric management essential. For several, the profit center philosophy proves effective. For others, the separation may be by geographic division, product, or a carefully controlled segregation of specialized activities.

The concept of "an idea whose time has come" certainly applies to physical distribution management. An era of organizational change, regrouping the activities necessary to such a function, though still a complex, sensitive task, becomes far more feasible than in the climate of 20 years ago.

A classic case of physical distribution management benefitting from broader organizational change took place a few years ago at the Noxell Corporation. This well-known manufacturer of Noxzema skin cream, Cover Girl makeup and kindred products turned to modern logistics practices virtually overnight as part of a carefully-planned total management restructuring. Since then, Vice President William F. Wendler's department has become well known as an innovator in the handling of small shipments while Director of Management Information William R. McCartin and his staff have gained similar recognition for their progressive efforts in order processing, inventory control and customer service programming.

An inspection of Noxell's physical distribution facilities and practices in the spring of 1967 follows:

Noxell Goes All Out for Distribution

RAPIDLY increasing business imposes new and different demands on the once-small company. Noxell Corporation, producer of Noxzema Skin Cream, Cover Girl makeup and related products, is a classic case. Sales, only $10 million in 1957, broke through the $38 million level in 1966. Management took careful self-measurement during this period and started organizational shifts to cope with its progressive expansion. Significant among these was creation of a physical distribution department under Vice President William F. Wendler.

This new unit is built on the foundation of a seasoned traffic department. The firm's steady growth led the traffic staff into broader areas of responsibility—areas too frequently unrelated technically, or in which responsibility was shared with other departments. The situation was becoming increasingly confused, with resultant cost and service penalties. These problems led to engagement of John F. Gustafson & Co., management consultants, to examine the entire distribution function and make recommendations for its continuing development.

Working with Administrative Vice President William C. Chester, the consultants thoroughly analyzed Noxell's plant-to-customer service, submitting a report in October, 1964. A number of specific distribution problems discovered and identified, include:

- Split shipment inconveniences

Distribution services staff meets to review program development. From left to right, J. L. Bortle, assistant traffic manager; W. H. Williams, inventory control manager; J. H. Hoffman, traffic manager; W. F. Wendler, vice president-distribution services; F. V. Schmidt, warehousing manager and J. P. Winterson, manager customer service.

- Excessive order cycle times
- Inconsistent order cycle times
- Delivery bottlenecks
- Lack of response to inquiries
- Errors in order filling
- Order form inconvenience

The above constituted principal difficulties, but not the total. Here were some other trouble spots noted:

- Damaged packages
- Thefts in transit
- Lack of formal provision for emergency shipments
- Poor order-status liaison
- Lack of packing slips
- Frequent code changes
- Inadequacies in package identification

A three-phase approach to this situation was suggested. Initially, it was proposed that the existing organization tackle the major trouble areas for short-term solution of problems lending themselves to it.

Phase Two called for launching of three basic programs involving fundamental changes to eliminate deeper seated problems. These programs were establishment of a distribution department, automation of order processing and expansion of electronic data processing in the distribution area. Once placed under way, it was felt that specific projects could be initiated as part of the distribution service manager's activities, including:

- — Establishing guaranteed customer service levels
- — Elimination of split deliveries
- — Installation of a modern inventory and control system
- — Development of innovations suggested by changing circumstances

Distribution's role is clearly indicated in this chart showing the department's relationship to other management services and duties comprising its own function.

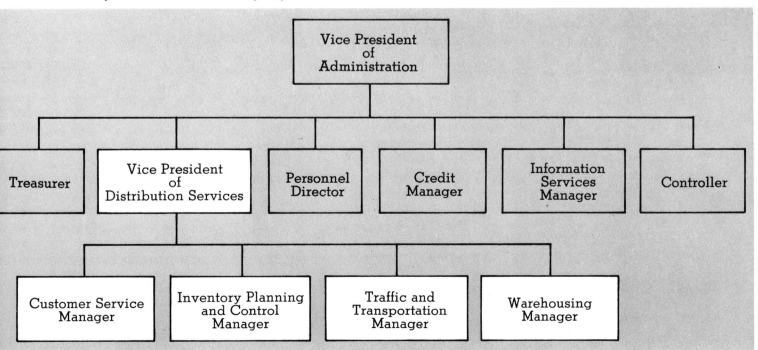

"The product should always be on hand wherever and whenever the customer wants it." . . . WITT

The third phase called for recognition of company-wide distribution improvement opportunities. These included:

1. A longer range customer-oriented distribution facilities plan integrated with future marketing-manufacturing plans, giving consideration to the distribution center concept.
2. An approach to the small order problem, correlated with such considerations as seeding, split shipments and minimum order quantities.
3. An overall, longer range approach to electronic data processing as a management tool.

Noxell lost no time in implementing plans based on these recommendations. Formerly general traffic manager of Alberto-Culver and before that supervisor of automated warehouse control at Westinghouse, Mr. Wendler was brought in as manager of distribution services. With first emphasis on improving customer service and secondary consideration given operating economies, he moved swiftly to build an organization and activate systems changes to speed the flow of goods. In early 1967, Mr. Wendler was made a vice president.

The chart on page 5 reveals that every distribution category cited formerly had at least dual reporting assignments. Order processing responsibility was split four ways. The right side of the chart indicates how distribution services revised lines of reporting to clarify responsibility. Of the group, only order processing continues to be split. Here, however, is an area where shared responsibility represents a minimum of confusion because the contrasting technical natures of the two affected units show clearly where each one's duties should begin and end.

Order processing automation has moved forward hand-in-glove with realignment of warehouse locations. The ten installations existing Jan. 1, 1966 have been reduced to five at present. Except for the Cockeysville, Md. headquarters facility, these are public warehouses. Dataphone service was installed between the headquarters computer facility and the remote warehouses for direct transmission of orders subsequent to electronic data processing. Closing warehouses and improving communications is expected to yield net savings of $78,000 annually. This represents warehouse and tax savings of $116,000 diminished by $38,000 increases for data transmission equipment and somewhat greater freight expenses. National average delivery time of 8.36 days will be reduced to 7.97 days. Although changes appear insignificant when viewed as a working average, customer service records indicate greatest gains will be in areas experiencing the longest order cycles. There will be an acceptable time increase in some regions that were most favorably treated under the former arrangement.

Under the new system, a normal order will be transmitted to an appropriate warehouse within one day of receipt at the computer center. All necessary inventory checks and adjustments, invoicing and shipping documentation will be computer processed. The resultant information, available the same day the order is received at Cockeysville, will be given in writing to the local warehouse or forwarded via Dataspeed to teletype receivers at the remote warehouses.

At present volumes, according to William R. McCartin, manager information services, it is most economical to translate order data from the punched card computer output to paper tape using Flexowriters. The punched tape is used to transmit information by AT&T Dataspeed equipment. As volume increases, it is anticipated that tape-to-tape transmission is likely, using magnetic tape output from the computer. Ultimately, an on-line operation with the computer feeding data directly via wire to appropriate warehouse receiving units is a possibility.

The present warehousing operation represents a marked improvement in service and cost, but it is intended to take a second look at the operation after the initial phase of distribution reorganization is completed. With the introduction of an IBM 360 computer and related data storage equipment in place of the previous 1401 system, information services intends to absorb inventory records of all warehouses at the central unit. A master file containing two years of customer sales history will also be developed, indicating accounts receivable and sales patterns. These data will be used by the department in building a distribution model for the benefit of distribution services in monitoring and improving their operations. In particular, it is intended to use such a model for evaluation of the distribution center concept as a factor in long range planning. "Even though we continue to operate in accounting and other areas," states Information Services Manager McCartin, "basically our function is distribution and marketing oriented."

The information services organization, like distribution services, reports directly to Senior Vice President Chester. Such units have more typically been responsible to a company controller, but placing this activity on an equal management footing with such functions as accounting and distribution provides more freedom to serve all without prejudice.

The changes in distribution and information services are indicative of an almost total revision of Noxell's management structure. Wholesale reorganization commenced in 1955, when Norbert A. Witt joined the company as vice president. His initial concern was sales, followed by marketing. Mr. Witt became president in 1963 and hit on other areas of management thereafter. Today's company finds itself in new physical facilities utilizing a healthy mixture of long-term managers and newcomers of specialized experience.

What does all this portend for the company and for its distribution services unit? "In a word, growth," states President Witt. "We are looking toward greater product diversification, new product development, international expansion and acquisition of firms whose products and services are compatible with our own." Because of this, distribution services is prepared for adjustments that such changes may dictate in its strategy. Upcoming programs are devised to allow for expansion.

Before-and-After Chart indicates duties and their reassignment after formation of a distribution department.

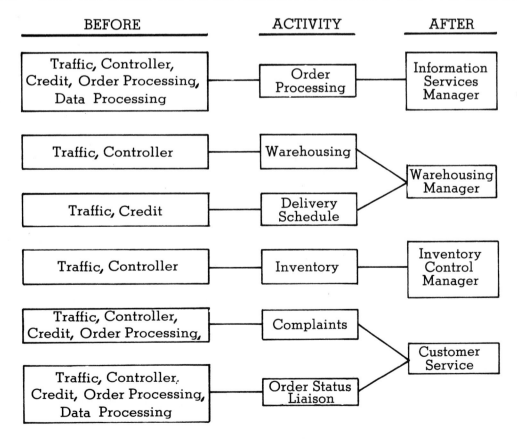

Looking beyond 1967, during which warehousing will be the major preoccupation, an inventory control project is anticipated for 1968. "We've set up a total distribution system in a short time that operates smoothly," says Vice President Wendler, "but more work is necessary to perfect individual components. The reorientation under way in warehousing represents considerable testing, research and development. Similar effort will be required in our approach to inventories. The computer can help a great deal in this, but computers have a lot in common with high priced sports cars. Owning the car does not guarantee winning races and, in fact raises significant potential dangers. We respect the computer in the same way. That's why we're tackling the bigger tasks one at a time in our drive toward a perfected total distribution program at Noxell."

The "new look" in distribution's relationship to other management sectors is also reflected within the department's structure. Line operations of traffic, warehousing and order processing are geared to give customer service that creates competitive advantage for Noxell. "Costs are kept under control and watched closely, but not at the risk of service deterioration," according to Mr. Wendler.

The Traffic Department's Part In Noxell's New Distribution System

The recommendations of the management consultant, the new warehouse-plant-headquarters complex and organization of the distribution services group have made a more effective unit of traffic. Freed of responsibility for extraneous and unrelated activities, staff members are putting concentrated pressure on the bread-and-butter traffic issues. Better shipping facilities and adequate space at the warehouse plus newer tools and improved management communication at the offices are further aids. This new climate is paying off in the continuing attack on problems pinpointed by the consultant's report.

One such problem—small shipments—is under intensive, continuing attack. Documentation has been eliminated or simplified on REA, U.P.S. and Parcel Post shipments. A study, completed in conjunction with the controller's department, provided the marketing department with accurate cost data upon which to base future decisions affecting

this area. By identifying specific factors affecting the costs of these shipments, it has been made easier for marketing and sales to decide in which directions to guide smaller customer buying patterns.

Centralized Traffic Unit Is Specialized, Computer-Oriented

Assistant Vice President-Traffic Manager J. Henry Hofmann has built his department to match the quickening pace of Noxell business. His specialized, computer-oriented staff of 11 is a far cry from the virtually one-man show that functioned in the old Baltimore plant two decades ago. The traffic unit is centralized, advising and assisting distant facilities from the Cockeysville location.

At present, traffic computerization is restricted to routing of shipments, with all routing cataloged on tape. Development of EDP tonnage reports, however, is under way, the traffic group cooperating with information services in assembly of suitable procedures. Subsequently, further programming will be developed for traffic and cost analysis of present or proposed shipping systems.

Motor carriers, including most of those serving Baltimore, handle a substantial volume of Noxell freight. The Baltimore & Ohio and Pennsylvania railroads also share in this traffic through piggyback operation. Plans are under development for possible installation of a siding, permitting direct rail car movement to and from the Cockeysville plant.

Some shipments move as well via Universal Carloading Company and part of the West Coast traffic is tendered to Sea Land Service. R E A Express, United Parcel Service and Parcel Post also receive significant amounts of freight due to the heavy movement of direct orders to small receivers.

Stock shipments to distant warehouses are moving about 85% in piggyback operation. Noxell currently uses Plan II and Plan III as well as combination Plan III-IV. Coloading with other shippers is common under Plan III.

Considerable use is made of consolidation arrangements and transit privileges, notably split delivery and stop-off provisions of motor carriers. A shippers association is employed at Chicago to get Plan IV piggyback service into a warehouse at Brisbane, California. Consolidations are regularly made to Columbus and Cleveland, Ohio, Detroit and Philadelphia as well as to a consolidation-distribution facility at Secaucus, N.J. The last two destinations in particular receive cage containers moved in solid truckloads without the carriers having to touch a piece of freight. "This yields rate and claim benefits to Noxell while offering operating convenience to affected motor carriers," says Traffic Manager Hofmann.

All products shipped are described as Toilet Preparations, and Shave Cream, taking a high classification. Rates are under constant surveillance, assuring service standard protection at lowest cost. Shipments do not normally require heating or refrigeration en route, but a degree of temperature sensitivity makes the use of reefer equipment advantageous, particularly in the winter. Efforts are being made to obtain year-round reefer utilization. Claim experience has been consistently good, none the less, as careful carrier screening coupled with long-time carrier familiarity with the products eliminates most potential headaches before they arise. In 1966, $32,000 in claims were filed, largely due to freezing damage in the winter months.

Traffic is also concerned with a small but fast-growing export operation. Much of the documentation is handled by the traffic department, while some is farmed out to a broker. Noxell maintains an international division in New York and has manufacturing arrangements in effect in 10 other countries. European shipments are moved, for the most part, in fibreboard containers on disposable pallets. These are delivered knocked down, being set up when ready for packing. Some

Uniformed work force at Cockeysville warehouse assembling orders on one of twin assembly conveyors.

European shipments are going in standard containers. It is anticipated that this means will be used more often as business increases.

Modern Systems, New Equipment Make for Effective Material Handling

Warehousing's greater autonomy under distribution services plus the acquisition of a modern 80,000 foot warehouse in lieu of old, cramped facilities has made progress easier for Warehouse Manager F. Vernon Schmidt. Shipping and warehouse supervisors, each with uniformed personnel under his control, work together to keep things moving, sharing or splitting their two work forces as conditions require.

Cockeysville warehouse uses 48 × 32 pallets, but 48 × 40 double-face pallets have been purchased recently. Replacements will continue in this size. Ultimately, Noxell will use either 48 × 40 disposable pallets or clamp handling. The latter is attractive, but virtually requires that it be used at both ends of the haul, posing problems where a receiving point may not have the proper fork lift equipment. Experiments are also under way with pallet racks. Further assisting these developments was the addition of five new lift trucks in 1966. Each is equipped to take all attachments with an extra 1,000 pounds capacity built in to handle a clamp or other alternatives. It is intended ultimately to put clamps on some of these trucks.

On parcel post shipments, some of the handling benefits of palletization are sought through use of wheeled hampers. With a capacity of 225 cubic feet or 3,000 pounds, they are expected to speed the loading and unloading of post office-bound trucks.

At first, the new warehouse used a single conveyor line for assembly of Noxzema brand products with a 350 order capacity daily. Two lines now feed the shipping area, increasing daily capacity to 800 orders. Installation of a viewgraph is planned to project orders on a large screen for use by "throwers" on the assembly line. Further assisting the throwers will be installation of roller-racks in lieu of the present system of supply by fork lift stock positioning.

Uniform Cosmetics Packs Assembled From Special Racks In Small Area

Cover Girl makeup orders are assembled in a separate area. Smaller shipments of wider variety are experienced, and the ratio of value per pound, Cover Girl versus Noxzema, is 7 to 1 in favor of the cosmetics.

Pack uniformity for the 12 makeup items and 14 lipstick shades made possible the use of Kwik-Pik racks permitting picking of the total line for order assembly within a span of only 4 linear feet.

Inbound freight is received at a large platform on the north side of the warehouse. Still greater area, encompassing a major portion of the building's south side, is available for outbound loading. This section has six automatic dock boards installed that can drop to a 31-inch level for loading of small pickup trucks.

Much inbound freight arrives by truck from local vendors. One major supplier, the Maryland Glass Company, delivers a continuous stream of the famous Noxzema blue jars which are the reason for the presence of a "de-palletizer" near the receiving dock. This unique machine removes the sleeve and top of large pallet-loaded cartons of jars, the pallet, sleeve and top being collapsed and returned to the vendor.

Noxell clearly recognizes physical distribution's role. Its orientation to sales and service, amply supported by a rapid, continuous growth rate, is expected to place increasing demands on this function. Improvements either currently in effect or soon anticipated are significant, but there is another, less obvious advantage that may prove most important of all. The new organization has an alertness born of modern communication and clear assignment of responsibilities. Even a subtle change in any phase of the distribution pattern can be sensed and evaluated in a hurry. Physical distribution's greatest gift to Noxell can come from "ailments" prevented rather than "cured."

Transportation: A Corporate Profit Center

Blue Bell is best known to the public as the manufacturer of Wrangler Jeans and a wide variety of other items of casual wearing apparel. More recently, it has captured substantial attention for its logistics innovations. The company employs the profit center concept in its overall management, carrying it a step further than most, to the benefit of the physical distribution function. Known as "Blue Bell Services," what would elsewhere be termed a department or division is treated virtually as an outside vendor. If any company unit finds an external service source and can justify its use economically in contrast to Blue Bell Services' fully allocated costs, then that division is free to choose the external alternative. Headed by a president with full executive responsibility, aided by his own controller, Blue Bell Services maintains a flexible, competitive management stance that keeps its own services attractive to other company divisions and shows a return on its facility investments fully justifying its operating costs.

The psychology of creating a "profit center," in contrast to the negative connotation of a "cost center," as such purely internal service operations are generally defined in other organizations, proves highly effective.

A detailed description of Blue Bell Services' organization and operations in the spring of 1970 follows:

THE profit center management concept meets considerable favor today among large corporations. Breaking increasingly unwieldy corporate bodies into simpler structures, spurring management initiative through greater delegation of authority and responsibility, major corporations find this approach can build an aggressive edge in competitive markets.

The physical distribution "fly-in-the-profit-center-ointment" too often gets shrugged off, however. Although the nature of this function's costs favors central control, many executives view the increased costs of divisionalized distribution as a minor trade-off against greater anticipated total gains from multidivision management.

Blue Bell, Inc. sees it differently. The firm's gross sales quadrupled in the last decade, reaching $239 million in fiscal 1970. Like others, the company introduced profit center management to cope with continuing

expansion, but unlike many others, it created a separate profit center to maintain centralized transportation and closely related functions.

On Oct. 1, 1970, Division President Frank R. Iler's Blue Bell Services division took over company transportation facilities. From the firm's Greensboro, N.C. headquarters, this unit now "sells" transportation services to other divisions which produce and market casual wear, utility clothes and uniforms.

"Our division fiscal policies closely parallel those of the other groups," Mr. Iler observes. **"Rates charged Blue Bell divisions for our services reflect the same return-on-investment goals that they seek in their own efforts. In this way, we must compete continually with external alternatives, seeking patronage where justified by our known costs, but referring assignments to external vendors where their charges are favorable. The result is a**

system which assures that final selection reflects the true economics of each situation."

Division services encompass a wide spectrum, including:

Private Air Service: A Lockheed Constellation, company-owned, ties Puerto Rican plants to the mainland complex with fast cargo service, while a Piper Navajo moves managers expeditiously among the 75 U.S. plant locations.

Private Truck Service: Centered in the Southeast, Blue Bell trucks perform substantial vendor-plant service in addition to moving finished goods toward their markets.

Material Handling Equipment: Plant trucks, fork-lift units and other material handling equipment are selected, purchased and owned by Blue Bell Services, which leases this equipment to the divisions for plant and warehouse activities.

Traffic Services: The division's traffic department, though primarily

BLUE BELL SERVICES brings the firm's Puerto Rican plants closer to vendors and distribution centers alike with this Super Constellation which symbolizes division objectives in serving the total company.

research-oriented, performs line export functions and provides guidance and procedures to govern independent local plant traffic activity.

Not only does each Blue Bell division have its own president, but, as the accompanying organization chart reveals, its own controller as well. **"My prime concern," notes Division Controller Euin Swafford, Jr., "is effective utilization of capital by the division at a targeted rate of return generally established by corporate policy."**

Reporting on a line basis to President Iler, Mr. Swafford also has a strong staff responsibility to Corporate Vice President-Finance G. Ervin Dixon. By working directly within the division, Mr. Swafford keeps closely acquainted with physical operations, thus developing a better understanding of any action's equity implications from firsthand acquaintance. Because he is part of the group management, he can function as an "instant consultant" concerning the specific financial implications of a suggested decision or investment.

The division controller works closely with operating center managers in preparing their annual budgets, these being derived from subordinate cost centers constituting the individual operating centers. The operating centers include cargo aircraft, executive aircraft, trucks, printing and leased equipment.

The operating center managers themselves develop initial annual budgets, which they review and revise in concurrence with division management. Their budgets in turn consolidate to a profit center budget for the

Blue Bell Services division, which then moves forward to the financial vice president for corporate budget development.

Performance compared to budget gets close scrutiny through a computer procedure. It starts with vendor invoices, which are coded and approved by cost center managers and passed to the division controller for review. Forwarded to Accounts Payable for disbursement, the data then enter the computer, where a management information system (M.I.S.) program produces an Account Summary by cost center format, sequencing these reports within a cost center classification grouping. The

data provide a basis for M.I.S. reports given each operations center manager that show his monthly and year-to-date performance compared to budget and any variances by individual account, segregated by cost centers.

Blue Bell's substantial printing operation at Greensboro may seem a strange companion for essentially transportation services, but there is much close coordination between printing activities and freight services. **"The major part of our output moves forward twice weekly by corporate truck," states Printing Manager Norman Reynolds. "Most of it goes to our Greenville, S.C. terminal,**

ANALYZING PROPOSED REVISIONS in coordinated truck-aircraft schedules are (left to right): Division President Frank R. Iler, Vice President Robert A. Ingram and Air Transportation Manager Frank A. Thompson.

where it is fanned out to the various plants throughout the Southeast. We also consolidate vendor material with our own print production to gain transportation cost and service benefits." A major printing task is the production of diversified garment tickets for the 75 U.S. plants. Company forms of many kinds are also a big factor in printing production.

Although Blue Bell is a heavy mover of small shipments by common carrier, some 95% of its outbound freight being of this category, it moves substantial volume freight in both common and private carriage. Its fluid private truck and air routings mesh into common carrier consolidation plans as well. In the ensuing pages, we examine these operations more closely.

CONTROLLER Euin Swafford, Jr. and Air Transportation Manager Frank A. Thompson discuss costs anticipated in an air service expansion proposal.

BLUE BELL SERVICES ORGANIZATION CHART. A notable feature is the inclusion of a divisional controller, aiding in cost measurement and the improvement of liaison with the corporate financial function.

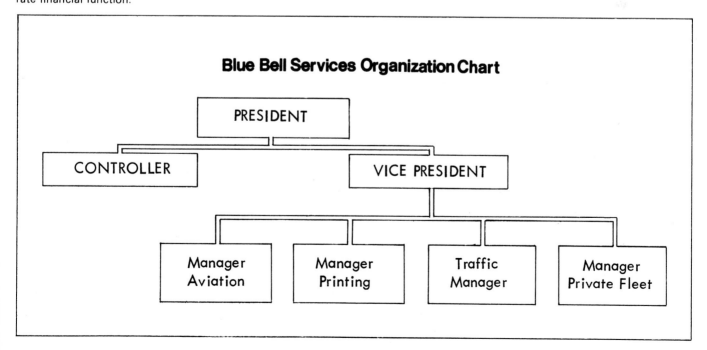

Blue Bell Services Organization Chart

- PRESIDENT
  - CONTROLLER
  - VICE PRESIDENT
    - Manager Aviation
    - Manager Printing
    - Traffic Manager
    - Manager Private Fleet

Company plane's role in intermodal service

"OUR AIR OPERATION really got its start from the 1968 dock strike," comments Vice President-Operations Robert A. Ingram. "We were forced to make several charter flights so that our Puerto Rican plants could maintain production, and they were a real eye-opener. What takes a week to 10 days by containership gets there in a single day by air. By marrying the plane schedule to the trucking services we operate, we maintain steady two-way movement that amply justifies our air operating costs."

Air speed lets one plane move a lot of freight. Blue Bell's Lockheed Constellation, purchased from Flying Tiger Line and slightly modified, regularly handles 40,000-pound cargoes, or a solid trailerload, both ways over two routes: San Juan-Greensboro and San Juan-Miami. The regular flight pattern includes two round trips weekly from Greensboro plus one from Miami.

Puerto Rico-bound flights pick up truckloads of vendor freight, consisting of 80% cloth and 20% hardware, taking them to San Juan and the waiting Blue Bell trailer for fan-out to the Mayaguez, Aguada and Anasco plants. The San Juan-Mayaguez truck run is a four-hour, 90-mile trip, but all three plants lie within 10 miles of each other at the western end of the island.

Before the plane departs from San Juan, a trailerload of Blue Bell's Wrangler jeans is loaded for the return flight. On its arrival at either Miami or Greensboro, it is off-loaded to a company trailer for delivery to distribution facilities at Wilson, N.C.; Luray, Va., or Seminole, Okla. The determinant of whether a flight will make Miami or Greensboro is the mixture of southbound vendor freight, rather than the Puerto Rican plant goods. Given a truck consolidation from the more southerly vendors, Miami is the preferred point of pickup, while vendors farther north will have their goods forwarded through Greensboro.

In addition to cargo handling, the Constellation carries three certified

THE BLUE BELL CONSTELLATION receives routine inspection and maintenance at Blue Bell Services' new airport facility located in Greensboro, N.C. Looking things over are (left to right): Flight Engineer Walter Dietrich, Mechanic and Loadmaster Joseph Kestner and Flight Engineer Donald Bowden.

bucket seats for company personnel, providing a valued direct service for management between the Greensboro headquarters and the firm's Puerto Rican facilities.

Equaling the importance of full loads in both directions is the consideration of ground time in determining operating costs. The plane is a big investment and idle time costs can mount fast. Air Transportation Manager Frank A. Thompson sees to it that maintenance work is carefully scheduled and handled speedily, while cargo handling gets close attention to minimize ground time at the terminals. An empty Blue Bell trailer kept at each airport assures prompt turnaround on the plane's arrival.

At San Juan, Blue Bell has its own load master, who is also the terminal manager for the total Blue Bell operation. When the plane is scheduled at San Juan, he brings three drivers to assure expeditious loading and unloading of the company truck. A commercial loading company, Interstate Air Service, handles on- and off-loading of the aircraft itself.

The entire Miami interchange op-

eration is handled by Air Agency, Inc. Its fast handling coupled with the shorter mileage make possible a complete San Juan-Miami turnaround in one day. San Juan and Greensboro normally are the scheduled points for overnight layovers.

Finished product leaving San Juan regularly moves in company-designed wooden containers. Weighing 70 pounds and carrying 1,200 pounds of cargo, they are double-stacked in trailers, but carried single stack in the aircraft, their high-density content causing the plane load to weigh out rather than cube out.

At Greensboro, unlike Miami and San Juan, all ground support functions fall to Blue Bell employes, including two full-time ground personnel and four part-time loaders. The two full-time men are both certified airplane mechanics, one of whom is also designated as load master. Most of the aircraft maintenance is done by these men, although Piedmont Air Lines occasionally provides assistance for some jobs. In addition, the three flight engineers who alternate in the plane crews are certified

"BIGGEST WASH JOB in Greensboro." Maintenance crew cleans up the Super Constellation at the new Blue Bell International Air Terminal at the regional airport.

THE NUMEROUS DIVERSIFIED PAPERS necessary for each flight are indicated on the flight envelope (at right) in which they are carried

BLUE BELL SERVICES COMPANY

THIS ENVELOPE CONTAINS THE FOLLOWING DOCUMENTS FOR FLT._____DATE _____

SHIPPING INFORMATION   INITIALS OF CREW MEMBERS

1. Weight and Balance Forms (2)   _____

2. Shipper's Export Declaration, Southbound (flights
   not originating North Carolina) (1)   _____

3. Shipper's Export Declaration, Northbound (1)   _____

4. Manifest Southbound, Signed by Receiving Agent (1)   _____

5. Short Form Bill of Lading, Northbound (1)   _____

6. Agricultural Clearance (1)   _____

7. Aircraft Loading Sheets, North and South (2)   _____

8. List of Cargo Loaded, Southbound only. (If not
   listed on Loading Sheet.)   _____

AIRCRAFT INFORMATION   (To be removed from folder and filed in
                         appropriate files in Air Cargo Office)

1. Flight Logs (2)   _____

2. Aircraft Logs (2)   _____

3. Pre Flight (2)   _____

4. Fuel Tickets (2)   _____

DATE RECEIVED: AIR CARGO OFFICE_____

FORM 4116 N9-70

air frame and power plant mechanics, with one of them a certified inspector as well. Between these people resources, there exists a capability to perform virtually any necessary maintenance.

"We farm out maintenance work not out of a lack of capability, but only as time and cost factors suggest," says Air Transportation Manager Thompson.

"Doubling in brass" in the air transportation section extends well beyond maintenance personnel. Department Manager Thompson himself, in addition to his managerial responsibilities, serves regularly as a pilot on the Constellation. The other three pilots include the chief of administration-air transportation, the air cargo manager and the assistant to the manager-trucking operation. Quite clearly, managers in the Blue Bell Services Division are anything but "deskbound." All pilots have college degrees and FAA air transport pilot ratings.

Each Friday, a new three-week schedule is produced for the air cargo operation. The first forward week schedule bases upon goods availability data supplied by the planning department. The additional two weeks represent estimated needs and the constraints imposed by the aircraft maintenance plan.

The Constellation, acquired in December, 1968, continues to prove reliable and well suited to its present assignments. Expansion planning looks to the addition of another plane and an expanded service or, alternatively, a switch to a high-capacity jet aircraft. The latter's additional speed and capacity must be weighed against the substantially greater investment, however, so careful evaluation of alternatives will be completed before a final decision is reached on air cargo expansion.

The big Lockheed offers a limited passenger-carrying capability, but most such service falls to the other unit in the Blue Bell air fleet. A Piper Navajo, based at Greensboro, serves primarily for getting corporate staff members to plant locations.

With some 75 U.S. plants, scattered primarily around the Southeast, manager travel is considerable in volume, and much of it flows to points with limited airline service for passengers out of Greensboro. Flights as far as El Paso are made by the craft.

The department's reservations clerk handles both private plane and regular airline reservations, building loads for the private plane to ensure efficient utilization of its five to six-passenger capacity. When four or more share a flight, the reservations clerk bills their divisions at the comparable tourist airline rate for the distance involved. When the party is less than four, there is a pro rata billing at the standard charter rate for the movement.

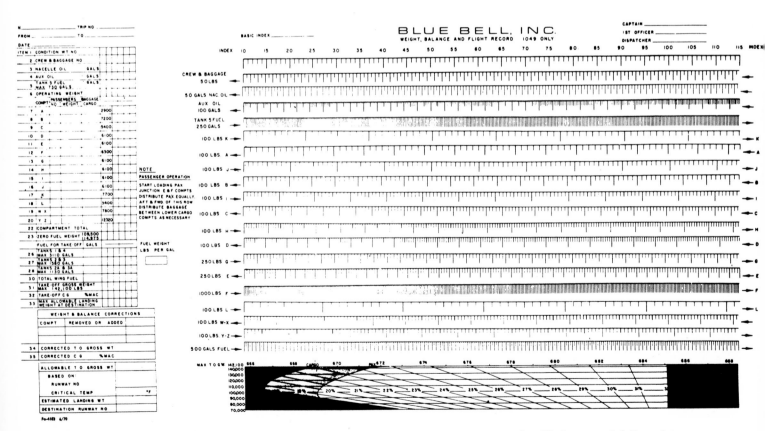

LOADING the Super Constellation in order to assure proper craft trim is far more complex than when loading a trailer. The above chart must be filled out and followed to assure proper weight distribution in flight.

BLUE BELL SERVICES' Greenville, S.C. terminal includes loading and transfer facility with attached offices (center) and a truck and material handling equipment maintenance shop (left). Substantial trailer parking is available.

Highway fleet performs regional services

COMPANY TRUCKING has a long history at Blue Bell. Initiated with two leased trucks in 1947, the fully-owned, over-the-road fleet now numbers 28 road tractors and 62 trailers. The operation is highly flexible, and where common carrier cost-service benefits prove greater, Blue Bell runs no trucks.

Notes Division President Iler: "We've always operated and still do under the philosophy that we're in the trucking business solely for economic or service advantages. When the common carriers can equal or better our standards, we're glad to turn over the freight. We once had four trucks running to the coast, but when piggyback and consolidation programs showed an advantage, we were glad to withdraw the private trucks."

Manager Private Trucking Charles R. Sample maintains his headquarters at Greenville, S.C., the focal point in system trucking operations. Satellite terminals are maintained in addition at Tupelo, Miss. and Greensboro, N.C. Greenville, however, was chosen as main base because of its proximity to a great many vendors and is the nerve center of the system. Trucks fan out from there, moving finished goods to Blue Bell distribution points and picking up vendor freight for plant delivery or transfer to other company trucks at Greenville.

With 75 plants to service and a myriad of vendors, routings must stay quite flexible, but five final destination points are regularly reached at least twice weekly from Greenville, including Luray, Va., El Paso, Tex.; Oneonta, Ala.; Tupelo, and Wilson, N.C., the latter enjoying from 8 to 12 trips each week regularly. A weekly Northeastern run serves a Blue Bell warehouse at Rahway, N.J., returning with piece goods and trim supplies.

In addition to vendor and plant services emanating from Greenville, trucking operations include substantial consolidation activity. Finished goods from various plants move to the Tupelo satellite terminal where consolidations are made. From here, solid piggyback trailers flow to the coast by rail, supplying the Far Western markets.

Close coordination with the Blue Bell air cargo arm is another feature. The dispatcher keeps close tabs on planned flights, assuring timely connections with landings at Miami or Greensboro. At the airports and at any other locations where traffic justifies preloading or trailer exchange, the division keeps trailers parked to expedite service.

All over-the-road operation is under the control of the dispatcher at Greenville. He is kept informed one week in advance as to the services the truck operation will be called upon to perform, planning his runs to fulfill these needs with the minimum of waste space or truck mileage. Dead mileage is kept well below 30% and is watched closely, as are all cost factors related to trucking. States Mr. **Iler: "We know our costs; we know the carrier rates, and the measured cost benefits are substantial."**

Private Trucking Manager Sample's force includes 30 drivers as well as eight mechanics stationed at Greenville, where a maintenance foreman and the dispatcher are also found. Greenville, Tupelo and Greensboro each have terminal managers reporting to Mr. Sample. Reporting to him directly are an assistant manager who handles the in-house leasing operation and a second assistant who doubles as a pilot on the cargo aircraft.

The fleet consists of 28 road tractors, including Diamond-T, White and Peterbilt units, standardized as to engines, transmissions and rear axles. All of these have sleeper cabs.

Trailers number 62 in three basic groups: 12'6" height, 40-foot units; 13'6" height, 40-foot units, and 13'6" height, 45-foot units. Most are Fruehauf or Trailmobile trailers at this time.

While initially operating a leased fleet, Blue Bell bought out its lessor 14 years ago. In Mr. Iler's opinion, based on subsequent experience, there is greater economy in full ownership and control with an operation of this size.

The Greenville trucking center includes two modern buildings: a 14-bay truck terminal built to carrier standards and a repair shop which handles maintenance on materials handling equipment and plant vehicles as well as the division's over-the-road fleet.

Both buildings occupy a substantial plot of ground with ample trailer parking space, plus room for major facility or trailer park expansion should that become necessary.

The terminal building itself is laid out for cross-platform handling of freight between trucks. It is here that considerable consolidating takes place, resulting in faster delivery of partial loads to plants.

A Blue Bell truck may arrive here with a trailer carrying vendor freight from, say, three sources in the eastern Carolinas, but consigned to perhaps seven different plants. The Greenville transfer arrangement yields truckload operating economies for this freight over most of the initiating line haul, while the transfer over Greenville will generally find the seven subshipments in turn merging with others from different arriving trucks to constitute outbound solid trailer loads. Leaving the Greenville transfer dock, therefore, the seven subshipments again move in an efficient manner, maintaining full-load economy levels for most of their total travel. Common carrier trucks also make pickups and deliveries at the Greenville terminal, thus participating in the consolidation operations.

The terminal facility stands apart from any other Blue Bell activities, conveniently located on a major highway. Should the company's needs spell out a change of terminal location or in methods of operating subsequently, the unit would prove well suited to the requirements of a common carrier or other fleet operator.

The repair shop, in addition to standard truck and trailer repairs, handles as well all work on fork-lift and other units which the Blue Bell Services division "leases" to other company divisions for their use. In addition to the force of mechanics at Greenville, the division also calls on the expertise of the aircraft maintenance force for some of this work. Their knowledge of the hydraulic systems and other devices common to aircraft as well as material handling equipment stands them in good stead to perform some operations while guiding mechanics in other phases of this work.

The equipment leasing operations of Blue Bell Services involve not only materials handling equipment assigned to other company divisions but 60 trucks or tractors of various types and 50 trailers. The term "leasing," of course, refers to an accounting convention rather than an actual payment of money. Blue Bell's divisions are integral parts of the corporation, so leasing and other arrangements among divisions represent a tool of cost measurement and analysis primarily.

Maintenance of plant trucks is left to the discretion of the users on maintenance items up to $50. Any greater expenditures must be cleared by Blue Bell Services. The division is developing standards for this purpose, and all such requests are cleared by personnel qualified in this area. Fleet maintenance history is being built up on all units for the continued refinement of cost control.

The leasing program yields substantial economies for Blue Bell. In-

PRIVATE TRUCK MOVEMENTS employ a five-part bill of lading that keeps each handling point informed on shipments flowing through, their nature, schedule performance and specific conditions. Form distribution is made en route by the driver, as denoted by copy indicator shown at the bottom of each form sheet.

stead of six different company divisions or their individual facilities purchasing equipment, concentrated buying power in the Blue Bell Services division keeps equipment costs down. A division can specify its needs in terms of specifications or performance requirements for a fork-lift unit or a highway trailer, but the actual supplier will be the Service Division's choice, making possible group purchases at reduced unit costs for much equipment. In turn, some degree of standardization can be realized through such a system, creating further subsequent economies in maintenance practices, notably maintenance of parts inventories.

LOOKING OVER one of Blue Bell Services' modern highway units are (left to right): Shop Foreman Deward Wilson (in cab), Fleet Manager Charles Sample, Terminal Office Manager Bedell Smith and Dispatcher Gordon Ray.

THIS YARD JOCKEY was rebuilt from a fully depreciated road tractor and is a highly effective "switcher" at Blue Bell's Greenville terminal.

MODERN MAINTENANCE FACILITIES at Greenville fleet terminal can handle full spectrum of vehicle repairs, as well as overhauls of materials handling equipment. Blue Bell's policy of purchasing rather than leasing makes this necessary.

Centralized Control Broadens Traffic Service

The Scovill Manufacturing Company, one of America's major firms, operates a number of modern logistics programs behind a deceptively conventional facade. On the surface, it would seem that the company organization chart contains only a traffic department operating in the somewhat insular fashion all too common before physical distribution management theories and practices attained business acceptance. In fact, thanks to exceptionally good communications and coordination with other departments, the traffic unit makes certain that company transportation and warehouse costs and services are fully optimized as portions of total company cost patterns rather than as isolates. A January, 1970 TRAFFIC MANAGEMENT case study of this company, presented on the following pages, literally bristles with innovative ideas and practices in a diversity of transportation-distribution activities.

Distribution dynamics at work: Scovill Manufacturing Company

SHOULD MARKETING or manufacturing control the distribution function? Scovill Manufacturing Co. prefers a strategic middle course. This expanding, diversified producer's traffic department reports to Vice President-Waterbury Services George A. Goss, whose responsibilities include purchasing, engineering and employe relations.

How does traffic benefit from this service organization concept? Several advantages accrue:

• Without direct reporting responsibility to either plant or sales, the traffic department enjoys a freedom to achieve the best cost-service balance from a corporate standpoint.

• Because the department reports to the same vice president as do purchasing and engineering, good communications and shared concerns widen its service scope as well as strengthen its control over inbound freight and distribution-related aspects of materials handling.

• Broad line responsibilities are paralleled by staff functions, such as facility studies encompassing a number of divisions and subsidiaries, unrestricted by organizational lines.

"Scovill recognizes a growing need for effective physical distribution control," Vice President Goss asserts. "The company's sales growth, from $152,700,000 in 1959 to about $430 million currently, with an annual freight bill nearing $6 million, indicates distribution's importance here, and

the sales dollar increase has been virtually matched by growth in product diversity. New subsidiaries and divisions, acquired or created to maintain Scovill expansion, steadily broaden a product line which continues to identify with the body of productive skills for which our company has long been known."

What kind of company has Scovill become? Initially a New England manufacturer of buttons and other small manufactured items, it expanded its mill activities to produce metal rod, wire and sheet at Waterbury, Conn. and tubing at nearby New Milford.

Subsequent additions broadened out Waterbury area production to include industrial couplings in smaller sizes, automobile parts such as dashboards and, at the Oakville location, various pins and notions, paper clips and formed wire items (Dritz and Clinton brands).

Subsidiaries add greatly to the variety. Among these, Hamilton Beach makes household appliances and soda fountain equipment. The former General Hose and Coupling Co. facilities produce a wide range of industrial couplings, while slide fasteners are produced in plants formerly operated by other acquired companies. A. Schrader and Sons, acquired in 1925, is now divided among three divisions in the United States. These include the fluid power products division at Wake Forest, N. C., the aerosol division at Manchester, N. H. and an automotive product section of the general products division at Dickson, Tenn.

All of these operations have a direct staff relationship with the Waterbury traffic department, says Director of Traffic Arthur

Display panels at Waterbury headquarters show samples of Scovill's varied product line. Appliances from Hamilton-Beach, NuTone and Dominion Electric; grippers and fasteners from the closure division, and auto parts, cosmetic containers and notions are among those shown.

Examining the traffic department's findings in a recent warehousing study are, left to right, Assistant Director of Traffic William J. Morrison, TM Executive Editor Jack W. Farrell, Vice President Waterbury Services George A. Goss and Director of Traffic Arthur M. Rogers.

M. Rogers, although some employ line traffic managers at their plant locations. In addition, the recently acquired NuTone Division, a manufacturer of built-in household appliances, maintains a separate traffic unit, as their marketing channels differ largely from those of most Scovill products.

The traffic department's position of interested neutrality in dealing with other company units reflects in its selection of modes and its forward planning. In several major areas, trade-off possibilities exist in variable degrees, and the department takes full advantage of them. These activities include:

Pooling and consolidation. Rail, common carrier truck and corporate fleet all handle combined shipments, large and small, keeping the cost-service mix at the best competitive level.

Corporate truck operation. Scovill's trucks supplement common carriage in some measure, but they perform unique services in the materials handling and special shipment area beyond the scope of the usual truck fleet assignments.

Warehousing. Forward warehouse planning and site selection relate strongly to envisioned transportation costs and alternatives.

Making big shipments from small ones

SMALL-TO-MEDIUM-SIZED shipments constitute a significant proportion of freight originating at Scovill's Waterbury plant complex. Upward spiralling costs on these, though a headache just as in other shipping firms, have been effectively minimized by the traffic department. Pool cars by rail, consolidations by common carrier truck and still further consolidations employing Scovill's own vehicles help to take the sting out of continuing small shipment rate increases and restrictions.

Pool cars handle a substantial number of outbound shipments from Waterbury. Chicago is the largest pool destination, with Los Angeles and San Francisco ranking close behind. In addition, there are occasional marriages to Texas.

The traffic department strives for 80,000 pounds per load in pool cars. Typical ladings include large less-than-carload or truckload size components. While generally routed to Scovill warehouses, some pool cars also move to heavy customers.

Truck consolidations, made up of many small shipments, average about 15 per day from Waterbury. An assigned traffic department employe has full responsibility for this activity. From each mill in the Waterbury complex, he receives a weekly anticipated shipment list, which provides information he requires to develop individual consolidations and determine their routing.

Each Waterbury mill has its own shipping facilities, so small shipments are gathered from these at the central shipping facility for consolidation in rail cars. If, however, an individual mill shipment portion is destined for truck movement, the procedure varies somewhat. Larger components may be picked up by the road truck at the individual mill shipping facility, while smaller units will be processed through the central unit.

Numerous small shipments, running about 100 daily, still remain that cannot move in the consolidations, notes Assistant Director of Traffic William Morrison. Of these, 20 to 30 will move via United Parcel Service, with R E A Express and Parcel Post accounting for much of the remainder. Very few of these shipments are in the minimum charge category, as most of the latter are absorbed in the consolidation program.

Scovill's own truck fleet helps control small shipment costs. A three-legged sleeper-cab operation originating at Oakville, Conn. typifies this operation:

A sleeper-cab tractor goes south to Fayetteville, N. C. with mill products in their original work pans, saving packaging and material handling costs, reducing transportation costs and minimizing inventory through faster deliveries. At Fayetteville, small shipments are picked up and consolidated with freight remaining on board for final delivery to the plant at Spartanburg, S. C. At Spartanburg, goods from both Oakville and Fayetteville come off, while any northbound Spartanburg small shipments fill out the trailer in combination with northbound freight placed aboard at Fayetteville. Similar efficient employment of return trailer space makes the Scovill fleet an effective small shipment cost-cutter.

Major portion of inbound materials reaches Waterbury in rail carloads.

Small shipments from Waterbury stock move on Eastern Express trailer.

Materials service with the corporate fleet

WHILE SCOVILL maintains substantial conventional, over-the-road trucking routes, a large part of its fleet serves essentially as a plant facility in the Waterbury area. Within the basic mill complex, two tractors and 14 trailers move freight between buildings without leaving the premises. The trailer fleet not only moves material, but provides effective wheeled storage as well.

An additional tractor and three trailers run between the box shop and the various mills with specially made boxes for shipping mill products. The same tractor also handles the transfers of three additional trailers that move metal between the Waterbury mills and the fabricating divisions.

Augmenting the conventional trailers that move goods within the Waterbury plant area is a single large flatbed that carries special racks for moving rod and wire. Capable of moving both within and between plant buildings, this unconventional vehicle sees ample use to justify its existence, sharply reducing the handling effort that would be needed to move the same materials in standard trailers or by other means.

Because in-plant trucking involves many short runs and frequent pickups and drops of trailers, the traffic department wants to reduce the needed effort for these tasks. A plant tractor has been equipped with a Jockey Lift which is in the "de-bugging" process. With the Jockey Lift, a tractor can pick up or drop a trailer without the necessity of raising or lowering the trailer landing gear, greatly speeding operations. When the operation proves fully satisfactory, a second tractor will get similar equipment.

For miscellaneous plant services, five straight trucks operate within the plant area. These vehicles pick up small inbound shipments from the receiving facility and peddle them to the designated plant locations. In reverse operation, they also gather smaller shipments for assembly at the central shipping facility. There are also two dump-body trucks that handle salvage and refuse disposal and two other similar units for construction work.

Partially a mill facility is a group of five tractors and eight trailers which deliver mill products to customers and return with scrap for smelting from points within adjacent states. Their radius is restricted to points where a round trip can be completed in one day. In direct plant service, this group makes from three to five round trips daily taking extruded tube and scrap boxes to the company's tube mill at New Milford and returning to Waterbury with scrap or tubing deliveries. Waterbury trucks have two-way radios tying them to the local dispatcher for maximum flexibility.

Corporate trucking also carries heavy over-the-road responsibilities. In part, specialized equipment and service advantages account for this. The greater consideration, however, is cost. "If we could get a common carrier to haul for 50 cents a truck mile, we would not consider private carriage," comments Director of Traffic Rogers. "Under prevailing circumstances, however, long-haul operations save us $285,000 a year compared to equivalent common carriage."

Most units in the fleet are on net finance leasing. All over-the-road trailers are equipped with Schrader tire inflation systems, which automatically maintain tire

Scovill's 40-foot open-top trailers, chosen to ease unloading, in the Waterbury plant grounds.

An open-topped Ohio Express trailer is unloaded by overhead crane. The 13,000-pound rolls of aluminum from Alcan's Oswego plant will be replaced by aluminum scrap for return from Waterbury to the upper New York source.

inflation while a trailer is connected to a tractor. A flashing cab light notifies the driver when a tire or tires are drawing air. Tires will normally draw air for about a half minute when a tractor first hitches up. In six years of operating this system, there have been no delays whatever due to tire leakage.

All conventional, closed trailers are equipped with Evans loading devices, protecting content from various forms of potential shock damage. Open-topped equipment operating between Waterbury and the Alcan aluminum plant at Oswego, N.Y. employs Aero-quip devices instead. They proved their worth in a recent accident, when a trailer turned over on a soft highway shoulder, sustaining $2,000 trailer damage plus $8,000 on the tractor. Nevertheless, the 13,000 pounds of aluminum coils remained securely fastened to the trailer bed thanks to the Aero-quip Duron strapping, specially designed for hauling loads of this kind.

In some instances, common and private carriage share traffic. Daily runs by two sets of Scovill equipment, each taking two days per round trip, assure that one load of reroll aluminum stock will make Waterbury from Alcan's Oswego plant daily, returning the following day with Waterbury aluminum scrap for remelting. These loads come in 40-foot trailers, as do other loads regularly received in common carriage via Associated Transport and Ohio Fast Freight.

Several other operations cover greater distances to middle-atlantic-area and southern plants from Waterbury or perform interplant services within the southeastern plant complex. Among these, the Waterbury-Dickson, Tenn. sleeper-cab operation makes two 3-day round trips per week with a one-day layover at Waterbury. The 2,230-mile round trip is carefully timed for a 20-minute turn-around at Dickson. A box on the trailer side contains related shipping papers, so that even the clerical chores cause minimum delay. The southbound load typically consists of 43,500 pounds of brass rod, occupying only 20-inch depth in the trailer because of its density. The return load is scrap for the Waterbury mills.

Truck fleet employment typifies the approach of the Scovill traffic department to the total distribution concept. At first glance, an inventory of department equipment appears conventional, even dull. Closer examination almost invariably reveals quite a

Letter space finders, replacing conventional drawer files, create greater accessibility in reduced floor space for bills of lading and freight bills. Reviewing some recent bills are Assistant Director of Traffic William J. Morrison (left) and Traffic Manager-Rates Richard M. Tice.

different picture.

Without fuss or fanfare, this organization makes effective use of equipment far beyond the scope its initial manufacturers envisioned. Mention trucks to most traffic men and they think purely in terms of transportation. At Scovill, innovative minds see anything that moves as a potential materials handling system. "After all," notes Assistant Director of Traffic Morrison, "just what is freight transportation if it is not an extended materials handling system?"

A multipurpose freight bill audit

FREIGHT BILL AUDITING is a key activity in the traffic department's rate and tariff section. As all freight bills are paid through the First National Bank of Boston freight payment plan, this traffic audit provides for the subsequent distribution of charges to the affected Scovill divisions, in the process determining their accuracy and disclosing shipping practices which might benefit from change for cost or service benefits.

"We recover between $130,000 and $140,000 annually in net transportation charges through the audit," states Traffic Manager-Rates Richard M. Tice, "so we benefit from direct financial return as well as from spotting ways of minimizing expensive transport practices by the divisions."

In 1969, the traffic department undertook a complete analysis of audit recoveries. The results confirmed departmental policy in filing for recovery on all detected errors. "I was particularly surprised," Director of Traffic Rogers noted, "to find that 35% of the dollar errors were less than $5 and 23% were between $5 and $10."

The remaining errors included 18% between $10 and $25, 17% between $25 and $100 and 7% in excess of $100. Because the rate and tariff section is equipped to process these audits expeditiously, a substantial proportion of the recoveries are pure gain.

Efficient auditing practices, while helped by a substantial incidence of common origin destinations, gain in great measure from sound systems practices. In addition to modern, easy-access tariff files, desk carrousels containing ready-reference rate cards make checking a large proportion of bills a fast and easy procedure.

Preventive maintenance yields material-handling reliability

THE manufacturing division at Waterbury operates its own internal materials handling equipment, but it seeks traffic department guidance in setting up specifications for forklift trucks and rolling equipment. These specifications are important to the traffic department because it has the responsibility for equipment maintenance, and materials handling equipment failures can mean expensive downtime on manufacturing production lines.

Controlled by Supervisor of Transportation Maintenance James Mitchell, the department operates a large repair shop on a three-shift basis. There is also a small separate facility within the manufacturing division's casting shop, where super-intense lift truck utilization demands rapid service. The latter repair shop handles preventive maintenance for its equipment, but sends units to the basic traffic department facility for heavy overhaul or repair.

The main repair staff includes 11 men on the first shift, five on the second and one man who works from 11 p.m. to 7 a.m. The latter normally works on routine chores, but is immediately available to cover any night-time breakdowns.

The shop, in addition to total servicing of forklift trucks and light maintenance of road trucks and trailers, maintains complete records of both repairs and hours of equipment operation. The resultant information provides a valuable index of performance for consideration when developing new equipment specifications or in selecting among competing manufacturers' products.

Standard procedure finds the shop notifying manufacturing units when their equipment should be brought in for preventive maintenance attention, advising as well when it will be returned. In the event of any equipment failure in service, a telephone call to the shop brings skilled help right to the trouble, frequently resulting in the prompt return of equipment to service, thus reducing costly delays in the movement of materials within the widespread manufacturing facilities.

The traffic department's maintenance shops handle widely varied assignments. In addition to full maintenance of diversified materials handling equipment, the facilities handle light work on road vehicles (heavier repairs of trucks and cars are handled by the lessor).

A **Hawker-Siddeley** DH-125 seven-passenger jet sees few quiet moments in Scovill service. Considerable management time savings result from plane's capability for making on-line points out of off-line ones, reducing multi-legged flight and ground transportation demand.

Personal transportation—
The traffic department's role

THE SERVICE CONCEPT at Scovill shows up nowhere more sharply than in the traffic department's concern with the movement of people. Employe transfers, business travel and control of the company aircraft operation receive continuing attention.

Most unusual is the thorough support provided for employes and families when position transfers mean moving to new communities. The traffic department tackles the complete job, including acquisition of the employe's present home and the processing of all benefits.

Any Scovill division can telephone the details of an employe transfer to the traffic department, which takes it from there. If a house owned by the employe is involved, the traffic department gets three current fair market value appraisals of the property and offers the employe the average of the three prices. A deal is worked out and the purchase is consummated through a lawyer, followed by negotiation of the home's resale.

The actual move is made with a mover of the employe's choice, but billed through the traffic department. In general, experience at Scovill suggests a minimum cost for a complete move of approximately $6,500. The maximum figure is in the vicinity of $12,000.

The company aircraft enjoys a high rate of utilization because of close traffic department control. Schedules are maintained by the department, adjusted to varying needs of management personnel, and every effort is made to fill available space. Company plants are widespread, so managers must move frequently and fast to keep on top of things.

At present, a seven-passenger Hawker-Siddeley DH-125 provides the service, replacing a somewhat smaller Aero-Commander jet. A staff of four captains maintains the operation.

Flight requests move through the traffic department which, in turn, makes known the planned movements of the craft. In this way, those contemplating visits to plants where the plane is scheduled to visit can time their own travel to take advantage of its flight plans, filling as many seats as feasible to hold down the passenger-mile costs of the operation.

The accompanying chart illustrates a typical one-day schedule for the craft. "A company plane is expensive transportation, but we feel the superior service more than warrants it," claims Mr. Rogers. "Management time is costly, too, and our aircraft saves hours and days in direct flights to so-called 'off-line' points where inconvenient connections or slower ground service would be necessary with commercial airline routings."

In fact, most flights do serve off-line or poor service points. They can be requested by any person who reports to a general manager or above, while others can seek "booking" on a space-available basis. A complete service is offered, including arrangements with airports en route to provide food for in-

November 10, 1969

Re: Scovill Flight Operations

Wednesday, November 12th, leave Battle Creek, Michigan at 8:00 A.M. with

> Mr. Stookes, Sr.
> Douglas Stookes
> Albay Paige
> Susan Hess

Fly to Cleveland, Cuyahoga Airport, ETA 8:30 A.M. pick up Dave Carter.

Fly to Waterville, Maine and discharge all passengers.

Fly to Richmond, Virginia for a 2:30 P.M. pick up of John Helies.

Fly to Washington, N.C. for a 3:15 P.M. pick up of Forrest Price and 5

Hamilton Beach men.

Fly to Bridgeport and discharge John Helies. ETA 4:30

Fly to Bradley, discharge remaining passengers.

Ferry to Waterville, Maine for a 5:30 P.M. pick up of *

> Mr. Stookes, Sr.
> Douglas Stookes
> Albay Paige
> Susan Hess
> Dave Carter
> Langdon Quimby

Fly to Battle Creek, Michigan E.T.A. 8:00 P.M., discharge all passengers except

Dave Carter and Langdon Quimby.

Fly to Cleveland, discharge Dave Carter and Langdon Quimby.

Ferry to Bradley.

                                    * Sandwich tray for one out
                                      of Waterville.

A.M. Rogers
vc

cc: Scovill Flight Operations
     Dave Carter
     Langdon Quimby
     Forrest Price
     Gus Wallin
     Jim Hahn

An actual day's log for Scovill's corporate aircraft. There are 10 separate flights, virtually blanketing the eastern area in a crisscross pattern that moved 27 people in just seven seats.

flight service.

Intercity air or surface travel, while under traffic department supervision, is handled externally. The department has selected a travel agency located in Waterbury to handle this activity and works with them to assure that reservations and ticketing are properly handled.

Local transportation, however, is another matter. Scovill's Waterbury area operations include not only a large group of facilities spread over its major in-town property, but it embraces as well operations on separate local properties, plus plants at New Milford and Oakville, Conn. To speed communications between plants as well as to local vendors and service agencies, the traffic department maintains and dispatches a fleet of 16 passenger cars. These are based at the main Waterbury headquarters and are kept under the truck dispatcher's control.

Actual operation of other private cars is the responsibility of individual division managers. Any heavy maintenance work, howev-

Dispatching by radio keeps vehicle utilization high. At the microphone is Supervisor Automotive Transportation James Mastrodonato.

er, must be cleared with the traffic department.

Because the Waterbury complex covers a substantial physical area, internal transportation poses people problems. Some 200 buildings occupy 60 acres, with considerable distances separating many of the facilities. The traffic department's answer is a 17-passenger Metro bus. Operated on a scheduled, 20-minute headway, it saves time and effort for people moving between facilities, as well as providing a means for quick transfer of internal mail among the divisions and mills. As is the case with local trucking and car fleet operations, bus service comes under the Waterbury dispatcher's control.

Warehouse planning with outside guidance

WHILE WAREHOUSING is essentially locally controlled, the traffic department sets routing policy and will recommend changes in such routings where bill audit indicates the necessity. In addition, the

About to start on its regular, every-20-minute trip, the traffic department in-plant bus picks up a passenger. Some 200 plant buildings covering 60 acres make essential a service of this nature.

DATE 8/18/69	STANDARD PRACTICE	NUMBER V-01-04	
WRITTEN BY A. M. R.	BRANCH OFFICE MANUAL	PAGE 1	OF 1
APPROVED BY General Managers		SUPERSEDES 9/6/68	
SUBJECT 1970 AUTOMOBILES FOR REGIONAL AND DISTRICT SALES MANAGERS		DISTRIBUTION	

A.   For Regional and District Sales Managers who drive 10,000 miles or more per year, the following vehicles are available in 4-door sedans or hardtops:

Ford Galaxie 500 390 cu. in., 265 H.P., V-8 Engine.
Chevrolet Impala 400 cu. in., 265 H.P., V-8 Engine (Regular Fuel)
Dodge Polara with 383 cu. in. Engine.
Oldsmobile Cutlass 455 cu. in., 2 bbl. carburetor Engine (Regular Fuel)
Buick "350" Skylark 350 cu. in., 250 H.P. Engine.
Pontiac Catalina 400 cu. in., 265 H.P. Engine (Regular Fuel)
American Motors Ambassador 360 cu. in., 245 H.P. Engine (Regular Fuel)

The Optional Equipment may include:

Automatic Transmission
Power Steering
Power Brakes
Air Conditioning
Tinted Glass
Pushbutton Radio
Wheel Covers
Foam Front Seat Cushion
Vinyl Upholstery

In New England, New York, Ohio, Pennsylvania, Indiana, Illinois, Michigan and Wisconsin: Positive Traction Rear Axle and Undercoating.

No additional accessories or extras can be supplied.

B.   For Regional and District Managers who drive 8,000 miles per year, but not more than 10,000 miles per year, based on previous useage, these individuals will be provided with a vehicle of the same model and type as used by salesmen and as otherwise covered by these regulations.

C.   For District or Regional Sales Managers who drive less than 8,000 miles per year Scovill will not furnish an automobile, but the District or Regional Manager may use his own car for Company business for a mileage up to 8,000 miles per year and Scovill will reimburse him for this use at the rate of 9¢ per mile, plus garage storage charges away from the District or Regional Manager's home base, and tolls. All of the remaining automobile expense will be the responsibility of the District or Regional Sales Manager.

Where a District or Regional Sales Manager uses his privately owned car for company business, the Scovill liability and property damage policy will protect Scovill against suit. It should be understood that Scovill does not carry insurance to protect the District or Regional Sales Manager against damage to his car or from damage suits.

Company automobile leasing policy information is given through standard practice pages such as the above, prepared by Director of Traffic Arthur M. Rogers and approved by the general managers.

Alfred Christiano, supervisor of receiving, and Assistant Director of Traffic William J. Morrison check the transit time performance on a group of critical inbound small shipments.

department has undertaken long-range warehouse rationalization studies, including one for the closure division, the data from which was turned over to Food Machinery Corp., a consultant, for further review. Both the traffic department and the consultant independently reached the conclusion that minimized branch warehousing would give the division significant cost benefits without impairing services.

Another similar project assigned to the same consultant concerned itself with modernized warehousing for the Hamilton-Beach Division. Both of these projects are essentially forerunners of major studies of broad central warehousing. The firm's continuing expansion, both through individual division growth and a continuing program of acquisitions, points up the need to establish a total corporate warehousing system and policy, assuring all divisions of service with a minimum of duplication.

Airfreight's growing share of daily shipments

AIR FREIGHT looms large in Scovill's future planning. Today's volume is small but steady. In the opinion of Director of Traffic Rogers, however, substantial growth is inevitable if present rate trends continue.

"Surface rates are increasing at a faster pace than the charges for air cargo," notes Mr. Rogers. "Under these circumstances, the time is coming steadily closer when prudence will dictate air movement on the basis of decreased warehousing that its greater speed makes possible. We see significant cost-cutting opportunities also in the reduction of inventory maintenance expenses and the time-value of money now tied up in such goods as well as goods-in-transit."

At existing rate levels, some air movement is already a routine' shipping procedure. "Standard air freight accounts for about six shipments a day from Waterbury," states Assistant Director Morrison. "Total daily weight currently runs from 50 to 500 pounds by this mode, and it is growing.

In addition to air freight, on which Scovill makes its own air bills, there is significant air movement in and out by other means. Wings and Wheels as well as the Air Express Division of REA make pickups and deliveries at Scovill regularly, as do various other air forwarders and services.

Air freight destined to or from Scovill at Waterbury moves through Bradley Field, the Hartford-Springfield international airport. Surface handling is performed for the various airlines from this point by Fournier Express, which provides a regular daily service.

The air volume comes from a number of sources. A highly diversified manufacturer, Scovill does a substantial business with the automotive industry, notably in the manufacture of formed metal parts. Such items as dashboards, for example, come forth in a great variety for numerous models of automobiles. Changed models, new or added types and revisions in existing models need to be checked prior to mass production, so samples flow back to the ordering companies. These and other comparable items go by air.

Various parts and fittings for use in the maintenance of existing equipment also take to the air, thus reducing the need for field warehousing of a great variety of materials for which demand at any one time would be minute. Inbound traffic runs somewhat parallel, including design samples and materials among other products.

While speed is a factor with much of this freight, it is nonetheless considered as routine, not exceptional, movement. "We do use air in various emergencies, of course," Mr. Morrison notes, "but emergency movements constitute the smaller part of our air shipments. The convenience factor looms large, however, particularly on the shipment of higher value merchandise in small quantities. Air shipment is an increasingly attractive element in answering the growing small shipment problem."

Scovill's steady expansion creates an internal role for air freight as well. Increasing occasions arise for between-plant transfers of items well suited to air freight.

How L&M Upgrades Distribution Through Centralized Control

In the intensely competitive field of tobacco products, Liggett & Myers maintains a tight grip on its distribution costs. As in the previously cited Noxell case, L&M brought together a diversity of functions that formerly operated in separate company sectors. Placed under the control of Roland C. Hendricks, a company veteran who had been director of the budget, the new department benefitted at once from the understanding of cost interrelationships engendered by Mr. Hendrick' prior experience. TRAFFIC MANAGEMENT's December, 1968 review depicts a uniquely flexible department operation geared to instill multiple skills in all staff members. In the short run, the flexibility benefits day-to-day operations considerably. Even greater values accrue from the resultant continuing upgrading of all distribution personnel in a field where external recruiting at any level is becoming continually more difficult.

TRAFFIC MANAGEMENT's Liggett & Myers case follows:

WITH ANNUAL SALES approaching the $600-million mark, Liggett & Myers has confronted the need to hold a tight rein on distribution costs incurred in moving its numerous brands of cigarettes and other tobacco products through one of the most competitive of consumer markets. Corporate management, seeking improved customer service and closer control of these costs, turned to centralized supervision in 1965. A department headed by Roland C. Hendricks, former director of the budget and now distribution manager, was assigned responsibility for four major elements at the Durham, N.C. headquarters three years ago. These include:

• Warehousing. Products flow from plant facilities to 65 public warehouses, carefully selected and closely supervised so that customers get fast delivery from fresh, quality-protected stocks.

• Order Billing. Largely computerized, this function coordinates closely with inventory control and traffic, minimizing paperwork while speeding goods and information flow.

• Traffic. Continuing development of specialized rates, revision of shipping patterns, packaging changes, pooling and consolidation programs hold L&M's freight cost line in the face of continuing inflationary pressures.

• Inventory Control. Closely-watched sales history, frequently adjusted, keeps stock investment at a minimum level but adequate to service customers quickly.

While these collective responsibilities indicate a typical modern operation, its staff is anything but conventional. Fluid is the word for L&M's distribution supervision. "Organization charts don't matter much when the team's members fully understand their department's total mission," states Mr. Hendricks. "Our people do a total job, not a string of separated specialties. Rate analysts

Warehouse shipment routings are reviewed by Distribution Manager R. C. Hendricks (far right) with (from left) Order Processing Supervisor Leroy Duke, Traffic Supervisor C. H. Gerling, Warehouse Supervisor Terence Mc-Cann and Inventory Supervisor Joseph Sommers.

tackle claims problems without any hesitation when need arises. The claims staff is quick to assist in rating or inventory control if those areas hit peaks. We are 50 flexible people aggressively determined to keep this a number one distribution department. We're moving freight efficiently and keeping inventories low. We take pride in today's efforts while seeking still better control for tomorrow."

This flexibility is reflected in both day-to-day operations and long-term assignments. Peak shipping days find the order processing staff helping to prepare shipping documents. At other times, traffic people jump in on the order processing action. No one gets concerned if someone must be absent from work. From top supervision down, every one gets enough experience to pull his weight on most of the department's jobs.

The longer view finds personnel moving between jobs at reasonable but regular intervals. Nobody stays in one spot long enough to go stale or get completely bored, yet neither are changes so frequent as to prevent development of maximum competence. Work loads are closely controlled to assure that, while slack time is minimal, harrassing duties or excessive individual responsibilities are also minimal.

Warehouse Supervisor Terence McCann

keeps a large field network tuned to distribution's requirements. The 65 public warehouses for which he is responsible assure deliveries to customers who maintain low inventories and stock competitive merchandise. "In this business," notes Mr. McCann, "back order is a synonym for lost sales. If a clerk tells the customer he's out of Chesterfields, that customer doesn't usually defer his purchase to the next day. He'll pick up a competitive brand instead. That's one reason field service means so much here. We watch costs closely, but getting the right product in good condition where the customer wants it, when he wants it is all important to us."

The plant at Durham, N.C., and Richmond, Va. serve as shipping warehouses giving same-day or next-day delivery to customers in their immediate areas. It is at the 65 public warehouses that most storage takes place, in a service system geared for same day, or at worst, next-day delivery to 5,000 customers at about 4,000 points throughout the states. This operation generates 8,000 to 10,000 bills of lading every week.

Public warehouse changes are infrequent. Sales territory realignments sometimes make them necessary, while an occasional change of warehouse ownership may adversely affect rate or service arrangements, thus re-

Inspection Report

DATE February 14, 1968

WAREHOUSE XYZ Warehouse Company   PERSON VISITING:

Anywhere, U.S.A.   Mr. Q. C. Black

RAIL SIDING: Southern Pacific

RATES: STORAGE & HANDLING .0001   MINIMUM .0003
        RECONDITIONING   .0002   MINIMUM .0004

ADT & SPRINKLER SYSTEM: Yes

TYPE OF CONSTRUCTION: Brick and concrete

WAREHOUSE INQUIRIES: REMARKS

BACK ORDERS & INVENTORY PROBLEMS	None None
MAIL DELIVERIES	Occasionally late
DAMAGED MERCHANDISE	Awaiting replacements
ADJUSTMENTS	No problems
CARRIER COMPLAINTS	None
ROTATION OF STOCK	Stock being rotated properly
STORAGE AREA & MERCHANDISE	Clean and neatly stacked
PACKING MATERIAL	Sufficient quantity on hand
TOBACCO ACCOUNTS	Three accounts
CONSOLIDATION PROGRAM	Yes, execellent coverage
ROUTINGS	Using carriers specified
TRANSMITTING ORDER	Teletype, TWX, and Telex
ORDER CUT-OFF TIME	12 Noon

PERSONNEL   Mr. A. B. Jones, President
                         Mr. D. E. Smith, Vice President
MANAGEMENT   Mr. G. H. Brown, General Manager
                         Mr. T. H. Green, Office Manager
HANDLING ACCOUNT   Mrs. Jane Doe, Clerk

COMMENTS: Our merchandise at this location was found to be in
good condition and all records were readily available and in
order. Mr. Jones, President, was instructed to caution his
Shipping Department in the handling of small shipments in order
that they be moved at the most reasonable cost consistent with
good service. It is to be noted that cigarettes and tobacco
products are stored in an area in which warehouse has installed
humidifiers in order to maintain a satisfactory moisture level
for the storage of tobacco products.

An actual copy of a recent L&M inspection report is shown above. Only the name and location of warehouse and personnel names have been changed.

quiring a shift.

How L&M Selects And Activates
Its Public Warehouses

In general, the decision to warehouse in an area will be based on competitive circumstances, customer service requirements and possibilities for distribution cost reductions. Then, the department will pick a specific location based on sales volume in the locality, carrier rates and services to the point chosen, and the effect of existing tax laws on stocked merchandise. Obviously, there must be one or more suitable public warehouses available for consideration.

Selecting and obtaining the specific facility involves several criteria. Single-story buildings with concrete floors and high ceilings get preference. Sprinkler and burglar alarm systems are a must. The management has to be reliable and their personnel clearly effective in their performance. A warehouse operating its own drayage services together with a good shipment consolidation program means much, as does an effective small-shipment recognition and handling system that holds down possible minimum-charge shipments outbound. Significantly, L&M prefers warehousing where competitive or similar products are also stored. This assures that handling requirements are already well understood and opens the door to customer delivery consolidations and other economies.

When a warehouse meets these conditions satisfactorily, the distribution staff checks out the firm's credit ratings and reviews its financial statement if possible. Assuming everything is in order, the parties negotiate a storage and handling rate on a 100-pound basis, the most practical for L&M's high volume and rapid turnover, minimizing paperwork for both parties. Once in accord upon a rate, the distribution department submits a written agreement for signature by both companies. This document, in addition to outlining rates and charges, defines liability of both parties and provides a broad outline of requirements for the proper handling of the L&M account.

After an agreement has been signed, activation follows promptly. Necessary forms go to the new warehouse, L&M people confer with warehouse management to initiate standard procedures, and a special "Instruction Guide for Public Warehouses," prepared by the L&M warehouse supervisory staff, is given to the warehouse management for their guidance. Thereafter, all affected L&M staff members in the company's various departments are notified on what date the new facility will go "on line," what the contract terms are, and any specific circumstances that are either unique or significant to this particular operation.

Clearly written and amply detailed, the Instruction Guide includes examples of all types of forms and letters regularly employed in servicing L&M's account by an individual public warehouse. A conscientious warehouseman of average intelligence should have no difficulty in following its instructions for any type of normal transaction or, in practice, many perhaps not-so-normal ones as well. It is in the exceptional case, after all, that a manual most often must prove its worth. The contents include these topics:

—Shipments to Warehouses. This section describes normal paper flow and goods movements from plants at Durham, Richmond and St. Louis, with instructions concerning protection in cases of delayed shipments.

—Reporting Loss or Damage. The manual instructs on the preparation of over, short and damage reports, inspection of shipments, and notification reports to the distribution department.

—Handling of Damaged Merchandise. This covers the handling and disposition of such goods under a variety of circumstances, as well as the related paperwork.

—Loss or Damage Caused by Negligence or Act of God. Such goods get somewhat different treatment than other defective merchandise under the L&M plan.

—Transmittal Report and Orders. Warehousemen are instructed on checking accuracy of these forms, which move forward from L&M immediately in advance of the actual shipments.

—Types of Orders. Broken down into eight categories, they are defined here and instructions given for correct processing.

—Transmittal Report Column Headings. This section details functions of the transmittal report beyond relationship with concurrent orders. This instrument provides both L&M's warehouse supervisory group and the individual warehouse with a running, up-to-date inventory.

—Monthly Inventory Report. Its preparation is described and the report is prepared by the public warehouse for L&M's use, providing a check against the running data from the transmittal reports.

—General Warehouse Procedures. Proper stock control, necessary protection from odoriferous goods, required humidity and other physical conditions, stock rotation requirements and related matters are covered here.

—General Office Procedures. This details normal clerical procedures needed to service the account, covering telephone order requirements, back ordering, cancellations, bills of lading and numerous other activities.

The manual includes just 18 pages of text plus possibly an equal number of forms and sample letters. Brief and clear, it makes a new warehouseman's initiation to L&M a straightforward matter.

"Picking a good warehouse and starting it off on the right track goes a long way toward avoiding problems," Mr. McCann observes, "but in a complex, competitive business, a little deviation from standards can give birth to a subsequent catastrophe if it isn't watched. Everyone of our public warehouses gets a regular visit by our staff, never less often than once yearly. New operations and key points get checked more frequently. If conditions turn up that don't meet standards, we report them, request correction and check again subsequently to be sure things are set right."

The 65 public warehouses handle such well-known cigarettes as Chesterfield, L&M and Lark, but most never see the company's specialized, slower-moving brands. With a flavor for every taste, many types move infrequently as small orders, a sure headache to a mass market-geared warehouse network. Restricting these stocks to eight central distribution points reduces manufacturing and inventory totals substantially. The savings more than offset minor freight cost increases.

The warehouse unit closely watches state and local taxes. Careful shipment scheduling, timed to keep taxable inventories at optimum levels, saves markedly on such taxes in many localities.

Recent packaging changes assist warehouse material handling considerably. Increasing shipping carton bursting strength

Stock stays only briefly at Durham. Carloads and truckloads depart in a steady stream to the firm's 65 field warehouses with fresh merchandise.

from 175 to 200 pounds per square inch, while reducing damage, also permits storage three pallets high without causing carton creasing from pressure in the lower tiers.

Important also are local climate conditions. Inventories cannot stay shelved too long where humidity is either inadequate or excessive. Stock rotation is significant because of this and is checked closely on warehouse visits.

Traffic — The Key Element

It is in traffic, however, where the new distribution department's payoff punch comes through most sharply. Formerly fragmented activities came together in one solid departmental section some three years back, creating a much-needed voice for carrier and industry dialogue. While certain distribution advocates appear to denigrate traffic's role somewhat, particularly in companies where it was once strongly emphasized, the L&M approach sees it as central to the distribution department's successful operation.

"Negotiating and refining rates coupled with pooling and consolidation programs, even if traffic did nothing else, should yield 5% to 7% annual savings on freight if the traffic manager does his job," comments Mr. Hendricks. "Too many companies still look at traffic as a necessary evil instead of as a positive, significant contributor to a healthy balance sheet."

Traffic's control is thorough. Inbound supplies are under its supervision as are out-bound finished products going to field warehouses and ultimate shipments moving from them to the distributors and retailers. Inbound control came in strong about six months ago, with the exception of tobacco moving from areas adjacent to plant facilities. Inroads are being made steadily here as well.

Some Inbound LTL Has Lead To Pooling And Consolidations

While much inbound freight is carload or truckload, there is heavy less-truckload movement from northeastern origins. Substantial savings arise here through pools and consolidations assembled at New York.

A case in point is aluminum foil, which formerly moved LTL from New York. Traffic worked out plans with the shipper to combine L&M's prepaid shipment with another firm's, stopping off en route at the latter's receiving point for partial unloading. By thus creating a truckload out of two former LTL shipments, all three parties have benefitted while giving the carrier a saving in reduced handling and paperwork as well. Studies have been completed to pool-truck raw materials into respective factories. This will save considerable freight expense for both shippers and L&M.

Consolidation programs prove particularly attractive outbound, however. Movements to warehouses usually are quantity loads, but beyond-warehouse movement is predominantly small shipments. Of the 65 public

Clearing its load, an Overnite Transportation Co. truck leaves while other trailers load. At adjacent platform, rail cars take on freight.

Warehouse Supervisor Terence McCann, center, meets with his assistant, John Van Roy, left, and Service Coordinator Robert Johnson to discuss proposed revisions of the firm's warehouse manual.

warehouses, eight have thus far established consolidation programs of major scale. The department wants to move fast and hard here, because the present eight demonstrate clearly that significant freight savings can be expected wherever consolidation programs go in. A department team is slated to visit other warehouses and sell them the consolidation idea.

Freight savings aren't the only consideration. Consolidation can mean "moving warehouses" that reduce or eliminate inventory-consuming stationary facilities for some regions. "Some competitors maintain storage in the Camden, N.J. area and ship LTL into the Washington-Baltimore area out of Richmond. L&M feeds this region via Washington-Baltimore-Philadelphia pool trucks from Richmond. This handling produces savings under LTL commodity rates that competitors now pay and eliminates warehouse expense," says Mr. Hendricks. "The customers get overnight delivery, easily matching what performance would be from a Camden warehouse."

In addition to consolidation developments, many other rate projects get departmental attention. One current major program is incentive loading. Because the company makes larger-than-average shipments regularly, it seeks to gain recognition for the good density and high equipment utilization that handling carriers enjoy. In lieu of typical 20,000-to-25,000-pound minimum loads, the rate group would like to negotiate lower rates based on minimums in the 35,000-to-40,000-pound range. There are already some commodity rates to New Jersey, Massachusetts, Maine and Ohio points as high as 33,000 pounds, plus some in the Southern Motor Carrier territory set at 35,000 pounds.

The many small shipments L&M moves go largely by United Parcel Service or parcel post. "Where UPS has rights, we much prefer it," states Traffic Supervisor Clarence H. Gerling."We find UPS particularly important on special and promotional sales to small customers served directly from Durham. They mean a lot, also, to our slow-moving brands. These go in LTL volume for the most part, with many minimum-size shipments."

As with most big shippers, containers and piggyback plans enter L&M's activites. Piggyback, however, dropped off considerably when rail "per car" rates became effective. The Southern, Norfolk & Western and Durham & Southern railroads move substantial volumes on these rates but Plan II piggyback still serves Birmingham occasionally as rates and schedules compete effectively with trucks. "At one time, Plan III figured heavily to several points, but it generated substantial

Forklifts and pallet trucks shift stock into cushion underframe boxcars while a company truck loads at platform.

claims problems," Claim Supervisor J. D. Wells observes.

One-Fourth Of Richmond Plant's Exports Shipped In Containers

Containerization, contrarily, figures heavily in L&M exports. The Richmond plant runs out 25% of its export shipments in containers, much of it going through Hampton Roads ports and via Sea-Land from Baltimore to Puerto Rico.

The Traffic Group recently recommended shifting two-thirds of exports formerly moving through New York to Hampton Roads, Va. This resulted in a savings on inland charges. Rate Analysts Bill Beard, George Outlaw and Harvey King feel certain that still further economies will be found in this shipping sector.

Carrier service gets continual close scrutiny. Car and truck reports covering every volume shipment come in daily, with multiple reports expected on "hot" cars. This procedure developed substantial schedule accuracy and reliability gains. When carriers don't make their time, they get called on to explain why. The reports come in by wire and phone. Pickup carriers alert the beyond carriers that such reports are expected.

Among his widely varied duties, Service Coordinator Robert Johnson rides herd on car reports, maintaining a list of bills of lading shipped daily for cross-checking carrier reports on a day-by-day, hour-by-hour basis. This data, summarized weekly in a routing book, provides a continuous performance record. These records quickly reveal the true performance of routes and carriers, helping considerably in rail-truck choice decisions and in rail routings.

Distribution Manager Hendricks brings his budget background to bear on freight cost measurement. Budgeted in cents per 1,000 cigarettes, these costs are measured by individual warehouse. A closely controlled annual budget, adjusted quarterly, gets further adjustments when major changes make them significant. "We're looking for considerable improvement through warehousing and consolidation savings with our acquired subsidiaries," Mr. Hendricks states. "One of these is joining our programs soon and others suggest mutually advantageous possibilities as well."

Inventory — The Physical Distribution Approach

More than any other single activity, inventory control made major gains when L&M

Reviewing an active first year's accomplishments at Liggett & Myers' new centralized Durham operations facility are Controller R. Haywood Hosea, left, and Roland C. Hendricks, distribution manager.

centralized its distribution. Drastic inventory reductions became possible soon after, promptly benefitting the balance sheet. Continuing systems refinements and service innovations made by Supervisor Joseph Sommers and his staff yielded still further improvements and promise more ahead. As yet, inventory control is fully computerized only to the plant warehouse door. Partial computerization in distribution department inventory control, however, speeds existing clerical procedures and a complete computer inventory system will be installed within another year. The big problem lies in revenue reporting to meet tax requirements.

At present, computer assistance is reflected in the Duration Report, also called the Stock Status Report. It derives from the company's pre-billing system, which produces bills of lading and invoices two days in advance of anticipated deliveries, permitting the closest match possible of goods and invoice receipts. The Duration Report is a by-product of the system and indicates the number of days' stock in the warehouses based on prior inventory modified by current sales.

Inventory planning bases on the prior four weeks' sales history modified by relevant holidays or anticipated special sales programs. Local climatic effect on stock and transit times affects inventory levels in varying degree, but the department generally maintains the following stock levels regionally:

East—Up to 10 days' stock on hand and in transit

Midwest—10 to 15 days' stock on hand and in transit

Far West—15 to 20 days' stock on hand and in transit

Stock levels set by the department cover over 100 brands of cigarettes as well as incidental smoking tobacco, chewing tobacco and miscellaneous commodities. At the company plants (Durham, Richmond, and St. Louis), very small inventory stays on hand. At least 85% of cigarettes, in particular, ship out within the day they come off the production line.

Looking ahead, Distribution Manager Hendricks envisions expanded computer employment, not only in line functions such as inventory control but in numerous management science applications that will speed planning and explore new alternatives. Installed at the company's spacious new operations center only since Oct. 1967, the two IBM 360-30 computers handle steadily increasing workloads, planning toward a total management information system that will greatly widen computer service horizons for physical distribution.

Computer coordinated order processing

The computer's emergence at L&M lends increasing support to physical distribution. A system employing three IBM 1401 units around the country gave way last year to centralized service at the company's Durham operations center employing two IBM 360-30 systems. Major order processing elements move through it in addition to numerous other company data functions.

Orders come in to Durham by mail, telegraph and telephone. The department has its own special post office box number to speed mail order handling. On receipt, clerks spread orders to individual state shelves. They are then reviewed and edited to batch quantities by standard L&M shipping case sizes. At this point, any emergency orders are telephoned direct to the affected ware-

houses, assuring prompt movement of goods to avoid stockouts at the consumer level.

Regular orders are numbered with the customer code. Operators then punch cards from these orders, entering six brands on each card while concurrently making a tape on an NCR machine. Subsequently verified as to customer, brands and quantities, batched tapes and cards proceed to the computer room.

Under normal conditions, computer material is ready at 11 a.m. each day. An hour and a half later, the computer cranks out the requisite bills of lading, invoices and transmittal reports. At 12:30 p.m., therefore, the order processing group commences its final check of billing against the transmittal reports. Checked and approved invoices are in the mail the same day.

Direct orders get the above treatment, but there are also many customers who have standing orders. Accounting for about 40% of total orders, these move somewhat differently. Data concerning them is in computer tape storage, scheduled for processing at the customers' required intervals. Each working day the necessary tapes are drawn and processed together with the day's direct orders so that both direct and standing order paper flows forth for final clerical checking and forwarding at the same time.

"Standing orders cut our work load considerably," notes Order Processing Supervisor Leroy Duke, "but we do have a problem with customers who make frequent changes in their orders. This necessitates considerable effort both in our section and the computer room to keep stored data current. On balance, though, it is more than offset by savings in direct order processing."

Emergency orders, of course, move in somewhat different channels. A six-clerk group processes these, notifying the affected warehouses promptly and ensuring that related paper goes through the system smoothly and rapidly. Once the day's emergencies are cleared, this group joins the rest of the staff in normal order-processing activites.

The credit department is not under Distribution's control but coordinates closely with the order processing group. They occupy adjacent floor space in the new operations center building, facilitating quick personal contact and sharing files needed by both.

New Style Distribution Serves a Textile Manufacturer

The William F. Carter Company, though a recent arrival in the field of integrated physical distribution management, has made rapid progress. Its product line and physical facilities differ markedly from those of the Noxell Company, but Carter's heavy reliance on computer programs is markedly similar. Like many other companies, it has converted its warehouses to modern distribution centers that make effective use of specialized handling systems. Unlike most companies, however, it is product, not geography, that determines center establishment. Like Blue Bell, the Carter company requires considerable interplant transportation over wide areas and operates a private fleet for much of this activity.

A review of this company's logistics activities as reported in the December, 1970 TRAFFIC MANAGEMENT, follows:

NEW distribution methods find favor with an old New England firm. The William Carter Company, a fourth-generation manufacturer of underwear for the family and infant apparel, feeds nationwide markets from its plants in Massachusetts and the Southern states. Currently grossing over $50 million annually, recent distribution betterments yield not only service and financial benefits, but assure further gains as the company continues its expansion.

Total logistics management here dates from 1968, when Distribution Manager Roy E. Schorer and Traffic Manager James P. Piepgrass assumed their current responsibilities. Ably supported by a computer network with substantial capacity, their operations encompass new and revised systems that keep inventories low and move goods fast. The major elements at this time include:

Automated order processing and inventory control: Specialized program regularly produces a 40% increase in the allocation of available stock to current orders over prior performance.

Distribution center order processing: Needham Heights, Mass. and Barnesville, Ga. facilities are product-oriented rather than area-oriented, with modern packaging and handling systems as well as improved transportation patterns that amply justify their establishment.

Mixed common and private carriage: Primarily common carriage in market service, but 80% company truck on interplant and plant distribution center services, the company fleet is believed to offer important time and reliability benefits as a virtual production-line extension.

Automated data processing has had a long history at Carter. Starting out with punched-card equipment in the 1920s, the company installed a Univac File Computer in 1958, programing a basic stock allocation/prebilling system and a production control system for this first-generation equipment. By 1965, increased sales volume and management information requirements needed greater capacity. These led to additions and changes resulting in today's configuration, which includes Honeywell H-1200 and H-125 computers at the Needham Heights headquarters plus an H-120 at the Barnesville, Ga. facility.

Orders, largely by mail, a few by telephone, enter the computer system on punched cards. Thereafter, magnetic tape, augmented by a direct access drum, takes over the work.

Employing a method termed "resolution programing," the automatic stock allocation/prebilling system allocates the maximum available stock to customer orders consistent with 120 different constraints established by management. It selects orders by priority and calculates work required to fill each order, reviewing weekly up to 30,000 future and current orders containing approximately 1,500,000 individual items.

Insuring proper order rotation, the computer upgrades each order's priority value regularly until it is fulfilled. With many advance or seasonal orders filed, programing can handle up to 30,000 such units at a time. It checks items on these orders in terms of long-range availability and can substitute or cancel in cases where it becomes appropriate.

The computer completely edits each order and prints an edit listing, showing garment sizes individually. On valid orders, it updates sales statistics, allocates stock and prepares a prebilled invoice and related shipping papers, with invoice items in picking sequence.

A certain healthy lack of the orthodox typifies this computer operation. Where most computer people shudder at the thought of using high-priced electronic equipment for simple printing press work, Data Processing Manager Ralph H. Harber does just that twice annually.

"We found," he notes, "that we could print a few thousand specialized style-color-size order forms twice yearly in lots of a few thousand at a direct saving of $8,000 per year. Small volume printing costs run high, and with the computer, there is the added indirect benefit of an ability to make last-minute changes or even in-season revisions."

These orders employ regular three-part tab paper in a snap-out form. The salesmen use them exactly the same as a standard printed Carter order blank. A further assist to this project: Only routine utility computer programing was used, so no expense was generated for programing whatever.

The newest computer area is traffic. In partial use at present, computerized routing is expected to be nationwide by the spring of 1971. The procedure breaks orders to three weight brackets, assigning specific carriers to customers based on a code, a three-position-type derived from the zip code with a single character alphabetic modifier. In operation, routings will be stored on the computer drum with permanent storage on magnetic tape.

2

4

3

A CUSTOM-ASSEMBLED packaging line at Needham Heights finds an operator placing precounted garments on a moving belt for packaging (1). Directly to her left, a unit opens plastic bags with an air blast (2), while garments feed in from the belt, dropping the units on another line for the next step. Bags then proceed through two steps in motion (3) in which one machine heat-seals the open bag ends and an immediately following device imprints size information on each bag as it passes. At line's end (4), another operator places bags in shipping boxes which are then imprinted with content information on a small press.

Looking ahead, Manager Administrative Services Edward C. Marzo foresees the use of simulation and other operations research techniques in future distribution center development. "We're already developing this in manufacturing areas, and our growing data base makes it highly suitable for this purpose as well," he states.

Product-Oriented DCs

Preceded by extensive studies, the Carter Co. opened a second major distribution center in the spring of 1968. Needham Heights, Mass. processes orders for underwear and layette items, with Barnesville, Ga. handling sleepwear and outer apparel.

At both locations, folded goods arrive from the plant complex and are packaged using modern equipment in configurations developed by the company's industrial engineering unit.

A typical operation, pant and shirt packing, finds a girl distributing goods for input to the packaging unit. A feeder girl inserts the garments in a predetermined multiple (one, two or three) into the machinery feed. In the first operation, an air jet opens a plastic bag and a pusher arm pushes the goods in. The pack then moves along to be hot-wheel-sealed, machine-priced and, at the end of the belt, placed in a box which a girl imprints on a small press with style-color-size data, finally loading the boxes on hand trucks.

The new Georgia facility represents a departure from prior Carter warehousing. "We got away from low, multistory buildings and went to high-cube storage with about 26-foot ceiling heights," Mr. Schorer observes.

Custom-designed or custom-configured racks serve the 6 to 10-week stock on hand. At Needham Heights, Rapistan Gravity Flow Racks with flanged wheels handle some 60% of the goods. Barnesville, however, has custom-designed gravity racks of a small, 30-inch-square pallet type. At both locations, bulk storage is in standard racks, which feed in turn to gravity racks for order assembly, other than for very large, single-commodity picking. Lewis Sheppard Order Master lift trucks, which handle much stock movement at Barnesville, are all radio-equipped. These trucks can thus

OVERHEAD MONORAILS permit speedy movement of trolleys carrying garments on hangers through warehouse areas, simplifying shipment sortation and assembly.

call the office for a location change if they find an initially assigned stock space already loaded.

At the other end of the operation, conveyor systems handle most material from the final packing stations to the shipping floor. Separate lines handle LTL traffic and REA-UPS-Parcel Post packages.

An assist for the customer, as well as for Carter, lies in an automated tab card reordering system. Each box of a specific item leaving a distribution center contains a reorder card, which the store returns following the last item's sale or removal from

PLANS FOR INTEGRATION of automated routing into a total order processing, inventory control, shipping procedure are discussed by (left to right): Distribution Manager Roy E. Schorer, Data Processing Manager Ralph H. Harber, Traffic Manager James P. Piepgrass and Manager Administrative Services Edward C. Marzo.

COMPUTER DEPARTMENT Operations Manager Victor Bonaceto (left) reviews work schedules in the computer facility.

stock, sending it back for a refill. This assures prompt order cycle activation and means, in effect, that Carter is maintaining the customer's inventory for him.

Actual orders break down into two types "at once" and "seasonal." The first type get stock-allocated the same evening received, distribution centers shipping the available goods immediately and back-ordering the rest. Other orders are seasonal with specific dated deadlines. These latter give the distribution centers an opportunity to smooth the work pattern. When time is available, the staff prepacks advanced orders and holds them in separate storage against the preselected shipping dates.

"We've designed our facilities for optimum efficiency at specified capacities," Mr. Schorer asserts. "Continued expansion of the Carter business will inevitably lead to additional distribution centers. At a certain point, adding capacity to a center tends to increase unit costs of operation, so business growth makes ultimate consideration of other centers a must."

Building Savings via Traffic

Traffic control, formerly managed at the local or regional level, became centralized at Needham Heights in early 1968. Primarily a staff function, it also has the line responsibility for private fleet operation. An intermill traffic coordinator, reporting directly to the traffic manager, is located at the Barnesville facility.

JOHN M. COX, private carriage coordinator, keeps his planning a full four weeks ahead through a handy magnetic wall chart, which shows where equipment is located, where it is needed and where load potential exists.

A SEPARATE, CONVEYOR-EQUIPPED shipping area speeds handling of UPS-REA-Parcel Post shipments at Carter's Needham Heights facility.

Small shipments prevail in Carter customer service. Of these, 60% move LTL with the remainder UPS-Parcel Post-REA. In the latter area, the traffic department instituted consolidations which include 3,000 to 4,000 pounds weekly moved from each of the major distribution centers as bulk shipments to Los Angeles and San Francisco for fan out west of the Rocky Mountains. "The savings over direct Parcel Post exceed 25%," claims Mr. Piepgrass.

In general, the department minimizes the number of carriers it employs. While following customer routing requests, it will seek to modify these when a non-Carter carrier is named, suggesting selection from a group of alternates, but complying with the initial request if the customer prefers not to change. This procedure minimizes the total number of carriers with resultant benefits in dock efficiency and customer service.

The private truck operations maintained by the company were established primarily to provide service between the company's facilities. The control function was uppermost among management considerations in establishing this service. In operations between the New England area and

THE COMPANY TRUCK shown at right shares dock space with several common carrier vehicles at Carter's Needham Heights distribution center.

the Southern mills, time savings on individual movements run as high as 10 days, while schedule regularity, fully as important as actual speed, has been materially enhanced. Though control was the basic motivator in this development, the private carriage program generates considerable direct savings in freight costs as well.

The total distribution concept is now the way of life at Carter. More than new equipment and procedures,

it represents rather the matching and meshing of these tools in a manner calculated to optimize customer service under controlled cost conditions. The successful blending of computerized inventory controls, innovative packaging and custom-tailored transportation can be expected to develop a still finer competitive edge as recently developed methods become further refined and carefully planned new procedures and facilities come into use.

CHAPTER II

Logistics in the Giant Companies

The sheer volume of business in America's largest companies necessarily assures greater-than-average attention to logistics costs. Contrary to the accusations of excessive conservatism frequently flung at the giants, TRAFFIC MANAGEMENT studies find several of them in the forefront of distribution management development. Heavy reliance on the computer, substantial employment of operations research techniques and much concentration on personnel development and advancement characterize many of these organizations.

The Eastman Kodak Company, a true pioneer in physical distribution management, must also operate one of the largest distribution departments in private industry. With over 2,800 employees, its responsibilities embrace virtually every category that the most utopian distribution theorists could wish for.

It is not sheer size, however, that makes Eastman Kodak's distribution notable. Far more important is its directed, measured control from mine pit or farm to consumer, world-wide. A major TRAFFIC MANAGEMENT study in November, 1971, presented herewith, describes the company's remarkable facilities as well as the physical distribution department's multitude of duties, many of them unusual:

Eastman Kodak Company

MOST concerns consider themselves veterans if their physical distribution departments date back 10 years. Eastman Kodak, America's 27th largest private firm in sales (according to the *Fortune* 500 annual survey) recognized this management discipline's potential long before that, establishing an initial distribution center and setting up a corporate organization in 1949.

"Our management foresaw growing activity in world as well as domestic markets," states Vice President-Distribution Robert E. Schellberg. "They decided that service had to match product quality under anticipated conditions and that gave us a head start in logistics development."

Sales of $1,153,500,000 in 1960 soared to $2,784,600,000 in 1970, illustrating an increasing market activity that requires continued expansion of distribution effort.

Virtually every duty generally associated with business logistics lies within the scope of the Eastman Kodak distribution division, including many that have only recently been generally recognized elsewhere.

PRESIDENT Gerald B. Zornow (right) of Eastman Kodak Company reviews a recently instituted international modular inventory program with Vice President Distribution Robert E. Schellberg.

Its functions include at least a few not commonly associated with physical distribution, but company experience proves that these assignments are effective and logical.

The day-to-day photographic product flow is illustrated in Chart One, showing movement of Rochester-manufactured products through the major distribution center in that headquarters city. Opening of another such center in Windsor, Colo. will provide similar support to the new manufacturing facilities at that location. In addition to photographic materials, the company manufactures and markets a widening number of organic chemicals, vitamin compounds and other products, primarily distributed within the same distribution systems.

Kodak's definition of physical distribution is refreshingly brief. **"We view it as the science of professional product management,"** states President Gerald B. Zornow. **"This is complete management of the product from the first estimate of sales to delivery to the customer."**

His view reflects clearly in a management organization of exceptional breadth. Chart Two shows Mr. Schellberg's management team, each member heading a substantial department or facility of his own. Greater than usual emphasis on short and long-range planning, as well as close coordination with manufacturing and marketing divisions, sets the structure's tone.

Initial steps in building up "The Big D," as the distribution division is known at Kodak, entailed control of the physical handling of the product after leaving the production lines, as well as total control of finished inventory throughout the world. Added scope came from the assignment of sales estimating and production planning responsibilities to the new department.

"Prior to 1949," notes Mr. Schellberg, "we had three separate estimates of sales in use: one was generated by the marketing and sales group; one was made by the factory, and there was one in between that was supposed to be the management estimate. **We replaced them with a single estimate, prepared within the distribution department under the guidance of a sales estimating council."**

This council, chaired by Mr. Schellberg, includes management, marketing, manufacturing and distribution representatives. Individual distribution, factory and marketing people meet weekly to review every facet of the estimates, while meetings of sales estimating subcommittees representing the five marketing divisions occur monthly. Twice each year, a major committee meeting reviews both five-year and long-range estimates.

Given sales estimates, the distribution division had the tools at hand for planning production in conjunction with the manufacturing and marketing divisions. Conflicts found in many firms between marketing and manufacturing forecasting concepts can't get off the ground at Kodak.

Warehousing then came into the distribution orbit, followed by order processing and customer service. Ultimately, virtually all field marketing activities that were not directly sales-oriented became distribution duties, including the management of field properties and the provision of supporting clerical and secretarial staffs for the marketing professionals.

With the building of such a logistics structure, it was clearly apparent that the traffic department was essential to this "family," and it, too, joined the group. Overseeing broadly diversified modal services, it plays an important role in the expanding import-export trade on which this firm places heavy emphasis.

Though its organization chart suggests primarily the division's role in the United States, there is a considerable responsibility overseas as well. Dotted line relationships exist between the distribution division at Rochester and the various "Kodak Houses" in other countries. Managers of these houses report to the international photographic division, the distribution division maintaining its dotted line relationship on systems development and assisting them in the development of facilities.

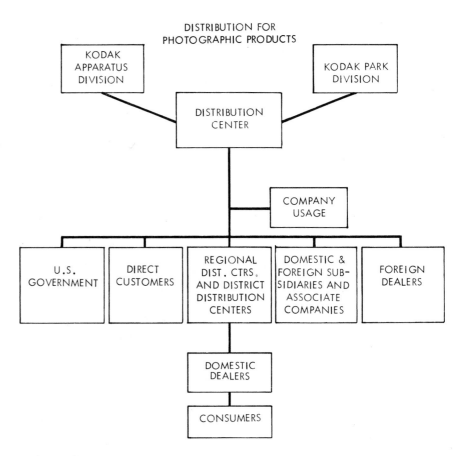

CHART ONE—Above is shown the distribution channels for movement of Eastman Kodak photographic products emanating from Rochester, N.Y.

CHART TWO—The Eastman Kodak distribution division's organization chart reveals a diversity of responsibilities among the seven management teams reporting to Vice President Robert E. Schellberg.

```
                          GENERAL MANAGER
                        DISTRIBUTION DIVISION
                    R.E. SCHELLBERG  VICE-PRESIDENT

   DIRECTOR          DIRECTOR          MANAGER          MANAGER
  MARKETING &         STAFF           ESTIMATING &      FIELD OPERATIONS
DISTRIBUTION FACILITIES SERVICES      PLANNING
  R. G. VAN DUYNE   D. M. KLADSTRUP   R. L. KOEHLINGER  G. A. SNYDER

            GENERAL TRAFFIC      MANAGER              MANAGER
               MANAGER        DISTRIBUTION CENTER  DISTRIBUTION CENTER
                                 ROCHESTER            WINDSOR
            K. H. JAMIESON     G. E. YEOMANS        W. E. HALLOWELL
```

CHART THREE—Specific duties of Eastman Kodak Company's distribution division are spelled out in this table of responsibilities.

DISTRIBUTION ORGANIZATION RESPONSIBILITIES

1. Estimate sales.
2. Schedule production.
3. Control inventory
4. Coordinate world-wide distribution.
5. Warehouse and handle product.
6. Handle and account for returned goods.
7. Warehouse and distribute advertising materials.
8. Account for production, inventory, shipments.
9. Develop business systems.
10. Provide transportation for product and people.
11. Develop facilities for marketing and distribution requirements outside Rochester.
12. Direct distribution operations in the Regional and District Marketing and Distribution Centers.

GATHERED INFORMALLY before a recent distribution division staff meeting are (left to right): W. Elmer Hallowell, manager of the new Windsor, Colo. distribution center; Kenneth H. Jamieson, general traffic manager; George A. Snyder, field operations manager; George E. Yeomans, manager of the Rochester distribution center; Donald M. Kladstrup, director of staff services, and Robert G. Van Duyne, director of marketing and distribution facilities.

Estimating procedures, established at Rochester, now apply in foreign countries as well. London, for example, has its own sales estimating council covering its internal British market. Their exports are controlled, however, from Rochester by the photographic resources committee, encompassing top management, distribution division representation, international division and factory representatives. In this way, worldwide planning assures proper market service while maintaining total production and distribution efficiency.

"Total distribution seems to be the term that is currently accepted," Mr. Schellberg observes, "but I feel that the better term, though not yet in common usage, is logistics. There are other terms for essentially this same thing, of course, and at least 10 colleges have majors in this area, whether they are called physical distribution, materials management or logistics."

Chart Three illustrates the responsibilities now assigned to the division. With some duties spread among several departments, while others are more specialized, close cooperation and continual liaison are a divisional hallmark within the organization, as well as in its relationships with other segments of Kodak. A significant part of the corporate management structure, the division is an important underlying factor in building competitive strength throughout the world as well as in the U.S. market.

"When mother goes to the store to buy film for a birthday party this afternoon," observes Mr. Schellberg, "she'll be looking for that familiar yellow box. If it isn't there, she won't wait until tomorrow, and a sale is lost. So we aim to make sure it is there. **Our company rightfully prides itself on its dependable product. Our division prides itself on keeping that product available to our customers where and when it's wanted.**"

The addition of further major functions to the division is not now anticipated. Instead of seeking or accepting new tasks, management currently looks instead to the continuing expansion and refinement of the duties it now has. Operating more than 40 distribution centers of three types within the United States, pro-

viding statistical and research support for marketing and manufacturing as well as top management and overseas operations, controlling worldwide product flow, "The Big D" sees its next phase as the refinement of an existing structure. Advanced computer applications already employed will be augmented by still newer procedures and hardware, easing management control and speeding response of divisional units to changing conditions, whether within the company structure or out in the marketplace.

On the ensuing pages, many of the present and anticipated ideas that give this firm's distribution organization its outstanding character receive attention.

Sales estimating and production planning

IN RECENT TIME, much attention has been given in distribution or logistics circles to what is termed the "materials management concept." Under this philosophy, a number of companies have recently commenced to perform volume estimating and production planning activities within the physical distribution, logistics or materials management sector of their organizations. Eastman Kodak's distribution division, however, has performed these functions since its inception following World War II. Estimating and planning were among the initial functions placed under the distribution umbrella when the division was founded.

Prior to this organizational development, there had been separate estimates prepared by manufacturing and marketing, with yet a third representing overall management as a sort of compromise approach. Centralizing estimating and planning responsibility in a single division within the distribution organization, therefore, produced a consistency of data valuable to all management user groups, while relieving other departments of this work load. The estimating and planning division's overall assignment today includes the following responsibilities:

• Propose and coordinate preparation of quantity sales estimates.

• Plan a "normal" stock of finished products in keeping with seasonal sales and production schedules.
• Schedule transfers of finished production.
• Control inventories of finished products.
• Coordinate worldwide sales estimates and sources of supply.

"The quantity sales estimates for which we are responsible fulfill many purposes in the Eastman Kodak Company," states Manager-Estimating and Planning Roger L. Koehlinger. **"They are used for expenditure purposes, for new product development, for inventory plans and for production schedules among others.** We build the quantity estimates and then these offshoots come forth. A dollar estimate, for instance, is nothing more than a quantity estimate priced out at the prices for which the affected goods will be sold. Accordingly, the dollar estimate must necessarily be consistent with the quantity estimate.

"When we refer to coordinating our estimates, we mean literally drawing on all the resources that we can in the Eastman Kodak Company to establish proper estimates and, once established, to measure our components against these estimates and to propose revisions in them individually when we believe they are necessary."

Many information sources

Information from the widest possible variety of sources is continually evaluated by the division in terms both of the effect on the total sales picture and on individual products or product lines. Direct personal contact with marketing and manufacturing staff members is a continuing source of information, as is a steady flow of information from field distribution people. Vital to the estimating activity is the heavy data input arising from existing systems of reporting activity, including daily and weekly orders and orders by types of product. Salesmen's comments coming in every month, reports from biweekly marketing meetings in consumer products and other such sources also contain data or significant information to the division.

A recent example of how the division watches a product's progress

EASTMAN KODAK COMPANY - PERIOD SALES COMPARISON REPORT
MARKETS DIVISION
Domestic (Incl. Gov't.) Sales

Report #DC-520

	Period 9, 1971 (Terms: Units)					Year-to-Date Through Period 9, 1971 (Terms: Units)					1971 Estimate (Terms: Units)				
	1971 Actual	1971 Estimate	Act/Est %	1970 Actual	% Chg. 71/70	1971 Actual	1971 Estimate	Act/Est %	1970 Actual	% Chg. 71/70	1970 Actual	Estimate Original	Estimate Current	Est/70	Date Of Est.
TOTAL PRODUCT GROUP	19.9	20.0	0%	20.5	- 3%	141.7	144.9	- 2%	145.8	- 3%	208.0	212.0	209.0	0%	1&9/71
SUMMARY															
Group A	3.6	3.7	- 3%	4.2	-14%	25.8	24.7	+ 4%	29.3	-12%	40.5	32.7	35.4	-13%	1&9/71
" B	5.5	5.5	0%	5.1	+ 8%	41.3	41.6	- 1%	39.0	+ 6%	54.5	59.3		+ 9%	1/71
" C	10.8	10.8	0%	11.2	- 4%	74.6	78.6	- 5%	77.5	- 4%	113.0	120.0	114.3	+ 1%	1&9/71
PRODUCT A															
Sub A-1	1.1	1.3	-15%	1.3	-15%	8.5	8.7	- 2%	10.5	-19%	15.0	11.3	12.4	-17%	9/71
" A-2	2.3	2.2	+ 5%	2.7	-15%	16.1	14.8	+ 9%	17.5	- 8%	23.5	19.7	21.3	- 9%	9/71
" A-3	.2	.2	0%	.2	0%	1.2	1.2	0%	1.3	- 8%	2.0	1.7		-15%	1/71
PRODUCT B															
Sub B-1	1.2	1.3	- 8%	1.0	+20%	11.6	12.0	- 3%	11.1	+ 5%	15.9	17.5		+10%	1/71
" B-2	1.2	1.2	0%	1.1	+ 9%	8.8	9.0	- 2%	7.8	+13%	11.3	13.3		+18%	1/71
" B-3	2.2	2.1	+ 7%	2.1	- 1%	13.8	13.4	+ 3%	13.5	+ 2%	17.9	18.1		+ 1%	1/71
" B-4	.9	.9	0%	.9	0%	7.1	7.2	- 1%	6.6	+ 8%	9.4	10.4		+11%	1/71
PRODUCT C															
Sub C-1	.7	.7	0%	.8	-12%	5.5	5.5	0%	6.9	-20%	9.5	8.7	7.8	-18%	9/71
" C-2	8.6	8.6	0%	8.9	- 3%	59.0	62.9	- 6%	60.3	- 2%	89.2	96.2	92.0	+ 3%	9/71
" C-2a	(5.0)	(4.9)	+ 2%	(5.4)	- 7%	(36.0)	(39.7)	- 9%	(38.5)	- 6%	(58.1)	(59.7)	(58.0)	- 1%	5/71
" C-2b	(3.6)	(3.7)	- 3%	(3.5)	+ 3%	(23.0)	(23.2)	- 1%	(21.8)	+ 6%	(31.1)	(36.5)	(34.0)	+ 9%	9/71
" C-3	1.2	1.2	0%	1.2	0%	8.0	8.0	0%	8.1	- 1%	11.3	12.0	11.4	+ 1%	9/71
" C-4	.3	.3	0%	.3	0%	2.1	2.2	- 5%	2.2	- 5%	3.0	3.1		+ 3%	9/71

MANY FORMS represent the efforts of estimating and planning personnel, but this period sales comparison report is the most universally employed, each one providing present and anticipated performance data on a variety of products.

ROGER L. KOEHLINGER (left), manager, estimating and planning department, reviews 1971 film sales estimates with Donald Brown, manager, film planning.

was demonstrated at a meeting with the consumer markets management, reviewing activity of a recent model camera. Mr. Koehlinger observes:

"We were able to give them a lot of new information about what was happening in their market. They expected us to, because we have taken all of the data that is constantly flowing in here and placed it under continuing analysis. We told them how many dealers had ordered this specific camera, as well as how many of these dealers have placed a first reorder for it. We told them as well the size of the first reorders and, additionally, how many dealers placed a second reorder and what the average size of that was. We then compared this performance against another product introduced two or three years ago at the same time, because seasonality is a factor, and indicated what reception that prior product had received. We then assessed in our own minds the external factors that could be affecting both of these sets of numbers to draw a conclusion, which was that this new camera is being received better in the marketplace and by the customers. In this instance, all of our conclusions were based upon internal data, without any input from salesmen or other personal sources."

Sales comparison report

A basic document to the division's operation is the period sales comparison report, a period at Eastman Kodak consisting of four consecutive weeks, with a total of 13 periods each year. This report reaches all appropriate marketing and key manufacturing people, covering the innumerable products for which the division makes specific individual estimates. A simulated page of this report is included with this article to illustrate the manner in which this data is presented. It is broken into three major sectors, the final one including a current estimate in contrast to original estimates released each October. On the average, for each item, estimates may change two or three times each year, but the division makes such changes only when it deems them appropriate from a demand or production standpoint. Also shown in this sector is the actual date of estimate, which tells the user how recent-

ly the estimating and planning division has made a change for a specific product. In some instances, no change may be shown at all, these being cases where, in the division's judgement, the initial estimates maintain their validity.

"We use a number of other reports as well," states Mr. Koehlinger, "but **if I had to pin down one basic document that we employ most consistently in our discussions with marketing and our own reviews with production people, this is it.**"

Estimates serve a diversity of purposes in other company areas, but for the estimating and planning division they are the opening step in establishing inventory objectives. Related as well are such questions as transit times, the time required to move goods out of warehouses, the variability of production and other factors related to individual products or product groups.

Inventory goals function

A look at Eastman Kodak's annual report reveals approximately $500 million in inventories, an important part of which is finished photographic goods. The responsibility for the latter lies basically in this division, establishing inventory goals to meet four principal objectives for the company:

• Service to the customer, assuring timely product availability at point of sale.

• Minimizing inventory size so that funds may find alternate employment.

• Maintaining level employment through inventory-building schedules that meet seasonal demands yet avoid repetitive hiring and firing plus excessive overtime.

• Perishability: Inventories must move properly to protect expiration dates on products such as film and paper.

Once an inventory objective is determined, the division is in a position to supply the factory with a schedule of needed production to match that goal. Dealing with 10,000 different products, division personnel are in constant daily contact with the factory and the regions, making changes to reflect current conditions.

On a more formal basis, the divi-

sion holds regular meetings to discuss the sales estimates, the inventory objectives and various problems. At these meetings, the division presents what has happened, what the division's needs are and what it is requesting, followed by mutual discussion. In a recent typical week, there were four such meetings held.

Worldwide coordination

Worldwide coordination is a significant part of the divisional activity, involving a group called world estimating. With plants in England, France, Germany, Australia, Canada and Mexico, any individual market may be supplied in a number of alternate ways. All of these plants except Germany make sensitized products in some measure, although not every one makes 100% of the line. In supplying Switzerland, for instance, a number of questions must be raised. Does a potential plant make the specific product wanted? If not, can it do so, and if so, will the demand be sufficient to justify the addition to its production? Does it have the current capability of employment in terms of the number of people and skilled persons? Also, what about the question of customer preference? Historical trade patterns as well as the emergence of the common market, EFTA, LAFTA, etc. all can affect such a situation, and all are evaluated.

With a staff of 160 people and an annual computer bill running well into seven figures, the estimating and planning division is a busy complex. Simulation techniques and numerous original mathematical and statistical approaches play an important role in the division's work. While the computer assists in these activities to some degree, it plays a greater part in maintaining inventory control through the automatic replenishment system. The computer also generates production schedules based upon decision rules and subsequently edited and reviewed by the staff.

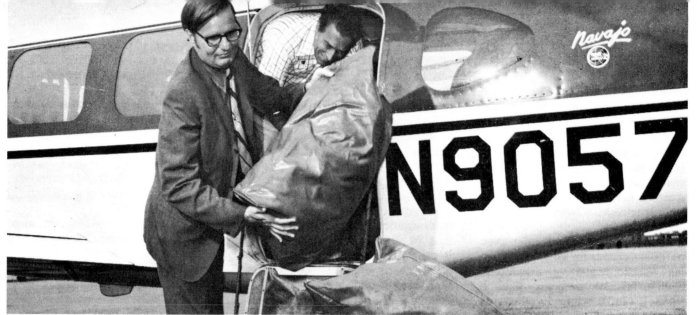

AIR TAXIS and specialized surface courier services, fulfilling schedules set up by Eastman Kodak Company's traffic de- partment, assure 48-hour turnaround of color film and print processing orders from consumers nationwide.

Traffic responds to market expansion

IN 1970, Eastman Kodak Company and its domestic subsidiaries experienced total transportation expenses of $74,850,745. The U.S. plants alone received and shipped a daily freight volume of substantial tonnage. Yet freight charges on almost all long-haul shipments from the Rochester complex remain the same or less than they were 15 to 20 years ago. The answer lies in a general traffic department which continually seeks overall transportation systems betterments while carefully policing individual movements and carrier performance.

A glance at the department's organization chart is a partial indication of its varied activities. What it does not show are such duties and specific projects as the following:

Site development: New locations for distribution centers and plants involve departmental consultation and negotiation both in actual site selection and in developing necessary transportation facilities, carrier arrangements and rates.

Computerized administrative and research procedures: Routing guides, claims analysis, shipping document procedures and several other program packages have been developed in conjunction with corporate data processing.

High speed shipping networks for color processing: Air taxi, special courier services and others have been selected and grouped to give customers a 48-hour processing service at a cost lower than first class mail.

Inbound controls: Though a part of the distribution division, the general traffic department nonetheless holds responsibility for inbound transportation to manufacturing units.

"We seek to control inbound routings," observes General Traffic Manager Kenneth H. Jamieson. **"We're successful in doing so in most cases. Economies here can be quite substantial."** Working closely with the purchasing department, the general traffic department promptly provides necessary routings covering any new suppliers. Subsequent audit checks route observance. Regular monthly meetings take place with the purchasing department, known as "counseling and liaison."

Traffic also conducts regular transportation classes for all new purchasing agents, explaining the department's function and the ways in which it can be helpful to purchasing personnel.

While Assistant General Traffic Manager Howard L. Verbridge han-

IMPACT of Eastman Kodak's recently developed computer claims analysis procedures is discussed by (left to right): Freight Claims Section Supervisor Robert C. Foy, Rochester Operations Traffic Manager Frank T. Rawls, Foreign Traffic Manager Joseph P. O'Donnell, Assistant General Traffic Manager Howard Verbridge and Assistant General Traffic Manager William W. Rhoton, Jr.

dles rate negotiations, auditing and the preparation of domestic and international shipping manuals within his department sector, he is responsible as well for the complex activities necessary in developing transportation into new company locations.

"We became involved in a most interesting venture when the Midwestern Regional Distribution Center was to be moved from Chicago to Oak Brook, Ill.," he observes. "The selected site was approximately two miles beyond the commercial zone of Chicago, and 30 of our carriers did not have operating rights to serve Oak Brook.

"In this instance, because all the transportation involved crossed state boundary lines, applications for extensions of operating rights had to be filed by the carriers with the ICC. We supported the carriers' requests on the basis of our needs and our long years of association with them."

Here is a chronology of the department's activity in this case:

May and June, 1961:
> Carrier applications filed.

June 31, 1961:
> Chicago hearing.

September 8, 1961
> Approval to serve Oak Brook granted to 28 motor carrier companies.

March 16, 1962:
> Approval to serve Oak Brook denied for New York Central Transport Co. and Rock Island Motor Transit Co.

August 10, 1962
> On appeal, previous decision was upheld by Operating Rights Review Board.

February 13, 1963
> On appeal, matter was reopened for further consideration by order of the ICC.

June 17, 1963
> Division 1 of the Commission reversed decision and granted permission to the two rail motor carrier subsidiaries to serve Oak Brook.

June 28, 1963
> Date of service of Commission order.

A similar procedure was followed in assisting motor carriers to obtain operating rights to serve Windsor, Colo.

CHECKING OUT a piggyback load of Kodak freight that is about to leave Rochester are Penn Central Supervisor Joe Hennessey (left) and Eastman Kodak Coordinator-Outbound Traffic Bert Lonngren.

As a rule, the general traffic department does not concern itself directly with day-to-day operations at Kodak origins. The notable exception is Rochester, where both the primary bulk distribution center known as "Building 605" and the Eastern Regional Distribution Center are serviced by Traffic Manager Rochester Operations F.T. Rawls and his staff. This unit is also responsible for inbound traffic, exhibits and household goods.

Traffic Manager Field Operations William J. Maher's unit concerns itself primarily with activities between the regional centers and customers in contrast to the Rochester operations unit's concern with movement between the major bulk distribution center and the regional locations. Both share an interest in the department's modern, computerized routing guide. This system was developed during 1968-69, producing its first outputs during 1970.

In its present form, the routing guide programing yields three outputs: a routing guide for direct use by regional distribution centers and others, a control routing guide with more detailed data for general traffic department use in analysis and research, and a consolidated destination report containing complete routing-related detail for a specific destination.

The basic routing guide is issued once each period (four weeks) unless changes are sufficiently significant to warrant an additional run. Sequenced by regional distribution center, state abbreviation and destination city name, it contains the service weight breaks for each mode for shipper use in manually routing shipments. It also contains motor carrier names, branch truck and leased truck information, county name, parcel post zone, parcel post class and United Parcel zone. A complete new guide can be requested at any time because of changes to one of the master input reports for a particular region.

The control routing guide contains cost and service weight breaks for each mode. With this guide, the department regularly analyzes differences in weight breaks between cost and service. If a particular mode is found superior for servicing a specific destination on some types of shipments, a request will be made to include it in the service weight breaks for the next period, as well as for inclusion in the routing guides sent to the regions.

The consolidated destination reports contain all routing information for a given destination. This information is an accumulation of six master data inputs and is used by traffic as a daily reference, an audit tool and a ready reference when changes are contemplated for a specific destination's routing pattern.

Pool trucks' role

Pool trucks play an important part in the regional distribution picture, consolidating many small shipments for an individual city in a single line-haul shipment, generally placed for delivery at the destination city with local cartage agents. Rochester and the regional centers together currently service 56 pool truck destinations. When traffic data suggests an opportunity, the general traffic department seeks to set up additional such operations whenever practical to do so, investigating and establishing further pools when proven practical.

A freight bill payment computer system was developed in 1964 and is administered by Office Manager Robert B. Anderson's group. This program produces a series of carrier analysis reports showing weight shipped and dollar amounts by carrier. This procedure incorporates microfilming of initial documents and subsequent key-punching. It is, in effect, a dual-purpose program, im-

FOREIGN TRAFFIC STAFFERS consider a routing change. From the left: Anthony J. Capozzi, James L. Lamb, Robert Marshall and Manager Joseph P. O'Donnell.

MEMBERS of the field operations staff update charter air routes handling Kodak color print and processing laboratories traffic, including, from left, Manager William J. Maher, Donald Goodrich, Eugene Acciari (standing) and Gerald LePage.

OFFICE MANAGER Robert B. Anderson (left) and Mrs. Mary Thorpe, section leader-freight billing, review current output. At right, Mrs. Vera Richardson operates a Friden Computyper used in the billing procedure.

proving freight bill payment control and acting as an analysis tool.

More directly research oriented is the regional distribution center transportation cost computer model. This program applies mathematical rate models to the product weights moving between established points in the distribution system and between other major metropolitan areas, measuring the costs by various modes. Data analysis permits the department to rapidly locate the most feasible alternatives for more detailed review.

Latest addition to the department's computer library is its claims system, producing reports covering all carriers. "Prior to this system," notes Mr. Jamieson, "claims were filed in numerical sequence, and it was an impractical, though not impossible task to gather information on a specific carrier. Computer sortation changed all that. **We are looking at carrier claim performance regularly now, and when any one of them is out of line, we'll promptly be asking why.**"

In a further refinement, the claims report can be run by product class, showing where the problem areas lie and aiding in determining their probable causes. "It's a remarkably productive tool based on a surprisingly simple computer program," notes Senior Analyst David Leidig. "We can do a number of other things with it as well, such as analyzing ratio of freight losses to carrier revenue and building histories of performance for carriers we use."

Color print transport system

Back in 1955, the color print processing division requested the general traffic department to develop a transportation system for color print and processing work that would bring it from dealers to Kodak laboratories and return finished material within 48 hours at a cost equal to or below first class mail rates. Assistant General Traffic Manager-Service William W. Rhoton, Jr. has done just that.

In the state of Ohio, as an example, two types of movement are necessary, with the laboratory at Findlay handling Kodachrome and other reversal processing materials, while print work must flow to the Rochester laboratory. When the system was started for that state, carriers were contacted in each major city to provide pickup and delivery service of processed film, which they did during the daytime, forwarding it by surface to Findlay or by air to Rochester, returning it again within 48 hours if everything worked correctly. This satisfied major metropolitan area dealers but did nothing for the suburbs. Accordingly, Mr. Rhoton obtained the services of a carrier who now has rights in some 42 states, American Courier Corporation, a primarily bank or nonnegotiable instrument carrier.

Covering the entire state of Ohio, this carrier works at night, bringing film into the cities and making essentially the same shipment pattern to the various laboratories. It is a nonexclusive operation, but basically any town that has a bank has this service.

"Our cost in this operation is equal to or less than first class mail throughout Ohio," states Mr. Rhoton, **"satisfying the initial objective."**

Up until 1966, commercial surface

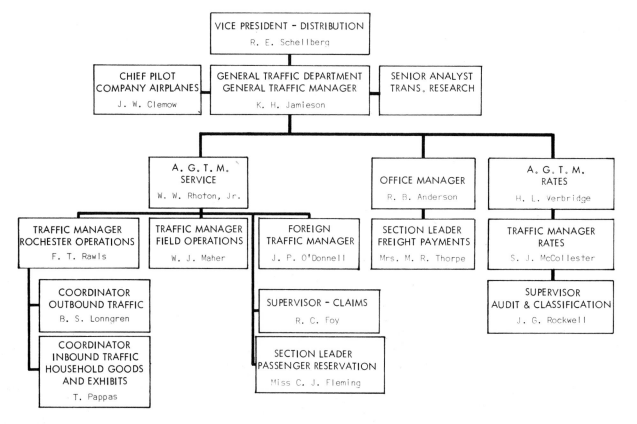

COMPREHENSIVE SCOPE of traffic functions in Eastman Kodak's general traffic department shows itself clearly in its organization chart, reflecting a heavy emphasis on forward development and fulfillment of day-to-day line functions.

transportation was used between major cities and the laboratory, with commercial air transportation tying the major cities and Rochester. A further refinement now finds the entire state of Ohio covered by charter aircraft—air taxi planes that are chartered each night, with two involved in the operation. One comes out of Detroit, stops at Cleveland and comes into Rochester five nights a week, Monday through Friday, returning the following morning. Another aircraft leaves Rochester, goes to Cleveland, pick sup work from Toledo, proceeds to Columbus, picks up work from Cincinnati, goes over to Pittsburgh and returns to Rochester. It leaves at approximately 11 p.m. and returns around 4 a.m.

There are several others, including a charter from Washington to Philadelphia to Bethlehem and into Rochester. Another comes from Boston, stops at Providence, New Haven, New York City and proceeds to Rochester. On that flight, because of high volume, there is an intercept when necessary that picks up work from the original charter plane in New Haven and flies it into Rochester, thus creating two flights coming in on such a night.

The Boston flight lays over at its home terminal each day, then makes pickups through to New York, at which point it drops Kodachrome film for New York processing, but picks up other freight for the Rochester laboratory in its stead and takes off. After unloading at Rochester, it follows the same route back to Boston, dropping the processed film.

During 1970, a year marked by substantial amounts of bad weather, only four flights in all were missed. The laboratory is able to count on having this film available to work on, so it schedules its production based on the arrival of these aircraft.

"It gets to look better every time the first class mail rate goes up," notes Mr. Jamieson.

Steadily expanding exports

With nearly a third of outbound movement from Rochester now exports—a steadily expanding business—this volume carries a particular importance to the general traffic department. Foreign Traffic Manager

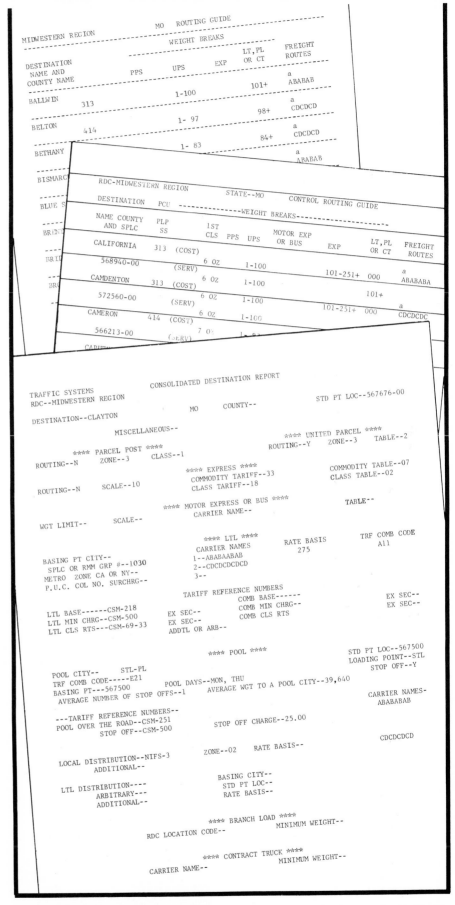

THE COMPUTERIZED ROUTING GUIDE programing employed by the traffic department produces data periodically in the above three basic forms. At top, a basic routing guide, produced each Kodak period (four weeks), supplies users, such as regional and district distribution centers, with modes and carriers to fulfill service requirements. The "control routing guide" (center) is augmented by cost data and is a traffic department working tool. For each destination, a consolidated destination report (at bottom) offers all pertinent information to assist traffic personnel in evaluating existing practices or proposed changes.

Joseph P. O'Donnell and his associates have been taking full advantage of newer methods in furthering this activity.

Containerization

Consider paper work, for instance. It was through this unit's efforts that a single product description was developed and approved for a major segment of export shipments, thus opening the door to a computerized export declaration. **"Our real goal,"** **says Mr. O'Donnell, "is elimination of the export declaration, replacing it with appropriate statistical data that will be sent to the Department of Commerce on a periodic basis.** We were one of a few companies involved in pilot studies to accomplish this, but a problem encountered in our drawbacks has prevented the change thus far. We will change over, however, as soon as we can create an appropriate statistical procedure."

Containerization found Eastman Kodak a pioneer user, thanks in no small part to the general traffic department's interest. It was not without its problems, however, for a major company some 400 miles from its principal port. A switch to neutral containers Interpool, ICS, CTI solved many of these.

"The neutral containers function like railroad cars; they're freely interchangeable," **Mr. O'Donnell asserts. "We often send a container out at night and get it on a vessel the following morning.** Previously, when using a specific container line's box, schedules were tight, and if a unit missed a sailing, it sat in New York for a week. Container lines are understandably reluctant to send their equipment via competitive vessels in these circumstances."

Air freight, like ocean freight, is booked for Kodak by a forwarder at the port of exit along with related ancillary services. By shipping air freight on scheduled day to volume destinations, many small shipments are consolidated with consequent substantial savings.

"From time to time, we have had sufficient volume, particularly to Europe, to charter aircraft," **notes Mr. Jamieson.** "We pay a flat charge for the charter, depending upon the des-

NOT EVERY SHIPMENT can follow traffic department standard routing practices. This oversized load is one of many requiring special planning in conjunction with carriers and others that recently was shipped to the new Windsor, Colo. facility.

tination. Complete utilization of the aircraft brings significant savings in the air freight charges in comparison to the lowest tariff rates."

Air freight accounts for 5.5% of Kodak freight moving in foreign transportation. Though still a high cost mode, the cost and service advantages of air and surface are under continual scrutiny as cost patterns continue to change rapidly.

Passenger service, too, is a part of the department's assignment, with a passenger reservation section handling this work. Additionally, the department controls the company aircraft operation, a Grumman One and a Grumman Two being operated out of Rochester. The chief pilot for this operation reports directly to the general traffic manager.

GENERAL TRAFFIC MANAGER Kenneth H. Jamieson (right) discusses recent systems improvements with TM Executive Editor Jack W. Farrell.

Specialized logistics for advertising matter

IN MOST COMPANIES, the distribution of advertising material or comparable printed matter is an adjunct function of the general distribution operations. Not so at Kodak. Heavy volume, diversified items, special services, closely coordinated with marketing activities, amply justify this firm's highly specialized advertising distribution department. Another of the management units reporting to Rochester Distribution Center Manager George Yeomans, its staff reports to Advertising Distribution Manager John G. Eckl.

"We perform two main functions," states Mr. Eckl. **"For one, we fill orders or requests from dealers, customers and others for advertising and sales promotion materials and technical information or pamphlets.** We process many orders from universities, schools, government agencies, book stores and similar sources.

"Our second function is the preparation of material for routine dissemination. We maintain approximately 300 large mailing lists to perform what might be termed automatic distribution. A large variety of magazines and newsletters, announcements of new products, and special promotions are among the items handled in this category."

For filling orders, the department has a regular order processing and billing operation, as well as stock handling, warehousing, packing and shipping units. In total, the department employs approximately 120 people, about 65 of whom are in the production area.

While Kodak distribution is generally broken down into regions, the advertising distribution department services the whole country. The rapid turnover of items and the need for precise timing of materials slated for specific marketing campaigns make this central control desirable. In 1970, the department processed 124,000 orders. Normal volume averages 400 to 500 orders daily. In the mailing area, 1970 volume exceeded 10 million pieces forwarded to some one million names on the department's mailing lists.

With shipment timing so vital in many of its operations, the department finds it necessary to keep close control over work cycles. All orders move on a schedule stipulating a maximum of six days for nonimprinted items, or a total of 10 days when material must be imprinted. These time levels provide a maximum of two days for order entry and processing plus four days for layout, packing and shipping. Normal cycles generally run somewhat faster, but time must be built in to allow for the considerable fluctuations in work load that the department experiences.

Imprinting is handled within the advertising department. It includes such services as placing dealer names on advertising or other materials, as well as the sequence numbering of photo finishing envelopes. The annual volume is in excess of 100 million pieces.

The department's order processing and various controls are computerized. Cards are key-punched and edited within the department, but processing is done on the Rochester Distribution Center equipment, with order cards forwarded to the electronic data processing facility twice daily. Cards are matched against master product and dealer files, after which the computer produces shipping tickets. Cards sent down in late morning are processed during the noon hour, and shipping tickets return to the department in the afternoon. Cards sent to the distribution center in the evening are run on the "B" shift at night, shipping tickets for these coming to the department first thing in the morning.

Because the department's widely varied materials have highly diversified life cycles, stock control is vital. Each item, therefore, has a "low stock point" established to maintain control over reorder or discontinuance options. When stock drops to the low stock point, the computer automatically kicks out a set of cards notifying the department of this condition. If the item is something under internal control, the department may assemble additional stock items, such as, for example, literature kits of

CAREFULLY TIMED simultaneous release of nationwide promotional materials demands precision distribution planning. The department team preparing just such a schedule includes (left to right): Supervisor-Customer Services John W. McCarthy, Supervisor Data Programing and Processing Donald J. DeVries, Department Manager John G. Eckl, Supervisor-Production William C. Heuer and Supervisor Administrative Services and Planning William J. Fackelman.

PACKING STATIONS that are strategically located along a belt conveyor are but one of several efficient materials handling tools employed in the advertising department's independent warehousing and shipping operations.

varying kinds. It will also follow through if it is a book that may be ordered from the distribution center.

Project proposal

If, however, it is an item that is controlled by marketing, the cards are sent to the appropriate marketing unit so they may decide on appropriate action. They may choose to reprint an item as is, reprint with appropriate modifications, discontinue when stock runs out if another item will replace the material in question or, finally, tell the department to back-order when stock runs out pending reproduction of replacement material.

When the marketing divisions place a new item in distribution, they are required to make out a project proposal listing the item's title, production group, quantity, delivery, inventory and other data. This "Markets Project Proposal" includes all information pertaining to the product, including cost information, selling price, sales class, etc. The advertising distribution department then makes out a master product sheet, which proceeds to the tabulating unit for computer entry into the master file tape so that orders may be placed against it. The computer supplies a print-out for each such entry, while computerized daily balance reports list all items and their stock balances.

Assembly and shipment

Bulk storage encompasses about 70,000 square feet of space, primarily employing pallet racks. As the product is fairly fragile and varied in form, pallet racks are essential to utilize storage space up to ceiling height. The department operates 13 pallet and fork-lift trucks. Lift truck maintenance is handled by the Kodak Park field maintenance division.

Orders picked from stock come to an assembly area where a group leader assigns work and watches shipping dates on the individual orders. Picking is aided by a stock locator system covering the more popular, faster-moving larger items.

Orders normally are small and are laid out in tote boxes. Once assem-

FORK-LIFT OPERATOR John Russi removes display material from a warehouse pallet rack prior to shipment as part of a carefully timed program.

ADVERTISING DISTRIBUTION DEPARTMENT'S warehouse employs conveyor lines extensively for order processing and assembly. At left, Thomas Furness draws material for conveyor movement to staging area, partially filling an order.

DONALD BURDICK, at right above, routes laid-out orders after checking for completeness, assigning them to packing stations.

bled, these will proceed on a conveyor line along the building's outside perimeter to the packing and shipping area. Complete orders arriving in the latter sector proceed direct to a checking and routing station.

Other orders, either lacking specific items, or scheduled to match with large, bulky items at this point, will be shunted to an inner conveyor line, which is "addressed" by an activating pin on the tote box. A station on the inside line functions to work out such orders and merge them back into the shipping flow.

Checking and routing involves the use of traffic department-supplied routing manuals. Depending upon size and service level required, the checker will apply the appropriate routing to the ticket and assign the shipment to one of the packing stations. From the packing stations, a rubber belt conveyor line on which they front feeds the shipping area in the following room; picking, packing and shipping are all partition-separated facilities, tied together by conveyors. In general, most of the 400 to 500 daily shipments end up as single cartons.

"If we get a large shipment bound for, say, the West Coast," notes Mr. Eckl, "including anything exceeding 20 pounds, we would seek to move it with the product truck as a branch enclosure through our regional distribution center at either San Ramon or Whittier. In such an instance, we forward the shipment to the product handling department, to be sent along with other freight to the appropriate regional center, which will, in turn, forward our shipment to the customer for us."

While pools out of the main distribution center handle these shipments to distant regional centers, the advertising distribution department also takes advantage of pools within the Eastern region by transferring such freight directly to their center located immediately adjacent to the department's own shipping facility. The Eastern region distribution center also takes care of all LTL shipments for the department, while the department deals directly with Parcel Post, UPS and REA Express shipments.

The advertising distribution handling facilities are located in a part of

MARKETS PROJECT PROPOSALS, prepared for each new item initiated by the marketing division, provide needed data to guide Eastman Kodak Company's advertising distribution division in making physical and control arrangements for the proper handling of the described material.

what was once the company's principal distribution center, now replaced by the huge modern location known as "Building 605." Equipped with rolling doors and load levelers at each dock position, the building is a thoroughly modern facility—ample for its present functions, although long outgrown by the demands now fulfilled at "605."

Speeding export shipments

AT EASTMAN KODAK COMPANY, overseas markets play an important role in distribution. As in most companies, the complex paperwork entailed as well as the vagaries of vessel schedules in the past represented substantial costs in time and money. The billing and order department of Kodak's Rochester, N.Y. distribution center, however, has made important strides toward conquering these problems. Systems, both material handling and paperwork, have been largely responsible for upgrading the department's service beyond levels possible under more conventional methods and procedures.

In particular, two elements created particularly significant benefits:

Containerization: A former 12-to 15-day cycle from packaging to vessel is now at the two-to three-day level, with other parallel advantages accruing as well.

Computer processing: Growing export systems computerization permits handling greatly increased order volumes without additional

personnel, improves paperwork reliability and reduces order processing cycle time by a full day.

"Before containerization," notes Billing and Order Manager Charles E. Thrasher, "we literally backed into our shipping schedules based upon dates that boats were scheduled to leave, as supplied by our traffic people. Typically, only one sailing a week was available for individual destinations, so a shipment coming up to the packing room after deadline would lose a whole week. To avoid this, we scheduled packaging for completion several days in advance of the paperwork closing date, creating a 12-day cycle from packing to boat.

"Now, thanks to containers, we have a whole new system. The material is packed promptly, and as soon as we have a containerload

CHARLES E. THRASHER, manager-billing and order.

ready, they spot one for loading. We inform traffic, and they give us the first available sailing. Moving a container is a lot easier than han-

WHO SAYS IT CAN'T BE DONE? Computerized export declarations pose a serious challenge to systems men, but Kodak's traffic and distribution systems men have put it together with resounding success.

DO NOT USE THIS AREA	Form No. 7525-V-Alt. (Rev. Aug. 1965)	U.S. DEPARTMENT OF COMMERCE—BUREAU OF THE CENSUS—BUREAU OF INTERNATIONAL COMMERCE			APPROVED BUDGET BUREAU NO. 41-R397.6			
		EXPORT SHIPMENTS ARE SUBJECT TO U.S. CUSTOMS INSPECTION CONFIDENTIAL.—For use solely for official purposes authorized by the Secretary of Commerce. Use for unauthorized purposes is not permitted (Title 15, Sec. 30.91(a), C.F.R., Title 50, U.S.C. App., 2026c). NOTE.—If a destination control statement is required on an Export Declaration, such statement must also appear on all copies of the bill of lading and commercial invoice.			District	Port	Flag	Country
					10	01		

DELIVERING CARRIER | Customs Authentication *(For customs use only)*

1. Forwarding Agent— ADDRESS— REFERENCE NOS.
ABC FORWARDING COMPANY

B/L NO.

2. Method of Transportation *(Check one)*
☒ VESSEL   ☐ AIR   ☐ OTHER (SPECIFY)

SHIPPER'S EXPORT DECLARATION
READ INSTRUCTIONS ON REVERSE SIDE

Declaration *should be made by authorized officer or employee of exporter or forwarding agent of exporter.*

3. Exporter *(principal or Seller license and address)*
► **EASTMAN KODAK COMPANY**   ROCHESTER, NEW YORK

21. I certify that all statements and information contained in this export declaration are true and correct.

(Signature)   *(Date)*

4. Consigned To
►

For **EASTMAN KODAK COMPANY**
ASS'T TO DEPT. MGR.

5. Ultimate Consignee/Arrival Notice Party *(Give name and address)*

KODAK A.G.

SCHARNHAUSEN, NEAR STUTTGART, WEST GERMANY

6. Intermediate Consignee *(Give name and address)*

22. Ultimate Consignee *(Give name and address if this party is not shown in item 5)*

7. Exporting Carrier *(If vessel give name and flag, if airline give name of airline)* | 8. Pier or Airport | 9. Port of Loading **NEW YORK**

23. Date of Exportation *(Not required for vessel shipments)*

10. Foreign Port of Unloading *(Vessel and air shipments only)* | 11. For Transshipment To *(If goods are to be transhipped or forwarded at port of unloading)*

24. Place and Country of Ultimate Destination
SCHARNHAUSEN, WEST GERMANY

MARKS AND NUMBERS (12)	NO. OF PKGS. (13)	Description of Commodities *in Schedule B detail, with export license number and expiration date (or General License symbol) below, description of each item See instruction IV on reverse side* (14)	MEASUREMENT (15)	GROSS WEIGHT (POUNDS) (16)	D or F (17)	SCHEDULE B COMMODITY NO. (18)	NET QUANTITY *(State unit)* (19)	VALUE *(Nearest dollar)* (20)
VAN 12345 SEALS 78600/78612	96511/13 13 CASES							
KA SCHARNHAUSEN NEAR STUTTGART VIA ROTTERDAM		STILL PICTURE EQUIPMENT PARTS AND ACCESSORIES N.E.C.		255	D	8616940	–	0000.
		X RAY FILM AND PLATES		311	D	862.4630	2083 SQ.FT.	0000.
		OPTICAL ELEMENTS UNMOUNTED		5	D	861.1120	304	0000.
LICENSE GDEST		United States law prohibits disposition of these commodities to Southern Rhodesia, the Soviet Bloc, Communist China, North Korea, Macao, Hong Kong, Poland (including Danzig), Romania, Communist-controlled areas of Vietnam and Laos, or Cuba, unless otherwise authorized by the United States.						

DC 255

Reference Notes a–b IMPORTANT—See Instruction No. IV on reverse side

NOTE—No validated declaration may be altered or amended without written authorization of the Collector of Customs   Instructions 11(d) and 11(e)

DO NOT USE THIS AREA

dling 246 boxes, so traffic can pick a sailing as early as the next day or the second day, if necessary.

"If we get something packed on Monday, we can have finished paperwork on Tuesday and will probably ship Tuesday or Wednesday, so we've gone from a 12-to 15-day cycle to a two-to three-day time. It's not entirely gain, as it sometimes takes a while to accumulate containerloads for smaller countries, but for the larger ones, we tend to move one container a week, which goes forward with great rapidity."

Computerization of the billing and order unit's paperwork is advancing steadily. Though billing and associated paperwork is far more complex than in the domestic operations, the computer now processes ocean freight shipments for finished products. Measured in terms of actual amount of product by case count, this represents 80% of the freight volume processed. Primarily because of this operation, department personnel remains stable despite substantially increased business in overseas markets.

"We're getting reports that quickly pinpoint problems for us," Mr. Thrasher observes. "Reports on material released but not packed, when such conditions arise, go to the shipping department with a request for explanation and correction. A packed-but-not-shipped report will go to our forwarding people asking why the described freight is not moving. We're getting a great deal more valuable information from the computer than we anticipated when we started working with it initially."

Orders from customers first flow through editing and control in the billing and order unit. From there, they move out to the planning department for processing through the daily balance system. The computer then generates handler cards that are used for product handling and export packing. Paperwork then flows back to the billing and order unit for completion of processing.

It is in this area that the most recent systems betterment has taken place. A new card order

entry system, under which people overseas now place orders by forwarding appropriate tab cards, employs a computer master file initially supplied and maintained from Rochester. All the overseas unit need do is punch quantity, routing and special instructions where appropriate. The accurate product coding and description is provided from the master file. Eliminating the editing and the other manual clerical operations, it saves a full day's time in order processing. Perhaps even more important, the new system reduces errors or delays through decreased handling in both the order processing and the handling units.

Centralized planning aids real estate development

A UNIQUE distribution division function is provided by the marketing and distribution facilities department. In effect, it is the real estate development arm of both the marketing and distribution divisions for properties outside of the Rochester complex. In conjunction with the field operations department, which fulfills the landlord functions once a facility is operational (see article in WAREHOUSE LOGISTICS section of this issue), the marketing and distribution facilities department frees marketing professionals to concentrate on sales without housekeeping concerns, fulfilling a comparable service role for other departments within the distribution division.

"Our function primarily is to coordinate space planning activities and to acquire space to fulfill these needs," states Director-Marketing and Distribution Facilities Robert G. Van Duyne. Working with him full time is a staff of facilities coordinators, augmented by the necessary engineering personnel to develop specific projects. As many as 16 or 17 project engineers and related staff personnel from the Kodak Park engineering staff may be working on specific department projects at one time, while

the combined efforts of a variety of industrial engineers represent the equivalent of three to four men in this category as well.

Smaller units in Dallas and LA

With facilities located in more than 40 sales districts, there is never a shortage of activities. "We have an expansion currently under way at Chamblee, Ga. (near Atlanta); we have a renovation project in Dallas; we're expanding the Whittier, Cal. facility (near Los Angeles), and we're renovating the marketing offices in San Ramon (near San Francisco). So we have four major regional projects now in progress," Mr. Van Duyne notes.

"We're also opening district marketing centers at Los Angeles and Dallas that will be fairly small units running about 5,000 to 6,000 square feet. Though they will have only business systems market division sales people located in them, our division will have the landlord responsibilities."

More on the drawing boards

On the drawing boards right now are another district marketing center, a relocation project and two district center renovations.

Field distribution facilities themselves are essentially of two different types, regional and district. The seven regional centers handle a broad spectrum of Kodak products, while some 40 district centers—smaller facilities—are restricted primarily to the selling and servicing of business systems products. At the regional level, with the exception of New York City, the company owns the properties. District facilities are mostly leased, the majority of them in free-standing buildings. These operations are largely an outgrowth of the Recordak Corp.'s activities, that subsidiary having been merged into Kodak a few years ago.

In dealing with leased rather than owned facilities, each one is necessarily a unique case involving, of necessity, individual owners and architects. Nonetheless, the department strives to maintain a number of standards. There are, for instance, standardized

REVIEWING PLANS for a proposed distribution facility somewhere in the United States are (left to right): Assistant to Director Marketing and Distribution Facilities Richard A. Vinchesi, Supervising Project Engineer Harold J. Swartout (standing) and Manager-Project Engineering Office Jack E. James.

designs for sales display areas to be installed in district locations, differentiated by size, an A, B or C unit being "plugged in" according to the size of the metropolitan area that the district services. A C unit measures approximately 1,200 square feet, while an A unit will represent a 3,000-square foot space. Working with such modules, facility coordinators can more readily anticipate the types of lighting that will be involved, the type of equipment to be included and other significant details.

The warehousing aspect of each district center must also take into account the variables imposed by differing building configurations. Typically, 4,000 square feet in size at most locations, they may have either one or two shipping docks, varying in shape as well. At a typical location, there would be a staff of eight distribution people, in contrast to a total staff of up to 40 or 50 people at some metropolitan locations, including sales, processing and customer service personnel. Material handling at these facilities is commonly oriented to pallet racks and fork-lift truck operation.

"Office landscaping"

A new concept in office design plays an important role in the marketing and distribution facilities department's forward planning.

Termed "office landscaping," it is already substantially employed in company facilities at Rochester. The concept generally involves a large open floor with movable low partitions made up of soundproofing materials or plants. The primary objective is to create functional work stations and to give privacy as needed.

Recently, the department applied the "office landscaping" treatment to the new facility at Dallas. Only conference rooms and one or two specialized units have floor-to-ceiling partitions there. The managers' offices are segregated by acoustical screens and such in the same manner as the space used by the sales and customer service representatives.

"The big advantage in office landscaping lies not in the initial cost, but in what you save when the inevitable changes become necessary," Mr. Van Duyne asserts. "Changes in layout can be made overnight. There is a real cost gain there, and even more so when renovation rather than reorientation becomes necessary. Our people state that their figures demonstrate such savings clearly and that, in addition, productivity rises where office landscaping is installed."

On the department's major projects, while engineering assistance comes from other Kodak units, an assigned marketing and distribution facilities coordinator from Mr. Van Duyne's staff has total responsibility for any specific project from inception to completion. The nature of the work, typical of most activities throughout the distribution division, nonetheless represents a team effort with other units in virtually all cases, with operating, systems, estimating and traffic people taking part, as well as industrial and project engineers.

"Clerk of the work"

On larger projects involving heavy construction, it is not uncommon to have an on-site representative from project engineering serving as "clerk of the work," maintaining constant vigilance to assure that ongoing construction conforms to agreed-upon specifications. The present Chamblee project is a case in point, and it is standard practice on all of the large, complex regional projects. Looking beyond the division, there is continual interaction with the legal and tax departments, and safety and fire prevention specialists, among others. Observes Mr. Van Duyne, "We try to utilize knowledge and expertise wherever it exists within the firm."

Coordination and support for distribution

FOR MOST COMPANIES, distribution management poses a dilemma: Because of its relatively recent emergence upon the business scene, staff and development work demand considerable attention, but day-to-day operational situations all too frequently monopolize the larger share of managerial attention. At Eastman Kodak, neither situation holds true, as the following indicates:

• Better than 20 years' experience as a "going business" has given the distribution division a level of sophistication well beyond the staff concerns of a fledgling or even a young distribution activity.

• The division's size readily lends itself to managerial specialization— the staff services unit assuming administrative and research and development duties in large measure, releasing other managers and departments to concentrate more fully on their own specialties.

"What we have here," notes Director-Staff Services Donald M. Kladstrup, "is a philosophy similar to that underlying the distribution division's own development. Just as distribution assumes various duties that release marketing talent to sales effort rather than administrative work, so the staff services unit performs functions that permit traffic, field operations and other professionals to similarly concentrate on their professional responsibilities."

Coordinator-Financial and Office Services C. H. Philbrick and his staff perform a function akin to that of a controller's group for the division. Developing measurement techniques, both performance and financial, Mr. Philbrick's staff assists division management with programs for evaluating service, operations and financial activities. His unit is responsible for coordinating departmental budget preparation, consolidating the division's capital and operating budgets, as well as performing diversified administrative duties.

Director-Personnel Development G. A. Semlak brings to the division a specialized understanding of its unique personnel requirements. States Mr. Kladstrup: "By having a personnel unit within the distribution organization, staffed by qualified people fully acquainted with the diversified requirements of our division, we feel there has been a significant advantage, notably in our ability to select and train professional distribution people."

Maintaining a personnel inventory of about 460 professional distribution people, the unit is in a good position to recommend personnel for placement opportunities within distribution and in other divisions, and at the same time it is in a favorable position to evaluate individuals elsewhere within the company who might prove well suited to distribution's needs.

Acting Director Laurence G. Locke's Distribution Systems Development group provides essentially staff services organized into several functional areas including:

• Rochester distribution systems and services, which provides methods and systems support to estimating and planning, Rochester Distribution Center, international photographic division and special project teams, fulfilling such assignments as systems development for the new Windsor, Colo. distribution center, integrated distribution stock system development and export computer systems.

• Field distribution systems and services fulfills the requirements of the regional distribution centers and district marketing centers. Responsibility areas include computer systems design and manual operating procedures development with primary emphasis upon order processing, billing and related administrative functions.

• Distribution operations analysis group, which provides the mathematical, statistical, computer and other scientific expertise to fulfill distribution's long-term information, decision-making and control system requirements.

Additional specialized units perform a diversity of functions—some permanent in nature, others set up for a specific long-term project that terminates upon individual project completion.

Professional mathematicians

The operations analysis group includes five professional mathematicians, most of whom have master's degrees or are working on them. One of their major concerns is in the area of estimating and planning. They make heavy use of computers, largely writing their own programs. In addition, they have recently started what might be called a mini-computer.

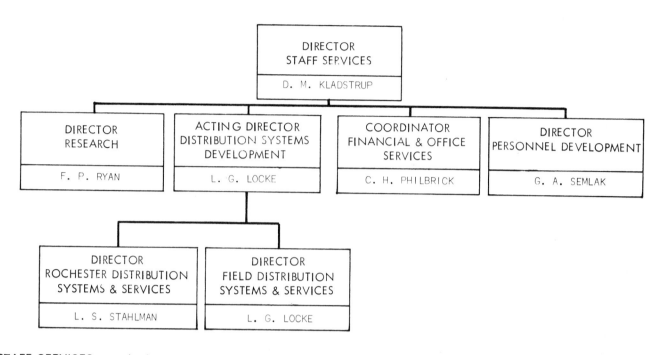

```
                        ┌─────────────────────┐
                        │      DIRECTOR       │
                        │   STAFF SERVICES    │
                        ├─────────────────────┤
                        │   D. M. KLADSTRUP   │
                        └─────────────────────┘
```

DIRECTOR RESEARCH	ACTING DIRECTOR DISTRIBUTION SYSTEMS DEVELOPMENT	COORDINATOR FINANCIAL & OFFICE SERVICES	DIRECTOR PERSONNEL DEVELOPMENT
F. P. RYAN	L. G. LOCKE	C. H. PHILBRICK	G. A. SEMLAK

DIRECTOR ROCHESTER DISTRIBUTION SYSTEMS & SERVICES	DIRECTOR FIELD DISTRIBUTION SYSTEMS & SERVICES
L. S. STAHLMAN	L. G. LOCKE

STAFF SERVICES organization chart demonstrates this unit's role, providing specialized talents and auditing performance.

LAURENCE G. LOCKE (left), director of distribution systems development, reviews the planning network for a complex new Kodak project with Louis S. Stahlman and Miss Carol L. Rosenquist of his department's staff.

Termed a Wang Calculator, it can be readily programed to perform various types of complex mathematical operations, including forms of simulation. Notes Mr. Locke:

"Calculating a reorder point in the stock system involves a lengthy formula requiring up to 15 minutes' clerical effort if handled on a typical desk calculator. Senior Analyst T. W. Schwegel programed the formula, and all he needs to do now is enter the raw figures for a specific product into the calculator, press about three buttons and "zap"—there's the answer."

In the international area, distribution systems development has large and growing responsibilities. Among these have been the creation of modular computer procedures that individual overseas Kodak Houses now employ for several purposes, assuring uniformity in their data production, thereby making comparisons and analyses simpler at the corporate level. SIMPAK, for example, denotes Scientific Inventory Management Package Kodak and is the procedure now used at a number of overseas locations. Somewhat similar to the IBM stock "IMPACT" system, it has several advantages for Kodak's particular requirements in Mr. Locke's view.

"We have the sophisticated routines required for our products; we selves, we really know what's in it and we know how it works," he comments. **"This knowledge and understanding really pays off when difficulties or misunderstandings arise at some location many thousands of miles from Rochester."**

Currently under development is FORPAK—Forecasting Package Kodak—which is being built into an overall international estimating and have incorporated other advanced techniques useful for our business, and by developing the system our planning information system, which is a current major project. There are about six to eight people assigned to international systems work in the division. Their efforts include not only activities at Rochester headquarters, but resident international analysts and others who provide on-site assistance in the installation and maintenance of new systems at some 50 overseas Kodak locations.

Domestically, a major current project in distribution systems development is the creation of a single integrated stock system. Called the "Stock Project," it has been attacked in segments. The department recently replaced the original RDC (Regional Distribution Center) stock system with a new procedure that will become a compatible portion of the total integrated system. The staff is progressing toward the marriage of this system to other new or revised elements representing tasks now performed under a "daily balance" program and a distribution center stock system.

Long-range objectives

A separate staff services unit under Director-Research Frank P. Ryan concerns itself with long-range distribution objectives. **"The job a research unit must do,"** asserts Mr. Kladstrup, **"is to help the distribution division to prepare itself, both in its objectives and in its organization, to handle a business becoming constantly larger in terms of dollar volume, quantity, array, variety and markets."**

To provide for such activity, it was deemed necessary that it be assigned to someone free of operating responsibilities. Previously, Mr. Kladstrup's personal assignment, Mr. Ryan became research director this year. In addition to several special products which receive his attention, Mr. Ryan chairs a research committee encompassing representation from 11 different management groups within the division.

"We believe that a long-term plan is particularly necessary, and we are working on this within the committee," Mr. Ryan says. **"Though we are attempting to look up to 25 years ahead in our thinking, beyond doubt the long-term plan will influence today's decision making."**

Building 605:
A special distribution center

THE BIGGEST THING in Eastman Kodak distribution is the mammoth distribution center known simply as "Building 605." At present encompassing approximately 1.2 million square feet of space, it will ultimately include four wings with a potential of about three million square feet of usable space on its Rochester site. The prior distribution center, itself a surprisingly modern unit by accepted standards, was obsoleted by the sheer growth of company volume.

"In the mid-60s," states Manager-Rochester Distribution Center George E. Yeomans, "increasing volume got us into a position where we were operating out of four different locations. This caused much extra handling and congestion, adding greatly to our costs. Productivity was moving in the wrong direction. **We are now in the process of getting back under one roof over a period of several years."**

Chart One indicates the planned layout as well as the specific portions currently in use and under construction at Building 605. During 1970, 960,000 orders, amounting to 326 million pounds destined for domestic customers and 121 million pounds for foreign customers, passed through this center.

With individual wings developed as 400 by 1,600-foot building sections, each wing unit is built up from a group of 80,000-square foot modules. An individual module approximates one year's anticipated growth. These modules lend themselves readily to subdivision into 40,000 and 20,000-square foot rooms where necessitated by environmental requirements of particular products or insurance considerations. Precast concrete panels make up the outside walls, a layer of insulation separating them from interior concrete block walls to prevent heat losses.

All interior doors, at fire walls and at truck docks, employ overhead rolling shutters, except where fire codes require sliding fire doors. Entrance and exit doors at loading docks use air curtains for climate control when these doors are open.

Mercury vapor lamps are used in the shipping areas, providing a 100-foot-candle light level. Because these lamps would cause discomfort for order assembly personnel looking upward in them in the course of picking, warehouse areas use fluorescent lights, maintaining a light level of 30 to 35 foot-candles, or 25% above normal warehouse standards.

Fan room complexes are located overhead at fire wall intersections throughout the building, conditioning recirculating air at approximately 70 degrees F. in most areas, with one 80,000-square foot portion maintained at 35 degrees and another 154,000 square feet at 50 degrees.

A computerized control center complex constantly monitors and records environmental and security conditions throughout the distribution center. A control center operator can check and adjust temperature, humidity and air pressure in any building location by pressing a few buttons. The center also contains a small weather station monitoring outside temperature, wind speed and wind direction.

A vital control center function is monitoring of the building for critical alarm conditions, checking fire alarms, smoke detectors, the volatile vault storage areas and all perimeter doors. A single cigarette's smoke in the warehouse area will cause an alarm to sound in the control center.

Chart Two represents a hypothetical tour of Building 605, its facilities and activities. Following the sequence

THE MEN who supervise operations at the Rochester Distribution Center include (left to right) front: Stuart Wahl and James A. Stover, and rear: Ronald A. Mazeau, Ed. Steck and Gordon McCrosson.

indicated in this chart yields an opportunity to demonstrate this center's present operations and capabilities.

At the receiving area, photographic products from the Kodak Park manufacturing plants arrive throughout the 24-hour day by plant truck. Pallet loads of goods are checked against applicable punched cards when unloaded

A TRAILER-CONTAINER marshalling yard handles all inbound and outbound common carrier equipment, units moving to and from loading docks at the warehouse proper behind plant tractors, radio-controlled by Kodak dispatcher.

to make certain that inbound material matches production delivery documents. The punched cards then go to the computer for entry at night on the "B" shift as additions to inventory. The goods are then moved to the warehouse areas subsequent to checking.

Approximately 1.8 million pounds of inbound material move daily to separate paper, film, motion picture, chemical and equipment locations in the warehouse. Building 605 can store 30,000 pallets on pallet racks and 48,000 additional ones in open bulk (floor) areas in its present configuration.

A six-digit stock location system is used for all products in bulk, rack and bin storage. The first two digits refer to room number, the third and fourth to aisle or row number, and the last two to section number.

The color paper products room is maintained at a 35-degree temperature to assure maximum life for the material's photographic characteristics. Pallet racks are used exclusively here for easy access to specific items of paper needed to fulfill customer requests.

The black and white paper storage room employs both pallet racks and bins to match the varying patterns of customer demand. Filling 4,000 orders daily for domestic and foreign customers here, stock keepers retrieve the necessary material and place it on a dragline cart in the warehouse for movement to the proper shipping area.

The chemical storage area employs the six-digit stock locater system throughout. Stackable materials are floor-stored, while the nonstackables are stored in pallet rack areas.

The Materials Handling System in-floor dragline is the keystone of Building 605's stock movement arrangement. It will move 300 carts per hour past any point in the building when cars are spaced 18 feet apart and travel at 90 feet per minute. Each cart will handle a 2,000-pound pallet load not exceeding 59 inches in height.

Cart fronts are equipped with a spur selector and an accumulation bumper. Varying the position of two probes in the cart's selector rack permits programing a cart from any building location to any other. Dragline spurs permit automatic cart sorting with fingers that project from the floor at switch locations. As a cart approaches, the selector probes on the cart line up with these fingers, if the cart has been addressed for this specific spur, and the cart is then diverted from the main line into the spur. Carts not addressed for this location will pass by without interruption. Carts programed for a full spur will circulate until an opening occurs, circumnavigating a loop in 20 minutes.

Spurs not located in shipping areas require manual return of carts to the main line. The shipping spurs permit automatic return by tripping an overhead switch.

Because film products, like paper ones, are sensitive to climate conditions, they must also be stored in a temperature-controlled environment. The major portion of film storage is in a 50-degree F. area. Some highly sensitive materials, however, must be stored at zero temperature to maintain photographic stability.

Adjacent to the film storage facilities lies the building crossover connection between the two existing major wings of Building 605. Through this crossover connection passes a dragline system link tying together the various

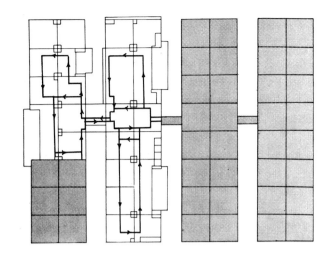

CHART ONE—In this plan of Building 605, the tinted area at lower left is a sector soon to be opened. The two wings at right are to be built in the future as demand requires. Shown within the existing building is the network of dragline loops, the principal material handling means.

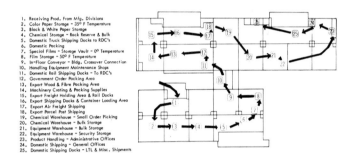

CHART TWO—A sequenced "tour" of Kodak's Building 605 at Rochester reveals many of its unusual features.

loops in the two wings for building-wide distribution of dragline carts. Carts programed for a particular loop will accumulate in this area until space is available on the loop for which they are programed.

The building crossover connection is also the location of a truck maintenance shop, where repairs and alterations to electric power handling equipment are made. Personnel carriers, hand trucks, ride-on counterbalance and outrigger trucks plus tractor-trains, representing an approximate $1 million investment, constitute a fleet embracing 200 pieces of equipment.

Each truck is periodically steam-cleaned and greased and the oil is changed. The tires and batteries are checked, and the truck is safety inspected. Water is added to batteries once each week, with 200 gallons of distilled water required for this task. Voltages run from 12 to 48 and the amp-hour capacity ranges from 143 to 850 hours. Battery average life is eight years.

Individual computerized truck records yield detailed cost reports. Only electric trucks are used in order to maintain cleanliness and minimize health and fire hazards.

Narrow-aisle, high-lift straddle equipment, largely with

triple telescopic masts, work all warehouse areas. The receiving areas use counterbalance machines primarily for unloading trailers. In addition, a tug pulls a two-trailer tractor train. Various counterbalance machine models are used in the shipping areas for truck and rail car loading. Battery charging stations for the many electric trucks are located at a number of strategic places.

Regional distribution centers, other than the Eastern region located at Rochester, regularly receive truckload shipments from Building 605's domestic truck shipping docks. These centers are at New York; Chamblee, Ga.; Oak Brook, Ill.; Dallas; Whittier and San Ramon, Cal. On the average, 18 trucks draw 500,000 pounds daily from this facility.

The truck pit area measures approximately 400 by 117 feet. The entirely enclosed docks have one entrance and exit to and from the building. These are equipped with automatic overhead doors actuated when approached by a vehicle. There are 28 dock doors, each equipped with automatic dock plates.

Trailers moving to and from the domestic truck shipping docks are handled by Kodak's own drivers with two radio-dispatched tractors under the Kodak dispatcher's control. Carriers deliver and pick up trailers at a marshalling yard adjacent to Building 605, thus avoiding much congestion.

THE BUILDING 605 DRAGLINE, a Material Handling Systems installation, features automated addressing that will move an individual cart between any two of the myriad sidings found throughout this 1.2 million-square foot facility.

THE MISCELLANEOUS FREIGHT AREA segregates outbound lots by overhead signs as pallet loads arrive by dragline for staging and ultimate forklift loading to outbound trailers at Eastman Kodak's Building 605.

"Under our former system," notes Manager-Product Handling Stuart A. Wahl, "we were totally dependent upon the carriers placing trailers at the specific times we requested. If trailers arrived late or in unacceptable condition, this would disrupt work schedules and create dock and loading difficulties. The trailer pool has done away with that.

"We can bring in trailers today for use tomorrow morning, and then our own drivers can spot them at our docks as we need them. This gives a desirable flexibility to our carriers as well as to ourselves. Moreover, while in the past, we experienced dock delays waiting for carriers to pull their loads, we can now clear a dock immediately upon closing a trailer's tailgate, moving it out to the marshalling yard for subsequent carrier pickup. **We can now make six to eight loads a day at a single dock and maintain a continuity of loading and productive effort that wasn't previously possible.**"

The completely enclosed train shed permits preheating of insulated cars for protective shipments during the winter months. The Chamblee, Dallas, San Ramon and Whittier regional distribution centers in particular receive regular rail shipments, approximately four boxcars moving daily with a volume in the 300,000-pound range.

Unit loads and palletized shipments figure significantly in these rail movements. In addition to other commodities regularly handled in this manner, the unit load program was recently expanded to include sensitized shipments to Chamblee and Dallas.

A special government packing area provides for the protection, marking and shipping of photographic materials for U.S. government agencies in various parts of the world. Shipments must be packaged in accordance with specifications set forth by the governmental agencies served. Personnel processing government shipments must maintain a broad knowledge of these specifications so that material they handle will pass the inspection performed by the resident government inspector.

Where once wood packing was the major procedure for Kodak overseas shipments, fully 90% of such movements

SPECIAL ROUND PALLETS bear rolls of photographic paper destined to the new Windsor, Colo. manufacturing facility.

are now containerized. The remaining 10%, however, are handled in the export wood packing area. Orders for export-associated companies and distributors, when the volume is not large enough to fill a direct load van, are packed for shipment here.

Various methods of packing are used:

Wood cases—These may be used to any destination.

Tri-wall/van-pack—Used to pack larger orders for customers with facilities capable of handling such containers.

Collapsible container—Employed to certain countries where the service is provided by the steamship lines.

When packed, cases are stored in the freight-holding area until documentation is completed and they are scheduled for shipment to the Port of New York for vessel loading.

A specialized machinery crating area employs approximately 15 men who pack and prepare for shipment machinery and electronic equipment from one-ounce diodes to 25,000-pound machines.

A major recent task was a 29-boxcar shipment of photofinishing equipment for Kodak Mexicana. The unit has recently completed a 60-truckload shipment constituting a complete paper manufacturing facility destined to Sao Paulo, Brazil.

At the export shipping docks, 15 operators currently

THE CENTER'S packing room is well equipped to make large crates for the movement of major items of equipment.

ROCHESTER DISTRIBUTION CENTER'S control room monitors climate, security, fire control and a variety of other conditions throughout the building. An operator at this console may rapidly check conditions at any point, check continuing record maintenance and communicate with persons who may be working at any one of innumerable control points.

load about 50 containers per week with 1.3 million pounds of product consisting of 4,000 items packed in 40,000 fiber cases. Those products requiring temperature control move in refrigerated containers.

Export shipments represent 25 to 30% of outbound tonnage. As in domestic shipping, a punched card order system is used, with essential differences due, in particular, to heavy documentation requirements.

Export packers may now write information directly on punched cards in a faster, simpler manner than was formerly necessary for conventional packing records. When the cards reach a girl in the computer facility, she enters the raw data directly, and the computer, which has stored size and weight information on all of the involved cases, readily calculates cube and other needed information in a fraction of the former time required by packers working with paper and pencil. It has materially improved productivity and service.

In the chemical warehouse, small order picking is an adjunct facility with rack and bin order picking locations for filling small orders, which constitute about 11% of chemical orders.

The equipment warehouse is divided into bulk and security storage locations. Kodak apparatus division products, including items ranging in size from Instamatic cameras and projectors to large photofinishing processors, are in the bulk storage area. The security storage mezzanine warehouses items that are stored in small quantities, as well as high value ones that require special security storage techniques.

Domestic shipping general offices are located at one end of Building 605, while not far from them are found the product handling administrative offices. The latter serves the manager-product handling, four operating supervisors, administrative staff members and industrial engineering staff assigned to product handling.

The domestic shipping offices prepare all shipment documentation. Bills of lading are typed on Flex-O-Writer units and transmitted to the dispatch office located adjacent to the trailer marshaling yard. The bills of lading are presented there to carrier drivers for signature. The shipping office prepared over 39,000 bills of lading in 1970.

Located adjacent to the shipping offices are the domestic shipping docks for LTL and other shipments that move by pool truck. Destined to district distribution centers, direct customers and cities throughout the country, between 25 and 30 LTL and pool shipments leave daily with a typical weight of 150,000 pounds. This area is served by a packing unit which also handles the packing of intercompany and other miscellaneous orders.

Because some of the chemical products stored at Building 605 are hazardous, they are kept in four 2,500-square foot rooms or "vaults." These facilities have special sensing devices to detect vapors, fumes and heat. Their inside walls are constructed of steel-reinforced concrete to guard against potential explosion damage. Only highly skilled operators with special equipment may work in this area.

In addition to Building 605, Center Manager George E. Yeomans' organization manages the previously described advertising distribution function, the central adjustment activity and what is termed the billing and ordering func-

tion, the latter essentially concerned with export shipping procedures.

Building 605 was designed by Kodak's own staff and, thus far, has met management's expectations. Proof of this is indicated by the fact that, in building the new Windsor, Colo. distribution center, which handles products from the firm's new major Western plant facility, the modular construction of Building 605 has been used again. Ceilings are slightly higher, however, and utility lines are internal. "We started limited operation in August," states Windsor Distribution Center Manager W. Elmer Hallowell. "We expect to be in full operation during 1972."

The 12-man starting staff at Windsor will expand to 50 during 1972. While substantially smaller than the Rochester Distribution Center organization, the new operation at Windsor will nonetheless be a sizable distribution center operation by any normal standards.

Central control for better field warehousing

RESPONSIBLE for managing seven regional distribution centers, 38 district ones and a specialized center in Hawaii, distribution division field operations is a major factor in Eastman Kodak's market service. In contrast to the Rochester and Colorado distribution centers, which serve primarily for initial bulk distribution of production, the field facilities concern themselves primarily with direct customer service.

Attuned to the individual and unique requirements of their specific market areas, the centers regularly serve approximately 100,000 customers. Included are about 25,000 dealers, who in turn resell to their customers, and 75,000 others who purchase items not distributed through dealers. An accompanying map illustrates the field operations division's geographic dispersion.

Total field distribution responsibilities extend well beyond the operation of physical facilities. Elements it controls include the following:
• Regional and district product handling, order processing, customer service, stock control and related services.
• Photographic products transportation from regional and district centers to customers with the aid of the general traffic department's consulting service.
• Field distribution administrative services with the aid of financial and office services and the distribution systems development group in Rochester.
• Industrial relations administration for distribution and marketing personnel in the regional and district centers with the advice and counsel of Kodak office industrial relations department.
• Management of all domestic marketing and distribution facilities for photographic products.
• Coordinating use of "outside Rochester" facilities for photographic products with other company divisions.

As the marketing and distribution facilities department plans and develops facilities for both marketing and dis-

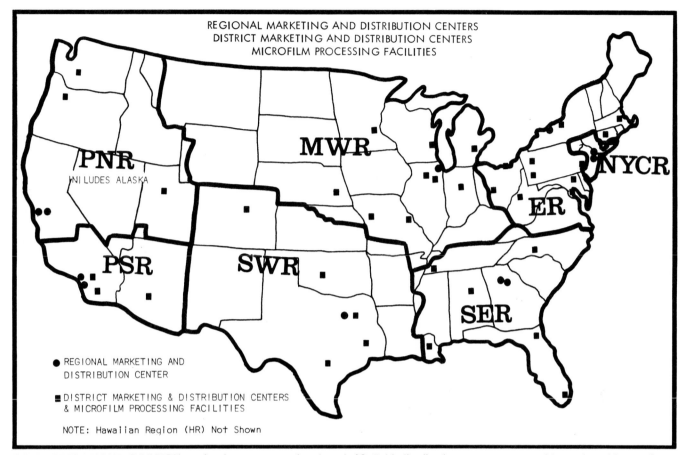

REGIONAL MARKETING AND DISTRIBUTION CENTERS
DISTRICT MARKETING AND DISTRIBUTION CENTERS
MICROFILM PROCESSING FACILITIES

PNR
INCLUDES ALASKA

MWR

NYCR

ER

PSR

SWR

SER

● REGIONAL MARKETING AND
  DISTRIBUTION CENTER

■ DISTRICT MARKETING & DISTRIBUTION CENTERS
  & MICROFILM PROCESSING FACILITIES

NOTE: Hawaiian Region (HR) Not Shown

FIELD OPERATIONS DIVISION maintains seven regional and 40 field distribution centers to provide nationwide service.

tribution use, so does the field operations division act as landlord. **"We provide the marketing division with not only real estate and related building services, but also with secretarial and clerical assistance in the field,"** states Field Operations Manager George A. Snyder. **"Thus, we free the sales people for their basic mission: to sell."**

Together, the regional and district distribution centers encompass three million square feet—more than 70 acres of space. During 1970, these facilities shipped 273 million pounds of freight, received about 1,250,000 orders and employed a total of 1,700 people, including more than 400 who serviced marketing and others, leaving a net distribution staff of approximately 1,300. Over a billion dollars' worth of sales were represented by 1970 field operations activities.

A wide diversity of products flows through the seven regional centers. They average about 7,000 stock items and handle many others ordered as required from central distribution centers in Rochester and Colorado.

When marketing and distribution were reorganized a few years back, distribution placed great emphasis on customer service improvement. Today, field operations is seeking to refine its procedures, maintaining high customer service levels but placing greater emphasis on cost control than in the past.

Growing experience coupled with improved performance measurement procedures aid the division in achieving a proper balance, yielding good service at the lowest possible cost. To fulfill this objective, management has

MANAGER-FIELD OPERATIONS George A. Snyder (left) discusses regional improvement program report with Eastern Region Distribution Manager Richard E. Ceder.

established a number of goals: service, accuracy, operating efficiency, financial and innumerable projects for the improvement of programs and systems.

"We are out to show a productivity increase in our sales per person ratio," Mr. Snyder notes, "and we are shooting for a 5% annual increase, which we are making."

Significant recent projects include a new stock control system and a district distribution center order processing and billing system. The latter involves putting additional billing operations upon the computer, paralleling in some measure systems now in use or under development at the regional level. Another new project is a computerized shipping ticket system for the regions.

Product handling, too, is the subject of much current attention. Unit load shipments from the Rochester Distribution Center to the regions and districts seem to offer a number of benefits and is under development. Bulk dragline systems are under study, following their installation at

AN EMPLOYE at a regional distribution center retrieves order information stored by the Kodak Miracode System, reviewing it on a Recordak Lodestar reader-printer.

the Eastern region center at Rochester. In the packaging area, field operations is currently testing shrink wrap.

While a multitude of individual projects are now under way within the regional improvement program, a single particular area has thus far proven the most fruitful for cost savings: transportation. Changes in modes and schedules, better leased truck utilization, expanded use of pool trucks and a variety of other aspects, being developed in coordination with the general traffic department, are expected to contribute markedly to improved regional distribution center efficiency.

Aiding these various transportation improvements is the fact that either a traffic manager or someone holding the general functional responsibility is resident in each region. While they report in each case to the regional operations manager, functionally, informally, they have a responsibility to General Traffic Manager Kenneth H. Jamieson. In effect, there is a "dotted line" relationship, comparable to the relationship between regional planning or stock control management and Manager-Estimating and Planning Roger Koehlinger.

Although the district distribution centers perform a more specialized, business products-oriented distribution function in general, a few of them are now supplying motion picture products and Kodagraph products as well. Last year, about 14 of the district centers moved a number of photographic items under a special Christmas promotion plan, and it is anticipated that the number of centers doing so will probably increase this year, thus getting stocks closer to dealers and improving the handling of emergency needs in the week before Christmas. "This is a temporary arrangement," states Mr. Snyder, "but it is a factor in our flexibility."

The regions work quite closely, supporting each other whenever necessary. A major conversion occurred at the Eastern region in Rochester early this year, and most of the other regions provided assistance to try to keep service levels at normal standards for the Rochester regional center. Assistance came as well from the company's Rochester Distribution Center—the huge bulk handling facility controlled by Distribution Center Manager George E. Yeomans and his department.

Distribution dynamics at work
Western Electric Company

Western Electric, the manufacturing and logistics arm of the American Telephone & Telegraph Company, has a simple basic duty: placing whatever material that telephone engineers and installers require in their hands precisely when needed anywhere in the United States. It may be a complex set of central station equipment requiring innumerable intermeshed moves over a period of months culminating in delivery on a specified date; it may be a single small insulater requested Tuesday by a rural lineman in West Virginia's mountains for Wednesday morning installation or it may be literally a total communication system made necessary without warning following a hurricane, flood or other natural disaster.

It is a system geared to handle emergencies, but nonetheless a system emphasizing efficiency. Western Electric knows well the potential economies of scale. As a huge shipper of small shipments, it has made a science out of consolidation programs. It is, like Eastman Kodak, a pioneer in distribution computerization, fitting programs to whatever functions reveal the necessary volume-complexity mix to justify them. New advances, such as cathode ray tubes, microfiche and modern data communications, all play major parts.

The company prides itself on its personnel training techniques and the continual advancement of individuals who demonstrate capabilities for upward movement. Training, both formal and informal, meshed with individualized personnel transfer and promotion programs, provides the transportation department with managers who know one another personally to a greater extent than is common among firms one tenth of Western Electric's size.

TRAFFIC MANAGEMENT's February, 1972 major case study of this company follows:

Matching transportation management to modern systems methods

MAINTAINING logistics for the Bell System telephone companies throughout the United States is a king-sized job. The transportation specialists of the Western Electric Company, manufacturing arm of AT&T, the world's largest public corporation, know it well. Their transportation organization is big by any standard. The staff numbers over 400, and the gross annual freight bill exceeds $135 million. Continuing expansion is a fact of life, as telephone usage increases because of rising living standards and increasing population.

Guided by Director of Transportation William P. Noonan, the organization is effecting major changes in its operating methods. Mr. Noonan assumed his present post in 1963 and has subsequently overseen changes in both organizational structure and departmental philosophy. These geared his organization to better handle the rapidly increasing day-to-day workload, while greatly expanding its staff role and forward planning capabilities. A once-orthodox traffic organization has become a

logistics-oriented unit fully attuned to its new role as a sophisticated user of modern management techniques in a computer environment.

Illustrated in the accompanying chart, the organization includes centralized staff functions coordinated closely with decentralized line activities. Regional assistant managers control much of the latter, reporting to Manager George Prill in the East or Manager Edward J. Dieter in the West, both of whom report in turn to Mr. Noonan. The assistant managers enjoy a considerable degree of autonomy in their territories. **"We feel," states Mr. Noonan, "that if you're going to hold these fellows responsible—and this is the name of the game—you've got to give them the authority to operate."**

The increasingly important staff transportation functions center at New York headquarters under Manager Planning, Development and Administration Alfred H. Odeven. He is supported in turn by three assistant managers. The first of these is responsible for planning, development and studies. The second is in charge of rates and routes, each operated as an individual department. A third assistant manager is responsible for claims, contracts and services. Passenger reservations, executive travel, expediting, tracing and household goods

moves with respect to headquarters operations are also within his purview.

The present revamped transportation organization has been carefully built up, piece by piece, reflecting the concern with personnel development for which Western Electric has been noted for many years. The remarkably extensive studies in industrial human relations conducted at the company's Hawthorne Works in the early 1930s remain to this day among the most significant ever undertaken in this field. A book entitled "Management and the Worker," written by Prof. F. J. Roethlisberger of Harvard University and William J. Dickson of Western Electric in 1939, a detailed analysis by two of the program's major participants, continues to be a highly respected reference text for academician and executive alike.

In refashioning his transportation organization, Mr. Noonan made heavy use of two tools that have become continually more effective: individual job reassignments to "round out" the experience of transportation management personnel and direct programs of training, both individual and group. It is quite common for transportation supervisory and technical personnel to be transferred or promoted frequently. Mr. Noonan's own background is a case in point. His 35-year Western Electric career, embracing several departments, has given him a broad background in total logistics as well as management.

The numerous position transfers, courses and workshops have an important side effect. Despite the organization's size and its nationwide scope, transportation people are pretty generally well acquainted with one another. Communications, therefore, are good, and team activity is effective. **"We're firm believers in 'job enrichment,' "** Mr. Noonan notes. **"Our people know they can have all the responsibility and authority they want to work for. When they're ready for more, we're ready to give it to them."**

The transportation organization's current thrust encompasses two primary areas:

Advanced data systems: Increasingly computer-oriented since installing several procedures in 1957-58, diversified new programs are building greater efficiency in most department activities.

Multilevel consolidations: A huge shipper of small shipments, computer-assisted consolidation development is achieving cost and service gains through three-stage consolidations, regional distribution and related techniques.

Elsewhere in this study, we review progress in both of these fields.

A manufacturing company by definition, Western Electric is perhaps even more a service company. The goods it sells to telephone companies invariably represent purchases timed for practically immediate use of material to keep investment down as well as cope with emergency conditions. Whether for the preplanned new installation or for service restoration following a hurricane, stocks must be available on short notice everywhere. Strategic stockpiles and effective transportation management hold the answer. Important, too, are outside contractor services. A wide network of public warehouses and transportation services, selected for proven capability, helps give the transportation organization its instant response capability.

Within the organization, while a development group concerns itself primarily with computer applications, a transportation systems research and design group works separately in furthering broader transportation concepts which may also call upon computer services as they develop. **"Our fellows represent a small traffic department within a major one,"** notes Transportation Supervisor **Nicholas J. Scocozzo. "They've been carefully selected to give a total transportation outlook to consideration of problems or proposals."**

Studies vary greatly, including the transportation economics impacting on site selection and analysis in conjunction with the company's long-range planning engineers, and development of total logistics systems for specific areas, as in a recent study reorienting procedures for the state of Virginia. A recent plan to consolidate three downstate New York repair facilities, reducing costs while maintaining or bettering previous turnaround times on repaired material represents another type.

Since 1967, this unit has conducted systemwide tonnage studies every second year. Covering all locations, it draws data from one of five forms filled out for every shipment during the chosen four-week sample period. An accompanying illustration shows the headings of these forms, several of which in the late 1971 study were

TRANSPORTATION ORGANIZATION'S basic structure appears in the above chart, reflecting the decentralization approach to which the department has moved in recent years. A major factor in this development has been improved communications and expanded computerization that effectively tie headquarters and field office operations together.

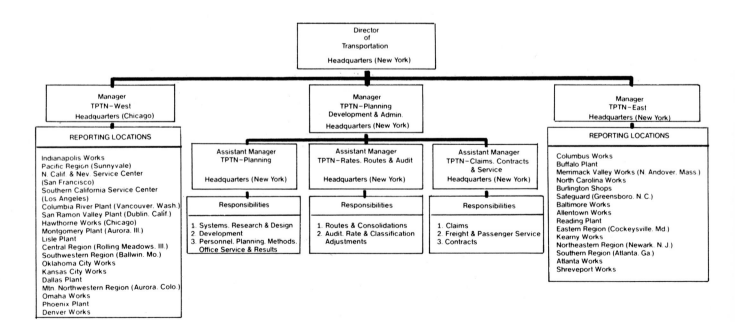

designed for reading by optical character recognition equipment to speed computer entry. A substantial task for field personnel, the payoff has been great in both direct cost benefits and in the development of new programs. Future such studies will be simpler as more of the needed data becomes retrievable through the department's proliferating computer systems.

Just how valuable these tonnage studies become is readily apparent in two of the many uses made of the 1969 study. The data made apparent the potential benefits of adopting a West Coast consolidation out of the Omaha Works. Implemented through the department's local office, it resulted in $200,000 annual savings—an ample return on a study costing $30,000.

The second case concerned a Southern Motor Carrier Rate Conference proposal to require that all cable on reels be lagged. "We were able to develop a quick claims ratio plus figures on where cable of ours moves in the South," Mr. Scocozzo states. "We were also able to compare our claims ratio on a national basis with experience in the South. **This by-product analysis from our tonnage study permitted us to go on record before the bureau to the effect that lagging our cable would have created an unnecessary hardship costing $1,750,000. This is a clear cost avoidance. It is just one more of many ways in which the tonnage survey pays for itself many times over."**

The 1969 tonnage study revealed that three million out of four million shipments were small, adding impetus to consolidation development and further research in this area. The 1971 study, extremely comprehensive, embraced approximately 500,-000 line items.

Good communication, a natural byword in a communications equipment manufacturing company, profits from a unique, inexpensive telephone procedure recently developed, tieing field locations with New York headquarters for broad-scale dissemination of priority information. TELFACT (Telephone Facsimile Transmission) started to work in the fall of 1970 as the result of a transportation workshop suggestion. Assistant Man-

TELFACT, a telephone "broadcasting" procedure, employs two telephone-answering equipment sets to deliver prerecorded bulletins nationwide among transportation offices. Assistant Manager Francis J. Rizzo "reads in" one of the twice-daily messages available to offices dialing the TELFACT number.

ager Francis J. Rizzo developed and now maintains the procedure.

TELFACT needs little equipment. A conventional telephone answering set will do the job, although the department uses two with the thought that ultimately there might be value in supplying different messages for specific regions. The 37 field transportation offices call the numbers assigned these sets in the morning and

again in the afternoon to pick up news, requests for information, special instructions or current information of general value. It has also been helpful in smoothing the way for subsequent individual calls for information.

Placing the message on the units is a simple procedure. The written text is read above the telephone headsets, which are lifted from their cradles to

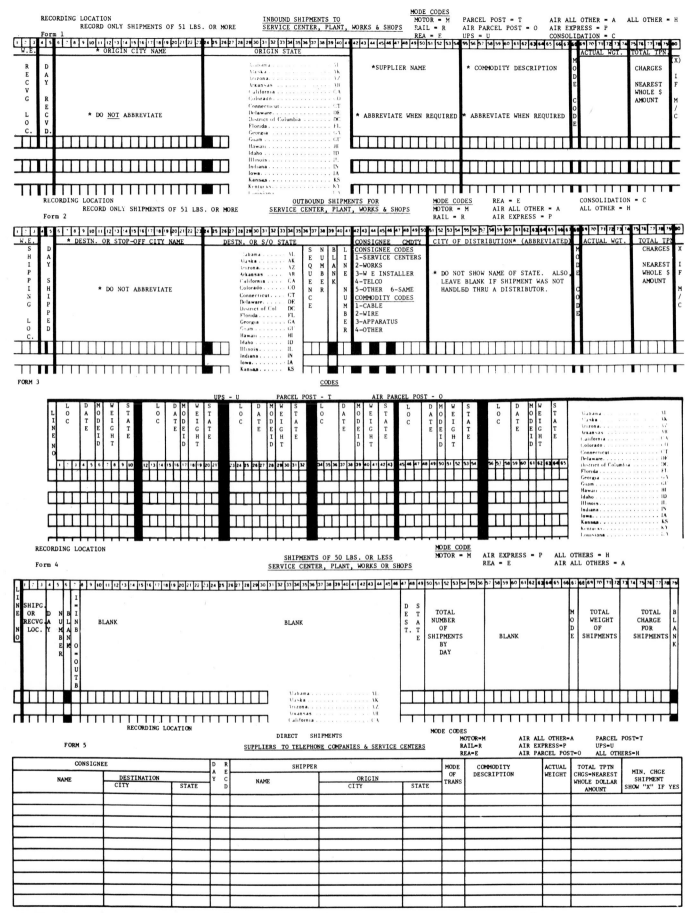

LATEST TONNAGE SURVEY performed by the Western Electric transportation organization employed five data retrieval forms, the headings of which are illustrated above. Their comprehensive nature was suggested by results of the preceding biennial survey, which indicated the vital significance of small shipments in the total picture. Of these forms, four were designed for computer reading through the use of optical character recognition equipment.

record the announcements, after which the messages become immediately available to callers.

"TELFACT has really paid off in many situations," states Mr. Noonan. "Our vice president, Paul Zweier, requested some data at 4 p.m. one day but did not indicate any particular urgency. He called just after 8:30 the next morning and said, 'Have you that information yet?' 'I didn't know it was that hot,' I responded, 'but I'll have it for you shortly.' We put it on TELFACT, and the whole country responded before 11 a.m. So we put it in his hands at 11:30."

With growing computerization, transportation organization attention is placed upon external possibilities as well as in-house systems. It was in 1965 that Mr. Noonan called a meeting of principal shippers to focus on the problem of computer data standards. Out of this was developed an ad hoc committee in the National Industrial Traffic League. This, in turn, captured the interest of other concerned groups and led to today's Transportation Data Coordinating Committee in which Western Electric is very active.

Systems innovations, diversified consolidations, controlled contract services, management development—these hold the keys to future transportation development at Western Electric. Their significance draws further attention on the pages that follow.

Training the experts

TRANSPORTATION managers gather no rust at Western Electric. Promotion within is a rule, and frequent job changes are fairly typical. **"We want our men to be all around transportation experts," states Manager Planning, Development and Administration Alfred H. Odeven. "Careful individual career programing facilitates this in significant measure.** Obviously, operating efficiency requires that people enter their new posts with sufficient prior training and orientation to perform effectively."

The department makes heavy use of diversified external courses and seminars as well as internal meetings to further staff training. In a recent instance, a special midday course in export traffic was given to a group at the Academy of Advanced Traffic. The major activity, however, is on-the-job training. It assumes many forms. The accompanying chart illustrates a number of training modules and some of the possible relationships between them.

In the case of a newly hired employe or a person promoted into the department at entry level, he will typically assume a C5 grade level under company standards. In the normal line of progression, depending upon his potentials and the available assignments, lines of promotion will lead up through grade C9, after which movement may be either into direct managerial promotional channels (section chief, department chief) or through specialist channels in graded administrative, nonsupervisory positions (ANS-1, ANS-2, etc.). At whatever level an employe is to function, the training modules provide a basis not only for immediate new instruction, but for reorientation and updating as well.

The program's introductory phase is being converted in some measure to take advantage of one of the newer teaching aids—prerecorded cassettes. With three separate 15 to 20-minute cassettes covering this phase, the trainee listens at his leisure during his orientation period and, more importantly, may listen to them several times, or repeat specific portions, thus insuring a thorough understanding.

"This offers a clear advantage," notes Assistant Manager, Planning, Development and Personnel Francis J. Rizzo. "The trainee now has the advantage of a sufficient, self-imposed time period to absorb information and to review specifics that would not be practical in direct discussions with department personnel. **The cassettes, therefore, offer a reduction in management time for instruction while materially enriching this phase of presentation for the trainee."**

These cassettes, in fact, can be of value to more than just beginners entering the department. They can speed transition for an employe "lateraled" in from another Western Electric department and can serve to refresh existing employes on current transportation department conditions.

The cassettes, in addition to the above-indicated advantages, offer a further benefit. By generating copies of these, they may be forwarded all over the country, and any new personnel will thus receive the same information as those entering the headquarters office. At most, only minor revisions or additions would be necessary to account for a few activities not performed at all locations.

In addition to the introductory cassettes, persons in the orientation phase receive what is essentially a "guided tour" through diversified activities within the department, becoming acquainted with not only transportation department management people, but those in adjacent parallel functions as well. Essentially, this is the total orientation program offered both transportation and non-transportation people. If, however, the trainee is to stay in transportation, still further exposures are provided.

Newcomers to transportation at the C5 level will get "basic training" in rudimentary traffic assignments designed to familiarize them with rates and tariffs, working procedures and the general flow of department activity. Subsequent progression may find them moving through grade C6 in the passenger service area or directly to C7.

"When we get a man into the C7 grade," observes Mr. Odeven, "there are two requirements we feel necessary for him to be an effective transportation man. He must have freight service and audit experience. Really, simply, rate training. Time permitting, we like people at C7 level to experience claims, passenger service and development as well. Some exposure to the specialized activities within classification and contracts is also beneficial."

If conditions do not permit thorough indoctrination in areas other than freight service and audit, Mr. Rizzo and his staff offer mini-programs covering the phases shown on the accompanying chart. Offering briefer exposure than normal work

DISCUSSING a proposed training "package" for a soon-to-be-promoted manager with Director of Transportation William P. Noonan (standing) are (left to right): Assistant Manager Francis J. Rizzo, Manager Transportation-East George Prill and Manager Planning, Development and Administration Alfred H. Odeven.

TRANSPORTATION TRAINING PROGRAMS

CUSTOM-TAILORED TRAINING, fitted to the individual's needs and potential, can be prepared in countless variations within the overall pattern charted here. Seminars, cassette-lectures, individual meetings, committee activities and hands-on experience assure that both updating and upgrading are available at every stage of personal career development.

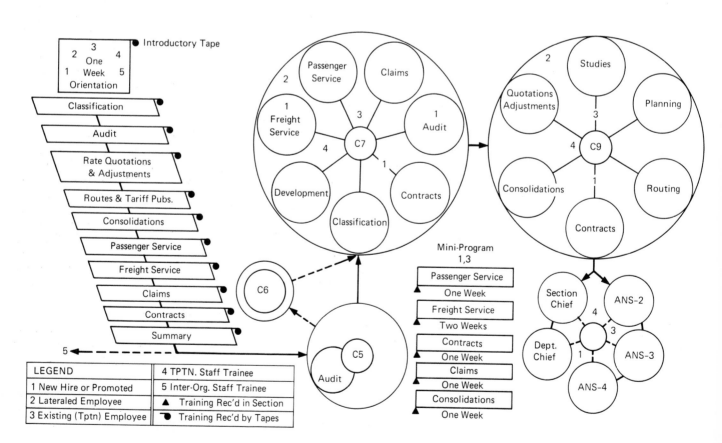

assignments, the mini-programs nonetheless assure sufficient "hands-on" experience to give transportation people the flavor of these activities.

At the C9 level, the highest grade prior to managerial or administrative nonsupervisory positions, there are six specialties pinpointed as essential to transportation personnel's continuing development. Similar stress is placed on all of these.

Normally, those entering grade C9 from within the department have had an adequate grounding in prior positions for their new assignments. Nevertheless, there are entrants, either from other departments in this grade or outside of the company, who may lack needed familiarity with department activities. Here, again, the initial introductory cassettes, as well as tailored-to-the-individual mini-programs, make the difference in building job effectiveness.

"Consider our rate men, for instance," states Mr. Rizzo. "We formerly trained them in audit. For this particular group, we found that training is more effective in the rate adjustment and quotation section. **In a recent example, a C9 went through this training, learning to check rates in all bureaus within six months. He never would have accomplished this training within such a brief period if he had worked instead on audit.** Now he will go on a production job in the audit function. He may not yet be a crackerjack rate man, but he can operate in any bureau. We've never been able to train a rate man that fast before."

Training administration is in all cases geared to the individual's capacities. Instead of an arbitrary three months here and six months there, management watches the progress of individuals and moves them forward at a rate to match their aptitudes and needs. The constant measurement of individual employe performance, coupled with regular, programed reassignments, effectively blurs the line between "training programs" and "career advancement." For transportation personnel, learning leads to greater responsibilities which, in themselves, advance learning.

Area teams manage a plant group's traffic

WESTERN ELECTRIC'S Hawthorne Works is an impressive industrial complex by any standard. Employing over 13,000 people at its suburban Chicago location, it is the largest manufacturing entity among the several the company operates.

As may be expected, transportation statistics here are on the heavy side: last year, 24 million pounds of outbound freight moved monthly; the annual transportation bill exceeded $13 million; passenger reservations numbered 20,000, accompanied by 10,000 hotel and motel reservations, and approximately 350 household moves were processed. A 31-man transportation staff, plus associates at the Montgomery, Ill. satellite plant and the Rolling Meadows Regional Center, has the full responsibility.

Hawthorne's recently reorganized transportation department operates on a regional basis. What amounts to a complete small traffic organization does the routing, expediting, auditing and other transportation tasks for freight destined to assigned sectors, such as Mountain-Northwest and Pacific territories. Another group covers the Eastern part of the United States, while a third controls Central-South-Southwest. A support group handles passenger reservations, some inbound routing, household goods, contracts and various administrative matters that are not regional. Each of the regional groups numbers approximately five to six people.

An important consideration in going regional was the new Merchandise Data Management (MDM) procedure recently developed for the merchandising department. "Under our former methods, transportation handled a large volume of manually prepared routing requests from the merchandising people," Resident Transportation Manager E. L. Johnson, Jr. notes. "The old system allowed three days for our people to develop these routings and return the papers to the merchandising department. With computerization, we're shortening the available time interval. **By regionalizing so that a trans-**portation group works with a smaller part of a total, we can live with the shortened time computerization permits us."

Is it worth it? According to John W. McCarthy, department chief, shipping, clerical and routing, who was largely responsible for developing this system in the merchandising department, savings on clerical effort alone will lie somewhere between $100,000 and $300,000 annually. In addition, several highly complex procedures that hid numerous clerical errors have been eliminated, indicating large unmeasurable potential savings plus important service benefits.

Substantial traffic data are included in the programing, the computer taking on preparation of carloading sheets, a listing of all boxes and cartons of freight, summarization of freight in terms of pieces and pieces-by-commodity-by-freight class, producing not only individual shipment-related papers but also management reports and summary information for an expanding data base.

The transportation organization's duties are broadly diversified, but one in particular sees maximum concentrated effort. **"We were able to reduce 1970's freight bill by $2.4 million through consolidation, so consolidation is our way of life,"** Mr. Johnson asserts. This growing activity encompasses 48 regularly scheduled surface consolidations, many operated twice or more each week—even daily—plus 18 daily air consolidations and innumerable on-the-spot ones—targets of opportunity—assembled to various points when shipping documents suggest the possibility. Increased shipment document computerization gives this latter type growing significance, with speedier data retrieval simplifying the selection process.

The 18 daily air consolidations move as regular cargo by scheduled airlines. Weights range from 200 to 4,000 pounds daily, with the three largest destinations being San Francisco, Los Angeles and New York. Western Electric pioneered the new LD-3 containers, designed for large-bodied jets, from Chicago in mid-1971. The Los Angeles shipment each day generally includes two such containers plus an accompanying outside piece going at the container rate.

TRACING/EXPEDITING REQUEST □ ORIGINATED □ SERVICED

FILE REF | CONSIGNEE | DESTINATION
ORDER NO. | SUPPLIER | ORIGIN
REASON FOR EXPEDITING | START DATE | ON JOB DATE | ROUTE
EXPEDITING REQ REC'D FROM & TEL NO | ORG./LOCATION | TIME | DATE | PIECES | WEIGHT | MATERIAL
NOTIFY | BUSI-NESS | CITY | PHONE | CAR NO.
| HOME | CITY | PHONE |
BILL OF LADING NO. | DATE | | STOP-OFF AT | PIECES | WEIGHT | ORDER NO.
PICKUP DETAILS
CARRIER NO. | DATE | TRUCK/CAR NO. | TIME | DATE
CARRIER NO. | DATE | DRIVER | TO STATION/AIRPORT | TRANSLOAD AT
| | | | HOLD AT AIRPORT FOR PICK UP

OUT IN	STATION	CAR. TRUCK. ETC.	TIME	DATE	TRAIN FLT. ETC.	CARDED	DUE TIME/DATE	RECORD REC'D FROM OR GIVEN TO NAME	TIME	DATE	BY
								FROM TO			TEL/TWX
								FROM TO			TEL/TWX
								FROM TO			TEL/TWX
								FROM TO			TEL/TWX
								FROM TO			TEL/TWX
								FROM TO			TEL/TWX

CARRIER	LOCATION/TEL. NO.	PERSON	TIME/DATE	BY	RECORD OF PERTINENT COMMENTS OR SPECIAL ARRANGEMENTS
CARRIER CONTACTS

FRONT AND BACK of Hawthorne's standard tracing-expediting forms. Numerous high-value, top priority shipments make effective expediting a must, greatly assisted by close coordination of effort among regional transportation offices.

From the destination cities, the component individual shipments fan out over wide areas. States Manager, Transportation Administration, Planning and Development Alfred H. Odeven: "The significant factor here is that when you hit 1,500 pounds, the air rate to the West Coast becomes $14 per hundred, while the truck rate is $14.20 at first class. This has the effect of placing a ceiling on the amount of ever-increasing labor costs the trucking industry will be able to pass on to the shipper in the future. We're slowly getting into the position where we may fly more of our freight. **Truckers are going to have to take a hard look at their costs and increase their efficiency to compensate for part of the increased labor costs. We think the time has come when they are going to have to quit passing on to the shipper 100% of what they settle for at the bargaining table."**

West Coast UPS material is metered at Hawthorne based on rates applicable from either San Francisco or Los Angeles to final destinations. Flown to these points in LD-3 containers, delivery is direct to UPS, where the contents are disbursed as individual shipments up and down the coast. This is a multiple cost reduction: the consolidation technique initially reduces costs, while the LD-3 container enjoys the benefit of a lower air cargo rate.

The Hawthorne warehouse works two shifts, with airfreight generally selected at night and delivered to the airport early the following morning. Freight moving in the scheduled consolidations, therefore, generally enjoys an afternoon delivery at the destination airport. In the case of dire emergencies, however, the freight will not wait for consolidation, but moves out as individual shipments on an expedited basis.

Surface consolidation, embracing rail cars, piggybacks and common carrier trucking, has been going through a "rolling readjustment." A long-time practice, the ways in which it is done are changing drastically out of Hawthorne. Before January, 1970, LTL freight left via local cartage company and was peddled to appropriate Chicago carriers, but growing volume coupled with street traffic delays pointed up the need for

A TRANSPORTATION SHOWCASE lies beyond office window as Resident Transportation Manager E.L. Johnson (right) confers with Department Chief, Transportation G. P. Nelson about further refining Hawthorne's consolidation procedures.

change. Accordingly, the transportation organization regionalized the country into 12 blocks, assigning each to an individual carrier for LTL pickup. Under this plan, a carrier spots his trailer, takes loads for all points in his area and then transfers the load through his terminal according to his own transportation pattern. Carriers were assigned individual states based upon normal tonnage flow, equating the business among them.

As Western Electric's volume continues to grow, additional problems come to view, and in October, 1970, a new solution evolved, based initially on the Tower Trucking Distribution operation at Elizabeth, N.J., but subsequently expanding through other similar centers at strategic points. Called Wide Area Distribution (WADS), it entails bulk movement of LTL as well as volume freight to distant regional locations where it may in turn marry Western Electric freight from other origins or move separately as conditions dictate for final short-haul delivery.

"We're shipping 12 to 15 piggyback loads a week to our New Jersey point," notes Mr. Johnson. "It worked so well that last February we went into Nashville for the states of Alabama, Mississippi, Louisiana, Tennessee and Kentucky. A month later, we went to Atlanta for Georgia, Florida, North Carolina and South Carolina. Our next will probably be somewhere in the Southwest. We had consolidations to these regions before, but of a different type that was not so all inclusive."

Benefits from the new system accrue to the merchandise organization as well as to transportation. Some of the gains include:

Direct transportation savings: On the New Jersey volume for the Northeastern area alone, an additional $50,000 cost reduction is realized annually.

CLOSE CONTROL over household moves means more than just making contracts. At Hawthorne, as elsewhere, follow-up keeps check on van line performance, assuring proper standards are maintained to minimize inconvenience for employe families while providing performance analysis for carrier selection guidance.

EIGHTEEN daily air shipment consolidations move from Hawthorne. Western Electric pioneered the use of these large jet containers in the Chicago area.

Van Line

To: Transportation Organization

Re: Household Goods - Appraisal of Carrier Service
 Origin Agent _____ City or Town _____
 Destination Agent _____ City or Town _____

1. Packing   Excellent   2. Courtesy and   Excellent
                    Satisfactory   Cooperation   Satisfactory
                    Unsatisfactory   at Origin   Unsatisfactory

3. Unpacking   Excellent   4. Courtesy and   Excellent
                    Satisfactory   Cooperation   Satisfactory
                    Unsatisfactory   at Destination   Unsatisfactory

5. Removal of Packing Material   Excellent
                                                            Satisfactory
                                                            Unsatisfactory

6. Was delivery accomplished at residence on the date promised?

7. Was the unpacking completed by the moving company? If not, please give details.

8. Was any portion of the shipment loaded on the tailgate of the moving van?

9. Did carrier provide satisfactory services at origin incidental to the packing and moving of your household goods and personal effects? YES___ NO___ At destination? YES___ NO___

10. Were any other services, not mentioned above, rendered unsatisfactorily by the mover.

11. COMMENTS:

 Van arrived at origin_____ at_____ AM and departed_____ AM.
                     Date   Time PM   Time PM

 Van arrived at destination_____ at_____ AM and departed_____ AM.
                          Date   Time PM   Time PM

 _____
 Employees Signature

 _____
 Date

Faster deliveries: Shipments no longer hold over even one day for additional weight. They also move over the road faster because more of them are in volume shipments, both out of Hawthorne and beyond the intermediate consolidation-distribution center.

Reduced shipping effort: For the affected regions, freight requires no staging, but flows directly to waiting piggybacks or over-the-road trailers. Holding freight to build specific loads for one or two days becomes unnecessary, eliminating dock overtime that arose when several loads would coincide.

Improved potential for secondary consolidations: Because Hawthorne freight arriving at a distribution facility meets freight from Omaha, Oklahoma City and other Western Electric origins, all these points mutually improve their chances to build beyond volume shipments for specific consignees and minimize smaller shipments, minimum charges, etc.

Paralleling the Kelly operation described elsewhere in this issue, Hawthorne benefits from a Chicago area consolidation contract operation for West Coast and other traffic. Tying its own flow in with Western Electric vendor material moving through this facility, from three to five batteries of carloads move to the coast each week, including from 4 to 21 cars in each battery.

Transportation has a big job on the inbound side, too. They receive about 3,600 carloads per year, as well as a substantial truck volume. Outbound approximates 270 carloads a month plus 450 piggyback or truckloads.

Expediting is particularly important in Western Electric traffic because so many shipments are scheduled to fulfill closely timed requirements in construction or installation projects, while others often are replacement materials bearing some priority. Though procedures vary somewhat around the country, different company units work closely to assist each other in tracing activities.

A "hot" shipment from the Kearny, N.J. Works bound for Denver will be watched en route by other transportation offices as well. People at Columbus will shepherd it through their area and inform Hawthorne of

SPECIAL YARD TRACTORS quickly move motor carrier and piggyback trailers between dock positions at Hawthorne's shipment-handling facilities.

the forwarding, while Hawthorne will in turn make sure it moves properly through its own sector, advising Denver of the forwarding. **"This way,"** **states Manager Transportation-West** **Edward J. Dieter, "the originator** **isn't trying to reach out all the way** **from Kearny, N.J. to talk to people.** **Fellows the beyond carriers know are** **talking to them about it."**

Hawthorne uses a special expediting form, a copy of which is illustrated, initiated by the consignor in all cases, although expediting may be at the consignee's request. "We originate 15,000 of these forms a year here," Mr. Johnson observes, "and have 5,000 that we get from other offices passing through Chicago going either east or west of us. On these 'passing through' forms, we'll alert the affected carrier and then subsequently check him, passing the information on to the next affected office for their follow-through."

Expedited bills are stamped with a big "X" and carry a telephone number which the carrier is to call upon receipt of such a bill. When the carrier calls, the information is recorded on a special device and stored for subsequent transportation personnel retrieval, thus minimizing the

number of individual telephone calls necessary to the department staff. Carriers like it because there is no delay waiting for an answer on such calls, or no problems with busy signals. They can "deposit" their information 24 hours a day.

The carrier's call is the first notification to the transportation organization concerning the expedited shipment. The expedite card is then filled out based on the forwarding recorded by the carrier, after which the information is passed to the next transportation office or the consignee.

Though logistics is not centrally managed, Western Electric maintains interdisciplinary staff activities that further the total cost concept. Many cooperative operations, some involving projects, some continuous liaison, further this cause. **"Our loading and** **packaging engineers are located adjacent to us at Hawthorne," Mr. Dieter** **comments. "They report into merchandise, but we work very closely** **with them. This neighborly placement** **was deliberate to facilitate close cooperation."**

A good example is an inspection team that includes a supervisor from transportation, a merchandise loading group supervisor, a packaging engineer and a merchandising division claims man. This group makes weekly dock area inspections to see that company procedures, local regulations and AAR rules are observed in preparing shipments. (Their "Inspection of Loading" form is illustrated.) They also conduct inspections at carriers' facilities, checking with them for problems at either end of a move and making certain that Hawthorne itself is providing material in proper order to the carriers. Periodically, test cars will move forward, and team members will meet them at the destinations to check conditions in the company of carrier representatives.

Regional distribution: Supplying the field

WESTERN ELECTRIC'S Atlanta Regional Transportation office, overseeing activities in the nine-state Southeastern region, operates in a different traffic environment than is found in the region controlled from Chicago. While Assistant Manager E. L. Johnson, Jr., located at the giant Hawthorne Works, necessarily devotes much of his organization's efforts to the needs of the Hawthorne complex, Assistant Manager John Ballard's principal concerns lie in the field. Destination control gets major emphasis, although the soon-to-be-opened Atlanta cable plant will significantly change the complexion of activities.

Administration centers primarily in the Atlanta transportation office, but there is a separate unit at Shreveport, La. as well and another subordinate traffic function at the Atlanta cable plant which is preparing to handle the heavy traffic this source will generate. Central office activity flows through two groups: a service unit does all of the auditing and claims work, expediting, tracing, passenger reservations, household moves and day-to-day traffic activities, and a separate unit handles the warehousing, distribution and hauling and hoisting contracts (see "Warehouse Logistics" in this issue).

Sophisticated consolidation procedures play an increasing part in the nine-state shipping pattern. As Manager Planning, Administration and Development Alfred H. Odeven notes: **"We recognize we are primarily a large shipper of small shipments. Our answer has been to work consistently toward making larger shipments out of them through consolidation and other effective plans. We believe the small shipment problem, insofar as our company is concerned, is one that it is up to us to resolve internally. We work steadily toward this end."**

Already enjoying consolidation benefits from two distant operations (Kelly Konsolidating at Kearny, N.J. and Modern Shipping at Chicago, servicing the Hawthorne Works), the Southeastern region has now established two new distribution centers within its area as well. Freight formerly moving LTL from numerous Western Electric and vendor origins to Southeastern points now funnels through Atlanta for North Carolina, South Carolina, Georgia and Florida destinations, while Kentucky, Tennessee, Alabama, Mississippi and Louisiana locations are served out of Nashville. Thus, a factory can load a consolidated truck with freight for four or five states to either point, enjoying substantial economies, and the regional transportation department will arrange the beyond distribution.

"I don't think we have anything running over a week's transit interval for cumulative legs of the shipment," states Mr. Ballard, **"yet we were running something like 16 days on LTL from Chicago to Miami prior to this development."** Transportation personnel check carrier performance regularly and closely.

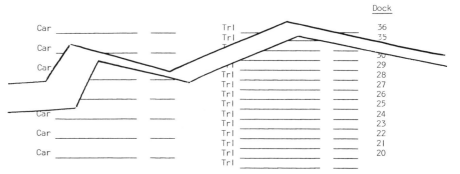

MEMORANDUM FOR RECORD

Re: LOADING - FILE 200 - REPORT OF INSPECTION OF LOADING

On _____, 1971, a joint inspection of Merchandise cars and trucks by representatives of the Hawthorne Warehouse, Transportation, Claims and Engineering Organizations revealed the following exceptions to good loading.

OTHER TRAILERS NOT INDICATED WERE LOADED PROPERLY FOR SAFE TRANSIT.

EXAMPLES OF EXCEPTIONS

1. Insufficient doorway protection.
2. Void space not filled with dunnage.
3. Blocking defective or inadequate.
4. Disregard of signs on cartons.
5. Separation not considered.
6. Beltrails not covered (cushioned).
7. Damaged cartons found in lading.
8. Improperly loaded.
9. Incomplete.

COMMENTS:

Inspected by:

_____ Transportation

_____ Engineering

_____ Claims

_____ Warehouse

FORM 200, "Inspection of Loading," is regularly completed on sample shipments by committee members from the transportation organization and other management units to assure proper performance by company personnel and carriers.

Setting up the Atlanta and Nashville centers materially improved services while holding down costs, but even greater benefits will soon accrue following completion of systems changes. The practice has been for each factory to make up its own bills of lading. While this will continue, changes will be made in payment procedures.

The distributors have generally done one of two things: either they have received shipments on bills marked for the carrier to bill the factory direct or, in most cases, the distributor has paid the freight charges, subsequently billing the origin for the cost. New procedures will change this. Hereafter, freight will come into Atlanta or Nashville with beyond addresses indicated, but billed only to the distribution point. Goods will leave on bills originated at these points, with the regional office handling both payment and paperwork.

"We don't have to worry about shuffling money back and forth within the company under this procedure," Mr. Ballard comments. "Also, it will relieve our distributors, who are primarily outside contractors, from having to tie up capital paying these bills and **thus will encourage a greater number of qualified people to quote on our distribution contracts—an important factor to us in our growing market.**"

The new procedure offers an opportunity for significant further economies through secondary consolidations. In the case of shipments moving to Dothan, Ala. on a given occasion, for instance, these might readily include a 10,000-pound one forwarded from the Northeast by Kelly Konsolidating, a second 10,000-pound shipment from Modern Shipping in Chicago and a third from Western Electric's large Omaha plant. Up until now, these would necessarily have moved forward from the distributor as separate LTL shipments, with billing to be paid by the origin locations. New 1972 procedures will see them move forward on one master bill of lading from Atlanta at truckload rates.

The same thing might well happen to other freight arriving with such Dothan shipments from the aforementioned origins in the building of

A NEW 50-TON LOCOMOTIVE shifts cars at the new Atlanta cable plant, where 4½ miles of track are operated by Western Electric within the plant area.

additional secondary consolidations to other Southeastern points. Clearly, this two-phase system offers substantial economies, but the service factor in an organization where so many goods move in connection with closely scheduled construction work may well mean more.

This procedural change means increased traffic activity at the Atlanta transportation office, as an additional $700,000 worth of distribution freight charges will pass through its hands annually. A still greater change will take place as the new cable plant comes on line. Its first outbound freight is scheduled for April 1, and its inbound raw materials requirements will exceed 215 million pounds per year.

Where rail figured comparatively little in regional traffic, the new plant will develop substantial rail traffic, both inbound and outbound. It will, in fact, include a railroad of its own, some 4 1/2 miles of track and a 50-ton diesel-electric switching locomotive servicing the heavy flow of shipments.

Facilities include a truck scale just beyond the plant entrance gate as well as rail car weighing facilities, thus assuring check weights for vehicles and cars, both light and loaded. Plastic bulk-handling facilities are being provided to take care of large inbound shipments of plastic insulating materials by both modes.

As in other Western Electric regions, the Atlanta transportation office handles all types of transportation requirements, including household moves and passenger traffic.

Household moves, however, have been particularly heavy in recent times.

"We normally run somewhere around 200 moves a year," states Mr. Ballard, "but the new cable plant has been creating an extremely heavy inbound flow at this stage. We had approximately 250 plant-related inbound moves last year over and above our normal flow. This really gets difficult, because if you have a heavy movement of people into an area, all the bookings are on the other end, and the big fee percentage goes to the origin booking agent. **You've got to do a lot of public relations work with your local carriers,** therefore, because their relatively small percentage for destination service may cause them to overlook the long-term benefit of future business deriving from our increased size and subsequent outbound moves which may be booked through them."

The department not only sees to the conventional moving aspects, but also arranges for minor modifications within the premises to existing utilities at the new home site to accommodate the family's appliances, seeing to it that they are properly installed and operative. More than that, they will make certain of the proper handling of possessions beyond the usual household items— boats and even a portable swimming pool.

Continuing methods refinement, a transportation trademark in this company, will soon reflect in yet another unique application: There will be no conventional tariff file at the Atlanta cable plant. In its stead, microfiche tariff pages and a microfiche reader occupying a minimum of space will serve in lieu of conventional, cumbersome rows of tariff files.

Automated consolidations from Northeast

SHIPMENT CONSOLIDATION is big business at Western Electric, but nowhere bigger than at Kelly Konsolidating, the contractor-operated consolidation center at Kearny, N.J. From this location, 91 different consignees receive 1,500,000 to 1,750,000 pounds of freight weekly. Some 1,700 shippers at 1,000 different origins in the Northeastern states feed into this facility for nationwide fan-out.

In a directly reverse operation, Tower Transportation, located a few miles away at the Elizabeth, N.J. Wheeling Warehouse, receives consolidated shipments from a number of Western Electric manufacturing centers around the country, distributing them over essentially the same area from which the Kelly operation draws its freight.

This operation has been under way at the New Jersey meadows location since August, 1969. Replacing previous centers handled by two separate contractors, the new location can handle significantly greater volume with maximum economy. The facility was built to Western Electric specifications and turned over to them under a leaseback arrangement. Kelly Konsolidating operates the center under a contractual arrangement with Western Electric.

Speedy paperwork handling despite high volume results from computerized consolidation processing, employing, up to the present, key tape units at the New Jersey location, tied to an IBM 360 computer at Western Electric's downtown New York City headquarters. Entering service March 1, however, is a new procedure employing cathode ray tube (CRT) equipment in place of the key tape units. The accompanying flow chart illustrates the sequence of events in processing a typical shipment.

JOHN F. BALLARD (left), resident transportation manager, reviews a computer-produced report with (l. to r.): Transportation Associate R. T. Wise, Transportation Department Chief M.A. Jedrzejak and Transportation Specialist M.C. Kelly.

Following the chart, a sample shipment and its delivery sheet, upon arrival at the consolidation center, are processed through the HIC (house inventory control) system, which assigns an HIC number, in this instance 11-1234—11 signifying November and the subsequent digits indicating this is the 1,234th shipment for that month. The freight is also marked with symbol 03, a numeric code for its destination (Atlanta), while the 12 below the HIC number shows there are 12 pieces in this shipment.

The delivery sheets, under the new procedure, are processed through the COPS (Coding of Priority Shipments) system, which sorts the freight bills by scheduled ship dates. With the advent of the new CRT equipment, a new system known as TOPS (Transportation On Line Processing System) will be instituted, whereby shipment data may be transmitted directly to the New York computer, with a dedicated portion of that computer validating instantaneously the information transmitted directly from the display tube. The new system requires less effort for the coding-transmittal operation and will greatly speed information flow, at the same time reducing unnecessary work at the New York computer unit, since the improved accuracy will eliminate daily transaction or validation runs previously necessary.

Even as the shipment itself is staged, selected and loaded on a trailer or rail car, the computer swings into action on related paperwork. It prepares the destination manifest for that particular consolidation, which is mailed promptly from the local post office, arriving at the destination in time to aid the consignee in properly unloading the trailer.

The computer rates each inbound shipment, feeding data into the APS (Accounts Payable System) for carrier payment. It also generates data to prepare a rail bill of lading which is submitted with a manifest to the originating carrier on West Coast rail shipments.

Motor carrier payments are made seven times a month based on freight bills produced by the Western Electric computer. An itemized statement accompanies the computer-prepared check—a summary of inbound charges—and is forwarded to each affected carrier without awaiting the carrier's statement.

Ordinarily prepared within the first five days of each month, a monthly accounting report covers each contributor into the consolidations, serving as the freight bill chargeable to these locations. In the case of Western Electric's Kearny Works, for example, the report will

Transportation On Line Processing System (TOPS)

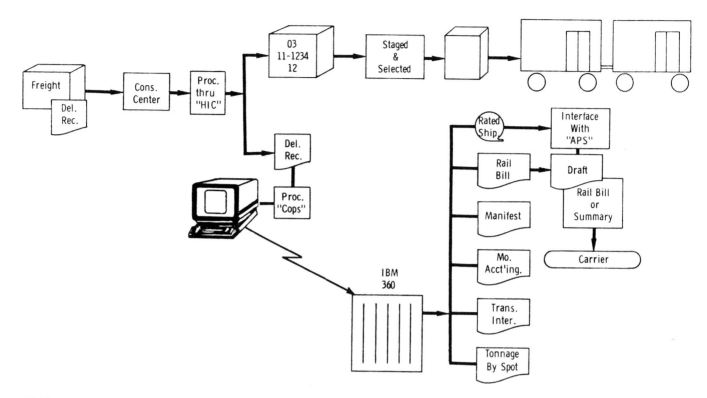

CHART illustrates shipment and paperwork flow in the "TOPS" system, or Transportation On Line Processing System, which speeds consolidations through a computerized procedure using a CRT terminal unit at consolidation center.

run typically about six pages in length.

The "tonnage by spot" report summarizes daily tonnage received for each destination point or "spot," including all consignees at each location. This data helps determine shipping schedules, suggesting changes in frequency or specific sailing days when patterns change.

Highly significant to management is the transit interval report, issued monthly, listing actual transit times for every shipment by carrier. This data is tested against computer-stored acceptable transit times, developed in conjunction with the carriers, and an exception listing constitutes report Part 2, summarizing all shipments that exceeded the proper transit times. Notes Assistant Manager John A. Miltenis: **"This is a very valuable tool. Our routing section writes carriers immediately when their performance slips. The report is also helpful as a reminder of carrier virtues or vices when solicitors call."**

Fast handling of the freight itself parallels computer efficiency in the

paperwork. "We try to get a carrier in and out as fast as possible," notes Transportation Specialist Peter Cuicci, who represents Western Electric at the Kelly operation. "That's the reason we went into a day-night operation, primarily.

"During the daytime, we receive

freight, mark and segregate it, and place it in its proper dock location. At 3 p.m., the night crew takes over, loading all freight possible onto waiting rail cars or piggyback trailers. This assures maximum utilization of mechanized equipment. Lift trucks need not be diverted from receiving

WESTERN ELECTRIC Transportation Specialist Peter Cuicci (right) reviews a scheduled rail car consolidation with Kelly Konsolidating Manager Phillip McEntee (left) and Kelly Dock Supervisor Duncan Gray. Directly behind them, a rail car planning board shows dock positions and currently assigned loadings.

operations during the day to load an odd trailer or rail car, while the night shift concentrates them similarly on efficient loading operations."

The Kelly dock has seven rail car doors on its south side and 30 truck doors on the north. Ample internal space provides for short-term holding of goods awaiting assembly into consolidations, as well as for direct transfer between trailers and rail cars. The double tracks on the south side hold up to 14 cars for loading, passing freight through cars on the inside track across steel bridging to the outer units.

Both DF loaders and refrigerator cars are favored. The DF cars handle all freight of unusual lengths or sizes because of their particular suitability for appropriate blocking and bracing. Reefers are preferred on cable and carton freight bound for the West. **"With their mechanical doors," Mr. Cuicci asserts, "all you have to do is turn these around and lock them into place, whereas standard boxcar doors require blocking and bracing, expending additional time and money."**

Constant upgrading with modern methods goes forward at the consolidation terminal as at all other Western Electric transportation operations. A highly successful innovation has been the use of a rayon strapping-reinforced heavy kraft paper, used to segregate shipments between consignees within a vehicle as well as to secure loads.

"This permits us to load high and tight instead of tapering the load, at the same time reducing space required because shipments thus become more compact," states Department Chief, Transportation Claims Joseph F. Jonish. "This in turn yields a higher load factor per vehicle and consequent cost reductions. **In 1970, the Kelly operation processed 78 million pounds of freight, yet claims were filed for less than $5,000. We feel this system contributed significantly to both cost minimization and claim prevention."**

STEEL BRIDGING between cars speeds dual-track loading at Kearny consolidation facility, permitting 14 cars to be worked at a time from seven rail loading doors.

In another damage-prevention move, Kelly dock personnel have received specialized training in blocking and bracing—what has been termed a "cooperage experiment." The selected individuals received hands-on instruction by packing and loading engineers at Western Electric's Kearny Works in addition to formal training through films or other training packages.

Signal benefits have been derived from observations made at the company's request by loading experts from the Santa Fe Railroad. They made a number of suggestions leading to more economical but effective blocking and bracing procedures for rail car shipments.

Also under study is shrink-wrapping of consolidated shipments. Preliminary studies suggest potential savings on labor alone of over $50,-000 a year on material from the Kearny Works routed via the Kelly operation. Forward planning envisions three phases: an initial Kearny installation, a subsequent one at the Merrimack Valley (Mass.) Works for Kelly-bound freight and, finally, shrink-wrap equipment on the Kelly dock for use in palletizing and shrink-wrapping freight arriving from external suppliers.

At the Tower operation in Elizabeth, N.J., Transportation Associate James P. Brennan distributes inbound consolidated car and truckloads through the Northeast, primarily via five motor carriers. **"We average about 21 to 22 trailers a week through here, with the beyond routing computerized,"** he observes. "The operation was conceived as a means of releasing floor space at various plants from staging activities for manufacturing or other purposes." Thus, while the facility develops effective economies through beyond consolidations, it also performs sorting operations that would otherwise be required at origin.

Economies of scale result from this one location doing the job for Hawthorne Works, Oklahoma City Works and Omaha Works freight, with Kansas City freight possibly soon to be added. Combining shipments to common destinations from multiple origins also reduces beyond freight costs. Early success at Tower

led to the establishment of similar operations at Nashville and Atlanta, with others likely to be established assuming continued success.

Freight moving through the Tower facility normally clears within 24 hours. The operation is largely palletized, generally employing 12,500 square feet of space, although more is available as needed.

Building capacity with a systems "package"

FOR THE MODERN transportation organization, a chart tells only half the story. Management as well as clerical duties assume a different coloration when computers, sophisticated data communication hardware, microfilm and comparable tools assist the effort. Though 400 people seems a large staff for transportation, Western Electric would need a far larger force without its extensive, modern information equipment and innovative, carefully developed working methods.

Electronic data processing became important to this department in 1957 and has assumed a variety of departmental tasks year by year, but its greatest progress is taking place at this writing. Recent programs, several more about to enter routine operation and yet others in the testing and planning stages spell improved performance and substantial economies ahead. More than that, at a time when company volume is growing and professional transportation-distribution people are hard to find, it means that the present staff may absorb an increasing work load without difficulty.

The systems now under way were designed with an eye to the future. All written in the same computer language — COBOL — to facilitate common usage of some components, they are being built up in modular fashion. By tackling one piece of work at a time, proving it out in practice, then proceeding to another segment, large systems have been automated without running the risks of disaster inherent in overnight conversions. Ultimately, several present

systems plus others to come should in turn merge into a single, unified transportation information system.

Not every possible task is automated just for the sake of computerization. **"We run a feasibility study to see which is going to pay off before we implement any computer procedure,"** states Transportation Department Chief, Development Organization Joseph B. Howell. "If we find that it's more economical to do a task manually, working with paper instead of microfiche or the computer, we'll work with paper."

Key systems in service and under development include the following units:

TIPS: Transportation Information Plant System, designed for automatic routing and rating of shipments from all company plants to any U.S. destination by all modes. Automatic payment of freight bills and the elimination of the audit function are the most important features of this system.

TRICS: Transportation Information Claims System, which seeks to provide guidance in developing claim prevention measures, necessary in-house claims reports and diversified interface action reports and devices.

TICS: Transportation Information Contract System, an analysis and control system covering the hundreds of warehousing, transport and hauling and hoisting contracts necessary to field activities.

TOPS: Transportation On Line Processing System, a refinement of the earlier TIS (Transportation Information System), developed for the expeditious processing of consolidations (see further details in the article "Automated Consolidations From the Northeast").

TIPS, flow-charted in Table 1, is being implemented in four phases, as indicated in the table. The plant route guide module, Phase A, is the conversion of manually prepared outbound routing guides into a computerized procedure. It derives from a data base consisting of routing and rating information via all modes, reflecting class rates, commodity rates and exceptions. Mode control and route assignment will be computer-optimized based upon rates consistent with transportation organization service standards. The guide it-

TRANSPORTATION SPECIALIST Michael Fugmann (left) and Transportation Analyst Theodore Gronski inspect engineering drawings portrayed on microfiche equipment that is utilized to assist in determining freight classification.

TABLE 1—A flow chart of "TIPS," or Transportation Information Plant System, illustrates the separate modules which will ultimately constitute the complete system, automating routing and rating of shipments from company plants.

Transportation Information Plant System (TIPS)

Purchased Data
- City/Code Translation
- U.P.S. P.P. Zone Info.

H.Q. Generated Data → **T.I.P.S. Maintenance System** → **T.I.P.S. Data Base**

Phase A — Plant Routing Guide Module
- Route Guide Module → Micro Film Routing Guide ⟶ Microfiche ⟶ Desk:Top Viewer

Phase D — On-Line Decision System
- T.I.P.S. On Line Decision System
- Open Order File
- T.I.P.S. C.R.T. Inquiry Terminal
- Shipment Construction Guides
- Shipping Documents

Phase B — Carrier Payment-Audit Analysis
- Carrier, Destination, Weight, Commodity
- Shipment Info.
- B L
- Payment/Audit Module →
  - Payment Tape
  - Hdq. Analysis
  - Excess Billable Charges
  - Audit Report

Phase C — Plant Consolidation Guide Module
- Open Order File → Consolidation Guide Module → Shipment Construction Guides

self will be available for review in microfiche form for desk top readers, rather than as printed hard copy, though the latter may be readily prepared if required. A unique computer maintenance system will allow the transportation organization to change data files by using a free form common language input for this purpose.

Phase B, the carrier payment audit analysis, will generate rates and charges from bill of lading data, comparing it with the carrier's invoice. Whenever there is a conflict according to the program's ground rules, the affected unit will be kicked out of the processing cycle for manual audit and correction. Phase B will also create management reports, audit reports and excess billable charges reports (showing differences between normal and premium charges when shipments move on the latter basis).

Phase C and D are essentially long-range applications. At this stage, under an open order file system, built-in consolidation guidelines will be able, where practicable, to consolidate single-destination shipments based upon weights available, scheduling requirements and alternatives available on any given occasion. Phase D, specifically, is an on-line decision system under which open orders will be displayed on cathrode ray tubes and transmitted via telecommunication lines to permit on-the-spot decisions. It will also have the capacity to produce shipping documents.

Substantial savings will accrue from the completed TIPS program. Plant tariff research and maintenance costs will be reduced by $275,000 annually, while plant rate and route request costs will diminish by $140,-000. These are savings for Phase A alone. For Phase B, taking into account audit control, accounting manpower savings at 19 locations and other factors, including management reports, estimated total annual savings represent $450,000.

With the Transportation Claims Department at headquarters receiving approximately 2,500 claims (out of four million shipments) annually for filing and pursuit of payment, representing about $2 million per year against a sales volume of $5.7 billion, substantial cost and effort is entailed

in claims administration. The TRICS program, illustrated in Table 2, seeks to reduce the administrative costs while concurrently furthering claims prevention practices and expediting claims processing.

It is anticipated that computerized analysis will aid in determining the cause of damage claims. Different printouts may suggest, for example, that a particular commodity requires investigation of its packaging by engineering staff members. The program may also highlight specific geographic locations as trouble spots, particularly helpful where more than one company source supplies the same materials. An analysis of claims frequencies or of carrier patterns may also spot such circumstances as inadequate security measures at a given company or carrier location, improper handling or the lack of necessary handling equipment.

Transportation organization management and Western Electric user organizations will benefit from diversified in-house reports as well as data files that will be available on call. Claims documentation will be logged from the time of occurrence through every step to their closing and maintained on current file for up to one year, thereby providing finger-tip information on current claims. Additionally, there will be provision for a history file that will reach back as far as five years, particularly helpful in reviewing individual carrier or location performance analysis.

Review of claim types by mode of transportation will be another tool to

aid decision-making as to specific commodity routing and shipping conditions. Important, too, will be a time interval analysis for each filing location. The value of prompt claims reportage in achieving satisfactory settlements makes such policing highly desirable.

TRICS will make possible reports tailored to the needs of accounting, purchasing, packaging engineering, security, insurance, routing and carriers. These may be developed periodically or on call, individually or jointly as circumstances and policy dictate.

The transportation organization's fast-moving systems activity has already partially obsoleted the illustrated TRICS flow chart. The large number of reports indicated as individual outputs at the table's right side have been substantially consolidated or modified for more efficient production. Moreover, several reports intended initially for regular, periodic presentation will revert to "on-call" status—readily available when needed on an exception basis, but not otherwise presented in hard copy.

"Computerized data can be a valuable tool," Assistant Manager Francis J. Rizzo notes, "but it is a costly waste if it is generated unnecessarily." All reports within the transportation organization, regardless of past precedent, are reviewed with indicated recipients before each issuance to make certain they are still necessary and valuable. Not only has the organization greatly reduced the total number of reports issued, eliminating

A SPECIAL CAROUSEL DESK at New York headquarters speeds travel and hotel/motel reservations activities for Transportation Analyst Peggy Monahan (left) and Reservation Service Coordinators Marian Salciccia (center) and Connie Kresback. Such specialized equipment, as well as computers, CRT units, microfiche and other modern devices, typify the direction of systems development in the organization.

Transportation Information Claim System (TRICS)

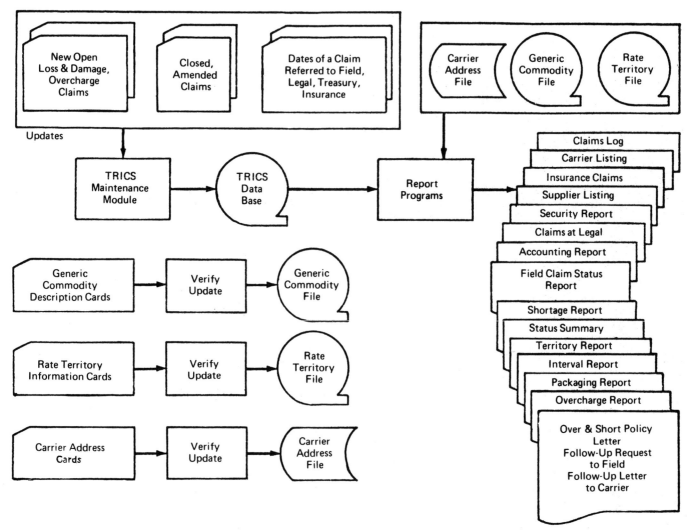

TABLE 2—This "TRICS," or Transportation Information Claims System, flow chart indicates the highly diversified information being computer-developed. In the course of refinement upon entering service, several of the individual reports are being consolidated, but all data indicated above will be made available from the resultant grouped reports.

some of them completely, but it has consolidated many others and changed the time intervals for their issuance as well.

A case in point is a major departmental report, TM-110, a monthly report of data concerning direct equivalent employes performing certain specified functions. A thorough analysis has led to its replacement by the new TQ-110 report. Issued four times yearly in lieu of the TM-110's 12-time schedule, it will save 80 man days' effort in its preparation. Moreover, it will incorporate data eliminating the need for six other reports,

resulting in even greater preparation savings, yet offering recipients a more valuable tool than were any of the preceding reports underlying this new instrument.

Computerized programing's success derives from close teamwork between the transportation development organization and the information systems development organization's programers and systems personnel who have primary systems area responsibility. The transportation development group's function essentially is the furtherance of computer programs, working hand in

glove with the systems research and design group in many instances. The latter unit, largely concerned with transportation field studies, makes substantial use of the computer where volume and complexity of input warrant it, but uses as well a variety of noncomputer operations research techniques in many applications.

PERT (Program Evaluation and Review Technique) is used frequently, for example, but generally in a simplified form that does not demand computer time. Western Electric recognized PERT's general value several years ago and set up a course for interested people to instruct them in some of its basic techniques. This provided the systems research and design staff with an initial exposure.

States Nicholas J. Scocozzo, transportation supervisor, systems research and design: **"We find PERT particularly useful when, on occasion, a substantial project comes along with a short interval to its assigned completion date.** I've got to figure out what my manpower will be to meet that date. Assuming the typical 10 or 12 major studies going on in our unit, a properly designed PERT chart will at once simplify the estimate of time requirements for the new program and indicate what priority rearrangements, if any, may be necessary to meet the new project's completion date. If the need is deemed sufficiently critical, staff members will either move to the new project from others, deferring the latter, or people from elsewhere in the transportation organization will be temporarily assigned to this study."

A significant advantage that Mr. Scocozzo finds in the application of PERT lies in the resultant form of presentation when the chart is completed. Rather than showing a single opinion as to the proper course of action, the finished PERT chart presents the various alternatives and a reasonable indication of the cost trade-offs entailed. This greatly aids management in reaching final conclusions as to policy in furthering individual projects and in reaching decisions as to changes in priority, if any, relating to other projects under way.

Elsewhere in the organization, several modern tools are assuming increasing importance. Microfilm, in rolls, cartridge and microfiche form, is proving valuable in several applications. Microfiche tariff files, stored in color-coded drawers, reduce costly space consumption and provide easy access to rate information at headquarters. Future plans envision the ultimate availability of such material, via conventional telephone lines tying into sophisticated terminals at other locations, minimizing the number of tariff files in any form required at regional offices.

Aperture cards containing 35mm. slides in addition to data relevant to innumerable individual specified line items provide a compact file for ready reference in the department's classification unit, speeding and simplifying analytical work. Teleticketing units and equipment such as American Airlines' Saber reservation system contribute to passenger traffic operating efficiency.

Contract control builds nationwide warehouse efficiency

PUBLIC WAREHOUSING plays a vital role in Western Electric field activity. Servicing telephone companies throughout the nation, local maintenance stocks and specially engineered equipment for expansion are held in reasonable quantities at many places.

Public warehousing supplements the company's own facilities. In Miami, serving the city alone, the Southern Region Transportation office has 40,000 to 60,000 square feet of warehousing in addition to a company facility. Other warehousing contracts cover Hollywood, Fort Lauderdale, Pompano Beach, Fort Pierce, Key West and Homestead in this southern Florida area alone. Warehousing and related contracts therefore demand considerable attention.

Contracts encompass such diversified activities as the following:

Public warehousing: Strategically located facilities assure prompt response to both routine and emergency needs of local telephone companies.

Hauling and hoisting: These cover the transportation of central office equipment from warehouses to telephone company buildings where the contractor effects inside delivery to the point of intended use, usually accomplished by hoisting large units into buildings by winch or truck crane. Contractor also uncrates the equipment and disposes of the packing material.

Distribution and local cartage: These involve break-bulk operations rather than full warehousing, plus provision for local deliveries.

Consolidation: Assembly and forwarding of small shipments.

Tractor-driver contracts: These cover transport of empty and loaded trailers between railheads, consolidation and distribution centers and company locations.

The great diversity of vendors performing warehousing and related services for Western Electric creates a substantial administrative burden for the transportation organization. In consequence, procedures have been established to facilitate contract administration, protect the integrity of quotations and simplify their development and evaluation. A typical contract lasts two years, although some span five years. Competitive quotations are solicited and impartially evaluated.

Contract awards are made on the basis of quotations submitted by interested parties in advance of a stipulated date. When the transportation personnel solicit a quotation from a contractor, they review the company's ethical code governing supplier relations and then deliver a form to him in person bearing instructions to mail the completed form to the quotation registrar at the proper office address with an indicated reference number.

The registrar receives these quotations in private envelopes, initialing each page bearing any figures to indicate their notation on receipt. This precludes the improper addition of a new page or quote at a later time. Any erasure or changes observed on receipt are initialed separately to assure their authenticity. Prepared quotes are not submitted to the assigned contract man until the date on which all quotes are released. With these safeguards, potential contractors are relieved of any doubts as to the integrity of their written quotations.

After quotations have been released for review, contract personnel prepare summary and evaluation forms which provide a direct comparison between the quotations on the proposed contract and the existing contract (if the quotations are on a contract being renewed). Accompanying illustrations show the standard summary and evaluation forms for warehousing contracts and for transportation services (including hauling and hoisting).

The great number of individual warehouse contracts makes necessary careful preplanning to ensure continuity of service at all locations. Under the normal schedule, there is a reminder to contact the using organization 120 days before expiration and, if a renewal is required, requesting past invoices and an indication of the tonnage that will flow during the new contract period. A transportation representative will survey the present or prospective contractor's facility and explain the requirements, at the same time determining which contractors are best suited to quote on the individual contract.

There is a 20-day interval in which the approved contractors may prepare quotes and submit them. The transportation office evaluates the data and recommends award 50 days prior to the effective date. The contract dollar value determines the level of management approval required. Contracts are transmitted thereafter to the chosen contractors 30 days in advance, allowing 10 days to sign and return the papers. The regional office transmits the original executed contracts to the headquarters corporate file in New York, with copies to the using organization.

After a new contract is awarded, a transportation representative meets with the contractor to further familiarize him with company requirements and to assist in any way possible in the establishment of a smooth routine. Visits may take place if it is deemed necessary either by the transportation organization, the Western Electric using organization or the contractor, if he has any problems. Inspection forms of the question and answer type are prepared during these visits, as shown in the accompanying illustration. A similar form is used for transportation hauling and hoisting contracts.

A further check on warehouse performance lies within the regional transportation office itself. There is a constant check on the paperwork handling end of these activities at the office, obviating in large measure the need for visitations.

In general practice, a particular individual will be assigned to the evaluation of quotations for a specific contract and will continue to service

SUMMARY AND EVALUATION OF QUOTATIONS FOR AWARD OF TRANSPORTATION SERVICES CONTRACT

(BASED ON ACTUAL ACTIVITY TAKEN FROM A STUDY OF THREE(3) MONTHS' INVOICES AND PROJECTED FOR APPROXIMATELY A TWO(2) YEAR PERIOD.)

FOR ACCOUNT OF THE INSTALLATION ORGANIZATION AT (JOB LOCATION) _____

QUOTATIONS SUBMITTED BY	QUOTATIONS DATED
1	
2	
3	
4	
5	

CONTRACT SECTION	PRESENT CONTRACT				1				2			
	RATE	UNITS	WEIGHT	VALUE	RATE	UNITS	WEIGHT	VALUE	RATE	UNITS	WEIGHT	VALUE
A TRANSPORTATION												
PER CWT												
MINIMUM CHARGE												
SUB-TOTAL SECTION-A												
B1 CARRY-IN												
A. PER CWT												
125 - LESS												
126 - 350												
351 - 499												
B. PER CWT												
MINIMUM COMP												
B2 CARRY-IN												
A. PER CWT												
125 - LESS												
126 - 350												
351 - 499												
B. PER CWT												
MINIMUM COMP												
SUB-TOTAL SECTION-B												
C1 HOISTING												
PER CWT												
MINIMUM COMP												
C2 HOISTING												
PER CWT												
MINIMUM COMP												
SUB-TOTAL SECTION-C												
D REMOVING REFUSE												
PER TRIP												
E SORTING												
PER CWT												
F HOURLY BASIS												
RIGGER FOREMAN												
RIGGER												
HELPER FOREMAN												
HELPER												
2-1/2 TON TRK/DRI'R												
WINCH TRK/DRIVER												
TRUCK CRANE												
NOTE 1 PER TRIP												
SUB-TOTAL SECTION-F												

	PRESENT CONTRACT	1	2
TOTAL STUDY DOLLAR VALUE			
TOTAL STUDY TONS			
TOTAL COST PER TON			
INSTALLATION FORECAST TOTAL TONS NEXT 2 YEARS			
TOTAL PROJECTED DOLLAR VALUE 2 YEARS			
DOLLAR CHANGE FROM PRESENT			
% INCREASE (+) DECREASE (−)			

SPECIAL FORMS help make quick work of quotation comparisons when contracts for hauling and hoisting services are established or are renewed.

that contract for its duration. At renewal time, however, it will be transferred to another staff member so that a decision among competitive bids cannot possibly be influenced by prior personal contact between the contractor and the Western Electric representative.

In continually changing the contact, there is the further assurance of a fresh viewpoint, as well as the natural competitive desire on the part of individuals to provide the best performance. This policy has been con-

SUMMARY AND EVALUATION OF QUOTATIONS FOR AWARD OF STANDARD WAREHOUSING CONTRACT

(BASED ON ACTUAL ACTIVITY TAKEN FROM A STUDY OF THREE(3) MONTHS' INVOICES AND PROJECTED FOR APPROXIMATELY A TWO(2) YEAR PERIOD.)

FOR ACCOUNT OF THE INSTALLATION ORGANIZATION AT (JOB LOCATION) _____

DATE _____

QUOTATIONS SUBMITTED BY:	QUOTATIONS DATED
1.	
2.	
3.	
4.	
5.	

CONTRACT SECTION	PRESENT CONTRACT RATE UNITS WEIGHT VALUE	1 RATE UNITS WEIGHT VALUE	2 RATE UNITS WEIGHT VALUE	3 RATE UNITS WEIGHT VALUE
A	HANDLING IN & OUT OF WAREHOUSE PER CWT..........				
B1.	ONE MONTH STORAGE PER CWT....................				
	ONE-HALF MONTH STORAGE PER CWT..........				
B2.	MINIMUM COMPENSATION-HANDLING IN & OUT OF WAREHOUSE INCLUDING STORAGE FOR 1ST. MONTH PER LOT.				
B3.	MINIMUM COMPENSATION SUCCEEDING MONTH PER ORDER NUMBER.........................				
C.	MISCELLANEOUS MANUAL SERVICES PER 1/4 HOUR.....				
D.	RECEIVING AND HOLDING MAIL AND PARCEL POST PER PIECE.........................				
	TOTAL STUDY DOLLAR VALUE...				
	TOTAL STUDY TONS...........				
	TOTAL COST PER TON.......				
	INSTALLATION FORCAST TOTAL TONS NEXT 2 YEARS........				
	TOTAL PROJECTED DOLLAR VALUE 2 YEARS..........				
	DOLLAR CHANGE FROM PRESENT				
	% INCREASE (+) DECREASE (−)				

STANDARDIZED COMPARISON FORMS aid analysis of quotations for warehousing services.

sidered an important factor in keeping Western Electric field warehouse costs at a satisfactory level and is conducive to the proper "strictly business" relationship.

Suitable warehouse costs are not necessarily the lowest ones, however, and the organization recognizes this. **"We don't want would-be contractors quoting below their actual costs, just to get the contract," comments John F. Ballard, resident transportation manager of the Southern region. "This only leads to dissatisfaction subsequently."**

The company's heavy continuing experience with innumerable public warehouse contracts makes normal cost patterns fairly apparent. In addition, continual cross-checking and analysis help the regional offices in developing cost data and in comparing quotations received on individual contracts.

There is a private listing furnished regularly showing every contract for hauling and hoisting as well as warehousing. With indicated information

as to their terms, it becomes relatively simple to develop a picture of normal cost patterns and to determine what conditions should be for pending new contracts. By having this data and relating it to labor scales in a specific area, transportation organization personnel experience little difficulty in estimating appropriate cost ranges for quotation evaluation.

An additional assist in determining specific costs lies within the contracts themselves. Many contain provisions

HAWTHORNE WAREHOUSE employs diversified forklift equipment for trailer loading from the shipping docks, which are fed in turn by stacker cranes.

Date of Inspection _____

TRANSPORTATION ORGANIZATION INSPECTION
STANDARD WAREHOUSING CONTRACT
INSTALLATION

Location _____ Contractor _____ Contract No. _____

Contractor's Address _____ Name & Title of Person Contacted _____

CONTRACTOR'S PERFORMANCE

I. Warehouse Facilities

1. Is Warehouse clean and dry?

2. Is all material stored inside warehouse?

3. Does warehouseman store material for other companies?

4. Is space utilized effectively?

5. Are combustibles such as paper, paint, chemicals, etc. stored in warehouse?

6. Is there evidence of careless use of material handling equipment?

7. Is general housekeeping satisfactory?

II. Receiving Material at Warehouse

1. (a) How is incoming material checked for correct count? (b) Is delivering carrier's delivery receipt and warehouse receipt noted if shortage occurs? (c) Is installation verbally notified immediately and confirming letter sent Registered Mail within 24 hours after receipt of material?

2. (a) How is incoming material checked for damage? (b) Is delivering carrier's delivery receipt and warehouse receipt noted if damage occurs? (c) Is installation verbally notified immediately and confirmation letter sent Registered Mail within 24 hours after receipt of material? If an inspection is necessary, installation representative should be present during inspection.

3. How is material checked off trailer; by load sheets, freight bill, etc? (Recommend check be made and warehouse receipt prepared before taking to permanent storage location. This usually saves time since material has to be moved only once.)

4. (a) Are load sheets received with or before shipment? (b) By what method do you receive these documents? (Obtain examples if not receiving.)

5. Do load sheets contain correct information, i.e., number of pieces, piece number, weight, etc.? (Obtain examples if not.)

II. Receiving Material at Warehouse (Cont.)

6. Is order number shown on carrier's delivery receipts for easier identification?

7. What is warehouseman's opinion of general condition of loads. If unsatisfactory, where does fault lie?

8. Are seal numbers recorded? If seal is missing or broken, notification to the delivering carrier should be made immediately in addition to being noted on the delivery receipt.

9. Are lot numbers clearly marked for identification?

10. Is storage location marked on warehouse receipt?

III. Storing Material in Warehouse

1. Is material stacked so box numbers are turned out toward aisle for easier identification?

2. Are aisles properly aligned and wide enough for safe storage and removal of material?

3. Is material stacked so mashing and damage will not occur?

4. Do stacking heights appear satisfactory for safe storage? (Heavy items should not be stacked on top of electric storage batteries.)

5. Do electric storage batteries show evidence of leakage? If so, see that damage properly noted.

6. Does warehouseman store material by "Lots" as prescribed in contract? If no, how and why isn't it being stored by "Lot?"

7. Is material received via a premium mode left in the warehouse for extended periods of time?

8. Is payment being received for all materials in warehouse? (Installation shall not be stockpiling.)

9. (a) Has any material been in warehouse more than six months? (b) How long? (c) Why? (d) How much storage charges have been paid?

IV. Warehouse Receipts

1. (a) Are warehouse receipts issued and mailed immediately? (b) What is schedule? (If less than once a day, action must be taken to have receipts issued and mailed every day.)

2. Do warehouse receipts contain sufficient information, i.e., warehouse receipt number, issue date, order number, lot number, weight, warehouse location, delivering carrier, delivery receipt number and warehouseman's signature?

IV. Warehouse Receipts (Cont.)

3. Is a separate receipt issued for each order number when a shipment contains two or more order numbers? (Specification if contract designates.)

4. When material cannot be identified sufficiently to issue a receipt, is the material held and the Installation supervisor advised?

V. Removing Material From Warehouse

1. Do you receive a Warehouse Removal Notice from installation 24 hours in advance of the required removal time from the warehouse? (Excepting emergencies and then always confirmed with written order.)

2. Does the Warehouse Removal Notice contain complete information?

3. Is the warehouseman preparing a delivery receipt and obtaining the carrier's signature for all material removed from the warehouse?

VI. Warehouse Invoices

1. Do warehousing invoices show complete information required, i.e., contract number, date of invoice, period covered, order number, lot number, date received, weight, handling in and out and storage by lot charge?

2. What schedule is followed? Invoice must be issued for first months handling and storage and subsequent months storage at least once a month?

3. Are charges being correctly computed? Are minimum charges applied correctly?

4. Is warehouseman receiving prompt payment from Western?

5. Is warehouseman issuing invoices for all service performed such as sorting, etc.?

INSTALLATION'S PERFORMANCE

Name and Title of Person Contacted _____

(In addition to following specific questions, verify with installation the information furnished by the contractor.)

I. Removing Material from Warehouse

1. Does contractor remove material from warehouse within 24 hours after receiving Warehouse Removal Notice?

2. Is Section C (Miscellaneous Manual Service) authorized when part lots are ordered from the warehouse? (This situation should be treated with caution as it is charged at the contractor's discretion.)

I. Removing Material from Warehouse (Cont.)

3. Are periodic checks made to be sure all material associated with closed orders is removed within the prescribed time limit?

4. Is the Warehouse Removal Notice properly completed and forwarded to the contractor within the prescribed time limit?

II. Warehousing Invoices

1. Are warehousing invoices processed and approved for payment immediately upon receipt? (This is necessary in order to meet the schedule of payment in the contract.)

2. Are sufficient records maintained, either recorded on Warehouse Receipts, Record of Warehoused Material (SR6-1) or similar forms, to verify invoices?

3. Are Warehouse Purchase Orders (SD-4-321-D) prepared and forwarded to accounting and the contractor in advance of the first receival?

4. (a) Is the contractor being requested to perform services not covered by the contract which he may not be paid for? (b) Does contract require amendment to correct this situation?

GENERAL DISCUSSION AND SUMMARY

Determine if there are any parts of the contracts which the contractor or installation does not understand. Volunteer to explain in detail if there are any areas of misunderstanding.

After conferring with the contractor, visit installation to discuss report, particularly situations wich cannot be verified during visit with the contractor; i.e., issuing warehouse receipts on time, etc.

If discrepancies were noted involving installation, they should be discussed thoroughly and corrective action recommended so as not to jeopardize our position with the contractor.

Follow-up with interested personnel, if necessary - contractor, installation, regions, manufacturing locations, etc., to be sure corrective action is taken.

If the contractor and/or installation are doing a good job, they should be commended. Verbal commendation to the contractor will be sufficient; however, a copy of this report when forwarded to installation, should include a comment regarding installation's performance.

CONDENSED from eight pages to four for illustrative purposes, the above rendering shows the detailed review made by Western Electric's transportation personnel when making inspections of present or proposed public warehousing.

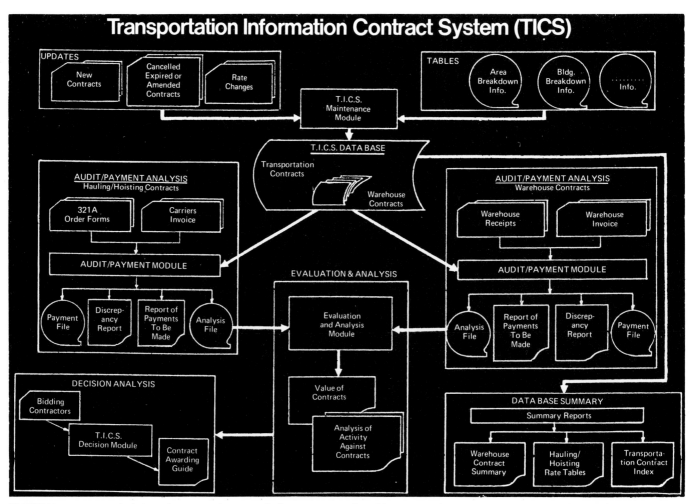

Transportation Information Contract System (TICS)

UPDATES
- New Contracts
- Cancelled Expired or Amended Contracts
- Rate Changes

TABLES
- Area Breakdown Info.
- Bldg. Breakdown Info.
- .... Info.

T.I.C.S. Maintenance Module

T.I.C.S. DATA BASE
- Transportation Contracts
- Warehouse Contracts

AUDIT/PAYMENT ANALYSIS
Hauling/Hoisting Contracts
- 321A Order Forms
- Carriers Invoice

AUDIT/PAYMENT MODULE
- Payment File
- Discrepancy Report
- Report of Payments To Be Made
- Analysis File

EVALUATION & ANALYSIS
- Evaluation and Analysis Module
- Value of Contracts
- Analysis of Activity Against Contracts

AUDIT/PAYMENT ANALYSIS
Warehouse Contracts
- Warehouse Receipts
- Warehouse Invoice

AUDIT/PAYMENT MODULE
- Analysis File
- Report of Payments To Be Made
- Discrepancy Report
- Payment File

DECISION ANALYSIS
- Bidding Contractors
- T.I.C.S. Decision Module
- Contract Awarding Guide

DATA BASE SUMMARY
Summary Reports
- Warehouse Contract Summary
- Hauling/Hoisting Rate Tables
- Transportation Contract Index

MANUAL contract administration procedures are being augmented and/or replaced by computer ones, as shown above.

for reopening upon changes in their costs under union wage agreements. When these occur, it is necessary for an affected contractor to demonstrate the nature and effect of such changes in order to justify the sought-for contractual revisions. Resultant data provides yet another statistical tool for cost evaluations and comparisons.

Warehousing needs are continuous, but do not remain static. Change is in the direction of constant growth. New technology, such as microwave transmission, and the movement of population into the suburbs are creating demands for service and facilities over ever-wider areas at increasing numbers of locations. The recent company history, therefore, is one of steady, overall growth in the employment of public warehousing throughout the country. Continued expansion of population and of the economy suggest more of the same in the days ahead.

Up until the present, manual pro-

INSIDE LOADING of rail cars as well as trailers assures protection of costly, delicate gear leaving Western Electric's Hawthorne plant.

cedures have monitored the extent and quality of service received, the analysis of tonnage and movement statistics and the evaluation of contract quotations. TICS, a new contract system under development, will automate these areas while providing a mechanized system for payment of contract charges. It will cover updates, new contracts, canceled, expired and amended contracts and rate changes. Through stored tables, it will provide area and individual building breakdown information and potentially other data for expansion of the system.

The accompanying flow chart illustrates the TICS system.

Separate audit payment modules govern the hauling/hoisting contracts and the warehouse ones. The former module is activated by order forms completed by field installers which are then compared to carrier invoices in the computer. Similarly, warehouse receipts, matched to warehouse invoices, activate the warehouse audit/payment module. Both provide for automated payments, payment reports, discrepancy reports and development of computer analysis files which, in turn, feed the evaluation and analysis module.

The latter module maintains a running check of activity against existing contracts. It can indicate

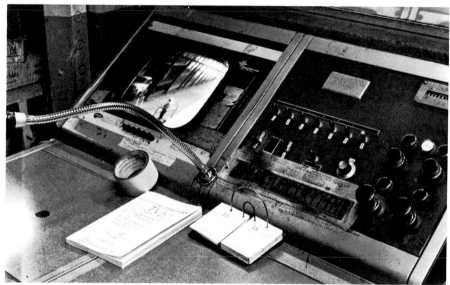

MODERN SYSTEMS DEVICES aid shipping activities in the warehouse, as well as in paperwork operations. At the Hawthorne facilities, the television unit that is shown above gives supervision a quick picture of activities "on the floor" without the necessity of leaving the unit's office location.

whether or not an existing contractor's volume is at the forecasted level and can provide ready answers when questions arise concerning minor revisions of individual contracts.

This, in turn, creates data for the decision analysis module, which is a contract-awarding guidance tool. While final decision-making necessarily remains in a responsible manager's hands, automated preanalysis can supply many salient facts in con-cise form, speeding and simplifying decision-making.

The final module will replace existing clerical procedures in maintaining warehouse contract summaries, hauling/hoisting rate tables and transportation contract indices. Need for continual update of the company's many contracts to keep these reports current creates a costly burden which TICS will materially reduce.

Phillips Petroleum Company

The Phillips Petroleum Company, like Eastman Kodak and Western Electric, places much emphasis upon computerization and personnel development. The transportation and supply department enjoys an advantage in the former area found in few other companies: Phillips' computers operate under the guidance of a former transportation manager, assuring a level of understanding and effective liaison found all too rarely in the logistics-computer relationship.

The transportation and supply department is unique also in having its own specialized personnel section, managing highly effective selection and training programs at all levels within the department as well as performing routine personnel functions necessary to a major company division.

Department computer programs embrace a diversity of line and staff functions, taking full advantage of the substantial capacity and unusual diversity of available computer equipment. Programs include inventory control, market forecasts, rail car fleet control and many more, keeping costs in line and assuring delivery reliability in a field where seasonal demand changes and variances in supply sources make timely information reportage crucially important to management.

TRAFFIC MANAGEMENT's major report on the Phillips Petroleum Company, initially presented in January, 1969, follows:

Phillips Petroleum Company—A different distribution climate

NUMEROUS BUSINESS JOURNAL articles depict the Phillips Petroleum Company as a successful, tradition-smashing giant, doggedly determined to keep its corporate home in a small Oklahoma city. Why yet another Phillips write-up? Because we feel that one of their biggest management stories is still untold—the story of a unique, strong and successful transportation-distribution operation. Vice President of Supply and Transportation Charles M. Kittrell directly controls virtually every business activity of this two billion dollar company associated with physical distribution.

At the Bartlesville, Okla. corporate headquarters, a staff of 200 operates the supply and transportation department headquarters facilities, in itself a substantial group as distribution departments go. The complete department, however, numbers over 2,100 employes worldwide. The pipeline section alone employs 1,300 people.

"The transportation man is tremendously important in the oil industry," Vice President Kittrell observes. "Transportation is the key to market entry."

The department's strong corporate position is nothing new or recent for Phillips. It dates from the company's beginning, long before such thinking was described as "Physical Distribution" or "The Total Cost Concept." When President Frank Phillips hired Charles Musgrave away from the Santa Fe Railroad in 1923 and created a pioneer modern traffic department, a ball started rolling

Where the action is in the Phillips supply and transportation

COORDINATION & PLANNING DIVISION J. E. ARNOLD MANAGER	TRANSPORTATION DIVISION J. E. DONNELLY MANAGER
COORDINATION H. J. CLASSICK COORDINATOR	AUTOMOTIVE LANE KELLEY DIRECTOR B. J. WEBB ASSISTANT DIRECTOR
NGL CORRELATION G. R. CARPENTER MANAGER	
CRUDE, PRODUCTS & PIPELINES L. L. HAYES MANAGER	RAILWAY C. W. HAAS DIRECTOR OPERATIONS H. B. PHILLIPS MANAGER MAINTENANCE R. E. PECK MANAGER
FERTILIZER, CHEMICAL & INTERNATIONAL C. HILL MANAGER	
PLANNING & DISTRIBUTION R. M. BERNER DIRECTOR DISTRIBUTION G. G. GREENE MANAGER PLANNING C. W. LEE MANAGER	RATES & SERVICES I. C. DICKERSON DIRECTOR D. E. FURNAS ASSISTANT DIRECTOR TRANSPORTATION RELATIONS D. E. MURPHY DIRECTOR

that gained momentum year after year.

Mr. Musgrave's continuing transportation and supply innovations anticipated a growing company's needs, paving the way for today's management science and computer techniques. When he retired in 1957, his successor inherited a department already employing these tools at the most advanced level feasible under the existing state of the art. This is no case of "discovering" distribution or "upgrading" traffic. Rather it is an account of continued and successful innovation by managers who consider first the total company objectives and second how best the supply and transportation department can serve these ends. With an annual freight bill alone exceeding $150 million the total distribution cost has significant impact when measured against $2 billion-plus annual sales.

Phillips management is organized functionally. Communication between departments and divisions within departments is kept strong as a matter of policy. An operating committee containing heads of operating and staff departments clears all proposals of any magnitude before they reach top management, assuring that representatives of all affected activities may bring their judgments to bear. "Our managers must be more than technical specialists," claims Chairman of the Board W. W. Keeler. "They must understand the company's business role, not just the details of their current assignment. Phillips managers are good generalists. Past and current performance proves their capacity for continued personal growth which benefits, in turn, Phillips corporate growth."

While oil and its refined products predom-

department. Organized on functional lines, teamwork on varied projects is a departmental characteristic.

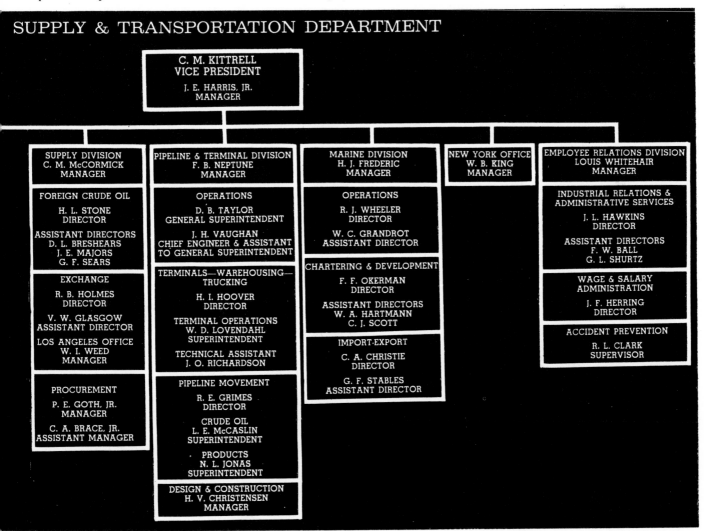

SUPPLY & TRANSPORTATION DEPARTMENT

C. M. KITTRELL
VICE PRESIDENT
J. E. HARRIS, JR.
MANAGER

SUPPLY DIVISION
C. M. McCORMICK
MANAGER

FOREIGN CRUDE OIL
H. L. STONE
DIRECTOR
ASSISTANT DIRECTORS
D. L. BRESHEARS
J. E. MAJORS
G. F. SEARS

EXCHANGE
R. B. HOLMES
DIRECTOR
V. W. GLASGOW
ASSISTANT DIRECTOR
LOS ANGELES OFFICE
W. I. WEED
MANAGER

PROCUREMENT
P. E. GOTH, JR.
MANAGER
C. A. BRACE, JR.
ASSISTANT MANAGER

PIPELINE & TERMINAL DIVISION
F. B. NEPTUNE
MANAGER

OPERATIONS
D. B. TAYLOR
GENERAL SUPERINTENDENT
J. H. VAUGHAN
CHIEF ENGINEER & ASSISTANT
TO GENERAL SUPERINTENDENT

TERMINALS—WAREHOUSING—
TRUCKING
H. I. HOOVER
DIRECTOR
TERMINAL OPERATIONS
W. D. LOVENDAHL
SUPERINTENDENT
TECHNICAL ASSISTANT
J. O. RICHARDSON

PIPELINE MOVEMENT
R. E. GRIMES
DIRECTOR
CRUDE OIL
L. E. McCASLIN
SUPERINTENDENT
PRODUCTS
N. L. JONAS
SUPERINTENDENT

DESIGN & CONSTRUCTION
H. V. CHRISTENSEN
MANAGER

MARINE DIVISION
H. J. FREDERIC
MANAGER

OPERATIONS
R. J. WHEELER
DIRECTOR
W. C. GRANDROT
ASSISTANT DIRECTOR

CHARTERING & DEVELOPMENT
F. F. OKERMAN
DIRECTOR
ASSISTANT DIRECTORS
W. A. HARTMANN
C. J. SCOTT

IMPORT-EXPORT
C. A. CHRISTIE
DIRECTOR
G. F. STABLES
ASSISTANT DIRECTOR

NEW YORK OFFICE
W. B. KING
MANAGER

EMPLOYEE RELATIONS DIVISION
LOUIS WHITEHAIR
MANAGER

INDUSTRIAL RELATIONS &
ADMINISTRATIVE SERVICES
J. L. HAWKINS
DIRECTOR
ASSISTANT DIRECTORS
F. W. BALL
G. L. SHURTZ

WAGE & SALARY
ADMINISTRATION
J. F. HERRING
DIRECTOR

ACCIDENT PREVENTION
R. L. CLARK
SUPERVISOR

Fast-breaking changes in the supply picture find Phillips managers ready for a quick response. A ship charter rate change announced at 2 p.m. finds a 3 p.m. managers' session laying groundwork for strategy changes by 8 a.m. the following morning. Participating are, from left, T. R.

inate at Phillips, greater diversification marks its recent growth pattern. Subsidiaries such as the Sealright Company, Inc., manufacturers of rigid packaging and Wall Tube & Metal Products Co., which produces metal furniture and tubular metal products are broadening the line parallel to internal developments in chemicals, plastics and other products. In general, the approach is toward development of Phillips as an extractive company rather than as purely an oil or energy company.

The company's vast oil holdings and the continuing improvement in its ability to supply widening markets will undoubtedly keep petroleum predominant in its activities. Discoveries of potential huge oil reserves in northwestern Alaska, among other elements, still further strengthens its role within the petroleum industry.

Physical Distribution Control Not As Evident Elsewhere

While other oil producers enjoy comparable geographic spread, concentrated physical distribution control is not quite so evident among them as at Phillips. John E. Harris, Jr., manager of supply and transportation comments: "Other companies in this field have more restricted supply and transportation departments. The pipe line function generally operates separately. It is also not a common practice to include marine activities under the transportation depart-

ment umbrella. The coordination and planning role generally is a separate corporate function to which transportation is only a contributor, whereas at Phillips planning centers in large measure within our department."

Just what the department's coordination and planning division does for its company is further detailed in ensuing pages. A major force in product strategy, it continually brings together other company departments while providing a comparable internal liaison among supply and transportation divisions that fosters company growth with minimum waste effort. Contributing markedly to its achievements as well as to those of other departmental divisions is a large and effective computing department, supplying both operations research expertise and electronic data processing hardware to amplify the planning staff's human potential.

Reviewed also are the supply division's activities in obtaining feed stocks for Phillips plants at minimum delivered costs. An unusual marriage of purchasing and quasi-traffic functions, this group comprises the merchants of the department.

The transportation division, in addition to standard traffic functions, carries heavy operating responsibilities for large rail and truck equipment fleets.

In the Phillips marine division lies a growing answer to successful overseas market

Wiggins, manufacturing department; J. E. Harris, Jr., manager, supply and transportation department; Vice President Supply and Transportation C. M. Kittrell; H. J. Frederic, manager, marine division; H. L. Stone, director of foreign crude oil supply; R. B. Holmes, director, commodity exchange; J. E. Arnold, manager, coordination and planning division.

penetration. Big and growing, its new cryogenic tankers are opening doors to economical gas exports from the United States and other sources.

Bulk shipment in high gear marks the Phillips pipeline section's role. One of the earliest major operators, the company's modern, largely automated network continually expands its continent-wide activities. Innovations in storage and terminal operations as well as in actual pipeline construction and maintenance suggest answers to bulk-handling problems beyond the petroleum industry.

In all of these divisions, reliance on modern cost controls and management science for research and development characterizes a continuing program of self-improvement.

This, then, is physical distribution at Phillips. Somewhat different both in specific answers to concrete problems and in its total approach to the distribution concept, its achievements suggest that these ideas might prove profitable beyond the boundaries of the petroleum industry.

Building tomorrow's distribution today

THE SUPPLY AND TRANSPORTATION department's broad mandate places heavy forward planning responsibilities upon it. Their increasing breadth and complexity, in a company whose 1957 $1 billion-plus gross income more than doubled in ten years, made a complete division devoted to planning and coordination essential. Not only does it provide heavy staff support to the supply and transportation department, it is responsible as well for both short- and long-range planning in conjunction with all operating departments. The planning and distribution section, while also working with other departments, particularly concerns itself with justifying all capital expenditures of the supply and transportation department.

How does the coordination function work? Company Coordinator H. J. Classick, in charge of and responsible for short-range company planning, produces an updated 12-month plan once each month. This plan recommends specific facility operating levels for the ensuing 30 days while depicting the following 11 months' anticipated conditions. It is submitted to the company's Operating Committee, whose membership includes representatives of all the affected departments. In general, the coordinator's recommendations on production levels are accepted.

In a company where rapid reaction to business opportunities is a watchword, even forecasts every 30 days are not considered, in themselves, sufficiently flexible. Accordingly, the coordination group does two jobs at once: it develops formal monthly plans while concurrently checking strategic data day-to-day and week-to-week. It thus produces instant information so that quick decisions can follow promptly when opportunities or imbalances occur, leading to trades, sales or other control measures. This flexibility not only stops many losses before they could happen, but frequently leads to profit opportunities not otherwise possible.

Coordination's role, then, lies in budgeting, forecasting and optimizing the total operation, providing quick reaction when opportunities present themselves. Supporting the company coordinator in this work are three correlation managers and their staffs.

Products Divided Among Three Groups

They cover the following specialties:
—Refined products and crude oil.
—Natural gas liquids.
—Fertilizers, chemicals and international.

The computer and related operations research techniques put the punch in coordination's report program. Minimizing staff requirements and speeding data assembly, they magnify available brain power by putting muscle where it's needed. Among other duties, computer programs provide fertilizer, propane and refined products sales forecasts.

In propane's case, individual customer data is stored in computer memory. The program picks up the latest 12 months' information, grouped by weather regions, to develop the monthly analysis. It also absorbs sales department data concerning customer and volume changes. Based on adjustments of preceding 12-month figures to a "normal" year plus the sales-provided data, the computer develops and prints out the monthly forecast.

A linear program optimizes this forecast, developing the mathematically most advantageous plan for fulfilling anticipated distribution requirements. This embraces origin points, supply availability, storage availability, seasonal demand variations, transportation costs by alternate modes and customer data information derived from the preceding forecast program. Linear optimization applies to fertilizers as well as propane in essentially the same fashion.

Refined products, while optimized and forecasted by computer techniques, employ a different statistical data system. Here, a few large refineries serve numerous terminals and have great capacity flexibility. Fertilizer and propane, however, move from many smaller plants of less flexible capacity.

What coordination develops, the distribution staff in the planning and distribution section progresses. Refined products, propane and fertilizer each have units within this group who schedule movements by all modes from sources to distribution terminals and customers based on the coordination group's plan. They maintain a continuing liaison with both the coordination section and the department's supply division. This pays off powerfully in the event of a problem such as a sudden pipeline blockage, for example. Distribution immediately swings into action with other affected groups to develop a product exchange, ship by an alternate route, divert consignments from other Phillips sources or establish other suitable alternative responses. "It is under such circumstances that our functional approach to organization really pays off," notes Coordinating and Planning Division Manager James E. Arnold. "Staff flexibility plus really exceptional communications mean a great deal when chance or nature shoot down a plan."

A major project series finds the division currently working with the computing department's operations research branch on central order system development, division by division. Project "POPS" (Plastic Order Processing System), now in its second year of evolution, sparked the idea. A similar procedure is to be instituted for fertilizer order automation. The development path chosen finds the central computer storing complete customer information. Orders will feed through consoles at sales points by direct wire into the computer, speeding invoicing, permitting more economical short-term transportation scheduling, bettering customer service and reducing communications as well as accounts receivable costs. "Something like POPS," observes Operations Research Manager Robert S. Gruel, "looks like a natural for Phillips Fibers Corporation as well." This subsidiary, like others in the corporate family, shares the freedom to develop its own pattern." Further in this respect, Vice President Kittrell observes: "Our company is actually in the process of management decentralization while continuing to emphasize coordination at Bartlesville.

The division's planning and development section, in addition to providing justification for supply and transportation department capital expenditures, works closely with the other divisions on economic feasibility studies. It also acts as an impartial arbiter among shipping modes where more than one division may be interested in handling specific movements.

The section is responsible for long-range departmental planning, guidelines for which come down from top management to each department planning section. These planning sections cross organization chart lines without hesitation to develop necessary joint programs furthering indicated goals for management consideration and action. Under present arrangements, the coordination section develops a seven-year forecast at mid-year as a basis for long-range programs and long-range capital expenditure budgets.

The seven-year forecasts from all departments go to the coordinator upon completion. He puts them through the existing 12-month planning program and produces a seven-year company forecast. This goes to all department planners, who then jointly formulate the most profitable system plans. They forward these to top management in late summer. Top management, in turn, does its strategic planning on the basis of this information, advising all departments thereafter of the selected overall objectives and the related funds allocations. On this basis, the department planners develop final plans fitting these objectives, submitting them to the coordinator. He assembles this material and arranges for the final production of a seven-year company plan in place of the initial seven-year forecast.

Within the planning and development section, one individual staff member and one alternate are assigned to one or more individual Phillips product lines. They devel-op relevant plans within the supply and transportation department and maintain continuing liaison with involved planners in other company departments.

The planning and distribution section was formed to consolidate economic development work and long-range planning under one unit. Major projects under way currently in tandem with other department planning units include a study of potential expansion of a large-diameter pipeline, a project tentatively priced at over $200 million.

Constant, alert watchfulness is essential in this highly competitive, sensitive industry. Weather and government are just two of many forces that can change plans in a hurry. Success or failure at out-guessing them are major determinants of profit or loss. If a winter proves to be warm and dry, liquefied petroleum gas and fuel oil sales drop sharply. Conversely, such an open winter sees a rise in gasoline sales as clear roads encourage more driving. If the Department of Agriculture sees fit to reduce acreages on certain crops, its decision is generally paralleled by increased fertilizer sales as farmers seek higher yields on remaining useful acreage.

Linear programming as a distribution planning method plays an important part in petroleum industry planning. The monthly natural gas liquid optimization program now employed represents developments over a period of 15 years. "Our first cut at this preceded computerization, in fact," states Vice President Kittrell. "We ran this one initially by hand successfully, but it took a year to complete. At our present state of development, it would be possible to optimize daily, but we'd be employing excessive computer time to do it. Monthly optimizing is the most practical present compromise,

Plastic Order Processing System
Estimated Total Annual Savings $495,000

Cost reduction and benefit analysis of "POPS"-plastic order processing system.

MEASURABLE SAVINGS $95,000

Faster Invoicing
Lower Communication Costs
Manhour Reduction

DIFFICULT-TO-ESTIMATE SAVINGS $400,000

IMPROVED OPERATIONAL CONTROL

Freight Savings
Fewer Invoicing Errors
Less Material Handling
Better Production Scheduling
Lower Inventories
Reduction in Unprofitable Sales
Timely Information for Planning

INCREASED SALES THROUGH BETTER CUSTOMER SERVICE

Faster Response
Order Status Information
Rail Car Location Information
Immediate Notification of Delays

but improved computers and continuing program sophistication should see us get to the daily basis."

Looking ahead five years, planning participates in an interdepartmental team effort aimed at a profit plan set up by product line. They are developing data necessary for computer simulation by appropriate statistical means; in the case of carbon black, for example, this will be a time-staged linear program. Ultimately, environmental models that statistically represent anticipated marketing conditions will make possible predictions such as the effect of additional research and development or increased advertising on specific products and product groups.

Setting the pace with high-powered computers

The computer today is an accepted, proven transportation-distribution tool. The managers who once were shy of it have come full circle and find, to their displeasure, that management is less ready for them to employ it than they might wish. Still further complicating matters is the too-frequent willingness of many computer chiefs to see themselves as high-speed bookkeepers rather than management information sources.

It's a different story at Phillips. Computing Department Manager Myron O. Johnson not only has abundant hardware, he also has a career behind him in the supply and transportation department, where he was manager before taking over his present position. Chairman of the Executive Committee Stanley Learned considered him the logical founder for this vital function because he was fully familiar with the company and its distribution practices and because his natural ability at mathematics indicated potential computer talents. Since then, he has presided over a major computer operation with branch facilities nationwide and a headquarters installation that puts in newer, larger hardware every second year, staying in the forefront of the latest computer technology.

This biennial computer upgrading is not without its problems. At present, Mr. Johnson's staff is finishing up de-bugging and program changeover for the new IBM 360-65/50 ASP computer system, but they are

Manager Computing Department M. O. Johnson, at right, checks out operation of the most recently acquired computer equipment at Bartlesville center with R. L. Peaster, supervisor, computer installation.

already casting an eye at the more powerful equipment that is about to be available. Right now they still run some of their work in emulation which, in effect, finds the 360-65 impersonating the former 7094-II equipment, but reprogramming has brought this down to only four hours daily out of the 24-hour, seven-day-a-week operation. The Bartlesville facility alone processes 900 to 1,100 jobs each day with substantial increases anticipated. Hourly messenger service to local Phillips facilities yields a two-hour turnaround on many jobs. Before long, input units right at the users' desks will yield real-time service, or the ability to interrogate the computer directly and get an instant response on the sender-receiver units.

Magnetic tape-encoder units provide the means for direct wire transmission of payroll checks and other information to and from Los Angeles. Running from tape to tape at

Message Switching Benefits

MEASURABLE SAVINGS $69,200

Man-hour Reduction
Elimination of Equipment
Reduced Stationary Supplies
Refined Products Invoicing

DIFFICULT-TO-MEASURE BENEFITS

More Efficient Line Usage
Timely Information Retrieval
Faster Invoicing Capability
More Rapid Communications
Reduced Voice Communications
Provision for Future Systems
Service to POPS and REDCAP

both terminals proved the lowest-priced practical approach of the feasible alternatives. The department also employs computer-to-computer Bell data phone connections between Adams Terminal (Houston, Tex.); the Sweeny, Tex. refinery; Borger, Tex.; Kansas City, Kans. and Bartlesville. Data flows to computer discs, then to the computer. The computer stores results with discs for transmission back to origins.

Both Borger and Kansas City have IBM 360-30 computers of their own, but the Bell lines make the central computer's power available to these and other points. The department staff totals 650 members, of whom 500 are in Bartlesville and 150 at other locations. Their numbers grow continuously as company growth increases its demands on both the personnel and the hardware at their command.

Continuous equipment upgrading anticipates not only expansion of real-time applications, but improved overall communica-

tions concurrently. Message switching within the computer rather than manual tape transfer is one instance of this, speeding up electronic data processing service, while saving money on handling other messages. This gives promise of growing benefits to supply and transportation as well as every other company department.

Minimizing goods movement to maximize profits

CRUDE OIL STOCKS are the lifeblood of a petroleum company. Their relative production or purchase costs, together with transportation expenses, determine whether any one source should be part of the company's raw material feedstock. Economic selection and employment of crudes is vital to a healthy balance sheet. Phillips, therefore, ties

Only a portion of the total computer facility at Bartlesville headquarters, this equipment is part of one available computer system which employs two complete computers interconnected for use as one.

the supply function to transportation, applying the physical distribution, or logistics, approach just as they do to the forwarding, stocking and marketing of their finished products.

This close supply-transportation relationship makes much easier the development of profitable trade-offs, both within the company and with other oil companies. Because crudes differ in their characteristics, different types are each best suited to specifically designed refining operations. High-sulphur crudes make bad input for some plants, while others swallow them happily. A sulphur-crude consuming refinery, on the other hand, does not necessarily digest a high-wax-content crude with similar efficiency. Matching out crudes to refineries and holding down transportation costs constitute a major responsibility.

The supply division's scope is worldwide. In addition to various types of crude oil, it obtains natural gasoline, propane and butane as well, supplying refineries in several countries from widely diversified sources. Supply Division Manager C. M. McCormick controls these activities through three separate, cooperating sections, including:

—Procurement. This group acquires crude oil and related products at the production site. Its U.S. purchases run about $1 million a day.

—Domestic Crude Supply and Product Exchange. This section acquires bulk crude (crude in pipeline systems) as opposed to purchasing at the original oil field site. They also sell or exchange crude oil.

—Foreign Crude Oil Supply. Supplies from foreign sources destined to either overseas or U.S. refineries are obtained by this section. It is also responsible for import quota paperwork between Phillips and the U.S. government.

The procurement section maintains offices in the major oil field producing areas. When new crude production is found, section personnel arrange for oil acquisition, setting up trucking programs to move the oil until a pipe line comes into the location. Phillips' crude oil production east of the Rockies is equivalent to roughly one-half of its refinery requirements. The balance is obtained by the procurement section through purchasing and trade activities.

Domestic refineries served include units at Sweeny (near Houston) and Borger, Tex.; Kansas City, Kansas; Woods Cross, Utah; Martinez, Calif. and Great Falls, Mont.

The foreign crude oil section concerns itself particularly with crude stock for five major refineries. San Roque, Venezuela draws primarily a wax-based local crude. Near Liverpool, England, the 50%-owned

Reviewing proposals for crude oil trades with other petroleum producers are Charles M. McCormick, supply division manager, left, and John E. Harris, Jr., manager, supply and transportation.

Eastham refinery also draws on Venezuela for a heavy, asphaltic crude well suited to the refinery's particular design. Another English facility, Teeside, is largely supplied from North Africa, using Phillips' resources as much as possible, but obtaining crudes from others as well. La Spezia, Italy at present is largely handled by the international department of Phillips in coordination with the foreign crude oil section, while Cochin, India is currently under a long-term purchase arrangement with a third party. At the latter refinery, the company hopes to start using Phillips crude in some part later on.

Besides the refineries, the foreign crude oil section sees to supplies for two overseas petrochemical plants. Phillips Puerto Rico Core, Inc. maintains an operation based on naphtha drawn from several Caribbean sources, with Venezuela predominating. Petrochim, S.A., a subsidiary in Antwerp, Belgium is also a heavy consumer of naphtha, most of which is obtained locally.

The United States Department of the Interior's oil import program places significant time demands on the foreign crude oil section. This program allocates annual import quotas to refiners and petrochemical plant operators based upon each such plant's crude oil consumption period. Rules and regulations designed to protect national security, including the development of a strong domestic crude oil production program, provide the basis for setting the overall import level. Import quota recipients, however, are permitted to exchange imported foreign crude oil for the domestic commodity. The inland refiner, with no access to foreign crude supplies, may trade his import allocation for needed domestic supplies. Only one Phillips refinery processes foreign crude oil, so the import quotas generated by Phillips' other U.S. refineries are traded for needed domestic supplies. The foreign crude section coordinates oil import activities relating to the company's operations.

The nature of these crude oil import quotas and the regulations concerning them involve the major oil companies and the government in considerable policy, administrative and legal negotiations, discussions and correspondence, most of which involves the foreign crude oil supply group. "The very complexity of this program necessitates changes from time to time in the governing laws, the quota-setting methods and the quo-

tas themselves," notes Foreign Crude Oil Supply Director Howard L. Stone.

The domestic crude supply and exchange section's basic job is probably the supply division's most unique physical distribution activity. Acquiring crudes from bulk sources, or above-ground stocks, rather than from direct production, the section also sells and exchanges Phillips bulk when conditions warrant it. Such trades, largely with competitors, may generate substantial marketing economies for all parties concerned. They take several widely varied forms, such as "borrowing" in the spring and "paying back" in the fall when a seasonality pattern can be smoothed by so doing, or direct quantity-for-quantity trades in which one type of crude is given to obtain crude of another kind.

These crude oil exchanges or acquisitions are a major element in transportation economies. In the event of down time at a refinery, trades filling the gap eliminate costly long hauls to other distant Phillips' refineries and subsequent back-hauls as well. A similar, longer range situation arises when the company and one or another of its competitors find themselves mutually producing crudes that better match each other's refineries than they do their own. Since Mother Nature concerns herself very little with oil company maps and plans, such occurrences are all too common.

The variety of trades possible or necessary keeps this division section continually active in the market. They constantly seek out stocks of crudes best suited to Phillips' refineries at convenient source locations while trading off Phillips' crudes of lower value to the company's plants.

Petroleum products are not alone in the exchange program. The finished product line includes about 30 different fertilizers as well, with plants at Pasco, Wash. and Borger, Houston and Hoag, Neb. Here, too, transportation costs are a major part of total product cost. A considerable variety of components goes into the manufacture of these fertilizers. Seasonal and year-to-year demand fluctuations occasioned by climate conditions and the market for agricultural products emphasize the value and necessity of trading arrangements.

Monthly computer runs show product exchange balances between Phillips and the companies with which this section trades.

At an East St. Louis terminal, one of the regularly scheduled refrigerated barges unloads anhydrous ammonia from Phillips' Adams Terminal on the Houston Ship Channel. This product, a major ingredient in fertilizer compounds, is an important factor in supply division's purchasing and trading activities.

The complex relations rising out of the widely diversified trading possibilities make such control essential. A similar computer program is under development for crude oil trading. These analyses help the section to maintain even ratios in their exchanges with other companies.

In a company where managers learn that they are merchants first and technical specialists only secondarily, the supply division becomes practically the classic example. The liaison with the coordination and planning division is close and continuous and both sections keep constantly aware of cost or service changes promulgated or required by other divisions to assure that company buying and selling prices fit market conditions as well as forecasted sales patterns.

The supply division is in effect, therefore, the major raw material purchaser in the Phillips company. Petroleum and its derivatives are the essential ingredients to most Phillips' products and this is the area of the supply division's responsibility. The physical distribution role is thus expanded significantly beyond its tentative boundaries in many other companies. As a result, age-old clashes between traffic and purchasing, all too common elsewhere, are totally absent here. In-

bound control is firmly vested in the department where it belongs; there is no conflict over whether purchasing terms should be collect or prepaid between independent managers seeking purely departmental budget advantage. Instead, continuing supply-transportation liaison, so necessary in the constantly changing crude oil situation, assures that the overall department result will be the lowest-priced delivery of supplies to the refineries, whether through direct extraction, trade or outright purchase from external sources.

Mixed modes, close service control, continued research: The Phillips blend for effective transportation

THE PHILLIPS TRANSPORTATION division in itself is big business. It maintains some 4,900 rail cars, 3,000 trucks and 2,000 automobiles. Its rates and services section pays freight charges exceeding $30 million annually while the employe travel service section spends $2,500,000 per year at Bartlesville alone for employe air travel. Nationwide, its staff numbers 400. Operating responsibilities absorb a large proportion of these people, but the sheer size of this division's assigned mission amply justifies a significant and growing staff and research activity at corporate headquarters.

Essentially, the division functions like a typical large traffic department, but with exceptionally heavy operational duties. As Transportation Division Manager John E. Donnelly states it, "There are days when we feel more like a carrier than a shipper. Everybody in this division wears two hats all the time." The division's section breakdown reflects this as well:

—Railway section. This group maintains and supervises the large and varied rail car roster.

—Automotive section. Operating and maintaining a nationwide highway fleet, it works through 21 company garages.

—Rates and services section. Common carrier shipments of a most diversified nature flow through this section's control.

—Employe travel service section. Pro-

viding travel service worldwide, it is also known for a unique over-the-road passenger service it provides between Bartlesville and Tulsa.

The railway section splits primarily between operations and maintenance. Much of the latter work is performed at company car shops in Borger, Tex. and Kansas City, Kans. "We also do some light repairs and inspections at Alvin, Tex.," stated Section Manager R. E. Peck. "Our nearby Sweeny refinery is a heavy loading point, so it provides an opportunity to spot a lot of our cars for a look-see all the time, minimizing dead mileage."

"REDCAP" is the magic word for Phillips rail services. An acronym signifying "Rail Expediting Daily Car Activity Program," this computer systems package provides information guiding rail operations personnel, helping salesmen in setting delivery dates and informing management concerning costs and condition of the rail car fleet. The company's 4,900 cars are essentially specialized equipment, including giant tank and hopper cars. Phillips, a user of this equipment, controls it closely to maximize loaded mileage

A pioneer in the mass-market development of liquefied petroleum gasses, Phillips also pioneered the use of jumbo tankers, such as this 30,000-gallon capacity car.

Computer activities of Project "REDCAP," automated system controlling movement of Phillips' 4,900 rail cars are reviewed by Computer Analyst D. R. Kirchman.

in relation to investment.

The basic Redcap report comes out daily, providing those concerned with a complete, up-to-the-minute review of car locations and conditions for the entire fleet. To date, over 40 railroads participate, with others joining the information flow as their own computer facilities expand. It was the combined expansion of both Phillips and railroad electronic data processing capacity that made the program possible.

The program's initial goal was a 3% improvement in car utilization. This would have meant annual savings of $125,000, ample to justify the plan. Results far exceeded expectations. In the pressure tank car fleet alone, utilization improved better than 9%. By January, 1970, 12% utilization gains are anticipated with readily measurable savings exceeding $500,000. Actual total cost reductions will go well beyond that, however, as less readily measurable savings are also substantial (see accompanying table describing current program economics).

Because railroads generally cut off input to their own computers each day at midnight, their data generally moves to Phillips via TELEX teletype circuits between 1:00 and 4:00 a.m. The Phillips plants generally cut off at 4:00 p.m., but report clearly anticipatable events of the night hours, thus keeping their day's input roughly parallel to railroad data on a time period basis. After transmissions to Bartlesville are completed, the night computer staff produces daily Redcap reports between 4:00 and 8:00 a.m.,

Anticipated benefits and cost reductions from the "REDCAP" car control system.

Economics Of REDCAP
Estimated Total Annual Savings Of On-Line System $743,000

MEASURABLE SAVINGS $463,000
INCREASED CAR UTILIZATION
Current Fleet Information

More Time to Optimize Fleet Operation

Information Available to Plants

Available Historical Information

Fewer Cars Assigned to a Customer

INCREASED CARBON BLACK PRODUCTION
Longer Production Runs on One Type Black
    Due to Better Information on Incoming Cars

REDUCED MAN-HOURS AND PHONE CALLS
Fewer Manual Reports

Calls from Field to Railroads

Calls from Field to Bartlesville

DIFFICULT-TO-ESTIMATE SAVINGS $280,000
INCREASED SALES (EXCLUDING PLASTICS)
Better Knowledge of Supply Situation

Automatic Notification of Abnormal Situations

Rail Car Location Information for All Products

OTHER BENEFITS
Immediate Error Correction

Ability to Monitor Rail Activity

Foundation for Future Information Systems

with delivery to recipients accomplished by the latter hour.

The basic report, covering 4,900 tank, hopper and box cars owned or leased by Phillips Petroleum Co., groups cars by shipping origins, car repair shops, or other assignment points.

Data for assigned points is further segregated to three sections. The first, empties on hand, starts with the smallest size cars and also separates the car types with totals by size and type as well as grand total empties. Additional pertinent data is included, as in the following Kansas City Report:

TV PSPX 000828 RE 06 09 03 67 SL KC 08 15 67 Diesel
PSPX 000830 RE 09 11 09 67 SL KC 10 18 67 66

Total Number of NC-8 Cars On Hand Empty at Kansas City—2

The foregoing shows two NC-8 (non-coiled, 8,000-gallon) tank cars on hand empty. The first entry line indicates that tank (T) and safety valve (V) tests are required before year's end for Phillips car (PSPX) 828. This car was received empty (RE) at Kansas City at 6:00 a.m. (06) Sept. 3, 1967 and was previously shipped loaded (SL) from Kansas City (KC) on Aug. 15, 1967. The final entry shows that on that occasion it carried diesel oil. The entry for car PSPX 830 reads similarly except that no shop work is due and the prior commodity was Phillips 66 gasoline rather than diesel oil. Comparing the last load date with the empty arrival indicates turnaround time; in the case of car 828, 19 days. Comparison of an empty arrival date and the current date shows how long a car has been sitting at a point inactive.

The second report section shows cars on hand loaded. Car orders and totals are set up as in the first section. As an example:

Kansas City NC-8 On Hand Loaded

PSPX 00870 LB 06 11 06 67 RE 11 01 67 Lube 007839

Total Number of NC-8 Cars on Hand Loaded at Kansas City—1

Here, a non-coiled 8,000-gallon car, Phillips 870, was loaded for billing (LB) at Kansas City at 6:00 a.m. (06) Nov. 6, 1967, having been previously received empty (RE) Nov. 1, 1967. The final two items indicate the car was loaded with lubricating oil in the amount of 7,839 gallons. The dates show that the car was on hand empty for five days before loading.

The final report section, Shipped or Returning, details cars shipped from a point either loaded or empty and the latest railroad location report, as shown in the following two Kansas City instances:

Kansas City 11.7M Shipped Or Returning
PSPX 16669 SL 09 11 07 67 RE 06 11 05 67 Propane
010549 Propane A. O. Smith Milw Wisc.

UP KC CMSTP&P MILW Savannah P 08 11 09 67 L
Diverted 11 10 67 Pac Pet Ltf Ft Whyte Canada Milw St. Paul
Soo Noyes CP

PSPX 16715 SL 09 10 30 67 LD KC 10 19 67 Propane 010560
Propane Comd Oil Co Hrvy Minn

UP COBL CMSTP&P Duluth DWP DWP Duluth J 16 11 17 67 E

Total Number of 11.7M Cars Shipped from Kansas City—2

The section heading indicates Kansas City as report point and car size as 11,700 gallons (11.7M). The first car, PSPX 16669, was shipped loaded (SL) at 9:00 a.m. (09) Nov. 7, 1967, having been received empty (RE) at 6:00 a.m. (06) Nov. 5, 1967, laying over two days before loading. The shipped product (propane) is followed by the quantity (10,549). The second propane entry indicates the last prior load in the car. Final entries in this data group are consignee and destination. There follows the railroad routing (Union Pacific to Kansas City connection with Milwaukee Road to destination) and the latest railroad record of this car. In this case, the Milwaukee (MILW) reports it passing (P) Savannah, Ill. at 8:00 a.m. (08) Nov. 9, 1967 loaded (L). In addition to passing reports and indications of whether a car is loaded or empty, railroad codes may show car at destination or turned over to another carrier at a junction as well as a bad order notation if a car is in disrepair. A further statement on this particular car reveals a diversion, instructing that the car be moved when empty from Milwaukee to Pacific Petroleum, Fort Whyte, Canada, via MILW-St. Paul-SOO-Noyes-CP routing. Subsequent daily reports would indicate when this car was emptied and diversion accomplished. The next car shown, PSPX 16715, carries the same type of information save that no diversion is shown. The last line of the report gives total cars of this class shipped or returned on the reporting date. A car remains continuously in this report section until received empty at an assigned point. Its arrival is then reported under the empty car report section.

When Redcap started, the division paralleled its output with manually developed data from Nov. 1, 1966 to Jan. 1, 1967, assuring that computer reports were matched out before becoming fully dependent upon the new system. It has expanded steadily as more railroads made computer data available and as Phillips expanded its computer flexibility and capacity. "We have an effective automatic accuracy check on the present daily reporting procedure," observes Division Manager Donnelly. "We look out the office window and spot one of our cars on a nearby siding. We then request a check of this car on the machine report and almost without fail it indicates that the car should, in fact, be currently on a Bartlesville siding."

Director of Railway Transportation Charles W. Haas, working with the computing department staff, keeps steadily expanding Redcap's scope, both fulfilling planned expansion and adding new reports or services whose values become apparent through the continuing development. "We built a three-phase approach for Redcap, looking to third phase completion in 1969," states Mr. Haas, "but we slipped into phase two-and-a-half this past year. Among other ahead-of-schedule items, we gave salesmen reports during the 1968 fertilizer season showing where ordered cars had most recently passed first thing each morning at sales offices. This gave a strong sales benefit by bettering customer service during the peak periods and cutting unnecessary telephone calls for both buyer and seller while easing customer inventory problems." Mr. Haas feels the brisk development tempo was helped no little because the computing department assigned a programmer to it, R. J. Scott, who himself was formerly with the supply and transportation department.

The daily action information, valuable as it is, may ultimately be matched by savings generated through accumulating trend data concerning maintenance, scheduling over alternate routes and car assignment practices. As Manager Railway Operations Howard B. Phillips observes, "Redcap smoked out quite a number of 'hidden' empties at plants and other locations where holding a little extra capacity can make things more comfortable at peak periods. It only takes a few places making themselves comfortable to

run up the car cost or, alternately, to starve the car supply for the total system. When any car sits in one place more than a reasonable period and it is not awaiting repairs, we see it on the reports and we want to know the explanation pronto. If a loading point is holding cars too long, it tells us that some of their equipment might be better assigned elsewhere."

Conditions such as the above, once brought to light, were one reason for setting up a non-activity report, showing cars not active, the circumstances and the cost to Phillips. Plant-held cars are checked directly, but held cars frequently are being delayed by customers, in which case they are reported to sales.

An annual run by car number develops a permanent record for each unit. This summarizes all activity of each car and is valuable for both maintenance and costing purposes.

Special reports give separate data on high-pressure tank cars and on 539 jumbo tank cars (30,000- to 33,500-gallon capacity). These reports are of particular value during certain peak seasons. The foregoing reports, by permitting faster planning and activation of diversions, make more effective use of this specialized fleet as well as a reduction in its size.

Similarly, an empty car diversion report gives valuable peak period information, summarizing cars diverted to plants running short in lieu of their regularly assigned terminals. This information helps in subsequent planning of car assignments.

Routing and scheduling benefits significantly from Redcap as experience with different routes and car types grows. Railroads and company plants become readily measurable in their performance. The department also maintains a diagnostic report on each of these concerning their reliability in car location and status reporting.

Until recently, Redcap ran on an IBM 360-30 computer. At this writing, however, 360-50 equipment of greater capacity and flexibility is taking over and message switching within the computer now replaces the former need for tape-to-card conversion on inbound data. The new arrangements open several avenues of expansion. They permit the Phillips computing department to interrogate railroad computers directly, not only daily, but whenever necessary for immediate hour-by-hour information. When necessary, this can be done multi-daily. "We've started phase three of the Redcap program with a broad, strong plan," comments Director Haas, "but we've kept it completely flexible. Past experience with Redcap proved that new pos-

In addition to shipping its products by air, Phillips' aviation products are sold to private aircraft owners and commercial airlines at more than 300 airports.

sibilities would spring from every addition, so we're holding our doors open for further improvements."

Private truck operations by Phillips are nationwide in scope, although the majority of routes are in the Texas-Oklahoma-Kansas area. Vehicle assignments are on an area rather than specific route basis in general, serving refineries, terminals and customers scattered over a region. An exception is a regular, daily Okmulgee-Bartlesville-Wichita route employing three tank trucks. As with the company rail car fleet, specialized equipment is the rule, with the engineering section devising trucking equipment specifications and working with other departments in designing to meet specific operating needs.

The decision to employ private trucks in any specific application takes into account potential costs versus available common carrier services and rates. In many instances, the need for specific services prompted the Phillips' decision. Once a route is installed, however, its costs are closely controlled. Director Lane Kelley's staff prepares a monthly Transport Truck Operating Statement which shows costs in detail for direct comparison to alternate modes and for indication of any irregularities. This statement, in turn, is analyzed and becomes the basis for an Annual Rate of Return Statement on capital involved by specific route. These returns average 30%.

In some instances, the combination of careful operation and thorough accounting serves as a means of showing common carriers correctible inefficiencies in their own operations. "Our operating statements are very helpful in rate negotiations," notes Transportation Division Manager Donnelly.

The question of inside or outside automotive maintenance arose for Phillips as it does for any company operating a fleet of highway vehicles. The decision was to do the job within where practicable and, again, watch costs closely in relation to costs outside. Monthly garage statements, therefore, not only present actual cost experience, but show as well what comparable costs in custom shops would be on each individual job, based on known area standards. Under the company's preventive maintenance program, recent figures reveal savings annually of roughly $500,000 over potential outside garage costs. The section's fleet control unit handles licensing and records of all automotive equipment in the United States.

Probably the most unusual automotive activity, however, is the Phillips Mail Service. Continued, increasing dissatisfaction with regular mail service in the region where so many company facilities are spread out led to the decision to try carrying its own correspondence for savings in time. Time they saved, but to everyone's satisfaction, money they saved as well—approximately $600,000 annually against alternate transportation, primarily U.S. mail.

Bulk-type storage tank is refilled from Phillips tanker with Philgas, Phillips' brand of liquefied petroleum gas, at a farm where it is used in a wide variety of ways both domestic and commercial.

Company mail runs move daily, either five or six days a week. In some instances, the runs are multi-daily. All of them are on tight, strict schedules and the level of performance is high. On one run, from Bartlesville to Borger, Tex., the assigned vehicle participates in a tire-testing program. This testing, if done independently, would cost in excess of $50,000 per year.

In addition to Bartlesville-Borger, seven other runs give coverage in Oklahoma and Texas, with one extending into Artesia, N.M.

The transportation division's rates and services section, centralized at Bartlesville, handles all domestic common carrier traffic activity within the United States. Fully equipped to do a complete orthodox line traffic job, it is nonetheless an unorthodox, increasingly sophisticated operation. Computerization relieves the section of many line duties, freeing the group for greater attention to research and advance planning. At the same time, automated tariff filing brings greater efficiency to internal operations.

"Our entire tariff file and any rate applications relevant to specific tariffs are stored in Remington Rand LEKTRAFILE units," notes Director of Rates and Services Irvin C. Dickerson. "We've used this system since 1963 with considerable satisfaction. Rate look-ups are easier and faster, particularly when something new or unusual is being checked and comparisons must be made among several modes or rate categories."

The three Lektrafile units store individual tariffs within rate bureau by number, with rate bureaus blocked out alphabetically. Each Lektrafile has push-button control with a button for each bureau. Pushing the button for a chosen bureau rotates the shelves automatically and places the required shelf at normal work level for easy access. The only operational problem is the need to keep tariff files back far enough on the 12-inch-deep shelves to avoid blocking the actuating electric eyes. All rail tariffs are color coded by various types within territories speeding both shelf searching and refiling.

Lektrafiles materially reduce floor space for the size library they contain. Their contents are stored all the way to the ceiling, well beyond arm's reach.

Numerous computer programs based on the rates and services section's input data keep company sales and operating departments advised as to common carrier costs and services affecting their activities. Customer data sheets for different commodities show individual customer destination, source, carrier, routing, rail or truck miles, freight rates and related information. Computerized rate studies detail and summarize product shipments information to selected states by specified modes. Distribution guides indicate the lowest freight cost distribution for specific products based on estimated demand by customer and destination. Master rail and truck routing codes are

Transportation division's plans for further rail car control computerization are discussed by, left to right, Director, Railway Transportation Charles W. Haas; Manager, Railway Operations Howard B. Phillips; TM executive Editor Jack W. Farrell and Transportation Division Manager John E. Donnelly.

summarized by computer from rates and services section information, as are master origin and master destination computer listings. These and other standardized report formats are readily augmented, as well, by special studies developed conjointly by the rates and services staff and the computing department.

While the employe travel service section's principle duty is providing travel service worldwide through its Bartlesville facility, it attracts most attention for a unique local service it operates. The section runs five limousines on an hourly schedule from Bartlesville to the Tulsa, Okla. airport on 15 daily round trips. Originating at the Phillips Transportation Center in Bartlesville, each trip makes a stop at the downtown Phillips Hotel and then proceeds to Tulsa, averaging 4½ passengers per trip for a 25,000 annual total. The service is free for anyone doing business with Phillips.

Continuing new developments resulting from oil field explorations pose ever-new shipping questions for the department. At this time, Alaska's limited transportation facilities and frigid climate necessitate some novel answers to getting goods to the huge new North Slope Oil Fields. The Alaska Steamship Company, working with the Alaska Railroad, recently opened a unique through service to this region. Containers and vans move via these two carriers to Fairbanks, then proceed by conventional highway some 50 miles further. Beyond this point, the truck operation is over a new "road" that is literally hacked out of solid ice from this point north and west, crossing the mountain barrier at Anuktuvuk Pass and proceeding into the oil sites. In this way, Alaskans convert a climate problem into its own solution for moving freight, speeding the development of huge new fields in which Phillips is a major developer.

Worldwide marine operations expedite refinery services while holding down expenditures

SET UP IN 1953 within the transportation division, the marine section got a real boost when Phillips acquired portions of Tidewater Oil Co.'s West Coast operations in July, 1966, adding a seven-vessel operating marine unit overnight. The present fleet, augmented by an even greater number of chartered ships, will expand during 1969 when construction of several additional units is completed.

Marine Division Manager Homer J. Frederic drew his present assignment late in 1967

At **Freeport Terminal** on Texas Gulf Coast, Mississippi River barges and ocean-going tankers load products from Sweeney refinery for domestic, overseas destinations.

after serving as assistant manager of the transportation division during the marine unit's expansion. "We wanted a supply-oriented executive rather than an 'old salt' for the job," notes Vice President Kittrell. "Rapid corporate expansion dictated a particular need for this unit to harmonize closely with supply activities rather than risk the discord that direct transportation preoccupation might have engendered under existing conditions." All ocean shipping as well as significant domestic inland waterway movements comes under the marine division. These three sections control activities:

—Operations. Manning, maintenance and scheduling of owned and chartered vessels get this unit's attention.

—Import-Export. Shipments other than those in bulk liquids are processed here, including varied small shipments and non-fluid commodities such as carbon black and others. Both air and ocean shipments flow through this section.

—Chartering and development. This group closely controls both the chartering of Phillips-owned or leased vessels to outside companies and the charter of other vessels for Phillips' use as needed.

The present Phillips-owned fleet includes two U.S. flag tankers and five large vessels of Liberian registry. While the term "tanker" generally describes all vessels in the fleet, many of these offer wider capabilities than this description suggests. Readily convertible for carrying such bulk products as mineral ores, their deadhead movements may be minimized by switching commodities for return loads.

The larger tankers, both owned and chartered, serve primarily from the Persian Gulf to Great Britian, Northern Europe, Japan and U.S. West Coast ports. The two small owned ships trade up and down the Pacific Coast. They run to Hawaii as well every three to four months, returning with molasses. They also bring occasional loads of crude from Phillips' Cook Inlet fields in Alaska to the West Coast refineries. In addition, a chartered ship runs exclusively between Cook Inlet, Alaska and Martinez, Calif. on about a two-week cycle.

A novel development slated for 1969 inauguration is the anticipated movement, jointly with Marathon Oil, of liquefied natural gas from Cook Inlet to Japan in two 33,470-ton tankers employing membrane-type cargo containment. The vessels are under construction in Sweden. This will mark the first export of this commodity from the Western Hemisphere and is intended to supply two Japanese utility companies with the fuel. While 70% of the gas will be Phillips-provided, vessel operation will be by Marathon. Phillips, however, anticipates delivery of a new liquefied petroleum gas tanker, the *Phillips Arkansas*, in 1969 for its own ac-

Proposed operating plans for tankers currently under construction are discussed by Marine Division Manager Homer J. Frederic, left, and James E. Arnold, manager, coordination and planning division.

A supertanker, the *Phillips Louisiana* comes into San Francisco Bay (above) with a cargo of crude oil for the firm's 120,000 barrels daily capacity Avon Refinery. Below, the *Louisiana* rests at anchor as part of its huge cargo is pumped into one of the smaller tankers the company employs in coastal service. The smaller tanker will move the crude oil to the Avon dock which the larger vessel cannot reach because of its deeper draft.

Loading oil from the company's Lot 9 in southern Monagas state, Venezuela. The Puerto Ordaz Terminal on the Orinoco River is 45 miles from the field by company pipeline.

count for general service.

The chartering and development section concerns itself with present employment and future expansion of marine ventures. This unit makes both short and long-term charters of Phillips' vessels. In turn, the section makes charters of other outside-owned tankers for Phillips' use as required. The philosophy here is the same as that behind the supply division's function: maximum utilization of Phillips' equipment traded off against the cost of outside services for specialized or unusual purposes. "By going both ways at once, we get the most for our marine dollar expenditures," comments Director of Chartering and Development Forrest Okerman. "We can respond quickly to rate changes in the charter market."

This section acts as agent for all plants and subsidiaries worldwide on international bulk movements. Crude stocks constitute most of these. Intercoastal and Puerto Rican movements are under the unit and expanded future operations are planned in these areas. Substantial coastal and inland barge operations similarly come under this group's control.

Continuing study of present and future petroleum demand is maintained in this unit. This bears particular importance in relation to reserve oil fields not yet opened up, where growing demand may indicate the feasibility of extracting and transporting the as yet locked-in production. Such projects as the Cook Inlet field and the gas movements from there to Japan typify these. In this instance, Manager Robert S. Gruel of the computing department's operations branch and his staff, working with the chartering and development section, simulated all conditions relevant to a 15-year service contract as part of the preliminary study. This and other management science techniques are increasingly employed by the group.

The marine division's import-export section provides central control of virtually all international freight to and from the United States. Import-Export Director C. A. Christie claims, "We handle everything from a suitcase to a complete factory."

This is no idle boast. The section moved all the material, both the plant itself and the necessary construction equipment, for buildings that constitute Phillips' Puerto Rico Core, Inc. This facility is a bustling petrochemical plant that underscores the company's growing product diversification worldwide.

Within a recent 18-month period, the section was called upon twice to assemble complete gas liquefaction plants for overseas movements. The most recent consolidated at Galveston and moved forward early in June as a single 2,800-ton shipment destined for assembly on a platform in Lake Maracaibo, Venezuela.

In the past, the company maintained offices at several ports, but economic studies showed outside brokerage more suitable. The section deals largely with international freight forwarders at Houston, Galveston, Los Angeles, San Francisco and New York plus custom house brokers at the same points.

Many export declarations are made "in house," nonetheless, particularly on items leaving Bartlesville directly or moving by air. A Tulsa air freight forwarder works with the department on some shipments, while inbound air shipments occasionally move through a custom house broker and the new customs office at Oklahoma City, which is a short highway run from Bartlesville.

While day-to-day operations keep the section busy, staff activities form an important part of its work. Subsidiaries seeking advice or assistance on import-export problems are assured of cooperation, the unit working closely with them developing rates and services on a regular basis.

A current project concerns a new carbon black plant in Colombia. The import-export section is developing rates and services adequate to move this traffic competitively.

Carbon black was featured in another research project that paid off in reduced packaging costs and shipping damages. The company moves many such shipments currently in 50-pound bags, 30 bags to a banded carton, which is glued or stapled to single-use wood pallets. With the top open, a second band is applied and loaded, covered by a large fibreboard "cap" which falls around the base carton sides as the bags settle.

Looking ahead, the marine division and the computing department are developing a marine scheduling and long-range planning system. Daily activity and historical data, merged with relevant cost and geographic information will blend to produce comprehensive forecasts of marine capabilities and costs as a basis for route development, vessel acquisitions and charter arrangements.

Pipelines: Underground movement yields bulk economies

PIPELINES RANK HIGH in the Phillips traffic pattern, but their development has been a cautious, long-term process. To be justified, the demand for their products must be very large and comparatively steady. Lines must be full at all times, operation is a 24-hour daily continuum, and substantial terminal storage investment backing them up is essential. When the conditions are right, however, pipeline shipping costs are remarkably low. Houston, for example, can move about ten gallons of petroleum product all the way to Linden, N.J., adjacent to New York City, for less than it costs to mail a letter. Savings such as this account for daily pipeline movement of 67,000 truckload equivalents by United States shippers each day.

At Kankakee, Ill., this 260,000-barrel products vault, mined underground in a bed of shale, was built for off-season storage of propane. Similar facilities mined in salt beds or shale deposits, or existing as natural caverns, provide low-cost storage for this product.

The Houston-Linden movement would use the Colonial Pipe Line, a common carrier partially owned by Phillips which is a strictly independent company, publishing its own tariffs. The line runs from Texas through the Southeastern states to northern New Jersey terminals, and each foot of its length demands over a barrel of product to fill it. This means that it contains a permanent underground inventory worth $40 million at refinery value. The trade-off, of course, is the very minimal cost of its operation.

With pipeline content moving at a brisk walk, roughly two to five miles per hour continuously, scheduling and dispatching require tight control from origin to destination and within the terminals as well. Either blockage or starvation create serious problems. The easy out would be to build maximum storage capacity so that inventory buildup at slack times would be no problem, but storage facilities don't come cheap. Gasoline storage averages about $1.50 to $2 per barrel. Propane, another major Phillips commodity that moves in heavy pipeline volume, however, runs about $20 per barrel for comparable storage. Very careful planning is necessary, therefore, to keep the product mix right in the pipe lines and, in particular, to avoid blockage through moving propane beyond the capacity of existing storage or customer demand.

While conventional propane storage runs exceedingly high, the company now operates some facilities that are reducing the figure significantly. When this liquid is chilled to 50 degrees below zero, it can be stored at atmospheric pressure for only about $6 to $8 per barrel. Recognizing this, Phillips engineers perfected a frozen earth "tank" that to date has proven a highly satisfactory storage vessel.

What they do is sink vertical pipe into the ground in a ring around the chosen area, filling the pipes with chilled propane. Excavation within the ring leaves a frozen earth retaining wall around the perimeter. A roof built up from the frozen wall completes the tank. The sidewalls stay safely frozen and tight as the tank is kept constantly filled with chilled propane.

Another proven method lies in underground storage. Caverns in salt beds and rock formations, both natural and man-made, offer substantial cost reductions over comparable capacity above-ground conven-

Pipelines, like all forms of transportation, require maintenance. Here, a new section of pipe is welded in at a field location.

tional high-pressure tanks.

Phillips started pipeline operation in 1931. Initially a strictly crude oil producer, the company acquired its first refinery at Borger, Tex. A line started from Borger ultimately reached Chicago in 1936. For some years, it handled only gasoline. Subsequently, it became a dual line, with gasolines and oils moving through one pipe while butane, propane and other so-called "light end" products filled the other. Today, on the Borger-Chicago operation, Phillips continues its original concept of pumping components rather than finished products, assembling specific products at terminals en route as local demands require. Such blending terminals are costly operations and are only feasible or justifiable when volume is very high.

Automation is a key factor in pipeline operation. As electronic and other controls continually improve, the justification for manned stations along pipeline routes becomes less and less. A single automated control console can effectively maintain proper operating pressures at every pumping station between Borger and St. Louis, to cite just one of many examples. A pipeline diagram, showing the route covered and the individual pumping stations and terminals gives instantaneous information as to pressure changes and other conditions that dispatchers must check in maintaining control. Even with automation, however, manpower remains crucially important to line dispatching. A wrong dispatcher decision can cost a great deal, while sound decisions, either logical or intuitive, can create

This remote control system provides for the automated operation of two products pipelines from Phillips Pipe Line's headquarters in Bartlesville. System controls these at 13 points between Borger, Tex., and St. Louis.

The Carteret, N. J. terminal operated by Phillips receives refined products via the Colonial Pipeline, in a never-ending flow, from the Sweeny, Tex. refinery, 1,500 miles away.

substantial savings that never identify their source in the books of account. When multiple products move through a single line, the effects on line pressure and pump station capacities are such that a dispatcher must develop the feel of a piano tuner if he is to get the most for the dollar out of line operation.

Moving multiple products creates more problems than pressure changes. Care must be taken to schedule products into storage at their terminals so that mixture or contamination is avoided. When two grades of oil move forward, there will be some mingling of these near the end of the initial shipment, so feeding of the initial "slug" into terminal storage must be stopped at the critical point where this mixing action commences. The flow following, wherein this blending occurs, is termed an interface and must be drawn off separately until the second slug of the other oil grade is running pure from the line. The interface is then sold, fractionated into its components by refining or, if its nature permits, blended within specifications with other products.

Drawing off the product at pipeline's end is a fairly straightforward operation, but removing shipments at intermediate destinations can be another matter entirely. Pressure must be maintained beyond the intermediate line point to avoid starving the line, creating vacuum locks and other difficulties that cost time and money to rectify. Depending upon circumstances, either of two methods can be used:

—Divert the main line stream fully into the intermediate terminal facility. This is feasible if pumping rates can be adjusted to maintain adequate pressures beyond the point of withdrawal for the time period involved.
—Strip off the needed quantity from the continuing main line flow. The stripping rate is set by the known length of the product slug, the flow velocity and the volume to be taken off.

Phillips pipeline activities vary from the comparatively short-run operations originating in the oil fields and drawing off crude stock to the high-volume, long distance carriers of varied petroleum products. The network embraces major market areas throughout the United States, but fanning out primarily from the major Texas-Oklahoma producing area.

The company is not alone, of course, in pipeline employment and operation. Virtually all petroleum producers, save perhaps the very small, employ the lines in varying degree. As new lines are built, representing substantial investments by petroleum producers, their competitive impact poses serious economic questions for each petroleum marketer's consideration. Chicago, for instance, already served by several pipelines, anticipates early completion of added crude oil and refined product lines from St. Louis and the Gulf Coast. The Interprovincial Line concurrently is being extended to that city from Canada.

Just what will happen to the affected market area when all of these and other possible carrier additions hit Chicago? Clearly, petroleum supplies from broader sources will be competing hard for a market which, while rapidly growing, does not appear to be expanding as fast as its sources of supply. The addition of high-capacity pipelines, capable of moving products at the highest rates of efficiency will, in any case, mean diversion of shipments from existing facilities in some measure. Cheap transportation from the North will also mean some potential diversion of patronage from other United States or foreign sources as well, so that existing modes will feel an impact, not merely of direct competition along their routes, but the indirect effect caused by customers shifting their purchases to entirely different shippers in previously unacceptable origin areas. The joint competitive impact of these upcoming facilities will be difficult to anticipate indeed.

Three views of a unique storage facility: Above at Phillips' Woods Cross, Utah refinery, the domed top of an underground storage pit for propane is shown during its construction. Diagram shows design of the "frozen earth" refrigerated propane storage pit which houses excess propane during the summer to level off sales surges in the winter. Below, the exterior of Phillips' unique storage facility after its completion.

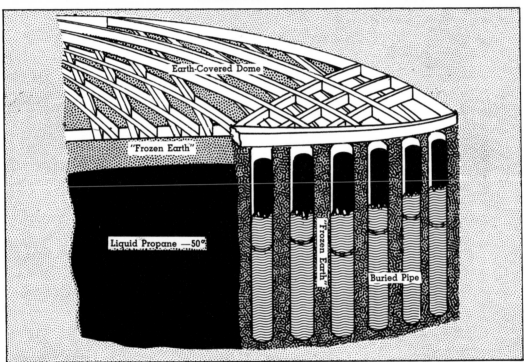

Earth-Covered Dome

"Frozen Earth"

Liquid Propane —50°

Frozen Earth

Buried Pipe

Discussing career prospects with two graduates of supply and transportation department's training program is Louis A. Whitehair, left, manager, employe relations division.

How supply and transportation's personnel department helps to build better distribution management

PHILLIPS' TRANSPORTATION and supply department gets good results from automation. Human brain power does more things faster because big electronic brain power capacity frees people from numerous routine chores. With each staff member able to carry greater responsibilities, matching men and jobs gains in importance. This consideration plus the department's sheer size (over 2,100 employes) lends increasing justification to its employe relations division. Reporting directly to Vice President Kittrell rather than an administrative or personnel relations vice president as in many other large corporations, the personnel staff profits from resultant improved intradepartmental communication and coordination. The payoff lies in steadily increasing job productivity from the top to the bottom of the organization chart, while recruitment becomes easier, thanks to a growing reputation for good jobs today and better careers tomorrow.

"Perhaps our most important task comes before a man joins us," states Employe Relations Divison Manager Louis Whitehair. "A new man must be more than a job-filler for a current opening. Departmental newcomers get up to two years training before actual job assignment. When it comes, man and department know each other well. The no-longer-newcomer, given a choice of job assignments, can decide more wisely because his actual experience with duties and people prepares him to select, not gamble."

The division doesn't depend on applicants knocking at the door. Seeking widely varied talents, department recruiters interview likely individuals at several colleges regularly. Following their schooling, selected applicants enter appropriate training programs. All expose new men to the total supply and transportation function, with assignment adjustments readily made where a man's needs or aptitudes suggest the advisability of such changes.

Plan "A" typifies the exposure provided. An "A" candidate gets 58 weeks' exposure, including 12 field weeks and 46 weeks divided between supply and transportation divisions at the Bartlesville headquarters. Plan "B", while similar, anticipates 4 additional field weeks for specialists more likely to profit from this specific exposure.

The Houston, Alvin, Odessa and Austin, Tex. areas provide most of the field exposure. Marine, manufacturing and chemical facilities see the candidate during nine weeks under Plan "A" or alternately 13 weeks under "B." Field gathering systems and the Pasadena terminal get appropriate attention. The Port Adams and Freeport, Tex. marine terminals offer marine operations indoctrination. Manufacturing know-how is inculcated at plants and chemical facilities. Importantly, much attention goes to electronic, mechanical and pipeline maintenance, the latter including station, terminal, gathering and main line equipment.

Next comes a week with the supply division. This involves customer contacts on raw materials and finished product sales, exchanges and purchases. Working with experienced Phillips supply people, a trainee develops insight into practical rather than theoretical trading relations.

The automotive division's widespread and diversified operations similarly get a week's on-the-spot attention, acquainting students with shop maintenance of vehicles and fleet operating practices employed by Phillips.

A final field week with the transportation division takes in attendance at actual rate hearings and other commission or regulatory activities. Following this, five or six days at Martinez, Calif. with the marine division includes background briefing on operating procedures, inspection and orientation aboard one or both domestically registered Phillips' vessels. The student also witnesses cargo loading and discharge.

While on the West Coast, four or five additional days offer contacts with terminal, automotive, rates and services, supply and coordination representatives in the Los Angeles office. Field trips to the Watson and San Pedro terminals may occur as well.

Major activity, however, spreads over 46 weeks at Bartlesville for the supply and transportation candidate. Each division keeps a neophyte busy for sufficient time in varied jobs to broaden his skills and knowledge while enhancing both his specific knowledge of Phillips' operations and his understanding of the company's managerial climate and philosophy. Employe relations, coordination and pipeline and terminal divisions each absorb an eight-week segment, while the supply division holds men in varied positions for 12 weeks.

By the time a man's training program ends, frequently long before, logical placement options become quite apparent. The new men have worked shoulder-to-shoulder with potential teammates long enough to know their work habits and their job conditions. They have tried, and been tried by, their possible bosses. Personnel, too has measured and compared their interests and performance. Placement, therefore, poses few difficulties and virtually guarantees against serious dissatisfactions for employer or employe.

The road does not end here, however. The Employe Relations Division keeps check on progress, coordinating with immediate superiors and department top management, assuring that continued development of personnel keeps capable men in motion. "We save our men from getting rusty or bored by timely changes," notes Vice President Kittrell. "Our growth rate, in fact, almost assures that we will have to, in any case. We like to move a man before he exceeds five years in a job, but the way we're going, it isn't often we have a job where a fellow stays that long."

The department's heavy operating activities create many carrier-type responsibilities for the employe relations division. Accident prevention finds Supervisor R. L. Clark busy advising employes as to safe procedures and observing operations. Moving millions of gallons of petroleum products by all transportation forms can prove costly to life and property unless everyone involved practices safe work habits and keeps alert to potential dangers.

Industrial relations and administrative services staff, under Director J. L. Hawkins, controls relations with unions representing employes under collective bargaining. They also handle general operations at the division's offices.

A third group, wage and salary administration, reports to Director J. F. Herring. This unit assures maintenance of company salary standards and equitable treatment of staff members. Its operations are one more assurance that careful selection and costly training will be followed through rather than forgotten.

Because the personnel staff are concurrently transportation men, they clearly understand the job requirements. Their vindication lies in a department of home-grown managers with advanced ideas, men who know they have a stake in their company and show little inclination to consider employment elsewhere.

Sharing Management Advances Under Decentralized Control

Mention Honeywell to any home owner and he instantly thinks of the ubiquitous round thermostats found wherever modern central heating systems are employed. These and other such control devices were the stock in trade of the Minneapolis-Honeywell Company, predecessor of today's diversified, multi-plant manufacturer. Computers, cameras, aerospace and ordnance materials are only a part of Honeywell's present-day product spectrum.

Much of Honeywell's growth results from major acquisitions in comparatively recent years. Largely maintained as independent divisions, continued separate operation of physical distribution departments is the rule. In recent years, these departments have worked increasingly together developing programs of joint cost optimization, aided in some measure by central headquarters at Minneapolis.

Honeywell makes notable use of electronic data processing. Many types of modern computer and communications equipment are employed by the various divisions, and substantial innovative programming can be found throughout the company. A particularly notable instance is the computerized inbound traffic control program of the ordnance division, a facet of traffic management all too frequently neglected in many companies.

In Chapter VIII, the unique and comprehensive logistics operations of Honeywell's Micro-Switch division are described in detail. In the pages immediately following, TRAFFIC MANAGEMENT's November 1970 major case study of Honeywell, Inc. is presented.

GIANT Honeywell's logistics become increasingly complex as sales soar and new divisions add diversity. Gross 1969 revenues reaching $1.4 billion, more than double the figure of five years earlier, reflect the efforts of over a dozen company divisions, each maintaining its own transportation-distribution operations At first glance a corporate conglomerate, a closer look reveals common themes among divisional activities. Virtually all Honeywell products represent precision manufacture, usually associated with measurement and control functions.

As the company expanded, corporate policy favored maximized local managerial responsibility. Thus, the company has proportionately an extremely small central staff, with purchasing, traffic, legal and financial functions among the few found at headquarters on even a limited scale. Purchasing and traffic, in fact, are the only operating functions thus represented at all.

"While we are highly decentralized, we nonetheless look for the best of both worlds," observes Director-Corporate Procurement Service Thomas V. Malloy. "We are building small corporate purchasing and traffic staffs to get an overview and to locate possible gains through joint ventures among divisions or in concert with these corporate units."

The initial move along this path set purchasing's corporate role as a service function under way in July, 1968. Early benefits from this step led to the thought of tackling traffic in July, 1969. The following month, therefore, Paul M. Lemieux assumed the management of corporate transportation services. Long experienced in managing Honeywell's international transportation, he brings to his new post a multinational viewpoint essential to the company's position as a world-wide manufacturer and marketing entity.

"We are fortunate at Honeywell in having already reached a high level of sophistication in divisional traffic activity," claims Mr. Lemieux. "Many divisions, for example, employ advanced computer procedures that keep service levels high at minimum transportation cost. Working from this solid foundation, we hope to help divisions achieve further gains through varied joint projects and through establishment of corporate measurement and performance standards."

Under corporate unit auspices, the possibilities of perfecting a uniform cost data system are materially enhanced. While the various individual divisions measure costs effectively for internal use, uniform overall standards become necessary for computer analysis of multidivisional distribution programs. Computer operating standards now exist company-wide within the United States; they will apply worldwide in the near future.

Given a new, high level of transportation data uniformity, the door opens to a total logistics approach,

SYMBOLIZING the company's worldwide distribution, a Honeywell 125 data processing system that was manufactured in Massachusetts passes the Doges Palace en route to installation at Venice Municipal Water Transportation Service office.

making possible use of simulation and linear programing to measure the impact of individual changes on the total transportation network. Such studies will, in fact, go well beyond transportation questions alone, ultimately becoming part of a complete computerized material system which will absorb some existing systems while setting the course for development of others.

The corporate unit has already undertaken one computerized cost study. Working with the Information Services Division, Honeywell's softwear marketing arm, an analysis of airline passenger travel was undertaken covering January-July, 1970, including aerospace division, ordnance division and general office travel out of Minneapolis. These three groups spent nearly $1 million for 9,026 trips. In themselves impressive figures, they became even more so when broken down to airline summary listings and airline destination summaries which covered hotel reservations in addition.

THOMAS V. MALLOY (right), director of corporate procurement service, examines proposals for developing uniform transportation cost data with Paul M. Lemieux (center), manager of international transportation, and Raymond R. Murray (standing), administrator of corporate transportation services.

"We found that 75% of travel dollars and 77% of trips involved just 18 destinations," comments Mr. Malloy. "Given this kind of information, we have a clear picture of where negotiation efforts would yield the greatest payoffs in hotel rates, car rentals and related matters."

Corporate transportation services anticipates extending these reports to other divisions, as well as other origins, in the near future.

Training of traffic management personnel in Honeywell's specific needs play a key role in the corporate group's activities. Various communication methods are currently under development, while a major transportation seminar recently brought together transportation-distribution personnel from most of the divisions.

"The session was planned for at least three-way communication," Mr. Lemieux notes. "We wanted to exchange views between the divisions and our corporate unit, but we were just as eager to start building stronger communications between the managers themselves. Important, too, was the opportunity to get both a consensus on several topics and separate individual manager opinions. We know a lot more about each other's operating environments now, and we think that all of us will benefit sharply in our individual communications hereafter. The seminar looks like a good method for generating worthwhile programs, as well as for evaluating existing and prior practices."

Computerization can be almost taken for granted with this major manufacturer of electronic data processing equipment. Employed at many levels, diversified programs for routing and inbound controls in particular substantially benefit several divisions. Order processing also leans heavily on the computer, with the latest in cathode ray tube (CRT) installations sharing increasingly in this work.

Unique, too, is the heavy use of premium transportation. Airfreight plays a large and growing role in this company's domestic traffic pattern, while international air cargo has played a substantial part for several years. On the following pages, these and other advanced phases of Honey-well distribution are reviewed and illustrated.

Computerized data builds distribution efficiency

MENTION Honeywell to a homeowner and he usually thinks of its ubiquitous round thermostat, a neat little device that controls so many of America's home heating units. The residential division's best-known product, it is just one of its many home comfort controls—the specialty of this division—covering heating, cooling and air purification installations. In addition, the division recently marketed a solid state control system for refrigerated truck trailers and is producing comparable modern equipment for some other nonresidential applications.

Because relatively small unit purchases characterize this highly competitive market, good service is essential and small shipments are characteristic. Distribution Manager Donald L. Bins, with a heavy Honeywell marketing background, knows this well.

"We're watching shipping costs both for our customers' benefit and our own, but we are at least equally concerned with developing delivery time consistency," Mr. Bins notes. "In some measure, transport modes set the pattern, but our choice of carriers and the ways in which we coordinate with them affect service importantly. A promised Friday delivery can inconvenience a customer as much if it arrives Wednesday—two days early—as it does if it shows up the following Monday. The division's delivery record is already good, however, and continuing innovations keep making it better."

System refinements, as well as totally new methods, keep residential traffic and distribution personnel flexible in their thinking and their work, shifting attention among numerous functions as better techniques evolve. These activities currently capture their particular attention:

Pooling and consolidation: A growing truck and piggyback network runs volume shipments to local delivery carriers, creating cost and shipment service gains.

Computerized routing and traffic analysis: EDP-prepared routing guides permit easy updating, while monthly machine-produced tonnage reports keep close, accurate check on route change effects.

Private truck operations: A small fleet on tight schedules, under residential division traffic control, keeps inventory levels down for three Honeywell divisions.

Computerized order processing: A CRT-based system automates many billing, credit, customer information and order assembly tasks.

Effective communications: An unusually comprehensive department manual and a monthly "Transportation Bulletin" keep in-house procedures current and inform those concerned of relative external traffic developments.

"We consolidate shipments whenever it is feasible," states Traffic Manager Rome C. Clinton. "Our computerized tonnage reports keep us continually aware of changing traffic patterns. Whenever the potential for volume movement begins to show up regularly between specific areas, we look into the possibilities for building full trailer schedules."

A typical instance found Philadelphia getting a new service from the Golden Valley, Minn. residential division plant starting last winter. Tonnage reports showed that trailers moving regularly to a New York area delivery carrier at Elizabeth, N.J. with a stop-off at Philadelphia could benefit both points. These trailers can load 12,000 pounds for Philadelphia plus 24,000 pounds to Elizabeth and move the total at a 36,000-pound volume rate. The affected Philadelphia traffic, now normally about 15,000 pounds weekly, develops substantial savings and moves with greater speed and regularity than in LTL form.

This shift was less simple than it looked, however. It required diverting some volume from an already effective consolidation program, so the trade-off between the two had to be carefully measured. Most New York metropolitan area freight leaves the Golden Valley distribution center on ITOFCA (Industrial-Trailer-on-Flat-Car Association) piggyback trailers,

A CONTAINERLOAD of residential division freight is bound for the East with consolidated domestic and export shipments.

going direct to Bilkay Express Co., Honeywell's pool delivery carrier at Elizabeth. The typical load includes 37,000 pounds of freight consigned to 54 individual consignees.

The Bilkay-routed shipments include much export freight, generally about 15,000 pounds in the average trailer, with numerous solid loads as well. For carrier convenience, the partial loads frequently go direct to piers in the road trailer, which benefits Honeywell also through reduced handling and the resultant minimized damage potential.

In addition to an average two ITOFCA trailers weekly to New York, the present arrangements find a regular weekly move between Gardena, Cal. and Minneapolis and one every two weeks between Minneapolis and Chicago. Both truck and piggyback consolidations may also be set up on a "one-shot" basis for anticipated tonnage or on temporary point-to-point arrangements where tonnage reports or business forecasts justify their scheduling.

Further consolidation programs within the residential division include diversified plans employing the private truck fleet plus an LTL program for parcel post shipments. In the lat-

ter case, where warranted by tonnage, arrangements provide for freight shipments to post offices for final delivery, yielding lower total costs plus substantial time savings.

Computer-Controlled Routings

Preparing a manual routing guide for a comprehensive, nationwide traffic pattern is a tough job, and keeping it current is no easier. At the Honeywell residential division, the computer not only takes the sting out of routing guide preparation, but takes over the actual individual routing tasks as part of the total order

PLENTIFUL COMPUTER DATA condensed to intelligible reports speeds performance analysis. Checking current conditions are (left to right); Distribution Center Superintendent Raymond Johnson, Traffic Manager Rome C. Clinton, Distribution Manager Donald L. Bins and Senior Traffic Analyst Hart C. Simonson.

processing system employing the company's own H2200 computer.

Under this system, the traffic department builds new routes on a form that spells out codes for the affected destination, identifying both the modes and the weight ranges they may handle, as well as the necessary point code data and customer information. This information is keypunched and goes to computer tape storage for later use as needed. Subsequent changes in rates or preferred carriers go easily into the resultant data bank through a "routing-maintenance" form on which traffic personnel enter only sort identification codes plus those items actually changed, checking them for keypunch operator attention. This permits quick revision of automated shipment routing while storing data for later revision of computer-printed routing guides.

Many of these route changes arise out of another computerized traffic activity—the tonnage reporting system, which includes quarterly reports showing individual plant tonnages segregated by carrier and tonnage given each carrier in a separate listing by source. A more detailed set of transportation indices, printed monthly for each residential division factory, shows figures by mode on shipments, tonnage, cost, average shipment weight, average shipment cost and average cost per pound. This data yields significant management control information, made available in the following forms:

Transportation location mode report: Indicates total volume of Honeywell residential division inbound and outbound shipments within one-day trucking radius of potential volume consolidation points.

Transportation index: Gives tonnage breakdown between prepaid and collect shipments for each mode.

Factory tonnage by mode: Shows total tonnage and weight average by transportation mode.

Transportation edit rejects: Lists items the computer did not include in the indices so errors can be detected, corrected and incorporated in subsequent reports.

Transportation duplicate payments listing: Points out shipments on which refunds should be obtained and indicates potential causes of payment

DISTRIBUTION MANAGER Donald L. Bins (right) observes operation of "VIP" (Visual Information Projection) unit, a cathode ray tube device that provides high speed computer access to residential division orders.

WHILE ONE COMPANY TRAILER pulls out for Toronto, Canada, a second readies to head for the Chicago area. The residential division's small but active truck operation speeds service between plants and divisions.

DUAL CONVEYORS serve Golden Valley warehouse packaging area. Stations at left may feed or draw from these lines, while wide chute at right diverts small parcels from outbound flow for separate handling from LTL and volume shipments.

duplication, while eliminating inflation of shipment data.

As important as the above described reports is the data base this procedure builds, facilitating numerous and varied traffic-distribution studies. Backed by ample computer working and storage capacity plus a diversified program library, residential division traffic analysts explore new ideas or variants of old ones with ease and speed, steadily reducing the gap between changing conditions and standard procedures.

Making Private Trucking Pay

In addition to diversified common carrier services, the residential division makes good use of a private truck unit. Operating only two over-the-road tractors, it provides priority-level services to three Honeywell divisions. The operation, domiciled in the residential division, owes much of its success to the interested, innovative attitude of Canadian Operations Traffic Manager W. Gordon Hipgrave.

"Rome Clinton and I recognized an opportunity to develop two and three-leg movements with minimal dead mileage," Mr. Hipgrave asserts. "Given this condition, you are well on the road to a direct cost trade-off against common carriage while enjoying substantial gains both in reliability and speed. When Fred Keefe (Fredric L. Keefe, distribution manager of Honeywell's micro switch division) sized up our plans and suggested adding tonnage from his Freeport, Ill. factory, we were convinced that setting up the current operation would materially benefit our individual budgets."

Trailers regularly load out of the Golden Valley plant, located in the suburbs of Minneapolis, carrying goods to the Toronto factory direct, or in combination with goods consigned to Micro Switch at Freeport, landing on specified days at these points to make both set-outs and pick-ups. Return hauls, in addition to Toronto and Freeport-originated freight, may fill out with vendor shipments. Similarly, regular deliveries of finished goods to specified Illinois-Indiana-Ohio locations matched by return loads of vendor material keep trailers well filled on a second circuit.

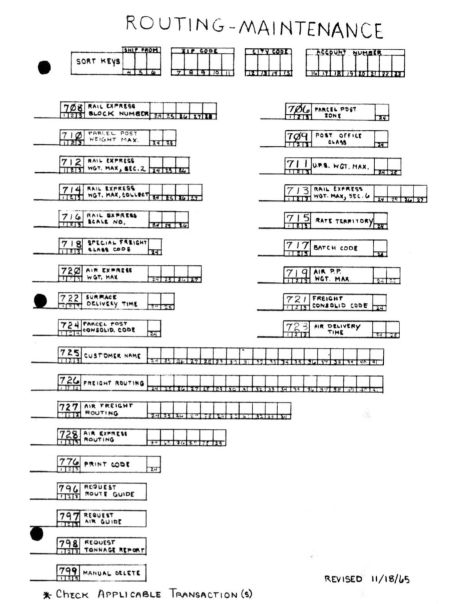

COMPUTERIZED ROUTING'S ADVANTAGES include easy change when need arises. Traffic personnel may enter any type of change on above form, checking items affected and entering data in spaces provided. Keypunch operators then cut new cards for each affected item that are fed to computer for instant data update.

"Deducting all relevent costs, the first run of the midwest trailer netted a $730 savings for the round trip," Mr. Clinton observes. "Subsequent runs showed continued substantial economies."

Equally important, indirect gains accrue in reduced inventories made possible by both the speed and the schedule reliability of the private truck operation. It has also facilitated a unique program in which certain Micro Switch products move from Freeport in combination work tray-packing units that serve on the Freeport assembly line and on the Golden Valley line as well, returning empty to Freeport for cleaning and recycling through the manufacturing operation.

Getting Message to Traffic

As in any large distribution operation, the residential traffic department faces communications challenges both in keeping its own staff abreast of current requirements and in apprising all concerned of external transportation circumstances that affect company practices and costs. Within the division, a remarkably comprehensive loose-leaf policies and procedures manual defines literally every specific line traffic task in full detail. More than that, it tells why each task is necessary, when it must be done and how it relates to other functions within and outside the traffic department. This tool gives a new man confidence, while speeding the instruction task for his supervisor. It generates personnel flexibility as well as skill.

Truly unique is the "Transportation Bulletin." Edited monthly by Senior Traffic Analyst Hart C. Simonson, it enjoys wide circulation through many company divisions, as its content serves all who are concerned with transportation-distribution matters. It is about the unstuffiest publication imaginable, presenting not only the facts but views as well. Frequently controversial, never dull, it keeps concerned people current and stimulates exchanges of viewpoint that lead to systems betterments reaching well beyond the residential division.

EDP-Expedited Orders

The customer service division seeks to bring the same efficiency to order paper work and fulfillment that engineers build into Honeywell production lines. "The intent is for the salesman to get the order and then get out of it," comments Manager Customer Service Peter M. Andrews. "From that point on, we want the customer to deal directly with our department."

Specialized account administrators handle individual domestic and international territories, getting involved in everything that relates to the customer. Expediting, order changing, telephone orders and liaison activity with the traffic department on shipment tracers fall within their purview. They will look into credit matters if they are causing shipment delay and will even go to the production floor to provide service for an account.

This specialist attention, on the one hand, becomes possible through the efficiency of highly automated, production-line order processing on the other. A separate group within the department regularly handles 800 to 1,200 orders daily. Order processing personnel number each incoming order and highlight significant information, passing the edited forms to the "VIP" (visual information projec-

tion) unit, where operators feed data to Bunker-Ramo cathode ray tube devices that input a Honeywell 1250 central processor located at the corporate office eight miles away. As orders pass through, this computer stores them on a large disc file for night processing by a Honeywell 2200 computer.

The latter computer automatically checks and applies credit, performing all pricing internally. It reviews all orders on hand, comparing customer requirements, stock availability and production schedules, updating inventory and releasing orders that meet set standards. On "future date" orders, it can make stock assignments or even commit upcoming production. Finally, the computer releases shipping documents and/or customer acknowledgements as appropriate, with nightly order status reports as well for account administrators' information.

The shipping documents, status reports and pick cards for each item cleared return by truck in wheeled metal containers. Return data flow by wire is considered unnecessary, as trucks deliver computer output before 8 a.m. After orders are assembled and shipping documents clear, the latter return to the customer service unit for "VIP" transmission to the computer for invoicing.

At the Golden Valley warehouse, batched orders and pick cards are built into four-hour picking cycles. Packing stations are assigned for each order and pick cards are then fed to a card sorter for grouping by picking locations. Based on a work-measurement chart, pickers handle 30-minute work units, confined where possible to a single aisle, and assemble the ordered material on four-wheeled Nutting trucks with shop-built superstructures. On more distant aisles, they employ Barrett "Power-Oxes" to pull one or more such units.

Loaded trucks then go to a marshalling area, where separate trucks assemble picked items to specific orders and move them to packing stations, based upon order form copies and picking card information.

Automation offers better inbound control

DISTRIBUTION is a different story in the ordnance division. Getting goods to consignees is the major job for most Honeywell traffic departments, but ordnance outbound moves essentially F.O.B. plant, so the customers, primarily the U.S. and foreign governments, route the freight. Elsewhere, Honeywell traffic men face heavy small shipment volume. At ordnance, small shipments are the exception. Rail carload freight constitutes the lion's share of a 100-million-pound inbound, 75-million-pound outbound annual flow. The five plants around Minneapolis plus a plant in Montgomeryville, Pa. all have sidings serving their needs.

"Rail service here is generally good," states Traffic Manager Robert J. Gallagher. "Moreover, despite the nationwide pinch, Burlington Northern car supply has been excellent. We've had no problems either with the Chicago & Northwestern, the Minneapolis, Northfield & Southern or the Minnesota Transfer at our facilities that they service. With 70% of our outbound going rail, this means a great deal to us."

Heavy inbound traffic including unusually diversified commodities and widely scattered destinations keeps the 11 staff members moving. Only a high degree of computerization makes it possible for them to not merely handle the day-to-day activities, but to steadily tighten control over this significant cost area.

While several Honeywell divisions employ computerized routing in some measure, the ordnance programs are especially comprehensive in their scope, constituting an important part of this division's purchase order information file, termed "P.O.I.F." P.O.I.F. programing encompasses requisitioning, ordering, receiving, recording and payment for vendor materials.

The division's H4200 computer, until the recent merger with the General Electric computer unit the largest Honeywell manufactured, provides the capacity not only to provide the required paper, but instantaneous visual review of purchase order status at any given point in process through CRT (cathode ray tube) auxiliary equipment. CRT units are being installed in purchasing, auditing, receiving and traffic locations for this purpose at present. With this change, EDP operations will switch from a cards-and-tape process to an all-tape system.

Purchase requisitions for goods moved F.O.B. vendor's plant are cued to either computer routing or traffic department attention when buyers make them out. On each requisition, a buyer enters in its designated space a six-digit code for the origin city that is supplied by the traffic department from a proprietary city-county-state code book. He then circles one of three numbers that determine routing procedure. No. 1 signifies normal surface routing; No. 2, normal air, and No. 3, a requirement for service or speed that normal routings cannot provide. Given a No. 1 or a No. 2, the computer will draw routing information out of storage and print it on the final purchase order which it develops based on the purchase requisition.

When a No. 3 shows up, it goes to the traffic department for route determination. Here, too, a split in methods exists. If one of seven relatively common specialized routings will do the job, traffic will insert an added code, known in the department as a "T" code, and the computer will draw this routing from the data bank as in the other cases. Traffic, however, has had the opportunity to review the need and to make a decision as to the proper routing.

The complete exception, where special treatment beyond the "T" code scope must be used, gets manual handling. The purchase requisition routing space is marked "see below" and traffic then manually enters a routing on the purchase requisition. This, in turn, is keypunched and fed to the computer for print-out on the final EDP-produced purchase order.

The obvious benefits of computeri-

TRANSPORTATION ROUTING & METHODS OF COST CONTROL OF INCOMING COLLECT SHIPMENTS

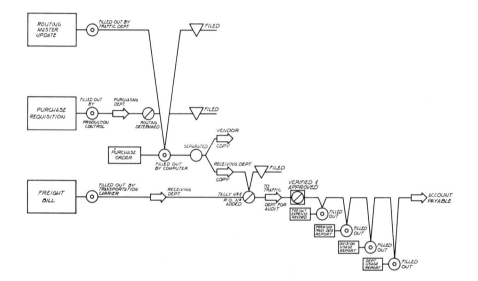

AT SEMIMONTHLY STAFF MEETING, members of the ordnance division traffic department review their inbound control procedures, as outlined in the control chart "blow-up" above. From left to right are Norman C. Grimme, analyst special projects; Charles W. King, plants coordinator; Frank E. Reckin, administrator; William P. Cirhan, analyst, New Brighton facility; Martha Hagberg, secretary; Robert J. Gallagher, traffic manager, and Robert D. Olson, administrator, St. Louis Park facility.

zation are speed and reduced effort in preparing and disseminating information. A still further gain can be the complete elimination of the need for some activities or data. Such is the case with ordnance routing.

Many traffic departments either review every purchase order, or wish they could, to ensure that purchasing staff members follow the best practices and to determine the reasons for exceptions. Thanks to EDP, the great majority of ordnance division routings which follow traffic standards get their review in the computer preparation process—exceptions automatically move to traffic. In this way, traffic deals with such cases before the purchase order is issued, enjoying the benefits of preview which prevents future problems rather than postmortems, which can only explain—but never cure—excessive incurred costs or lost service advantages.

As in most computer procedures, a substantial one-time manual job built the foundation. The traffic department established economical and serviceable air and surface routes from all known origin cities to the Minneapolis area plants. In addition, the procedure lends itself to additions and updates on a daily basis.

"We supply the purchasing department with a 'routing master printout' that details all existing routings by origin," Special Projects Analyst Norman C. Grimme states. "If they find that an origin point they need is not listed, they call us and we supply the needed F.O.B. point code number. We then fill out a 'routing master update' detailing our preferred routings and shoot it through to the computer center, keeping their stored data right in line with expanding point coverage developed by the purchasing department." These forms must clear the computer center by 3 p.m. daily.

A somewhat different form permits daily update of the special instruction "T" codes when needed. The standard routing master update may also be used to revise routings or weight breaks on traffic department initiative when rates change or new rates become effective.

Just as the computer puts push behind initial routing, so does it follow through on checking adherence. A computer-prepared receiving log summary flows to traffic daily, supple-

ORDNANCE DIVISION'S St. Louis Park facility has 16 doors handling up to 32 cars, based on two switches daily to support the plant's three-shift operation.

mented by a weekly overall summary. Serving several traffic purposes, its routing value lies in the quick spotting of deviations from purchase order-specified instructions. The traffic department follows up these cases with a routing deviation form which goes to the affected buyer with a carbon copy to his superior, asking if the deviation was made by the vendor or at the buyer's request, and whether the vendor should be charged back for excessive costs incurred.

In some instances, a "first offense" by the vendor will be met with issuance of a new routing letter reminding him as to ordnance division preferences. Repeated failure to meet Hon-

TRAFFIC MANAGER Robert J. Gallagher (left) and TM **Executive** Editor Jack W. Farrell inspect a loaded boxcar with palletized cartons protected by inflatable dunnage.

eywell requirements, however, means issuance of a chargeback, which informs the vendor of the cost differential experienced and advising that this amount will be deducted from his billing on the affected purchase.

Computerized receiving data also makes possible close check on carrier performance. Periodical transit time surveys based on this data are standard procedure. The computer-prepared form shows the origin points, separate modes, number of shipments during the affected time period and average time experienced in these movements. With this tool, the traffic department can give purchasing and other concerned people a clear picture rather than an educated guess as to what the carrier performance has been and what can probably be expected barring significant near future changes.

Another report regularly prepared by the traffic department spells out shipment costs for general merchandise in weight brackets from 10 to 1,000 pounds from various origins to the Twin Cities. This small shipment data covers all normal modes and includes average transit times, giving buyers a handy quick reference when ordering. The department is looking ahead to computerizing rate data for use by cost estimating, procurement and auditing staffs.

The high level of computerization makes traffic department operation pretty much "management-by-exception" in its work. Because traffic analysts encounter primarily the very poor or the exceptionally good treatment of shipments at their desks, these instances are graded and summarized regularly, employing a simple form showing the number of exceptional vs. poor citations by carrier. A monthly carrier rating list keeps management current, giving not only the basic statistics but explanations as well for the individual ratings. "It comes in handy in determining who will get our business on specific runs," observes Traffic Manager Gallagher.

Another important "after-the-fact" report is a twice-weekly computer print-out of paid freight bills. This is supplemented by copies of check vouchers covering carrier payments furnished at the same interval by the audit disbursements section. Through these means, the traffic department

TRAILERS OF RAW MATERIALS ready to move to the manufacturing area. The St. Louis Park facility is geared to operate directly from carrier's equipment to production lines, minimizing warehousing of both incoming materials and outgoing finished product. Tractors used are radio-equipped for efficient dispatching.

has immediate access to payment information without any lengthy manual investigations. Computer control greatly simplifies auditing procedures, notably with regard to duplicate payments.

All freight bills to the division are audited and, where indicated, "freight bill correction" forms go to the carriers, stipulating the amount shown on the bill, the corrected amount and the nature of any correction; that is, computation error or rate error. If the latter, tariff authority for the change is quoted on the form.

In addition to intercity common carriage service, the traffic department ties together the division's Minneapolis area facilities through a dedicated fleet operation. Sterling Cartage Co. men and equipment operate under ordnance division dispatchers on a two-shift basis. Service is provided by seven tractors and 23 trailers, plus straight trucks with power tail gates for handling explosives and a conventional straight truck for pickup work.

The fleet dispatcher, located at one

UNIQUE temperature and humidity-controlled containers, measuring 12 by 2 by 2 feet, stack four high, four wide and four deep in a 50-foot rail car, posing a tricky handling operation for forklift operators.

fixed location, can reach any truck at his pleasure through transistorized transmitting and receiving equipment in all cabs, as well as at the dispatcher's office. No fixed routes enter the picture, but there is steady, heavy movement on an area basis.

A space-age traffic department

THE rules change a little when every shipment is rush, every package is worth substantial cash and every item is a low-volume, high-precision product, specially created for a vital purpose. That's the aerospace division's traffic climate. It's a business that transcends national boundaries, with exports and overseas activities demanding much attention. It's also a growing business, where plants added today bring logistics complications, with tomorrow finding these new facilities already bursting at the seams, leading to still more new plants and more logistics complications.

Air services, passenger and cargo, figure big in this division's scheme of things. Not only must valuable products move swiftly, but a lot of restless aerospace technicians constantly prowl the world providing customer service, and the travel volume extends to substantial movement of their families and belongings as well.

Notes Traffic Manager James T. Welty: "Sample data on past overseas transfers showed that an average air move took 13 days, compared to 62 days by surface, from Minneapolis. Assuming $40 per day costs for a family of four, the trade-off clearly demonstrates air's cost benefit, while the employe morale value is at least equally important. For overseas moves, therefore, our policy is to specify air."

A pioneer in air consolidation within Honeywell and a major user of this service in combination with other Honeywell divisions at Minneapolis, the aerospace division receives numerous shipments daily by this mode from Boston, New York and Los Angeles destined to its Twin Cities plants. Jet Air Freight handles the

traffic, which is split between two procedures. If third-day delivery is fast enough, the traffic department will specify "surface consolidation," in which case UPS or another local package service makes the initial pickup at its prevailing rates. Where greatest speed is essential, the air forwarder is called on to handle the whole move, which reduces elapsed time in return for a higher charge.

On international traffic, which flows entirely by air, the aerospace division normally employs direct airfreight. Every night a full igloo container of such cargo leaves Minneapolis routed Northwest Airlines c/o Lufthansa for Frankfurt, clearing customs at the Twin Cities Airport. Today's igloo makes Frankfurt tomorrow night, with goods broken out and delivered to all other European destinations by the following morning.

Heavy travel activity—9,000 airline tickets issued by the travel section each year—justifies specialized forms, equipment and procedures. The division headquarters travel center, operated by the traffic department, has a

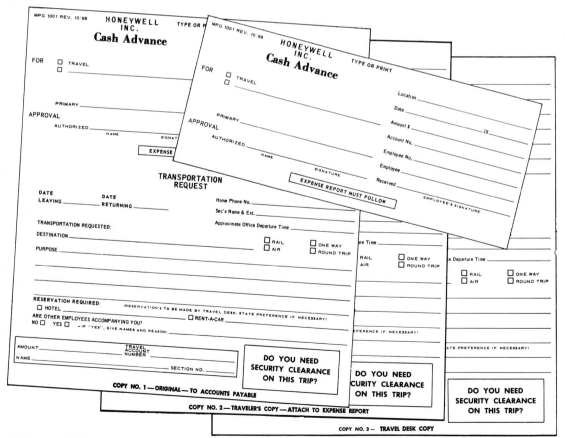

THE FOUR FORMS ABOVE constitute a single manifold on which transportation requirements, hotel reservations, car rental arrangements and cash advances may be processed, greatly simplifying travel administration procedures.

teleticket machine tied directly to airline reservation centers via telephone wire. A single form now speeds trip preparations, combining in one manifold the formerly separate car rental, cash advance, trip authorization and accommodation request forms.

"What we're seeking now is a completely automated reservation system," states Assistant Traffic Manager Thomas Jackson. "While the Holidex, Sheraton and other automated services operate satisfactorily, they are completely independent from one another. Since we use all of the alternative accommodations available, under today's 'state of the art' our travel center would look like a major computer installation and would probably prove similarly expensive if we bracketed all of the available systems."

Local passenger service also gets traffic department attention. A regular-route bus service and a fleet of 10 cars serve the five Minneapolis area plants, employing leased equipment domiciled at the Ridgeway facility. The bus service started in 1965, handling 1,352 passengers in its first year. By 1969, the figure had grown to 28,314.

Vehicle selection was developed using statistical probability tables and queuing theory—two management science procedures that many full-fledged transit companies have yet to discover. As a result, however, the schedules selected and the vehicles filling them have proven a near perfect fit to the demand pattern.

The two Ford custom wagons in a special 15-passenger configuration maintain a 30-minute headway between locations in Como, Roseville, Ridgeway and Stinson. In addition to passengers, they handle such items as briefcases, art work and priority mail. Their schedule is printed on a pocket-sized timetable. These vehicles have substantially reduced payments for employe car mileage and eliminated severe parking problems.

In common with several other Honeywell divisions, aerospace traffic employs computerized routing, with programing fitted to its particular needs. A unique feature is a single code combining both mode indicator and origin point in a four-position, alpha-numerical format based on the first three digits of the zip code. The

TRAFFIC MANAGER James Welty (right) checks air consolidation shipment with Traffic Administrator Tom Jackson (left) and Procurement Section Manager Eugene Ziehart.

THE TRAFFIC DEPARTMENT'S unique bus operation between the Twin Cities area plants cuts vehicle mileage costs and also solves parking problems.

A JET AIRFREIGHT TRUCK loads consolidated small shipments from the Los Angeles area aboard a Western Airlines flight for early delivery at Honeywell's aerospace division complex located in the Twin Cities.

department also makes generous use of the computer for research studies, as in the aforementioned transit vehicle selection study.

Improved logistics in a new facility

HONEYWELL'S commercial division is basically in the construction business. Its headquarters-plant-distribution center at Arlington Heights, Ill., an ultramodern facility, services the nation through a system of branch locations and a growing number of distribution centers. Typical customers include the World Trade Center in New York, Chicago's John Hancock Building and the U. S. Steel Office Building in Pittsburgh, all of which employ commercial division environmental protection equipment extensively.

This division's physical distribution recently underwent a major reorientation. Formerly headquartered in Minneapolis, the activity now centers in a Chicago suburb with a largely new logistics pattern governing its activities. Manager Administrative Services Louis F. Flagg and Traffic Manager Richard D. Abrahamson saw in this situation not only a necessity for change, but an opportunity to improve conditions as well. During the past year's course, therefore, significant developments arose in several key activities:

Computerized shipment control: Goods moving separately or in consolidations from commercial division plants at Arlington Heights, Ill. and Wabash, Ind., as well as from residential division sources in Minneapolis, get their papers through a multiple-computer communications network, speeding both goods and information flow.

Improved material handling: The new headquarters distribution center employs modern packaging equipment and in-house goods movement systems to full advantage.

Small shipment system refinements: A division small shipment committee chaired by Traffic Manager Abrahamson developed recommendations that led to significant cost benefits,

not only in freight charges, but handling costs as well.

While Arlington Heights and Wabash, together with an Akron, Ohio plant, manufacture exclusively for the commercial division, significant material flows into the division from the residential operation at Minneapolis as well. Basic control lies at commercial headquarters, but shipping papers, or "shippers" as they are known in the division, need to be available at the points of origin. Facilitating this is a unique EDP system which shares the Arlington Heights H2200 computer's capacity with Wabash through direct line connection to the latter's remote line printer and key tape units. For Minneapolis, an opposite approach applies, with Arlington Heights buying warehouse service and computer time from Minneapolis, feeding and withdrawing data by direct wire into the residential division complex.

"Our operations are fully compatible," Mr. Abrahamson states, "with Minneapolis distribution also processed by H2200 for both residential and commercial division shipments. All communication is based on Honeywell key tape equipment hooked up by a Bell dataphone network at the present time."

The new distribution center employs an underfloor tow line system for assembling small items plus modern lift trucks and lift jacks to handle palletized material and large cases. Modular steel storage racks, in varied configurations, stock goods so that fast-moving items lie in easiest reach with shelving designed to suit divergent pack sizes. Even space above some aisles yields stock storage capacity.

In the new operation, a major packaging step yields substantial gains. All standard units, about 60% of outbound flow, employ shrink packaging. The exceptions are large bulk packs and certain miscellaneous small parts which do not lend themselves efficiently to the process. Substantial weight savings in cartons and dunnage lead in turn to transportation cost savings through this process, with comparable savings in packaging material costs. Labor savings alone more than equal the sum of transportation and packaging material cost reductions.

TRAFFIC MANAGER Richard D. Abrahamson, at commercial division's Arlington Heights, Ill. computer facility, gets reading on order progress via direct-wire connection with Minneapolis computer center.

"Between the three elements, our Weldotron packaging system should pay for itself within a year," claims John S. Sisulak, manager of the Arlington Heights Distribution Center.

In common with other parts of the division headquarters complex, the distribution center benefits from two Honeywell electronic protection systems—a Delta 2000 environmental control system and a Honeywell security system.

The Delta 2000 constantly monitors nearly 500 points throughout the building (it has a potential capacity of 39,000) to make certain temperature and humidity stay at specified levels, providing both an audible and a printed indication when any point checks out improperly. At its console, it provides audio contact with any of these points so that mechanism sounds can be heard, or a mechanic dispatched to the location can confer from the site with personnel at the control center. Important, too, is its display tube on which circuits of the many climate control units may be displayed for instant analysis and diagnosis of any irregularities or for guidance in changing specific demands on equipment.

The Honeywell security system console, adjacent to the Delta console, keeps tabs on all means of access to the building, with bulbs on its graphic display panel showing entrances open but protected by personnel. These may be locked or unlocked directly from this center. Closed circuit TV equipment can display entrance areas for a watchman at the console, and separate "telephoto" units may be used for checking ID cards of people at entranceways, who must first call the guard by telephone prior to gaining entrance. This system also had audio contact throughout the building, as well as permanent record capability for noting any alarms, their locations and times of occurrence.

A small shipment committee does a big job for the commercial division. Chaired by Mr. Abrahamson and including representative managers from branch locations, distribution centers and division customer service, the committee uses a minimum of talk to achieve maximum action. On one recommendation alone, consolidation of nonemergency branch shipments to weekly, fixed-day schedules, they expect to accrue direct transportation savings annually of $25,000. Additionally, this change will permit better receiving practices at affected locations.

Other areas capturing committee attention include inventory control procedures keyed to building economic order quantities, greater standardization of parts packs and broad scale consolidation of shipments. The division already makes good use of piggyback consolidations in movements to its Edgely, Pa. distribution center and a similar new facility at Toledo, Ohio.

EDP traffic blends new and old methods

SHIPPING computers is tricky business. They're costly. They require careful handling. Shipments tend to be large and bulky. Customers usually want them in a hurry. For Honeywell's fast-growing computer division, there is the added complication that new systems for a client require assembly of components from among several plants in a wide radius around Boston, much of it destined for export.

Traffic Manager Joseph R. Concannon and his staff number about 50 people, approximately 15 of whom regularly work exclusively on export shipments. Administration Manager

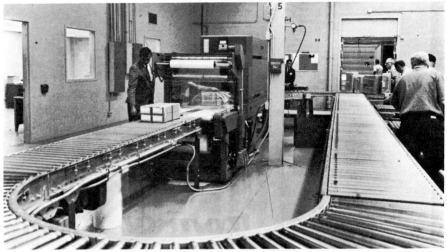

SHRINK-PACKAGING with a new Weldotron unit means material, labor, transportation and claims savings for Honeywell's commercial division.

AN UNDERFLOW TOW SYSTEM, augmented by high-reach lift trucks and other varied handling devices, gets goods in and out of the new warehouse in a hurry.

LOUIS F. FLAGG (seated), manager administrative services, and Traffic Manager Richard D. Abrahamson at the console of the Delta 2000 environmental control system, which maintains temperature and humidity levels as required and promptly indicates any deviations demanding attention. In the background, a Honeywell security system employs varied audio-visual means of protecting facility access.

AT AN ELECTRONIC DATA PROCESSING DIVISION computer center, Raymond R. Murray (left) of corporate transportation services and Joseph R. Concannon, traffic manager, inspect data input that is used in summarizing scheduled releases of complete computer systems for shipment.

TRAFFIC MANAGER Joseph R. Concannon and Administrative Aide Helen Kelly discuss arrangements for one of over 750 worldwide household moves arranged annually.

Herbert K. Davis and his associates control staff activities, relations with carriers, auditing, rate analysis and, in general, the paper work facets of traffic. Operations Manager Donald P. Cronin's section schedules department truck movements, handles export packaging, performs the physical work of shipping-receiving and overseas office relocation transportation. Administrative Aid Helen Kelly, who also reports to Mr. Concannon, numbers employe household goods moves among her major assignments, this rapidly growing Honeywell division having experienced 757 such individual operations, both domestic and international, during 1969.

As in many other Honeywell Divisions, although the company is a major computer producer, there is a refreshingly practical approach to EDP employment. Where cost-time factors justify it, the division goes all out for automated management. Conversely, where other, more prosaic means suit the needs better, they are unhesitatingly accepted.

Consider the paper work that activates a computer system shipment. Each day, a computer report termed a "finale" reaches the department showing the projected computer system releases as of that date for the current month. Part of a broad division control system, this information

concurrently reaches accounting, production planning, production control, field service and marketing management. From this information, traffic develops a form for office use detailing source plants for each system's components and scheduled pickup times plus other relevant data.

While triggered by a modern EDP program, this traffic work paper itself flows from partially computer-, partially hand-prepared hectograph masters, one of the oldest and still most economical methods of limited-run duplication. "It yields clean copies rapidly," notes Mr. Concannon, "and our total duplicating equipment investment consists of one fully amortized tray of gelatin."

Traffic's multiple information sheets enter process five full days prior to proposed shipping dates, with an initial "authorization to perform service" form set up for approval. Once approved, triplicate forms go to the affected carrier, an individual specific computer system file and to the shipment history file. Because multiple pickups among division plants occur frequently, the traffic department does its best to assure that shipping arrangements will get carrier pickup vehicles in and out of any plant dock within an hour of arrival.

As might be expected, premium transportation's role here is big.

During 1969, some 2,498 computer systems moved in padded electronic vans to U.S. destinations, with an additional 124 systems going by air. Export, exclusively airfreight, totalled 1,352,897 pounds for 1969 and a cool million pounds in the first six months of 1970.

Much overseas airfreight uses IATA standard corrugated containers. Recent experimental shipments employing the regular jet "igloo" container directly from the factory floor proved encouraging, and the department is checking with Honeywell facilities in Scotland to see if this would be a feasible standard practice. It requires special trucking equipment, but the department feels the vehicles are readily available at the Boston airport.

A fleet of five straight 2½-ton trucks and six panel trucks keep things moving between the Boston area EDP division plants. They also make vendor pickups, airport shipment deliveries and pickups of miscellaneous Honeywell equipment destined to division locations. The panel trucks handle company mail as one of their principal activities. An eight-hour day shift requires six vehicles for base service, with two vehicles operating a double shift for evening requirements.

In its unique mixture of "way out" and orthodox traffic management tasks, the department's freight auditing policy reflects a practical approach to one of traffic's long-standing concerns. "Until recently, we went the easy way, splitting returns with outside auditors," Mr. Concannon states. "Study suggested we give internal auditing a good look. In the first half of this year, with one man working at it full time, returns were over $34,000. This was far ahead of recaptures through external audit, and it amply justified our work investment. In addition, with only a minor traffic department time commitment, we realized nearly $6,000 savings through check-out of vendor compliance to our routing instructions."

The communication-conscious attitude characteristic of Honeywell reflects in two handy traffic department brochures. A single sheet folder in handy pocket-fold form details briefly the traffic department responsibilities and services. For Honeywell personnel, vendors, carriers and others, it is a convenient way to find out "where the action is" when shipping questions arise.

A similarly constituted folder, entitled "Honeywell Hints for Moving," guides personnel and their families in every facet of physical transfer of their homes and property. From the initial paper work through a moving day check list to the hopefully unnecessary subject of subsequent claims, the facts are here, including such indirectly related but significant details as a check list of people, services and bureaus that should receive the moving family's change-of-address notices.

A young traffic department proves its worth

TRAFFIC is a comparative newcomer with a growing role in Honeywell's computer control division. Until 1966, separate receiving and shipping functions existed, while two trucks served a few of the division plants in yet another separately con-

WITH PRODUCTION spread over a number of Boston area plants, the traffic department's truck fleet becomes virtually a production line extension.

trolled operation. September of that year saw these activities assembled under Manager Traffic Services Henry J. Wilayto, and expanded traffic management under his control generates continuing service and cost gains for the division.

While the Honeywell electronic data processing division assembles complete computer systems, the computer control division concentrates on auxiliary devices, control units and specialized parts. Its 15 plants in a 75-mile radius around Boston are tied together by a private truck operation, but customer shipments move almost entirely in common carriage with an almost even three-way split between air forwarder, truck (mostly vans) and combined UPS-parcel post.

HENRY J. WILAYTO (right), traffic services manager, and John McGill, vehicle coordinator, demonstrate the sliding panel on a production kit pallet box which has facilitated the loading of heavy material.

Attach To Package By Using Preglued Surface On Reverse Side

PAPER PAT'D BY N C R CO SPEEDISET® MOORE BUSINESS FORMS, INC. Q J

INSTRUCTIONS

ORIGINATOR.
1. COMPLETE FORM.
2. NOTIFY TRAFFIC RECEIVING SECTION OF DESIRED MOVE.

TRAFFIC
3. SIGN FOR MATERIAL, CHECK CONDITION OF PACKAGE, RETURN WHITE COPY TO ORIGINATOR.
4. DELIVER MATERIAL.
5. AT DESTINATION OBTAIN SIGNATURE OF RECIPIENT, WHO SHOULD CHECK CONDITION OF PACKAGE.
6. RETURN PINK COPY TO TRAFFIC VEHICLE OPERATIONS FOR FILING.

MATERIAL DESCRIPTION-IDENTIFICATION NO.		NO. OF PKGS.	DATE
FROM			
ORIGINATOR		DEPT. NO.	M/S
TO			
RECIPIENT		DEPT. NAME	
DEPT. NO.	EXT.	BUILDING NO.	M/S
TRAFFIC-RECEIVED BY		DATE	CONDITION OF PKG. GOOD / POOR
AT DESTINATION			
DESTINATION-RECEIVED BY		DATE	CONDITION OF PKG. GOOD / POOR

ORIGINATOR

A THREE-PART material transfer form with an adhesive edge controls private truck shipments. Affixed to one piece of each shipment, the three parts provide complete records for originator, consignee and the division's traffic department.

Premium transportation is a must for many movements, but even here economies can be attained. "We save $13,000 annually, for example," cites Mr. Wilayto, "by making our own airport pickups. We also find that better handling and faster service result when we can get goods aboard all-cargo planes and time our airport drops so that night freight handlers do the loading."

Protective packaging is a major concern of this traffic department. High cost components, frequently needed for prompt customer use, demand greater-than-normal assurance of immediate serviceability on arrival. All packaging for 10 different company locations is bought through a single central buyer, who prescreens every request with the traffic department, which is itself the largest single purchaser of packaging materials.

With traffic carrying heavy packing responsibility, Traffic Manager Wilayto maintains close liaison with Packaging Engineer James Flanagan, who provides staff support to the traffic department packaging operation. In Mr. Flanagan's opinion: "Any packaging man should spend at least two months in the shipping area. He should be fully conversant with all carriers and all modes of shipping."

Careful packing and economy nonetheless run hand-in-hand. The shock-mounted disposable skids of wood and Ethafoam that move many items cost just $5 apiece, replacing units costing $50 for substantial annual savings. Another innovation finds a standard slotted carton with a foam pad and a die-cut corrugated insert yielding substantial savings over prior custom-fitted, foam-lined boxes for shipping digital product omnibloc hardware. A single design of the new pattern successfully handles three different forms of this product line.

Air Cap, a plastic sheeting with entrapped air bubbles, sees growing use. It replaces a paper product at 10% lower cost while materially reducing damages.

Economy arises from a Box-O-Matic machine that can make up to 50 cartons an hour from corrugated stock. In general use, runs of 35 are more common. The machine is similarly valuable for making pads, pallets and other needed items. It can build special size boxes in a matter of minutes for custom work. Typically, the machine is operated during early hours and off-peak periods, turning low value labor time to productive benefit.

With substantial volume flowing steadily between the division's numerous plants, consideration of material handling tools for this purpose also gets significant attention. A particularly suitable unit now in use is a home-built "kit box." Made of plywood and angle iron corner braces with built-on skids for forklift handling, they cost approximately $30 each. Their average life has proven to be three years, making 100 trips per year at a per-trip cost of one thin dime.

These kit boxes lend themselves to an effective, simple paper-work procedure controlling their movements. The originator of an interplant transfer fills out a "material transfer" ticket, a three-part form with self-adhesive backing on each unit. He keeps the original white copy while the rest of the set is affixed to one of

FOAM AND WOOD, caster mounted pallets speed computer component movement within and between the computer controls division plants.

AIR BUBBLE packing material, plastic foam and diversified fiberboard elements are used to assure ample, yet economical protection of delicate shipments.

BUILT-IN logistics equipment and protective blankets simplify the strapping down and protection of costly, fragile equipment in the division's trucks.

the kit boxes or other packages constituting the movement. On arrival at the destination facility, the consignee takes a goldenrod copy for his own file and returns the remaining pink copy to the traffic department, which holds it on file for two full accounting years. Some 18,000 form sets are used annually on interplant moves.

The division's truck fleet includes three 20-foot straight trucks plus a small panel truck, operating a composite of regularly scheduled runs and special purpose trips. A single truck works both the regular day shift and a second evening shift, while two others operate day shift only plus overtime as required. The larger straight trucks employ logistics equipment and pad-

ding to protect electronic component shipments and are equipped with power tailgates with a capacity of 4,000 pounds.

Though traffic is a comparatively new function to the division, Mr. Wilayto has made substantial gains in an area too often neglected. Traffic screens all purchase orders, which have been previously routed by buyers using a traffic department-prepared routing guide. The guide itself resulted from a one-year study which revealed that all inbound shipments over 100 pounds came from just 160 origin points, making possible a concise, compact guide that lends itself to easy employment by purchasing personnel and others concerned.

What about automation in this automation-manufacturing division? "Coming soon," claims Mr. Wilayto. By the end of the year, he anticipates the start of outbound traffic data computerization. Soon thereafter, automated billing is expected to follow.

Important, too, in the forward viewpoint of the department is orientation of other management areas to the duties and benefits lodged in its jurisdiction. Mr. Wilayto has run seminars for field engineers and field marketing people with encouraging results. "Since we've had a better opportunity to get to know each other," he states, "opportunities have risen with increasing frequency to lick shipping problems before they start."

CHAPTER III

Where Management Science Plays a Major Part

While modern logistics management can operate effectively in some instances with little or no computer support, most distribution departments use electronic data processing in some measure. Numerous straightforward paperwork and accounting functions within logistics commonly fall in the computer orbit.

It is in the usage of operations research techniques, however, that many distribution departments achieve the greatest benefits to their companies, largely in conjunction with the computer. Some of these management science techniques, such as PERT (Program Evaluation and Review Technique), can perform effectively in manual form as well, but for most, data volumes and complexities require computerization.

Site selection for plants or warehouses, optimized vehicle utilization, sophisticated inventory controls and many more such programs typify the management science-oriented logistics department systems library content.

At the Carrier Air Conditioning Company, linear programming and simulation techniques have proven helpful in site studies as well as in the optimization of distribution center territory allocation. Through simulation, the physical distribution unit can rapidly and reasonably consider suggested system changes as well as monitor performance regularly to assure the continued efficiency of existing arrangements.

Important, too, is an integrated order processing-inventory control-shipping procedure. More than just a paperwork cost saver, this system tightens inventory administration, minimizing stock requirements while substantially improving customer service schedule reliability.

This company is noted for other significant distribution innovations also, as outlined in TRAFFIC MANAGEMENT's June 1970 case study presented on the following pages:

Organizing Logistics for Service Benefits

FAST-GROWING sales volume puts constant pressure on Carrier Air Conditioning Company's distribution system. The major division of Carrier Corporation, whose total corporate volume soared in 10 years from $256.8 million to beyond $535 million in 1969, "C.A.C." today faces challenges to distribution management and methods far greater than it experienced in earlier years.

Largely specializing in air conditioning and climate control equipment manufacture, this division finds growth in greater demand and more intensive coverage of its market. Moving its merchandise effectively requires increasing attention.

C.A.C.'s William J. Bailey recognized early the company's need for enhanced logistics capability. Taking the helm in 1967, he immediately set out with a management team to confer with the company's distribu-

tors. In a series of nationwide meetings, the president and his associates took a pulse reading of the company's logistics. What they found was a service operation that fulfilled its obligations by running at 100% of capacity, but was clearly incapable of absorbing any further workload expansion. Distribution functions operated under split control, several within the marketing area, but organizationally remote from one another.

Mr. Bailey, who early in his career was traffic manager of the Day & Night Manufacturing Co. division of Carrier Corporation, saw the picture clearly. "Under today's competitive conditions," he states, "the effective manufacturer knows that his service is as important as his product. Even the best equipment's value becomes minimal if dealers can't get timely deliveries to fulfill customer demand. Our logistics must match our products in quality and reliability."

Suiting deeds to words, the company made a thorough study of all distribution-related activities. Some immediate temporary changes were made in existing manual procedures while automation developments commenced and major organizational changes took place.

Symbolizing the new approach, a whole new management unit came into being under Vice President-Logistics Robert F. Allen. While Mr. Allen's title recently became vice president-administration, this change represents the addition of certain other services, such as purchasing and business statistics, in no way inferring a diminished logistics commitment.

"Our primary objective in upgrading distribution was service reliability to match sales growth," Mr. Allen observes. "Shortly after we got under way, however, significant opportunities for cost improvement became apparent. The more we learned about this area of activity, the more such opportunities came to light."

In Mr. Allen's opinion, better communication among managers as well as improved technical capabilities contributed markedly to this trend. As indicated in the accompanying organization chart, managers responsible for both distribution and distribu-

Organization chart of Carrier Air Condition-

Plans for a specialized purchasing traffic unit are discussed by (left to right): Manager-Physical Distribution Edmund R. Piesciuk, Vice President-Administration Robert F. Allen, Director-Materials Department Victor H. Pooler and Traffic Manager Anella Vaccaro.

An organization chart of the _____ing Co.'s administrative and logistics functions overlays a view of rail and truck-loading facilities for heavy climate control equipment.

VICE PRESIDENT
Robert F. Allen

BUSINESS STATISTICS
Harold Bonneville

ADMINSTRATION BUSINESS SYSTEMS
John L. Ayer

INFORMATION SYSTEMS
George McDonough

CUSTOMER SERVICE
Eugene W. Ward

MATERIALS
Victor Pooler

PARTS CENTER
Walter J. Drew

PHYSICAL DISTRIBUTION
Edmund Piesciuk

CREDIT & COLLECTIONS AND TREASURY FUNCTIONS
Richard Travers

tion-related activities share a unified line of report.

Coordination in this vital area gets strong support from the basic management approach. "Management by Objectives," instituted formally in 1969, gives each manager the broadest freedom to run his own shop, yet establishes clear-cut accountability that eases top-level control and pinpoints significant developments for prompt attention. Manager-Administration Business Systems John L. Ayer's initial responsibility following his appointment was to get this activity under way.

"What we've done is to develop with each major manager the elements for which he holds responsibility," he states. "We then sought to quantify these objectives in terms of costs, time periods or other significant terms of measurement." In distribution's case, for example, there are such continuing elements as freight factor responsibility, departmental expense, salary administration

and personnel administration. In addition, certain needs or improvement possibilities arise at specific times, such as contract carrier operations that are currently being developed, which make necessary continuing changes in the department's objectives pattern.

While all objectives are reviewed on a yearly basis, monthly meetings with each department keep Vice President Allen in close touch with continuing progress. Employing charts of performance, each manager within a group reviews his specific functions, while the major manager reviews general considerations affecting his whole department.

Important values derive not only from control of immediate circumstances, but from a balanced historical perspective as well. Charted objective records indicate past performance and provide a continually improving, experience-based tool for forecasting and budget control. Each major manager's manual of charts reflecting his operation's controlled facets is filed with Vice President Allen, providing a running picture of departmental conditions and pointing up interrelationships among them.

Greatly aiding expense control are seasonalized budgets, taking into account the considerable monthly variance in sales of climate control equipment. While a basic sum represents anticipated annual expense, statistical procedures break it down to differing monthly amounts that reflect shifting expenditures. If a specific department has a $1.2 million budget, but November is a slack month in its operation, it may rate only $50,000 in expenditures. Conversely, heavy July activity in the same department may tip the scales to a $180,000 figure. In both cases, the figures derive from a rational trend curve.

The "Management by Objectives" approach stimulates contacts among managers as well as between them and top management. Their growing awareness of mutual problems and goals leads them to greater teamwork and more effective joint effort on such forward programs as distribution procedures computerization, warehouse location revisions and necessary expansion plans that this fast-growing business requires.

Seeking total control of distribution

THE physical distribution concept, though a comparatively recent arrival at Carrier, has already made substantial progress. Building on the foundation of a capable traffic department, a larger physical distribution group was able to move fast on several fronts. Most important, too, were the newly available computer capacity with its related programing potential and the opportunities for efficient teamwork with other departments in the new logistics organization.

"We got off the ground about two years ago," observes Physical Distribution Manager Edmund R. Piesciuk, "and tackled two vital jobs at once: We developed interim procedures to further distribution activities manually and we trained and organized a staff with the interests and capabilities that automated, closely controlled distribution requires."

In Mr. Piesciuk's opinion, his departments are about to conclude the second of three distinct developmental phases. Phase I found major effort expended in preparing for automation while striving for efficiency within a conventional manual procedure framework. Phase II, the refinement era, currently finds automation easing many routine jobs while broadening planning and expansion horizons. Phase III will place growing emphasis on anticipative management, harvesting the fruits of data increasingly available from the computer and benefiting from additional skills within the division, developed through training of present management plus the addition of specialists to the staff.

Systems progress moves steadily forward on a broad front. Among the division's many diversified activities, the following selection illustrates both its accomplishments and its intentions:

Computer-assisted consolidation procedures: Augmenting prior manual systems, the initial year's added savings exceeded $500,000, with further gains anticipated through expansion and refinement.

Computer distribution model development: Through the electronic data processing techniques of simulation and linear programing, proposed facility or systems changes of any magnitude can be analyzed rapidly, speeding improvements while avoiding potential costly traps.

Staff development through personnel interchanges: Temporary staff intertransfers with the computer group benefiting divisional automation progress while creating clearer understanding within the information systems department of physical distribution data requirements.

Customer - oriented route selection (CORS): In cooperation with the company's distributors, the traffic department has developed and now maintains alternate routings, yielding required service levels for diversified shipments consistent with reasonable costs.

Controlled shipping cycle times: Through careful scheduling and operational improvements, goods now move through warehouses on standard time cycles, with performance measured on every shipment.

Material-handling innovations: Custom-designed in-house roller-bed tractor-trailers and expanding disposable pallet employment aid warehouse economy.

Computer-Aided Consolidation

To most traffic people, the term "consoli-

Traffic and systems personnel review computer programs that create physical distribution models. From (l. to r.) are: Traffic Analysts Anthony Reichel and Douglas Adams, Distribution Systems Analyst Charles Wright, Systems and Programing Supervisor Jack LaForse, Mathematician Adolph Uryniak, Traffic Manager Anella Vaccaro, Programing Supervisor Richard Gorney and Manager-Information Systems George McDonough.

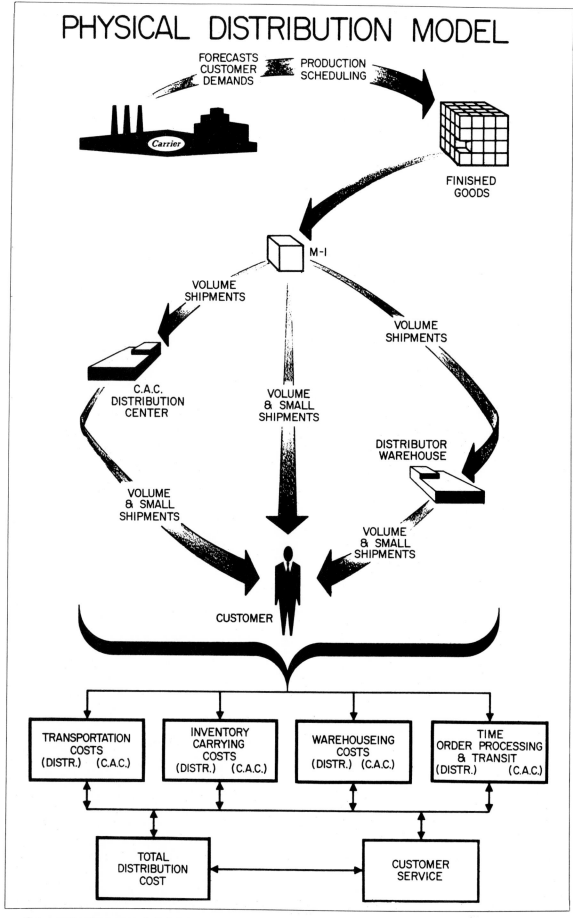

PHYSICAL DISTRIBUTION MODEL

FORECASTS
CUSTOMER
DEMANDS

PRODUCTION
SCHEDULING

Carrier

FINISHED
GOODS

M-I

VOLUME
SHIPMENTS

VOLUME
SHIPMENTS

C.A.C.
DISTRIBUTION
CENTER

VOLUME
& SMALL
SHIPMENTS

DISTRIBUTOR
WAREHOUSE

VOLUME
& SMALL
SHIPMENTS

VOLUME
& SMALL
SHIPMENTS

CUSTOMER

| TRANSPORTATION COSTS (DISTR.) (C.A.C.) | INVENTORY CARRYING COSTS (DISTR.) (C.A.C.) | WAREHOUSEING COSTS (DISTR.) (C.A.C.) | TIME ORDER PROCESSING & TRANSIT (DISTR.) (C.A.C.) |

TOTAL
DISTRIBUTION
COST

CUSTOMER
SERVICE

Schematic diagram of C.A.C.'s new physical distribution model shows basic routing alternatives from the McMinnville, Tenn. warehouse in symbol form at top, while below appear the interrelated costs that are measured and compared by the computer.

TRANSPORTATION COMPANY	NUMBER TRACTORS	NUMBER TRAILERS	OPEN TOPS	40 FT VANS	45 FT 13'6"	FLAT	OTHERS	DAILY AVG LOADS OUT-IN	WEEKLY AVG LOADS OUT-IN	MONTHLY AVG LOADS OUT-IN	TOTAL - EQUIPMENT			SPECIAL COMMODITIES	
											TRACTORS	TRAILERS	STR TRKS	TRACTORS	TRAILERS
FIVE F TRUCKING	13	15	2	13	0	0	5	14-10	70-50	260-200	789	1,507	224	-	-
FIVE G TRUCKING	7	14	2	12	0	2	8	7-7	35-35	140-140	40	80	40	-	-
FIVE H TRUCKING	4	7	0	7	0	0	3	4-3	20-15	80-60	514	829	298	4	4
FIVE I TRUCKING	5	12	1	11	0	2	5	4-5	20-25	80-100	10	20	10	2	2
FIVE J TRUCKING	29	38	4	24	10	2	12	20-22	100-110	400-440	298	674	145	-	-

Overlaying a view of the Carrier Air Conditioning Co.'s Syracuse trailer park is a sample of a home-created equipment register, wherein the traffic department details all equipment that each local trucking company has available for service from Syracuse. This data assists in the location of special equipment for special movements.

DAILY DISPATCH CONTROL - VOLUME SHIPMENTS

| WAREHOUSE | | | | | | | | | | | | DATE: | | | | | |

Daily Dispatch Control Sheet records not only the specific common carrier shipment assignments, but measures on-time performance at the shipping dock as well as of the transport company.

dation" suggests the assembly of freight from several origins for through movement in one lot to a destination or, conversely, the movement of a single large shipment containing freight for multiple consignees to one or more destinations for delivery fan-out, in both cases seeking the advantage of a volume rate differential.

At Carrier Air Conditioning Co., the latter form of consolidation is common, but there is a further type which looms large in its service pattern. This is a consolidation of orders to a single distributor that is created by holding them for a sufficient period of time, within understood limits, to reach adequate weight or volume for efficient carload or truckload shipment.

What would prove a tricky manual procedure in developing these single-consignee consolidations becomes fast, easy and accurate under computerized procedures. Once the computer is alerted that a specific distributor wants goods shipped at Carrier's carload terms, it will hold "shipper release"

data received from order processing in storage until enough tonnage is accumulated to meet volume load standards, or until the maximum days of permissible hold time have been attained. At the selected tonnage or time point, the computer will prepare a "shipper" (C.A.C. term for packing list), which cues the warehousing and shipping department to prepare a shipment for the specified distributor.

Under this system, the physical distribution department enjoys considerable flexibility in seeking transportation and warehousing economies while meeting prescribed customer service standards. The number of days that freight may be held in accumulation of volume loads can be changed and percentage of vehicle capacity that must be met before volume is considered adequate for shipper release can also be shifted. These standards may be changed to suit idiosyncrasies of particular warehouses or different conditions in various parts of the market area.

ANNUAL VOLUME	$_____	SIMULATION NO. _____
(Sales Value)		
PLANT ORIGIN	_____	DATE _____

CAC DIST. CENTERS

1. _____
2. _____
3. _____
4. _____
5. _____
6. _____
7. _____
8. _____

DISTRIBUTION PROFILE

Direct to Cust.	Thru Dist. Center	Thru Dist. Whse
____ % Mode:	____ % Mode:	____ % Mode:
CL ____ %	CL ____ %	CL ____ %
TL ____ %	TL ____ %	TL ____ %
LTL ____ %	LTL ____ %	LTL ____ %
	To Customer:	To Customer:
	Mode:	Mode:
	CL ____ %	CL ____ %
	TL ____ %	TL ____ %
	LTL ____ %	LTL ____ %

| COSTS | CAC | | | | DISTRIBUTOR | | % OF |
	PLANT	DIST. CTR.	TOTAL	% OF SALES	WHSE	% OF SALES	TOTAL SALES
INVENTORY							
WAREHOUSING							
TRANSPORTATION							
CAC DIST. CENTER							
DISTRIBUTOR							
CUSTOMER							
T O T A L							

| TOTAL DISTRIBUTION COSTS | CAC | | DISTRIBUTOR | | TOTAL | | |
	AMOUNT	% OF SALES	AMOUNT	%	AMOUNT	%	

CUSTOMER SERVICE LEVEL

% OF MARKET (Incremental)	NO. DAYS

Frequent use of the computer distribution model led to standardized input and output forms to speed data flow. In requesting a simulation of a proposed system, the requester details on the two-page form at top of page 155 a proposed distribution system that he wishes to measure. After this data flows through the computer, the abstract form at right is completed and returned, illustrating the effects that the suggested system might be expected to have if installed.

There are distinct advantages in varying the percentage of capacity at which the computer will release a shipper. Depending upon traffic patterns, shippers released at sufficiently low percentages of capacity may provide opportunities for manual consolidation with other freight blocs bound for the same destination or geographical area. These consolidations as well as LTL shipment assemblies and drop-off loads are regularly developed by the warehouse and shipping department traffic coordinators, who daily review the computer's shipper output to locate such economies.

"The combined effects of the traffic coordinators working with the new order system and the computerized consolidation procedure conserved well over $500,000 last year, while concurrently improving delivery performance, Mr. Piesciuk notes.

Physical Distribution Model

During 1969, the information systems department conjointly with the physical distribution department developed a mathematical model to optimize product distribution at the company's McMinnville, Tenn. plant, with the intent of expanding such model development to all company facilities. The need for a powerful analytical tool to explore not only the wide-ranging distribution possibilities within the existing company structure, but the potential of new or revised facilities and systems made this step essential.

Employing linear programs and simulation techniques, the model can illustrate actual or proposed system conditions including variant flow patterns of finished goods and all cost elements depicted in the accompanying physical distribution model chart. It

PHYSICAL DISTRIBUTION SIMULATION REQUEST

Request Date_____   Dist. Simulation No._____

1. CAC BASE WAREHOUSE OR PLANT ORIGIN:_____ SOURCE CODE_____

2. DISTRIBUTION CENTERS (8 Maximum on 1 run)

   (1)_____   (5)_____
   (2)_____   (6)_____
   (3)_____   (7)_____
   (4)_____   (8)_____

3. PRODUCTION SCHEDULE:

   Total Annual Units_____

      (a)   Level   (b)   Seasonalized to_____

      (c)   Other (Specify)_____

4. SHIPPING SCHEDULE:

   Total Annual Units_____

      (a)   Level   (b)   Seasonalized to_____

      (c)   Other (Specify)_____

5. MOVEMENT SCHEDULE: _____

6. TRADING AREA SALES VOLUME: Table No._____

7. PHYSICAL DATA: A.   Table No._____
                             New Table Attached
                             Special Product

                        DIMENSIONS (Inches) L_____ W_____ H_____

                        WEIGHT: _____ SALES VALUE_____

                    B. PRODUCT CLASS: A   B   C   Special Product

8. FREIGHT RATES: TABLE NO._____

9. WAREHOUSE RATES: TABLE NO._____

10. CAPITAL RATES: TABLE NO._____

2.

11. SCOPE OF SIMULATION: Total U.S. Market
                              Distributor Franchise Territory - Dist. No._____
                              Distribution Center - Location_____
                              Other: _____
                                     _____

12. DISTRIBUTION PROFILE:

    Base/Plt Whse to Job Site/Dealer: _____%
                                          Via CL _____%
                                              TL _____%
                                             LTL _____%

    Base/Plt Whse to Specified
          Dist. Centers: _____%
                                          Via CL _____%
                                              TL _____%
                                             LTL _____%

             Dist. Centers to Job Site/Dealer: Via CL _____%
                                                          TL _____%
                                                         LTL _____%

    Base/Plt Whse to Dist. Whse: _____%
                                          Via CL _____%
                                              TL _____%
                                             LTL _____%

             Dist. Whse to Job Site/Dealer: Via CL _____%
                                                          TL _____%
                                                         LTL _____%

14. SPECIAL INSTRUCTIONS: _____

    _____

    _____

    _____

    _____

                                        Requested by: _____

    Date Simulation Completed: _____

    Verified· _____

---

will respond to changes in markets, customer demand, production schedules, freight rates, shipping modes, production locations, warehouse locations, delivery times, inventory carrying costs, warehouse rates and handling rates.

"We can capture any separate cost or combination of costs to Carrier or to our distributors through the model, separating transportation costs into required segments," Traffic Manager Anella Vaccaro states, "including from the plant specified to any warehouse, from plant to company distribution center or distribution center to customer." Miss Vaccaro notes that it will also segregate warehouse storage and handling costs to Carrier Air Conditioning Co. or to a specified customer at any point in the distribution system.

While the distribution model program is being steadily expanded to embrace the total system, the initial simulation has already been run some 35 to 40 times, greatly assist-

ing in the future planning of McMinnville plant product distribution. Accompanying this article are copies of simulation request forms which are filled out to trigger a computer analysis, as well as a form copy showing the fashion in which computer data output is summarized for the requesting party.

In-House Training

Recognizing the need to learn each other's business, Information Systems Manager George McDonough and Physical Distribution Manager Piesciuk took a unique step to build bridges between their departments. For a six-month period, Distribution Systems Analyst Charles Wright worked on the computer unit staff, while Programer Sebastian Mandolfo came over from the information systems department and worked on a variety of traffic and distribution assignments. Both men returned to their normal duties with a far better understanding of the values and

Distributor	Type	Sq. Ft.	Stack Clear	Outdoor Storage Space Sq. Ft.	Rail Siding	No. Cars Accom.	No. Car Doors	No. Truck Doors	Type Leveling	No. Fork Trucks	Type	Lifting Capacity	Type Forks	L & W of Forks	Rail or Trk Pref	Tent. Plans Sq. Ft. & Year
FIVE A	Pvt	12,000	20'	None	None	None	None	3	Iron Plate	1	T.M. 350#	1,500	Chisel	36"x3"	Trk	None
FIVE B	Pvt	7,500	12'	None	None	None	None	2	Metal Dock Boards	1	Clark	2,000	Std	46'x30"	Trk	None
FIVE C	Pub	25,400	14'	None	PennCen	4	2	14	Normal	10	7 Gas 3 Elec	3,500	Std	44"x36"	Trk	None
FIVE D	Pvt	15,000	13'	4,000	None	None	None	1	-	3	Yale	1,500 3,000	Steel	48"x5"	Trk	50,000 1970
FIVE E	Pvt	1,400	9'	None	None	None	None	1	-	1	-	1,000	Tapered	4'x23"	Trk	None

An annual survey in the above format keeps tabs on handling conditions at regular consignee locations, typifying the distribution department's close watch over shipping conditions.

Spacious indoor loading dock affords speed and protection for handling of rail carloads.

the problems to be anticipated in future distribution program developments.

In addition, traffic and distribution personnel have received substantial computer orientation, while at the present time, Mathematician Adolph Uryniak of the information systems department is instructing affected traffic analysts in the vagaries of the distribution model programs so that they can make full and direct use of the model.

Under a plan that will give added service to another department, traffic personnel will soon receive exposure to the workings of the purchasing group. By assigning a traffic analyst and a rate assistant to the purchasing department, Mr. Piesciuk and Materials Department Director Victor H. Pooler agree that substantial benefits will accrue in tighter inbound transportation control. Commodity managers and their staffs will have instant advice both in planning specific inbound freight moves and in developing purchasing strategies to take maximum advantage of transportation rate and service conditions.

While it is anticipated that assignment of this traffic unit will be on a steady basis, the possibility is being considered of "rotating" one or both positions from time to time. In this way, distribution personnel may develop their understanding of this vital function, while the host department would gain the benefit of fresh viewpoints periodically.

Customer-Oriented Routing

A manual, but modern, routing system, currently working effectively at Syracuse, is being extended to other C.A.C. origins as well. In keeping with physical distribution department policy, while basic routes are set up and controlled by the traffic department, this system is administered in daily use by traffic coordinators in the warehouse and shipping department. This frees traffic spe-

Checking current physical conditions at one of the company's warehouses in Syracuse are (left to right): Manager-Warehousing and Shipping Donald E. Serens, Supervisor-Shipping Services Robert Ripberger and Superintendent-Warehousing and Shipping Raleigh Petrocci.

cialists for research and development work, while the warehousing and shipping staff can make "spot" routing decisions with consequent time savings.

To initiate or modify specific customer routing, the Carrier traffic department forwards a questionnaire to the affected firm, usually a distributor, indicating six alternate routings, the first three of which are currently active. The customer is asked to confirm the arrangement's suitability, or to indicate on the form a preferred order of precedence. Present volume shipment mode is shown with space to indicate any desired change, as well as the drayman of the customer's choice, plus space for naming alternates or suggesting any change. Any known route or equipment restrictions are noted separately, again with space provided for modification.

When customers complete and return such forms to the traffic services supervisor, the updated information goes on a routing card with a second copy provided for the customer's information and files. The basic card then goes on a "wheeldex" file in the shipping office, giving traffic coordinators a speedy reference when routing shipments and making consolidations.

Regularly updated from time to time by the traffic department, a customer can also instigate route changes by filing a request form with the department, indicating desired changes and the reasons requested.

The C.O.R.S. program supplies the best combined routing judgement of both C.A.C. traffic experts and the individual customers with their on-the-scene knowledge. It offers a means of forecasting traffic patterns, benefitting C.A.C. and its common carriers alike because volume by mode between specific destinations will be more readily predictable.

SHIPPING CYCLE TIME

WEEKLY AVERAGE

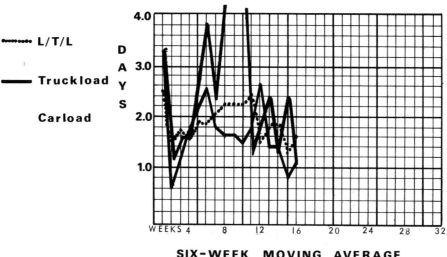

- •••••• L/T/L
- ——— Truckload
- Carload

SIX-WEEK MOVING AVERAGE

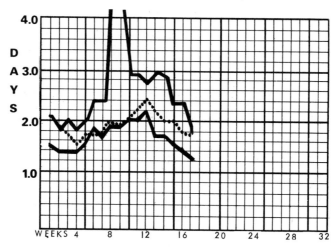

A dual-graph of shipping cycle times is typical of numerous control charts in physical distribution's management by objectives. Left chart indicates actual weekly performance. Though accurate for specific week-to-week comparisons, a clearer trend picture comes from second chart, which shows for each week the average of the most recent six weeks. By thus smoothing momentary shifts, a clearer trend picture becomes apparent. In both cases, however, a serious hardship, caused when several carloading crew members were ill, shows up in a sharp line deviation.

Controlling Shipping Cycles

Warehouse shipping cycle time—the elapsed period from receipt of shipping paper to the departure of the goods—receives close watch at the Carrier Air Conditioning Co. A few years ago, the company recognized a need not only to improve cycle times, but to establish effective means of measuring and policing them.

"We're at the point now where we can set and maintain appropriate cycle times without difficulty," claims Manager-Warehousing and Shipping Donald E. Serens. "We're now entering into another phase, refining procedures to optimize our cost per shipment."

The physical distribution division assumes that if a cycle time matches the needs specified by the marketing group, the resultant service level will satisfy customers and preclude sales losses attributable to time consumed in getting goods in motion.

Basic to performance maintenance is an

Carrier *Air Conditioning Company*
A DIVISION OF CARRIER CORPORATION

			SHIPPING PERFORMANCE STATUS				DATE	SHIPPING WORKLOAD PLANNING							DATE	(O) WAREHOUSE LOCATION	
A	B	C	D	E	F	G	H	I	J	K	L	M	N			(P)	
NO.	CHANNEL OF DIST'B'N	SHIP MODE	WORK ON HAND	WORK COM-PLETED	WORK LATE	CYCLE (STD=2) ACTUAL	WORK ON HAND	OLDEST RECEIPT DATE	MAN-POWER REQUIRED	PERM MP AVAIL	% WL TO PMP AVAIL	MP AVAIL ASGND	% WL TO ACT MP			DETAILED ACTION	
01	UEG	LTL															
		TL															
		CL															
02	MSG	LTL															
		TL															
		CL													(S)		
06	SPG	LTL													MANPOWER REALLOCATION	No.
		TL													a Temporary Transfer	
		CL													b Housekeeping	
03 04 05 07	MISC	LTL													c Sick	
		TL													d Sick Leave	
		CL													e Vacation	
	FSO	LTL													f Personal	
		TL													g Late Arrival	
		CL													(Q)	
	TOTAL	LTL													EXTRAORDINARY ACTION	
		TL													1 Casual Overtime	
		CL													2 10 Hour Shifts	
STATUS	DUE	7:30 AM	Completed			TOTAL →								3 3 Shifts	
ACTION	"	8:00 AM	"											4 Saturday Overtime	
REPORT	"	9:00 AM	"											5 Sunday Overtime	

(R) OLDEST SHIPPER NUMBERS ON-HAND				
UEG	MSG	SPG	MISC.	FSO

The shipping work load planning report, prepared each morning from a planning work sheet form, gives a clear, running picture of warehouse productivity and operating conditions.

adequate system of records and controls. At the end of each day, records become available to the second shift control clerk, whose duties include preparation of a shipping performance work sheet. Based on closed transmittal cards, he can identify shipments that have been processed and determine cycle performance levels on freight moved. His completed work sheet plus a partially filled out work load planning report are available to the warehouse superintendent at 7:30 a.m. each work day. He, in turn, confers with the warehousing office and completes a detailed work plan to initiate action by the foremen by 8 a.m. Completed work sheets and work load planning reports go forward by 9 a.m. to the physical distribution manager, with copies of the latter also going to the warehouse-shipping manager, the warehouse superintendent and the shipping offices supervisor. A sample work load planning form accompanies this article.

While daily paper work keeps line operations moving, close watch is kept on the trend of performance as well. Among the "management by objectives" control charts the physical distribution division maintains is the accompanying shipping cycle control chart, delineating performance of individual work crews. In the instance illustrated, both the week-to-week chart and the six-week moving average chart show the effect most strikingly of a severe illness problem over several weeks for the carloading crew. The chart points up as well the gradual improvement of productivity as new men learned their work and the regulars commenced to return. Perhaps most significantly, it provides a historical perspective should a like condition arise later, indicating what to expect and plan for in such a contingency.

Better Handling Speeds Shipping

In addition to warehousing and shipping chores, the warehouse-shipping department also transports much finished production from the end of the manufacturing line to warehouse storage locations. A great deal of this movement is on four-unit trailer trains hauled by leased Clark tractors. In addition, however, four unique, company-designed trailers handle large volumes of material.

The trailers each carry a roller bed which may be raised, lowered and tilted either toward the front or rear. At the production line end, the hauling tractor spots the trailer for loading, using heavy-duty hydraulic lift equipment to level the trailer roller bed. Palletized units roll forward onto the trailer, which is then lowered to the running position, tilted forward to hold its contents against a bulkhead by gravity. On arrival at the warehouse location, the hydraulic mechanism lowers the bed and tilts it rearward, at the same time pulling ahead so that the combined action of gravity and the tractor moves the load off onto the floor for subsequent lift-truck placement.

These units have been in operation for a substantial period of time, proving both efficient and reliable, while reducing time from plant to warehouse, as well as man-hours.

At the Syracuse location, a recent change to external storage for some types of heavy machinery led to savings exceeding $100,000 in public warehousing costs as well as in space released for production purposes. This was made possible through the lease of a 50-ton crane for use in a carefully selected and prepared area adjacent to the warehouse facilities.

Self-adhesive preprinted labels have replaced hand stenciling product identification on cartons. The labels speed stock selection through improved visibility for fork truck operators and other warehouse personnel. Errors have been reduced through this means as well. The color of labels is changed every three months, employing five colors in all. In this way, stock age becomes readily apparent, and the practice of "first in-first out" is most readily observed.

To the greatest extent practical, Carrier Air Conditioning Co. warehouses are palletized. There is also a clamp truck operation for certain products at the Los Angeles warehouse. Recently, however, steps have been taken to substantially extend pallet employment beyond the warehouses themselves. As described in comments on C.A.C. packaging elsewhere in this issue, "Buckboard" expendable pallets are currently being tried out and, if their performance continues to satisfy both the company and its distributors, a major portion of all freight will move on these units.

Loads, carefully blocked and braced when necessary, are photographed with Polaroid camera

before departure, establishing a record in the event of subsequent damage or claims following shipment.

Unique, in-plant-designed roller-bed trailers (above), loaded directly from end of a production conveyor line, carry merchandise on a bed tilted to hold packages by gravity against a forward bulkhead. On arrival at warehouse staging area (left), trailers are lowered hydraulically, tilted toward rear and unloaded by gravity and a forward pull by tractor.

A four-trailer train, hauled by a tractor, brings goods from the production line to the distribution warehouse, where final spotting is handled by fork-lift units.

A Look to the Future

Improving data supply through C.A.C.'s computerized finished goods control system makes forward planning both easier and more desirable for the physical distribution group. With many further refinements yet to come, the ability already exists to determine from 75% to 90% of warehouse work load a week in advance, for example. This allows affected foremen to prelocate merchandise and preplan much of their work forces' activity. Such information, growing in variety and accuracy, means that traffic and distribution planning can seek to develop new and better systems more rapidly.

To gear for this, Mr. Piesciuk will soon add a distribution engineer to his staff, establishing a full-time liaison between various packaging engineering groups, product engineering personnel, manufacturing and product design people. He can be both an interface with them and, when distribution has concepts to "sell," an instigator of them.

This new staff member will have heavy responsibilities in materials handling, issuing manuals and instructions on such matters as loading, blocking and bracing of heavy shipments and working with the traffic specialists on the reduction of damage claims of every variety.

Also anticipated is the addition of an industrial engineer to the warehouse and shipping manager's staff. "Ultimately," Mr. Piesciuk states, "we envision forming a single planning group based upon these soon-to-be-added engineers and our systems analyst. They will work together on such things as optimum shipping cycle development, distribution center site selections, physical facility configurations and overall systems betterments."

Operations and planning: Computer's growing role

AS LOGISTICS PLANNING and operations steadily increase their demands on computer capacity, new and better computer equipment becomes a continuing necessity for the information systems department. Personnel development and communications capabili-

Discussing test runs of a simulation program on the main computer are (left to right): Jack La Forse, systems group supervisor; George McDonough, manager-information systems; Richard Callahan, computer room supervisor, and Richard Gorney, systems group supervisor.

ties as well must be augmented to match these growing needs.

At the company's Syracuse data center, Manager-Information Systems George McDonough took a major expansion step recently through purchase of an existing large-scale computer, currently on lease, and the leasing of a second to replace a smaller unit.

"Not only will this increase capacity," Mr. McDonough notes, "but the new arrangement will permit the smoothing of work flow between the twin facilities. They

Instruction cards for a linear program produced by a new high-speed key punch unit are reviewed by (standing, left to right): Betty Elliott, key punch supervisor; Richard Gorney, systems group supervisor, and Adolph Uryniak, mathematician.

can share much peripheral equipment, such as tape drives, card readers, printers and discs, while programing will be simpler because staff members won't be concerned with choosing between two ways of handling material to fit differing model requirements."

Further computer expansion finds a new small unit now in service at the McMinnville plant, which can exchange logistics data with the Syracuse installation. Initially, data transfer will be off-line, employing tape-to-tape data transfer. When the need develops, the Univac will be tied by direct line to the Syracuse computers for remote batch processing.

A very specific distribution application now under study envisions a terminal computer to be installed in the distribution department. This unit can transmit, receive and "massage" data.

As one operation, the main computer would forward a "tentative shipper" to the terminal unit, which would in turn be fed any corrections or modifications required by the distribution department operator. The terminal unit would feed this information back to the main computer with instructions to print the final "shipper." Final copy would be printed out by the terminal unit on the regular bill of lading, or "shipper" format. Because the terminal unit can carry two forms side by side in the printer under separate control, the operator can review correction copy on one side against the shipper set on the other to make an accurate check. The speed of correction and verification will shorten both the shipping and invoicing cycles.

On the communications front, TWX teletype circuits are in use, tying order processing and distribution at Syracuse to other plants and warehouses, as well as distributors. Under consideration are more sophisticated data terminals, including cathode ray tube (CRT) equipment.

Automation speeds order scheduling and processing

THE BEST logistics system accomplishes little unless it is supported by adequate merchandise and prompt processing of customer orders. When total logistics came to Carrier, therefore, a customer services department was an important part of the new organiza-tion. The department's ability not only to process customer requests, but to predict their wants and develop related production schedules contributes markedly to the Carrier Air Conditioning Co.'s service image.

The department's activities fall in two distinct categories:

Day-to-day operations—These include processing of new orders, matching of merchandise to orders for distribution and related customer correspondence.

Forward planning—In this category lie the forecasting of sales and scheduling of production to match anticipated demand.

Typical distributor orders arrive daily by means of TWX teletype lines. These are processed by the availability group, who determine the appropriate shipping source and the availability of the requested products. While the availability group works with a hard copy taken from the TWX machine, a tape copy is also received. The latter goes through a tape-to-card converter, with the resultant card copies then held in the department's own key punch room. After the availability group marks up the hard copy, the data as to goods available are punched into the cards, and a card deck for each order goes to the computer, where it is booked, creating a formal record of the order. The computer extends the order's sales value for financial records and prints out a copy for the customer, with source and date shown for each item to be shipped, which then moves forward by mail.

In the event of a production schedule revision, the availability group feeds this information to the computer, and another notice goes to the affected customer advising him of change of date. Backlog items are reported as an activity takes place in the production record of the part number until matched to available production, at which point they transfer to a released status, but remain on the report until actually shipped.

An important control is the weekly customer order status listing, which shows all released orders in process as well as backlog orders which are open by distributor. Through this means, service levels provided to any one distributor may be readily checked, while any order irregularities are highlighted for needed attention.

When orders are released, punched cards from the order processing department flow to the computer for the development of indi-

Reviewing customer demand patterns are (l. to r.): Donald Bryant, order services manager; Eugene Ward, manager-customer services; Leo Rodgers, manager-distributor sales forecasting and scheduling, and H. F. Schoonmaker, manager-direct sales forecasting and scheduling.

vidual shipments or inclusion within consolidations. It is at this point that the traffic department assumes control.

In addition to the foregoing simulation program for developing comparisons, there is parallel linear programing available.

"With linear programing," states Vice President Allen, "we're optimizing our production against the cost of inventory and the cost of distribution. In letting us examine each piece of this, the linear tells production people what problems they can anticipate, and it also tells us how much we have to carry month by month in inventory."

Because the linear runs quickly on the computer, Mr. Allen finds it can readily be tested against a number of different forecasts. Whereas in the past such comparisons were laborious and difficult, he now finds it a simple matter to examine three or four alternatives, determining what may be the best, the worst and the most likely patterns of cost and activity. Instead of attempting to live with a single annual forecast, they are actually being run monthly to better keep up with seasonal fluctuations as well as

to keep close tabs on a business currently employing a high proportion of its productive capacity.

Based upon monthly national forecasts of sales, the customer services department develops production schedules which indicate goods that must be made available at a given time to support sales activity. Scheduling and control are split between what are termed "forecast" goods—standard equipment sold through distributors as stock items—and "to order" materials—largely heavy machinery, termed "applied products."

In determining the materials required at a given time point, cognizance is taken of a number of factors. Thus, a May total availability must support sales expected through August, including a safety factor, on items which have a three-month inventory lead time. In all cases, production adjustments must be made consistent with economic run quantities in the manufacturing operations.

Because both organizations have strong, continuing impact upon distribution schedules and reliability, the customer services and distribution groups work closely together on many activities. They share strong common concerns on such matters as facilities planning, the setting of terms on volume sales and the scheduling of shipments for individual distributors, job site deliveries and individual major customers. Such a program as the distribution unit's palletization project holds strong interest as well for the customer services group because it represents a change in the nature of delivery to the customer.

Computer-Assisted Planning

Because the customer services department is charged with the responsibility of matching production to anticipated product demand, computer simulation models and linear programing lend an important assist in correlating the company's highly seasonal demand pattern to available production capacity. Involved are such questions as whether to build substantial inventories in advance of season, to operate additional shifts and/or overtime rather than prebuild inventories and, from a longer range view, whether economics justify plant expansion.

"We have computer programing to evaluate trade-offs between all of these possibilities," notes Customer Services Manager Eugene Ward. "Through this means, we can check alternatives in comprehensive fashion. Such often-neglected costs as the expenses incident to hiring and firing in addition to wages of new personnel are considered, plus other costs relevant to starting or halting an additional shift and all the variant possible applications of overtime." Also measured is unused potential capacity, as when a second shift goes on but is only used to partial capacity, and other similar marginal costs.

Cooperative research develops better packaging

DISTRIBUTION's communication-oriented approach to improvements shows through strongly in packaging development work. Distribution, traffic and warehouse-shipping managers join with engineering personnel, including particularly the packaging engineers of the machinery and systems group (MSG),

in furthering packaging and handling betterment programs. Constituting a packaging task group committee, regular monthly meetings find participants evaluating present or proposed methods, assigning projects to committee members, reviewing progress of previously assigned projects and working with managers or staff members from other concerned departments in furthering distribution improvements through advances in packaging and handling.

A typical cooperative effort developed following the committee's March 4 meeting. Traffic Manager Anella Vaccaro and Manager-Warehousing and Shipping Donald Serens were designated to develop a project analyzing unitized quantity shipping procedures employing disposable pallets. Their project team will include representatives from engineering, marketing, customer service and physical distribution. They will jointly examine unitized shipping's costs as well as benefits in regard to their effects on sales, warehouse handling, vehicular loading and transportation expense.

Specifically, the unitizing project envisions standardized shipping on expendable pallets. The Menasha Corp.'s "Buckboard" pallet, employing a die-cut corrugated deck and nestable plastic pallet legs, is one of the types already undergoing tests by Carrier. The nesting feature builds pallet shipping efficiency, with a full 100 pallets stacking in just 48 inches of height. Pallet shipping weight is about five pounds.

Packaging Engineers Lee Daugherty (left) and William Bohall (right) prepare test equipment for attachment to a vibration table for simulation test of proposed packages, as Manager-Warehousing and Shipping Donald E. Serens looks on. Package improvement is a cooperative effort.

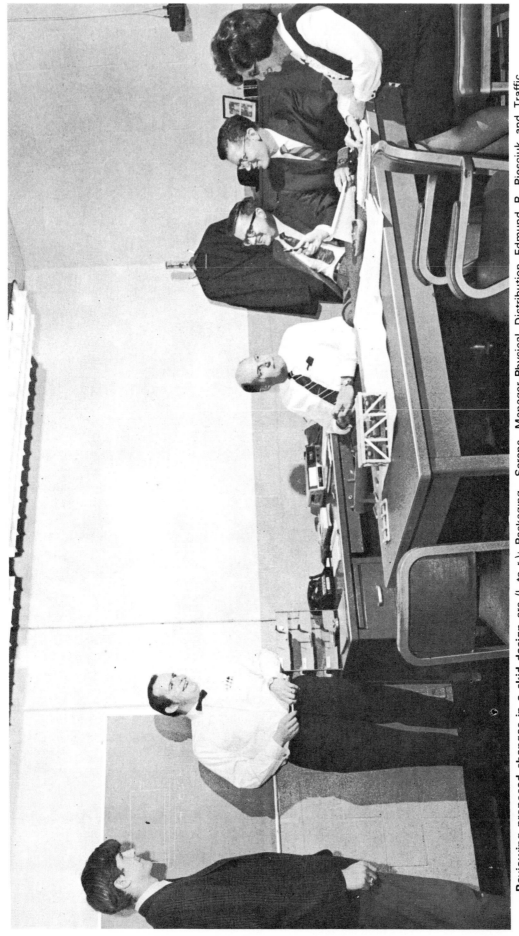

Reviewing proposed changes in a skid design are (l. to r.): Packaging Engineers Lee Daugherty and William Bohall, Manager-MSG Engineering Services Gordon Coupe, Manager-Warehousing and Shipping Donald E. Serens, Manager-Physical Distribution Edmund R. Piesciuk and Traffic Manager Anella Vaccaro at the regular monthly meeting of the packaging task group committee.

Unitization at Assembly Line End

At present, several of the predominant high-volume company product lines move on disposable pallets from plant to distributors. Assuming satisfactory evaluation of potential expansion by the committee, many more will be added to the list. The goal is unitization at the assembly line's end in standard shipping modules which will be maintained in movement to and through finished goods warehouses and on to the distributors. Applicable to most volume-sale products, some items will be excluded from the program either because of their physical nature or because of unique aspects of their sales patterns.

"Disposable pallets make unitization practical for us," states Mr. Piesciuk. "Unit-loading with conventional pallets has too high a nuisance value in a system working with numerous distributors. With the disposables, we eliminate not only the back-haul headache, but all of the problems related to pallet inventory and maintenance as well.

Upcoming are in-service tests of mixed commodity piggyback shipments in conjunction with the Penn Central Railroad. Specially assembled and routed shipments containing measuring devices will test packaging and shipment-bracing systems.

Independent parts distribution assures expedited service

THE Carrier Air Conditioning Co. has maintained a separate parts department for over 25 years. "Even though it requires some degree of inventory duplication, service makes it mandatory," claims Parts Center Manager Walter J. Drew. "The ebb and flow of parts demand, as well as the number of emergency shipments, represent an utter mismatch with a production system geared to preestablished market forecasts. There is a trade-off savings, however, in the segregation of obsolescent items that are essential to parts supply activity, but only waste space in a factory operation."

Highly automated, some 400,000 line items flow through computerized order processing and inventory control. The parts center has available its own computer, oper-

Rider-Stacker units make quick work out of picking from multilevel pallet racks in the parts center warehouse located at Syracuse.

ating largely with tape and discs. While this unit handles all day-to-day activity as well as some research and development, the center also makes use of simulation and linear programs available at the company's main computer center.

The department's huge parts variety calls for continuing review so that nonessential items stay off the shelves. Stock is sorted and placed for most efficient movement and inventory control on the heavy movers. Computerized inventory analysis reveals that just 21% of parts stored move in volumes of 100 or more units per year. This information together with a pick frequency report aids in determining both stock locations and stock levels.

Aiding the above are many of the parts center marketing activities. Marketing Manager Richard Gockley maintains studies on a two-man basis in such areas as motor standardization. If, for example, 110 different fan motors have been supplied with different Carrier units in the past decade, this team will seek to determine suitable alternates or

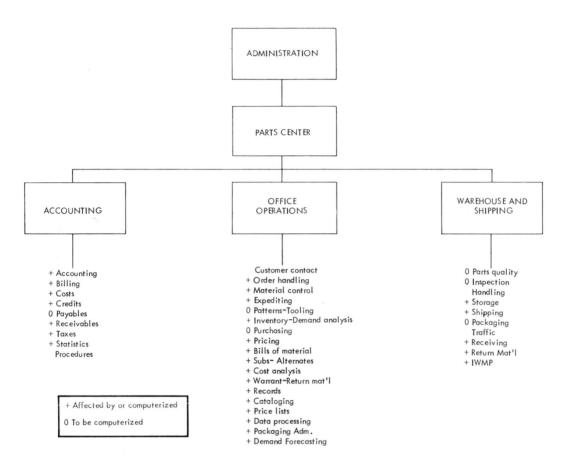

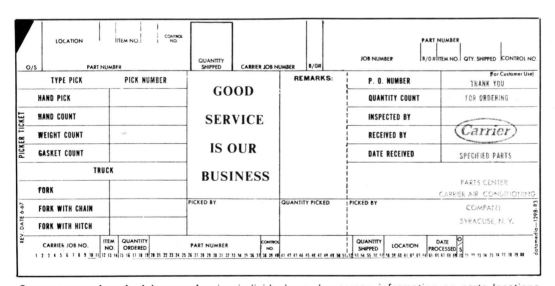

Automated procedures keep parts service levels high without forcing staff expansion despite increasing business. Table shows high degree of computerization achieved and anticipated.

Computer-produced picker cards give individual warehousemen information on parts locations and equipment needed to expedite their work. A second part of same form provides a basis for pay.

substitutes so that a stock of only 40 types will cover all contingencies. In this area, as well, computer procedures speed study.

Purchasing, too, functions independently within the parts center. Materials Manager John Dudley's organization purchases its needs both within the company and from outside vendors who supply items that the company does not manufacture. In addition, parallel buying is practiced in some measure, with goods purchased both inside and outside to suit time and cost conditions. Thus, when

Spur conveyors are used to speed small parts shipment assembly following picking operations in the parts center warehouse.

all company output is required for a new product or due to a seasonal condition, there is no problem of needed parts diversion. In fact, the parts center will on occasion sell parts to production to ease peak period conditions in the plant.

As might be expected, orders received get different priorities for processing. Emergency orders arriving up to 1 p.m. leave the same day with better than 95% performance, while regular orders from the same time period are shipped the following day. In addition, weekly stock orders from distributors, which have no emergency connotation, take one extra day.

While the center operates on a normal work week, there is a seven-day, 24-hour assured emergency service. A telephone call to

an order staff member on a Sunday will "open up" the parts center in a hurry.

Fully 80% of all orders arrive by TWX teletype lines. Eventually, it is hoped that virtually all orders will be routed by this means, removing the dependency on the mails as well as the problem of transposition errors which frequently arises in the handling of telephone orders.

Following initial review, orders are keypunched for data processing. The computer edits the order cards on an initial pass and loads the data to tape, at the same time checking information against disc-stored data, including parts information, current inventory and specific customer information (ship-to and sold-to addresses, tax information, etc.). Any back order information de-

Manager-Parts Center Walter J. Drew (right) discusses expanding role of the department's computer with Manager-Data Processing Joseph Arrigo.

veloped is retrieved and stored on the "ship-to, sold-to" disc during a subsequent tape pass to create sales orders.

While developing sales orders, the computer concurrently develops picker tickets, color-coded by day. These two-part forms give pickers needed information for efficient stock assembly on one part (included in this article), while a second form part is held as a basis for pay.

In making the sales order, shipping paper is created as well. When completed, these "shippers," as they are known within C.A.C., and the picker tickets flow via pneumatic tube from Data Processing to the warehouse office.

At the warehouse, picker tickets are batched in work groups and passed through a card sorter which places the batched cards in location order, after which they go in color-coded folders for routing by the shipping clerk.

Next move is the warehouse floor, where tickets flow to nine picking zones, five of which have bin storage serviced by a Lamson conveyor system. Rider-Stackers serve most of the remainder. Conveyor spur adjacent to the Rider-Stacker staging area simplifies the assembly of complete orders following the pick. In all cases, the picker ticket for each item is affixed to it when it is drawn from stock.

While weekly stock shipments to distributors normally contain substantial numbers of parts, fully 50% of actual shipments are individual pieces or small groupings that are best moved via parcel post. In the case of weekly distributor stock orders, greater size opens up alternatives.

"We are working with the C.A.C. traffic department on consolidation possibilities," notes Warehousing and Shipping Manager Donald Powers. "There is every reason to believe that combining parts with regular finished goods shipments could cut costs with no diminution of service."

Linear programing, proving its value in the physical distribution department, has caught the attention of parts center management as well.

"We are working with the information systems department currently to fit the existing physical distribution linear to a study right now," states Mr. Drew. "By employing an independent compressor rebuilder in the Southwest, we have cut down expensive back-hauls on compressor rebuilds. The plan appears worthy of expansion. For studies to

Walter Schermerhorn (left), service office methods analyst, discusses procedural revisions with Bob Piedmonte, manager-order services.

determine proper locations and their number, in a situation such as this, linear programing is an excellent method."

Another important "staff" job that the computer within the department tackles regularly is an annual review of individual distributor activity. This study analyzes the orders that have been placed during the preceding year and develops stocking policies, reorder points and reorder quantities for them to use in their dealings with the parts center.

While a nominal charge is billed to participating distributors for this service, it makes it possible for them to get the maximum benefit out of employing weekly stock orders, on which they receive a discount if filed on a specific day, with assured shipment immediately thereafter. Among other benefits, the parts center itself has enjoyed a considerable equalization of its work load.

In its daily operations, the parts center warehouse does a substantial volume of packaging of outbound shipments. It also does considerable parts crating on inbound merchandise. This step assures protection of merchandise while stored in the warehouse, frequently for far longer intervals than typical new goods inventory. It can also save valuable subsequent time, notably as when a hurried emergency call comes for such an item on a hot summer Sunday.

Largely computerized since 1960, located in part of a new, single-floor, 243,000-square foot building since 1966, the parts center is a growing organization. Only through computerization has the staff, still the same in numbers as in 1968, been able to cope with an approximate 40% increase in volume during this period.

As the Carrier Air Conditioning Co's own business increases, the business in necessary equipment for its product maintenance must be expected to grow, too. In a service-oriented company, its significance cannot be overstated.

Specialized logistics serve a world market

CARRIER'S concept of specialized distribution services, exemplified by the parts center, prevails in export activities as well. Carrier Overseas Corporation employs its own physical distribution services department. A staff of 69 fulfills the specialized requirements of the non-U.S. markets in such areas as order processing, traffic, customer service, inventory management and production scheduling control. Here, as in the parts center operation, some incidental duplication is willingly traded off against service benefits that accrue and the elimination of procedural complexities which arise when two dissimilar functions coexist under one roof.

"Syracuse is our home base," notes Manager-Distribution Services Richard K. Newmiller, "but we have a staff relationship with distribution people overseas as well. We recommend and specify distribution methods and procedures for our facilities at Montluel, France and Kuala Lumpur, Malaysia. Through uniform methods, we greatly facilitate communication."

While Carrier Overseas Corp. employs forwarders at ports of exit, the department prepares its own documents to speed goods flow. Most shipments clear through the port of New York, where three forwarders serve the company. Shipments originating at McMinnville, Tenn., however, pass through New Orleans, while Tyler, Tex., plant materials go to the port of Houston. Shipments are largely finished goods, but a sizable traffic in components moves through this company's channels as well.

General Traffic Manager Peter P. Bonito specifies the routing of export shipments from sources to ports of exit. He also has the responsibility for selection and control of forwarders employed at these locations. Through the pipelines he maintains, approximately 39 million pounds in export orders flowed forth to foreign destinations during 1969. All indications are that a continued accelerating growth in this volume can be expected.

Though employed by a separate entity, Mr. Bonito and other managers on Mr. Newmiller's staff work closely with their

Heavy equipment destined overseas leaves Syracuse in special open shipping containers for ocean movement.

Carrier International Limited staff reviews European shipment patterns. From the left are: Manager-Scheduling Fred Ludwig, Manager-Distribution Services Richard Newmiller, Manager-Order Services Department Robert Mattis and Traffic Manager Peter P. Bonito.

counterparts in the Carrier Air Conditioning Co. In Mr. Bonito's case, he meets monthly with the domestic traffic group on mutual concerns as well as having more frequent informal contacts during day-to-day operations. He works closely as well with the domestic organization's packaging engineers in resolving questions about packaging for specific overseas conditions or destinations, plus anticipating changes arising out of product redesigns or changing transportation conditions.

"Actually, packaging represents a three-party interest," Mr. Bonito observes. "We tie in also with our insurance company in our search for packaging improvements."

How Distribution Centers Build a Business

The Martin-Brower Company's specialty is supplying non-perishables to franchise food service locations and similar operations throughout the United States. The computer played a vital role in its operations from the start. Its present equipment represents a substantial advance in capability over more conventional "hardware" previously employed, affording efficiency gains comparable to those experienced when shifting from manual to computer procedures.

In day-to-day activity, the company's central computer works in tandem with a system of distribution center data terminals that have in themselves certain computing capabilities. Consequently, daily data accumulation and return activities for order processing and inventory control in the field have been reduced from a matter of hours to minutes. The new field terminals also greatly simplify clerical tasks at individual distribution centers, minimizing personnel training necessary and freeing the staff for the more usual duties fulfilled at these points.

Vehicle scheduling and vehicle maintenance also fall to the computer. Initial route studies, daily schedules and route revisions are all within these program packages.

TRAFFIC MANAGEMENT's March, 1971 Martin-Brower study follows:

MARTIN-BROWER CORPORATION'S business is physical distribution service. More than a material source, it maintains inventories and forwards varied products tailored to each customer's needs, feeding back market data to aid customer management. These customers include fast-food, drug, department store and supermarket chains, mail order houses and industrial plants.

Current gross sales in the $80 million range are more than double the figures of four years earlier. Expansion reflects similarly in company facilities: since 1966, distribution center space grew from 6,798,228 to 15,096-430 cubic feet at 11 centers, with two more under construction.

The company distributes some 5,000 different items in four major categories: disposable packaging, nonperishable food products, maintenance supplies and small food preparation equipment. Dealing with more than 600 firms, including such franchising giants as McDonald's, Baskin Robbins, Dunkin Donuts and Tastee Freez, Martin-Brower services over 14,000 retail outlets in all 50 states, Canada and Puerto Rico.

This multitude of products constitutes only a part of what Martin-Brower sells its customers, however. Working closely with them to determine the items best suited to their businesses, the company helps develop, design and contract for all these products in a complete program. Those selected then flow through Martin-Brower's distribution centers for scheduled deliveries as needed.

"Our services relieve chains from the burden of buying hundreds of items from numerous suppliers, arranging their deliveries and maintaining inventory," states Board Chairman Louis L. Perlman. "At the same time, the individual outlet is not concerned with storage problems and gains the price advantage of volume orders not possible if the outlet were ordering only for itself."

Scheduling and controlling this huge, diversified goods flow is a king-sized job. Management early recognized the potential handling and paper work bottlenecks inherent in its rapid growth rate and instituted several programs that now successfully hold down costs while making further service improvements, including the following:

• Computerized order processing and inventory control through a single central computer serving sophisticated data terminals at the nationwide distribution centers.
• Continuing distribution center expansion with standardized building designs and specialized handling equipment assuring rapid, efficient order fulfillment.
• Computer-controlled local and long-distance fleet operations with standardized equipment maintaining schedule reliability.
• Close coordination with common carriers, assuring maintenance of high service standards while planning operations to minimize inconveniences and costs for the carriers as well as the company.

DATA SYSTEM is discussed by (l. to r.): President Melvin Schneider, Executive Vice President Leroy J. Lanktree and Vice President-Operations James R. Bragg.

HARVEY N. MEDVIN, vice president-finance, works closely with distribution management in planning new distribution center sites.

With growth rates running better than 20% annually, year after year, physical expansion forward planning is a must. Vice President-Finance Harvey N. Medvin, Vice President-Operations James R. Bragg and Distribution Manager Charles Y. Buford look continually ahead to determine where new distribution centers will next be needed to absorb the added work load consistent with financial requirements.

The new company-owned centers can be built with ease and speed because they employ a standard design, well fitted to operating requirements while lending themselves readily to modern construction methods. Stated Toledo Contractor Carl Mockensturm upon completing one of the centers: "I never put up a building so easily in my life."

Martin-Brower operations place exceptional emphasis on computerization. Vice President Bragg, today in charge of operations, exemplifies the company philosophy, having joined the firm initially after serving as its computer consultant a few years ago. While computers were employed over a substantial period of time, they did not always do the satisfying job they now perform.

"What we had here a few years back was a near disaster," observes Mr. Bragg. "We were fighting work through a data processing configuration that didn't suit our requirements at all. There was nothing physically wrong with the equipment, a medium-sized disk pack operation, but it was like asking a dentist to transplant kidneys when placed in our work environment."

The present computer, a Honeywell 1200, employs five magnetic tape units and ties directly to COMPAT computer terminals at all distribution centers. In terms of "K," "computer-eze" for a thousand digits of information, the 1200 affords 32 K storage, while the five mag tape units have a speed of 64 K per second.

"We bought Honeywell because they had ample working softwear—specialized computer programing—that fitted a variety of our requirements, plus a subsequently proven capacity for not only routine service but continuing support on innovative projects involving systems design and equipment refinement," Mr. Bragg asserts. "They have also proven willing to make midnight 'house calls' on the few occasions when the equipment developed indigestion."

What are the success secrets in such an operation? "As in most jobs that are done right," claims Mr. Bragg, "there really are no secrets. As soon as an order, for example, enters the system, we establish a control on the number of documents, cases and dollars involved. This control is then completely balanced and is tied out every step in the operation, so that we don't expect errors. Very important is the fact that our programing staff is not only highly competent, but its members keep their training up-to-date. In today's market, really adequate computer managers are a lot harder to obtain than the computers themselves."

Despite heavy computerization, operations research programs for site selection projects and other studies have not yet assumed a major role here. "With substantial business data readily at hand from our routine computer operations," states Vice President-Finance Medvin, "we have literally a running analysis of factors influencing a variety of major decision types. Ultimately, sheer size alone will probably lead to greater management science employment. Up to the present, thanks to early computerization, we've kept decision-making far simpler than is common in a business of our present size."

OBSERVING traffic activity at Martin-Brower Corp.'s Chicago headquarters

Martin-Brower includes four manufacturing plants within its present operations. Prince Castle, Inc., Addison, Ill., manufactures specialized fast-food industry equipment. At Jackson, Tenn., the Jackson-Edwards division makes specialty paper bags and grocery sacks, generally imprinted for the user and designed for specific applications. Comet Packaging Corporation of New York City provides varied flexible plastic film packaging products for supermarkets, fast-food service industries and produce packers. A new plant, M-B Plastics, opened at Jackson, Tenn. in 1970, extrudes polyethylene, converting it into plastic bags, both clear and colored, and liners for cans, drums and plastic refuse cans.

"While manufacturing has been a growing factor," notes Executive Vice President-Manufacturing Leroy J. Lanktree, "we view distribution as the company's true main function. Any manufacturing operations are viewed as ancillary to a total distribution service."

In any forward movement by this company, the continuing service concept is its guiding philosophy. As President Melvin Schneider observes: "You can build a better mousetrap and have people beat a path to your door, but you'll sell a lot more mousetraps, if you deliver them at the moment the potential customer needs them."

and distribution center are (l. to r.): GM&O RR Trainmaster K. P. Bonner (at boxcar), Martin-Brower Vice President-Operations James R. Bragg, Distribution Manager Charles Y. Buford and Vice President-Finance Harvey N. Medvin.

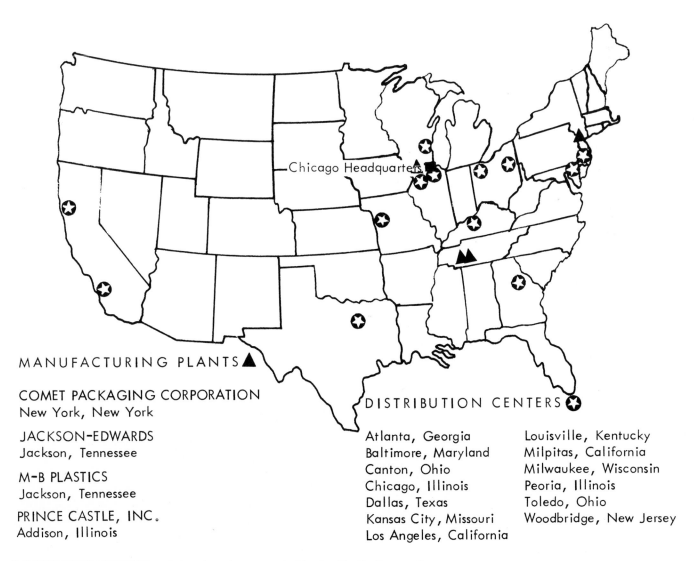

Chicago Headquarters

MANUFACTURING PLANTS ▲

COMET PACKAGING CORPORATION
New York, New York

JACKSON-EDWARDS
Jackson, Tennessee

M-B PLASTICS
Jackson, Tennessee

PRINCE CASTLE, INC.
Addison, Illinois

DISTRIBUTION CENTERS ✪

Atlanta, Georgia   Louisville, Kentucky
Baltimore, Maryland   Milpitas, California
Canton, Ohio   Milwaukee, Wisconsin
Chicago, Illinois   Peoria, Illinois
Dallas, Texas   Toledo, Ohio
Kansas City, Missouri   Woodbridge, New Jersey
Los Angeles, California

DISTRIBUTION CENTERS and plant locations operated by the Martin Brower Corp.

Computer-aided traffic speeds deliveries

FOR TRAFFIC, as for other distribution activities, computer control plays a major part at Martin-Brower. Common carrier freight, constituting 50% of company volume, operates under computerized bills of lading and related paper work. Similar forms route freight moving in Martin-Brower's own trucks, while other computer procedures route the vehicles themselves, measuring driver productivity, creating necessary internal and external reports, and determining total operating costs.

Inbound freight at all 11 distribution centers arrives predominantly by rail. An additional portion comes to these points as company truck return loads. Outbound freight flows entirely in trailers, including common carrier truck, piggyback and company fleet units. The latter are domiciled at each center, and plans call for fleet additions whenever new distribution centers open, including those now under construction at Louisville, Ky. and Milpitas, Cal.

"Generally, we find that cost and service conditions favor our own fleet operation in major metropolitan areas," notes Distribution Manager Charles Y. Buford, "but we make no arbitrary decisions on that basis. We determine proposed route suitability by comparing our anticipated costs with common carrier LTL rates between the affected points on approximate minimum loads of 22,000 pounds. Costs per truck mile for long haul and per hour for local deliveries, consistent with service requirements, determine our choice in each instance."

Martin-Brower's seven-part computerized shipping papers benefit carrier and company alike. Printed out for each order, the computer provides shipment routing and a bill of lading plus picking tickets for the warehouse and a stencil for marking the order's component pieces.

A copy of the bill of lading accompanies this article. Listed on this form are all stock items, accompanied by reference codes and the item numbers of these commodities in the motor freight classification. Thus, when a carrier rate clerk receives a bill of lad-ing, he cross-checks the printed reference numbers to find the specific commodities, obtains the item number citation and thereby saves a look-up in checking the rates. The roughly 100 item descriptions included cover an actual 5,000 items stocked (such as different types of paper cups which are adequately described under a single entry).

It formerly took as long as 30 minutes to produce a B/L manually. Now, it is a "free" by-product of the computerized picking ticket. A typical B/L includes 3,000 pounds of freight in approximately 15 freight classes.

The private truck operation requires no bills of lading, with picking, delivery sheets and driver manifests sufficient for dispatch of these shipments.

Routings and average rates to specific customers are computer-stored at Chicago and regularly updated by General Traffic Manager Arnold J. Vess and his staff. These rates are based on the average weight of individual customer shipments. Carried in computer memory, estimated cost for each shipment is automatically computed and compared to the carrier-submitted freight bill. If the carrier bill is within $2 of the estimate, no further check is deemed necessary. Given a variance either way exceeding $2, the traffic department checks the bill to determine if it is in order. If so, it is approved for payment. If not, it is paid on a revised basis. Over 90% of all freight bills clear automatically for payment, greatly diminishing audit costs.

At Chicago, where outbound volume is highest, common carrier trailer pickups and drops are made by a local cartage company. Started three years ago, this practice did away with three-block-long waiting lines and greatly reduced dock congestion.

A heavy user of stop-off shipments and consolidations, Martin-Brower

NATIONAL FLEET MANAGER Russell M. Race, General Traffic Manager Arnold J. Vess and Distribution Manager Charles Y. Buford.

loads the common carrier trailers, assembling shipments through computerized picking so that all common destination point shipments stage in a group. This helps the carrier in transferring freight and minimizing handling costs and attendant damage risks.

"We call the carrier and tell him the destination volume," Mr. Vess states, "and he can tell us the right loading order to give him the best-handling trailer load. If he wants to send a trailer through to Detroit, we nose-load the Detroit freight. We can frequently work out loading so that he doesn't even have to touch the lading at his local terminal before it leaves Chicago."

Consolidations keep costs down on several regular common carrier routes, such as Kansas City-St. Louis and Chicago-Minneapolis-St. Paul. Depending on total weight, cost reductions on the latter run are typically $125 to $200 per shipment. Computerized order processing greatly simplifies the development of such consolidated loads.

Building a Company Fleet

Major fleet operation commenced in 1968. Some 50 tractors and 70 trailers serve nationwide. The fleet employs White and Ford tractors, with the former predominantly assigned to long-haul routes exceeding 150 miles. Both tractors and trailers are highly standardized, meeting state requirements nationwide for ready transfer of equipment. In addition, this standardization minimizes driver familiarization problems. A substantial additional group of tractors and trailers, now under construction and on order, will augment this fleet during early 1971.

While 40-foot Gindy Volume Vans represent the basic standard, both for local and long-haul service, recent additions included 26 units of 27-foot length for tandem operation. National Fleet Manager Russell M. Race favors 35-footers in the Chicago area operation, however, due to the prevalence of narrow street situations where greater maneuverability is an asset. Tandems also handle much Los Angeles traffic.

All new vans, in addition to conventional rear access, have a side door halfway back on one side and one-third of the way back on the other. "This permits ready handling of cargo anywhere in the truck." says Mr. Buford, "and eliminates problems that nondelivery of a load in any truck bed sector might pose during the unloading of subsequent deliveries." Trailers carry conveyor equipment to speed handling.

In addition to conventional over-the-road operation, Martin-Brower employs piggyback. Quite frequently a tractor hauling freight to an outlying city, for example, will move a company trailer for an initial peddle route, then park it and pick up a railroad trailer or rented trailer that came forward by rail, peddling its contents similarly. In some instances, two trailers will be coordinated into such a delivery plan, with one driver and his tractor handling all three loads, returning to the distribution center with the company van.

From the start, the company deemed scheduled truck service essential. "Customer cooperation has been excellent in developing these sched-

MARTIN-BROWER'S computerized bill of lading form, one element in a computerized seven-part shipping manifold, includes classification item numbers for all commodities shipped, expediting the carrier rate clerk's work.

AC	STOR	DRV	TRK	HRS	DELV-DOLL	DELAY	DOLLAR	REA	WT.	TRAVEL$	TOTAL$	CWT$	CODE	DATE
BB	ABC	7	3000	.3	3.00			3	520	3.80	6.70	1.00	D	3/27/71
ACCT TOTAL				.3	3.00				520	3.80	6.70	1.00	1	6.70
AA	WXYZ	7	3000	.3	3.00			2	194	5.60	10.55	5.44	E	3/26/71
AA	WXYZ	7	3000	.2	2.00	.2	2.00	3	368	6.92	10.12	2.75	E	3/11/71
AA	WXYZ	7	3000	.1	1.00	.1	1.00	3	250	7.75	10.55	4.22	E	3/07/71
AA	WXYZ	7	3000	.9	9.00			2	1975	8.84	11.58	.60	E	3/01/71
ACCT TOTAL				1.5	15.00	.3	3.00		2787	29.11	42.80	1.54	4	10.70
CC	D111	7	3000	.2	2.00				182	5.60	7.60	4.18	E	3/10/71
CC	D112	7	3000	.3	3.00			3	161	3.16	6.16	3.83	E	3/14/71
CC	D113	7	3000	.3	3.00	.2	2.00	3	296	5.67	8.67	2.93	E	3/09/71
CC	D113	7	3000	.2	2.00	.1	1.00	2	168	2.67	6.67	3.97	E	3/10/71
CC	D118	7	3000	.4	4.00	.2	2.00	12	1331	5.67	11.67	.88	E	3/01/71
CC	D119	7	3000	.5	5.00				3660	7.78	11.78	.32	E	3/22/71
ACCT TOTAL				1.9	19.00	.5	5.00		5798	30.55	52.55	.91	6	8.76

MONTHLY delivery cost analysis reports, computer-derived from automated daily driver reports, break down delivery costs by individual store and total account.

ules," notes National Distribution Manager Buford. "The customers, in turn, benefit from assured schedule deliveries."

Setting Up the Routes

Establishing Chicago area computerized routing entailed substantial advance preparation. Mr. Buford and staff commenced this task using a neighborhood area map book from the Chicago Board of Trade. Regular customer locations were listed, including their parcel post zones, and plotted on these maps.

With this information, it became a relatively simple matter to group stops in a rational number and sequence, plotting the complete routes on a large area map. Splitting Chicago city runs to the north and south sides, those north received numbers one to eight, southside runs being 9 to 16. Northside suburban runs were numbered in the 30 series, with southside suburban service in the 50s, leaving adequate gaps should additional runs be created later on.

The resultant 60 runs per week, each assigned to a specific day, keep a 12-unit fleet occupied while an extra unit covers warehouse assignments. The runs are carefully scheduled so that in the event a delivery cannot be effected on the assigned day, another route on the following day's cycle will be able to absorb such an added stop with minimum waste mileage or time.

On each route, sequenced stop numbers spread five digits apart—for instance, 1 - 5 - 10, etc.—to provide for subsequent added stops, emergencies and redeliveries.

With all of this data prepared, routes were key-punched to read as follows: Division, branch, account, store, day, run, stop, delivery; each element is represented by assigned numbers. This information, meshed by the computer with current orders, yields a card deck showing the warehouse the proper trailer loading pattern for all affected orders.

Computer-printed driver manifests, completed by the drivers during the course of their work day, go nightly to the key-punch unit, where data is abstracted for subsequent computer preparation of monthly reports by driver, by account and as needed. A

CLAMP TRUCKS that pick up freight the full width of a trailer speed loading.

INBOUND FREIGHT, arriving at distribution centers largely by rail, is unloaded by forklift equipment for movement into storage and subsequent order assembly.

DRIVER REPORT FORM, initially prepared by computer, returns for the subsequent capture of data entered manually by the driver each day.

monthly delivery cost analysis clearly illustrates both hourly and individual delivery costs for each account. Samples of these forms accompany this article.

The success of this system in Chicago led to a program of installation at the other distribution centers. Fleet Manager Race recently completed similar arrangements at Baltimore and in the New York metropolitan area. Other centers will follow.

Advanced data network improves customer service

ELECTRONIC AGE management permeates every Martin-Brower activity. The computer got off to an early start here with a disk-oriented installation handling such tasks as accounting, payroll and order entry. An initial upgrading brought in a Honeywell 200 computer working in conjunction with a teletype network. This sped up order processing through wire instead of mail communication, as well as through benefits inherent in the magnetic tape-oriented computer programing.

Now, another breakthrough speeds service further, while cutting costs and simplifying paper work at many levels. A Honeywell 1200 computer, working through distribution center COMFILE data terminals, each in itself a mini-computer, saves up to a full day in many order-related activities. While doing this, it stores and analyzes vital inventory information, maintaining assured customer service reliability without building up excessive stocks.

A softwear technique called PROFIT (Programed Reviewing, Ordering and Forecasting Inventory Technique), developed by Honeywell and Martin-Brower, does the job. Combining 13 computer programs, this inventory management system merges traditional inventory control with advanced mathematical forecasting techniques, producing data in two major forms:

Forecasts: PROFIT reviews previous demand on the 5,000-item inventory and estimates future demand for each distribution center from current market trends and seasonal fluctuations, producing a monthly forecast.

Status Reports: PROFIT reports two or three times weekly on demand rates for all inventory items, placing asterisks beside those where demand exceeds forecast.

The status report answers the questions: "Should we order?" or "Can we wait?" If the answer is "order," the computer recommends how much, based upon the forecast for the rest of the month.

"Management-by-exception results from this procedure," comments Mr. Bragg. "Instead of 'eyeballing' those 5,000 individual products, we just scan down the list and look for the warning flags. The PROFIT forecast keeps the bulk of our inventory under control for us while we concentrate on the special situations."

The computer yields a customer service as well, providing each with

STANDARDIZED order forms ease editing and clerical effort.

IBM typewriters tied to data terminals feed Chicago computer.

regular reports detailing amount of each item ordered by each outlet from the individual distribution centers.

For many companies, a move to wire transmission of orders would mean a major speedup. Martin-Brower's shift from conventional teletype to batch transmission through data terminals was a step equally important in speeding the process. The COMFILE data terminal's magnetic tape magazine at an outlying point feeds the Data Central at Chicago in only 20 minutes the equivalent of three to four hours throughput under the former transmission system. In addition, it eliminates the need for translating paper tape to magnetic tape, saving one computer hour daily and eliminating an inconvenience for EDP personnel.

Each COMFILE Random Access Magnetic Tape Magazine gives its data terminal storage for 64,000 characters, requiring less than 0.5 second average access time for editing or correction. Operating like a disk system, it provides magnetic tape system economy and simplicity. A softwear package called COMENT that the manufacturer, COMPAT Corporation, provides controls data entry, positioning the electric typewriter carriage to conform to predetermined formats and minimizing operator errors by accepting only specified letters, numbers or their combinations in each data field.

The workings can be best demonstrated by following an order through the new system:

• The nearest Martin-Brower distribution center receives the order.

• The center codes the order by product and customer number, entering the data into the COMFILE data terminal. A single typist handles a distribution center's entire input up to a normal daily level of 10,000 characters. The unit itself can accept 64,000.

• As the operator stores input on the COMFILE magnetic-tape magazine, a paper copy is printed concurrently for backup reference.

• Batch transmission from the unattended data terminal takes place over Bell System WATS (Wide Area Telephone Service) lines upon polling by the Chicago Data Central.

• The COMFILE Data Central receives this information, error checks it, converts it to Honeywell BCD language, stores it on magnetic tape and loads it into the central computer through a standard tape drive, completely eliminating prior manual and computer steps required for data conversion.

• The Honeywell 1200 computer sorts and assembles all input, assigning customer addresses, shipping classifications, weights, invoice number, bill of lading and other shipping information. It arranges items automatically in picking order by carrier for sequential assembly in the distribution center. All orders are stored on a master "open-order" tape until ship-

ment is advised. The computer accumulates inventory control data concurrently. At day's end, inventory status of each item at every distribution center is automatically printed out for management review.

• The central computer records this information on magnetic tape, formatting for return by the Data Central to the originating COMFILE data terminals.

• Transmission follows, the distribution centers receiving the data at high speeds and recording it on the COMFILE cartridges. This transmission out to the centers takes 1½ hours, compared to 16 to 22 hours by former wire procedures. After transmission completion, the remote terminal automatically prints out order data on a seven-part print-out form at normal typewriter speed. The printing unit at each terminal is a standard IBM electric typewriter.

• The COMPAT system makes picking documents available by midafternoon, compared to the prior overnight schedule. Distribution centers now schedule the next day's work much earlier and can ship emergency orders the same day without manual bypass procedures.

• After assembling orders for shipment, each distribution center transmits a list of shipped orders to Data Central, which clears them from the "open-order" file and invoices the same day. The billing system handles adjustments to the original order as well, billing the customer only for what was actually shipped.

"What we've done for the distribution centers with these computer procedures parallels in nature our service to individual customer outlets," President Schneider states. "Our customer service package frees the storekeeper to do the things in his shop that yield the best return. Our computer procedure frees the distribution staff to build and move orders, unfettered by paper work complexities."

In reviewing the overall impact, Vice President Bragg draws particular satisfaction from the personnel effects. "We've eliminated a continual training and retraining problem for distribution center office staffs. The job is pleasanter and easier; turnover has dropped, and the system has created a clear capacity for absorbing substantial volume increases. In this business, that is extremely important."

Standardized warehouses aid growth

WITH COMPANY GROWTH continuously exceeding 20% each year, Martin-Brower faces two distinct challenges: running the existing operation efficiently while increasing throughput and developing additional distribution centers when and where they will do the job best.

Vice Presidents James R. Bragg and Harvey N. Medvin work closely in determining the areas for new distribution centers and control the site selection. Supporting them in the latter activity, National Distribution Manager Charles Y. Buford puts substantial effort into locating specific potential properties suited to company purposes and developing terms and contracts for their procurement. Company policy favors ownership rather than leasing of such land and buildings.

"Quite frequently, we find railroad-owned property the most suitable," Mr. Buford asserts. "Our operating practices make a siding for inbound freight essential. A large amount of our goods arrives in carloads."

After opening five new centers in as many years, two additional units under construction will soon join the group, with plans for yet others advancing. Standardized facilities contribute markedly to construction speed and costs.

"Five years ago," states Vice President Bragg, "an architect-prepared building cost us $10 per square foot. Our new Toledo facility, built by the contractor from our standard plans, cost only $7 per foot, despite interim material and labor cost increases. We anticipate our new Louisville facility will run about the same."

The standard unit measures 50,000 square feet, with a 24-foot clear ceiling, a three or four-car rail siding on one side and a truck-loading area on another with six truck doors and Kelley dock levelers. Building site functions may be shifted to accommodate terrain, siding location or other site features. One side wall is a "knock-out" sector for easy expansion. Each building has a standard office sector.

Joining with Mr. Buford after site development, Noah Thomas, manager of warehouse practices, defines material handling equipment requirements at new locations. He and his staff make certain, too, that shelving and other interior arrangements measure up to operating requirements. Notes Mr. Bragg: "Because of tested, standardized procedures, we can move into a 50,000-foot standard distribution center, stock it with $300,000 worth of 500 different items and make it fully, routinely operational within 30 days."

These centers average about 12 to 14 employes plus a supervisor and a lead man. The warehouse supervisor also has local fleet operating responsibility, reporting directly to Fleet Manager Russell Race in Chicago. Common carrier traffic control remains centralized at Chicago due to the computerized procedures employed.

Computerization also aids internal operations. Picking tickets list goods in the most efficient sequence, saving much labor. Average orders contain 30 different items totaling 3,000 pounds.

Each standard center works two or three lift trucks plus about four order-selecting equipment units. Adjustable shelving readily accommodates carton or system changes, which occur about 10 times each year systemwide.

Chicago's center is a different story. With 266,000 square feet of floor, a higher ceiling and over four times the standard unit activity, other methods are mandatory. High-reach fork trucks keep upper shelves and space

AT OUTBOUND DOCK, Guide-O-Matic train pauses while a clamp truck removes goods from pallets for trailer loading.

BARRETT GUIDE-O-MATIC operatorless train pauses while lift truck removes pallet of inbound merchandise for storage.

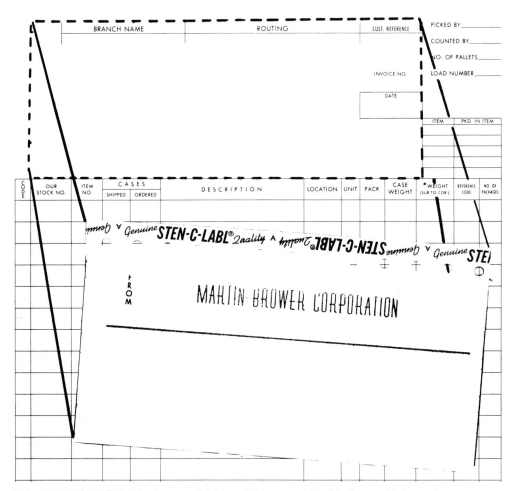

MARTIN-BROWER'S shipping manifold, in addition to a bill of lading and information copies, includes a computer-prepared picking ticket and a stencil. Picking ticket lists all items in most convenient assembly order, while computer-prepared stencil simplifies marking of the 26 pieces in the average M-B shipment.

active, while clamp trucks that lift loads the full width of a trailer interior make for quick palletizing and depalletizing at the dock.

A unique automated handling system contributes most importantly to the Chicago warehouse efficiency. The structure, built in 1967, handled 40% more merchandise by early 1969, operating on a three-shift basis. Initially, forklift trucks moved incoming merchandise to storage and back out for shipment. "If we continued this way and volume grew at the prevailing rate, aisle congestion would make it almost impossible to keep materials moving," Mr. Bragg asserts. "That's why we looked to driverless train systems."

Extensive feasibility studies led the company to install a Barrett Guide-O-Matic tractor system. Its two tractors normally each tow four two-pallet carts, 40 of the latter being purchased initially, with another 40 added upon finding that they would expedite handling. They permit advance loading and unloading, building greater flexibility into the total operation.

Separate loops through three warehouse sections have a combined 2,250-foot length. Each train completes a circuit in about 10 minutes, varying with number of stops required and time spent at each. The combined routes include 17 possible stops.

A train handles eight pallet loads in the space and time it took one fork truck to handle just one pallet. The system also frees aisles of handling equipment clutter and offers more timing flexibility in loading and unloading material moving within the warehouse. These Barrett trains replaced five double pallet trucks and saved the cost of three additional fork trucks otherwise necessary at the time. In addition, the service life of the remaining forklift fleet has been extended through diminished unit work loads.

Because cart loads range from 400 pounds per pallet up to 2,800 pounds, the riding characteristics vary significantly, making load stabilization and smooth floors essential. The Chicago warehouse floor was in good condition, so only minor crack-filling was required prior to system start-up.

When tractors and carts arrived in January, 1970, a typical train was driven around the desired route pattern to check clearances. These were noted and scribed on the floor. Beacons and holding stations were then installed, and the system entered operation at the end of the initial month.

The tractors have a width of only 34 inches, while pallets run 40 inches, so Martin-Brower specified that tractors should have sensing equipment to prevent entry into spaces narrowed by goods or equipment. Accordingly, a set of wire "feelers" was designed which project from the tractors. If they touch anything adjacent as the tractor proceeds over its route, the equipment automatically halts. A dual-braking system provides a normal smooth stop for the unit plus a rapid emergency stop.

Making Operations Research Pay

Stop & Shop is a large and growing supermarket chain in the Northeastern states. Its continuing expansion entails the regular addition of new store locations and the building up of needed logistics capability to supply them economically.

Many kinds of modern mathematical and statistical techniques, largely computer-oriented, aid site selection of warehouse facilities and store locations alike. Complex PERT charts govern all construction schedules, while company delivery fleet services function under a computerized delivery scheduling program that greatly eases the dispatching work load at critical hours while substantially improving vehicle utilization. This results in reduced driver hours and lower equipment investment.

So important are management science activities that the company maintains full-time staffing for this work, much of it directly oriented to logistics. A case study presented by TRAFFIC MANAGEMENT in March, 1970 follows:

IN THE TIGHTLY competitive consumer-retailing field, New England-based Stop & Shop is a standout. Annual sales in the $700 million range reveal vast growth from 1960's gross figures of some $240 million. Still largely a supermarket operation, substantial drug and general merchandise divisions contribute increasingly to the chain's success. Expansion has been geographic as well, with a number of stores added during recent years in New Jersey and New York.

Its industry's narrow profit margins, coupled with Stop & Shop's rapid expansion rate, demands meticulous cost control as well as the utmost sagacity in preplanning the numerous facility investments that company growth rate demands. A busy research department, backed by ample computer capacity, employs many advanced management science techniques to keep daily operations, as well as expansion activities, moving with optimum efficiency and economy.

"We cannot afford guesses in this business," notes Executive Vice President Avram J. Goldberg. "When we commit bricks and mortar to a huge new warehouse, we must be absolutely certain that its operation will yield the greatest output per dollar possible consistent with today's state of the art."

Director of Research Raj K. Dhanda makes good, practical use of operations research procedures that elsewhere are more frequently discussed than employed. In his own department, as well as in coordination with Director of Distribution Richard Silverman and his staff, widely varied applications provide payoffs that pack a punch right through to the balance sheet. Many of these procedures bear strongly on physical distribution, such as:

Warehouse design simulation. A new 340,000-square foot warehouse at North Haven, Conn. will yield substantial first cost savings plus operational advantages derived

through refinements suggested by a mathematical model.

Automated fleet scheduling. Computerized truck dispatching, a proven service-builder, brings cost reductions as well.

PERT (Program Evaluation and Review Technique). This proven control system for scheduling and guiding complex projects sees many applications at Stop & Shop, notably in the development of physical facilities, including stores and warehouses.

Backing up the many operations research activities, a powerhouse computer operation employs not just one, but three large computers, including an IBM 360-40 plus two IBM 360-30 systems—one of 65K capacity, the other rated at 32K—supported by, among other units, an optical scanner and six disc drives.

Even these resources have their limits, however, as huge daily turnover of Stop & Shop's myriad products creates an ever-increasing data flow through the headquarters computer facility. Accordingly, some work moves through time-sharing services as well. Both General Electric's Schenectady computer facilities and Dial Data's operation in Boston regularly augment Computer Center Manager Frank O'Sullivan's equipment capacity, precluding any delays in either staff activities or operational computer services.

"We've employed management science extensively and, we feel, successfully for the past four years," states Assistant to President Paul Kelly. "It serves us well. We foresee a continuing broadening of its planning and operational roles."

"Expanded use of operations research techniques in the inventory area lies in the

Stop & Shop's management science programs get a boost from ample computer capacity.

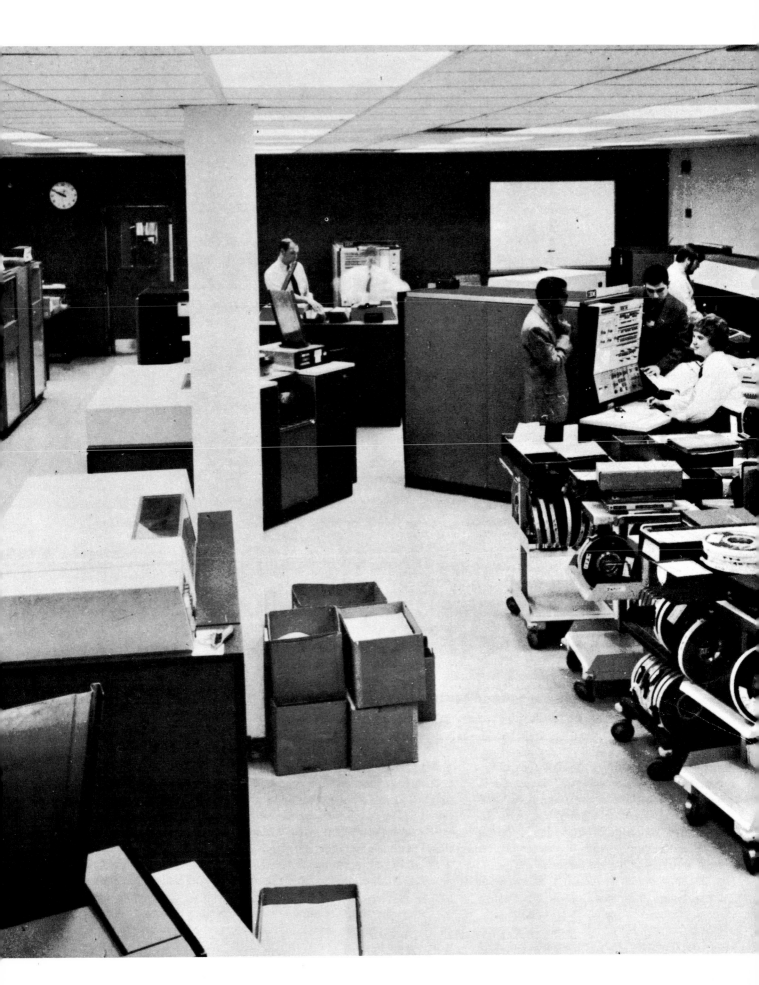

Analysis of computer-developed data simulating proposed operations at the new North Haven warehouse draws the attention of, left to right, Director of Research Raj K. Dhanda, Executive Vice President Avram J. Goldberg and Assistant to President Paul Kelly.

cards," Director of Research Dhanda notes. "We also intend to develop mathematical location models for the placement of new stores."

Techniques of various sorts, once proven in any one division of the company, lend themselves to expansion into other sectors, with appropriate revisions to match operating circumstances. After all, it matters not to the computer whether it works for Stop & Shop food stores, Medi-Mart drug units or the Bradlees group of self-service department stores, all of them company components that share in the available management science expertise.

Simulation builds a better warehouse

A HIGHLY MECHANIZED, 340,000-square foot grocery warehouse at North Haven, Conn. serves Stop & Shop stores in the New York-New Jersey-southern Connecticut area. Inaugurated officially in mid-March, partial prior service has already demonstrated the value of many of its new features.

The North Haven facility's planning and development depended heavily on management science techniques. In particular, simulation showed the road to substantial cost and service benefits. Separate mathematical models of two major system components yielded significant gains, including:

• Reduced accumulation conveyor investment. By simulating system operation, an alternative approach was developed at a cost 60% below the best estimate under conventional planning methods.
• Shutdown prevention. Simulated manpower and supporting equipment needs suggested greater-than-anticipated pallet-loading conveyor spur requirements, avoiding conveyor system congestion in operation that would lead to shutdowns and potential expensive equipment alterations.

Because North Haven represented a new approach, no previous experience afforded guidance in measuring various fundamental requirements. Stop & Shop's consultant, a firm with substantial grocery warehousing experience, made initial cost estimates that appeared reasonable, but could offer no pre-

At North Haven, Conn., finishing touches are put on an innovative warehousing system for a March, 1970 debut.

WHERE COMPUTER SIMULATION HELPED TO ELIMINATE THE UNKNOWNS IN AN ADVANCED WAREHOUSE DESIGN

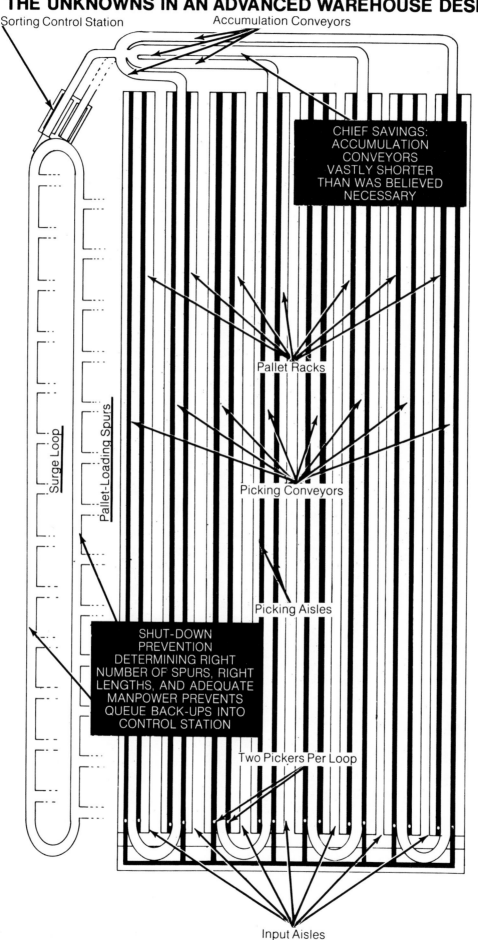

Sorting Control Station

Accumulation Conveyors

CHIEF SAVINGS:
ACCUMULATION
CONVEYORS
VASTLY SHORTER
THAN WAS BELIEVED
NECESSARY

Pallet Racks

Picking Conveyors

Surge Loop

Pallet-Loading Spurs

Picking Aisles

SHUT-DOWN
PREVENTION
DETERMINING RIGHT
NUMBER OF SPURS, RIGHT
LENGTHS, AND ADEQUATE
MANPOWER PREVENTS
QUEUE BACK-UPS INTO
CONTROL STATION

Two Pickers Per Loop

Input Aisles

cedent as proof of accuracy. The stakes were too high to move forward on guesswork. A required initial investment in the multi-million range, coupled with a critical need for goods flow reliability to preclude expensive shutdowns, clearly demanded greater validation of both costs and specifications.

Resorting to simulation, Director of Research Raj K. Dhanda and his staff developed mathematical models representing the proposed operation. Following tests of numerous variations in equipment and manpower assignments, the models led to estimates that differed strikingly from those postulated by the company's external consultant. The initial simulation, testing accumulation conveyor requirements in proportion to standard conveyors in the picking aisles, revealed an initial overestimate of 60%. As the simulation-suggested requirement itself was well within the six-figure cost range, investment savings from this initial simulation alone were considerable.

The second simulation looked at operations beyond the picking area, determining equipment and manpower required to keep goods flowing from the accumulation conveyors without danger of costly shutdowns. In this case, the model forewarned the need of substantial conveyor capacity to feed pallet-loading personnel. While this meant a probable cost increase in contrast to initial savings suggested for the picking area conveyor installation, the assured service reliability and maximized manpower efficiency made the extra conveyor costs in the pallet-loading area eminently worthwhile.

What was the need for this huge new facility in the first place? The company had two goals:

Accommodating expanding business. North Haven supplies stores in the newly developed New York-New Jersey region, plus speeding service to existing southern Connecticut stores. The facility will also absorb anticipated continued expansion.

Controlling store service. The new warehouse and its related systems seek to eliminate pilferage as well as losses arising from inadequate warehouse-to-store stock control.

These losses require a "store allowance," which can cost up to $1 million annually for the company.

Store service requirements create grocery warehouse design complexities. Goods must move from the warehouse properly assembled to avoid resorting in the back room at the receiving store. These goods, some 7,000 warehouse items, fall into family groups and commodity classes, including 60 of the latter. A typical family group is cereal, which subdivides as two commodity classes—hot and cold. All told, Stop & Shop handles about 60 grocery commodity classes.

Actual shipment assembly, therefore, finds family groups and commodity classes placed to feed store aisle arrangements with minimum in-store handling. The outbound warehouse dock moves freight to suit the stores' convenience. At the same time, efficient warehousing demands balanced work loads in the stock-picking operation. The final design, significantly affected by the simulation studies, achieved both ends.

The first model, which measured accumulation conveyor requirements and the speed at which the system should operate, was based upon volume flow and picker performance data. Historical records yielded information to analyze nine weeks of movement spread through the year period. Picker data, however, required direct measurement of actual performance.

Prototype picking aisles were set up so that picking time could be checked for taking a case from a rack, labeling it, walking to and placing it on the conveyor. Varied case sizes were tested because conveyor space employment was a critical factor in determining queue lengths. Times established for each operation were converted statistically to produce an overall average time and standard deviations from that average. Given movement data, operations sequence and picker times, the computer simulated complete picking cycles.

From this computer-developed information, three important statistics were recorded: average length of each queue, maximum length the queue reached and time a queue

Advance computer programs simulated North Haven warehouse conditions in advance, employing historical volume and movement data augmented by accurately timed test operations. Simulation objectives were excessive investment avoidance and conveyor shutdown prevention. The schematic diagram illustrates their relationship to a portion of the complete operation.

Inbound rail traffic feeds heavy volume to North Haven facility at its indoor unloading dock.

Numerous common carriers bring freight to North Haven, while company vehicles draw shipments for individual stores from similar freight docks situated on opposite side of the building.

Research Department members pool their brainpower on new store sight selection. From left to right are Location Research Analysts Janus Roht and Robert Cuzner, Marketing Research Analyst William Sullivan and Location Research Analyst Arnold Burke.

was at its maximum length. The average lengths determined how long the accumulation conveyor sections should be.

Further testing in this simulation employed such variations as a five-minute shutdown of the control station. In this example, the resultant delay increased a two-hour work cycle by as much as 20 minutes in order to clear the resultant congestion.

The second simulation determined how the pallet-loading men and equipment should handle the 600 to 700 cases per hour flowing from the control station. It determined the number of men necessary, their required work speed, length of required conveyor spurs and their number. Here, again, physical tests established standard pallet-loading times.

Because queues cannot be permitted to back up from the loading spurs to the control station, this simulation's primary mission was to determine the maximum queue length that might be anticipated. This was determined by testing the operation under varying operating conditions.

The ability of simulation to answer the unanswerable for Stop & Shop in the North Haven operation unquestionably sped facility planning operations. That it will be similarly employed when other such projects present themselves is a foregone conclusion.

Computerized dispatching improves delivery service

TRUCK SCHEDULING, under the best of conventional situations, remains a difficult and imprecise activity. At Stop & Shop, however, conventional dispatching situations are rapidly becoming a thing of the past. Computerized truck scheduling lifts the burden of too many decisions demanded in too short a time period from the dispatcher's shoulders. The sheer bulk of clerical effort removed, he can concentrate on the problems and exceptions where experienced judgment is most essential.

Automated scheduling fulfills many company objectives. First-class service in an intensely competitive market holds primary rank among them, with all stores in the food division receiving daily truck deliveries, and the merchandise they order being placed at their premises regularly within 24 hours after the computer releases an invoice. In some instances, the turnaround time is as short as four hours. Both improved paperwork and a greater flexibility in vehicle employment result from schedule automation, significantly benefiting service patterns.

Close to service betterment goals come cost considerations. Operating experience in the produce division during the past year clearly demonstrated transportation savings capabilities in the 10% range. As full activation spreads to the complete food service area, such a savings spread over a fleet approaching 200 trailers will be considerable. Materially aiding this prospect is the ability to move away from former fixed route patterns. "We've almost said 'fixed routes have no meaning,' " states Director of Research Dhanda.

Under existing procedures in the produce division, store orders come in daily by telephone line to paper tape readers, responding to calls initiated at headquarters. These feed to the computer, which develops a triplicate invoice to activate warehouse order assembly and the necessary accounting functions.

Following bill production, the computer proceeds to run the automatic truck-scheduling program. In doing so, it draws on conversion factors which translate specific commodity orders to piece counts and pallet loads. The resultant information is married to stored data on rolling stock to develop truckloads. In addition, the computer develops the best sequence of trailer loading, taking into account store constraints, dock restrictions, fleet limitations, whether or not power tail-lift-gate equipment is required, etc.

Actual truck routes are not spelled out, but the setup of loads and the order of stops is fixed, as is also the total time for the individual run. Time is not fixed for any one store in the individual run consist, however, store time for all stops being indicated only as a route total figure.

Work commenced on automated truck scheduling in mid-1968, based initially on a stock IBM program called VSP (Vehicle Scheduling Program). Radical changes were made in this system rather early, and continuing revisions dictated by experience have resulted in a virtually custom computer application that is well suited to the high-speed, high-reliability requirement's that the company's operations demand. Because Stop & Shop possesses an extremely complete and accessible management information system,

ZONE NUMBER	CUSTOMER NUMBER	QUANTITY 1ST SPEC.	QUANTITY 2ND SPEC.	STOP TIME HRS. MINS.	CALLING LIMITS DAY HOUR	DAY HOUR	TYPE/CAPACITY RESTRICTIONS	REMARKS
ROUTE NUMBER	39							
7721	W. FOX	3	85	0 31			VEH. TYPE 1	
7723	MEAT	2	52	0 32			VEH. TYPE 1	
4311	RCSLND	3	209	0 31			VEH. TYPE 1	
4313	MEAT	7	130	0 50			VEH. TYPE 1	
4312	RCSLND	4	209	0 34			VEH. TYPE 1	

ROUTE SUMMARY

ASSIGNED VEHICLE TYPE	= 1			EARLIEST STARTING TIME	=	DAY 1	HOUR 18.00
	1ST SPEC.	2ND SPEC.					
VEHICLE CAPACITY	= 20	1100		LATEST STARTING TIME	=	2	9.59
TOTAL LOAD	= 19	685		MILEAGE BASED ON AVERAGE SPEED OF 30 KM/H	=	31.5 KMS	
				TRAVEL TIME	=	1 HRS. 3 MINS.	
				ROUTE TIME	=	4 HR . 1 MINS.	
				NUMBER OF DELIVERIES	=	5	

Daily route delivery data produced by computer. At top is information covering each stop. Underneath, a summary statement reviews productivity elements of day's total route format.

necessary movement figures and other relevant data were readily available at the outset to back initial studies with amply detailed history prior to automated scheduling's adoption.

While the new system's day-to-day benefits show clearly in improved services, decreased costs and minimum ulcers at the loading docks, gains accrue as well in longer-range planning. The possibilities for greater vehicle standardization, as well as the determination of the proper mix among types, become more obvious as data accumulates from the new flexible routing experience, suggesting further possibilities for maximum vehicle utilization as well as store facility revisions where cost trade-offs might yield significant net gains in reduced specialized vehicle purchases.

Controlling major projects through management science

THE MANAGEMENT SCIENCE technique termed PERT, an acronym for "Program Evaluation and Review Technique," grows steadily more popular in physical distribution activities. As more managers learn its value in cutting large project control problems down to more easily workable size, both manual and computer versions of PERT handle project control on increasingly diversified assignments.

At Stop & Shop PERT is a fully matured working tool with a history of successful applications. So heavily is it employed that a full-time corporate PERT engineer, Wayne Boie, now handles this activity, developing project schedules for the various company

Corporate PERT Engineer Wayne Boie reviews preliminary plans for a major facility development with Operations Research Analyst Shri Talwalkar before designing a PERT network.

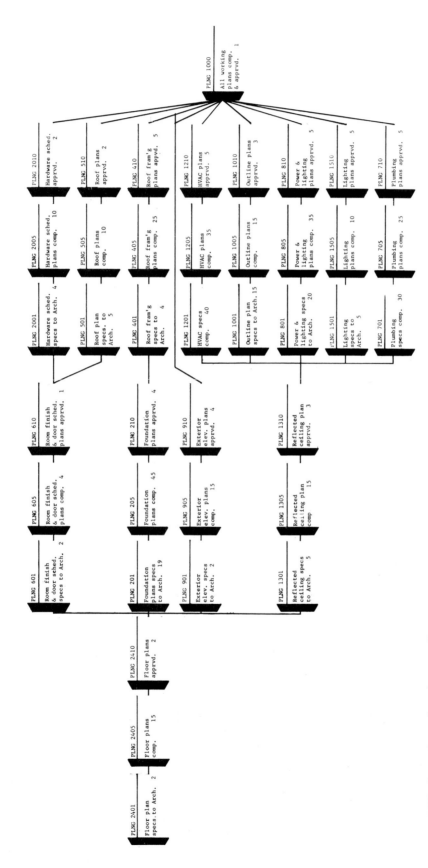

The PERT chart above is only a small segment of the total task pattern for the development of a new store. Representing the planning phase, each box describes a single task, with numbers at end showing the number of days per task anticipated. A heavy line coursing through the chart indicates the "critical path," a group of tasks whose relationships and timings dictate total days necessary for the project.

PCS - MASTER PRIORITY SCHEDULE BY DATE   12/16/69

EARLY START WORK ITEM DESCRIPTION DURATION STORE TYPE LOCATION EARLY FINISH LATE START LATE FINISH CRITICAL

OCT 31	CCN 2467	FLOOR MAT SAMPLES APPR'D	3	C220	W.CALDWELL	NOV 4			
OCT 31	CCN 2467	FLOOR MAT SAMPLES APPROVED	003	C223	HILLSDALE	NOV 04			
OCT 31	SEC 1004	AWARD ALARM CONTRACT	1	C223	E.BRUNSWICK	OCT 31			
NOV 03	SEC 1005	ALARM SYSTEM FABRICATED	27	C223	E.BRUNSWICK	DEC 11			*
NOV 04	CCN 1006	DROPS	6	C220	W.CALDWELL	NOV 12			
NOV 04	CCN 1006	DROPS		C223	HILLSDALE	NOV 12			

NOV 07	CCN 2115	LAST HARDWARE COMP	1	C220	W.CALDWELL	NOV 7			
NOV 07	CCN 2115	INSTALL HARDWARE COMP	001	C223	HILLSDALE	NOV 07			
NOV 07	CCN 2575	MAJOR DECOR COMPLETE	5	C223	E.BRUNSWICK	NOV 14			
NOV 07	DRUG 9999	FIRM OPENING DATE SET	001	D208	DARIEN CON	NOV 07			
NOV 07	DRUG 1013	OBTAIN NAMES OF DOCTORS	5	C223	E.BRUNSWICK	NOV 14			
NOV 07	DRUG 1102	PERS ASSEM CARPET EQUIP	3	C223	E.BRUNSWICK	NOV 11			

While computer output shows complete task schedules for each project separately, the master chart above gives top management a complete picture by period of all tasks under way or anticipated. Similar charts give localized data to department and division managers.

departments and supplying current data regularly on individual projects as well as in summary form at corporate and divisional levels.

What is PERT and how does it work? Essentially a performance time-charting procedure, it illustrates both the time allocations that specific tasks require and their relationships to each other in developing a completed project. The accompanying illustration, for example demonstrates various steps necessary in planning a store facility. Still to be "timed" in relation to full program scheduling, the "critical path" has been plotted manually for illustration purposes, indicating the key interrelated activities for the project. To reduce total project time, therefore, it becomes necessary to make any gains in functions on this "path" or no total performance improvement will be possible.

As with so many computer procedures, perhaps the most difficult task precedes computer entry. "Finding out just what specific jobs need to be done can be challenging in itself," comments Mr. Boie, "but determining interrelationships is no easier. It isn't enough to know that we'll need six days to accomplish an item. We need to be certain that we have identified every other job that must be accomplished before the one in question can start. We've also got to determine what other work is dependent upon the completion of the specific task under measurement. Only then can we start to manually plot a project chart or feed a computer to develop a project schedule."

Computer output includes three standard PERT reports:

Individual project reports. These tell managers specifically concerned what performance may be expected under specified activating dates assigned.

Departmental or divisional priority schedules. Representing specific time periods, such reports enumerate all tasks on all projects within the report unit that have been established and scheduled.

Corporate priority schedules. Similar to department schedules, they differ in that total corporate activity under PERT coverage is included.

A sample report accompanies this article. As indicated, provision is made for keeping track of any tasks that may have deferred starting dates, as well as those whose timing is critical.

Easing the path to PERT on major projects, a stock program, IBM Project Control System, Version 2 (PCS-360), processes the input and develops the previously described reports. While employed on many kinds of construction programs at Stop & Shop, it lends itself well also to such considerations as budgeting and diversified physical distribution projects. In developing the company's new meat-packing facility at Marlborough, Mass., many of the PERT applications are nonconstruction-oriented. Several such sub-projects share a heavy physical distribution emphasis, including a program to develop optimum delivery vehicle-loading patterns and other operational procedures.

Innovative Logistics Aid Hormel's Forward Thrust

The George A. Hormel Co. keeps close watch on several of its distribution assignments through computer programming. Fleet control, including passenger units and company trucks, benefits from such computer procedures. The distribution department also makes good use of simulation techniques in its site selection studies.

A particularly significant operations research application has been its employment of IBM's VSP Vehicle Schedule Program, modified by the company to fit its specific conditions. Initially employed in the Minneapolis-St. Paul area, it regulates the operations of an unusual containerized delivery fleet within that metropolitan region.

The program has been subsequently employed successfully in the Los Angeles territory and Director of Physical Distribution Robert A. Propf, under whose aegis these innovations have taken place, anticipates further expansion based upon the proven success of these initial installations. All computer operation necessary to VSP is provided at Hormel's Austin, Minn. headquarters, communicating with Los Angeles via Bell Dataphone for timely schedule deliveries.

These and other logistics activities at Hormel, detailed in TRAFFIC MANAGEMENT's March, 1972 issue, are described in the following report:

HORMEL'S 1971 annual report reveals net sales exceeding $686 million—a healthy gain from $385 million 10 years earlier. Net earnings growth, however, is even more impressive: almost $17 million in 1971 versus $3 million plus in 1962. Clearly, this Austin, Minn. management team made good use of its resources in the past decade.

Nowhere is this more sharply reflected than in transportation-distribution activities. Recognition of this function's vital role is implicit in the accompanying organization chart, which shows Director, Transportation-Distribution Robert A. Propf reporting directly to President and Chief Executive Officer I.J. Holton, coordinating his division's activities with those of every other company unit. An enlightened management's support makes numerous progressive and innovative logistics approaches possible, such as:

Domestic containerization: Started in July, 1959, containerized truck deliveries subsequently proved themselves in three locations and may soon be inaugurated elsewhere.

Computerized routing and maintenance: Daily computer vehicle routing, serving two major metropolitan areas, will be expanded, while company truck fleet maintenance also benefits from computerized data retrieval and analysis.

Site selection studies: A regular participant in prior surveys, the division's successful completion of a total analysis for a proposed distribution plant suggests a precedent for other similar studies.

Import-export developments: The division's forward planning activities increasingly involve expanding overseas sources and markets.

"Our transportation-distribution division is basically a staff function concerned with policy and administration, plus operational support where needed," Mr. Propf asserts. **"We develop and perfect programs or operations, but routinized day-to-day activities become local line tasks, audited by our division regularly to maintan proper service and cost levels."**

Accordingly, while there are transportation managers at the Austin, Minn.; Fremont, Neb.; Fort Dodge, Ia., and Atlanta, Ga. plants with administrative responsibility to plant managers, they also have functional "dotted line" responsibility to the director of transportation-distribution. At Atlanta, Austin and Fort Dodge, the purchasing department is under the transportation manager. For the seven smaller plants that have no resident transportation managers, Traffic Supervisor A. Clyde Vollmers acts as liaison and provides long-range planning assistance.

"The biggest problem for many of these plants is load imbalance," Mr. Vollmers observes. "Several are in sparsely settled regions, although service levels currently are pretty good."

In recent years, there have been substantial changes in physical facilities. **"We are looking to open more company-operated distribution centers,"** states Group Vice President-Prepared Foods Raymond J. Asp, **"preferably tied to production facilities."** Though 8 to 10 local warehouses were discontinued when the Atlanta plant opened, the company continued to maintain a 72-hour area delivery standard. Present policy favors satellite activity over large center production.

Site Selection Study

Such considerations as the foregoing led to the division's recent site selection study. Sales projections reaching 5 to 10 years ahead pointed up the need for additional capacity in the grocery products division. Sensing a demand within the central region, this division presented its re-

I.J. HOLTON (right), president and chief executive officer, discusses Hormel Co. forward distribution planning with Director of Transportation-Distribution Robert A. Propf.

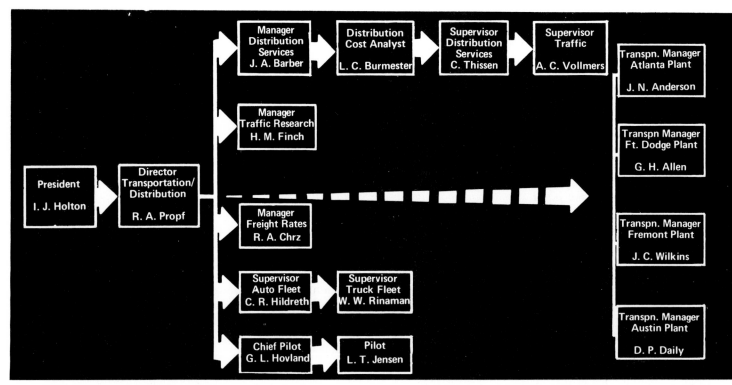

ORGANIZATION CHART indicates transportation-distribution division reports directly to the president on a level with other company functions, facilitating interdivisional communication and logistics program coordination.

quirements to the transportation-distribution division, which constructed models that considered sites throughout the area using simulation techniques. "We have locked our choice within a state," comments Vice President-Grocery Products Division James A. Silbaugh, "and anticipate a decision on the specific point shortly."

Conducted under Manager Distribution Services James A. Barber, the study is designed to show the preferred point and alternatives, cost justification, anticipated return and customer service objectives. "We have also considered the effect of intermovement among Hormel plants," Mr. Barber notes. Input from many departments was necessary to develop the required data. The company's continuing expansion indicates the probability of further such studies ahead.

Substantial modal changes have occurred in company shipping during recent years. Though a major portion of outbound traffic moves by truck, considerable rail tonnage splits between the grocery products plus nonperishables generally moving in GMA (Grocery Manufacturers Association), standard design, cushion-underframe boxcars and perishable products moving increasingly in mechanical rather than iced refrigerator cars.

In over-the-road operations, Hormel depends largely on irregular route carriers of specified commodities, having found that general commodity ones could not meet the stringent schedule requirements. Some 50 specialized carriers, such as LCL Transit, Midwest Coast Transport and Ellsworth Freight Lines, handle heavy tonnage.

The division supports motor carrier authority applications in specific cases where such service is needed. "These usually concern areas rather than individual locations," Supervisor Distribution Services Christopher Thissen states, "as in the Southeast, where we have a particular need for this."

Consolidated techniques also help. When the three-year-old food service division established a frozen entree line of about 45 items, Manager Freight Rates Richard A. Chrz set up a distribution program to optimize the situation. "We needed an adequate storage point in a location with broad carrier services," Mr. Chrz states, "so we went into Ajax Transfer & Storage Co.'s frozen warehouse facility at St. Paul. We ship consolidated loads from the manufacturing plant to Ajax, fanning them out via carriers offering frozen LTL service."

Export-Import Developments

Manager Traffic Research Harold M. Finch, largely concerned with division forward planning activity, works increasingly on export-import matters. "We are working closely with marketing on such studies as intermodal movements to San Juan and Honolulu for meat shipments as an example," he notes. **"We have also worked closely with marketing for the past 2 ½ years due to constant transportation labor problems, both domestic and transocean. Our many perishable products make this a serious matter, particularly so with pork, which ages even under ideal conditions."**

The company has lost no products due to strike interruptions, but the costs have been notable. During the fall longshoremen's strike, Hormel airlifted 250,000 pounds of manufactured sausage and hams from the West Coast to Honolulu at premium

TRANSPORTATION-DISTRIBUTION DIVISION STAFF CONFERENCE—Supervisor of Auto Fleet Chester R. Hildreth (standing at left) reviews a fleet control report with Hormel Co.'s Director of Transportation-Distribution Robert A. Propf (seated, center) while TM Executive Editor Jack W. Farrell (standing at right) looks on. Others are (l. to r.): Distribution Cost Analyst Lambert C. Burmester, Supervisor of Truck Fleet W. Wilson Rinaman, Manager of Traffic Research Harold M. Finch, Manager of Distribution Services James A. Barber, Dept. Secretary Jean King, Supervisor of Distribution Services Christopher Thissen, Supervisor of Traffic A. Clyde Vollmers and Manager of Freight Rates Richard A. Chrz.

cost. In some weeks, Mr. Finch puts 70 to 80% of his time into strike-related tasks. On call 24 hours a day in crisis periods, he makes hour-by-hour changes in the game plan as conditions dictate, keeping affected plants constantly apprised.

Strike costs involve more than premium freight and extra effort. "One obvious, albeit expensive, antidote is building up inventories," observes Treasurer Elwood C. Alsaker. "When this is done, there is a secondary cost penalty that students of labor problems frequently overlook. Hawaiian stockpiling required terms of sale to be adjusted last year so that payments were averaging 60 days in lieu of a norm approximating 20 days, or 44 additional days before receipt of payment."

Product perishability alone makes claims a major factor. The whole transportation-distribution staff is virtually a claims prevention committee. Close materials handling control, careful packaging and unitization help to minimize claims, however.

A significant asset is the 18-month-old packaging committee, which meets whenever a problem arises. Members drawn from the transportation-distribution division, purchasing, production and sales organizations define requirements, submit them to suppliers through the purchasing department and review submissions developed thereafter to be certain they fulfill needs. Anyone concerned can request a committee meeting. Purchasing is the focal point for assembly.

In one instance, vendors supplied a carton in which one of them made slight changes that caused difficulties. The committee took three actions: (1) It tightened basic package specifications; (2) it went to product unitization, and (3) it specified Angleboard to protect the units.

Unitization and Angleboard play growing roles in Hormel shipping. Before Angleboard, 1970 grocery product damages alone ran $400,000. After applying Angleboard, a fiberboard formed similarly to angle iron,

to unit pack corners, an early two-month sample period showed a 35% damage reduction, making 50% savings appear likely as plants develop their expertise. Significantly, two plants not using Angleboard had a 63% increase in claims during the same two months. Tape (3M) banding from a hand dispenser holds An-

ON A REGULAR CHECK-OUT, the company plane receives a once-over from Chief Pilot G.L. Hovland (right) and Pilot L.T. Jensen.

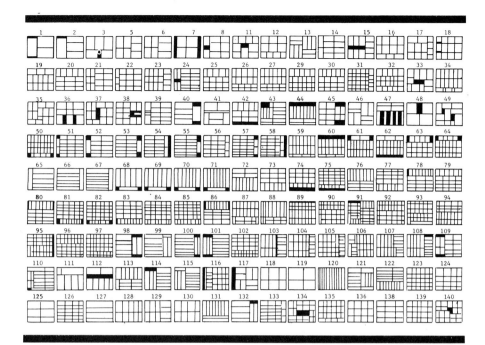

THIS PALLET PATTERN NUMBER GUIDE is included in a computer-prepared product listing (Palletizing Item List by Commodity Sequence), which stipulates recommended pallet configurations for all commodities, thus expediting unit loading.

FINAL PHASES of a distribution plant site selection study are discussed by (l. to r.): Manager of Distribution Services James C. Barber, Distribution Cost Analyst Lambert C. Burmester and Supervisor of Distribution Services Christopher Thissen.

gleboard in place with an absolute bond.

A palletized item list given the production staff, warehouse supervisors and sales staffs encourages unit load development and reduced labor costs. These computerized lists include a pallet pattern number applicable to each commodity which relates, in turn, to a chart showing specific loading patterns. These use not less than 80% of pallet surface, allowing three-inch overhang on a standard 48 by 40-inch GMA pallet. The list also permits sales people to figure gross and net weight on unitized loads.

In addition to palletization, slip sheets see extensive use for grocery products. The company is also currently running tests of possible shrink wrap applications.

Travel and Household Moves

The transportation-distribution division is charged with the scheduling and control of the company aircraft as well as the normal passenger travel reservation activities. The plane sees extensive use by sales and engineering personnel in particular, although other departments frequently employ it as well. While executives have some priority in its scheduling, it is basically a workhorse performing everyday chores for a company with a substantial share of "offline" points among its major plant locations.

"Our plane is a Beachcraft King Air," states Chief Pilot G.L. Hovland, "with essentially a seven-passenger configuration." The company has maintained a plane for 11 years, operating it generally within an 800-mile radius. For the limited priority

A MILWAUKEE TRACTOR spots a Seatrain container for rail movement to San Francisco and, ultimately, Honolulu. Manager-Traffic Research Harold Finch (left) and Milwaukee Road Freight Agent Edward Applebury observe the loading.

ANGLEBOARD protection of unitized loads minimizes palletized shipment claims, Hormel tests indicate.

OVER-THE-ROAD refrigerated trailers plus railroad piggyback units await loading at Hormel's Austin, Minn. trailer park.

travel beyond that distance, it has proven practical in large measure to use the plane for making connections with common carrier air lines, thus keeping the plane available for more intensive use within the region where most company facilities lie.

Flight plans generally base on any combination of five passengers for a round trip, although any division head can authorize a flight for even one person or an important package. Thus, if four prospective passengers are bound for Fort Dodge, where another wants to go to Austin, the quota of five exists, and the flight is scheduled. All reservations for the company plane are handled through Departmental Secretary Jean King.

Household goods moves, handled by the division, benefit from a fortunate regional circumstance. There are so many heavy computer movements out of plants at Minneapolis and Rochester requiring van service that many vans are available on regular schedules over long distances. Observes Traffic Supervisor Vollmers: "Some van lines have three or four regular East Coast runs a week, with service almost as good to some other population centers."

The bulk of the household goods moves are handled through two booking agents, with much of the activity emanating from a Fremont, Neb.-Fort Dodge, Ia.-Austin, Minn. triangle.

Substantial forward planning and research activities typify Hormel's approach company wide. **"It works well for us in product and market development," asserts President Holton. "Our experience suggests that it works similarly well in logistics."**

Containers augment trucks for better delivery service

COMPANY fleet operation has a long history at Hormel. With the exception of the Austin, Minn.-Fremont, Neb. interplant operation, one of the few true line-hauls, the service, however, is essentially delivery oriented. It consists largely of "country" runs, peddling to many accounts

INTERIOR of three containers on a 40-foot chassis, each with its separate refrigerating unit. Picture shows them open front and back for loading similarly to a regular trailer, with all three containers loading as a unit.

over an area on a schedule, plus comparable services within metropolitan regions.

Delivery activities assume an unusual character at three locations. Since July, 1959, virtually all of the distribution business within the Minneapolis area has been handled by reefer container units. Successful operation here led subsequently to partial containerization out of the Los Angeles plant as well as to a "country" container operation extending northward from Charlotte, N.C.

At Minneapolis, 10 local trucks equipped to carry the containers perform most deliveries. A trio of tractors and semitrailers shuffle containers for this service between the Austin plant and Hormel's transfer facility on the edge of Minneapolis. The Austin plant loads nine containers nightly for next day Minneapolis delivery, while nine others return daily from Minneapolis carrying inbound supplies.

Observes Director, Transportation-Distribution Robert A. Propf: **"The container program was seen as a need initially at Minneapolis due to the costly transfer situation plus a favorable back haul potential. The Minneapolis transfer point, therefore, is both a consolidation and a distribution center."**

A single 11½-foot container can handle 13,500 pounds legally when carried alone, but averages 12,000 pounds in service to avoid exceeding total allowable gross weight on a trailer when three units are carried. The trailers are equipped with collapsible mid-chassis "dock boards" which are hydraulically positioned to create a level floor between the mounted containers during loading operations at Austin. All of these containers have front and rear sliding doors so a three-container trailer may be loaded as a unit, much in the manner of a conventional "40-foot box." The specific container placed at the rear of the road trailer has a full-width back door so that in these particular units pallets may be readily fork-loaded.

So successful has the Minneapolis operation proven that when the time came for container replacement, the company purchased equipment of the same basic design. Johnson Truck

Bodies of Rice Lake, Wis. has supplied 22 containers within the past year for Hormel operations.

The Minneapolis group includes 12 11½-foot containers plus four larger 18-foot units, constructed essentially of fiberglass. The only metal is in the lights, door hardware and a floor of all-welded extruded aluminum. Insulation is polyurethane foam-in-place, with front and rear doors of molded fiberglass. The front door of each unit opens from the inside only. As the fiberglass is color impregnated, painting is never required.

"We maintain these containers at both Austin and Minneapolis," states Supervisor, Trucking Operations W. Wilson Rinaman. "Half of the units are 'owned' by Austin; the other half, by the Minneapolis plant, but both are expected to perform necessary maintenance chores indiscriminately as the need arises."

Reefer container units tank up with liquid nitrogen refrigerant for their individual Polarstream units at the Austin plant as needed.

Transfer between the road trailers and Minneapolis local delivery trucks is handled rapidly by a large forklift for the smaller containers. In shifting the larger containers, hydraulic equipment on the trucks and supporting, removable steel legs do the job. When the supporting legs are positioned, the road trailer is detached and driven from beneath the container so that the local delivery unit may then move under it, after which the container is locked in place; the legs are removed, and it is ready for its route.

The latter type of operation is also employed at Los Angeles. Here, a container trailer and six containers speed the local San Diego delivery operation from the Los Angeles plant.

In contrast to the Los Angeles and Minneapolis operations, the Charlotte container fleet covers a broad district in northern North Carolina-southern Virginia. In this instance, a single container trailer and six containers deliver loads to each of three locations about 50 to 80 miles apart daily. At each transfer point, the road trailer places its delivery for the day on legs and concurrently picks up the return container from the preceding schedule.

The container operation, in addition to its proven service economies, offers a product benefit as well. **"Reduced handling assures top shelf quality to our dealers,"** notes Vice President, Distribution Plants N.D. Gahagen.

These container services are lineal descendants of a successful rail car operation pioneered by Hormel some years ago. Additional similar operations are foreseen in the light of favorable service and cost experience at both Minneapolis and the newer container installations.

Belt-Bed Trailers

Unique, too, are the belt-bed trailer operations found at Austin. Each day, one such trailer picks up loads at the Owatonna Canning Company, 35 miles north of Austin, with considerable time and labor savings on both ends of each trip. At Owatonna, freight is fork-lifted to the trailer's rear, then moved forward on the floor belt using a plug-in electric drive controlled from the trailer rear. At the Austin warehouse, this freight is unloaded to a live roller conveyor leading into the warehouse for final movement by forklift to storage. The north-bound run hauls raw materials and supplies for the Owatonna Canning Co., which does Hormel business on a contractual basis. A second similar unit plies between the Austin plant and the canned goods warehouse.

Design, specification and purchase of equipment through competitive bids are the responsibility of Supervisor, Trucking Operations Rinaman. Though various equipment makes are used, Chevrolet and GMC currently account for the major share of the current fleet, primarily due to the highly satisfactory engine life with recent models.

A complete preventive maintenance program with very rigid standards maximizes vehicle life and utilization. A report comes in to Mr. Rinaman on every repair. Field locations must ask advice on any major overhauls so that "repair or replace" decisions may be made at headquarters. At 11 major Hormel locations, the company's own shops do the work. Austin, Fremont and

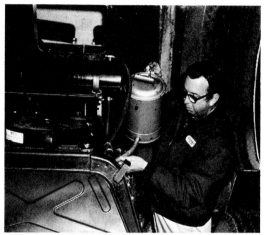

THIS CAB-OVER-ENGINE delivery unit, its cab tilted upward, is serviced between assignments at Hormel's garage-transfer point in Minneapolis, Minn.

AT AUSTIN CANNED GOODS WAREHOUSE, a power belt-bedded trailer stands ready to feed out its content to a powered platform conveyor, which feeds cargo into the building for subsequent forklift pickup. Powered equipment on trailer and dock greatly speed trailer turnaround, reducing labor costs and number of vehicles required for plant-warehouse shuttle service.

the Fort Dodge, Ia. shops maintain company-owned automobiles as well. "We foresee adding further shops where new plant facilities may be remote from adequate dealer services," notes Mr. Rinaman.

In general practice, company trucks are owned rather than leased. Leasing has been tried at several locations, and bids have been frequently solicited, but costs have not proved competitive with direct ownership. Observes Treasurer Elwood C. Alsaker: **"Because Hormel is a prime customer borrowing at the prime rate, ownership is preferable to leasing, not only on much of our rolling equipment but on facilities as well. There just isn't enough margin available for leasing companies to work on with us."**

Fleet operations in general are plant-based with the exception of Minneapolis, where the delivery fleet handles the previously described container service. There are also 25 trucks at a number of towns where one or two units are operated by the sales division.

Except for the few tractor-trailer units cited earlier, the fleet consists of two- and three-axle trucks. The two-axle units carry either 12- or 17-foot bodies, the latter being cab-over-engine units. The three-axle trucks carry 20- and 22-foot bodies, the latter preferable where palletized loads are carried.

Each plant location doing any warehouse deliveries has at least one truck set up for pallet handling with full-opening rear doors to permit forklift loading and unloading. All 20-foot trucks and any new trailers are being equipped with Type E Logistic Rail, an Aeroquip device, to permit subsequent double-decking of pallets when and if desired.

In fleet operations, as elsewhere in the division, computerization aids administrative activity. Its benefits to truck scheduling and maintenance programs are described in the following article.

Both owned and leased automobiles constitute a substantial Hormel fleet separate and apart from the trucking operation. "We have several hundred leased cars," comments Supervisor, Automotive Fleet Chester R. Hildreth, "divided between finance lease and full maintenance lease. These primarily serve our salesmen. In addition, we own about 165 cars operated by our livestock procurement people and carrying company identification."

Leasing, in the case of salesmen, proves practical due to the wide dispersion of such equipment. While salesmen generally drive leased cars, many at their own election use their personal vehicles on a car allowance of 10 cents per mile for the first 300 miles each week and four cents per mile beyond. In addition, the company provides public liability and property damage insurance. Leased cars can be used for unlimited personal operation based on a flat monthly charge to the individual plus a mileage fee. On company-owned cars, the employe can use the assigned vehicle for personal purposes within the home community.

Turnover of cars is carefully scheduled. Leased cars contractually are assigned for 24 months, but the division negotiates early renewal on extremely high mileage cars. For owned cars, the policy is to use them for four years or 60,000 miles. The cars are four-door sedans in the middle line of standard size "Big 3" cars. The cattle procurement cars operating over wide areas, plus a few other units, carry two-way radios as standard equipment. All cars have power steering, power brakes and automatic transmission, while air conditioning is provided on cars operated more than 500 miles per week.

Computerized equipment control

MODERN, even unusual, rolling stock handles much of Hormel's diversified traffic. The transportation-distribution division's several EDP administrative and operational procedures are similarly innovative. Already proving their worth, they offer a significant future asset through their capacity to absorb substantially greater work loads while creating minimal additional demand on division staff time.

Three areas benefit particularly from such computer procedures at present. These include:

Delivery routing: IBM's System

ZONE NUMBER	CUSTOMER NUMBER	QUANTITY 1ST SPEC.	STOP TIME HRS.	STOP TIME MINS.	CALLING LIMITS DAY	HOUR	DAY	HOUR	TYPE/CAPACITY RESTRICTIONS	REMARKS
1383	424743	100	0	8						
1317	422237	70	0	7						
1352	424169	120	0	8						
697	413846	50	0	7						
942	422864	70	0	7						
691	413...		0	9						
	413977	33		7						
850	414600	100	0	8	11.00	17.00				
694	413843	200	0	10						
1322	422248	24	0	6						

ROUTE SUMMARY

				DAY	HOUR
ASSIGNED VEHICLE TYPE	=	2	EARLIEST STARTING TIME =		8.19
VEHICLE CAPACITY	=	7000	LATEST STARTING TIME =		13.36
TOTAL LOAD	=	1481	MILEAGE BASED ON AVERAGE SPEED OF 30 MPH =		40.5 MILES
			TRAVEL TIME =		1 HRS. 21 MINS.
			ROUTE TIME =		3 HRS. 34 MINS.
			NUMBER OF DELIVERIES =		16

AT MINNEAPOLIS TRANSFER POINT, a large fork truck shifts 11 ½-foot containers, triple-mounted on a road trailer, to separate truck chassis for local delivery. Larger 18-foot units, as at left, are transferred by raising them on their own legs from road chassis with the local unit, then backing under, as here, to assume burden for local deliveries.

FLEET UTILIZATION SUMMARY   01/09/72

VEHICLE TYPE	CAPACITY 1ST SPEC.	MAX.VEH.TIME HRS.	MINS.	NO. OF VEHICLES	NO. OF TRIPS	ROUTE NUMBER	TOT.LOAD 1ST SPEC.	TOTAL MILES	TRAVEL TIME HRS.	MINS.	ROUTE TIME HRS.	MINS.	NO. OF DELS.
2	7000	8	0	1	4 *								
						1 **	2687	39.0	1	18	4	10	20
						2 **	3341	68.5	2	17	5	31	21
						3 **	4845	103.5	3	27	7	50	28
						4 **	1481	40.5	1	21	3	24	16
1	10000	10	0	9	0								
TOTALS	97000						12354	251.5	8	23	20	55	85

* MORE ROUTES THAN AVAILABLE VEHICLES
** ROUTE CONTAINS ONE OR MORE RESTRICTIONS
*** TIME ERROR

VSP COMPUTER OUPUT for each truck route is printed daily, much as the sample day's pattern for Los Angeles Route 4 shown above at top. In addition, the VSP computer program supplies a fleet utilization summary (above at bottom).

360 Vehicle Schedule Program (VSP), modified to fit specific local and/or company requirements, provides greater efficiency to individual delivery route scheduling while reducing dispatching effort.

Truck fleet control: EDP programs keep close check on individual vehicle mileage and maintenance history, permitting ready audit of specific conditions and creating a data file to aid in planning future truck acquisitions or replacements, as well as revisions of existing maintenance or operating procedures.

Rail car control: Computer control of mileage, rental charges and utilization for individual units assigned to each plant, reported monthly, yields necessary information for planning the most efficient employment of rolling stock.

While IBM's VSP program has been receiving increasing attention from a number of companies recently, Hormel has operated its Minneapolis delivery services successfully with VSP since 1969. Satisfaction with its performance in this pilot operation suggested the possibilities of further expansion. "We decided to tackle our largest delivery operation next," Director, Transportation-Distribution Robert A. Propf comments. "We felt that if it handled the job for Los Angeles, it would prove itself for use anywhere in the company." It did just that.

Operational since March, 1971, Los Angeles deliveries for a five-month period required 85 less loads—the equivalent of one extra truck daily—than would have been dispatched under prior manual procedures. The mileage reduction was estimated at 5,600 during this same time spell.

Once established, VSP becomes a pretty straightforward computer procedure. Computation and printout of the daily Minneapolis VSP schedules take normally but 15 minutes, while Los Angeles requires 22 minutes for average daily activity. The underlying stored computer data for each operation is in itself a model of the controlled distribution network. As such, these separate "packages" can serve for simulation should the division wish to pretest changes in the operations at Minneapolis or Los Angeles.

Success of both programs thus far led the division to recommend three additional locations for VSP. Ultimately, it is hoped to employ the program at all delivery fleet locations. Installation, however, is a complex task. It requires careful, painstaking assembly of geographic, customer and equipment data, which, in turn, must be processed through a network analysis program to build the basis for daily schedule development. Once this is completed, occasional revisions pose little difficulty, and day-to-day maintenance is simple.

Los Angeles offers a good case in point. Before VSP could be activated

THE VEHICLE ANALYSIS SYSTEM WORK SHEET shown above captures data for each individual maintenance event in a form that permits rapid, accurate key-punching for computer input and subsequent analysis.

DENVER DAILY (right), plant traffic manager, and Robert L. Brabbit, assistant plant traffic manager, check a recent update of the Minneapolis Vehicle Scheduling Program (VSP) map. Pins show numbered delivery zone locations and geographic reference points termed "nodes," which are generally major intersections.

there, Manager, Distribution Services James A. Barber and Supervisor, Trucking Operations W. Wilson Rinaman spent three solid months assembling necessary data for input to the computer at Austin.

What they did was develop customer locations, as well as distance relationships among them plus the plant location, on a large map. Individual isolated customers and groups of closely spaced ones were termed "zones" and were denoted by pre-numbered pins. Differently coded pins were placed to identify significant geographic reference points, usually major intersections, termed "nodes."

Every logical connection between each single such point (zone or node) and those adjacent was individually measured for computer input, these point-to-point measurements being called "links." Los Angeles required 6,000 such measurements. The computer, through the VSP Network Analysis Program, then combined links to develop distance measurements from each point to all others, expanding the 6,000-link input to over one million point-to-point measurements.

As might well be expected, a few illogical links representing erroneous or duplicated numbered pins showed up in the final stages of development. Assistant Controller Don J. Hodapp, informed of this problem late one day, developed a tracking program overnight in conjunction with Supervisor, Computer Analysis Vance C. Knutson. It cleared up all three problems the following day.

Manual recheck of the vast sea of four-digit numbers resulting from the initial computer test run would have been totally unfeasible. The tracking program, however, made short work of the noted three errors, identified an additional nine exceptions and provided an effective tool for future policing of additions or changes.

Orders for tomorrow delivery are coded and taped by NCR Add Punch machine at Los Angeles, then transmitted via Bell Dataphone to the Austin computer center by 6 p.m. daily. Processed against stored data reflecting not only geographic network data but also the equipment limitations, individual customer stipulations concerning delivery hours and other specialized conditions, printed truck loading schedules feed back to Los Angeles by teletype at 7 p.m. or earlier (Los Angeles time). Printout shows truck stop sequence and time at all points.

Significantly, the procedure employs conventional communications hardware, assuring dependability in this function and suggesting that VSP processing at the Austin center need know no geographic limitations

---

VEHICLE NUMBER: 04189
VEHICLE TYPE: TRUCK
ASSIGNED LOCATION: ▮▮▮▮▮

	MILEAGE	TONNAGE	ROAD FAILURES
CURRENT MONTH	2,894	202,974	1
YEAR TO DATE	96,320	2,413,813	10
LIFE TO DATE	96,320	2,413,813	10

DIRECT COSTS	CURRENT MONTH				YEAR TO	
	PARTS	LABOR	TOTAL	PER MILE	PARTS	LABOR
FUEL	126.01		126.01	.044	1,762.40	1
OIL	3.48		3.48	.001	41.22	
DIFFERENTIAL	3.65		3.65	.027	17.·· 58.47	59.10
ELECTRICAL	3.89	19.80	23.69	.008	62.45	281.60
CHASSIS & ACCES	17.06		17.06	.006	275.51	800.80
TIRES	112.14	33.00	145.14	.050	173.48	73.20
REFRIGERATION		52.80	52.80	.018	12.41	362.50
TOTAL DIRECT COSTS	298.62	496.10	794.72	.275	2,925.54	5,386.14

MOTOR TRUCK EXPENSE ANALYSIS

LOCATION

TRUCK NO	MILEAGE		TONNAGE	FUEL	MPG	OIL
	PERIOD	YTD	PERIOD	PERIOD	YTD	PERIOD
CMR7X	0	0	0	0.0	0.0	0.0
00007	3,041	8,681	249,790	0.0	4.6	0.0
03510	1,638	3,404	113,108	263.0	6.3	2.0
03728	1,382	2,901	90,834	275.0	5.4	1.0
03807	1,648	3,027	125,035	278.0	6.0	10.0
03893	1,793	4,476	115.760	289.0	6.4	10.0
03895	998			198.0	5.2	1.
	1,365		991,273	272.0	5.5	1.
		5,691	111,592	20...	5.3	3.
04256		7,705	176,650	506.6	5.7	16.
04259	1,574	7,832	17,999	513.6	7.1	15.
04289	1,654	3,872	98,480	238.0	6.4	14.
04290	3,477	7,441	131,090	542.0	5.2	17.
04291	3,041	8,681	76,810	582.0	6.5	46.
04308	1,904	4,430	721,332	217.7	6.8	9.
TOTAL	46,881	102,816	3,836,048	8,492.0	5.8	197.

COMPUTER-PRODUCED Vehicle Expense Analysis reports, published monthly for each vehicle, as in above samples at top, keep close tabs on individual truck performance. The computer also develops fleet reports by location (above at bottom), al-

---

in accepting other new area programs about the country.

Another effective computer program keeps a watchful eye on truck operating costs. An accompanying illustration shows the vehicle analysis system work sheet, the source document for this procedure. Laid out to facilitate accurate key-punching, the form records data concerning all phases of maintenance and operating costs. It becomes a source for computer-prepared vehicle expense analysis reports on each individual truck, as well as for the summary by fleet entitled "motor truck expense analysis."

Through these statements, the division keeps close tabs on individual unit performance as well as any unique conditions, either good or bad, that may arise among individual company fleets at specific locations. Comparative analysis of performance among differing unit makes or models, for example, is facilitated by such information.

Similarly valuable is the division's computerized car control procedure governing rail equipment. Input data for this system is developed from bills of lading and from car movement reports initiated at the affected plants. Distribution Cost Analyst

EL MILES PER GAL	QUARTS	CIL MILES PER QUAR
6.3	12	241.2
15.2	141	683.1
15.2	141	683.1

MILE PARTS	LIFE TO DATE LABOR	TOTAL	PER MIL
1,762.40		1,762.40	.018
41.22		41.22	
		824.54	.009
62.45	281.60	344.0?	
275.51	800.80	1,076.31	.011
173.48	73.20	246.68	.003
12.41	362.50	374.91	.004
2,925.54	5,386.14	8,311.68	.086

/08/72   09:00AM   Page 4

MPQ YTD	ROAD FAILURES	TOTAL COSTS PERIOD	PER MILE YTD
0.0	0	0.00	0.00
0.0	1	0.10	0.06
83.6	0	0.05	0.06
63.7	1	0.24	0.22
75.1	0	0.19	0.22
79.7	0	0.10	0.10
71.5	0	0.10	0.13
59.2	0	0.16	0.10
	1	0.?	
33.4	0	0.06	0.25
70.0	0	0.08	0.07
03.7	0	0.08	0.11
25.4	0	0.13	0.13
87.6	1	0.15	0.14
66.8	3	0.06	0.11
73.3	9	0.10	0.11

ASSISTANT CONTROLLER Don J. Hodapp (left) checks computer output of a Hormel Co. transportation program with Manager of Distribution Services James A. Barber (center) and Supervisor of Computer Analysis Vance C. Knutson.

lowing comparison of local conditions and a quick check on efficacy of changes in practices.

Lambert C. Burmester, who controls this activity, was formerly transportation manager at the Fremont, Neb. plant prior to November, 1970, so he benefits from field experience with rail car operations.

"I use the system reports to check on payments made to car companies as well as for overall cost analysis," Mr. Burmester notes. **"The program is particularly helpful in analyzing the efficiency of car utilization by individual plants, while providing a sound measurement of the cost merits of differing equipment types or makes."**

A monthly utilization report by plant shows rental charges by car type, car company or railroad. It also shows average turnaround by car type and degree of utilization during the reporting period and year to date. Individual car reports, also issued monthly, show the whereabouts of each unit on the last work day of the reporting month, car assignment and related detail.

Adding the computerized palletization procedures and the simulation techniques used in the recent site selection study, both described earlier in this issue, to the above-mentioned programs creates an impressive roster. The individual programs, effective for their present tasks and increasingly valuable sources of historical data for research and planning, suggest still further possibilities through combinations or comparisons of their data content. They put effective muscle behind Hormel's increasingly vital logistics activities.

Advanced Logistics:
Steelcase's Total Commitment

The Steelcase Company of Grand Rapids, Mich. operates an extremely comprehensive computerized management system. Distribution as well as many other functions benefits from a substantial investment in computer hardware and ancillary equipment. Routing guides, order processing, shipment scheduling and many other aspects of logistics activity are embraced by a management information system that tracks every individual order from its inception through manufacture of order components to final delivery.

Because of this comprehensive treatment, it is possible at any time to determine status of any order component instantly. Aiding this and other chores are cathode ray tube communication units found in several departments. Tied directly into the computer, a query through such a unit's keyboard will cause the computer to feed back immediately a display of the requisite data on the tube face. Corrections or additions to computer-stored data also flow through these units, at once speeding and simplifying the updating of stored information.

Described in TRAFFIC MANAGEMENT's December, 1969 issue, a detailed account of these and other distribution activities at Steelcase follows:

BUSINESS IS GOOD at Steelcase. Annual sales of this Grand Rapids, Mich.-based firm, the nation's largest manufacturer of steel office equipment, currently exceed $100 million.

Continuous plant expansion, equipment modernization and administrative refinement characterize this company's progress. All departments work closely in developing unified operating systems that integrate activities from raw material purchase to dealer deliveries. The traffic and shipping departments, working in harmony with marketing, manufacturing and computer functions, move steadily to keep ahead of growing customer demand. Currently, three important areas capture their particular attention:

Electronic data processing: New cathode ray tube (CRT) units and optical character recognition (OCR) equipment speed distribution data in and out of two IBM 360-40 computers with high data storage capacities.

Materials handling automation: Tow lines, conveyor installations and automated sorting systems speed order preparation in the shipping department's 320,000-foot Grand Rapids facility.

Private trucking: While three-quarters of the shipments move in common carriage, private fleet size has been steadily expanding. With packaging costs and carrier charges moving ever higher while competitive circumstances make better service increasingly imperative, Steelcase trucks fulfill a steadily widening role.

The company splits physical distribution duties between two units. Traffic and Distribution Manager Phillip T. Catalano's department runs the essentially staff activities, such as rating, routing, claims, carrier relations and related matters. Shipping Manager Rolland J. Varner operates the physical facilities, including a highly mechanized warehouse, packaging, a large private truck fleet and necessary supporting activities. Both men report to Vice President-Manufacturing Frank H. Merlotti. The question of marketing vs. manufacturing orientation does not apply, however. "In all of our departments," comments Mr. Merlotti, "Steelcase people are market-oriented."

Divided physical distribution responsibility pays off in progressing advanced programs. Both managers can concentrate full attention upon their essentially dissimilar specialties, joining forces whenever it becomes advantageous to a specific program. In the ensuing pages, we review some of these activities.

Large-scale computerization speeds traffic flow

MOST COMPANIES approach computer systems expansion step by step. They nibble a little at first, then gradually increase the work load as management finds its confidence growing. Steelcase took a different route. Backed up by $2 million worth of IBM hardware, the company expanded its management compu-

The mechanized Steelcase shipping facility includes a 22-spur conveyor sortation system, controlled by an Edon analog memory unit. Cartons are sorted and spotted automatically by the operator in foreground. ▶

Two high-capacity IBM 360 computers put the punch into automated systems for distribution and other functions. Disc storage (above) feeds data to the unit.

terization commitments heavily in 1968, bringing massive systems changes to many departments. Distribution and distribution-related activities were particularly affected.

Steelcase's "Project Scope" (Steelcase Coordinated Operating Plan for Efficiency) program is building a complete computer-oriented management information system. Distribution's role in it is a big one. Phillip T. Catalano, manager, traffic and distribution, devoted 70% of his time to this effort from March 1 to Dec. 31, 1968. Teaming with Supervisor of Systems Frederick H. Monson, Jr., he shared in program developments destined to reorient much routine department activity while at the same time providing a needed data base for distribution forward planning. A nine-system package, "Project 11" within the Project Scope program, resulted from this work, and spring of 1969 found the new methods phasing into action.

How will this affect the traffic department? In Mr. Catalano's opinion: "Project Scope

will reduce our need for additional help during the next four years despite predicted company expansion. At the same time, it will convert a fine clerical staff into a superior analytical group as we build our data base for research and forward planning. We will create an improved forecasting capability based on cost and sales trend data that until now was available only through expensive, tedious manual review and less certain statistical sampling techniques."

Just what specific ingredients make the Project 11 mix? Several programs now at work or under development encompass diversified traffic and shipping activities. These include:

Traffic routing system. Customer routes are computer-stored, with direct on-line access for supplementation, correction or revision by traffic personnel.

Purchased parts pickup system. Coordinating outbound private truck dispatch with inbound raw materials pickup, this computer procedure can capture more return loads faster than manual methods, increasing fleet efficiency.

Shipping unit development and balancing system. Separate orders bound for common destination points are grouped in shipping units that assure their production schedule coordination to develop ultimate shipping pools or consolidations after manufacture.

Volume measurement system. Measures each product in terms of both cube and proportion of vehicle that a product unit represents, such as fraction of carload or truckload, simplifying consolidations and shipment scheduling.

Stripped orders in process system. Reports this program generates will go to the shipping department three days before individual shipping units are scheduled for completion, showing full status of each order and indicating the completion state of all components, thus giving the shipping department ample notice for properly scheduling common and private carriage.

Shipping document and planning system. Destined to automate bill of lading preparation based upon existing order entry and sales information computer files, this procedure is also a basis for transportation-distribution planning.

Traffic-shipping load pattern analysis. From data generated in other programs, this procedure analyzes geographic delivery patterns to assist in common and private carrier route selection and development.

Freight damage and miscellaneous cost system. More than just a claims summary, this system's reports compare damage performance among carriers on the basis of frequency, shipment volume, revenues of carriers and carrier claims payment performance.

Computerization Speeds Routing

Project 11's heart is the computer routing system. "Total order processing time drops between two and eight hours on each order, depending upon time of receipt," Mr. Monson states. "This gain includes reduced time lag in paper movement as well as reduced clerical hours."

Part of Steelcase's routing went into the computer some time ago. This earlier procedure offered a single preferred routing for "sold-to" customers only. The newer system offers not only routing choices, but covers both "ship-to" and "sold-to" destinations. The "ship-to" and "sold-to" categories recognize that a customer billing address may differ from the specified delivery address.

In the spring of 1969, this initial computer routing program reached its peak, with 80% of customers so routed. Today, a broad-span approach encompassing the order department and other company elements finds all orders computerized, including exceptions, rush orders and other special situations.

Cathode ray tube (CRT) direct access provides the key. A Sanders 720 CRT unit in the traffic department ties directly to an IBM 360-40 computer, permitting instantaneous inquiry and response plus immediate update of stored routing information which the traffic department wants to change.

Following the concept's formulation by Messrs. Monson and Catalano, Mrs. Ruth A. Rich, traffic assistant-rates and routes, shared in the project's development. After learning required operating procedures, and developing master routing files for computer memory storage, Mrs. Rich trained her associates in the new procedures. As a result, when the CRT went "on line" in the spring, transition moved smoothly and departmental efficiency rose promptly.

Under the new system, postal zip codes identify destinations. Computer disc storage maintains "ship-to" and "sold-to" address data, related zip codes and traffic department-supplied routings to current accounts, covering varied shipment size ranges and alternative carriers.

Automated Routing for New Customers

What about new customers? When the order department enters an order for an unregistered "ship-to" address, the computer promptly tests stored data for existing routes to other customers sharing the same zip code. Quite commonly, one is found and applied, the new customer then being added to the stored route file, subject to traffic department audit.

When the computer finds no route, it holds this information for print-out in frequent summaries that go to the traffic department. At this juncture, traffic personnel take over, selecting applicable routings and feeding them back via CRT to computer storage. Each time a new destination goes into storage, the zip-coded data bank increases its

Cathode ray tube displays a customer order retrieved from computer storage by Mrs. Ruth A. Rich, traffic assistant-rates and routing, seated at console. Manager-Traffic and Distribution Phillip T. Catalano (left) and David C. Wittenbach, traffic assistant-administrative, compare with initial order data.

ability to route other new customers without calling on the traffic department.

The CRT offers unparalleled data entry speed and accuracy. More common "off-line" procedures require the writing of data for transfer to the electronic data processing section. At the latter, it must be keypunched to cards or tape and then fed to the computer. At every stage, error possibilities arise and multiply.

Not so with CRT. A router, after determining carriers required and any limiting conditions, enters the information through the CRT unit directly to computer storage, receiving visual confirmation of his exact entry on the cathode ray tube's face. Any errors noted can be "erased" at once and corrected through the CRT keyboard.

This also means instantaneous update of all other stored routing data. A needed carrier change takes place immediately. There is no time lag whatever, once the decision is made, because new routings become effective the moment they enter the keyboard. Time once spent on filling out forms or passing paper now goes to true research effort, speeding new ideas into action and simplify-

ing strategy revisions when rate, service or commodity changes make them necessary.

Speeding Customer Information Via CRT

The CRT unit is not restricted solely to routing functions. Probably one of its most effective gains lies in the rapid processing of customer requests for shipment information. "The typical case is a customer who telephones us for a shipping date, but has no Steelcase identification number for his order," notes Mrs. Rich. "Under manual procedures, this meant somebody had to search files in the order department, guided only by the customer's order number. Since the files follow the assigned Steelcase number sequence, this typically meant up to an hour's search. In some cases, it also meant even more time expended, only to find that the form was not there. CRT, on the other hand, can accept the customer order number and locate the proper order in computer storage immediately, displaying it in full (less detail line items) on the tube face. This means much in faster customer service. At the same time, it saves the department about a dozen hours of clerical time daily for other work."

Instant report of assigned shipping dates is but one of several kinds of information available in this way. The CRT expedites tracing following actual shipment by making available data reported from the shipping department. Once the goods move, the unit can display all prior order information plus the bill of lading number, pieces shipped, carrier or carriers used and shipped-to/sold-to address information.

"Our ability to make routing changes up to the last minute is also significant," claims Mr. Catalano. "While computer-assigned routings go on customer order early in its processing, we can catch the order at any point up to final shipping stage and reroute. A customer with an emergency can call us for a change in his shipment's destination or a switch to priority transportation, and thanks to CRT, we can make either or both changes at once, letting him know the action taken while he's still on the line."

Forward Look at Computerized Traffic

Claims, as yet under manual control, will soon enjoy computer efficiency also. "Given frequent detailed reports on damaged shipments, their location and the modes involved, we can speed our reaction time in identifying and eliminating the causes," notes Traffic Assistant-Administrative David C. Wittenbach. While the new program looks particularly at the several railroads plus 19 prime motor carriers regularly serving Steelcase, it can similarly reveal any damage patterns developing under private truck operation. This is expected to prove helpful not only in spotting individual, specialized problems, but in selecting or developing future equipment as well.

Looking further ahead, Manager-Traffic and Distribution Catalano foresees several worthwhile added applications. Data already at hand will permit a growing amount of computer simulation, while a growing data base will lend itself to other management science techniques such as linear programing and PERT (Program Evaluation and Review Technique).

"We've already employed PERT manually," observes Mr. Catalano, "charting projects by hand to decide on a proper sequenc-ing of activities and to forecast phase completion dates. Our new tools will make it easier to tackle some of the bigger jobs and to speed the smaller ones through appropriate operations research techniques."

An immediate possibility is freight cost comparison. Faced with a rate increase, the CRT can interrogate the computer and in relatively short order the department can learn the effect on specific destinations as well as alternative costs if modes are switched. On a more positive note, it also speeds cost studies when reductions, commodity rates or other favorable arrangements come under consideration.

Total distribution control characterizes company policy. Steel, for example, a major input, arrives in 10-ton coils instead of cut, flat sheet. Formerly purchased in the latter form, the company installed an automatic conversion line, cutting and flattening its own sheets. The trade-off among purchase prices, freight costs and material handling techniques resulted in savings that earned back the conversion line cost within two years.

While substantial outbound volume moves carload or truckload, much of this freight represents pooling and consolidation. Fully two-thirds of rail carloads are pools, while eight motor carriers leave trucks daily for next morning pickup on loads of 7,000 pounds of LTL and over. The company runs truck consolidations regularly on Iowa-Nebraska distribution and employs stop-off privileges heavily on both rail and truck shipments.

As the company expands, the Steelcase traffic department maintains parallel capacity increase. In 1959, Mr. Catalano's staff consisted solely of Mrs. Rich, whose heavy carrier traffic experience subsequently proved beneficial in training newcomers. Departmental expansion commenced in 1961, and in the spring of 1969, personnel numbered eight.

In-house training and internal promotion are strong company policy, which this unit practices steadily. Traffic people know each other's jobs, and new programs, such as the CRT operation, come to their attention well in advance of activation. Comments Mr. Catalano: "Every department member recognizes in the CRT-computer installation a vital new support for personal professional growth."

What CRT brings to traffic

The accompanying diagram outlines information flow between the traffic department's cathode ray tube (CRT) and the IBM 360-40 computer system at Steelcase. Arrows indicate the direction of data flow, while the shaded area at lower right encompasses three cylinders symbolizing disc storage electronic data files. Customer order information, also on discs, constitutes the remaining direct data input segment.

In addition to direct inquiry from the CRT by wire ("on-line"), "off-line" requests can be made by feeding properly keypunched cards to the computer for development of printed reports or summaries, as shown by broken-line figures at left.

While we've discussed many CRT functions in the accompanying story, a check of the specific data it can produce may suggest still further potentialities.

On demand, the CRT will display a specific customer order, including bill of lading number, shipping date (actual), scheduled shipping date, traffic route, ship-to and/or sold-to address(es) and shipping condition. If the shipment has not yet moved, traffic personnel can make changes in an order's traffic instructions directly, instantly, via CRT. There is also a capability for off-line selected data retrieval for analysis purposes, yielding printed summaries in the computer room of material too voluminous for CRT transfer or where lasting record for study is needed.

The CRT, on request, draws sold-to/ship-to data from disc storage, displaying standard traffic routes for an account, any routing constraints and linking to: All possible routes to a destination (zip file) and description and constraints of carriers. Through CRT, traffic personnel can change, add or delete traffic data in the sold-to/ship-to disc storage file. As with customer orders, capability exists for data search and off-line retrieval for analytical purposes.

From the zip destination (routes) file, CRT can display shipping points via zip code search key, including all possible routes, modes and alternatives to each point. Up to 36 possible routes may be provided for each area. The file encompasses some 4,000 shipping points. As in the other categories, direct data revisions may be made by traffic per-

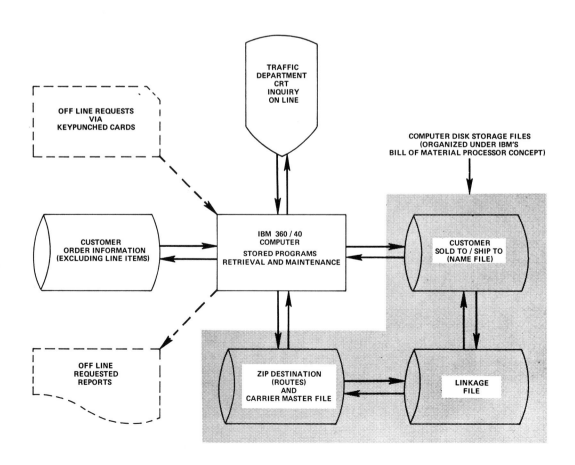

sonnel. CRT can search, with selected zip codes, for all carriers involved with a specific destination, all ship-to customers and all relevant orders currently in the Grand Rapids plant, responding directly on the tube face or off-line in a printed summary. The system's off-line capability permits cost analysis on tariff changes within given zip code areas, measuring in conjunction with sales history and customer order file data in disc storage.

The carrier master file, like the others, is subject to direct CRT changes, additions or deletions, based on an augmented National Motor Freight Classification four-digit alphabetic code, which includes all Steelcase carriers. Both CRT (on-line) and printed report (off-line) responses can indicate carriers serving one or many cities/areas. Off-line capabilities include determination of customers affected by carrier/rail mergers, tariff increases, carriers going out of business and related matters. Both off-line and on-line capability exists to massively change carriers on existing orders and any incoming business.

Department publications help employees and customers

Strongly communications-oriented, the Steelcase traffic department issues two booklets that make policies clear while offering sound advice for consignees and for company personnel changing their locations.

"Steelcase Shipping Data" tells customers what its traffic department practices are in making shipments to them, advising how best to handle problems that arise and soliciting their cooperation in solving mutual problems. Obviously, no two shippers are alike in their customer relations and shipping practices, but the 10 points stressed by Steelcase suggest a good guide for other traffic managers in developing comparable customer service manuals:

1. Shipments received in damaged condition.
2. Damage discovered after receipt of shipment.
3. Filing a claim for loss or damage.
4. Freight overcharge claims.
5. How to file an overcharge·claim.

6. To trace or expedite freight shipments.
7. If a shipment is received with a shortage or overage.
8. If transportation company's service is unsatisfactory.
9. Steelcase truck deliveries.
10. Return of merchandise.

Under each heading, the text covers points in simple outline form occupying six pages, accompanied by two pages of illustrations. "When traffic people find themselves frequently repeating the same information to customers by telephone or by mail, it's a good indicator that a pamphlet or bulletin can do a job for you," Mr. Catalano notes.

The seven-page text of "Policy Guidelines for Household Moves of Steelcase Employees" similarly fulfills a recurring information need. Some of its topics include:
—The traffic department's handling arrangements for personnel moves.
—Timing your move.
—What expenses will the company pay for?
—Some expenses not covered by the company.
—Unpacking your goods in your new home.
—Damages, lost articles, claim procedures.
—General information and moving check list.
—Important tax information about moving expenses.

While this booklet, like its companion consignee publication, reflects one company's special approach, there are several excellent guidelines available for traffic managers seeking to develop company manuals of their own. Published by leading van lines, they are readily available on request to those interested. These include the following:

• "Making the Right Move" (Marketing Dept., Allied Van Lines, Inc., P.O. Box 4403, Chicago, Ill. 60680)
• Series of Sample Suggested Policies (Marketing Services Dept., Greyhound Van Lines, Inc., 13 East Lake St., Northlake, Ill. 60164)
• "A Moving Policy Guide for Traffic Managers" (Advertising Mgr., North American Van Lines, P.O. Box 988, Fort Wayne, Ind. 46801)
• "Corporate Personnel Tansfer Poli-

cies 1968" (Advertising Dept., United Van Lines, Inc., 1 United Drive, Fenton, Mo.)

- "Personnel Moving With Management Control" (Bekins Moving & Storage, 1335 So. Figueroa St., Los Angeles, Calif. 90015)

- "Corporate Moving Policy Manual" (Jack Thorne, Atlas Van-Lines, P. O. Box 509, Evansville, Ind.)

Other publications can be obtained from the following:

William E. McCrain, Neptune World Wide Moving, 55 Weyman, Ave., New Rochelle, N. Y. 10805.

Aero Mayflower Transit Co. 863 Massachusetts Ave., Indianapolis, Ind. 46204.

How automation speeds handling

STOCK MOVES FAST at the Steelcase warehouse in Grand Rapids. The 320,000- square foot shipping facility stocks only about 10% of the most common company products, moving all other goods through within three days of receipt from the plant. Handling well over 40,000 pieces per week, 1968 saw some 2,400 boxcars and nearly 5,000 trailer loads clear through the company's loading docks.

Representing production from the existing 1,356,000-square foot plant, these shipments reach the docks through a materials handling system that employs considerable automation and mechanization, including:

Automated conveyor lines. Each of three main product lines enters the shipping area from the plant via automated conveyor equipment which extends through packaging facilities prior to final sort.

Automated sorting. A Rapistan sort system controlled by an Edon analog memory unit places goods on separate conveyor branch spurs for each individual carrier.

Underfloor tow lines. Two separate drag lines move floor trucks from the sorting system to truck and rail loading facilities.

Goods emerge from the plant labeled to move on a specific order save for the small portion consigned to stock. The computer-prepared labels stipulate full data covering the shipments affected, except for warehouse row location, bill of lading number and actual shipping date. The conveyor systems move goods directly to packaging stations, where each unit is packed to assure proper protection, helping to maintain Steelcase's low-for-this-industry damage rate of only ½%.

Packed goods again move by conveyor to the sorting operation. At this location, 22 conveyor spurs spread finished cartons in groupings by carrier. An Edon analog memory unit controls this operation, its operator choosing the appropriate conveyor spur for each case as it passes his position by depressing the spur numbers on the sorting keyboard. By entering a "19" as a carton passes him, he alerts sensing equipment that spots the affected container at the head of spur number 19 and operates electro-mechanical equipment diverting it into this spur.

Freight gathered in the spur conveyors next moves on carts over one of two underfloor tow lines. These two systems, which include 52 spurs for cart loading and unloading, feed rail and truck loading facilities separately as well as the storage areas. Rail tracks within the building can handle 14 cars, while 27 shipping doors at the facility's opposite end service trucks entering the fully enclosed dock.

Final loading of rail cars or trucks calls for completing transmittal slips which provide a quick update method for the central computer installation. These slips constitute a notice of loading, indicating shipping date and bill of lading number. Forwarded to the computer room, optical character recognition (OCR) equipment feeds the information directly to the computer, which promptly updates its stored order data and provides a basis for notifying customers that their shipments have moved.

Cathode ray tube equipment, installed earlier in the traffic and order processing departments, recently came to the shipping department as well. It provides a direct, instantaneous check of order data in the computer, simplifying decisions as to direct versus consolidated shipment of individual orders and alerting shipping personnel when an ahead-of-schedule production lot requires earlier documentation than initially anticipated.

Packaging is an important shipping department function. Corrugated material costs run close to $1.5 million each year. Crating and other materials build this figure to still higher levels. "We certainly prefer purchasing quality materials to facing losses

While goods arrive from the plant on conveyor lines, sorted cartons move to storage and shipping locations on floor trucks moved by underfloor tow lines.

Shipping Foreman Albertus Hooyer and Shipping Manager Rolland J. Varner discuss new handling equipment.

At the outbound Steelcase dock, a piggyback trailer awaits its load, fully protected from the weather.

Packaging, like most shipping and traffic operations, enjoys automation's greater speed and reduced labor.

and damages that would come with cheaper packing," observes Packaging Engineer Kenneth H. Brown. "We also want to keep customers happy with the reliable deliveries proper packaging assures. Damaged goods mean more than just replacement costs—they can mean sales losses or diversion at the dealer level as well."

Package design is a continuous activity at Steelcase. Upgrading packaging for present lines and developing new packs for new models and special orders makes this necessary. Substantial testing moves forward at a

vendor laboratory in Grand Rapids, with designs checked not just to meet, but to surpass the standards set by the National Safe Transit Committee.

"Our Steelcase fleet does the greater share of package testing for us," Shipping Manager Varner notes. "We can incorporate test pieces in regular loads or make special moves where necessary, simulating conditions that our packaging engineer is trying to counteract through specific pack patterns."

A growing factor in Steelcase shipping lies in uncrated movements. "At this time," Administrative Assistant-Shipping Neil Ezinga states, "roughly 40% of all shipments move uncrated and blanket-wrapped. We expect this figure to continue growing." Making it possible are the private fleet operation, the specialized services of five Grand Rapids-based furniture carriers, damage-free rail cars with protective equipment and over-the-road trailers with similar protection. In the case of railroad equipment, Manager-Traffic and Distribution Catalano has arranged with the Burlington, Northern Pacific, Santa Fe, Great Northern, Cotton Belt and M-K-T railroads to supply 40-foot DFB cars plus some 60-footers exclusively for Steelcase use.

The company's shipping facility handles its heavy duties smoothly, but it is gearing up for further challenges. Soon to open is a new plant addition of 800,000 square feet directly across the tracks from the exisitng complex. When completed, conveyor lines will feed into the shipping area over a high-level, enclosed bridge. Ultimately, three separate conveyors will be installed in this link. "We look forward to it," General Shipping Foreman Albertus Hooyer says. "Our present handling equipment has ample capacity and flexibility for absorbing the new plant's added burden. In this company, absorbing growth is practically a habit."

Company fleet serves widening market

PRIVATE TRUCKING started at Steelcase over 20 years ago. Until the early 1950s, the operation was small, with services covered by two tractors and four trailers. Since that time, increased needs for fast service and growing savings possibilities in the face of rate hikes made expansion attractive.

Today's operation finds 15 tractors and 27 trailers handling over 25% of the company's outbound tonnage and 50% of inbound vendor freight other than steel. Outbound service needs and increasing freight rates spurred private trucking's growth, but inbound tonnage built the savings potential that made it economical.

Truck operation comes under the shipping department, while traffic cost analysis and route selection are traffic department activities. Careful studies precede the setting-up of new destinations, and every trip is checked against comparable private carriage to determine savings or loss against prevailing tariff charges. A typical sample trip sheet accompanies this article, showing calculations of savings for both goods delivered to customer and supplies brought back to Grand Rapids. In February, 1969, 53% of private truck savings developed on the return legs of runs.

During earlier years, private trucking stayed fairly close to home, making deliveries on a catch-as-catch-can basis within 200 miles of Grand Rapids and handling a minimum of back hauls. Today's normal radius is about 400 miles, but with some runs reaching 1,000 miles. This greater area, while not affecting the Los Angeles plant, does put the Steelcase Toronto facility within reach, further broadening load possibilities.

Recent years also saw the introduction of scheduled deliveries for many dealer destinations. Actual routings remain flexible, but major cities receive service no less than once weekly, while some have a minimum of twice weekly service or better. Effective stop-off scheduling helps to maximize these delivery frequencies. By combining partial truckloads instead of holding trailers for full loads to single cities, affected points see Steelcase trucks more often, to the benefit of the dealers concerned. Since this service aids the dealers in holding down their inventories, frequent service gives a competitive edge wherever Steelcase private truck service can be practically provided.

It is in the return load operation, however, that the traffic department finds unique and varied benefits. Working closely with the purchasing department, the traffic department makes it possible to generate better prices where goods will move F.O.B. vendor's dock in Steelcase trucks. At the least, such planning can mean reduced transportation costs and quicker deliveries, which in turn lead to inventory savings.

The shipping department handles return loads on a dual-priority basis. Drivers going out with loads for dealers get vendor lists where they can pick up if they have space available when they return. They may also be assigned specific pickups which they must make, thus protecting any rush material on order. With schedules set up only for destination points rather than for specific highway routes, the drivers pretty well blanket

Adjacent to 27 shipping doors serving outbound Steelcase freight, ample storage space serves a constantly shifting fleet of common carrier and company trailers.

vendors within a 400-mile radius during a typical weekly operating cycle.

Steelcase owns and maintains its entire vehicle fleet. The power includes 14 over-the-road tractors and one city unit, the latter doing local work at Grand Rapids as well as spotting or shifting trailers at the shipping docks. As older road units are retired, the company replaces them with new sleeper cabs. Those purchased to date have proven themselves by increasing delivery speed and total mileage in recent years.

All 27 trailers are standard high cube, volume furniture vans. These 40-footers measure 474 inches inside length, 92 inches in width and 96 inches in height, offering a 2,432-cubic foot capacity. Chosen with the proper protection of furniture and lowest operating costs in mind, their capacity suits them well for the return load function at the same time.

A Grand Rapids-Toronto interplant service keeps two tractor-trailer sets busy constantly. Handling varied cargoes, they make

feasible an in-house container operation, reducing packaging costs and speeding the physical handling of numerous parts. The containers are steel tubs that can carry a wide variety of parts, lending themselves to varied materials handling techniques.

Looking back at the private truck operation's history gives a good clue to what lies in its future. The fleet size doubled in the last five years. Messrs. Varner and Catalano are in agreement that expansion will continue.

The traffic department foresees no break in the rising common carrier rate spiral. The shipping department anticipates increasing packaging costs. These two forces, working steadily in unison, continually build more leverage for private carriage. In consequence, private trucking, which had been growing roughly in proportion to company sales, has taken on a greater momentum. At present handling 25% to 28% of outbound shipments, this proportion is clearly destined for expansion.

Management Science Sharpens Canadian Distribution

Canadian Canners Limited faced a number of significant distribution choices in its operations a few years ago. Partially because of acquisitions, partly through continuing expansion of the Canadian market, the company found itself outstripping the capacities of its existing distribution warehouses.

Canadian Canners turned to a proven operations research technique in reorienting its warehousing. IBM's stock program for the simplex method of linear programming, revised to fit the circumstances, took the measure of existing capability and provided a ready means for mathematically testing the potential alternatives.

Since that time, the program package has served regularly to program warehouse utilization and determine sourcing for the widespread market areas that the company supplies within Canada.

These and other aspects of Canadian Canners logistics efforts, as reported in the October, 1968 issue of TRAFFIC MANAGEMENT, follow:

GROWING PAINS are an accepted, almost welcome, phase of daily living for Canadian Canners Limited. This Hamilton, Ont.-based Del Monte Corporation subsidiary grossed $53 million in 1968, up 23% in four years. These increasing sales suggest heavy demands on distribution, with sweeping production changes causing further complications in a highly competitive market.

With business climbing steadily, modernization dictated the consolidation of several company facilities, creating many storage problems. Where 48 plants supplied Canadian Canners' market in 1957, only 15 production facilities handled a bigger job in 1964. Today a still greater burden falls on 11 modern plants.

Since 1964, the firm has developed a strong physical distribution function. The new department provides full logistic support to the total company effort, keeping inbound materials costs and services under full control—storing and shipping a wide variety of finished goods in a manner maximizing customer service, yet holding down costs to keep prices competitive nationwide. In a country of Canada's extreme breadth, the latter becomes a major challenge.

Both planning and operation find the distribution department liberally employing computerized procedures and sophisticated but proven systems technology. To cite a few instances:

- Linear programing. Storage space control and transportation cost comparison get frequent, comprehensive review through this computer technique.
- Standardized materials handling. Economical palletization and compatible alternates keep warehouse and trucking costs down, but do not impede goods flow.
- Electronic order communications. In cooperation with the Bell System, a new TWX-based order processing system speeds deliveries while assisting the accountants.
- Company truck operation. A wholly-owned subsidiary gives private truck benefits, but furthers efficiencies through concurrent service as a common carrier within the province of Ontario.

Few fashionable topics get described glowingly more often by seminar-exhorters than linear programing. Accounts of miracles it can perform are rarely followed by a rush of converts to make them work, however. The plucky few that do check out those "manufacturers' stock programs" all too often spot traps that discourage them early in the game.

Canadian Canners Limited, however, puts linear programing to work in a number of worthwhile applications. Resource allocation and ingredient mix problems as well as a number of distribution procedures work well with a "canned" program from the IBM library. The company's present IBM 360-30 computer offers ample capacity for these purposes, although earlier successful linear runs were on an IBM 1401 of more limited data storage capability.

The company's first employment of the linear programing method was a storage space study for the evolving distribution department. Storage was a critical matter for Canadian Canners in the early '60s. When

48 plants dropped to 15 for more efficient production, warehouse space diminished as each plant closed. Growing business clearly called for careful allocation of remaining space as well as utmost discretion in building new warehousing during a period of accelerating construction costs. A four-man committee, chaired by Assistant Controller Eric R. Berndt and including Distribution Manager Thomas C. Norwood, tackled this problem in 1964. They carefully weighed the circumstances and, recognizing the inadequacy of conventional methods to measure the innumerable alternatives, chose to employ linear programing.

The resulting analysis guided the study committee in developing recommendations which they submitted during the spring of 1966. In the interim, substantial data development effort was necessary to fulfill the linear program's requirements. The committee found a growing volume of statistics needed for long-range planning unavailable, so their project involved creating a movement data bank as well. Among other elements, a uniform storage space definition did not exist. Traditional measurement in "cases" was inadequate because case sizes vary. In consequence, all existing storage was measured in terms of space available for 48 inch-by-40 inch four-way entry pallets.

The data, when assembled, went into the computer, which printed out an analysis that guided decisions on three questions:

—Which existing facilities required priority treatment in revising or expanding warehouse space?

—Where should new warehousing be built?

—What size should any new facilities be?

Immediate results were more effective allocations of warehouse space. Subsequent closings of four more plants, therefore, placed no serious strain on the total system. The program is run at least once each year, adjusted to most recent storage conditions. The resultant "matrix," a portion of which has been presented with this article, guides the physical distribution department in getting the most out of existing storage facilities. Supplementary program runs also take place when changed cost factors or new proposals for capital expenditures arise, giving a quick audit of any change's effect on the existing system.

More than storage is subjected to linear measurement at Canadian Canners. Messrs. Norwood and Berndt have their departments

Contrasting methods of material handling: At left, pallet loads move into storage on standard 48 inch-by-40 inch pallets at Toronto distribution center. Right, new clamp truck places goods at Exeter, Ont. warehouse, where successful clamp truck operation may lead to reduced pallet investment.

conjointly expanding a series of procedures which yield freight rate data and costs by individual product. The operations analysis section, working with distribution personnel, now seeks to key in such circumstances as crop availabilities and fixed costs of individual factories. The production planning staff is also participating in this effort.

"The new linear will yield practical solutions to distribution problems," Mr. Norwood observes, "recognizing existing facility limitations. At the same time, it will point the way to possibilities for new investments or new strategies that can create a more nearly optimum situation."

Every order is rated under this program, even if sold F.O.B. plant. Without this information, total cost of the complete physical distribution system cannot be determined. Even though the customer pays part of the bill, total cost data is essential to tell Canadian Canners its current competitive position. The final, landed cost to the customer is the critical factor. "Proper cost identification and segregation are vital, continuing necessities," states Mr. Norwood. "Traditional accounts are not always adequately segregated to identify distribution costs properly. Effective, continuous liaison with the accounting function is essential in broadening distribution's knowledge and control."

Another management science or operations research technique gets occasional use in the distribution area; PERT (Program Evaluation and Review Technique), a charting procedure for scheduling and controlling complex projects, worked out well for the initial storage study committee. Although PERT is commonly regarded as a computer-oriented method, Canadian Canners found it well suited to manual development for coordinating data assembly and development in the initial linear programing project.

Palletization—An Industry Standard

At Canadian Canners, Ltd., as in many other companies, the standard grocers pallet is an increasingly important marketing tool. More and more customers seek deliveries on these 48 inch-by-40 inch four-way entry pallets, a situation leading to growing pallet shortages. Pallet control is a full-time job, therefore, of growing importance.

With 120,000 standard pallets on its books, the company inaugurated a pallet control program in October, 1968. The first

phase of this program entailed a complete initial pallet physical inventory at all Canadian Canners locations, after which a comprehensive manual record was maintained, tabulating every pallet going in and out of each point. Subsequently, a physical check was made as well with five major wholesalers who accounted for about 80% of previously outstanding pallets, thus adjusting totals for a more nearly exact inventory.

The present manual procedure, in addition to keeping track of pallets released to customers, helps to forecast requirements, controls pallet costs and keeps customers from creating exchange imbalances. Nonetheless, computerized pallet control will be installed in the not-too-distant future. The computer's greater speed and lower cost is expected to assist greatly in developing pallet budget requirements. The company hopes to project pallet requirements by year by plant and/or warehouse, minimizing day-to-day shortages while at the same time holding down the total pallet inventory.

Palletized product movement is standard within and between the 11 plant warehouses and the company's five distribution centers, except at the Exeter, Ont. plant warehouse. Pallet loading patterns that assure maximum shipping efficiency are set by the distribution department in conjunction with the production department. Forklift operators and others face few surprises, therefore, when goods arrive at any facility from another company point

At the Exeter plant warehouse, however, something new is in progress. When the 63,000-square foot facility was inaugurated, clamp trucks went in service alongside the standard forklift units. While goods move to or from Exeter on pallets, actual stacking within the warehouse is pallet-free, the clamp trucks grasping complete pallet loads by controlled side pressure for ready movement, stacking or unstacking. "This operation is being closely observed to determine handling cost reduction and space saving potential. We have already determined that it saves at least $10,000 in pallet purchases annually," Mr. Norwood notes. Assuming continued successful operation at Exeter, it is quite likely that clamp trucks will appear subsequently at other company locations.

Electronics Comes To Order Processing

Order processing, for some time a dis-

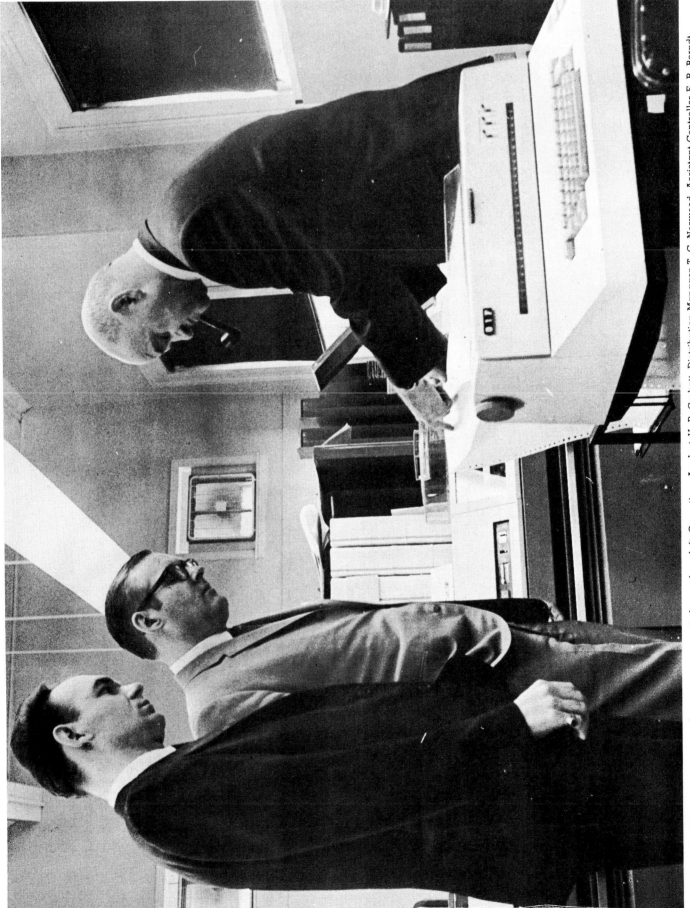

Checking computer output from storage space study are, from left, Operations Analyst V. R. Corbett, Distribution Manager T. C. Norwood, Assistant Controller E. R. Berndt.

Peak season operating strategy is subject of discussion at meeting of Canadian Canners distribution staff members. These include, from left to right, Herbert Wagstaffe, supervisor of distribution order services; Michael E. Biro, administrator of distribution planning and control; Russell W. Mueller, supervisor of transportation services; Dennis Payne, distribution research analyst, and Thomas C. Norwood, distribution manager.

tribution department function, entered a new phase in September. A new INFAST (Information Assembly and Transfer) system, developed in conjunction with the Bell System, now employs the latter firm's TWX services, reducing the invoice cycle time by one to three days in contrast to conventional procedures. The TWX teletype circuits are for order processing exclusively, with the company continuing its prior teletype network for other communications.

In the current stage, Toronto, Ottawa and Montreal order via TWX to headquarters at Hamilton. Orders will be by product code number only, without descriptions, a step permitting elimination of multitudinous forms. Hamilton then sends TWX orders to the Toronto distribution center which in turn returns TWX delivery slips to Hamilton as a basis for invoice preparation and mailing to customers. The plan includes enough slack to provide commodity description as well as code for up to 25% of customers if they request it.

Once this project is running on a routine basis, the next step anticipated will find orders run into the computer, yielding a daily inventory update. The company also hopes to develop automatic replenishment of the western warehouses at that time. "We anticipate further refinements in the actual order processing as well," Assistant Controller Berndt comments. "Our plans envision a paper tape-to-card procedure which will further speed the order-invoice cycle, benefitting both our customers and ourselves."

Company's Private-Common Carriage

While Canada and the United States follow similar patterns in many transport matters, differing regulations afford some freedoms on one side of the border not necessarily found on the other. In private truck operation, the greater stringency lies on the U.S. side of the boundary. Canadian Canners, through its subsidiary, Walmer Transport Ltd., enjoys the best of both the common and private carrier worlds. Walmer Transport operates throughout Ontario in private carriage for its parent. In addition, it holds somewhat more restricted rights in common carriage.

Walmer terminals are located at Hamilton and at the Rexdale distribution center, adjacent to Toronto. In private carriage, cans are hauled from the mill in Burlington, Ont. to parent company plants at Dresden, Amherstburg, Leamington, Waterford, Simcoe, St. Davids and St. Catherines, all of which are within the province. Cans unloaded, the trucks take on finished products for delivery to the Rexdale distribution center. An additional private carriage operation delivers steel from Ontario suppliers to the Burlington can mill.

The truck fleet represents a substantial investment. The operation employs 52 tractors and 80 trailers, 15 of which are vans. Most of the tractors have tandem axles. Another eight miscellaneous vehicles round out the rolling stock.

Operated as an independent subsidiary,

Ample inbound and outbound truck handling facilities speed stock into and deliveries out of the Toronto distribution center, one of a growing number the company operates throughout Canada.

Walmer Transport Limited, a Canadian Canners subsidiary, offers both private and common carriage services. The trailer carries the Aylmer herald, a Canadian Canners brand name.

Walmer Transport is none the less wholly owned by Canadian Canners Ltd. Distribution Manager Norwood serves on the Walmer board of directors, thus enjoying a dual relationship, being both a manager and a customer.

Inbound Controls A Significant Factor

While much company production comes from crops within easy reach of its plants, a significant proportion arrives from far distant origins. Imports play a big role in building the catalog. Polish fruit pulp, Italian cherries in brine, Sardinian zucca melons, Spanish olives and onions from Holland are among

them, shipped in varied packs conventional to the individual trades. Palletization, however, is beginning to become more prevalent and is now standard on shipments of French glace cherries, Portuguese tomato paste and Phillipine pineapple. California fruit is imported by rail in carload lots. These latter are now moving in some measure to the Rexdale distribution center on 48 inch-by-40 inch slip sheets for testing.

As currently organized, Supervisor-Transportation Claims and Imports Ron Duce routes all imports arriving by sea, thus covering virtually all other-than-U.S. freight. Customs Supervisor Les W. Hill handles custom clearance documentation procedure,

Indoor rail unloading facilities at Toronto distribution center assure weather protection for inbound goods.

auditing and approval of customs brokerage accounts. In the case of water shipments direct to Hamilton, Mr. Hill clears the shipments directly, acting as his own customs broker.

Physical distribution, as a finite staff function, is a comparatively recent development for the firm. Yet in its year of life it has already seen substantial progress and a high level of innovation within the company. Externally, the department gives a similar good account of itself. Supervisor Transportation Services Russell W. Mueller and other staff members are active in both traffic and distribution organizations in the area, while Distribution Manager Norwood, in addition to being current president of the Canadian Association of Physical Distribution Management, is chairman of the Grocery Product Manufacturers of Canada's Distribution Council.

A Growing Role For Linear Programing

Looking ahead, linear programing and related techniques will obviously play an expanding role at Canadian Canners. Operations Analyst Vincent R. Corbett, whose technical support is an important factor in these endeavors, feels that increased electronic data processing capacity will affect this significantly. "While we now enjoy greater speed and capacity thanks to our new IBM 360-30 computer," he states, "we are still somewhat hampered by the existing 'stock' program. It is actually a program

designed for the 1401 computer, but which is compatible with the 360 as we have it set up. The present program can develop a matrix of 96 rows and 600 columns. On some of the jobs we are running, keeping within the 96-row data limitation gets a bit sticky. What we're really looking forward to is a promised 'canned' program for the 360 itself which will allow for 200 rows rather than the present 96. That added capacity will open the doors to broader applications and faster results in many areas."

It takes considerable confidence and a lot of energy to tackle totally new ways of doing business. In many cases, the issue is either skirted or "farmed out" to other organizations. At Canadian Canners, opinion holds that knowing the company first is perhaps more important than prior experience with a specific technique. This attitude seems to be paying off well. In the words of a principal participant, Assistant Controller Berndt, " 'Hands-on' learning is the only way."

Exploring storage alternatives through linear programming

For Canadian Canners, linear programing determines mathematically the best courses of action under specified restrictions among the available solutions to many of their problems. The company keeps storage alternative costs clear for planners and managers through this means. The accompanying

Storage Problem Matrix
(Partial)

| | | | | #1 Dresden | | | #10 Kingsville | | | #49 Ridgetown | | #31 Amherstburg | | | #51 Exeter | | | |
| | SPACE REQUIREMENTS | Demand Quantity (Pallets) Period 40 | Pres. 011 | Exp. 013 | Cans Only 014 | Pres. 101 | Aux. 102 | Cans Only 104 | Pres. 491 | Cans Only 494 | Pres. 311 | Aux. 312 | Exp. 313 | Pres. 511 | Exp. 513 | Aux. 512 | Cans Only 514 |
Plant No.																	
01	5 Direct & Reserve	18,449	0000	475		557	1269		381		499	1012	1097	673	1212	1414	
	6 Western Whses	2,142	0001	475		557	1269		381		499	1012	1097	549	1088	1115	
	7 Via #2 Rexdale	10,007	0002	475		557	786		381		499	890	1097	207	746	624	
	8 Advance Cans	6,016	0003	475	0000	272	501	272	226	226	294	685	872				
	9 Can Float	735	0000	475	0000												
10	5 Direct & Reserve	1,149	499	974		0000	586		831		324	837	902	774	1313	1414	
	6 Western Whses	22	499	974		0001	586		831		324	837	902	649	1188	990	
	7 Via #2 Rexdale	1,996	499	974		0002	586		581		324	715	902	242	781	746	
	8 Advance Cans	-	196	671	196	0003	586	0000	236	236	193	584	771				
	9 Can Float	344				0000		0000									
49	5 Direct & Reserve	1,109	283	758		557	1194		0000		524	1037	1103	674	1213	1564	
	6 Western Whses	40	283	758		557	1194		0001		524	1037	1103	549	1088	1265	
	7 Via #2 Rexdale	801	283	758		557	711		0002		524	915	1103	224	763	729	
	8 Advance Cans	141	162	637	162	289	518	289	0003	0000	312	703	890				
	9 Can Float	-							0000	0000							
31	5 Direct & Reserve	3,446	508	983		357	1244		831		0000	561	578	799	1338	1665	
	6 Western Whses	437	508	983		357	1244		831		0001	561	578	674	1213	1265	
	7 Via #2 Rexdale	3,029	508	983		57	786		581		0002	561	578				
	8 Advance Cans	-															
	9 Can Float	5									0000		578				
51	5 Direct & Reserve	4,328	658	1133										0000	539	1089	
	6 Western Whses	104	658	1133										0001	539	1089	
	7 Via #2 Rexdale	4,870	783	1258										0002	539	915	152
	8 Advance Cans	971	260	735	260									0003	539	585	152
	9 Can Float	141												0000	539	585	

sample of the complete system "storage problem matrix" compares handling costs at five western Ontario plant warehouses for a single week (Demand Period 40).

At its left, the chart shows plant numbers and the pallet quantities requiring space at each point in five categories. This breakdown splits pallets between different consumer regions for production plus can stock.

The five subsequent major columns compare cost differentials per pallet among alternatives. In the first row, for example, Plant #1 (Dresden, Ontario) required space for 18,449 pallets in category 5 (Direct & Reserve). Because space exists and is already assigned at Dresden for this stock, there is no incremental cost for holding it, so under #1 Dresden in the columns, a cost of 0000 appears as the present condition (Pres.). Should conditions require plant expansion to accommodate this or any other category, either in whole or in part, however, the additional cost per pallet under existing conditions appears under Expansion ("Exp.") —in this instance $4.75 per pallet.

Additional sub-columns show cost penalties for alternative or auxiliary storage where feasible and for space restricted by nature to can storage only.

In the "Present" category, while cost differentials are nil at the same warehouse, a minute cost is shown for the three categories following "Direct & Reserve." These arbitrary figures are too low to affect program solutions, but serve to avoid confusion within the computer.

Looking further, the chart shows that penalty storage costs for storing these same pallets at Kingsville would be $5.57 at present, or $12.69 in auxiliary storage. At Ridgetown, the differential drops to $3.81, while Amherstburg finds it at $4.99. Exeter shows no cost in this category because of a management decision. The data can be printed out if needed, but it is not deemed a feasible solution. In the next category, Western Warehouses, however, Exeter does show costs, indicating a differential of $6.73 for storing Dresden pallets in present space compared to storage at Dresden.

This "five-by-five" matrix only samples the 20-warehouse, ten-plant storage problem matrix, which includes some further related information. In this configuration, it is handy for comparing alternatives in planning meetings and such. The available data also makes possible matrices of other types for differing studies, including total cost rather than differential cost comparisons and revised systems studies that consider the effects of specific proposed changes in facilities or methods. Messrs. Berndt and Norwood agree that the mathematics operations concerned are, in themselves, simple. Their huge, repetitive volume in working all but the smallest linear problems, however, makes linear analysis impractical by manual rather than computer procedures.

CHAPTER IV

Materials Management: Broadening Physical Distribution's Scope

Generally, physical distribution is the term commonly applied to business logistics. More recently, "materials management" finds growing usage. Companies with a particularly strong marketing orientation tend toward physical distribution, while those with a more pronounced manufacturing orientation in their managements tend toward materials management. The latter, in fact, represents an outward expansion of an in-plant management concern, whereas physical distribution departments generally represent growth from external warehouse and traffic management toward internal logistics functions.

A good case in point is the Micro-Switch Division of Honeywell, Inc., surveyed in Chapter VIII, where Distribution Manager Fredric L. Keefe operates a comprehensive materials management program within a single-plant logistics system.

Drug manufacturing and marketing, which demand the closest of controls in both aspects, lend themselves particularly well to the materials management philosophy. Abbott Laboratories and the Warner-Chilcott Division of Warner-Lambert have both chosen this management approach recently for their logistics control, calling in recognized experts to develop their programs.

Vice President Roland W. Puder's department at Abbott Laboratories encompasses purchasing and internal materials management as well as all the duties normally associated with distribution. A special characteristic of its organization is the thorough segregation of line and staff functions, freeing each for more thorough concentration on its specific and proper responsibilities. Initially presented in the TRAFFIC MANAGEMENT of May, 1972, this company's case follows:

Aggressive Management Builds Logistics Productivity

AS WITH THE computer, physical distribution management's presence no longer in itself marks a firm as uniquely progressive. Computers today are accepted tools, and the new measure of electronic data processing progress lies with improved equipment, sophisticated techniques and broader applications. So, too, with logistics management.

At Abbott Laboratories, these management techniques have been recognized and used for some time. Nevertheless, the past year and a half witnessed the birth of something new and exciting in this area—a "second generation" management structure, the corporate materials management division, which brings broader responsibilities and higher standards of efficiency under the logistics umbrella.

The key word is management. With 1971 sales exceeding $458 million—substantially more than double the figures of a decade earlier—this North Chicago-based company braces itself today in anticipation of still greater expansion ahead. Since Vice President Roland W. Puder assumed divisional control in December, 1970, much stress has been placed upon development of a management structure that carefully segregates staff and line activity, ensuring proper attention to both.

At least equal regard has been given to the continuing development of individual managers, including Abbott personnel previously assigned to logistics activities, those joining the unit from other company divisions and carefully chosen newcomers. The latter's particular skills speed the development of responsibilities most recently incorporated within the corporate materials management function.

"Abbott Laboratories' 'total research' philosophy applies as much to materials management as it does to product development," comments President Edward J. Ledder. "The most carefully made health product loses its value unless it is available where and when need exists. Effective logistics, therefore, is a vital ingredient of everything we make."

The accompanying organization chart contains some activities not commonly found together elsewhere. It also illustrates a unique duplication of interests, with virtually every line function paralleled by a staff activity under Director-Materials Management, Planning and Analysis Peter E. Reisner. Inclusion of a materials management controller's department within the division greatly benefits planning and measurement of costs and productivity.

Another recently added responsibility, purchasing, affords the po-

A TIME EXPOSURE lends a surrealistic note to interior of large new Abbott Park distribution center.

tential for signal gains through inbound materials control in coordination with traffic activities as well as beneficial support to warehousing and distribution center operations, optimizing costs of packaging supplies, material handling equipment and other purchases furthering the logistics function.

At present, three of the corporate materials management division's major activities symbolize its forward thrust. They are:

Productivity Improvement: Annually established productivity goals measure individual distribution center and warehouse performance through a management technique termed IMPACT (Integrated Management Planning and Control Technique). This manpower development and planning program permits rolling readjustment of responsibilities, checks progress and authority as manager capabilities increase and new responsibilities demand attention.

Variable Budget Plan: Each manager is developing an individual plan for matching cost performance to varying activity levels.

Staff Support to Other Divisions:

Materials management teams perform studies and submit recommendations for distribution and purchasing improvements at the request of other company divisions.

Developing Management

The IMPACT program is a multi-purpose tool for seasoning individual managers, enhancing the management team's overall productivity and monitoring progress toward specific department goals. Each manager initially completes an IMPACT form (see accompanying illustration) detailing his regular responsibilities and specifying both results expected and dates by

PRESIDENT Edward J. Ledder (left) and Vice President-Materials Management Roland W. Puder confer at center's enclosed rail docks.

which they should be achieved. A separate portion covers similar information on special project assignments.

The form provides for six-month and year-end reviews, taking into account any changes in circumstances hastening or detaining progress. The form also provides a "skills inventory update" which summarizes the individual manager's new work, education and training experience since prior review and a "career goals restatement" which stipulates further training or job experience deemed necessary to the individual in attaining his current career goals.

Though the standard form presumes semiannual review, Vice President Puder in fact surveys these responsibilities quarterly and revises them wherever necessary with involved staff members. Typed form summaries, attached to large charts with adjacent blank space at the right, make easy work of writing in changes at these quarterly discussions.

These individual reviews are supplemented by monthly management meetings to check division progress. At these, each manager summarizes the current state of his stewardship, after which there is general discussion of overall department activity. Emphasis is placed on the team approach, encouraged in great measure by various dual interests of line and staff managers.

Positive motivation arises from a management incentive program initiated in 1971. As a result of early successes in reaching goals originally set, Mr. Puder has been permitted to broaden this plan recently. It gives those achieving established goals significant rewards. Important, too, are the long-term career gains resulting from planned manager development, the discovery of previously unrecognized talents through assignment diversification and selective manager transfers that broaden capabilities while improving the cross-disciplinary communication essential to team-oriented management.

Measuring Performance

A program such as IMPACT makes close performance measurement essential. Toward this end, the corporate materials management division has under development a variable budget program. "A fixed budget represents what you thought might happen," observes Mr. Puder. "A variable bud-

get measures operating results in terms of what actually did happen. **If business volume runs higher or lower than a fixed budget suggests, it becomes an inadequate measure of productivity."** The variable budget, however, calls for specified performance levels that relate directly to actual business volume.

Each manager in the division develops an individual variable budget plan for his unit. In the near future, all of these will be completed and in use. The variable budgets augment rather than replace fixed budgets. Further information concerning variable budget procedures and installation by the division controller and his staff may be found in the "Distribution Systems" section of this issue.

Overseas Logistics

Overseas business plays a growing role at Abbott Laboratories. With plants in 27 countries on all continents plus export-import movement involving the United States, overseas logistics are widespread and complex. At the request of International Division President George Young, the corporate materials management division is providing in-depth support to develop materials management within the

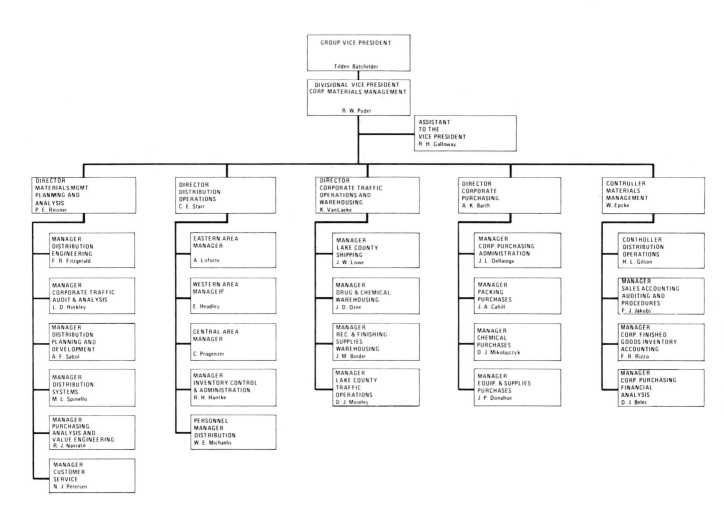

ABBOTT'S materials management division organization chart encompasses broader logistics responsibilities than normally are found within either a physical distribution or materials management orientation.

international division.

The international function will be serviced initially by a small unit in the planning department, providing for close control and careful measurement of progress. Careful scrutiny and evaluation has found considerable savings in purchasing and distribution for the various international affiliates, with further potential economies anticipated down the road.

Among other considerations are the possibilities of free zone assembly work overseas and a centralized European distribution center, consolidated freight forwarder usage, larger shipments, shipping via standard modes, improved container design and correlation purchases worldwide to get optimum prices. Not international, but nonetheless overseas, the concept of moving soybean oil from the Midwest by barge down the Mississippi River and then by sea to San Juan,

Puerto Rico is being checked against present overland movement to New York and container beyond.

Building New Division

Divisional restructuring and a host of special projects account in great measure for this function's 20% productivity improvement since February, 1971. The "big push" under way currently foresees a 78% gain over the February, 1971 levels by the end of 1972. Clearly, this is a transitional era for the corporate materials management division. Planning and analysis activities, therefore, create an exceptionally heavy current load.

"We have over 150 projects in the planning and analysis department at any given time," asserts Director Peter E. Reisner. "Individually, each of our specialized managers carries up to 60 assignments in his unit."

The department employs simulation techniques intensively in studies aimed at optimizing the present distribution system. Numerous other operations research techniques and diversified computer programs assist planning and development efforts as well.

In general, the department develops and tests new logistics programs, including actual operation of new facilities or procedures through the "debugging" phase, after which line units within the division assume full responsibility. Planning and development, for example, handles public warehouse selection and negotiation when such facilities are found necessary, but actual operation and control reverts to the distribution center manager in the affected geographic area.

Planning managers coordinate closely with line managers in developing programs. There is also

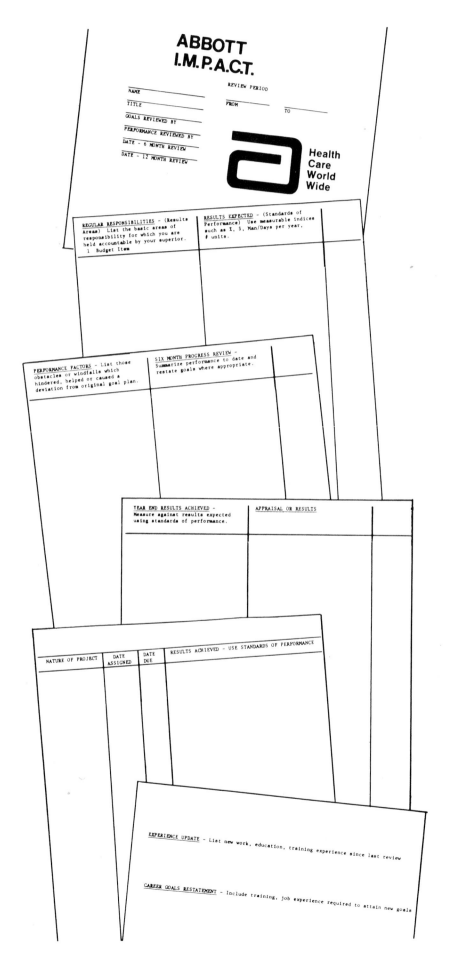

THE DEPARTMENT'S "Impact" program for scheduling and evaluating individual performance records progress regularly on this form.

considerable interplay among the planning management team members. Manager-Distribution Engineering F. R. Fitzgerald, for instance, in addition to working with both regional and headquarters management in the distribution operations department, maintains close ties with Manager-Distribution Planning and Development A. F. Sabol and other managers within the department affected by such activities.

The engineering group supplies materials handling inputs, warehouse layouts and other materials management engineering elements that importantly affect distribution center systems and facilities. Among many such projects, a program to improve case picking is expected to yield $60,000 in cost reductions during 1972, while implementation of an automatic weight check system suggests an $80,000 gain. The latter program involves comparison at the weigh station with weight and price data placed on orders by computer. If actual weight does not match, the affected order is kicked off of the line for manual determination and rectification of the problem.

"The advantage of an improvement such as this," notes Mr. Fitzgerald, **"lies in the fact that, once proven at an individual distribution center, similar benefits can probably be realized at 19 additional locations."**

Manager-Corporate Traffic Audit and Analysis L. D. Hinkley's section concerns itself with negotiations, carrier selection, straightforward costing and, within a specialized two-man unit, international traffic matters. During 1972, the latter unit expects to achieve a $200,000 cost reduction in international division export and overseas shipping—a significant factor in a firm where a quarter of total sales lies beyond the continental U. S. borders. Another $200,000 is expected through development of improved freight consolidations, modal optimization, rate negotiations and suspensions. Substantial savings are envisioned as well working in connection with other divisions.

At present, the traffic analysis section has operational responsibility for the company's private truck fleet, including peddle trucks generally operating within a 100-mile radius of distribution centers and over-the-road units serving currently out of the North Chicago and Rocky Mount, N. C. plants. The latter forward finished goods to distribution centers, returning with vendor freight. Van-type peddle trucks serve the distribution centers, while conventional 40-foot trailers operate over the road. The private truck operation is slated for ultimate transfer to a line operations group.

RONALD J. NAVRATIL, manager-purchasing analysis and value engineering, at department staff meeting, spells out detailed proposals for a 1972 $800,000 cash flow savings in his area.

The distribution planning and development section seeks overall improvements in distribution center operations. More than just a cost-cutting activity, Manager Sabol and his staff seek to develop physical distribution and marketing innovations during 1972 that will lead to a minimum of $100,000 in additional sales.

The purchase analysis and value engineering section under Manager R. J. Navratil necessarily coordinates activities with virtually

PETER E. REISNER (seated, left), director-materials management planning and analysis, and Manager-Corporate Traffic Audit and Analysis L. D. Hinkley respond to a floor question at a staff session.

every division of Abbott Laboratories. Among many areas of current interest, Mr. Navratil is working closely with Manager-Packaging Purchases John A. Cahill in the development of packaging system improvements keyed to economic purchases of packing material. Mr. Navratil's section examines every aspect of what, how and why everything is bought by Abbott Laboratories.

Manager-Customer Service N. J. Petersen and his staff are working with the distribution centers to improve order cycle performance and other service-related factors.

This area is currently under heavy study.

Computers and other system tools carry an increasing portion of the logistics burden.

The corporate materials management division is one of two cost divisions which, together with four profit divisions, report to Group Vice President Tilden Batchelder. **"The materials management concept has already proven itself at Abbott through successful implementation of numerous important programs," states Mr. Batchelder. "It is slated to play a major part in improving Abbott's profitability as business expands."**

AL SABOL (right), manager-distribution planning and development, reviews order cycle systems with Operations Researcher Jerry Scott.

HANDLING PROCEDURES for a new company product are discussed by (left to right) Director-Corporate Traffic Operations and Warehousing Kenneth R. Van Laeke, Director-Corporate Biological Quality Assurance James Lonergan, Director-Corporate Quality Standards and Audits Dr. Robert Rivett and Director-Distribution Operations C. Edward Starr.

Distribution/traffic: Revised operations

DIRECTOR of Distribution Operations C. Edward Starr and Director of Corporate Traffic Operations and Warehousing Kenneth R. Van Laeke, as well as their departments, epitomize the fast-paced changes under way in Abbott's corporate materials management division. Messrs. Starr and Van Laeke switched jobs last November. The traffic operations and warehousing unit was in itself newly structured as of June, 1971. The distribution operations department is at present undergoing important changes, placing area managers physically within their regions instead of headquartered at North Chicago as in the past.

For traffic, there were both gains and losses within the department. Formerly embracing both line and staff activities, the latter were diverted to the materials management planning and analysis department. In their stead, new operational responsibilities were acquired from other entities. Prior to January, 1971, receiving as well as drug and chemical warehousing were under the purchasing department. These now report to a separate management. Shipping and finished goods warehousing, once distribution operations department

responsibilities, are also shifted to the traffic unit.

These additions saw the transfer of new managers into the department also. Manager-Shipping and Finished Goods Warehousing James W. Lowe was Cincinnati distribution center manager for many years, while Manager-Drug and Chemical Warehousing J. D. Ozee was formerly in quality assurance activities before accepting his present assignment in October, 1971. Recently, Manager-Receiving

and Finishing Supplies Warehousing J. M. Binder came aboard. Prior to Feb. 1, he was materials management manager at the Ashland, Ohio plant of the consumer products division. Today's department, therefore, benefits from diversified field experience in its management background.

The department makes good use of newer methods in surface transportation. Both unitization and containerization are found here, with Sea Land containers moving

VICE PRESIDENT Roland W. Puder (center) and Director-Materials Management Planning and Analysis Peter E. Reisner survey traffic-distribution goals as Departmental Secretary Connie Roger takes notes.

regularly between the San Juan, Puerto Rico and North Chicago plants. A previous diversity of pallets has now been replaced by Grocery Manufacturers Association standard 48 by 40-inch four-way entry pallets, greatly simplifying development and handling of unit loads. Largest outbound tonnage is in rail movement, with substantial use of piggyback as well, particularly to points without sidings.

Most rail shipments are in Abbott's own leased cars—a fleet of specially insulated boxcars plus a few tank cars, giving Abbott a controlled fleet of 258 cars in all. "We have been receiving certain bulk commodities in hopper cars," Mr. Van Laeke observes. **"We hope to expand our bulk receiving in the future as it affords substantial economies in both transportation and handling."**

In managing truck shipments, schedule reliability and protection against freezing are two primary requirements. **"Uniform protection against freezing is vital to us because of our mixed loads,"** notes Manager-Lake County Traffic Operations D. J. Moseley. "There may be only a small segment in à whole truckload of freezing-sensitive materials, but its needs will govern."

J. MORRIS BINDER, manager-receiving and finishing supplies warehousing, uses forklift radiophone for intra-warehouse communication.

FLOW RACKS, conveyors and other modern equipment speed order selection and assembly at the Abbott Park distribution center.

PALETIZED SHIPMENT being assembled in a carrier trailer typifies movements from North Chicago plant.

JERRY D. OZEE (left), manager-drug and chemical warehousing, and his staff at Abbott Park keep a close check on quality of the sensitive materials passing through their facilities.

Distribution Network

With 20 distribution centers, supplemented by 28 public warehouses serving the nation, area stocks assure prompt response. Individual distribution centers may handle 2,000 stock-keeping units or more, but this varies. The five largest installations (Chicago, Los Angeles, Dallas, Atlanta and New York) handle 50% of the volume, moving items from all Abbott sources.

Most of the other distribution centers do not handle the full spectrum, although all handle goods from the two largest divisions—hospital products (HPD) and pharmaceutical products (PPD). Specific area need is the governing factor. Additionally, the Ross Division, which markets a line of pediatric nutritionals and pharmaceuticals, funnels some of its products through the 20 distribution centers, although its greatest bulk moves through public warehouses.

Public warehousing serves essentially to supplement distribution center operations, handling volume movements from locations close to specific markets. This saves freight costs and at the same time minimizes Abbott's investment in bricks and mortar.

Organizational changes currently under way find functions flowing in two directions at once. Regional line management is decentralizing, with the manager-Eastern region moving from North Chicago to Philadelphia and the Western region manager slated for an early transfer to a major city in his own region. Conversely, the new central control administrative staff group will henceforth support these field managers from North Chicago, handling personnel matters, reports, general communications and overall liaison activities with North Chicago organizations. "It is a reconstitution of prior small individual groups that reported to each regional manager while all were resident at North Chicago," notes Mr. Starr.

Manager-Inventory Control and Administration Richard H. Hantke has assumed the responsibility for this centralized support group activity. His unit's primary function,

RICHARD H. HANTKE (standing), manager-inventory control and administration, checks status of a critical item with Reimbursement Specialist Robert Priebe. Blackboards in background detail current low stock items and estimated arrival times for replenishment stock at the various distribution centers.

however, is distribution center inventory control. This centers basically around the two main divisions—HPD and PPD. The computer plays a growing role in this area, lending itself well to a product orientation.

Individual reimbursement specialists in the department are each assigned specific groups of distribution centers for their particular products. A weekly computer-prepared distribution center reim-

locations. At each distribution center, there is also a blackboard showing low stock items and estimated time of arrival for replenishment stock. The centers report nightly on "low and out" stocks. **"We find these visual reminders an effective tool for keeping both reimbursement specialists at North Chicago and distribution center personnel aware of any critical inventory conditions," Mr. Hantke asserts.**

from centralization of expediting and various administrative duties, freeing them to concentrate upon their specific skill areas.

Following its reorganization, the department has sent its experts to field locations for exhaustive study of individual point needs and methods. Subsequently, it will develop specific purchasing modernization programs as part of an overall effort to control and direct purchasing dollar commitments.

At the Rocky Mount, N.C. plant, the department has gathered data concerning potential annual requirements for diverse commodities.

"From this data," states Mr. Barth, "we will then prepare solicitations for bids by local suppliers on a when, as and if basis, either annualized or fitted to some other sufficient time basis to make it worth their while."

The new procedure will require only a single purchase order for the time stipulated. Thereafter, dealings will be direct between the authorized requisitioner and the vendor at the time of need. Ven-

D. J. MOSELEY, manager-Lake County traffic operations.

bursement report, accompanied by concurrently prepared shipping tickets for appropriate central warehouses plays an important part in inventory maintenance procedures.

Adjacent to the reimbursement specialists' desks at North Chicago are large boards showing low-level item conditions at the various field

Purchasing joins the logistics team

SINCE June 1, 1971, Purchasing Department Director A. K. Barth and his staff have reported to Vice President Roland W. Puder of the corporate materials management division. Mr. Barth, a newcomer, assumed his duties in October, 1971 and proceeded thereafter to make important changes in the department's organizational structure.

An accompanying chart compares former and present arrangements. The prior functional breakdown is still largely respected, but individual buying units now benefit

A. K. BARTH, director-corporate purchasing, makes a point in describing his department's changing methods.

OLD AND NEW organization charts of purchasing function illustrate the greater segregation of specialized duties to improve performance.

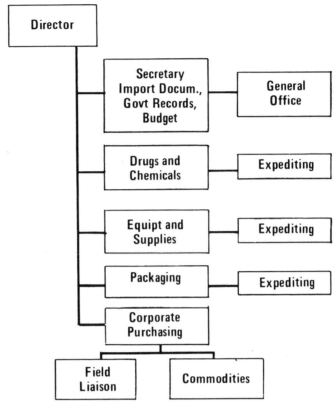

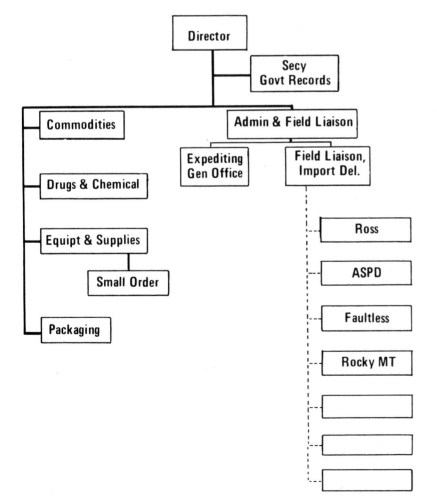

dors will bill monthly with a copy to the purchasing agent so that he may ascertain that his stipulations have been complied with.

This method will at once reduce costs for both vendor and Abbott. Additional cost-saving techniques will include the reduction of single source items, development of additional sources, changes in commodity packing and long-term contracts among others.

A newly established computerized management information system also assists the department. It can break out items by vendor, by item or by buyer as needed, thus simplifying analyses and comparisons of present or proposed purchases. It is intended to standardize identification of all items for computer input using the Federal Commodity Classification, a four-digit code.

Purchasing, like traffic, finds small lots causing cost and service problems. The recently established small order unit handling requisition-purchase orders for under

$100 values at North Chicago effectively minimize this burden. It relieves buying personnel in three areas, as well as the typing pool—a work load reduction of 15 to 20% at both levels.

The requisitioner initiates a small order on a six-part, no-carbon form, inserting the proper account number and adding his prefix code to the preprinted requisition-purchase order number. It is then signed by the small order buyer and officially approval-stamped by the purchasing department. This arrangement parallels standard requisition procedure, but the form eliminates need for retyping. This is an interim system that accomplishes its main purpose—relieving buying staff of time loss on small orders, yet assuring proper control. Small orders generally turn around in 72 hours.

Material management information system: Second generation

ELECTRONIC data processing came early to Abbott Laboratories' distribution activities. Initial systems, significant improvements over prior methods, today in their turn are being questioned. Should certain existing equipment be replaced? Will different devices or computer configurations do some jobs better? What further departmental activities lend themselves to modern systems improvements? Considerations such as these guide Manager-Materials Management Systems Michael J. Spinello and his staff in the continuing upgrading of corporate materials management division methods and procedures.

A key unit in the materials management planning and analysis department, the systems group, in addition to monitoring and control of day-to-day activities, has significant additions and improvements planned for 1972. Among these are the following:

- Implementation of a new Abbott Billing System (ABS).

SMALL ORDER unit handling requisition-purchase order forms, recently employed at North Chicago, help relieve buying staff of time loss on small orders while maintaining proper control.

- Development of a purchasing management information system.
- Revision and improvement of finished goods reimbursement (stock replenishment) procedures.
- Development of a finished goods inventory program.
- Cost-cutting innovations in materials management information systems.

Computerized Billing

In the past, distribution systems people were largely concerned with developing computer procedures to replace prior manual systems. At Abbott, the need for revision or replacement involved a centralized computer system already in existence. Their billing system, initially satisfactory, employed Computypers. These units entered billing data on paper tape at the distribution centers which was mailed to North Chicago daily. Converted there to magnetic tape, the data was processed through a computer program which audited format and accuracy before release to accounts receivable, inventory and sales. The procedure took three to five days following preparation of invoices at the various centers. After several years, Computyper maintenance problems arose. At the same time, the need to further reduce the processing cycle was becoming increasingly apparent.

"We decided to buy some time by rebuilding the best of our Computypers as an interim step," states Mr. Spinello. "This avoided locking ourselves into an existing system, freeing us to consider numerous other order entry billing system configurations."

After considering a dozen methods, it was determined that the local small computer approach was best for Abbott. North Chicago's new Honeywell 115 computer and its supporting units entered service in November, 1971, followed by an Atlanta installation in February of this year. The Dallas center was slated to follow on April 3 and the

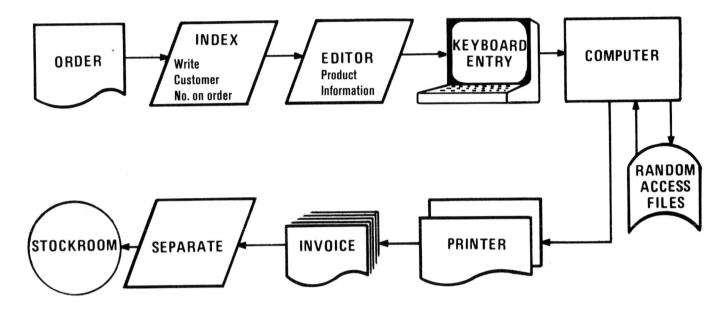

FLOW CHART illustrates in simple form current order handling procedures employing CRT units (labeled "keyboard") in conjunction with individual Honeywell computers at the distribution centers.

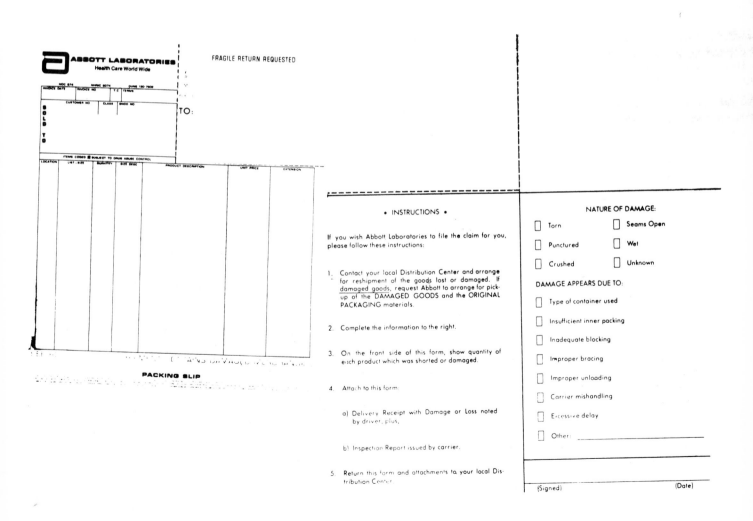

COMPUTER-PRODUCED shipping papers include a packing slip in the manifold form which includes claims and damage handling instructions for receivers on packing slip's rear, expediting claims processing and control.

New York distribution center one month later. All distribution centers will be functioning by the end of 1972, fully replacing the remaining computer units.

This new procedure wipes out the three-to-five-day time lag under the former system. Cathode ray tube units at each distribution center input sales data which the local computer audits instantaneously and stores. This data flows nightly over conventional telephone lines via Bell Dataphone to the North Chicago computer, which switches from its daytime role of distribution center activity to become a communication center for the network.

Each night, the North Chicago operator polls the other centers and draws in the data from unattended computers at the distant locations. In addition to receiving the invoice material, the North Chicago operator feeds back file update information concerning customers, products and prices to the individual distribution centers. As his final chore, the night operator delivers magnetic tape summary distribution center data for the day to the corporate computer unit at North Chicago. The latter then inputs accounts receivable, inventory, reimbursement and sales, much as under the preceding arrangement.

An accompanying flow chart illustrates the local computer systems. Equipment at each distribution center includes one Honeywell Model 115 computer with a capacity of 24K (24,000 digits), one disk drive, one standard tape drive, one Honeywell Model 112 line printer and Honeywell Model 775 cathode ray tube (CRT) units. North Chicago has 8K additional capacity in its computer, plus other minor equipment necessary for data collection. All of the distribution centers have Bell Dataphone sets.

In processing an order, the index clerk enters necessary customer information. The order editor enters size code and verifies that information is complete. Customer account number and any exception condition that the computer program must use is entered by the keyboard operator. The program performs necessary validations and

audits, displaying an error message to the operator when improper entries are made. It assigns the invoice number, performs price selection, discounting and tax calculations, and, lastly, resequences the

individual items into an efficient warehouse picking sequence.

The average operator can enter 50 orders per hour via CRT in contrast to only 15 to 18 per hour under the former method. More-

MICHAEL L. SPINELLO, manager-distribution systems, checks out a new systems presentation just completed by Chartist Bonnie Ploskee.

NEW ON-LINE cathode ray tube installations at 20 distribution centers have sped order and inventory operations while reducing costs over a prior system employing Flexowriter units in an off-line application.

over, whenever billing lines were defective, they required manual correction in the past. To date, the new system error rate has been only fractional and has been dropping as operator proficiency increases.

Fully operational at three large centers, the billing system is under continuing development. The computer-communications network created for this activity will open the door to other distribution applications as well.

New tools for distribution's financial control

THE National Council of Physical Distribution Management places great stress on the need for improved logistics cost measurement and control. Many professionals today believe this function benefits greatly when an in-house controller, sympathetic with the unusual requirements, is on the departmental staff, but few companies as yet have made such an arrangement. Abbott Laboratories is one of the fortunate few.

"Our department continues a 'dotted line' functional relationship with the corporate controller's organization," notes Controller-Materials Management William Epcke, "but our basic responsibility is to the divisional vice president-materials management. Working within the department, as we have since November of last year, greatly eases communications in this complex area. **We're learning a lot from our new associates about this division's business and we feel that they, in turn, benefit significantly from the 'instant controller consultation' now available to them."**

Manager-Financial Analysis-Procurement Don J. Belec concurs. "We previously took care of the division's financial matters satisfactorily," he states, "but **the new organization structure lets us tackle procedural problems more effectively."**

Inventory accounting is a major

Materials Management Controller's Department

Controller
Materials Management
William Epcke

Controller
Distribution Operations
Harold L. Gilson

Manager-Sales Accounting
Auditing and Procedures
F. J. Jakubs

Manager-Corp. Finished
Goods Inventory
Frank R. Rizzo

Manager-Corp. Purchasing
Financial Analysis
Don J. Belec

departmental responsibility. Fully computerized, the system maintains accurate measurement in both units and dollars. **"The new CRT installations that will service the billing system will benefit our inventory accounting as well,"** observes Manager-Inventory Accounting Fred R. Rizzo. "When the change-over is completed later this year, we will reevaluate data and report impact at the center level, making procedural adjustments to take full advantage of the new equipment's capabilities."

Inventory management performance has been improving steadily due to closer communication, management field trips and regional meetings. The department seeks to achieve a 3.1% recount goal for 1972—for every 1,000 items counted on inventory, only 31 will be permitted to exceed a specified level of variance requiring a recount.

In purchasing as in inventory accounting, the controller's department looks to further automation. Recently installed Friden Flexowriters have aided this process, serving as the first step in developing a purchasing management information system employing computer programming to measure vendor, buyer and purchasing performance. Typical of so many other corporate materials management division projects, this particular activity finds no less than three departments working to achieve a common goal: the planning and analysis department, the corporate purchasing department and the controller's department.

A vital controller's device that is rapidly being applied to all divisional management structures is the variable budget. Initially developed in 1970 for distribution center control, it sought to measure performance, identify costs and provide a means of charging profit divisions for distribution expenses while assisting in planning and fitting budget requirements to changing volume requirements.

Under older, fixed budgets, measurements of actual performance required comparison to an estimated figure rather than to actual conditions. This automatically created

VICE-PRESIDENT Roland W. Puder (right) discusses the gains achieved through incorporation of a controller function within his department with TM Executive Editor Jack W. Farrell.

variances in some degree on innumerable items. The variable budget approach, however, compares performance to standards applicable at any level of throughput. A variance would exist and require management review, however, if output per man-hour or other relevant measurement went outside of the established standards and tolerances.

After initial planning and research, the program was first installed at the St. Louis distribution center. Thereafter, three management teams went forth to the other 19 centers, literally spreading the gospel to both the managers and the personnel who perform the necessary measurement and reportage the system requires.

"Our two-man teams covered the country in one month, spending a day and a half at each center," comments Controller-Distribution Operations Harold L. Gilson. **"Prior to these visits, the newly completed distribution center variable budget plan instruction manual was forwarded to all centers, preparing them in advance for constructive review and discussion. In consequence, transition to the new procedure went off smoothly on schedule."**

Key to variable budgeting's success is the establishment of realistic work standards, relating task accomplishment to time units (cases per hour, etc.) and these, in turn, to cost factors. Thus, the new system is at once a financial tool and a comprehensive productivity measuring procedure.

The variable budget system permits prompt corrective action on specific problem areas. Importantly, it also provides justification for additional labor and equipment when volume increases. Under older systems, justification of such additions was an arduous procedure for both local and divisional management. Under the new arrangements, justification becomes virtually self-evident.

Physical Distribution — and More

Manager-Materials Management Robert M. McIlwain brought to Warner-Lambert's Warner-Chilcott division a diversified experience in distribution and materials control. With both manufacturing-oriented and market-oriented logistics assignments behind him, his department's orientation reflects this harmonious duality.

The company's modern plant in northern New Jersey has been arranged internally for the orderly movement of goods-in-manufacture between individual steps. More than simple movement efficiency is involved, for here, as at Abbott, tight precautionary controls are essential to ensure highest standards of sanitation and positive protection of materials that are delicate, sensitive and of high value.

Careful observation of governmental handling and marking regulations, effective packaging and efficient, modern handling systems characterize the Warner-Chilcott operation, reviewed by TRAFFIC MANAGEMENT in May, 1971 and presented on the following pages:

LOGISTICS MANAGERS, whatever their titles, seem to be broadening their responsibilities further. Growing numbers of companies now entrust internal material flow to their command as well as the customer service and inbound goods movements they have supervised before.

TRAFFIC MANAGEMENT's January issue noted this in viewing Manager-Traffic and Materials Administration Jon Page's role at the Recognition Equipment Company. Our April issue found Manager-Distribution Fredric L. Keefe with parallel responsibility at Honeywell's Micro Switch Division.

This month, we observe the practice in a major ethical drug firm. Warner-Chilcott Laboratories' Robert M. McIlwain, manager-materials management, watches over the goods from actual sources of supply right through to the customers, as he also did previously as the Singer Company Consumer Products Division manager of materials and distribution.

Mr. McIlwain's present assignment embraces line services to the Warner-Chilcott and the General Diagnostics divisions of the Warner-Lambert Company's Professional Products Group, with staff services offered as well to other divisions within the group on request. His department reaches this large ethical drug manufacturing entity's market through a unique combination of public and private warehousing in contrast to the fully private operations typical of other concerns in the industry.

"Rather than dealing solely with finished goods in the commonly accepted physical distribution sense," states Mr. McIlwain, "a full materials management approach tracks everything we use from its very source. We have the ability to determine where we're going to keep our inventories, be they in vendor plant, in raw materials, in process or in finished goods. As to finished goods, we can select as well between central locations and branch distribution centers, setting the ratio for optimum benefit.

"This puts a premium on doing a very professional job. You've got to know your cycle times all the way through—cycle times in the total sense. Transit time, for instance, is really another cycle time. You have to consider purchase lead time, cycle times for going through your various key stages of manufacture, cycle times for customer deliveries and any other relevant time-related activities. When you can measure and adjust these cycles, controlling them fully from beginning to end, there's a real payoff."

Mr. McIlwain's operations encompass not only inbound and outbound flow, but in-plant handling as well. At the Morris Plains, N.J. divisional headquarters, warehousing and manufacture become largely integrated activities within a single building. The materials management department placed inventory and production planning, warehousing, distribution, traffic, purchasing and package engineering under one authority upon its inception three years ago. Order entry, though a sales department function, coordinates closely. Its offices, located adjacent to the materials department, assure easy communication.

VICE PRESIDENT MANUFACTURING F. H. YEOMANS (standing left of chart) visits a materials management staff meeting conducted by Department Manager Robert M. McIlwain (standing, right). Seated are (l. to r.): Package Engineering Supervisor Richard C. Belthoff, Traffic Supervisor Carle Leslie, Purchasing Manager Lloyd Magai, Supervisor-Warehousing Ralph Amato and Manager-Manufacturing Planning F. William McCoy.

Soon after the new department's formation, the present distribution centers were created. Morris Plains, the basic manufacturing facility, proved also to be a logical Northeastern distribution center. Anaheim, Calif., which shares a consumer products group computer unit and other local company services, similarly lent itself to private warehouse operation. The three other centers chosen, however, are all public facilities.

How were these public facilities selected, and why? Several factors governed the choice:

• Public warehousemen experienced in the exacting quality and precise controls required in the handling of ethical drugs could lend instant expertise. Their market area knowledge, familiarized personnel and existing specialized facilities were important advantages.

• Public warehousing offered greater flexibility. Changing market conditions or unsatisfactory performance can be rapidly cured by shifting to more suitable vendors or locations. A private facility inevitably means a longer-term commitment to a site.

• Efficient labor utilization derives from the multiple-account activities at a public warehouse. Peaks and valleys in Warner-Chilcott requirements can be "averaged out" by the differing cycles of other warehouse customers.

At Peoria, Ill., Midwestern business moves through a public warehouse handling a large volume of compatible goods. In Dallas, while other Warner-Lambert proprietary drug products flow through a large public facility, the Warner-Chilcott division chose a smaller unit 15 miles distant operated by a proprietor with lengthy ethical drug warehousing experience. The third such unit, in Jacksonville, Fla., though operated by the same warehousing company that handles proprietary drugs, is also housed separately. In this instance, the warehouseman recognized the significantly differing requirements and took over a

MODERN flow-through picking racks include overhead bins for easy disposal of emptied boxes. Racks are equipped with drop fronts for quick cleanup.

facility formerly owned by another drug company to better match Warner-Chilcott's needs.

These needs differ markedly from the typical manufacturing-marketing complex. From start to finish, materials and products must maintain a clear identity, with quality control exercised at every step of the way. For the public warehouse, this means relating specific batch numbers to orders and maintaining rigorous records. In the plant, it means quality control measurement of not only raw materials coming in, but every batch of material after each individual manufacturing step. Company standards as well as Food and Drug Administration regulations make this mandatory. More than that, records must reflect not only test results but disposition of product through to the customer.

Control, then, is the key, and a control orientation characterizes materials department organization. A planning unit, under Manager-Manufacturing Planning F. William McCoy, plays a critical role, not only scheduling production for the manufacturing facilities from sales forecast data, but also controlling both raw and finished goods inventory and supervising branch distribution center operations. In close coordination with Mr. McCoy is Manager of Purchasing Lloyd Magai and his staff, under whose scrutiny purchases of every kind and magnitude must pass.

Fully a fifth of purchase activities involves materials meeting the requirements and specifications of Package Engineering Supervisor Richard C. Belthoff and his staff. At the Morris Plains facility, a materials handling department under Supervisor-Warehousing Ralph Amato operates shipping and receiving facilities in addition to highly diversified storage sections and all in-plant materials handling operations. Traffic Supervisor Carle Leslie's staff services all distribution centers, plus export movements and direct deliveries to consignees.

**Purchasing's role in the materials department is a vital one. "We view our suppliers' receiving platforms as the start of our production line,"
states Mr. McIlwain, "so the purchasing function is a primary element**
in our overall control pattern. By operating the purchasing element under the overall materials management umbrella, we can also assure that purchase costs trade off properly against other cost factors for full system optimization, instead of suboptimizing for lowest purchase cost at the expense of other sectors which would lessen total gain."

The purchasing staff includes seven buyers and 10 clerical employes, the buyers and their individual secretaries each specializing in particular product areas. **"This specialization not only builds superior product knowledge," Mr. Magai asserts, "but it similarly builds a continually improving rapport with both our outside suppliers and our internal customers."**

Computerized purchase forecasting builds increasing negotiation effectiveness. In use for some period, Mr. Magai recently asked the computer unit to array commodities in order of dollar magnitude, easing buyer's work in doing A-B-C analyses to determine where major purchasing effort may best be exerted.

After three years of operation and continuing development, what is management reaction to the materials management concept in action? **"In general, it's doing the task well," Vice President-Manufacturing F. H. Yeomans observes. "The department does a good manufacturing support job while maintaining a perceptive sensitivity to marketing needs. Our experience appears to prove that the functions which we believe should be**
under common management have demonstrated this point through substantially improved performance. Other parallel functions, such as customer service and systems, remaining under separate jurisdiction, but placed in physical propinquity to the materials management activities, have also shown that better communication rather than outright control can spell further gains in optimizing our logistics."**

Planning builds better inventories

WHY would a planning unit supervise public warehousing? At Warner-Chilcott, where inventory control is a major planning section responsibility, it makes a lot of sense. The line activities, after all, are the warehouse owners' responsibilities—the only tasks that the planning people need do regularly are audits of their performance.

Helpful, too, is the intercommunication system based on Mohawk Data Science terminal units at each of the three public warehouse locations. Through these, such tasks as inventory adjustment, shipping paper preparation and shipment scheduling can be kept centralized at the Morris Plains computer, which flows this needed material instantaneously to the centers for action. Decision-

PLANNING SESSION discusses a new product introduction schedule. From left to right: Manager-Manufacturing Planning F. William McCoy, Manager-Materials Management Robert M. McIlwain, Supervisor-Systems Vincent Novak.

HEAVY TRAFFIC at the inbound dock of Warner-Chilcott's Morris Plains facility. With five of six unloading doors occupied, fork trucks move briskly to get raw materials placed for quality control inspection and subsequent storage.

making activity stays at headquarters, therefore, with the public warehouse staff role basically being in muscle-power supply.

The planning group keeps a close watch on these external facilities, nonetheless. At least once every six weeks, a staff member visits the three individual locations and checks out both physical facilities and operational performance. They particularly review sanitation conditions, accuracy of record control and individual warehouse inventory procedures.

Product control, in particular, draws heavy attention to ensure that "good manufacturing practices," as specified in Food and Drug Administration Regulation 133, are observed to the letter. This regulation covers every phase of product handling from its initial formulation through sale to ultimate customer and the maintenance of full records on every lot manufactured.

"Anyone in the drug business must have instant capability to locate a specific batch," notes Planning Manager McCoy.

"Planning," he adds, "is basically an information system supporting day-to-day decisions in this department. These day-to-day decisions, however, can involve highly variable time commitments for the manufacturing and quality control activities. Manufacturing cycles for some products can measure as much as six months, necessitating extended-range market forecasting." Frequently, the major time factor will derive from quality control requirements; one four-month cycle product entails a 90% quality control factor. Both planning efficient work loads for such cycles and seeking ways to achieve cycle reductions are major planning responsibilities.

Important, too, in scheduling production, is maintaining the best possible inventory levels. On the one hand, Warner-Chilcott seeks to provide a near 100% service level for most material and a positive 100% level for lifesaving drugs. On the other, judicious purchasing and production scheduling maximize the inventory portion held in lower value raw materials obtained at prices-on-delivery schedules that yield the best employment of company funds. Mr. McCoy notes: "We try to order large quantities to gain price benefit, but in split deliveries, so as to keep inventory levels as low as possible."

Inventory control also benefits from the computerized shipping procedures the division employs. The computer which creates shipping documents also adjusts distribution inventory figures on all stock items. "Computer-stored information maintains not only a physical balance of total goods at each warehouse," notes Supervisor-Systems Vincent Novak, "but a separate availability balance as well, reflecting the physical balance diminished by stock committed to orders."

An accompanying chart illustrates how computer procedures adjust balance figures to reflect the order itself and subsequently the related shipment. This maintains a continuously accurate picture of goods available, assigned and in transit at all branch operations. It is an important tool of the manufacturing planning operation, which is charged with the setting and maintenance of inventory levels.

The planning section works hand in glove with purchasing, developing

	Physical Balance	Available	Pending	Shipment	Back Order
Order No. 1	1,000	1,000			
		− 100	+ 100		
	1,000	900	100		
Shipment No. 1	− 100		− 100	+ 100	
	900	900	0	100	

ADJUSTMENTS in computer stock-balancing figures resulting from an order and from the subsequent related shipment are illustrated in the above chart.

QUALITY CONTROL inspection of all inbound material is mandatory. A QC "man in white" is about to check drums of chemicals for purity.

the timing and quantity of purchases. Purchasing stipulates economic buying quantities, selects vendors and schedules deliveries.

Varied techniques determine specific inventory plans. In the case of labels, for instance, the planning staff's chart procedure compares purchasing cost (including vendor setup), receiving cost (including quality control) and inventory carrying cost. The chart gives a quick and easy reading of proper purchase quantities to achieve optimum total cost.

Looking beyond regular production requirements, the planning unit faces major assignments when new products come into existence. PERT (Program Evaluation Review Technique) assures that all required steps are considered in getting a proposed product from research through manufacturing to market.

Modal diversity speeds nationwide service

WARNER-CHILCOTT'S traffic department splits its work into sharply differing categories. "This is not basically a tonnage industry," says Traffic Supervisor Carle Leslie. "We do, however, manage to develop some **economies of scale through the consolidation opportunities inherent in distribution center operation. Distribution center outbound freight to customers goes parcel post, UPS, motor carrier and air in about that order. From Morris Plains to the distribution centers, it's another story. Truckload, carload, sea container—quite varied means—move freight bound for the branches."**

The Peoria distribution center commonly draws stock in truckloads or by piggyback, while Jacksonville bulk shipments move substantially via Sea-Land from Port Elizabeth. The Anaheim center gets both rail shipments and containerized coast-to-coast sea movements, with high speed supplementation via Navajo Red Ball 72-hour truck service. Dallas, too, enjoys multimodal services chosen to match speed and economy requirements for the individual lots. The department keeps an open mind about new modes and methods.

Overseas shipping is a growing traffic responsibility. One company plant overseas ships inbound materials to Morris Plains, while the same region draws other products from Morris Plains as well, generating formance evaluation. The system bases upon a multipart, computer-produced form generated following order entry. The form parts include a warehouse copy (pick and pack), packing list, original bill of lading, shipping order (carrier copy) and freight audit copy (attached to freight bill and sent to the bank by the carrier under the freight payment plan). The orders flow from Morris Plains into other centers through Mohawk tape-to-tape units with coupled IBM selectric typewriters at the warehouses. This same equipment serves to print out the transmitted shipment information from the central corporate computer facility.

The shipping manifest, in addition to conventional information, shows customer product unit orders converted to cases, shelf packs or other standards. It shows case weights, shelf weights, loose weight and the movement by container in both directions. Other overseas freight consists primarily of palletized exports moving in conventional stowage, including both finished goods for marketing divisions and process materials for company plants in other countries.

Specific mode and carrier selection on larger shipments is conditioned in some measure by loading speed and loading problems at both Morris Plains and the destination centers. How effectively a common carrier handles loading and unloading strongly influences selection.

"We can get our docks tied up terribly by one common carrier coming in and dogging it all day," notes Mr. Leslie. "Given equal point-to-point performance, good dock performance will govern our carrier selection."

Computerized shipping procedures greatly facilitate both day-to-day traffic operation and subsequent performance evaluation. The system bases upon a multipart, computer-produced form generated following order entry. The form parts include a warehouse copy (pick and pack), packing list, original bill of lading, shipping order (carrier copy) and freight audit copy (attached to freight bill and sent to the bank by the carrier under the freight payment plan). The orders flow from Morris Plains into other centers through Mohawk tape-to-tape units with coupled IBM selectric typewriters at the warehous-

SEA-LAND containers call regularly at Warner-Chilcott Laboratories, serving Florida, Puerto Rico and Texas points.

es. This same equipment serves to print out the transmitted shipment information from the central corporate computer facility.

The shipping manifest, in addition to conventional information, shows customer product unit orders converted to cases, shelf packs or other standards. It shows case weights, shelf weights, loose weight and the total of all three, expediting carrier choice. **"Subsequently, cube as well as weight will be shown, with the ultimate thought of using cubes and weights jointly in determining branch order shipments,"** states Mr. McIlwain.

Routing is computer-entered as well, based upon regular routing file updates supplied by the traffic department. Initially based on an individual customer file, point routing information is changing over to a zip code procedure. Individual updates go to the computer room on a special form with data entries made to simplify accurate key-punching of the additions or changes.

Data derived from computerized shipping ease subsequent cost and service measurement. Regular reports compare distribution center (branch) movements by destination and mode, actual versus optimal,

showing any variances and comparing to prior year performance. States Mr. McIlwain: **"We watch this closely in terms of both per hundredweight and per order costs."**

Air movement expedites many of the higher value, more delicate shipments. Several air forwarders, one primarily, regularly move diagnostic products which need temperature protection. **"We cut our own bills and make them 'delivered at airport,' "** notes Mr. Leslie. **"These shipments are consolidated for delivery to Newark airport at substantial savings over**

conventional air pickup services."

A current problem for this department as well as other traffic units is the growth in accessorial charges. States Mr. Leslie: **"The carriers apparently find accessorial charges an easier way to up their rates, but they are skyrocketing our paper work costs in ways that don't happen with conventional rate increases. I wonder, too, if the parallel jump in their own paper work costs doesn't more than offset the gains from some of these accessorials."**

CAREFULLY SEALED DRUMS constitute an export shipment bound for Venezuela waiting to clear through the Morris Plains facility's export packaging area.

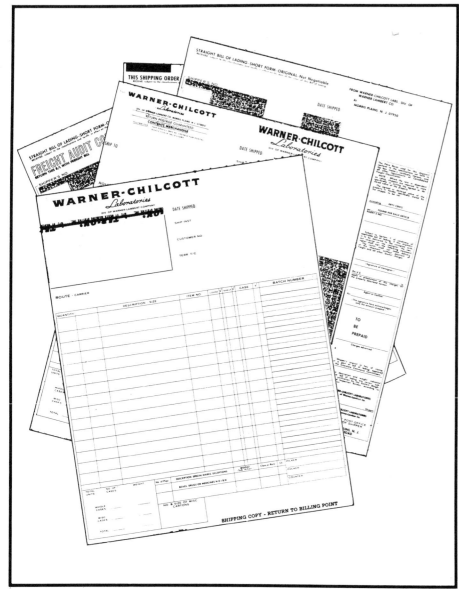

COMPUTER-PREPARED six-part shipping manifold speeds shipment preparation, aids traffic control and assists in picking order components from stock.

In-house testing keeps package standards high

SHIPMENT PROTECTION gets close attention at Warner-Chilcott. Package Engineering Supervisor Richard C. Belthoff's full-time staff and a substantial package testing laboratory confirm this interest. While the company's marketing arm develops the package graphics, physical aspects are entirely under materials management. **"Our prime objective is to design a package that will meet marketing's needs," comments Package Engineering Supervisor Richard C. Belthoff. "Package engi-**neering is also vitally concerned with product protection, package material costs, handling and productivity."

Backing up package design and development is an impressive laboratory, encompassing many test devices not commonly found among shippers. Drop test, compression and vibration test units may seem conventional, but a number of stability cabinets are quite unique.

What a stability cabinet does is provide a predetermined atmosphere for measuring temperature and humidity effect on both the package and its contents. The goal is not to develop an invulnerable package, but to protect the contents, and it is the ability of the two to survive together

that measures success.

Varying in size from a counter cabinet to a near walk-in, both small and large packs can be tested for substantial time periods with chosen humidity and temperature levels maintained inside continuously. Freezable, meltable or spoilable products, as well as their packaging, can be quickly checked for individual package design validity.

At present, an 18-inch drop test is standard for most new packs, but a test shipping program using Impactographs to measure actual shocks in travel may modify this procedure. Mr. Belthoff anticipates fine-tuning the drop test standards to match Impactograph-recorded shipment experience.

Among various projects currently occupying Mr. Belthoff's attention, the conversion of many products from glass bottles to polyethylene containers particularly captures his current interest. Much more than just a shift in the basic container is involved: changed handling procedures and external packing must be considered at the same time.

"Glass is subject to breakage through shattering, but nonetheless, it can handle a lot of weight, and our present packs stack well in storage," notes Mr. Belthoff. "With poly, on the other hand, we escape from shatter breakage all right, but it reacts differently in stacking, with a danger of buckling or failure and thus a need for stronger external packaging if we want to maintain stackability. On balance, though, the polypropylene container looks clearly like a better cost-and-service pack than glass for our liquid products."

An important design consideration in the liquid product area, too, is a postal regulation requiring sufficient absorbent packing to take up the complete liquid content of any bottle or tube that breaks in shipping.

In any packaging design, the specialized requirements of the ethical drug manufacturing business make vital demands. For example, extensive label information is required, often necessitating a package insert which must be attached to the container. Every label bears a coded batch number which can be used to trace the history of the specific manufacturing conditions, ingredients and customers to whom sold.

Unified material handling eliminates bottlenecks

THE total material control system virtually eliminates the usual distinctions between plant and distribution center warehousing at Morris Plains. From receiving dock to shipping platform, unified management makes the most of available space and equipment.

Handling chores require 15 lift trucks, all electric, split between 2,000-pound counterbalance trucks for heavy work and 2,000-pound reach trucks for low volume items stored in 7 1/2-foot aisles, plus two rider-transporters working the separate inbound and outbound docks. An employe reporting to the assistant supervisor of warehousing works full time on maintenance of the lift truck fleet.

Lift truck operators carry substantial responsibilities in this operation. Specific men and trucks are assigned to individual production or handling areas, operating exclusively for these functions. Each man must be familiar with the specific products to be moved in and out of various production phases and storage, but must be certain also that quality control stickers are properly affixed at each stage, that each product batch is correctly identified and that he knows where needed materials are stocked.

Although random storage is standard practice, certain slow-moving items are location-cataloged. Such materials are largely in double drive-in racks, trading off added handling time against substantial space savings. The refrigerated warehouse and a section of the finished goods area have these racks, as do a few other locations. Numerous packaging items are among their contents.

Each day, lift truck operators assigned to specific manufacturing operations receive lists of materials which they will bring to their specified production lines. The materials generally move in pallet lots, and any

PACKAGE ENGINEERING SUPERVISOR Richard C. Belthoff inspects a stability cabinet which measures the effects of preselected temperature and humidity conditions on packages and their contents over specific time periods.

portion not used is subsequently picked up following the manufacturing operation and returned to storage. The lift truck operator's responsibilities, therefore, include feeding and returning supplies plus moving the finished goods from the operation to quality control inspection. Lift truck operators not only work to move goods under specific batch control numbers, but see to it as well that strict stock rotation practices are followed.

"In process" storage is maintained adjacent to walled-in production facilities, with goods moved back and forth from storage for each individual operation. Following each step, the production batch must be checked by quality control. When the subsequent step is scheduled, the fork lift truck operator must be certain that all containers in the lot have the prior step's quality control sticker applied and that the batch number corresponds with the manufacturing

DIAGNOSTICS DIVISION MATERIAL, located in racks adjacent to one of the division's enclosed manufacturing laboratories, is inspected by Supervisor-Warehousing Ralph Amato (right) and Assistant Supervisor George Taylor.

unit's order. Assigning one man full time to this task assures his familiarity with the diversified requirements of this post.

Similar lift truck positions support other operations. The diagnostic packaging and processing area lift truck runs many loads between the fully-enclosed work space and a 2,500-foot special refrigerated storage room in addition to conventional adjacent rack space. Uninterrupted handling service is essential here, as many items must be temperature-protected and must return promptly to the refrigeration section after specified times in the processing facility.

The liquids area as well enjoys a full-time lift truck service. This is the heaviest tonnage sector among the manufacturing-support lift truck assignments. A full-time truck also serves the similarly heavy tablet packaging operation.

At the completion of manufacture, two lift trucks service finished goods. A counterbalance truck picks up production dropped at the outbound door of manufacturing and places those loads destined for storage. A stand up reach truck supplements the first unit, supplying the professional service area, the export area and the pick and pack area. The smaller truck not only matches the somewhat lighter volume movements in these instances, but is essential to maneuver in the 7 1/2-foot aisles found in some of these sections.

The present manufacturing operations, though devoid of conflicting material flow patterns, offer opportunities for handling procedure refinement. **"Our long-range goal,"** Supervisor-Warehousing Ralph Amato states, **"is a continuous flow pattern, with goods entering interim storage locations placed in a direct line between operating sections. They will flow, for instance, from the north end of a production unit to storage and quality control, with the next production station, in turn, placed to the north of the interim storage-quality control area. This will reduce lift truck effort significantly. It will take time, but changes in this direction are already under way."**

Input for the total plant-warehouse complex crosses a fully enclosed dock area. Six trucks can be served at indi-

CARTS MADE UP from shelving and stock casters function as picking racks, in addition to serving a transport function for goods kept under refrigeration.

A KOREA SHIPMENT is prepared at one of six export packing stations.

vidual loading doors with the parking area in turn fully enclosed, thus providing double weather and sanitation protection. An average day finds 35 trucks making deliveries here, serviced by a rider-transporter whose easy maneuverability speeds unloading, augmented by counterbalance trucks during peak periods. With dock utilization running 60%, it is common to find as many as five trucks being unloaded at once.

The initial move from the dock is not far—everything coming in must clear through quality control. Brightly lit areas lie adjacent to the inbound center for this purpose, manned by

quality control "men in white."

At the finished goods end of things, most products move through the pick and pack area, except for volume shipments to the other distribution centers. In addition, some shipments are in case quantities or LTL-size lots. Back-load gravity-fed racks stock the small items area, while roller-equipped flow racks handle the full cases.

Because the small items area generates a lot of empty cartons, their disposal could create congestion. Warner-Chilcott licked this problem with overhead slanted bins having drop fronts. Pickers toss empty cartons in them as they deplete their stock, and at shift's end, they are opened up to gravity feed their contents into refuse carts. The carts themselves are one-piece bodied, Rubbermaid plastic units on four casters. Shaped for efficient nesting, they store easily, are light in weight, yet well suited to hard use.

For some time, a "supermarket" picking procedure has cared for small shipment assembly, pickers working with carts essentially similar to those in shopping centers. More recently, a specialized hand cart entered this service.

"These new units offer greater picking efficiency," claims Assistant Warehousing Supervisor George Taylor. "Our pickers now have two tote boxes available on the work-shelf level instead of one. This reduces trips to and from the packaging line and maximizes time for picking. We found the initial design had a slight balance problem, but overcame this easily by counterweighting the bottom shelf."

Packing and assembly work through conveyorized lines. With one line devoted to case lots, another handling the small shipments, the conveyor system can dispatch packed material over either route.

Pickers roll their loaded carts to the packing stations adjacent to the conveyor lines for order preparation. The units destined for the small shipment line pass working positions equipped with meters for UPS and parcel post, which account for the handling of most such orders. Final departure sees lift trucks taking over and feeding carrier trucks at a fully enclosed dock similar to the receiving facility with six truck doors.

POWER CONVEYORS speed case lots from picking areas to outbound dock.

LARGER PALLETIZED SHIPMENTS move on a separate conveyor system.

AT THE OUTBOUND DOCK, as at the inbound one, a rider-transporter operates full time, moving goods in and out of trailers and shifting stock in the dock area.

Logistics: A Materials Management Approach

Recognition Equipment Company manufactures optical character recognition devices that can input written or printed matter directly to computers or other electronic units. Differing radically from the drug companies described on the preceding pages, its need for effective materials management is fully as urgent.

It is not uncommon for this company's individual customer orders to run into the millions of dollars. Values such as these placed on highly sophisticated, custom-prepared electronic equipment demand the utmost in care and preplanning throughout manufacture, installation and subsequent servicing of the equipment.

Recognition Equipment's materials management unit, therefore, fulfills assignments world-wide as well as in-plant. Materials management people may be found at customer locations in any place where major systems are being installed, making certain that receiving conditions are right and that the schedule and physical conditions of delivery are properly fulfilled. On the other end, the department closely watches the inbound scheduling of vital elements for incorporation in new equipment that is produced under the most rigid of schedules.

TRAFFIC MANAGEMENT's January, 1971 study of Recognition Equipment follows:

WALKING THROUGH Recognition Equipment's production facilities, Traffic and Materials Administration Manager Jon P. Page (left) and Director of Materials Robert C. Warford discuss plans for new handling systems at firm's Dallas facilities.

TRAFFIC — Distribution — Logistics: these terms symbolize varying approaches to goods flow and storage management. At Recognition Equipment Incorporated, all these elements and several more get unified treatment. "We're applying a materials management concept," claims Director of Materials Robert C. Warford, whose responsibilities, in addition to inventory control and purchasing functions, embrace a traffic and materials handling department that literally achieves the more than a decade old distribution man's dream—complete physical control from raw material source through manufacture and distribution to the final, positive installation of finished goods in a customer's premises.

Just nine years old, Recognition Equipment Inc. today enjoys a $40 million gross income and the promise of continued rapid growth in its field of optical character recognition (OCR) equipment and related computer components. Banks, credit card services, airline reservation systems and a growing variety of other applications, several distribution oriented, now employ Recognition Equipment systems or feed work through the company's affiliate, Corporation S, which operates OCR service bureaus known as optimation centers. Where volume document flow warrants this specialized equipment, company systems cut computer input costs and greatly diminish entry time requirements because keypunching to cards or tapes is no longer necessary.

Why this close control of material

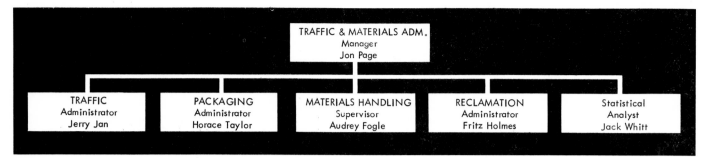

TRAFFIC & MATERIALS ADM.
Manager
Jon Page

TRAFFIC
Administrator
Jerry Jan

PACKAGING
Administrator
Horace Taylor

MATERIALS HANDLING
Supervisor
Audrey Fogle

RECLAMATION
Administrator
Fritz Holmes

Statistical
Analyst
Jack Whitt

STAFF CHART above indicates the diversified functions housed within Recognition Equipment's traffic department.

flow in this young Dallas-based company? For one thing, even the raw materials entering its electronic components are expensive and delicate, demanding utmost care in handling and storage. For another, minimized inventories and timely goods movement at all stages help maintain a strong cash flow, a characteristic that the company has maintained through the recent tight money period as it has throughout its history. States Mr. Warford: Effective E.D.P. employment and economical materials management largely account for this fortunate condition.

In great measure operating with leased systems rather than out-and-out sales, Recognition Equipment users are virtually 100% under maintenance contracts. Thus, in all cases, a firm employing these systems represents not just a one-time shipment, but a continuing traffic demand. Though customers number only slightly over 100, they blanket North America and Western Europe. Every new system leased or sold, in turn, adds one more destination to the traffic department's clientele. With individual systems typically worth $1 million and up, preplanning, shipment surveillance and delivery inspection demand concentrated traffic attention.

Overseeing the many related physical handling activities, Traffic and Materials Administration Manager Jon P. Page operates a uniquely comprehensive department. The accompanying organization chart shows not only the orthodox traffic bases neatly covered, but several unique duties in addition. The materials-handling responsibilities include not only shipping and receiving, but in-plant handling as well. The latter function became a department responsibility in September, 1969, a few months after Mr. Page became the company's traffic manager. Even more unique are the reclamation and the intercompany business functions, the former of which involves returned or reusable items as detailed in another portion of this survey.

Intercompany business concerns the sale of incidental manufactures to subsidiaries or external companies. "In the course of manufacturing our major system units, we can economically produce a substantial run of components useful in many other applications," states Mr. Page. "Printed circuit boards, for example, lend themselves readily to this. In dealing with our own affiliates, we bid for their needs on the open market, leaving them free to buy from us or from other sources purely on the basis of price and quality. With outside vendors, we seek to develop a similar relationship. Through this means, we develop improved total costs for both our own production and that of our customers for these in a sense incidental products."

The company's systems, because of their size, have generally required a level of use that precluded distribution employment except through optimation centers or in high volume operations such as mail order house applications. A bright new star now shines over the Recognition Equipment horizon for distribution management, however. A new terminal unit, Input 3, recently became available which lends itself to practical, smaller scale distribution applications. This equipment reads widely varied printed and handwritten materials, translating them directly to computer input for such computers as the IBM 360, 370 and others. Renting at about $1,000 monthly, it is intended to eliminate the need for keypunching or other forms of retyping, thus materially reducing labor costs wherever remote terminals feed a computer. "Such applications as freight docks or distribution centers which tie into a central computer by wire typify the applications we have in mind," observes J.E. Ashby,

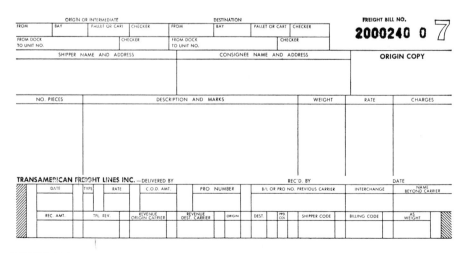

TRANSAMERICAN FREIGHT LINES' new pro is designed for reading by the equipment of Recognition Equipment's affiliate, Corporation S, thus eliminating the necessity for key punching or retyping for computer access.

vice president-North America sales.

Carrier applications of Recognition Equipment systems are receiving close attention, too. Corporation S, in conjunction with Transamerican Freight Lines, Inc., recently developed a pro manifold form which lends itself to efficient handling by Recognition Equipment machines. The accompanying illustration reveals a form that differs little from other typical pro sheets, but the bottom two lines of format are set up for maximum reading efficiency. Such forms can be read directly into a computer at a speed of 1,200 documents a minute, greatly speeding data access while concurrently eliminating keypunching costs.

Under development is another system with distribution overtones: a mail sorting system that will cover a wide range of envelope sizes as well as varied forms of machine printing. To be used by the U.S. Postal Service, it may well point the way to major service benefits throughout the postal system.

TRAFFIC MANAGER Jon P. Page (left) and Traffic Administrator Jerry Jan review plans for a new Recognition Equipment system's installation in Tokyo prior to Mr. Jan's departure for Japan.

World distribution from a single plant

FOR TWO YEARS NOW, the traffic and materials administration department's role has grown steadily at Recognition Equipment. In a business where many shipments run exceptionally high in value, require careful handling and are moved under serious time pressures, it is all too easy to treat every one as a "special case." Manager Jon Page recognized this condition early and strives continually to build up standard practices covering the broadest portion of potential shipment circumstances. For both domestic movements and exports, standardized forms and instructions ease handling and assure performance reliability for field engineering personnel at delivery sites and affected traffic staff members at Dallas as well as on site.

The traffic department takes responsibility for systems equipment on the test room floor of the Dallas plant and follows through until installation is completed on customer premises, including any problems involving access to customer premises due to size, weight, etc. Shipment practices fit two basic categories—routine and emergency.

Routine domestic shipments move forward to major metropolitan areas in weekly consolidations. These shipments include varied equipment and supplies, with complete systems moving separately and individually. European shipments are being brought into a similar procedure, much of this freight flowing through the company's own service supply center at Frankfurt, West Germany for fanout to European customers. This location also maintains a stock of various items for speedy response to regional customer requirements.

1500 West Mockingbird Lane Dallas Texas 75222 Telex 073 2342 Cable Address RECOGROUP (214) 637 22°.

PLEASE RETURN TO THE TRAFFIC DEPARTMENT - MAIL STATION 32
PERFORMANCE CHECK LIST

CARRIER_____
AIRBILL NUMBER_____
DATE SHIPPED_____
SITE_____
EMERGENCY: YES_____NO_____
- TIME SHIPPED/FLIGHT NO._____
- TIME NOTIFIED _____
- TIME PICKED-UP_____
- FLIGHT INFORMATION TO FIELD ENGINEERING_____
CONDITION AT RECEIPT:

PERFORMANCE CHECK LIST helps Recognition Equipment keep tabs on carrier service for future selection and instruction.

DATE_____

SHIPPER_____ CITY_____ STATE_____

LOADING FOR:_____

ADDRESS:_____

CITY_____ STATE_____

CONTACT:_____ OR _____

TELEPHONE NO:_____

I.   LOADING OR UNLOADING AREA

DESCRIBE CONDITION:_____

_____

_____

DOCK HEIGHT:_____ NUMBER OF STEPS:_____

RAMP?_____ SURFACE CONDITION_____

II. ELEVATOR SIZE_____ BY_____

ELEVATOR DOOR_____ ELEVATOR CAPACITY_____

CAN CAPACITY BE INCREASED IF NECESSARY?_____

TO WHAT CAPACITY?_____

III. CITY ORDINANCE OR RESTRICTIONS:_____

CAN PROPER CLEARANCE BE OBTAINED?_____

FROM WHOM?_____

TELEPHONE NUMBER:_____

IV. IS HALLWAY CLEARANCE AMPLE:_____

V.   IS MASONITE REQUIRED FOR FLOOR PROTECTION?_____

VI. NUMBER OF MEN REQUIRED FOR INSTALLATION:_____

VII. IS RIGGING OR HOISTING REQUIRED?_____

HAS APPROVAL BEEN OBTAINED FROM RECOGNITION EQUIPMENT, INC.?_____

FROM WHOM?_____

DESCRIBE HOISTING REQUIREMENTS:_____

_____

NAME OF RIGGING COMPANY:_____

ADDRESS_____ TELEPHONE NO._____

CITY_____ STATE_____

CONTACT:_____

VIII. ROOM FOR INSTALLATION

DOORWAYS AMPLE?_____ FLOORING:_____

IX. SPECIAL EQUIPMENT REQUIRED

FORK LIFT_____

POWER GATES_____

HYDRAULIC JACKS_____

X.   ESTIMATED TIME:_____ ESTIMATED COST:_____

(Signature of Division Manager or Agent)

TRAFFIC AND ENGINEERING personnel use this form on new system site studies to assure proper installation.

On emergency shipments, consolidation has no application. The sole concern is reliable speed. The traffic department has an agreement with the field engineering division that two hours from the time traffic physically receives a part, it will be packed, delivered to the airport, flight booking made and all information concerning flight, waybill number and related matters forwarded to concerned company personnel at destination, generally a field engineer. At present holding true on domestic shipments, a similar formula is under development for export emergency shipments.

Careful stocking of customer system locations and a network of parts depots help to keep emergency shipments trending downward. In addition to the Frankfurt facility and a new Tokyo center for overseas customers, North American parts depots can be found in Chicago, Los Angeles, Philadelphia, Houston and Toronto. Nevertheless, the Dallas plant still experiences some four to five rush shipments in an average day.

Whether routine or emergency, precision handling of shipments is vital. "One scratch," notes Mr. Page, "and I've got to buy a new panel or a paint job." For this reason, carrier performance means much to the company, both as to time and condition of shipments. States Mr. Page: "We've installed a carrier performance evaluation procedure developed from a similar approach described in TRAFFIC MANAGEMENT'S survey of the Macklanburg-Duncan Co. in the February, 1970 issue. These case studies frequently suggest methods and procedures for solving some of our particular problems."

In another such instance, Mr. Page recently submitted to his management an analysis of the travel function and future plans matched to anticipated growth based upon TRAFFIC MANAGEMENT'S survey of representative corporations in the November, 1969 issue. The description of varied current practices and recommendations based upon them gave Recognition Equipment executives clear-cut choices covering future travel administration plans.

The company's traffic department provides two different routing guides. Those for buyers cover all vendor locations. Compliance is reenforced by traffic department monitoring of purchase orders and receiving reports, with charge-backs to vendors who deviate improperly. In addition, a "compressed" routing guide goes to field engineers. While similar in construction to the buyer's routing guide, the engineer's version covers only points where Recognition Equipment installations currently operate.

Export volume was sufficient to make this company the Dallas "Exporter of the Year" in 1969. Easing its overseas shipping tasks is a service supply license obtained for the company by Mr. Page. "Only about four other companies have as yet obtained such licenses," he notes. A thorough study and resultant brief, hand-carried to Washington, led to the sought-for licensing. It covers the following activities:
• Export to countries of spare parts without import certificate or export license.
• Export to Germany for stocking.
• Reexport from Germany to any site in Western Europe.

TRAFFIC MANAGER Jon P. Page (left) and Purchasing Manager Arthur Paulsen discuss proposed revision of a standard vendor routing.

• Reexport from sites in Europe to Germany for repair and restocking.
• Reexport between sites without U.S. authorization on individual moves.

Mr. Page finds the latter two waivers to be unique. In all, this licensing represents a major gain in shipping efficiency, cutting time and costs through paper work simplification.

Internal export methods benefit as well from another recent project. In March, 1970, Mr. Page visited each affected European country and developed individual import-export procedures. Coordinating with company marketing and finance staff members in these countries, as well as with Dallas headquarters, he has developed standards covering each activity from the writing out of equipment orders through to final deliveries.

While all European systems' shipments move via air, the major share of domestic systems' shipments employ padded vans with logistics equipment installed. Comprehensive check lists cover each system movement, including a site check list, a van check list covering the actual point-to-point movement and a follow-up list to be certain that schedules were met, deliveries were com-

plete and installation was properly accomplished.

Traffic Administrator Jerry Jan maintains a folder for every equipment order to ensure the fulfillment of procedural requirements. On the more complex export shipments, he maintains a "Traffic Check List of Events" form in the file, recording the planned shipment arrangements thereon, dating and initialling each event as it occurs.

How to handle million-dollar shipments

MATERIALS HANDLING Supervisor Audrey Fogle has a two-pronged responsibility: the proper physical handling of material from plant to ultimate destination and, similarly, proper handling of materials from receipt through manufacture to the test room floor, where traffic takes over for shipping. At the moment, big changes are taking place in the former section, with a new plant about to open momentarily.

While the present location has "made do" with restricted shipping space, small four-wheel trucks and

pallet jacks, a greatly expanded, well-equipped dock will soon be placed into operation. Internal handling will benefit from addition of forklift equipment as well as two Plant-Cats, small electric units with one or two seats and a rear flatbed for handling material. Provision has been made as well for the subsequent addition of multiple power and gravity conveyor lines as growth makes them necessary at the new Dallas location.

Department Manager Jon Page involved himself deeply in designing the new plant's shipping dock. His particular concern related to the problem of ground clearance on company units. This is typically in the range from one-half inch to 1½ inches, yet many of the units are up to eight feet long, so sills, ramps or floor slopes assume a considerable significance. The new dock has five loading doors equipped with Kelly dockboards, with a built-in Precision scale adjacent and a rolling door-protected port for the projected conveyor line. Ample access to the large adjacent stock facilities is provided, and dock width permits easy movement of long or high units preparatory to loading or unloading of trucks or vans.

The careful handling of complete system shipments is a major concern

MATERIALS HANDLING SUPERVISOR Audrey Fogle prepares a system-loading simulation for a proposed vanload shipment.

of the materials handling section. Some three weeks in advance of such a move, a van line agent and a Recognition Equipment engineer or systems analyst complete an "Installations Site Survey" at the actual installation point, sending a copy of this form to Dallas. Analyzed by the traffic staff, decisions are then made as to whether a traffic representative should accompany the shipment and what special arrangements may be necessary.

Mr. Fogle and his aides must determine whether an existing elevator can handle the system weight and if not, whether its capacity can be temporarily increased through rigging or other arrangements. Barring that, the question of opening a wall or going through a roof must be explored and provisions made to follow through on the ultimately chosen approach. On all domestic shipments valued at $1 million or above and export shipments of $100,000 or above, the insurance company must be notified. In the case of van shipments, not more than $1 million worth of material may move in one van.

Those shipments that do move by van are carefully plotted on simulation charts in the Dallas office. A chart for the specific size van employed provides a base for placing scale-sized templates of system units to develop the loading pattern. "This pattern must not only provide for efficient cube utilization, but proper weight distribution as well, assuring that weight does not exceed legal limits on any one axle," notes Mr. Fogle.

The materials section also operates a local transport service. A minibus provides scheduled service between plant and office facilities, moving personnel, data and small items on a once-hourly schedule, making occasional airport shuttle trips during its layover time as well. In addition, a two-ton truck takes care of most pickups and deliveries at the airport, plus any rush vendor pickups in the immediate area.

Perhaps the most unusual function of this department is its reclamation activity. Parts Reclamation Administrator Fritz Holmes initiated this operation in January, 1970 and by the end of October had already chalked up an impressive $145,000-

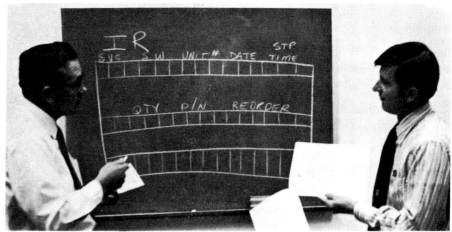

DIRECTOR OF FIELD PROGRAMS Rex Darling (left) and Director of Field Engineering Administration Robert McWhorter review module for field usage reports.

plus in recoveries for the traffic budget. Mr. Holmes enjoys virtually complete freedom to locate useful items that can be put to good use or converted to cash. Old systems or obsolete units coming back from the field, for instance, release many kinds of electronic elements and hardware that can provide further service within the company or without. Already, three testing units have been assembled employing just such items. Employe sales at very low percentages of initial costs also earn a return from such used materials.

The "Blue Barrel" program initiated by Mr. Holmes brings increasing gains right from the plant floor. Large metal barrels painted bright blue with an orange stripe are spaced at convenient intervals throughout production areas. When assembly personnel encounter mislabeled or misplaced parts, they put them in the nearest such receptacle rather than either discarding them or going through a paper work procedure that consumes productive time. The reclamation section readily sorts and identifies such materials, channeling

RECLAMATION ADMINISTRATOR Fritz Holmes among some of his "finds." At left are power supplies ready for reuse or sale. In foreground are connectors ready for stripping and reuse, while resistors are stored on shelves at right rear.

them back to proper uses. Not only does this create material savings, but data on specific items showing up in improper locations help to pinpoint trouble spots as an event pattern develops.

Quite naturally, the company generates substantial computer output in its payroll department, much of which enjoys only a short useful life and then becomes refuse. By shredding this material and placing it in plastic bags supplied by the reclamation section, free packing fill is generated for the many fragile shipments originating at the Dallas plant.

A special program also sees to the collection and segregation of ferrous and nonferrous metal scrap, as material thus segregated gets higher prices. Scrap solder is also separately accumulated and sold at 70 cents per pound whenever 500 pounds are accumulated. Scrap wire, even small cuttings, are accumulated to merchandisable lots. On this and other items, Mr. Holmes watches market prices regularly to dispose of the materials at greatest advantage.

GRAND OPENING will soon take place at the new Recognition Equipment plant, where five doors, Kelley dockboard-equipped, will serve a large shipping area. Initially set up for conventional operation, there's provision for conveyorization.

SENIOR ENGINEER William E. Viering (left) and Traffic Manager Jon P. Page discuss handling requirements of new equipment designs that are currently in production.

"The traffic sector is a particularly suitable spot organizationally for effective contact with all company departments," Mr. Holmes asserts. "A vital part of this job is knowing who has both material and information, permitting you to act as go-between in developing parts uses, locating specific items and identifying the many things that turn up out of the blue."

Effective packaging cuts costs

MODERN packaging control got its major impetus when Packaging Engineer Horace Taylor joined the company in February, 1968. In addition to specialized packs for standard company items, he provides expertise for the movement of custom products, both in their packaging and their handling, either packed or unpacked. Working closely with Materials Handling Supervisor Audrey Fogle, he frequently visits sites when installation problems arise, arranging for and designing specialized rigging whenever required for the safe installation of Recognition Equipment systems and equipment.

At present, Mr. Taylor is working with American Airlines to develop prototype weatherproof containers with logistics equipment, padded like standard vans. "On international shipments," he notes, "this could save 5,000 pounds tare weight plus crating costs. The crating alone runs $2,000 on an average system. In 1969, we spent $45,000 on crating for overseas that this container would have eliminated. Add to that the transportation savings from reduced weight and you can see why we're interested." With preplanned container loads secured by logistics strapping, the only additional packing requirement would be some simple cushioning under the units, such as urethane foam. Such a container could greatly increase the airline's share of systems moving to domestic locations also, in Mr. Taylor's opinion.

Home-designed shipping braces and shipping slings now protect many internal parts of company system units. Through these devices, many elements formerly shipped in separate accompanying cartons now reach the customer in their normal working location. This procedure saves several hours work for company field engineers during field installation operations in addition to reducing cubic shipping dimensions and eliminating the costs of separate containers and related packaging material.

With all international shipments routed by air, efficient placement of the many units making up a typical system is important to both carrier and Recognition Equipment alike. Braniff Airways and the company together recently developed a cargo plane hold simulator to aid preplanning of individual system component placement. The simulator, a scale model, works with scale size balsa blocks representing specific components, assuring both maximum security of this freight and the most effective use of available cargo hold capacity. With overseas systems shipments running at least $1 million or more in value individually, careful preplanning is amply justified.

By no means does all of the packaging activity concern itself with huge systems and seven-figure values, however. For Recognition Equipment, as for most companies, proper handling of smaller, high-frequency items yields substantial payoff. With some 12,500 products stocked by the company, there is ample opportunity to check specific units and apply packaging standards where gains through damage prevention or cost reduction may accrue.

Some of these individual gains can be quite dramatic. Consider the company's Ink-Jet Printer, an item that prints numbers in bar code form for subsequent computer reading after an initial printed-character reading by optical character recognition equipment. Machined to close tolerances, these printers formerly traveled in small wooden cases with internal foam protection. Each case represented a $24 expense.

Mr. Taylor sought to eliminate these specifically tailored units and came up with a standard package and a slight modification that proved fully satisfactory under test. The new pack is a Compress-O-Carton made of conventional fibreboard with urethane foam built into its top and bottom members, while an inner corrugated sleeve is added for further projection of the Ink-Jet Printer. Total cost: 94 cents. Contrasted to the $24 item it replaces, the savings on even a few shipments are substantial.

Another system component, a read drum, formerly moved in a kraft paper wrap with a patented protective paper filler between the wrap and the finely finished drum. The new pack for this unit represented roughly comparable costs, employing a full-telescoping corrugated carton with Ethafoam end caps, the latter grasping the drum by one inch at each end.

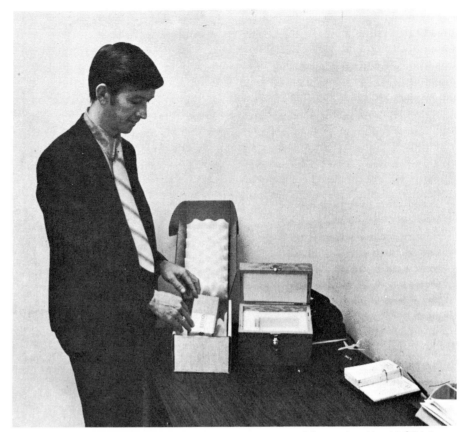

PACKAGING ENGINEER Horace Taylor compares new 94¢ pack with old $24 item.

A COMPRESS-O-CARTON with fitted end blocks of urethane foam saves $5,000 annually in shipping these finely finished read drums.

In this case, the goal was not packaging savings, but greater protection. Annual savings from reduced damages currently run about $5,000. Fully as important, since this is a vital part in Recognition Equipment systems, is the greater delivery reliability, since a damaged drum will not put equipment back in action if the particular shipment is emergency in nature.

Also benefitting packaging economy is a Box-O-Matic machine recently acquired by the department. This box-maker takes about two minutes to make up cartons in custom designs for specific equipment. It not only assures that packaging can be prepared promptly, but it also saves about $50 to $60 weekly in the process.

Important, too, is the department's materials handling manual. Cataloging the various parts, it provides numbered, detailed, illustrated packaging and handling standards to guide engineers in the plant or the field.

Con Edison Improves its Supply System

While materials management is viewed as manufacturing-oriented and physical distribution is more marketing-oriented, there is a third face to logistics: Consider the chores of a major receiver.

New York city draws its supply of power from the world's largest privately held utility, the Consolidated Edison Company. Familiarly known as Con Edison, the maintenance of its numerous huge generating stations, gas plants, supply systems and other facilities requires a substantial annual input of specialized as well as conventional supplies.

As part of the company's program to update management and operating practices, Con Edison merged a number of functions previously handled within separate divisions into a single materials unit. Centralized warehousing and truck fleet operation brought cost benefits plus substantially bettering response capability to the demands of company divisions, improving total service reliability for the system. Innovations at the company's giant Astoria warehouse and storage center in particular have done much to benefit the total system, while continuing expansion of computerization assures still further improvements. TRAFFIC MANAGEMENT's May, 1971 Con Edison presentation follows.

CON EDISON'S name gets quick recognition as a major utility, and well it should. Its 12 generating plants feed a 630-square mile area encompassing virtually all of New York City and most of adjacent Westchester county. Few would think of a utility company as a major logistics operation, however—nobody inventories electricity.

Yet, Con Edison maintains a steady $55 million inventory that supports its power, gas and steam production. Encompassing over 90,000 items, everything from tweezers to transformers, from penny pins to intricate, highly-machined valves worth thousands of dollars, transportation and supply department stocks give massive support to diversified operating and maintenance functions.

The size of this function is only one measure of its significance. Fully as important is an ability to offer instantaneous response to emergency demands. The ability to locate any item promptly on demand, coupled with the capacity for rapid emergency delivery anywhere within the system, gives maximum assurance of uninterrupted utility services to millions of customers in the New York metropolitan area. Even parts required less frequently than once in 10 years can be confidently requisitioned by authorized company field personnel.

The concept of centralized logistics service represents a comparatively recent development within the system. Previously, individual divisions of the company fulfilled these needs within their own sectors or functions. Company recognition of both service and cost gains inherent in a total logistics system, however, brought changes, and the past 1½ years have seen a strong transportation and stores department developing its role. Under its banner, duties formerly split between the purchasing department, the construction department and a smaller transportation department now enjoy the benefits of integrated control.

Attesting to the department's significance is a staff of 830 people who operate stores bureau facilities, transportation bureau equipment, a transformer shop for the rehabilitation of equipment, a property disposal unit which produces handsome salvage dividends and an equipment operator training and accident prevention unit that keeps vehicle performance levels high for this major fleet user in one of the world's toughest traffic congestion areas.

"Our goals are to concurrently improve service, build revenues, reduce costs and improve storage efficiency," states Assistant Vice President-Transportation and Stores J. Frank Burgess. **"We've made a few short-run strides already, but we're seeking greater gains from such programs as a three-year plan to reorient 100,000 tons of materials stored in Astoria that we activated in 1970. Actually, we're looking ahead 20 years in our overall logistics planning."**

Some of those short-run programs have had impressive results. Consider these:

Reduced gas cylinder demurrage: Improved storage and distribution practices brought this cost below $5,000 monthly, compared to a previously normal $12,000.

Improved receiving report processing: Good systems work cut cycle time from 10 days to three, yet overtime dropped concurrently from 11,000 monthly hours to under 2,000.

Reversed cable reel damage trend: Improved procedures in detailed written form saw cable reel loss and damage diminish 25% in 1969; an additional 21% in 1970.

What about salvage? A function showing up increasingly under logistics and distribution management control in many companies, it plays a significant financial role for Con Edison. Just how significant shows up particularly in scrap copper disposal. With copper selling at 68½ cents per pound in 1969, the department recovered $4,029,000 from scrap sales. In 1970, though copper scrap fell to 40½ cents per pound, sales from recovered copper jumped to $4,654,000.

Modern storage facilities, backed up by heavy computerization and continuing systems betterments, yield high service levels at diminishing costs, but more ambitious improvements are coming. Mr. Burgess now chairs a Materials Management Steering Committee representing various affected company departments that seek greater cost-service gains through a sophisticated total approach. Characteristics of such an integrated materials management system would include:

- Daily processing of all transactions.
- Computer-initiated and produced documentation.

IN A SPECIAL BAY of the Astoria warehouse, larger, heavier items are moved by a 100-ton overhead crane. Special racks hold complete boiler flue replacement sets for specific installations, speeding maintenance and repair assignments.

- Direct interrogation of computer.
- Automatic stockage list maintenance and stock reservation.
- User-manager catalogs.
- Requisition priority system.
- Service level of 90% or more on nonemergency material.
- Integrated management/accounting reports.
- Financial inventory management and control.
- Automatic inventory.
- Automatic matching of all data needed for payment of suppliers.

"In developing these elements," notes Mr. Burgess, "we hope to create reports that will give timely performance data for management, rather than just dollar data for accounting information. We want stronger emphasis on the positive side—better performance—rather than looking at costs alone. Both ends must be served, but changes in computer-support equipment and total system orientation will be necessary. That is why Executive Vice President William W. Lapsley established the steering committee earlier this year."

Complex production of essential services through extremely costly facilities typifies the public utility enterprise. New plants come high and maintenance demands commence the day a power plant goes on line.

"We strongly believe in sharing our expertise with other public utility companies," asserts Executive Vice President-Divisional Operations Bernard E. Gallagher, to whom Mr. Burgess and his department report. A case in point is Con Edison's Arthur Kill No. 3 plant on Staten Island. "With equipment comparable to Detroit Edison's Trenton Channel station, our companies are developing a cooperative logistics program supporting both plants." Similar activities

REVIEWING performance measurement charts are (left to right): Assistant Vice President-Transportation and Stores J. Frank Burgess; Rudy Vcelka, assistant to Mr. Burgess, and Manager-Central Stores Andrew Gaydos.

may be expected to reflect a growing trend for the transportation and supply department.

Centralized storage cuts inventory and handling costs

HEART OF Con Edison's transportation and stores operation is the Astoria Central Warehouse. Encompassing not only a modern 7½-acre building for widely diversified materials, it includes 35 acres of outside storage and other specialized enclosed facilities as well. Its location is virtually at the center of the company's service region, yet sufficiently "off the beaten path" to ease truck movements in and out of the area.

Computerized order procedures and picking forms, coupled with teletype units at the Astoria location and supplemented within the warehouse by pneumatic tube

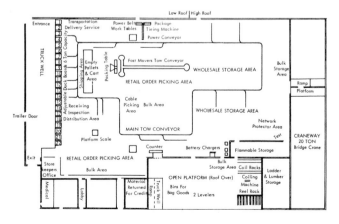

ORIGINAL LAYOUT of Con Edison's modern Astoria warehouse. A large storage wing at right has since been added.

paper handling, help hold down delivery cycle times. Goods handling itself goes rapidly, employing two separate tow conveyor systems supplemented by lift trucks. Adjacent power conveyor installations and packaging machines, strategically placed, complete the automation picture in the main warehouse area. In a separate bay, having a special high ceiling, a 20-ton crane makes fast work of moving large generator parts, boiler tubes and other heavy materials.

Why so much mechanization? **"It buys time, for one thing," states Manager-Central Stores Andrew Gaydos. "Normal field orders reach requisitioners within two days, while turnaround within the warehouse occurs within 24 hours."** A Monday order, for example, leaves by truck Tuesday for satellite warehouse delivery and actual field use on Wednesday. Only effective material handling can get goods in and out of a 7½-acre warehouse on schedules such as this.

The major building is one-story high with no divider walls. Support columns, carefully located, offer no storage space interference. At its south end, a fully enclosed dock, entered through two electronic doors, offers 22 unloading positions. In addition to six-ton-capacity automatic dock boards, a 20-ton truck leveler is available here. The building's east side has a somewhat smaller exterior loading dock with semiprotected storage space. Here, also, automatic dock boards speed transfer operations. Docks handle both inbound and outbound freight, with the scheduling of movements minimizing any conflicting patterns.

Though the warehouse has three shifts, the midnight-to-8 a.m. one primarily is an emergency service coverage. The service cycle essentially occurs during the "day" operation (8 a.m. to 4 p.m.) and the "night" shift (4 p.m. to midnight), with the normal cycle starting early on the latter shift. The following morning, the day shift assembles this material for outbound movement, with the freight ready to depart at shift close. The 4 p.m. to midnight crew loads this material at the start of its shift and then commences picking the second day's requirements. A typical day's operations finds from 800 to 1,000 separate requisitions filled.

Goods storage breaks down within the warehouse between "wholesale," stored in a high-roofed area, and a "retail" zone, which includes a separate area for 1,400 fast-moving items. A few additional separate areas, broken down by goods type or use, house specialized items.

Most important warehouse areas are on the 1,200-foot Link Belt tow conveyor system. More than 150 four-wheel pallet carts equipped with tow pins circulate on this system. The carts, having multiple magnets that activate reed switches at siding locations, can be "programed" to enter spurs for partial or complete unloading by forklift trucks, including 16 high-reach units for the high roof section and more conventional units from the 45-unit fleet for service elsewhere.

In the area for fast-turnover items, a separate 300-foot tow conveyor loop keeps goods moving. This installation uses smaller trucks, or "T-Wagons." No sidings or shunting devices are employed here. The lighter trucks are easily placed on or off the line manually. Through this segregated assembly operation, however, substantial time savings accrue in processing these fast-moving items, largely destined to the Construction Department.

A unique feature of the warehouse operation is its stationery function. Employing 14 people, its stock includes widely diversified papers, forms and office materials. Recording instrument charts in some 840 varieties must be stocked, while each month close to six million forms and four million envelopes come from here for computer processing. Each year 380 million tab cards flow through this facility for computer operations as well. Assembled through the tow conveyor system, all such freight gets to its destinations through the department's closed van trucking operation.

While inbound and outbound freight segregation at the docks is at least partially a function of schedule, there is also a segregation of on-dock facilities to help this out as well. At the east end of the enclosed dock is the basic receiving, inspection and distribution area. Here, a Lektrafile unit housing purchase orders for inbound shipments and tub files indexing stock locations are located, as well as tow-line spurs holding empty carts that can absorb material destined for storage subsequent to acceptance.

The enclosed dock's western section includes a large shipping area. This includes several tow-line spurs conveniently separated for easy unloading of material coming out from storage. Space is provided for holding the pallet carts following unloading, and an adjacent packing sector is serviced by a powered conveyor section. Ample dock space makes loading or unloading of a truck at any position practical.

The present material requisitioning system involves a telephone-computer-teletype system. Authorized individuals place their orders by telephone call to Con Edison's to the order pickers for the purpose of stock selection.

Outside Storage a Major Activity

Much diversified construction material lends itself to external storage at Astoria. While it includes such unusual items as preformed concrete manholes, electric cable in tremendous variety constitutes the greatest single commodity concentration. In this exterior location, known as the "pipe and cable yard," about 9,000 reels of cable on 70 varied sizes of drums can be found. The stock generally represents a three-month cable supply, depending on the production lead time for each item.

In addition to stock items, the yard also holds reserve cable assembled in advance for specific construction work and contingency cable for emergency use in the Con Edison system. In some unique applications, where a "one time only" cable was required for a specific project, extra lengths are held as a reserve, since subsequent replacement by repurchase is highly impractical.

Special cutting equipment and heavy-duty forklift trucks adapted to handle cable reels can be found at Astoria. Cable handling, however, is undergoing significant changes. The old practice of leaving cable reels on the main offices in downtown Manhattan. From this call's information, a key-punch operator prepares an individual card for each item, employing a self-checking, seven-digit number by which the item is identified, the number being

REMINGTON RAND Lektrafile units store purchase orders, cutting shelf space while speeding file access via automation.

A CONSTANT STREAM of four-wheel pallet-bearing carts services the main tow-conveyor system, bringing in stock and taking out goods that are destined for final delivery.

PACKING STATION at the foot of the separate fast-moving item tow-conveyor system employs conveyor sections to clear the work station, feeding to pallets and wire containers that move goods to satellite warehouses or project sites.

ENCLOSED DOCK at Astoria facility's south end has 22 loading positions, each with automatic dock boards.

MUCH MATERIAL, including cable drums and construction specialities, is stored outside on 35 acres at Astoria.

supplied by the requestor from a computer-prepared catalog.

The computer, given the individual item cards, checks each against the history, description and location information in storage for stock items stored at Astoria, adding further detail necessary to the requisition and printing the latter out on the warehouse data terminal printer. In addition to printing out the individual item descriptions on the requisition, the computer indicates warehouse aisle and bin number for each item in proper picking sequence, while updating inventories and maintaining stock records. As order forms come through complete on the warehouse printer, the operator strips them off and then sends them street at construction sites is being eliminated over a one-year period, and the problems posed by the huge reel variety is being tackled as well. Reels on the street have been reduced from 1,000 on any given day to 250, with complete elimination intended by year's end. **"We're working to get the reel types down from 70 to 10,"** states Assistant Manager-Stores Operations Len Morey, Jr.

The king-sized job of handling cable reels demands a variety of techniques. Though reel and cable sizes may sometimes be awesome, the cable itself may nonetheless be readily subject to damage and must be properly protected. Trucked-in loads are carefully checked on arrival for proper chocking and bracing, with the cable itself inspected subsequent to unloading to assure its condition. Loading and unloading of much of this material takes place at a special cable and transformer platform. A heavy 15-ton Wright crane augmented by several large lift trucks handles a variety of major units as well as cable shipments here.

Just as in the warehouse proper, goods flow from the pipe and cable yard through Con Edison's standard requisitioning system. Goods located outside are spotted in coded locations that are as easy to find as the bin locations in the warehouse itself.

In general, while shipments from inside storage flow through the satellite warehouse locations in the metropolitan area, pipe and cable yard orders flow direct to specific construction sites. Their sheer bulk makes a direct truck drop decidedly preferable handling. Not only cable and certain other electrical equipment move from this source, but virtually any of the materials common to a field construction move from this source to job sites as well.

Specialized cartage creates reliable field service

BY FAR, the majority of the 100-plus daily inbound shipments to Con Edison's storage complex arrive by common carrier truck. Outbound shipments to satellite warehouses and construction sites find the situation reversed, with the company's own vehicles doing the job, employing both innovative equipment and unusual scheduling to achieve efficiency. In addition, units will occasionally make vendor pickups where critical timing or other factors make it necessary.

For some time, the department has been running two 40-foot trailers, each carrying two 20-foot containers for satellite warehouse and other deliveries in addition to conventional equipment. The special trailers can drop a container at one destination and then "shorten up" the undercarriage through a hydraulic mechanism, converting the unit instantly to a 20-footer with the single remaining container. This containerized operation proved quite satisfactory in recent operations, but it is only a precursor of things to come.

The "new look" will employ straight trucks rather than tractor and trailer combinations for this local delivery service. The standard 10-ton trucks to be used will haul custom-built containers measuring 8 ½ by 8 by 5 feet, two at a time, for satellite warehouse deliveries on the night shift. In addition, the same trucks will handle single 20-foot containers for street drops at construction points during the day. Construction is such that in the event a truck becomes disabled, it will be possible for it to drop its container in the street for subsequent pickup by another similar unit. The one-man hydraulic system represents a clever conversion from the familiar "Dempster Dumpster" units in common usage with other types of containers.

Somewhat similar technology lies behind another vehicle whose importance is growing rapidly at Con Edison. This "Load Lugger" truck is an adaptation of a sanitation department vehicle which uses a hydraulic arm device to lift refuse containers. In this case, however, the burden is cable reels. With a Load Lugger, cable crews can pull cable without the need to drop reels on the street, working directly from a reel suspended from the truck. Loading and unloading will be eased as well by this unique vehicle's "self-help" features. Just how important cable handling is to the department is evidenced by the fact that in 24 hours, vehicles handle an average of 150 reels.

The total transportation and supply department fleet includes 278 vehicles. Work assignments are 80% scheduled, 10% anticipatable special work and 10% emergency services. Normal operations encompass the metropolitan New York City area plus Westchester, but trucks sometimes get as far afield as Boston or Pennsylvania, occasionally in fulfilling sudden needs of other utility companies.

For special material, such as pipe-type cable, special 85-foot trailers do the job. **"These extra-high voltage lines require careful handling,"** asserts General Foreman-Equipment Assignment Edward Noury. **"When loaded, the carrier is completely covered with canvas, with the reels themselves in sealed waterproof paper coverings that must not be broken until cable crews are ready to pull the lines."** At times of high humidity levels, lines of light bulbs are placed in such trailers and turned on to heat the air and hold down the moisture.

An accompanying illustration shows such a trailer being loaded with pipe-type cable of the 138-KV variety for a line extending more than 90,000 feet from the Farragut Switching Station to the Brownsville area in Brooklyn. This pipe-type cable will be pulled, three lines at a time, through a pipe which is then filled with oil for insulation between the cable members, sealed and pressurized.

SUCCESSFUL TESTING of warehouse deliveries with these two 20-foot containers and an expandable trailer has led to the ordering of a series of specialized containers for satellite warehouse deliveries employing straight trucks which will handle both the new 8½-foot units and the 20-footers.

TRAILERLOADS of braced and blocked cable make frequent, scheduled arrivals at Astoria cable dock.

LEN MOREY (right), assistant manager-stores operations, checks organization chart with Storekeeper Edward Curran.

HIGH-CAPACITY fork-lift trucks move cable reels between the cable dock and various outside storage locations.

CUSTOM-DESIGNED, 85-foot trailers handle high-voltage, pipe-type cable requiring protection from the elements.

Some 20 tractor-trailer units employed by the department serve largely for construction assignments, while a number of stake-bodied trucks and smaller enclosed trucks handle varied delivery work. Upon the arrival of the new container units in the near future, some of these burdens may be shifted.

While the daytime pipe yard loads can end up anywhere within the company's operations area, the night shift operation dispatches trucks to quite specific destinations. In addition to two satellite locations each in the boroughs of Brooklyn and Manhattan, there are single satellite warehouses in Queens, Bronx, Staten Island and Westchester. As a general rule, these facilities have been placed adjacent to properties where company line trucks are parked at night. In this way, line men can pick up their needed materials the following day with a minimum of lost motion.

The satellite warehouses maintain small stocks of a few most commonly used items, but primarily they serve simply as staging areas for material requisitioned out of the central supply source at Astoria.

Perhaps the most surprising part of the department's fleet is a number of buses. Because the large Astoria facility, which encompasses several functions in addition to transportation and supply, is at some distance from suitable public transportation, the department operates an employe transportation service to and from the nearest New York City rapid transit station. The buses are also useful within the 300-acre grounds at this location and on occasion serve to bring large groups to out-of-the-way construction sites.

Looking to the future, Con Edison is working within transportation as well as its other departments to further the cause of reduced pollution. Project Manager Harolde N. Searles of the company's vehicle pollution reduction project is pressing forward on studies of vehicles powered by liquified natural gas (LNG) and compressed natural gas (CNG). In the near future, 18 vehicles of widely different types in the company's Westchester Division will be converted to LNG from gasoline operation.

CHAPTER V

Diversified Approaches in the Food Industries

The food industry, like the drug industry, requires careful controls of product purity with due regard to its sometimes perishable nature. Firms in this business generally are high-volume operations with minimal profit margins on individual product units. Distribution costs, therefore, assume a critical importance and those engaged in these enterprises have accordingly had longer and deeper involvement with business logistics than has been true elsewhere in the economy.

Typifying this attitude is the particularly effective activities of food distribution professionals exercised through trade associations and professional societies. Unlike many other highly competitive fields, companies supporting the Grocery Manufacturers Association, in particular, have worked together in logistics advancements, offering great benefits to firms far beyond this specialized sphere as well. Many companies gain from using the GMA standard design of four-way entry, 48" x 40" pallet to hold down handling costs, while the GMA-standard rail car assures companies manufacturing products other than groceries of specifications they may stipulate to maximize protection for myriad other goods.

Hershey Foods Corp., a household word for chocolate products for many years, is today a more diversified manufacturer of foodstuffs. Characterized by its employment of effective handling techniques, strong vendor-carrier communications and efficient paperwork, it is similarly notable as a company in which a continual, long-term upgrading of physical distribution has been under way. Typical has been its approach to computerization. Many companies making the changeover stay with obsolescent manual procedures until a 100% computerized system is ready to go when a switch is thrown. Not so at Hershey. General Traffic Manager Howard J. Gabriel commenced making rolling readjustments in manual procedures as individual pieces of a total distribution program were developed, tying unique office equipment and diversified communication modes to both computer and shipping facilities, upgrading clerical efficiency on yet-to-be converted manual procedures. This feature is but one of several unusual sides to Hershey's physical distribution climate. TRAFFIC MANAGEMENT's November, 1970 review of Hershey logistics follows:

Tailoring Tools and Systems for Better Customer Service

SUPPLYING CUSTOMERS at 65,000 destinations from its main plant alone, Hershey Foods, Inc. nonetheless keeps tight control over individual account service. Distribution is big business here. With annual sales of almost $300 million, the total freight bill alone ranges around $15 million. Both figures are trending upward.

"For commodities such as ours, bought largely on impulse by consumers," noted General Traffic Manager Howard P. Gabriel, "first class service is a competitive essential. We have to move over 100,000 pieces daily, and we have to make certain they move on schedule with proper care. Late deliveries or damaged stock automatically mean lost sales.

"At the same time, we control costs closely. Pennies quickly become dollars on a volume such as ours. We spend willingly to give customers good service, but we make very sure that full value comes from every expenditure."

Traffic and distribution face continuing change at Hershey. New methods and changing rates account for this in part. Growing business and the acquisition of subsidiaries that revise market geography and product mix also make different approaches necessary. A 1968 survey would have varied significantly from today's examination. Present developments-in-progress guarantee similarly important changes later on.

A look at Hershey distribution today, therefore, reveals a traffic department on the move, handling heavy daily operations effectively while planning toward still higher efficiency. Improving methods reflect themselves in such areas as these:

- Centralized traffic control: Hershey's growing number of plants opens the door to consolidations and other joint services. Local traffic managers work with the Hershey, Pa. corporate staff on such planning activities, yet enjoy autonomy in daily operations and most local matters.

- Broadening computer employment: Rates, routes and bills of lading are largely computerized. Other routine department activities are slated for electronic data processing, as well as numerous forward-looking research projects.

- Market-oriented rate analysis: Hershey's rate staff develops new rates and watches its competitors' rate activities as closely as it does the carriers' proposals, assuring that rate changes in any part of the nation do not adversely affect the company's competitive position.

- External traffic activities: The department joins competitors in cooperative action to protect the total industry's costs and services through trade associations. It works closely also with regional and national traffic groups.

- Pooling and consolidation: Fully 50% of all orders leave Hershey, Pa. in scheduled pool trucks. Partially computer-controlled, additional developments in this area will speed service still further while easing the traffic department's work load.

- System-tailored office design: A custom-built carrousel, surrounded by work positions relating to order flow, cuts wasteful paper movement, as do pneumatic tubes that flow paper between the traffic, computer and shipping facilities.

- Inbound traffic controls: Working closely with the purchasing department, fully 90% of inbound freight moves on standardized, traffic department-specified routings. All purchase orders clear through the department, which contacts affected vendors directly when routing deviations appear necessary.

- Specialized equipment: Fully 200 modern insulated cars are leased by the company for rail deliveries. A fleet of stainless steel tank trucks handles inbound milk deliveries.

In the opinion of Corporate Secretary Richard L. Uhrich, to whom Mr. Gabriel reports, such continuing changes are essential concomitants of the company's present expansion phase. "Sheer volume alone would dictate the need for distribution modifications," he notes. "Even more significant, however, is the diversification element. New products mean a broader inbound material mix to more numerous plants as well as a more complex product flow to the markets. Our traffic department's early recognition of this circumstance has kept the transition smooth."

More than short-term transition occupies traffic department planning. A major project in the drawing board stage envisions a highly automated distribution center to be built a mile from the main plant. Connected directly by rail, stock will move by fully automated trains between the facilities.

"Such progressive thinking continues a company tradition," President Harold S. Mohler observes. "Milton S. Hershey, our founder, was an inventor and innovator of considerable repute. He set a fast pace. We intend to maintain it."

Integrated traffic serves widespread facilities

MENTION HERSHEY and most people think of the ubiquitous chocolate bar. They may also consider in passing the pleasurable tourist attractions surrounding the company's major plant at Hershey, Pa. or the numerous philanthropies of Milton S. Hershey, the parent company's colorful founder. These impressions grow increasingly short of a full picture under today's conditions. Recognizing this, the company changed its name in 1968 to Hershey Foods Corporation from its former title, Hershey Chocolate Corporation. With good reason. Consider some of its present-day subsidiaries:

—Cory Corporation (Chicago, Ill.). Known for its coffee-making and food service equipment, it also manufactures writing instruments, air treatment equipment, stainless steel cookware, home appliances and giftwares.
—San Giorgio Macaroni, Inc. (Lebanon, Pa.). Its macaroni, spaghetti, egg noodles and spaghetti sauces are marketed along the Eastern Seaboard.

Founder Milton S. Hershey's home, at center, is today a facility of the Hershey Country Club. To the right, two tall stacks bearing his name serve the plant producing the products that he originated.

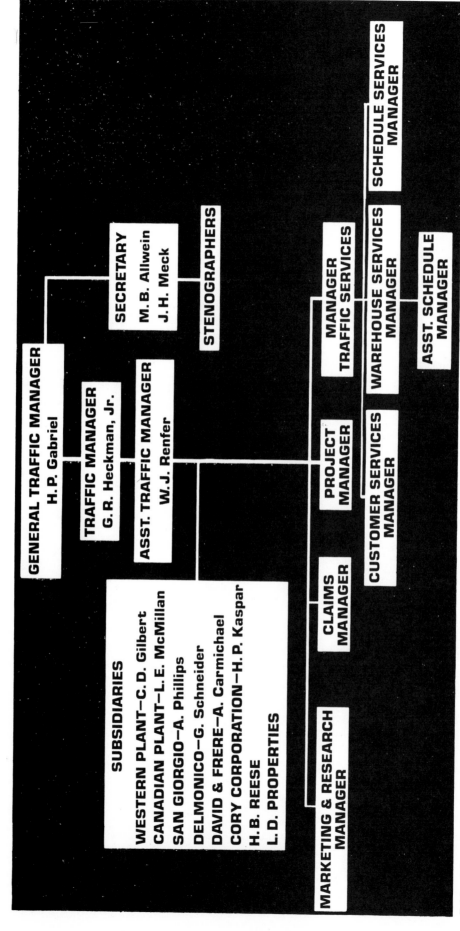

Table of Organization for Traffic Department of Hershey Foods Corp. at corporate headquarters.

Traffic department control of inbound material requires good communications with plant management. General Traffic Manager Howard P. Gabriel (left) and Plant Manager Robert M. Bucher meet frequently to assure that freight flow matches production requirements despite changing conditions.

—Delmonico Foods, Inc. (Louisville, Ky.). This organization markets products similar in scope to the San Giorgio line, primarily in Indiana, Kentucky and Ohio.

—David & Frere Ltee, 1967 (Montreal, P.Q., Canada). One of Canada's largest sweet biscuit and cracker manufacturers, it also imports and markets candies.

—H. B. Reese Candy Co., Inc. (Hershey, Pa.). "Down the road a piece" from the parent company's main plant, this unit specializes in chocolate-covered peanut butter cups.

In addition to these, the company also operates Hershey chocolate plants at Smith Falls, Ontario and Oakdale, Calif.

While the Cory Corp. has its own general traffic manager, H. P. Kasper, each of the other units has a local traffic manager or traffic supervisor assigned. Monthly reports come to General Traffic Manager Howard P. Gabriel from four of the outlying managers for consolidation into a monthly department report. The Oakdale, San Giorgio and Delmonico facilities also submit daily shipping reports, eliminating much searching for bills of lading and shipping records. All freight bill audits and approval for payments for all locations (except Cory) are made at Hershey, Pa.

The plant traffic manager's first duty is to his customers and his plant. He takes independent action on their behalf without consulting headquarters, but within basic guidelines established by the traffic department.

There is a growing amount of interaction toward developing mutual economies, notably between the Hershey chocolate plant and the San Giorgio and Reese units. These three facilities lie only a short distance from one another, making pool truck assembly as well

Forward planning is reviewed by General Traffic Manager Howard P. Gabriel (second from right) with left to right: Assistant Traffic Manager William J. Renfer, Traffic Manager Guy R. Heckman, Jr. and Department Secretary Margaret B. Allwein in the traffic department's conference room.

as carload and truckload consolidation development feasible.

In Canada, the company anticipates the possibility of significant distribution benefits through coordination of the Smith Falls chocolate plant and the operations of David Frere. The latter operates a factory at Montreal plus warehouses at Ottawa, Toronto and Quebec City. Its private fleet based at Montreal serves the western Quebec region plus offering stock replenishment service between Montreal and Ottawa. Ottawa-based David & Frere trucks serve eastern Ontario, while a separate fleet of vehicles covers local Toronto deliveries and southern Ontario points.

Under consideration is a merger of warehousing into Smith Falls, with an expansion of local fleet operation to cover both present duties and Hershey's chocolate deliveries. "We're looking at the pool truck potential also," states Hershey Assistant Traffic Manager William J. Renfer. "As the Smith Falls plant serves most of Canada, possibilities arise in any David & Frere market where sufficient tonnage moves."

Electronic data processing— A growing force

FORWARD DISTRIBUTION planning gets increasing help from the Hershey computer center's activities. Already processing orders and producing bills of lading, the IBM 360

series computer facilities create a growing data base for analyzing traffic data, testing new ideas and studying changes in demands placed upon existing procedures. The traffic department, working with the computer group, looks forward as well to expanding daily line functions performed by the computer within traffic's scope.

"We've got two major activities under review right now," Traffic Manager Guy R. Heckman, Jr. observes. "Computerized freight payments offer interesting potential-

Communications between electronic data processing and traffic department operations benefits significantly from high-speed pneumatic tube document transfer. Serving the shipping room as well, the traffic department tube terminal at the picture center does much to cut the time between the receipt of orders and the subsequent forwarding of shipments.

Hershey Foods Corporation
Hershey Chocolate & Confectionery Division

AT _____ DATE _____ SHIPPER'S NO. _____

Consigned to

Destination   State   County

Routing   Car or Vehicle Initials & No.

No. Packages	Kind of Package, Description of Articles, Special Marks and Exceptions	*Weight (Sub. to Cor.)	Class or Rate	FREIGHT CHARGES	
					R E C O B.

R E C O B.

* RETURN COPY OF BILL OF LADING

NOTICE TO CARRIER — IMPORTANT —

TO INSURE PROMPT PAYMENT PLEASE RETURN THIS FORM
THIS FORM MAY BE USED AS YOUR FREIGHT BILL BY INDICATING THE
RATES AND CHARGES IN THE B/L DESCRIPTION ABOVE.
IF YOU MUST SEND US YOUR FREIGHT BILL, PLEASE ATTACH SAME TO THIS FORM.

RETURN TO: **Hershey Foods Corporation, Traffic Dept.**
Hershey Chocolate & Confectionery Division Hershey, Pa 17033

Hershey's EDP-prepared bills of lading include the above return copy (termed "RECOB"), which carriers may use for billing. When carriers return these as requested, both audit and freight bill payment are simplified.

ities and faster, easier pool truck consolidation and scheduling also appear promising."

The existing computer billing operation at the Hershey main plant processes orders on the eight basic product classifications shipped. These products generally fall within three rate levels. The rate data itself occupies disc storage with customer destinations keyed to the rates. Thus, if Hershey-Binghamton traffic enjoys the same rate as Hershey-Richmond movements, Binghamton and Richmond share the same disc address for computer search. This same program also prints rates from the various field warehouses and plants.

Given an order to process, the computer prepares a complete bill of lading manifold, listing and rating all items and providing sufficient copies for invoice preparation, carrier use, consignee and necessary company controls. In addition, it will print a pool truck "load list" on a single bill of lading manifold, summarizing all individual B/Ls for each truck in groupings designated by the pool desk personnel. Completed bills return to the pool desk for final check and distribution on release of loads.

Following shipment, the department returns an original bill copy to the electronic data processing unit. The computer then prepares an invoice plus a B/L summary card ("B"-card). The B-cards go in storage for possible traffic studies. Because September is a heavy Hershey shipping month, its traffic yields a maximum number of destination points that can be used for an annual traffic study.

The traffic department's marketing and research section developed, and finds reliable, a percentage factor relating September performance to a full year. "Tying this factor to data for a given warehouse or plant gives us a good basis for study predictions," Marketing and Research Manager Richard L. Dows notes. "We make heavy use of the B-cards for distribution analysis, rate studies, point comparisons and like matters for any or all months, however."

The computer employs the B-cards in building daily warehouse freight reports, sequenced by document number. Since carriers must bill the company by document number, this speeds auditing, as carrier bills are compared to this report on receipt. If charges agree, the numbers are checked off the report, the carrier's addition is checked and correct bills go forward to the accounting department for payment.

A return copy of the B/L (termed the "RECOB"), included in each manifold, can further hasten the above process. If a carrier uses the RECOB as his own freight bill, or returns it with his bill form, checking the daily report becomes unnecessary. Agreement between RECOB and freight bill constitutes a sufficient check, as the computer-created RECOB in itself contains all necessary check data.

A unique traffic department feature, symbolic of the computer's growing value, is a position devoted to computer-traffic liaison. The full-time EDP coordinator's primary job involves computer rate updating and making revisions in service area boundaries which re-

quire disc address changes for affected destinations. He watches rate supplements constantly so that computer rates get prompt updating. He checks problems arising when carrier bills and EDP copy disagree, determining whether carrier or Hershey data require correction and arranging to rectify errors discovered.

The EDP coordinator serves other, growingly important purposes as departmental research activity expands. Special studies by traffic personnel that draw on computer data find him heavily involved as a go-between, translating for each department the capabilities and limitations of the other in areas related to a given study.

Traffic-computer coordination reaches well beyond the usual constraints. An open-minded traffic department, while seeking new ways, wants to be sure they are also the best ways. Accordingly, Assistant Traffic Manager William J. Renfer has visited several other companies heavily employing computerized distribution, comparing present and proposed methods, sharing experiences and developing new ideas that can help Hershey and the host companies alike.

"This approach clearly saved us from walking into some traps," Mr. Renfer believes, "but it opened as many doors as it closed. It added appreciably to our already healthy respect for the computer. At the same time, we feel certain some of our own prior experience suggested further EDP possibilities to the firms that were visited."

Inbound controls—
A major responsibility

PHYSICAL DISTRIBUTION means considerably more than a consumer product pipeline to Hershey Foods. Inbound materials are heavy and varied, with seasonability playing an important role in setting storage and transportation requirements.

The most important inbound freight is cocoa beans. These seasonal movers can come by the shipload in 140-pound bags. A single vessel may contain over 100,000 of these. A carload of them runs to 500 pieces.

Between the seasonality effect and other uncertainties, the traffic department is placed at the mercy of the market and the buyers. It must plan strategy, therefore,

Refined sugar arrives regularly in covered hoppers for unloading directly inside the plant. Sanitary unloading facilities reduce labor costs, as well as yielding savings through bulk rather than bag purchases.

under conditions that change daily. Heavy arrivals from December to March necessitate storing large quantities in concrete silos adjacent to the plant which have a 90-million pound capacity. Most of this freight comes from Philadelphia, with additional tonnage arriving via port of New York.

Another major commodity, almonds, creates substantial inbound movements. Through its subsidiary, L. D. Properties Corporation, Hershey Foods harvests almonds from 5,500 cultivated acres in California each year, making it the world's largest almond grower.

Peanuts, a similarly significant ingredient, move in large volume by rail and truck. These include Spanish peanuts from the southwest and "runners" from southeastern origins.

Sugar plays an important production role. Most refined sugar shipments arrive by rail from Philadelphia in covered hoppers as bulk. There are some shipments as well from other origins, including some shipments in bags.

Coal, too, is an important item. The company's own electric plant has five boilers running generators that serve not only the factory, but the entire town of Hershey. Most coal arrives by rail from West Virginia origins.

Locally, a company fleet of 14 stainless steel tank trucks picks up over one million pounds of milk daily from five area milk stations. Fresh milk is an important ingredient to several Hershey products.

Fully 90% of inbound freight moves on fixed, specific routings. All purchase orders clear through the traffic department, however, and if any deviations from specified routings appear necessary, the traffic department will contact the affected vendor directly.

Rate control— A marketing concept

THE SIGNIFICANCE, scope and nature of the traffic department's rate activity is best exemplified by a typical weekly rate meeting. Department management and affected personnel meet at 8:15 a.m. and confer however long it takes to cover the agenda—one determined by new ideas generated "in house" and by external rate developments in the preceding week.

More than the company's origin-destination moves get consideration. On the date when we sat in, reductions granted some competitors in certain regions were noted. The decisions, based on specific merits of the individual cases, were not to oppose any of the instances cited provided comparable relief was offered to Hershey Foods Corp.

Certain other rate changes of a broader nature clearly demanded lengthier scrutiny than the meeting offered. These were assigned to staff members for study, their reports to indicate whether or not they deemed action necessary, and if so, what action they would recommend. A few simpler revisions were discussed, and decisions were taken di-

Effective consolidation programs keep rail shipping costs in line. At Hershey plant, shipping personnel fill out a carload with Reese peanut butter cups from the affiliate's nearby facility, supplementing a shipment of Hershey products for a single destination, creating carload economy without service loss.

rectly at the meeting regarding appropriate follow-through.

The meeting concerned itself with the total national, as well as local, picture. This assists in developing mutual information exchange with competitive traffic managers as well as in cooperating with industry traffic groups. While a south-to-southwest rate increase may not directly affect the company at present, its potential effect on national rate structures gets a serious examination, as does the direct effect on the total industry competitive structure.

At this particular meeting, a report was made on efforts of the Eastern Manufacturing Confectioners Traffic Association to achieve uniform minimum weights and acceptable bill of lading descriptions in Middle Atlantic tariffs. A committee from this group has submitted its own suggestions for revision of Middle Atlantic Tariff No. 2. The tariff bureau has accepted the committee's proposed format, reducing total text to less than five pages in lieu of 37 separate page entries, and eliminating such odd items as "syrup in paper bags."

Traffic Department's Unique Dualism

"On the one hand, this may look like an obsession with detail," Traffic Manager

Heckman states, "but consider the clerical hours we've wasted wading through 37 spread-out items, trying to find needed facts in an obsolescent verbal jungle."

The traffic department's unique dualism, then, finds it protecting the company from damage to its competitive position through rate benefits gained by competitors, yet at the same time cooperating with these entities in protecting the total rate-service framework within which all must operate. In addition to the aforementioned eastern group, the company works also with the Manufacturing Confectioners' Traffic Conference nationally, and in the Midwest with the 40-manufacturer body entitled the Confectioners Traffic Association.

"These organizations," observes General Traffic Manager Gabriel, "have collectively made themselves totally aware of their responsibility to their managements and act as 'watchdogs' for the industry on the growing problem of small shipment rates."

Pooling shipments for service and savings

THE ACCOMPANYING schedule, illustrating one day's pool truck plan, at once demonstrates the high service standards and the rel-ative scope of this activity at Hershey. Small shipments, a major fact of life in the candy industry, account for the largest part of company orders. Fully 50% of these leave the Hershey, Pa. plant in pool trucks, however, minimizing through movement of small shipments and concentrating much of this activity in movements beyond the nearly 30 field warehouses servicing the nation.

Working from the daily pool schedule, two pool clerks start their day at 7 a.m., going to the order approval department and marking all orders slated to move the same day for priority treatment. Separated for prompt computer processing, these orders go from the computer to the pool desk by pneumatic tube at 9:30 a.m. The pool clerks then set aside other work and assemble these individual orders to logical shipment groupings, returning them to the computer for B/L and load list preparation. Again returned from the computer, the pool clerks check the documents and perform an initial split, holding white copies for the computer unit and yellow copies for the traffic department. White copies are then "tubed" to electronic data processing; yellow copies are held for next-day match against line haul B/Ls prior to filing, and the remaining shipping papers move by pneumatic tube to the shipping department for shipment assembly and release.

A **specially designed** work station on the traffic department carrousel, shared by Pool Clerks Florene Altobelli and Louella Edris, is fitted specifically to speed their tasks and provide ready communication. Directly adjacent to them is a pneumatic tube terminal facility, providing rapid paper transfer to and from the shipping room and the electronic data processing facility. The carrousel itself simplifies and speeds up Hershey's intra-department pool paper transfer.

POOL TRUCK
SCHEDULE

EFF. 4/11/69

Copies to:

Pool Desk
E. Spangler
E. Yocum
H. Winters
D.P. Glenn
MEW
MLR
WFW
GRH

MAKE UP POOL	SEND TO I B M	SEND PAPERS TO SHIPPING ROOM	TRUCK ARRIVAL	TRUCK RELEASE	
8 AM Prev. Day	8:30 AM Prev. Day	2 PM Prev. Day	6 AM	10 AM	Charlotte
8 AM Prev. Day	8:30 AM Prev. Day	2 PM Prev. Day	6 AM	10 AM	Columbia
1 PM Prev. Day	1:30 PM Prev. Day	4 PM Prev. Day	6 AM	10 AM	E. Hartford
1 PM Prev. Day	1:30 PM Prev. Day	4 PM Prev. Day	9 AM	2:30 PM	Charleston
2 PM Prev. Day	2:30 PM Prev. Day	7 AM	11 AM	2:30 PM	Buffalo-Rochester
4 PM Prev. Day	4:30 PM Prev. Day	7 AM	10:30 AM	2:30 PM	Altoona
7:30 AM	8 AM	2 PM	8 PM	11 PM	Philadelphia
9:30 AM	10 AM	1 PM	6 PM	10 PM	Charlton
9:30 AM	10 AM	1 PM	3 PM	6 PM	Baltimore
10:30 AM	11 AM	1 PM	6 PM	10 PM	Scranton
10:30 AM	11 AM	Noon	4 PM	8 PM	Cleveland
11:30 AM	Hand Post	12:30 PM	6 PM	10 PM	N. Bergen
1:30 PM	2 PM	4 PM	8 PM	11 PM	Washington

Pool truck schedule (sample day): Each day, Monday through Friday, pool trucks move to a number of metropolitan delivery points. The Wednesday schedule, illustrated above, is typical in size and complexity. Not only are truck departures pre-scheduled, but the whole paper flow sequence shares in timetable discipline. In this way, the traffic department knows exactly what performance is possible or may be anticipated on any specific order at any time.

Future date pool orders receive essentially the same treatment as the "same day" orders, save that this work is performed after processing is completed on the latter.

Specific carriers handle each scheduled pool run. In some cases, a different carrier serves the same destination on different days, but the days are fixed so that carriers know in advance the equipment necessary and the time it must be spotted at loading dock.

Speeding the pool truck development is an unusual office equipment installation. This "carrousel" operation is detailed in the following article, accompanied by a schematic diagram of the pool truck clerical operation.

The continuing increase in pool truck activity places growing pressures on the existing staff and system. Future computer programing, however, is expected to alleviate this condition significantly. "Ultimately," states General Traffic Manager Gabriel, "we would like to relieve our two pool clerks of much routine paper handling, reserving their efforts to the making of nonroutine judgments and the checking of computer-supplied data prior to shipment assembly. In this way, we can both reduce pressures now inherent in their positions and increase their ability to absorb the growing pool truck work load."

The existing pool truck procedure, then, is essentially an interim operation. Significantly more efficient than earlier conventional practices, it nonetheless is geared to anticipated further changes. With the introduction of additional computer programing in this area, both the timing and nature of steps needed to assemble pool loads will change markedly. The existing personnel will continue to function as before on the carrousel. Time pressures on their jobs, however, will be materially reduced and their productivity will grow, creating a desirable capacity increase in the face of Hershey's expanding sales.

While growing business might seem to indicate the possibility of more large loads, thus diminishing pooling activity, such is not the case in the candy industry. Most receivers require small shipments, and increasing business is generally reflected in more customers and more shipments, rather than in any change in the nature of shipments themselves. Pooling and consolidation, as a vital element in the total Hershey traffic picture, will undoubtedly continue to be the major operating consideration that they have been in the recent past.

Unique office equipment improves shipment processing

A "FIRST" recently scored by Hershey's traffic department suggests interesting possibilities for other companies as well. Taking a cue from railroads and airlines in their high-speed reservation processing systems, department management recently installed a large carrousel to speed data flow within its service section. Personnel handling pooling, consolidations, stock control, customer service, routing and scheduling have to be able to move paper among themselves rapidly. The carrousel meets this need admirably.

"We took this idea up with Acme Visible Records, which manufactures carrousels used by many carriers for processing passenger reservations," General Traffic Manager Gabriel stated. "Their people in Harrisburg, Pa., worked with us to determine the specific requirements, then developed an initial design. We looked it over and discussed it at length within the department and found it quite feasible after a few minor modifications."

What evolved was a group of desks and specialized paper-handling facilities built to fit a large, circular, table-height unit surmounted by a two-level, rotatable set of tray spaces or pigeonholes. The upper deck holds supplies of forms and other materials in some spots, provides for deposit of file materials in others. The lower deck has "in" pigeonholes for specific people or functions sharing the facility. Paper flows from one desk to another simply by the "sender" putting it in a proper pigeonhole for a "receiver" and rotating the carrousel with his fingertip to his position.

Faster and easier than conventional paper-walking, staff members around the unit find that it offers individual facilities and conveniences exceeding that formerly available at more typical desk locations.

Customer Services Manager Walter F. Wyld and his staff, including pooling, routing and tracing personnel, share the carrousel with Schedule Services Manager John U. Gruber, whose staff includes equipment sche-

Heart of the traffic department's day-to-day operations is this unique, custom-designed carrousel, supplied by Acme Visible Records, Inc. Action-oriented functions sharing its periphery benefit from speedier paper flow and simpler intradepartmental communications. Recently installed, the unit has contributed markedly to departmental efficiency. Staff members as well as department management appreciate the gain in convenience over conventional systems.

duling and consolidation shipping personnel. Pooling activities, described in the preceding article, are illustrated as well in the accompanying schematic diagram.

Coming around the carrousel counterclockwise from the pool desk, we find Customer Service Manager Wyld who, in addition to supervision of routing and tracing, also maintains a preshipment checking service. Under this procedure, each consignee in several eastern major metropolitan areas is telephoned prior to release of his individual shipments. This step virtually eliminated truck detention, redelivery and related customer service problems in these localities, benefiting customers and sales department.

"It certainly does no harm to our competitive posture," comments Mr. Gabriel. "We're starting to expand this function to other regions with the ultimate probability of nationwide application."

Schedule Service Manager Gruber is particularly watchful of stock conditions, keeping pool clerks, consolidation shipping clerks and all others concerned advised as to items that may or may not be available for shipping at any particular time. Daily stock reports from the computer arrive in Mr. Gruber's carrousel sector, reflecting conditions as of 6 a.m. that same day. These are checked daily against a customer back order file for immediate shipment possibilities. As stock becomes available, Mr. Gruber establishes priorities with General Warehouse Manager Floyd E. Deppen for back order release. This sector controls rail carload processing as well as truckload and less than truckload shipments slated to move separately from the pool truck LTL shipments.

The schedule services group includes the four consolidation shipping clerks. As pooling helps cut small shipment costs, so Her-

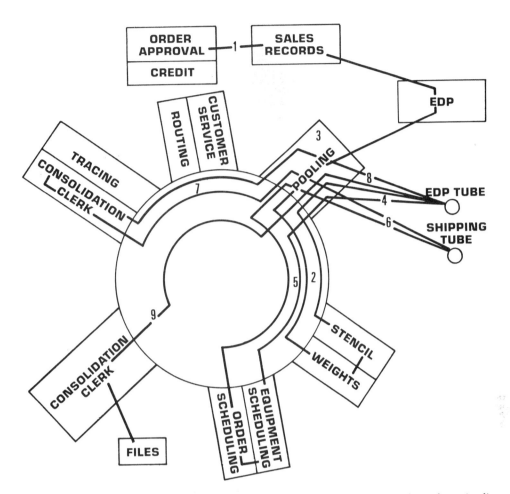

Pool truck paper flow in the traffic department carrousel operation is illustrated in this schematic diagram. **Step One:** Orders destined to pool trucks clear initially through the order approval, electronic data processing, sales record and credit units before hand delivery to pool desk. **Step Two:** Pool clerks interchange orders with the stencil-weight desk (adjacent on carrousel) for changes, back orders and/or stencil preparation, if any. **Step Three:** Pool clerks total individual orders to determine truckload weights, and add requisitions, if any, making certain stock is available for orders and any other necessary adjustments. **Step Four:** Pool clerks forward orders via pneumatic tube to EDP, which processes the orders and returns them with pool truckload lists to traffic. **Step Five:** Pool clerks inform equipment scheduler of pools assembled so that carriers may be advised in advance of weights. **Step Six:** Pool clerks send load list copies via pneumatic tube to shipping room for staging and loading. **Step Seven:** Shipping room returns load list copies after vehicle is loaded so pool clerks may complete bills of lading, then return to shipping room for carrier signature. **Step Eight:** Order copies return via pneumatic tube to EDP for invoicing. **Step Nine:** Additional order copies are attached to a load list copy and routed to file via consolidation desk.

shey employs consolidations to get more efficient truckloads from small T/L shipments and larger LTL shipments, filling out weights to maximum advantage. Consolidations, after assembly, pass to the routing desk to assure that original routing is still in order. They then return for final inventory confirmation and transfer to the equipment scheduler, who arranges with carriers for pickup.

The equipment scheduler maintains a running log on a "Schedule to Truck Shipments" form, showing the exact information telephoned to a carrier on each ship-

ment—what he is required to do at both origin and destination, keeping a record of the specific carrier employee contacted. If something goes wrong, therefore, records show and confirm initial action and are used to show changes made or action taken to alleviate negative conditions wherever possible.

Consolidation and scheduling also cover significant amounts of traffic from the nearby Reese and San Giorgio plants, which participate in Hershey carload and truckload assemblies as well as the various pool trucks.

The consolidation shipping clerks prepare master bills of lading which cover stop-offs

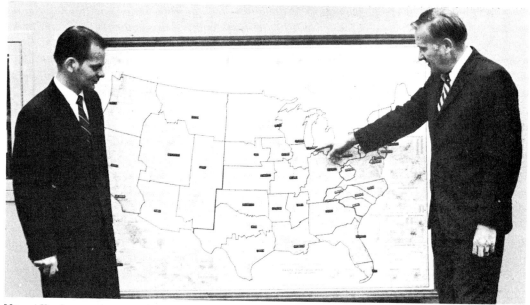

Map of Hershey service areas is examined by Marketing and Research Manager Richard L. Dows (left) and Assistant Traffic Manager William J. Renfer. Changing transportation patterns encourage forward planning.

and other special circumstances. These are made by hand based on initial computer B/Ls, building consolidations from individual orders.

The carrousel, then, concentrates departmental service functions in an effective pattern for intercommunication, further extending its efficiency by adjacent placement of pneumatic tube terminals for lines leading to the computer facility and the shipping room.

More conventional desk arrangements serve Claims Manager Russell C. Flowers and his staff on one side of the department space, with similar facilities provided at the opposite end for the marketing and research staff. A high lighting level in the new area, it is generally agreed, benefits everyone. Thus, the carrousel is restricted to those functions that place two specific demands on the office environment: a need for fast, same-day action on specific tasks and a requirement for rapid intercommunication between functions to accomplish specific assignments.

Special equipment and service assures reliable deliveries

IN ADDITION to its local fleet of stainless steel milk tank trucks, Hershey Foods employs other specialized forms of transportation to keep critical movements on sched-

Typical of Hershey's modern equipment is this Alvey automated palletizer. Fully mechanized, the unit will operate only when a load is removed, at which juncture it draws boxes from production line end for next pallet.

Anticipated rail car arrivals are discussed by General Traffic Manager Howard P. Gabriel (center, with hand on railing) and Traffic Manager Guy R. Heckman, Jr. (at bottom step) with Reading Engineer Charles Hummelbaugh (in cab window) and Fireman Robert Dinger (left). Heavy rail shipments in and out of the Hershey plant keep a Reading locomotive and crew busy. Leased equipment and conventional rail cars are used.

Cooling down trailers prior to loading. Water spray assures they will be properly conditioned for chocolate shipments, permitting use of conventional trailers.

The traffic department sends posters out each spring reminding carriers and warehousemen that a few precautions can eliminate potential damage problems. Created at the plant, they keep handling personnel alert.

Some of Hershey's 200 modern insulated cars await loading adjacent to main plant.

ule. A major portion of stock destined to warehouses moves in Hershey's own leased fleet of 200 modern steel insulated cars. Handling solid warehouse or customer shipments, the 150 44-foot cars and 50 50-footers have three inches of urethane insulation in their sides and four inches in the ceilings. This setup equals in effectiveness 10 inches of fiberglass insulation on each surface.

While insulated rail cars assure maximum protection, common carrier truck movements in conventional equipment pose no problems, providing proper schedules are observed and subsequent warehousing is in facilities where reasonable temperatures are maintained. Hershey's regular, heavy ton-

nage gets good service because carriers know well in advance when shipments are available, where they are going and when delivery is anticipated. Pool trucks move on a written time schedule that clearly defines both Hershey's role and the carrier's in timely vehicle dispatch.

During the summer, adequate temperature control is assured through precooling of trailers awaiting loads at the Hershey loading docks. Before cartons go on board, external water spray equipment cools down the vehicles, creating a proper trailer environment for the lading.

Each year, when the mercury starts to soar, the traffic department sends notices to truck companies calling this problem to their attention. In poster form, they may be readily placed on carrier bulletin boards as reminders to drivers and handlers. Samples from recent years accompany this article.

Because breakage may cause problems where rough handling occurs, carrier performance is carefully monitored in this respect. Checking on both temperature control and shipment handling is regularly performed by a group of temperature and shock recorders maintained by the company. These are shipped frequently without prior announcement via the various outbound transportation modes. "These instruments tell us in a hurry where rough handling or improper equipment is creating claims problems," states Claims Manager Flowers.

Effective Distribution for a Fluid Product

They still don't call it physical distribution at Welch Foods Co. Perhaps this is because Transportation Director Frank Barry was already doing the logistics job there 20 years before the total cost concept became fashionable. A company once entirely oriented to grape products, Welch Foods enters increasingly into other food production fields as its expansion continues. Palletization, slip sheets and other material handling methods that expedite carrier and warehouse handling play an important role here as they have for many years. The company also makes substantial use of bulk shipping and was largely instrumental in the development of specialized food carriers, many of whom assist the company in minimizing distribution inventories by providing fast, reliable services between plants and distribution centers.

The company has employed simulation techniques for several years in its forward distribution planning as well as for monitoring current costs. The full program is run periodically by an outside data processing service organization, but a simplified version for "in-house" purposes can be used at will in measuring the potentials of planned distribution system changes.

TRAFFIC MANAGEMENT examined Welch's distribution activities in April, 1967, as follows:

COMPETING with diversified giants, a specialized producer has more than held its own in what many class as the most competitive industry of them all—food. A coordinated physical distribution program has helped the Welch Grape Juice Company to boost its sales from $9,000,000 in 1946 to a 1966 total of $64,000,000.

Among this program's notable features:

#Specialized equipment for rail and over-the-road shipments

#Drastic reduction of warehousing

#Centralized control of transportation-distribution operations

#Development of specialized motor carriers

#Application of an E.D.P. distribution model to forward planning

The "new look" in physical distribution started early at Welch. Keeping pace with the post-World War II retailing revolution, a centralized Traffic Department was established in 1949 at the company's Westfield, New York headquarters. Under Director of Traffic Frank Barry, sweeping changes were effected in services and facilites, creating a sensitive, responsive system that has minimized field inventories, transportation costs and time losses in the order cycle.

Present physical facilities are a radical departure from the pre-1949 operation. All warehouses, totalling 400 at the time, were eliminated, with storage reverting to plants. Each of these became a semi-autonomous distribution center, manufacturing and retaining a complete variety of Welch products for servicing its area. All are in the midst of grape-producing regions, minimiz-

ing inbound hauls. In the northeast, the Westfield plant and an adjacent facility at North East, Pa. process goods for markets from Maine to Florida. Springdale, Ark. serves much of the South and Southwest. Lawton, Mich. distributes to the Midwest. Kennewick, Wash. handles most of the Far West.

Plant-to-market service is almost entirely by motor carrier. Over the years, Frank Barry and General Traffic Manager John Burks participated in more than 200 proceedings before the Interstate Commerce Commission to establish rights for specialized food-handling carriers to serve their needs. Rates charged by these carriers are generally lower than those published by general commodity truck lines. As a through movement is provided without lading interchange, minimum standard packaging materials are used and breakage is reduced. The resultant improved performance has made possible plant-to-market deliveries normally within 48 hours to all U.S. points. These services and related rates are under constant surveillance to maintain both reliability and economy.

Market service is of primary importance, but there is also significant farm-to-plant and interplant tonnage. While whole grapes move by truck, a large volume of juice and concentrate is shared by leased rail tank cars. A fleet of 18, varying from 6,000 to 10,000 gallons capacity, are now in use. Four additional cars of 20,000 gallons capacity have been contracted with General American Transportation, custom tailored to Welch's requirements. These

Management team of Traffic Department shown at one of the meetings held periodically for evaluation of shipping procedures. From left, John W. Burks, traffic manager; Frank Barry, director of traffic; Anthony R. Canella, supervisor-transportation; and Joseph T. Calarco, supervisor-distribution services.

units greatly reduce the cost of transferring fluid between production points, with savings accruing from reduced handling as well as from quantity rates. Tank trucks are also used to augment the rail service.

Unusual or original equipment is virtually characteristic of Welch's traffic operations. Because receivers of finished products buy mixed lots and hold shipment size down to minimize inventories, the necessity of delivering "hot" (non-refrigerated) and "cold" merchandise concurrently to achieve truckload lots was a continuing problem. Accordingly, in 1956, Mr. Barry suggested the development of an inflatable rubber bulkhead to separate "hot" and "cold" half-truckloads in the same trailers. Perfected with the cooperation of U.S. Rubber Co. and Worster Motor Lines of North East, Pa., the inflated units fit tightly into irregularities of the trailer structure to prevent air circulation between frozen and non-frozen products. Inflation is accomplished using air from the truck brake system. When deflated, the bulkhead could be folded into a compact package for storage. As manufacturers subsequently developed built-in equipment to accomplish this purpose, use of the device has diminished.

While the Traffic Department eliminated field warehousing and its related inventories for most products soon after its formation, the very nature of frozen products continued to require minor public warehousing in several areas distant from supply points. Improved distribution control made possible the elimination of small but annoying losses

"Distribution's role grows continually broader in our type of business." NED M. BROWN, Senior Vice President, Manufacturing

Reviewing test output of a "static" simulation program from Welch's IBM 360 computer are, left to right, A. J. Brewer, manager industrial engineering; Frank Barry, director of traffic; R. L. Judell, vice president-treasurer; and D. E. Cook, manager information service. Full model is run on larger computer by consultant organization.

on the affected operations. "Such savings, though individually small, are part of a continuing healthy pattern that I have watched developing here over the years," states Ned M. Brown, senior vice president-manufacturing. "Distribution's role grows continually broader in our type of business."

In addition to nationwide U.S. distribution, an expanding overseas market is being served. Regular shipments move to the Far East from San Francisco and Seattle. Containerized movements are made via New

York to European destinations while Latin America is served through the Gulf ports. Continued and expanding use of standard containers has materially reduced pilferage and damage. Distributors have been sold on the virtues of this mode because of reduced insurance premiums. The Traffic Department is seeking to develop through rates and complete origin-destination service.

A vital feature of Welch distribution is the use of operations research techniques for development and control of a total sys-

FRANK BARRY

Frank Barry has managed Welch's traffic function for 17 years. He started his traffic career as assistant traffic manager of the Gurtler Electric Company. During World War II, he served as transportation adviser to the U. S. Navy Bureau of Yards and Docks. Subsequently, in addition to activity as an independent consultant, he was employed as assistant to the director of traffic, American Home Products Company and traffic manager, Viking Chemical Company. He is licensed to practice

before the ICC and the FMC. He has also served on the faculty of Traffic Managers Institute.

Although he was a polio victim at age four, rigorous exercisé and sheer strength of will have made him fully mobile since the age of twenty. Active and prominent in many traffic and civic functions and societies, he sets a remarkable example for others who have experienced similar difficulties. He is fully in accord with TRAFFIC MANAGEMENT's program to encourage distribution as a career that the disabled may consider. "Backs we can always find, but brains are expensive," states Mr. Barry. "An alert, willing man can find a job and a challenge in our field."

Fibreboard dividers braced by fiberglass straps prove a simple, effective means of segregating drop shipments.

tem. With the assistance of a major electronic data processing consultant, a distribution model of Welch was developed in 1964. This analysis included such factors as plant capacities, operating costs, relevant freight rates, sales history, raw materials availability, raw material costs plus many other elements necessary to a complete system simulation. Three test runs were made of the model, followed by full activation in 1965. Since then, the model has been run on five occasions to audit distribution system performance and to consider the feasibility of proposed changes.

"The Distribution Model has given excellent proof of the validity of our current distribution practices," states John Burks. "In virtually every case, computer output has specified identical consolidation groupings to those we had previously selected manually using more limited data plus seat-of-the-pants judgement. Continued use of the model will make possible faster, more economical analysis of future distribution plans. Prior manual audit was necessarily restricted to transportation and interplant transfer costs plus a few key production costs. Computer utilization permits quick analysis of

the total cost complex, yielding conclusions of far greater statistical reliability."

In conjunction with A. J. Brewer, manager industrial engineering, arrangements are being made to develop a "static" simulation technique using the IBM 360 equipment at Welch's Westfield headquarters. While the full model must be run on a larger computer by the consultant organization, a simplified approach "at home" will measure individual proposed changes against the most recent prior run of the total system model by the consultant.

Use of the model in forecasting is anticipated as more related company functions are added as data sources. At present, five years of sales history are on tape, providing a reasonable base for projection in conjunction with other pertinent statistics. Improved forecasting will enable the Traffic Department to anticipate demand patterns, scheduling leased rail car utilization and plant-to-store consolidations well in advance of actual needs with a lessened safety margin requirement. Given the possibility of a reduced crop in one region, use of the model in tandem with advanced forecasting would substantially reduce the time and ef-

Part of a special 10-truck "convoy" is shown assembling to move a record shipment of fruit drinks from Welch's North East, Pa. plant to the New York City area.

fort required to adjust shipping plans. It would also open the door to early negotiation of satisfactory carrier arrangements for shipments that, if handled on an obviously emergency basis, would move at higher cost.

Traffic Manual, Special B/L

Another aspect of traffic activity has been development and maintenance of a comprehensive transportation manual for plants and brokers. Revised at regular intervals to keep its information current, procedures are outlined for expeditious customer services consistent with minimum costs. Brokers are shown how to order to minimize delays. They are shown what points should be consolidated, how much weight to include, how many stops can be made by affected trucks, how to combine frozen and dry shipments, how to order warehouse stock and numerous other details. Careful observation of these regulations is a major factor in maintenance of a nationwide three-day order cycle from order initiation to shipment delivery.

Related to the manual and an important element in order cycle performance is a specially imprinted bill of lading. Included are a number of features designed to speed and simplify designation and routing of stop-off shipments. Separate sections are provided for canned and frozen foodstuffs, listing commodities and specifying the contents of standard cartons. Special carrier instructions are an integral part of the form to ensure the maintenance of proper temperatures in vehicles. With this built-in guidance, it is difficult for brokers to overlook salient points in preparing shipping orders.

"Tools are important," says Frank Barry, "but it's people that make them work." Messrs. Barry and Burks are convinced that careful selection and development of capable personnel are paramount departmental responsibilities. Both men have substantial academic backgrounds—both have taught outside of the company as well, Mr. Barry at Traffic Managers Institute in New York City and Mr. Burks at Gannon College in Erie, Pa. Staff members are encouraged to further their educations, both general and traffic. Most have graduated from or are attending traffic school, while several are candidates for college degrees. The Welch tuition refund program returns 50% of costs to employes for successfully completed courses. Company policy sets high product standards and maintains similarly high standards in personnel selection and development. The pay-off is reflected in the tendency for people to move ahead at Welch rather than to move out in search of growth.

Welch's gross sales are running seven times their 1946 volume. Indications are that this growth rate will accelerate in the future. Such past product additions as frozen concentrates required substantial revisions in systems and procedures as well as in traffic department organization. New products, new producing locations in the future may signal far greater changes. "For the past seventeen years, change has always meant growth at Welch's," says Frank Barry. "With the tools now available to us, growth problems become opportunities."

Customer Service:
The Special Ingredient

Gerber Products Company, though only in existence since 1928, enjoys a reputation and a tradition that makes its image seem as old as the Republic. This may be due in part to its major product, baby foods, which leads increasing generations to believe that those life-supporting glass jars must have been there to meet the first man upon his creation.

At Gerber, as at Welch Foods, modern distribution management enjoys a long history. Actively supporting Grocery Manufacturers Association and other external groups promoting logistics betterments, Gerber's internal distribution accomplishments set a similarly enviable track record.

Palletization, pooled shipments, bulk handling and containerization all play parts in expediting goods flow. The company also marries effectively a number of plant-located distribution centers with regional public warehousing operated under standards carefully set and regularly audited.

Long-term computerization plans have already brought substantial automation to current paperwork as well as forward planning, with further progress anticipated as internal resources become available and external standardization of tariffs makes possible the simplification of its already computerized rate files.

TRAFFIC MANAGEMENT's February, 1971 review of Gerber Products Company follows:

THE Gerber Products Company today enjoys the distinction of being a recognized American institution. Any mother assumes its baby products have always been available. Surprisingly, Gerber baby foods came to market only in 1928. With sales in fiscal 1970 exceeding $217 million, it is easy to see why the company's acceptance as an "old reliable" is an established fact.

"We've won our recognition by fulfilling two basic customer requirements," Chairman of the Board Daniel F. Gerber asserts. **"We produce the best product possible, and we make certain it is available when it's needed. Research and quality control**

assure our product's excellence. Effective traffic and distribution management build in that important added ingredient — dependable customer service."

Famous for its baby foods, Gerber today serves additional markets. Its food products now include specialties for children up to preschool age, and the company is expanding into institutional food service also, while such nonfood products as infant wear and baby necessities have come into the fold through a program of acquisitions.

In the midst of this burgeoning activity is the company's general distribution department. Located · at the Fremont, Mich. national headquarters, it plays an important field role as well through five associated plant traffic managers. A department enjoying strong recognition within the grocery manufacturing industry since the early days of physical distribution management, it evolved from a prior traffic department of similarly strong repute. Evidence of traffic's major role is the group of seven Interstate Commerce Commission practitioners on the staff.

Our survey reviews some of the general distribution department's comprehensive traffic and distribution activities. Areas of particular current emphasis include the following:

Specialized Rolling Stock: The Conditionaire car and its role in creating more effective product handling systems.

Pool Shipments: Rail car, piggyback and truck shipments, carefully merged to get timely deliveries at minimum cost.

Warehouse Development: Selecting sites, setting up facilities, establishing procedures are among this department's capabilities.

International Traffic: Growing overseas business finds the department negotiating rates, seeking out routes, developing containerized, palletized movements.

Warehouse Productivity: How plant traffic managers participate in planning daily operating schedules to assure timely shipping without incurring excessive costs.

Public Warehouse Control: Maintaining proper physical conditions and performance standards where contractors perform the tasks.

Internal Freight Payment Plan: What Gerber seeks from an in-house, bankless freight payment procedure.

Multi-Facility Inventory Control: How the department keeps inventory investment down and service up despite widely varied products flowing from and between more than 20 distribution locations.

Company Aircraft Operation: How three fast aircraft keep management close to the whole country despite headquarters being at an "off-line" point.

Strong emphasis on staff responsibilities characterizes this department. Delegating much of the line activity to the plant traffic units, the central staff concerns itself in important measure with control functions, forward planning and systems development. Much of this work is in a transitional stage, moving toward a very high degree of computerization, but currently employing mixed manual and computer procedures designed to optimize available data processing capacity for distribution purposes.

"We are moving forward as fast as resources become available," notes Director of Distribution Peter J. Sullivan, **"but like many companies, we are limited by time available for such projects."** In the Gerber case, the distribution department at least enjoys the luxury of knowing not only what computer capacity is available, but the specific priority level of each of its projects. Department heads meet as a group four times yearly with Information Planning Manager Robert Bristol and his associates to review project status. "In this way, each department knows where its programs stand and can plan accordingly," Mr. Bristol observes.

Certainly, the hardware is there. In addition to an IBM 360-40 computer at Fremont headquarters, each plant has its own 360-20. At present, the plant computers produce concurrent bills of lading and shipping orders. In the near future, they will be interlocked in a highly computerized order processing system. By February, fully half of all orders will clear through the headquarters computer from district office teletype units. The Fremont computer will then feed data to the plant computers for preparing bills of lading, while the Fremont computer will handle the invoicing. Typical of company programs, this procedure has been under test by two district offices on an interim basis for a year, assuring that debugging has progressed a long way before making the procedure standard. By June, 1971, normal order processing will be on this basis 100%. Comments Distribution and Customer Service Supervisor Milton G. Daenzer: **"We've been partially forced into telecommunication by the deteriorating mail services. This condition has hastened our conversion."**

Rate computerization is making long strides as well. Better than 50% of rates, including pool trucks, class rates and other fixed rates, are now computer-available. Next on the agenda are the more complex rates, such as commodity rates, exception rates and other such elements. The department is looking forward to computer production of rate charts from this material. Distribution Manager Sullivan is an active member of the National Industrial Traffic League's Tariff Construction and Improvement Committee, which is working with the carriers toward tariff computerization.

While such sought-for distribution tools as a complete simulation of Gerber's U. S. market are not yet employed, the department makes good use of a computerized tonnage report, available when needed on an "ask for" basis by price brackets by customer. The department benefits as well from a computerized Consignment Report which shows costs between warehouses on shipments, both by individual move points and in summary, and from an Outbound Freight Costs by Line report showing product-line totals of shipments to customers by sales district. This report provides district managers with average cost per dozen by district, in effect guiding managers toward creating customer economic order quantity level determination and minimizing their need for premium transportation.

Good management communication extends well beyond the computer decisions. Mr. Sullivan chairs a distribution committee which meets at least monthly. Including sales managers from the East and West Coast plus manufacturing, marketing and sales people, this forum makes speedy decisions possible when distribution conditions change or new strategy possibilities arise.

In addition, Mr. Sullivan is on the company's packaging committee. He has direct responsibility for the company's unit-loading program. Through this committee's efforts, continual improvements are developed in product protection. Recent experiments at the Asheville warehouse proved that five-ounce glass containers may be shipped "stagger-packed" safely without internal dividers. A year's successful operation in the Southeast now makes this economy available nationwide. Further experimentation is currently underway with the use of eight-ounce bottles.

Physical distribution's role in this company has always loomed large.

CHAIRMAN OF THE BOARD Daniel F. Gerber (right) says: "Effective traffic and distribution management build in that most important added ingredient—dependable customer service." With him is Director of Distribution Peter J. Sullivan.

Looking ahead, it appears destined to assume even greater importance. **"Our products enjoy a rapidly increasing acceptance in overseas markets,"** states President John Suerth. **"The greater complexity of servicing these diversified countries with our traditional reliability places increasing demands upon our general distribution department's proven expertise."**

Modern technology expedites traffic

RAIL AND TRUCK carriers both figure heavily in Gerber movements, the forces of economics as well as service criteria setting the pattern. On inbound produce, trucks deliver to Gerber plants generally from points within a 300-mile radius, while rail takes over on longer hauls. Finished products move by pool car in large volume, with piggyback pool truck and irregular route motor carriers also carrying their share. Overall tonnage is about evenly split between rail and truck.

Today's trend is to freeze the crops in their picking areas, moving them by reefers, either rail or truck, to the plants as required, thus diminishing production seasonality at plants and leveling their work loads. In consequence, new and better refrigerated equipment means a great deal to Gerber. Recent highly successful tests with the ACF Conditionaire cars point toward a new era in bulk handling of much Gerber produce.

The Conditionaire car is a closed hopper unit with insulated walls and mechanical heating and refrigeration equipment. Bulk loading under controlled temperature conditions means a different approach to shipping pears, carrots, peaches and other crops. A single car hauls 89 tons of pears in bulk, the equivalent of three conventional mechanical reefer loads. Unloading takes 19 1/2 man-hours, compared to an average of 63 hours for the conventional equipment. **"On test,"** claims Mr. Sullivan, **"these new cars unloaded 40 bushels of pears per minute, or 20 to 30 tons per hour. We've got studies under way now to determine the best method of developing the needed Conditionaire car pool for early service in handling several of our raw materials."**

For nonrefrigerated, packaged goods moving in distribution channels, all plants have assigned pool cars. Railroads involved in the regular routings supply these cars, all of which are equipped to GMA (Grocery Manufacturers Association) specifications. Pools are generally established by plant traffic managers under corporate supervision, while corporate staff develops pool patterns between plants where necessary.

THE ACF CONDITIONAIRE CAR hauls 89 tons of pears in bulk, which is comparable to three standard mechanical refrigerator cars. The unloading time of 19 ½ hours compares favorably to 63 hours with use of conventional equipment.

PALLETIZED INTERNAL HANDLING with diversified forklift equipment typifies operations at Gerber plant warehouses.

The GMA cars are cushion under-framed boxcars with side fillers. They are insulated and carry logistics equipment for secure loading.

From the California plant, most interstate freight moves piggyback, representing 70% as compared to 30% carload freight. Within the state, however, 90% of all movement is by intrastate motor truck. Piggyback serves in other areas of the country as well. Gerber, while employing ITOFCA services in some instances, makes its own piggyback trailer marriages wherever it proves feasible.

In the motor freight area, because produce is an exempt commodity, negotiated rates are commonplace. General Traffic Manager-Rates Robert Bayle handles long-distance cases, while plant traffic managers cover regional rate negotiations. All work closely with the produce department in this regard.

The irregular route carriers employed are specialists in canned goods. "We find them well suited to volume moves," states Mr. Bayle. "They give us reliable, reasonable and fast deliveries."

While much rate activity concentrates upon pooling patterns, piggyback marriages and other line activities, forward research plays an important part in traffic duties. The department is consulted on all new products to determine service requirements and anticipated distribution costs. The same holds true on studies of company acquisitions, new plant or warehouse sites and other such matters.

"We want to build a complete United States model for simulation studies in the future," Mr. Sullivan states. "Our department today employs much computer-produced material to perform studies of a wide variety.

Through simulation and other operations research techniques, we anticipate shifting much of the remaining clerical burden still incident to these studies onto the computer's broad shoulders."

Plant location studies, in particular, have found the department heavily involved. The traffic overview has kept freight costs down, kept service up and minimized site obsolescence. The department's continuing resurveys show that existing distribution centers represent the best alternatives from a total cost viewpoint.

Overseas business in particular plays a large role in Gerber's continuing expansion. Company plants now operate at Queretaro, Mexico; San Jose, Costa Rica, and Maracay, Venezuela. In Canada, a subsidiary operates the facility at Niagara Falls, Ontario. Licensees now make Gerber products additionally in Japan, Australia and Europe.

The general distribution department's role in this expansion is a big one. The complete Puerto Rico warehouse was set up by the department. While operation is in the hands of local personnel reporting to Gerber Products-Puerto Rico, Inc., automatic stock replenishment remains a distribution department function, Puerto Rico getting a fully palletized flow from the Rochester warehouse, containerized as well.

In developing this operation, the general distribution department selected the actual warehouse site and negotiated the leases. It set up materials handling specifications, bought needed lift trucks and established necessary procedures for the line operation. Continued consultation between the department and the Puerto Rican management assures efficiency, just as does the similar relationship between the central distribution staff and other Gerber facilities.

"Containerization has been a great boon to us in overseas movements," Mr. Sullivan asserts. **"We ship all Hawaii traffic this way in addition to the Puerto Rican traffic."**

Nor does department responsibility end with Hawaii and Puerto Rico. International as well as domestic units of the company look to the general distribution department for such traffic services as routing, rating and related matters that concern increasingly diversified worldwide destinations.

LOADING COSTS AND DAMAGES are both held down through the use of rail shipments employing unit loading of fibre sheets for customer deliveries.

ALL GERBER PLANTS have forklift equipment that includes special push-pull attachments. With this type of materials

handling equipment, goods may be depalletized and loaded onto truck trailers without the further handling of cases.

Traffic-warehouse coordination— The branch traffic manager's function

THE branch traffic managers play a major role in keeping transportation service levels high for Gerber. Working with and for their individual plant managers on a line basis and reporting to the general distribution department on staff matters, they enjoy a professional cooperation with central traffic staff members and among themselves that significantly benefits cost and service standard maintenance in the traffic and distribution arena.

Cooperation is similarly strong between branch traffic managers and their warehouse management counterparts. Working together at each branch location on a daily basis, all plant traffic managers and warehouse managers meet at least biennially at the Fremont headquarters to compare notes and develop ideas in conjunction with the general distribution department staff.

Externally, all plant traffic managers are active in regional traffic organizations. All are either ICC practitioners, certificated members of the American Society of Traffic and Transportation or both.

Because each plant makes the majority of Gerber products on a self-sufficient basis, most tonnage fans out to field distribution directly. In addition, certain specialized items are made at individual plants. These products make necessary significant interplant movements to fill out stock for servicing the field public warehouses in each region.

Internally, the branch traffic manager's office plays an important role in the daily warehouse activity planning. Based upon the labor standards that warehouse management agrees are feasible, stipulated in a Standard Data Conversion Chart measuring cases per hour by product categories that two-man crew units can handle, the traffic department supplies the warehouse with a Daily Load Schedule. It shows a breakdown by truck or rail car and a total for the day. Working together in this fashion,

THE CLOSE WORKING LIAISON between Warehouse Manager Willis Bohmbach (left) and Traffic Manager Charles Benes at the Asheville, N.C. plant characterizes the coordination that is found at all Gerber production sites.

GERBER PRODUCTS COMPANY FREMONT, MICHIGAN						
DAILY LOAD SCHEDULE				DATE OF SHIPMENT _____		
S/SO NUMBER	DESTINATION CITY	CUSTOMER	REQ. MAN HRS	NUMBER OF CASES	WEIGHT	METHOD OF SHIP

WORKING WITH warehouse-supplied productivity standards, branch traffic units develop daily load schedules meshing labor needs with scheduled customer orders.

both warehouse and traffic management readily spot any potential bottlenecks and can prepare their resources to eliminate them.

How distribution works today and plans for tomorrow

SPECIFICALLY distribution-related efforts split generally between staff and line units in Gerber's general distribution department. The staff role involves continuing analysis of service and facility adequacy, both for present performance and in the light of forecasted market growth. In its line activities, a department unit maintains close control over day-to-day inventory conditions. In both areas, maintenance of competitive service levels gets close attention.

Distribution and Customer Service Representative Milton Daenzer's title understates his actual scope. Largely concerned with staff work, he is, in effect, generally charged with departmental research responsibilities. While directly handling specific individual customer requests, he also develops plant location studies, warehouse forecasts and other similar projects.

With some 50% of volume packed seasonally, warehousing is a big factor. Mr. Daenzer maintains a five-year forecast of commodity and warehouse needs, subject to constant update. He negotiates for space with public warehouses and controls these operations, setting standards to be observed as established by Gerber's quality control staff. Public warehousing's role has been growing here. "Rising LTL costs make this necessary," observes Mr. Daenzer.

To assure that storage space is adequate, but used economically, plants keep Mr. Daenzer advised when they divert warehouse space. He visits plant warehouses regularly, making regular on-the-spot peak period checks to determine the adequacy of existing storage arrangements at these locations.

Computer Freight Payment Plan

An important plus for distribution research is the company's internal freight payment plan. **"We anticipated no actual cost advantage from it," Mr. Sullivan comments. "The major reason for developing the plan was to assemble data for distribution analysis."**

In action, the computer kicks out a rating sheet from each shipping order, showing pounds by freight class and related identification. This sheet comes to the traffic department, which enters rate data and other needed traffic information manually. It then returns to the computer, which extends the rates and spreads cost information to each product, concurrently producing checks, a freight payment memo and a check register. The carrier gets a memo copy, while the original goes to traffic and a third copy to accounting.

The freight payment plan is strictly internal. It employs no outside banking facility. Tested for five years, it has now served Gerber for just one year. Messrs. Bayle and Daenzer find

CHECKING distribution strategy are (l. to r.): Distribution and Customer Service Representative Milton G. Daenzer, Traffic Manager-Rates Robert D. Bayle, Distribution Supervisor Richard G. Vredeveld, Director of Distribution Peter J. Sullivan.

PACKD BY	ITEM	FOR	AVAIL	SCHED PACK	UNSHIP	INTRANS	TOTAL	SALES RATE	MOS SUPPLY	ALLOT	MINUS INV	MINUS INTR & UNSH	N S
33	2032	73	32,861				32,861	6.9	3.8	33,690	32,861		
		39	12,389				12,389	3.3	3.8	11,030	12,389		1
		28	14,748				14,748	3.5	3.8	30,580	14,748		15
		09	77,931				77,931	12.3	3.8	42,810	77,931		35
	TOTAL		137,929				137,929	26.0	3.8	118,110	137,929		19
33	2033	28	5,555			9,032	14,587	2.6	3.1	16,280	5,555	9,032	1
		09	21,234				21,234	4.5	3.1	23,360	21,234		2
	TOTAL		26,789			9,032	35,821	7.1	3.1	39,640	26,789	9,032	3
37	2034	73	13,658				13,658	4.4	5.1	28,032	13,658		14
		39	25,480				25,480	8.1	5.1	25,260	25,480		
		28	15,932				15,932	4.6	5.1	15,932	15,932		
		09	63,720				63,720	16.5	5.1	36,220	63,720		27
	TOTAL		118,790				118,790	33.6	5.1	105,444	118,790		13
37	2035	73	33,780			2,001	35,781	6.4	4.5	32,821	33,780	2,001	
		39	40,824			928	41,752	6.9	4.5	37,380	40,824	928	3
		28	13,632				13,632	3.3	4.5	25,380	13,632		11
		09	1,221			44,320	45,541	7.1	4.5	3,301	1,221	44,320	2
	TOTAL		89,457			47,249	136,706	23.7	4.5	98,882	84,457	47,249	9
25	0610	33		44,231			44,231	.0	2.5				
		39	6,625				6,625	1.3	2.5	8,010	6,625		
		09	2,133				2,133	.3	2.5	7,090	2,133		4
		28	12,032			2,250	14,282	2.6	2.5	12,039	12,032	2,250	
		66	11,822				11,822	2.4	2.5	11,822	11,822		
	TOTAL		32,612	44,231		2,250	79,093	6.6	2.5	38,961	32,612	2,250	6

COMPUTER-PREPARED inventory allotment work sheet shows stock moved, scheduled to move or available to be order out, aiding in short-term forward planning while showing stock available for immediate emergency transfers.

one problem in the plan's operation that is still difficult to control: the failure of rate bureaus to provide timely change information. They note that supplements, suspension notices and related items frequently arrive as much as two weeks beyond their effective dates, with the result that the payment plan makes erroneous payments on affected shipments during that period. In general, however, the plan works well, simplifying paper work and yielding needed data for forward distribution planning.

Distribution Supervisor Richard Vredeveld's unit keeps inventory levels up to standard at all distribution centers. These include the plant warehouses and some 15 public warehouses.

AT GERBER'S FREMONT PLANT, Assistant Traffic Manager Jack C. Gillette (left) discusses the effects of packaging changes with Director of Distribution Peter J. Sullivan (center) and Traffic Manager Charles F. Holbrook.

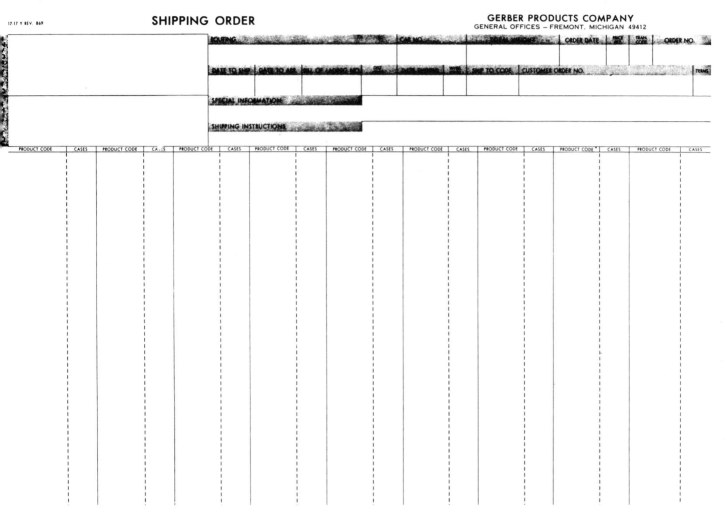

SHIPPING ORDER FORMS, too, are computer-produced. Detailing all pertinent order information, they yield a manifold which includes the bill of lading and accounting forms that speed both deliveries and invoicing.

As in several other instances within the general distribution department, inventory control currently mates computer and manual procedures for optimum use of present data processing capacity. Working tools include a complete computerized inventory report made available every Monday. In addition, daily exception reports from the computer cover items that fall below minimum stock level for that week, supplementing the overall Monday report. From these sources, the unit builds its shipping plan, moving public warehouse shipments during the same week, with plant warehouse shipments scheduled for following week movement.

Because there is a diversity in production among the Gerber plants, interplant shipments play a significant part in the company pattern, and an inventory allotment work sheet reports all items packed at one location for other Gerber plants. This sheet indicates what stock has moved, what will move and what remains to be ordered out. The latter is then tentatively assigned on the basis of sales and inventory history, but is available for transfer in emergency situations. In addition to this work sheet, a recap is developed. This recap expedites carload formations, making it unnecessary to explore the whole allotment work sheet in performing this particular task.

"We keep close watch on numerous factors in planning our specific warehouse movements," says Mr. Vredeveld, "raising or lowering stock levels to suit the circumstances." Warehouse space problems, carrier strikes, tax assessment regulations and a variety of other conditions affect day-to-day planning.

Making "on-line" points out of small airports

A MARKETING and service-oriented nationwide business requires much executive and employe travel to keep things running smoothly. An important traffic function for any such company, at Gerber this activity receives particular attention. With national headquarters at an "off-line" point, timely people movement demands careful planning and resourceful administration.

Transportation Supervisor Clare Van Emst exercises tight control over company travel. Hotels, rental cars, airport transportation and related miscellaneous items get his attention, as well as the booking of commercial airline flights. More than that, he is literally the traffic manager of a three-plane "airline," owned by Ger-

TRANSPORTATION SUPERVISOR Clare Van Emst and his assistant prepare the final version of a daily flight schedule for Gerber's three-plane private air fleet.

THE COMPANY'S three Beech King Air 90 jet-prop planes assure prompt arrivals for management appointments anywhere in the country.

ber, which primarily serves to move people, but handles a modest volume of rush "cargo" items as well. **"Between commercial airlines and our own planes,"** notes **Mr. Van Emst, "we book in excess of 500 flights monthly."**

Company planes enjoy a long history at Gerber. The fleet reached its present size in 1962 and today includes three jet-prop Beech King Air units, planes well suited to the service. They can carry six passengers plus pilot and copilot. Owned outright by the company, they are serviced by flight personnel and mechanics who work directly for Gerber, supervised by a chief pilot who reports to the top executive level.

Biggest share of plane movement is Detroit and Chicago shuttle service from the Fremont, Mich. airport. On flights from here, company men can make a downtown New York City appointment in 2 3/4 hours. **"The best common carrier flight combinations available to us on this run can't even come close,"** Mr. Van Emst states.

Numerous additional flights reach varied destinations where common carrier air service is limited. Controlling these latter flights is a requirement of three or more people as a minimum group to a single point, thus keeping the planes from being tied up unduly by out-of-the-way flight patterns.

While this three-man-minimum stipulation may appear to preclude needed service for some company staff members, the scheduling procedures generally make it easy to assemble minimum or larger-sized groups for practically any Gerber destination at reasonable intervals. For one thing, Mr. Van Emst and his assistant maintain an "open" request register from people wanting trips to various points. Matching up such potential reservations as they develop, the travel unit not only can get the needed threesomes, but can generate many full planeloads in this manner, with minimal delays to those traveling and with beneficial effects on flight costs.

A running two-month in advance airplane schedule, updated continually, keeps the planes moving steadily. Each day's schedule is maintained in pencil, permitting ready upgrading of individual moves and the total flight pattern until actual movement date. On Friday of each week, the chief pilot gets the full rundown of the next week's schedule by telephone, making his operational plan accordingly.

Physical Distribution:
A Major Receiver's Approach

At the receiving end of the food business, as in manufacture, a competitive edge requires close logistics control. Earlier, in Chapter III, the specialized efforts of Stop & Shop were explored in their Northeastern states market area. Another progressive firm, Giant Food, Inc. serves a portion of the Middle Atlantic states with a similarly expanding chain of supermarkets and shopping centers. Its operations centralized largely in a complex located above Washington, D.C., it makes life easier for both its common carriers and the company stores by accepting all deliveries at company warehouse facilities, then fanning out material by company truck for scheduled deliveries employing specialized handling equipment and procedures.

For the carriers, the system eliminates multitudinous stops and unloading delays. For Giant, the economies of consolidation, better internal handling and reduced inventories are at least as important as are the eliminated handling expenses and congestion at the store level.

Unique, automated material handling with remote controlled picking units in the company warehouses adds a further electronic touch to a system operated under substantial computer controls.

What Giant Food accomplishes through centralized distribution is explored in the following presentation, which appeared initially in the September, 1971 issue of TRAFFIC MANAGEMENT:

WHEN a major food retailer's sales move from $162 million in 1962 to almost $477 million in 1971, distribution development faces ever-broadening challenges. Top it off with other retailing activities such as pharmacy, auto and general merchandise sales through diversified stores and centers, and you get the picture at Giant Food, Inc. Operating a chain of 94 supermarkets and shopping centers throughout the Baltimore-Washington-Richmond corridor, company planning involves still greater expansion.

This heavy market concentration can mean economies of scale in product distribution not available to smaller or less-concentrated operations. Vice President-Distribution Alvin Dobbin and his associates make good use of this opportunity. Consider some of their specialized approaches:

Electronic material handling and data processing techniques in distribution center management: Electronics not only means computerized order processing and stock location; it means remote control of picking cart power units, speeding operations with a minimum of labor.

Centralized traffic control: A shift to corporate traffic management means new service gains, greater economies through broadened consolidation programs, systematic inbound control and effective coordination of multidivisional shipping and receiving programs.

Effective store delivery fleet management: Specialized company trucks mean faster, easier service for the individual stores. At the same time, initial large shipment deliveries to a modern distribution center in lieu of myriad small shipments to stores make Giant Food a more attractive customer for the common carriers feeding the chain.

Distribution activities employ a force exceeding 560 people at present. The accompanying organization chart indicates that more than day-to-day operational concerns occupy this department. While the traffic, fleet and warehousing operations reporting to Mr. Dobbin are in great part operational functions, with some additional regard for, and participation in, staff development, he also enjoys the support of a project manager and a chief industrial engineer, whose units are necessarily preoccupied with staff concerns and forward planning support in large measure.

"Giant Food is more than a seller of goods; it is a strongly customer service-oriented company," claims

ALVIN DOBBIN (second from left), vice president-distribution, confers with fleet maintenance staff members, including (l. to r.): Inspector William Heffiren, Supervisor-Fleet Maintenance Robert Hartman and Assistant Manager James Chrabot.

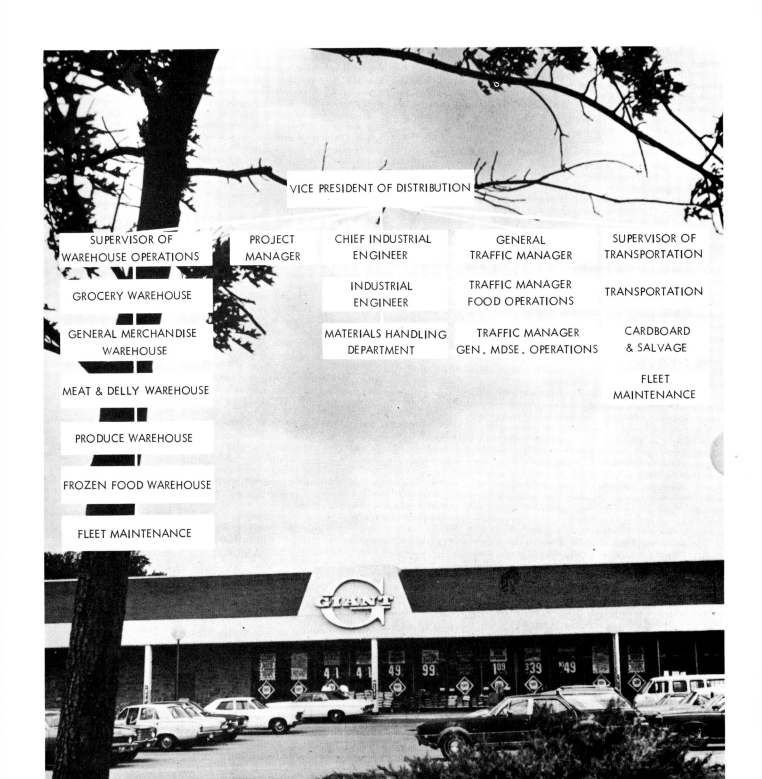

VICE PRESIDENT OF DISTRIBUTION

| SUPERVISOR OF WAREHOUSE OPERATIONS | PROJECT MANAGER | CHIEF INDUSTRIAL ENGINEER | GENERAL TRAFFIC MANAGER | SUPERVISOR OF TRANSPORTATION |

GROCERY WAREHOUSE

INDUSTRIAL ENGINEER

TRAFFIC MANAGER FOOD OPERATIONS

TRANSPORTATION

GENERAL MERCHANDISE WAREHOUSE

MATERIALS HANDLING DEPARTMENT

TRAFFIC MANAGER GEN. MDSE. OPERATIONS

CARDBOARD & SALVAGE

MEAT & DELLY WAREHOUSE

FLEET MAINTENANCE

PRODUCE WAREHOUSE

FROZEN FOOD WAREHOUSE

FLEET MAINTENANCE

GIANT FOOD'S distribution department organization chart, illustrating the diversified functions under its control, overlays typical scene at one of the firm's 94 modern shopping locations in the Baltimore-Washington-Richmond corridor.

Mr. Dobbin. "Effective, reliable service demands this kind of forward-thinking attention. It is also the reason we perform so many tasks within the organization that others might assign to contractors or vendors. We have our own maintenance facilities, painters, millwrights and several other support elements in the company's direct employ. Working this way, operational schedules as well as expansion timetables are readily met or even bettered, to customer advantage as well as our own."

Centralized traffic management benefits a major chain

FOR RETAILERS, in many cases, traffic management is a passive function, making the best of vendor-controlled routing and easing day-to-day problems as smoothly as possible. Giant Food sees it another way. Late in 1969, separately controlled traffic functions were brought together in a corporate traffic department and placed under General Traffic Manager Chris Balodemas, reporting directly to Vice President-Distribution Alvin Dobbin.

The new organization, in addition to achieving better carrier coordination and superior inbound routing control, plays an important internal part as a coordinator between the warehousing, buying and transportation aspects of the business.

"To the greatest extent possible, our buyers now order on an F.O.B. vendor basis," notes Mr. Balodemas. "In this way, we have the opportunity of routing as much of our inbound freight as possible. This allows us to reduce the total number of carriers calling at our docks, thereby minimizing congestion and material handling costs for ourselves as well as reducing delays for the carriers. We thus become both a larger and a more desirable customer for the carriers serving our facilities."

Traffic Manager Frank Esparraguera, who handles the general merchandise sector of the traffic department, echoes this approach: "We currently route all general merchandise purchase orders within the traffic

department to ensure proper control, but intend giving the buyers their own traffic-maintained routing guides in the future. We set up appointments with the carriers so that their trailers will come to the right door at the right time for expeditious handling."

Procedures differ slightly among the company units on routing. While general merchandise is manually processed, grocery division order processing, including routing, is computerized. The computer-stored routings are updated by the traffic department as necessary.

This essentially new department is moving ahead with several ambitious programs, including various consolidation operations. At present, contract carriers handle vendor freight

consolidations in the New York metropolitan, greater Philadelphia and Baltimore areas.

Among further consolidation plans under study is one for a Southern area consolidation of goods from numerous ready-to-wear vendors. Tonnage distribution and potential rates via a number of key cities are being considered in reaching the final determination.

Located on the Penn Central, substantial inbound traffic arrives at the Landover distribution center in carload lots. "We've noticed a recent sharp service improvement on this," Mr. Balodemas asserts. "Our lead times are now under review with the thought of possibly shortening them if this condition holds up." Large tonnage also arrives by various forms

FRANK ESPARRAGUERA (left), general merchandise traffic manager, and Chris Balodemas, general traffic manager, review plans for servicing shipping centers.

GIANT FOOD'S position as a largely inbound traffic operation requires much external contact and careful interplanning of arrangements with vendors and carriers. Much of this activity is handled by (left to right): Traffic Coordinators Carol Peak, Dorothy Wright and Shirley Brown.

A CONTAINERLOAD OF OLIVES fresh in from Europe is about to be unloaded at one of the weather-protected truck-receiving doors. Containers moving via Baltimore play a growing role in supplying Giant Food.

of motor carriage, including common, contract and private. There is also a significant and growing movement of import containers arriving over-the-road from the Port of Baltimore. Tonnage by all modes inbound exceeds one million annually and is growing steadily.

In addition to direct rail carloads arriving at Landover, the traffic department makes extensive use of piggyback services, notably on meat arriving from the Midwest and frozen concentrates coming from the South. In both cases, reefer units are necessarily standard equipment.

On the communications front, so important to the success of any traffic department, several projects are under way. Just recently, a new bill of lading form, specifically tailored to Giant Food's particular needs, was put into use. In a parallel development, a complete set of written procedures is being documented for both department personnel and others in the company concerned with traffic-related activity.

Backing this up is a mini-traffic course to be given buyers and others, acquainting them not only with the department's duties and functions, but orienting them as well to newly developed traffic tools for their more effective future employment. Additional mini-seminars have been run and will be in the future for receiving personnel, keeping them alert to the necessities of checking merchandise condition on arrival, proper notations

on delivery sheets and related matters.

Largely a palletized operation in common with much of the grocery industry, external affairs with regard to pallet exchange are handled by the traffic department. Pallet exchange programs as well as slip sheet ones are being pursued increasingly with significant numbers of Giant Food suppliers.

On the general paper work front, the traffic department has relieved the accounting department of freight bill payment and now audits and pays bills itself. The new payment setup greatly simplifies a number of procedures, as well as speeding up bill payment. It assists as well in the department's auditing program, an in-house procedure that not only finds bill errors for correction, but spots trends such as misapplications of specific rates at a carrier terminal that may be called to their representative's attention, thereby eliminating a whole class of errors in a single step.

The department's liaison role between buyers and warehouse operation is an important one. Profit margins are close in the food chains and minimal inventory is a big factor in maintaining favorable cash flow. It's a tricky scheduling job to buy just when something is needed, get it into the warehouse on time, flow it out to the stores as they order and then repeat the cycle so that there is never a stockout, yet never a significant sur-

plus. Giant's total traffic approach is doing just that. As the traffic staff develops new programs, additionally speeding service while reducing costs, it will still further vindicate the department's role as both a service and a profit-builder.

Electronics comes to the warehouse

GIANT FOOD'S Landover, Md. distribution center differs a little from traditional concepts. Instead of fanning out products over a wide area, it funnels goods from widely dispersed vendors into the 125-mile radius wherein the company's 94 stores are located. Keeping turnover high through modern management and equipment, it is more transfer point than warehouse. Nothing sits still long at this facility.

Several innovations here keep stock on the move, yet concurrently relieve destination stores of much handling work or the need for the traditional "back room" storage. Among these are the following:

Computerized order processing: Data phone lines permit stores to key-punch orders via telephone circuit, speeding computer preparation of stock selection and delivery papers.

Radio-controlled tuggers for order assembly: Order selectors employ Barrett-Cravens Radox units, remote controlled from belt-worn transmitters, that haul several carts for a selector's use as he walks through the warehouse section aisles.

Collapsible carts for direct store delivery: Roll-on, roll-off carts, loaded at the warehouse and delivered by company trailer, may roll directly onto a store floor for shelf delivery or for direct use as temporary display or shelving space.

Order processing for groceries initiates with key-punching of data at the store at a scheduled hour. Replenishing innumerable items in trailerload lots, punching the information for transmission via Bell dataphone may keep a store's model 1094 communication unit on its call for up to one-half hour.

First order-processing step is hand preparation of an initial hard copy. A

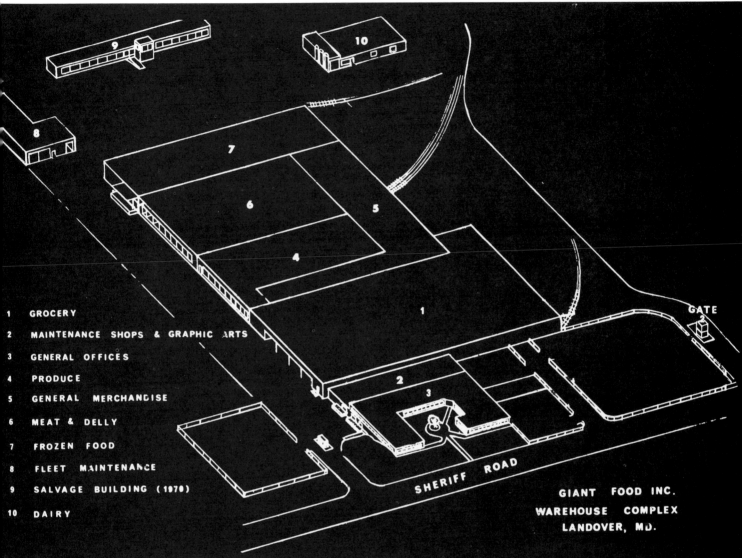

1 GROCERY

2 MAINTENANCE SHOPS & GRAPHIC ARTS

3 GENERAL OFFICES

4 PRODUCE

5 GENERAL MERCHANDISE

6 MEAT & DELLY

7 FROZEN FOOD

8 FLEET MAINTENANCE

9 SALVAGE BUILDING (1970)

10 DAIRY

SHERIFF ROAD

GIANT FOOD INC.
WAREHOUSE COMPLEX
LANDOVER, MD.

A SCHEMATIC DRAWING of the Giant Food distribution center and other company facilities at Landover, Md. reveals the diversified activities controlled from this single location. Several innovations here keep stock on the move.

catalog book with blank columns for quantity entries by day expedites this step, with entries made in day-columns opposite commodity descriptions. Replacement catalogs go to the stores every four to eight weeks as required—sooner, if necessary. Supplements are also issued for intermediate updating.

The catalog provides both an input for punching and a hard copy record for the store of current and prior orders. Only page, line and quantity of goods is punched, thus speeding transmission. When the computer prints out hard copy subsequently, it supplies complete description from its disk memory files.

At Landover, incoming dataphone transmissions flow directly through IBM 024 key-punch units equipped with communications devices, fed directly via conventional Bell system telephone line. These cut individual tab cards representing each catalog page and the standard 24 items per page.

Batched cards flow about four times daily to computer processing, generally performed on an IBM 360-40, although an available 360-30 may be used as well. The computers match orders against their disk inventory records and print out a complete order in two hard copies, adding the storage slot location number and full commodity description to the punched card data. Order pages print out in the proper slot sequence for expeditious picking, and the store copy is used by the stock selectors, returning to the store in the trailer with the order.

The order pages go to selectors in sufficient number to constitute a normal 200-piece work unit, representing a "run," set up to preclude cross-picking. Selectors pick from one side of an aisle only, a move down one aisle being termed a "trip." A run may constitute either one trip or several, depending upon movement necessary to achieve a 200-piece assembly.

Remote control tuggers

A string of four-wheeled, steel flats accompanies a selector on his rounds, hauled by a Barrett-Cravens remote control Radox tugger. On a special belt, the selector wears a small button-actuated control unit with which he controls the Radox. Picking his

UNIQUE, FOLDING KWIK-KARTS flow from warehouse direct to store floor. They are easily loaded to delivery trailers using Barrett-Cravens Radox units. A handle at left front, installed on the Radox unit by Giant Food maintenance personnel, permits uncoupling from the cart without the operator leaving his platform.

FULLY-ENCLOSED DOCK SPACE for 11 rail cars gets inbound goods into storage rapidly. Pallet jacks and fork-lift trucks speed inbound handling in the essentially palletized operation at Landover, Md.

TUGGER UNITS move freely throughout the warehouse under individual operator guidance. Selectors, when assembling orders, "lead" these units and their trains with belt-mounted radio controls, moving them down the aisles from place to place without having to board the units, freeing their hands and saving time.

way steadily down an aisle of pallet racks, he "walks" his train along by actuating the button controls, eliminating any need to mount or dismount the unit or to manipulate its auxiliary manual controls.

Though an unusual installation in many ways, it is not a new one. Some of the tuggers are now 14 years old. As their radio control parts wear out and replacements for these earlier models become unavailable, they are being converted to plain, manual-control tuggers, with every indication of yet further substantial service life ahead. No longer suitable for order assembly, they prove highly satisfactory for trailer loading of the new type delivery carts now serving a growing number of stores. They serve as well for various switching chores on the loading dock.

At the close of a run, a selector's piece count is entered on the back of the order sheaf he turns in. These papers ultimately are assembled for delivery with the merchandise, a typical order representing up to 10 to 15 selector runs.

Each selector carries a pad for use when he fails to find an item at its indicated slot. In each instance, he makes out a slip detailing store number, item and other necessary information. At run's end, he turns in a "pull down" sheet listing these entries. A forklift operator then searches out missing items, replenishes the affected slots and fills out the affected order at the dock or on the trailer.

Collapsible carts

Substantial steel carts weighing 240 pounds with two large shelves now service 16 Giant Food stores, with an additional two locations added to the schedule each month. These "Kwik-Karts" carry substantial quantities, yet may be folded to a slim eight-inch width for storage.

Stores may unload a trailer of these in 25 to 35 minutes, substantially better than the normal time with conventional palletized loading. Additionally, their use eliminates the need of maintaining power jacks at the affected stores, thus cutting material handling costs.

Not only do the carts ease unloading at the stores, but they provide as well a convenient in-store handling system, rolling right onto the floors

CONFERRING adjacent to IBM disk pack units holding inventory data, are (l. to r.): Data Processing Operations Manager John C. DiDomenico, Supervisor Systems and Programing David J. De Waters and Warehouse Superintendent Herman Millman.

AT THIS DATAPHONE CENTER, vital to Giant Food's rapid store stock replenishment, 10 key-punch units with telephone auxiliary equipment receive orders punched directly by the stores on a scheduled program, with the resultant cards being fed directly to the computer for order processing.

and usable, when necessary, as display units. Loading at the distribution center is also fast and easy.

Company fleet deliveries cut handling and inventory costs

A MARKET-ORIENTED truck fleet has been part of its service package from the day Giant Food opened an initial Washington, D.C. supermarket in 1936. The company saw here an early answer to several problems. It eliminated the expensive storage and handling encountered when innumerable vehicles make nonscheduled deliveries to the typical store "back room"; it made possible large-scale carrier deliveries to distribution centers to obviate the small

shipment problem for both parties, and it made far more effective use of total inventories, with the central source making store backup stock minimally necessary due to scheduled, reliable company truck deliveries.

The traditional bugbear of such private fleet operations, deadhead return movements, is tackled head on by the company in a novel way. Transportation Manager Elwood Berger's department, in addition to its fleet control duties, operates an effective recycling program based at the Landover distribution center in a new building. Trailers once brought in empty from store deliveries may now return with used boxes, corrugated materials, crates and baskets that formerly presented a huge disposal headache.

At the new facility, a huge machine, designed by Giant Food per-

sonnel, takes all the corrugated material and compresses it into bales through a fully automated operation. This machine thus creates a readily handleable product for reprocessing to pulp and, subsequently, into new boxes. Resalable crates and baskets are disposed of intact. Their volume runs 9,000 units per week, while the baling machine produces 350 tons of baled fiberboard during the same period.

Backhauls profit, as well, from increasing vendor pickups where these can be effectively scheduled. Recent substantial gains out of the Baltimore area have benefited the backhaul totals importantly.

With a fleet haulage capacity of 8,000 tons, the end of 1970 found typically 46,000 tons moving every four weeks from the Landover facility. This contrasts sharply to just four years earlier, when 21,000 tons would move in a comparable period. Some 95 tractors and 370 trailers handle this work. Built to carefully chosen specifications, their number increases steadily. Of the trailers, 182 are reefers including 72 nitrogen units. Trailers are 40- and 42-footers.

The latest fleet units are 42-foot Brown trailers. Their aluminum bodies ride on Parish slide tandem suspensions employing Rockwell-Standard axles. They have galvanized steel inside liners, while laminated oak floors ease forklift loading. Because these trailers line up closely for efficient warehouse handling, they include special reinforcements to shrug off the inevitable "body contacts" expected in such close spotting.

The newest tractors in the 95-unit fleet are International Harvester-built with Cummins diesel engines powering Rockwell-Standard 411:1 ratio rear axles through Fuller RT 906 Road Ranger transmissions. All tractors receive scheduled preventive maintenance at the Landover shop, where a 40-man force keeps reliability records high, checking out the trailers similarly at three-month intervals. Weekly wash-downs make certain that outer appearance matches inner security so that a Giant Food's truck is a rolling favorable image as it passes company customers going to and from the places where they shop.

A SMALL PART of the Landover distribution center trailer parking area, as well as varied company equipment and, in the background, a portion of the warehouse facility, are seen through a window of the transportation department office.

THIS GIANT-DESIGNED compacter and baler, located in a separate building at the Landover center, is key to firm's carton and fiberboard reclamation program.

Good equipment does a better job when good hands guide it. Transportation Manager Berger is a strong exponent of careful driver selection and constant upgrading through effective training and orientation. Vice chairman of the American Trucking Association's Council of Safety Supervisors, he is also a qualified instructor of defensive driving courses, an attribute put to good use within the operation.

Proof of the pudding lies in outside recognition: Giant Food's fleet has won the District of Columbia Safety Award for one million or more miles of accident-free driving every year for seven in a row. There were two Giant Food drivers who made it to the 1971 National Truck Roadeo finals in Houston as well.

The company also adds a direct incentive on the job. Safe drivers re-

TRANSPORTATION MANAGER Elwood Berger places great emphasis on driver selection and training.

ceive an incentive premium for each month of safe driving plus an added

bonus for a full year of accident-free operation.

In addition to services to and from Landover, the truck fleet provides deliveries from the bakery distribution center at Silver Spring, Md., from which stores receive deliveries Monday through Saturday. Canned goods and dry groceries flow from Landover typically four times weekly to a single store, but up to six times where volume warrants it. Dairy products reach the stores five times weekly, while perishable service is uniformly on a daily basis.

Largely palletized at present with forklift loading at the distribution center and pallet jacks at the stores, the growing use of novel carts in warehouse-trailer-store movements, described elsewhere in this issue, still further reduces turnaround times on deliveries.

Single-Source Distribution:
Reliability, Economy, for Food Servers

What the supermarket is to the housewife, Foodco is to the hotel, restaurant or institution providing on-site meal service—and more. Offering a total service, including inventory control at the customer location, total accounting service and portion-packaged food units that greatly simplify necessary kitchen work in a labor-short era, Foodco services assure reliable operation of dining facilities under conditions that might appear substantially less than favorable.

The company leans heavily on computer support, literally checking customer pulse day after day to assure timely deliveries of perishables, yet never overloading the limited storage facilities characteristic of such operations and always respecting specific constraints such as limitations on hours of delivery, size of packages acceptable or other unloading restrictions. At its Bronx, New York headquarters, the computer plays a similarly important part in maintaining warehouse productivity, both as to space utilization and labor employment. Few firms have better or more timely information instantly available on every phase of physical and financial activity than does Foodco.

The systems employed and the equipment maintained were initially presented in TRAFFIC MANAGEMENT's March, 1969 issue as follows:

Is THERE AN ANSWER to the growing problems hotels, restaurants and institutions face in serving their customers the meals they want when they want them? Foodco, Inc., a unique young food supplier, thinks so. By removing headaches for both the kitchens and the accounting departments of large institutions, it built gross annual sales exceeding $25 million in less than five years. Generating 25% of this business overseas, the company's vigorous expansion aims at still broader areas of market penetration while building higher revenues.

The typical large hotel obtains foods from at least 12 to 20 sources. Its chef contends with multiple deliveries and, consequently, multiple possibilities for delivery failures as well as too-frequent changes in actual sources. All too normally, delivery schedules tend to suit supplier convenience rather than the chef's. On another floor, the hotel's management and accountants contend with paper flow from these sources representing varied terms of sale that demand differing treatments to suit each vendor's convenience.

Foodco's three-pronged approach diminishes these difficulties:

—One-stop shopping for virtually all major food items. The five principal product groups—meats, frozen foods, dairy products, produce and groceries—are assembled to customer specification and moved to the waiting kitchens in single shipments.

—Custom-tailored order processing. Shipments, both in form and frequency, fulfill customer schedule needs, matching his receiving capacity and minimizing his paper work.

—Total cost control. Sophisticated systems and procedures keep the customer fully informed on all related expenses. The complete food and service package is cost-competitive with alternate sources, yet provides faster, more reliable input where it counts—at the kitchen door.

"Complete physical distribution control from a California strawberry patch to the Caribe Hilton's dining room in San Juan, Puerto Rico is the answer," in Vice President Theo. J. Van Amstel's opinion. "Our entire management staff are food professionals with heavy hotel and institutional experience. We look first for quality in the raw material, but we know that getting it where it's needed in top condition is the make-or-break factor in our business. Otherwise, the chef must watch the receiving platform more than the stove. This inevitably means disaster at the dinner table."

How does this company set up its individual accounts for the specialized services it provides? Several steps are necessary:

—It develops an individual service plan for each account, based on customer product specifications, storage capacity, required delivery frequency, and customer accounting requirements.

Checking choice beef into the aging room: Choice cuts, aged to customer specification, assure uniform quality at the stove and on the table.

At console of Foodco's computer, Operations Manager Peter Drummond and EDP Operations Manager Robert Warren review schedules of distribution-related reports.

—It backs up the customer plan with substantial inventories at the Foodco warehouse, maintaining fresh stock as required by customer demand patterns.

—It moves shipments by first-class transportation to assure arrival on the day and hour agreed upon in the service plan. Modes include common carriers of proven reliability as well as a private truck fleet. Air freight, both domestic and international, figures prominently, as do containers for overseas moves.

—It coordinates all activities with electronic data processing. Multiple computer programs keep operating and accounting data current, schedule the customer orders, develop required shipping papers, invoice each account monthly and, as a by-product, provide both Foodco and its customers with clear, concise control reports.

Everything funnels through Foodco's single modern facility in New York City's Bronx borough. Under one roof are warehousing and processing facilities, computer

operations and sales, accounting and executive offices. Drawing from world-wide food resources, it serves domestically a primary area stretching from Philadelphia to New Haven, Conn., plus some individual accounts at significantly greater distances.

Its principal overseas bailiwick is the Caribbean, with 60% of area activity centered in Puerto Rico. Both Europe and the Far East provide large accounts for meats. Vice President Van Amstel notes: "We export ribs, strip loins and short loins to Europe by air, taking advantage of the 18 cents-a-pound commodity rate. The idea of the American steak house is very big and growing in many countries. Pan Am handles this traffic as well as weekly broader-line foodstuffs shipments to Barbados, Trinidad, Antigua and Jamaica. The latter places get everything but groceries this way. We find it more efficient to move them by ship once monthly."

Gathering the goods in is a major task. Great amounts are imported, such as fancy peas from Germany, white asparagus from

Monthly summary computer report is examined by Vice President Theo. J. Van Amstel and Export Coordinator Gerard Goldblatt before it is sent to customer.

Special telephone equipment and order forms that match rapid communications to computer capabilities help order processers speed fulfillment of customer requests.

Japan and truffles from France. Most fruit comes in from California or Florida, the fancy varieties regularly by air. Seafood and frozen vegetables come in by rail, delivered either to the Bronx plant siding or to a separate additional freezer facility in downtown New York.

A full spectrum of common carriers participates in delivering numerous other products. The company's own trucks, however, pick up 80% of the dairy products and grocery specialty items as well as 75% of the produce from suppliers in the immediate area. Once received, many products require sorting, packaging or processing operations before they can move forward to customers. In other cases, certain large customers draw commodities which may simply go in and out of the highly palletized warehouse on the pallet that brought them in.

Meat, in particular, must match customer specifications. At one New York hotel, for example, orders call for hundreds of beef loins weighing between 22 and 24 pounds. Because Foodco respects this requirement, the chef's roasting procedure becomes a

Meat cutting and packaging, accurate within one-quarter ounce, assure needed uniformity for meal preparation in large kitchens.

smooth, assembly-line job, freeing attention for other matters. Other meats, including steaks and individual hamburger patties, are portion-controlled to customer order. If a restaurant wants 14-ounce steaks, the meat cutters provide just that, carving to weights within a ¼-ounce tolerance. Such product uniformity not only eases kitchen burdens but avoids the kind of customer annoyance created when four people at the same table receive steaks in four different sizes.

"We're selling service values on a systems basis," claims Marketing Vice President Robert T. Belden. "Our competitive posture predicates a lower actual purchasing cost for the customer, taking into account all of the related costs, not merely the purchase price alone. Because we are the only United States company offering essentially a single-source food supply, we compete successfully even when our selling price is the same as or slightly above an alternate source's." The company trades off very effectively against reduced handling and accounting costs while providing customers with a sales dollar-creating edge through superior service.

Foodco's typical U.S. account places $200,000 worth of orders per year. When a new account is acquired, specialists perform substantial preliminary work to develop suitable shipping patterns and to establish mutually satisfying accounting procedures. They assist the customer in developing adequate and efficient systems for getting the most out of his storage space and for development of effective materials handling.

Based on storage and material handling capability, delivery frequency requirements are established. Company specialists, working with the customer, develop an individual order book at this point which reflects all food items that would be normally required. This, in conjunction with a specific customer service plan covering his delivery requirements, accounting procedures and any special arrangements, sets the stage for operations.

Paper promises and goods delivered are not the same thing, however. That is why a Foodco account manager is assigned to the new account, visiting its premises no less than once each week when things are running smoothly and living with it when any problems arise. Good day-to-day service is not enough. The customer paying $60-plus a day for his resort accommodations doesn't want to hear about dock strikes. When he orders bacon and eggs, he expects to get it. Foodco sees that he does.

In addition to its routine air movements, the recent dock strike found Foodco shipping 82,000 pounds by air to Puerto Rico each Sunday morning in lieu of unavailable container freight. Though not a complete

Checking out part of an export shipment bound for the airport are, from left to right, Peter Drummond, Foodco's operations manager; Gerard Goldblatt, export coordinator and Franklin M. Thalheimer, distribution supervisor.

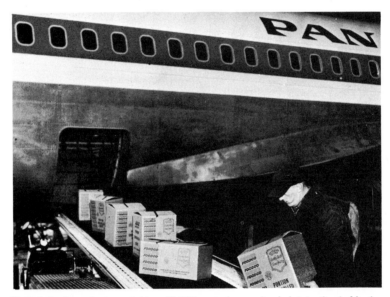

Varied food products weighing 82,000 pounds are loaded into the hold of a waiting Pan Am jet freighter for swift movement from New York to Puerto Rico, easing pressures on resort dining rooms caused by longshoremen's strike.

service substitution, it did mean that numerous resort managers were saved much embarrassment without purchase cost penalties, because no special charges were assessed. Such when-the-chips-are-down service as this explains why the company and its clients enter into no contracts. Reliability under fire is all the assurance customers need, in the opinion of Vice President Belden.

Centralized Export Control

Export as well as domestic service operates from the Bronx headquarters. While Vice President Van Amstel maintains staff activities and supervises worldwide services from this base, the operational tasks fall locally to Export Coordinator Gerard Goldblatt. He in turn maintains liaison with Foodco agents on several Caribbean islands through Lee Shaffer, customer service manager, Caribbean, in Santurce, Puerto Rico.

At Puerto Rico, Sea-Land Service delivers an average of two dry trailers and four reefer units each week. Local deliveries move by contract carrier, while Berwind Lines takes Virgin Islands-consigned trailers by barge from San Juan to St. Croix and St. Thomas. Assistant Customer Service Manager Tony

Caceres controls all of these transportation operations. His office checks each container on its arrival at the Sea-Land Puerto Rico terminal to make certain that Foodco's own seal, installed upon loading in the Bronx, is intact on arrival. In the nearly five years of operation, no broken seals have been found.

As on the mainland, company agents establish strong personal relations with hotel management, purchasing agents, accountants and chefs to ensure that service requirements are met. "Our company is the only food purveyor in the Caribbean giving a full invoice showing FOB price at New York, transportation rate, delivered price and actual issue price—the price for one item from a case when issued from the hotel storeroom to its kitchen," claims Vice President Van Amstel. "By being frank about terms we save accountants from problems. We make no effort to hide any part of our profit in transportation or other ancillary costs as so frequently happens with export shipments. Whether a customer checks our individual bill or his complete purchase report, prepared for each one individually on our computer, his costs are readily apparent in every category," Mr. Van Amstel explains.

Computerized Warehouse Control

Warehouse operations depend significantly on computer-developed information. An IBM 360-30 unit, in addition to developing account information for both customer and Foodco use, prepares as well a number of special reports that spell out current inventory status, trucks needed and personnel requirements for upcoming shifts to provide day-to-day service. In addition to providing routine daily information, the computer builds experience that maintains and revises productivity standards for the performance of various warehouse tasks.

Each night at 6 p.m., a report is released forecasting truck and labor needs for upcoming shifts in the 24-hour-a-day operation. This proves particularly important when absenteeism or other problems arise, indicating where feasible labor reassignments can be effected. There is a substantial variance in productivity in the warehouse jobs, even for ostensibly comparable chores. It takes two men eight hours, for example, to pick 13,000 pounds apiece of frozen foods for orders. In the same period, one man selects 20,000 pounds of groceries. Similar variations exist among other categories in the stock.

A companion computer report, issued for each of the five major food categories, consolidates all activities for the day, yielding data for buyer planning of purchases to maintain inventory levels.

The computerized customer orders provide information specifically for warehouse use as well as for the customer. The selection ticket shows loading supervisors the commodity order in which the delivering vehicle should be loaded, the time delivery should be made, whether to use skids or pallets and any driver equipment required. This information assists not only in the proper staging of individual loads, but in the selection of truck-loading order as well.

Daily productivity records from the computer show whether labor has been assigned effectively, so that no men are unfairly burdened while others coast. This data proves helpful in the continuing refinement of nightly labor requirement forecasts, so that the build-up of performance history yields progressively improved forecasting capability.

A computer "slot run" comes forth on request showing what merchandise should be in each storage slot in the warehouse. Daily checking assures prompt and proper replenishment. Slot numbers on each bin come from the computer as well. When goods are shifted from one slot to another, the responsible foreman submits a change report to the computer section, assuring that a weekly inventory report by slot numbers is not distorted by changes.

Another report reveals the routing of movement for each item as picked for shipment within the warehouse. Through these reports, proper rack locations are determined to minimize worker movement in picking fast-moving items. In consequence, 68% of items picked to fill orders can be selected in the first five aisles of the grocery section. Warehousemen shift these items to match seasonal demand variations, thus maintaining this ratio continually.

A final report breaks down items ordered by specific accounts to determine if particular items are moving, are expected to move, or whether the customer should be checked to determine if the affected goods should continue to be stocked. Close watch is maintained through this means on odd or unusual items requested by only one or two accounts.

"We tend to take the computer for granted," observes Operations Manager Peter Drummond. "This is probably because

A **Sea-Land ship** drops containers at a terminal in Puerto Rico, where Foodco shipments are received regularly for ultimate delivery to numerous hotels and institutions.

we've employed it steadily since we opened for business, so the novelty element is not present as it would be in older companies. Its value grows steadily for us, and we anticipate still wider computer applications in the future. For example, we anticipate developing a substitution program so that when a customer orders something momentarily out of stock, the computer will tell us immediately what substitutions can be made that will satisfy his needs." At the present time, substitutions are part of the customer coordinator's tasks. While relying in some measure on his own judgement, he also consults with customers to determine their opinions and, in the event of any order problems whatever, whether shorts, substitutions or delays, keeps them informed and works with them to solve any resulting problems.

Distribution center operations require 71 employes who report to assistant foremen in charge of the specific warehouse areas. They report in turn to either a day or night foreman, both of whom are responsible to Frank-

lin M. Thalheimer, distribution supervisor. In addition, Mr. Thalheimer supervises the trucking operation which supplies accounts that are directly serviceable from the headquarters location.

The warehouse space is split between the five major commodity groups, all of which have direct access to a large staging area inboard of the loading platform. This sector is kept clear of everything except orders in process of assembly for immediate loading. In each product area selectors assemble segments of individual orders and hold them within their areas until the foreman announces that a particular load is to be assembled. At that time, all five sections bring in their order segments on pallets or semi-live skids, assembling goods in designated areas for specific trucks and placing pallets in accordance with a loading diagram on the wall in the assembly location. Forklifts, Rider-Walkies and other units perform the transport function internally. When the load has been staged and checked, the trucks are

Foodco trucks assure prompt deliveries to hotels, restaurants and institutions located from Philadelphia, Pa. to New Haven, Conn., who depend on this service.

loaded and released. The night foreman starts moving trucks out at 3 a.m., acting as dispatcher until the regular dispatcher comes on duty at 7 a.m.

Internal transport equipment includes eight Hi-los, 23 hand transporters, two Rider-Walkies, one reach truck and several hand-hydraulic trucks. "We're moving increasingly to Rider-Walkies in the selection area," notes Distribution Supervisor Thalheimer. "Not only do we cut fixed costs by 75% per unit, but their improved maneuverability yields sharply higher operator productivity in order picking and assembly."

Part of Foodco's sales package to its mass-feeding customers is the reassurance of sanitary food handling afforded by continuous U.S. Department of Agriculture supervision. A resident inspector, changed every four months to assure objectivity, sees to it that federal food handling standards are strictly complied with. All floors in the warehouse are scrubbed daily by an Advanced Scrubbing Machine, which tours the complete facility in two and one-half hours. As standards require, Foodco trucks are washed inside and out weekly, while trucks carrying meat are scrubbed out daily.

The truck fleet consists largely of leased vehicles, although two 40-foot reefer trailers, a step van, two panel trucks and a station wagon are owned. Leased equipment includes one tractor, one trailer, 23 delivery trucks and three market trucks (two meat, one produce). The leasing companies keep four more straight jobs on standby as well to protect Foodco service.

Each delivery truck is insulated, has a reefer unit and a 4,000-pound capacity tail-lift. Because most loads combine diversified food products, refrigerated equipment is essential. Both gas and diesel trucks serve the company at present, but remaining gas trucks are being phased out in favor of 20-foot diesel units.

Management watches truck utilization closely. While first emphasis goes to giving good service, every effort is made to develop optimum truck loadings and, where possible, to get more than one load per day moved by individual trucks. At present, about 30% of the fleet moves at least two loads per individual truck daily, with some units doing even more. The remaining trucks carry at least one full load daily.

Because delivery plays an important part in Foodco costs, actual customer charges take into account the size and frequency of such truck deliveries. Controls are pound-oriented rather than dollar-oriented up to the point of actual cost allocation, with rates predicated upon pounds per delivery and delivery frequency. A customer whose storage space makes a once-weekly drop of 10,000 pounds feasible, therefore, enjoys somewhat lower costs for his merchandise than one who gets the same amount of goods, but in five 2,000-pound shipments, necessitating increased handling and added trucking expense.

Truck loads change their character depending upon the type of institution served. While the quality of food remains the same, a hospital's order will run only half as many cents per pound as a hotel order. Several factors account for this, principal among them the fact that patients most assuredly receive three meals a day, while the hotel's dining room tends largely toward dinner menus.

"With over 8,000 food items under one roof,

providing in-season and out-of-season delicacies in addition to the most prosaic of groceries, Foodco's business literally is physical distribution," notes President Robert D. Peterson. "Not only does it relieve operating pressures on food service accounts, it relieves financial and administrative management as well of a variety of costs and clerical activities." Where competent labor and clerical personnel are in acutely short supply, a service such as Foodco's can justify dining operations not otherwise feasible.

CHAPTER VI

Where Bulk Shipments Spell Economies

At first glance, it would be hard to imagine two companies with less in common than American Smelting and Refining Company and Hiram Walker Limited. Copper ingots and Canadian Club have little in common. Yet both firms face the problems of transporting heavy volumes of raw materials to and between plants and both are deeply concerned with international distribution.

American Smelting and Refining Company, commonly known as ASARCO, faces notable engineering challenges in developing logistical support for mining operations, frequently found in remote locations about the world. Building railroads, developing ports and setting up ocean transport arrangements are just a few of its unusual tasks in the materials management area.

Because the value per pound of its raw material is low, transport costs loom particularly high in ASARCO's production cycle. Efficiency here is critical, with the result that much planning and engineering go into both equipment and systems for handling ore initially and refined products as well with the least possible labor or material. Bulk shipping is important and specialized rolling stock for this purpose as well as special vessels for sea movement do much to keep ASARCO production costs within reason.

How the company has developed its ore and metal handling systems was explored by TRAFFIC MANAGEMENT in July, 1969 as reviewed on the pages that follow:

The huge Mission mine and smelter operation in Arizona, shown at left, is a major source of copper, silver, molybdenum and zinc. Above, policies concerning the transport of these products are among subjects discussed by Asarco's Executive Advisory Committee.

Asarco: Traffic at the Top Level

THE "PHYSICAL DISTRIBUTION Revolution," currently creating much managerial interest elsewhere, rates only polite smiles at American Smelting & Refining Company's New York headquarters. With a $40 million bill for freight alone, this major metal producer's top executives readily recognize the role of logistics in building and supporting annual gross sales exceeding $100 million.

"Transportation has always held major attention in our company's highest councils," states Vice President—Traffic Frank L. Merwin. "More than that—our executives are extremely knowledgeable in the field. E. McL. Tittmann, chairman of our board of directors, was responsible for the construction of a 120-mile, first-class railroad for the company across the Andes Mountains in 1956-1958, so you can see that transportation know-how means more than just checking freight bills in our company environment." Board Chairman Tittmann rose through various posts in company plants, at which levels traffic and transportation play major roles.

Top traffic men have always been part of the executive inner circle at Asarco. The company, founded in 1899, soon thereafter appointed its first transportation vice president. Since that time, management's transportation interest has been reflected in many ways. Consider the following:

#Company Policy—An advisory committee consisting of all general officers and comparable level specialist executives meets weekly to consider and recommend to the company's board of directors action to be taken on matters affecting future developments. As a vice president, Mr. Merwin is an active team member, participating in major corporate decisions.

#Facility Development — Site locations, plant erections, warehouse selection or construction invariably mean thorough study of alternatives by the traffic staff. Subsequent construction or acquisition finds the department directly involved in activation and refinement of relevant logistics equipment and materials.

#Interdepartmental Liaison—Traffic managerial personnel work closely and continually with their opposite numbers in engineering, marketing, mining and other major company functions. In consequence, knowing intimately the economics of the total business becomes even more important than their specifically traffic capabilities because they constantly take part in programs involving broad, complex cost interrelationships.

Asarco's primary business lies in the mining, smelting and refining of copper, silver, lead, zinc and other non-ferrous metals from basic ore. While copper bulks largest among company products, substantial amounts of silver, lead and zinc flow through the refineries as well. Asbestos and other products more recently came into the company's orbit, reflecting a decision to diversify into areas analogous to traditional corporate activity.

In addition to smelting and refining material from its own mines, Asarco is the world's largest custom smelter and refiner. This custom activity is the processing of ore from outside sources. The relative importance of such custom work, however, is diminishing. The company seeks a more fully integrated production system and has made strong, continuing effort during the past decade to expand the role of its own mines.

Heavy Emphasis On Staff Activities

Because traffic participates amply in the company's highest councils, Vice President Merwin sees little need for his department to control routine, day-to-day transportation activities at every level. When changes are needed or new ideas come up, effective liaison assures consideration regardless of which specific department or unit controls a given activity.

Take the case of warehousing. As new facilities are needed or existing warehouses prove inadequate, the traffic department lo-

Frank W. Archibald
Vice President, Smelting and Refining

cates new units, determines that equipment and space meet the requirements, and negotiates necessary terms for reliable services at a fair price. Traffic stays on board a while longer to be sure that things run right, but it turns over administration to the sales department. Thus, facilities meet traffic department requirements, while the sales department enjoys full authority in the field, devoid of confusions that can arise when two departments must share control at the local level.

Similar thinking prevails in another area —private truck operation. "We were virtually forced into this by continuing rate increases and specific customer service requirements a little over five years ago," notes General Traffic Manager George Cantwell. Here, too, the traffic department offers its assistance to local entities in establishing service, but not in providing the continuing operation. The initial idea for a truck route may originate with a plant manager, or it may be suggested by the traffic department itself if conditions favoring such an operation come to its attention. In either case the same procedure ensues. Traffic personnel determine schedule and tonnage demands, seeking out any possible return load arrangements at the same time for inclusion. They determine what equipment will be required, negotiating lease terms that assure service coverage.

At this point, the affected plant manager and the traffic department confer. If the manager concurs in the arrangements, traffic personnel establish the operation, clear up any starting problems, and turn it over to the plant manager for administration. While it then effectively leaves department control, traffic personnel will review the operation again at any time the plant manager feels

changes may be necessary. The department will also suggest later changes, expansions or eliminations on its own initiative at any time changing conditions suggest it, as when a route change may yield additional return loads or a change in assigned equipment may offer greater efficiency.

Inbound shipments get careful scrutiny at Asarco. Here, too, close interdepartmental coordination pays off. All purchase orders come to the traffic department to have routings inserted, and any invoices containing freight factors are also cleared before final processing. Significantly, construction contracts must also get a check-out from traffic, assuring that all transportation considerations are in order. Working this way, the purchasing department has the needed traffic advice and protection with a minimum of procedural complexity.

Many Shipments Needed
To Create Final Products

Producing a ton of copper, lead or zinc creates numerous collateral movements of diversified materials. In addition to the ore itself, the smelter must bring in coal, coke, limestone and fuel oil. On completing its work it ships out not only metals but numerous by-products, including silver, gold, sulphuric acid, cadmium and other residual elements. These add up, typically, to over a dozen separate movements aggregating 15 tons total for each final ton of metal. In one instance study proved that a ton of ore from a Colorado mine instigated 29 different movements.

Domestic traffic moves preponderantly by rail, primarily on commodity rates. Privileges such as smelting-in-transit and refining-in-transit also loom large in Asarco's traffic accounts. Riding herd on these matters, Traffic Manager-Rates Charles W. Kane and Traffic Manager-Service Alex Hunter work closely with General Traffic Manager Cantwell, responding quickly to carrier tariff change proposals and initiating requests for more satisfactory rates and services where their studies and surveillance suggest worthwhile possibilities. Underlying staff support, nominally split between line activities and research functions, swings readily back and forth between them as conditions change.

While running the traffic department's headquarters requires 34 people, there are others sharing total responsibility. District Traffic Manager Curtis R. Merritt at San

At the Glover smelter, giant storage bins receive hopper-delivered raw materials. Fed by gravity, an overhead crane moves material as needed to feed the furnaces.

Francisco and his counterparts, Gordon W. Dokes at Houston and Russ Van Howling at Whiting, Ind. plus Federated Metals Division Traffic Manager George Carr, have full line traffic responsibility for specific areas. In essence, while reporting to the central unit, they operate complete traffic departments. This arrangement reflects Vice President Merwin's firm belief in delegation, not just of responsibility, but of authority.

While rail matters weigh heavily in traffic's workload, alternatives also come into the act. Barge movements play an irregular but important role. The lengthy non-ferrous metals labor strike which ended in April, 1968, however, deterred such moves until backlog orders caught up and time pressures diminished. Because barge movement is slow and requires 1,200 tons of cargo per load, several conditions must be met to make it efficient. "When economic production circumstances permit the longer transit time plus time needed to accumulate barge loads, however, it works out well," claims Traffic Manager-Service Alex Hunter. "Common

carrier barge lines can carry our freight from Corpus Christi and Amarillo to Chicago, Pittsburgh, Cincinnati and St. Louis quite readily."

The department also considered employing a pipeline to move copper concentrates in Arizona. The ore would have moved as a slurry with a 65% solids mix. Study showed, however, that not enough traffic was available to keep the proposed line operating more than one day each week and, in the absence of any other potential traffic, the project was dropped.

Plants And Investments Are Huge

New mines and processing plants come in only one size range for the copper industry: huge. There is virtually no such thing as a small investment. Accordingly, much executive time and effort in this company goes to careful forward facility planning and subsequent development. Vice President Merwin's opinions weigh heavily in these efforts. The new lead smelter and refinery at Glover, Mo., for example, could have been built on

Vice President-Traffic Frank A. Merwin, second from left, discusses ore movement with General Traffic Manager George Cantwell, left, Export Traffic Manager Adam Hunter, center, and James G. Cox, assistant manager, ore department. Mr. Merwin is also a vice president and director of the NIT League.

Copper wire bars, one of the major products from Asarco's Baltimore refinery, are criss-cross stacked to prepare load for movement by overhead crane.

At Perth Amboy, N. J., large Asarco smelter produces silver, gold, copper. Here, copper bars are being assembled for shipment.

any one of three sites to the satisfaction of other departments. Mr. Merwin suggested the Glover site, however, to assure more satisfactory rail service than that offered by the alternatives. "In examining all of our U.S. plant operating costs, one of our biggest single bills is freight," Vice President—Smelting and Refining F. W. Archibald notes.

How distribution helps build markets

Traffic management means more than cost control at Asarco—it means sales building and profit boosting as well. The company's subsidiary, Lake Asbestos Company of Quebec, Ltd., fully appreciates this. When it encountered warehouse space shortages at Canadian outports in its first active winter, the traffic department solved the problem and created an effective marketing advantage at the same time.

With the problem recognized, the export traffic manager headed straight for the European market area. Working with regular company freight forwarders, he established regional asbestos warehousing in facilities already housing Asarco metals. Comments Vice President Merwin: "We moved our shipping platform from Black Lake, Quebec to Antwerp, Bremen and other European locations."

This did far more than alleviate the temporary Canadian warehouse shortage. It brought stocks closer to customers, reducing order-cycle length and speeding deliveries while avoiding shipping delays due to winter ice in the St. Lawrence River. On the cost side, bulk vessel movements to European warehouses in lieu of separate shipments to individual customers meant reduced ocean shipping charges.

In the domestic area, too, traffic works with production and marketing to build more sales in many cases. Typically, this three-way approach paid off with one northeastern asbestos purchaser. This potential customer's interest grew when the sales department brought in production specialists who demonstrated that a lower-priced, shorter-fibered asbestos could meet the same manufacturing demands as a competitor's product. The clincher came, however, when Asarco's traffic department came on board. They reworked the routing of the raw material, negotiated new rates and came up

with a cost-service package that helped to reduce any remaining customer resistance.

Custom cars cut costs

WHILE ASARCO enjoys growing product diversification, copper and copper concentrates continue to be its major freight items. This volume makes equipment tailored to these products increasingly attractive as labor costs spiral upward and inflationary pressure makes intensive equipment utilization more essential.

Thus far, two specialized car types regularly serve the company's distribution:

—Copper concentrate cars. These replace conventional hopper or gondola cars, speeding and simplifying unloading at destinations.

—Copper anode rack cars. These cars carry greater weight per car and are more readily loaded and unloaded than conventional boxcars or gondolas.

Copper concentrate is sticky stuff. Loaded in a conventional hopper, it proves most uncooperative when it arrives at destination and the hopper bottoms open for unloading. This leads to much expensive shoveling, pushing or other manual urging to make it stop clinging to car sides and yield to the open hopper's gravity.

After some study, Baldwin-Lima-Hamilton built a single test car which differed radically from regular hopper units. The whole car bottom was, in effect, two doors. With car sides canted slightly inward as they rise from the frame, concentrates could cling to no surface when the bottom dropped out. The load fell freely, completely eliminating tedious manual labor required with the standard hoppers.

Continued testing showed consistent success. The Southern Pacific and Santa Fe railroads now own substantial fleets of these cars, while Asarco itself keeps eight of its own busy entirely within its large lead smelter property at Glover, Mo.

Jointly developed by the Santa Fe, Southern Pacific and Asarco, the copper anode rack car also fits conditions unique to the copper industry. The anodes are unrefined copper forms of uniform weight and shape. The rack cars hold these anodes in fitted racks, three anode cars replacing five boxcars, with a resultant 40% reduction in car movements. The railroads enjoy increased potential carload earnings, therefore, while

Special "barn door" hoppers unload sticky copper concentrates with ease, materially reducing labor costs in contrast to conventional hopper cars.

At the Mission smelter, a small shifting locomotive prepares to spot an ore gondola. Shown here moving on the rails, this locomotive can use retractable rubber-tired wheels for road movement as well.

being in a position to offer more competitive rates.

Volume shipments move from the El Paso smelter to the Baltimore and Perth Amboy refineries. Plant managers at all three locations were consulted before design adoption, in this way seeking to avoid any local cost penalties negating anticipated lowered total costs.

The Perth Amboy plant's experience proved that the new anode cars made possible $15,000 annual savings in handling costs. At El Paso, loading costs dropped $32,500 annually. While one man loads an anode rack car in 20 minutes, it takes three men a solid hour to load a conventional gondola.

These cars are a short 33 feet in length because of railroad weight restrictions, but this design element also means positive advantages for shippers and receivers. The cars offer space savings and greater maneuverability, both important in getting the most out of busy industrial plant freight handling facilities.

Rail car development at Asarco, then, ties together the traffic department, the engineering department, the railroads and the car builders. "Typically," observes Vice President Merwin, "new rail car development takes about two years from the concept's birth to fruition in an operating fleet."

At El Paso smelter, two special cars for transfer of molten metal are shifted by company-owned locomotive.

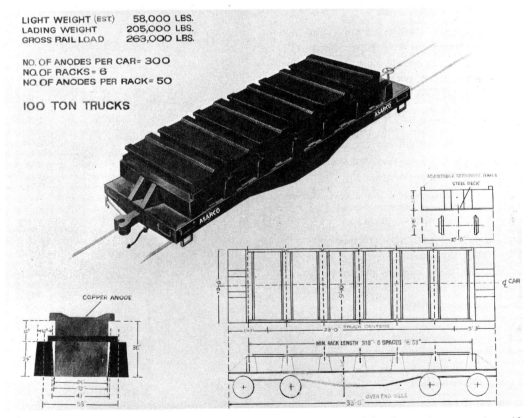

LIGHT WEIGHT (EST) 58,000 LBS.
LADING WEIGHT 205,000 LBS.
GROSS RAIL LOAD 263,000 LBS.

NO. OF ANODES PER CAR = 300
NO. OF RACKS = 6
NO. OF ANODES PER RACK = 50

100 TON TRUCKS

Diagram shows interesting features of copper anode rack car, developed by Asarco in cooperation with the Baldwin-Lima-Hamilton Co. and the Santa Fe and Southern Pacific railroads.

Worldwide control gains better market service

COPPER PROCESSING is a world, rather than a national, business. The ore shows up in widely scattered deposits, all too frequently remote from refining and supply facilities or from ultimate end-product consumers. Moves between three countries, shifting ore from mine country to a smelting country, followed by transport to a market country, are by no means uncommon for Asarco.

Because copper ore discoveries often occur in arid, sparsely populated territories, the company must move every conceivable type of supply into its development sites. Exports, therefore, are more than just sales to customers.

The vast Southern Peru Copper Corp. operation accounts for over 50% of export traffic department activity. Similar projects require traffic support in such assorted areas as northern Peru, Nicaragua, Canada, Mexico and northeastern Australia.

Steady procedural refinement keeps internal costs down despite growth in both volume and complexity of overseas shipments. While the Toquepala, Peru mining operation was under construction, the export staff expanded to 28 members during 1956-1958. Once the new mine was completed and operational, lessened pressures yielded

ar positions wire bars for lowering into vessel's hold at pier in Baltimore. Much of the copper, tellurium, selenium, silver and gold here is exported.

time for a thorough revamp of systems. The staff, reduced to 14 people under the new procedures, subsequently absorbed rapidly growing workloads with such success that they now handle Toquepala shipments in even greater volume than during heavy construction with half the earlier staff.

Such continued efficiency accounts in large measure for Asarco's long-standing preference for doing most of its own documentation, vessel space-booking and other ocean freight forwarding tasks. "We regularly compare in-house processing costs with outside forwarder services," observes Export Traffic Manager Adam Hunter. "We consistently find savings of 25% to 33% over the best they can offer. More than that—we're convinced that our own people, knowing the nature of our own business, can give and get better service."

Peruvian copper moves into the United States through New Orleans, Baltimore and New York. The export department also controls shipments going directly from Peru to Antwerp and Belgium for European refineries. Asarco copper exports from United States origins normally clear through the ports of New York, Baltimore or Tacoma.

Because this company is the world's largest custom smelter and refiner, it handles substantial movements from and to other companies in various nations that provide ore for processing and seek refined copper in return. They buy this service to avoid investing in their own smelter or refinery capacity.

"Minimum shipping costs are vital in this custom work so that, for example, the Corpus Christi electrolytic zinc refinery can compete effectively against Belgian, German and other firms," Mr. Hunter states.

A specific case arose with a Peruvian custom source. Freight costs from Peru to San Francisco were spiralling steadily upward, hurting competitive capabilities in comparison to available European custom processors. The cost hikes resulted directly from rapidly increasing stevedore charges at the Selby lead smelter and refinery on San Francisco Bay. In this instance, the cure was more drastic than a rate negotiation, but it proved highly effective.

A new, two-phase material handling system provided the answer:

—Gantry cranes replaced ship's gear to speed unloading.

—Conveyors supplanted trucks from the pier to the furnace storage area for off-loaded cargo movement.

The installation meant a large investment —$1,500,000—but it promptly cut stevedoring costs 60%, sharply improving the competitive situation.

Asarco Mexicana, a company in which Asarco has a 49% interest, ships silver bars through Tampico, Mexico, in addition to refined lead and zinc. They also forward some copper from Tampico to New York.

While most shipments move by vessel, there are a few exceptions. Silver bar exports from the United States, generally routed by

Loading a vessel at Asarco's Baltimore pier with wire bar from the nearby smelter. Smelter production moves from the plant to the pier on a narrow gauge industrial railroad.

Palletization simplifies handling of materials, such as this caulking lead at Toronto warehouse.

water from Baltimore or Perth Amboy, now move on occasion to Great Britian in charter planes from New York.

A by-product metal from the zinc process which also moves in significant volume is cadmium. A material of growing space-age importance, it flows from plants at Corpus Christi, Tex. and Denver. The former source ships over Gulf ports, while Denver cadmium destined overseas clears through New York.

In doing all of its own vessel booking, the export traffic department builds a growing knowledge and understanding of water carriers and shipping conferences. Over the years, it has established an impressive record at keeping ocean freight costs in line. The anticipation of movements, so crucial to cost control in the Toquepala project, is an important element in the successful negotiation of ship space charters at suitable rates. The export traffic unit, accordingly, maintains a close liaison with the purchasing department. They know well in advance, therefore, when unusual shipments such as locomotives, 100-ton trucks, ball mills and payloaders can be expected to develop. Similarly close communication prevails with all overseas properties and other company departments that may occasionally have unusual overseas shipping requirements.

Liasion within the department plays an important part, too. The district traffic managers at San Francisco and Houston, who report to Vice President Merwin directly, have export as well as domestic line responsibilities in their areas. While not showing up on an organization chart as adjuncts of the export traffic unit, their offices contribute markedly to the successful coordination of export programs.

Unlike many shippers, Asarco has mixed views concerning the container revolution. "Container lines are forming as consortiums of old conventional lines," states Export Traffic Manager Hunter, "restricting themselves to one or two ports. The result is a drying-up of conventional hold stowage and an increasing problem in bulk shipping. This points toward a need to go container eventually on many metals shipments for want of adequate hold space and services." Conventional-hold ships carry the annual 140,000-ton flow of copper from southern Peru.

Recently, much Asarco freight has been palletized for ocean shipment. Further palletization is under study along with the development of a company standard pallet for such shipments.

While export shipping activities essentially move through the export traffic group's control, the department makes an exception in one area. It does not handle customs brokerage. The traffic department selects the brokers, but turns actual day-to-day work with them over to the accounting department. Under conditions which arise out of international tax and accounting complexities, this arrangement undoubtedly minimizes potential duplications and confusions. It reflects, as well, Mr. Merwin's determination that traffic line activity be restricted to essentials, maintaining focus on the department's staff role instead.

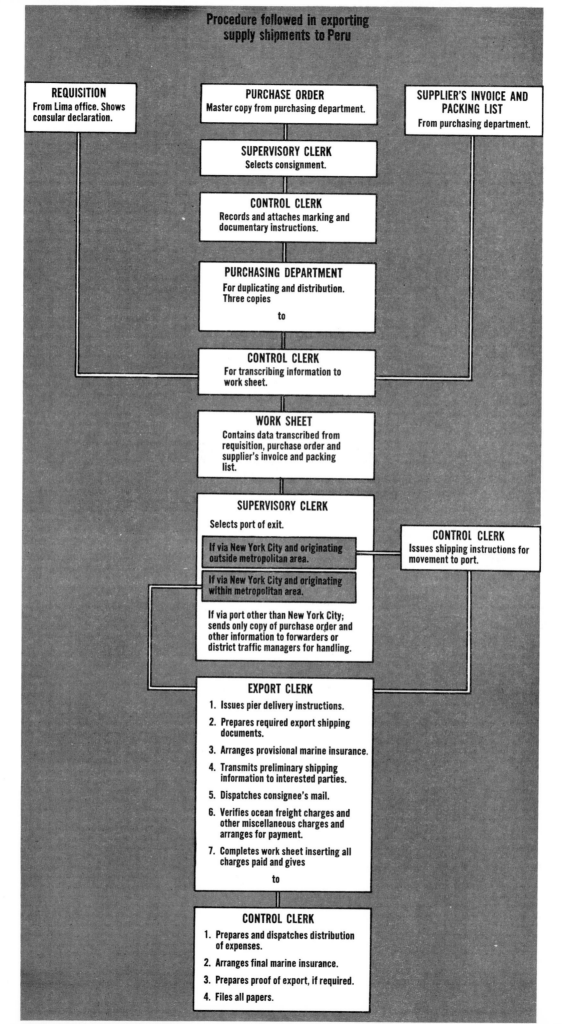

Procedure followed in exporting supply shipments to Peru

REQUISITION
From Lima office. Shows consular declaration.

PURCHASE ORDER
Master copy from purchasing department.

SUPPLIER'S INVOICE AND PACKING LIST
From purchasing department.

SUPERVISORY CLERK
Selects consignment.

CONTROL CLERK
Records and attaches marking and documentary instructions.

PURCHASING DEPARTMENT
For duplicating and distribution. Three copies
to

CONTROL CLERK
For transcribing information to work sheet.

WORK SHEET
Contains data transcribed from requisition, purchase order and supplier's invoice and packing list.

SUPERVISORY CLERK
Selects port of exit.

If via New York City and originating outside metropolitan area.

If via New York City and originating within metropolitan area.

If via port other than New York City; sends only copy of purchase order and other information to forwarders or district traffic managers for handling.

CONTROL CLERK
Issues shipping instructions for movement to port.

EXPORT CLERK
1. Issues pier delivery instructions.
2. Prepares required export shipping documents.
3. Arranges provisional marine insurance.
4. Transmits preliminary shipping information to interested parties.
5. Dispatches consignee's mail.
6. Verifies ocean freight charges and other miscellaneous charges and arranges for payment.
7. Completes work sheet inserting all charges paid and gives
to

CONTROL CLERK
1. Prepares and dispatches distribution of expenses.
2. Arranges final marine insurance.
3. Prepares proof of export, if required.
4. Files all papers.

Chart shows how Export Traffic processes supply shipments from the U.S. to Southern Peru Copper Co.

Sunset sees no stoppage in smelter operations at Port Ilo, Peru, where ore from the Andes Mountains is refined for overseas shipment.

Establishing logistics in an underdeveloped region

ASARCO'S TRAFFIC department faced its greatest challenge when the Southern Peru Copper Corporation project started its development high in the Andes Mountains. Commencing with a 17-ton shipment for use in constructing a pier at Ilo, Peru on Dec. 2, 1955, the department controlled many hundreds of sailings during the four-year construction period. "It was the largest single transportation job ever undertaken by our department in its 70-year history," observes Vice President Merwin. "It presented a challenge to Asarco's traffic men—a challenge they eagerly accepted."

Southern Peru Copper Corp., jointly owned by four major copper producers (Asarco, Phelps Dodge Corp., Cerro Corp. and Newmont Mining Corp.), is operated by Asarco. Its large mine, 11,000 feet above sea level, is over 120 miles from the sea coast. The company had to build a railroad to supply it and develop a seaport for outbound blister copper and inbound supplies as well. Construction, besides the aforementioned,

included complete town facilities at both Port Ilo and Toquepala, plus a smelter at Ilo and an ore mill at Toquepala.

Substantial economies resulted through the traffic department's early and continuous involvement. Long before the first shipment left New York, negotiations took place between the company and the steamship conference to develop freight rates suited to the project's needs. Thorough study of all costs as well as comparison among competitive choices ensued. The initial estimate that 167,000 tons of freight would go into construction meant heavy expense for Southern Peru Copper Corp. and an attractive piece of traffic for the carriers. The two parties concluded a mutually beneficial agreement on Aug. 11, 1955. By contract's end, the estimated volume swelled to an actual 300,000 tons. Net savings under the agreement approached $4 million.

After negotiating the freight agreement, the department set up appropriate procedures for contractors covering materials and equipment to be shipped by them. Copies of the agreement were provided to affected contractors and meetings were held with those concerned to fully acquaint them with

Asarco's requirements in the preparation of shipping documents as well as those posed by Peruvian customs regulations. These contractor representatives also learned of the company's overall system of issuing instructions to suppliers with particular view to consigning materials via the port of exit offering lowest through costs to Ilo consistent with favorable transit times.

In the case of the Morrison Knudson—Utah Construction Co., the prime contractor, the traffic department arranged to keep them currently informed of materials lined up for delivery on specified vessels. This enabled their expediter to maintain an up-to-the-minute record of expected arrivals of all materials consigned to the project.

Some Toquepala shipments originated in Europe as well. Arrangements for these were handled directly by Mines Trading Co., Ltd.,

guided by Asarco traffic department instructions covering preparation and distribution of shipping documents.

During the construction period, coordination among these varied elements was a continuing major responsibility of the traffic department.

The initial harbor at Ilo was an open roadstead, cargo being brought ashore from ships by lighters. These in turn discharged to a mole. Before heavy port operations could get under way, this arrangement clearly had to be improved. Phase One found a crane sufficiently powerful to handle heavy equipment under way on ship's deck to Ilo. The available lighters could not take it to shore, so the unit was unloaded by ship's gear onto a specially constructed raft. The raft was then beached alongside the mole and the crane moved to shore on its own power.

Large ore vessels deliver ores and concentrates regularly from Peruvian sources and Australia to Asarco's smelter at Selby, Calif. on San Francisco Bay.

At Toquepala, a locomotive moves side-dump cars carrying ore through the mill's unloading facility. Inside the shed, cars are tilted, dropping their burden for subsequent processing and rail movement to Port Ilo.

Progressively heavier cranes were delivered to the port so that heavier equipment could move ashore readily and finally, in October, 1957, a pier was completed and vessels commenced mooring alongside for direct discharge.

In addition to operating responsibilities covering shipments to the project, the traffic department participated heavily in staff activities and continues to do so as it does in other company activities where traffic and distribution is involved. On numerous occasions it has assisted in matters concerning construction and operation of the company railroad, aiding in the procurement of both materials and expertise as needed. The railroad currently employs five main line locomotives and 237 pieces of rolling stock while the mine itself operates a substantial fleet of cars with over a dozen locomotives providing power. A large fleet of trucks also serves the pit, with individual capacities to 100 tons.

Port Ilo today is a bustling port with substantial tonnages moving out regularly from the adjacent smelter. Inbound freight includes everything from desalinization plants to tooth brushes, including many exotic items peculiar to living requirements in southern Peru. "We've even shipped out orange golf balls," notes Traffic Manager-Rates Charles W. Kane. "There is no green grass up high in the Andes, and you can't find a white golf ball when you drive it onto a lava field."

Under present arrangements, Asarco accumulates stores in a New York warehouse for movement by container to Port Ilo. Customs are cleared at that point and the freight is stripped for movement to final destination.

Outbound copper shipments move in heavy volume from Port Ilo's pier. It is shipped on a "free-in" basis, the company doing its own loading at the company-owned pier. This operation works out to carrier advantage also, because the well-equipped and supervised operation speeds vessel turnaround time while reducing shipper costs. Over a nine-year period, production rates have improved at the pier by 35% through equipment betterments and the development of trained, experienced personnel.

The prior construction experience may soon stand the traffic department in good stead for another round. At the present time negotiations are under way with the Peruvian government for a bilateral agreement which, if successfully concluded, will permit development of the Cuajone ore body at an estimated cost of $335 million. This will require a 35-kilometer extension to the railroad's present 186 kilometers, with 27 kilometers in tunnels. Building the tunnels alone represents a four-year job. At the present planning stage, Vice President Merwin contemplates the use of piggyback service to bring in construction materials, moving trailers from Ilo to Toquepala over the railroad.

A Canadian Distiller's International Distribution

For Hiram Walker Limited as for ASARCO, raw material movement creates important cost considerations. Bulk handling in this company takes place at several levels. Inbound raw grain arrives in bulk, while spent grain resulting from the distillation process also lends itself to bulk handling. Neutral spirits may be moved in bulk from distillery to drain-and-fill facilities for barreling and subsequent aging. Matured whiskies in turn go forward to bottling facilities as bulk shipments in certain instances, adding yet another bulk handling transport cycle to the total picture.

For Hiram Walker, then, a complex of rail hopper cars and tank cars, comparable highway units and barges do much to minimize both transport and handling costs. Equally important is the existence of in-house handling systems designed to take full advantage of bulk handling techniques, while comparably modern procedures keep costs down through mechanized and, in several instances, automated handling systems for the movement of packaged goods within finished goods warehouse facilities.

A survey of Hiram Walker logistics activities, first presented in the June, 1972 TRAFFIC MANAGEMENT, follows:

WHEN physical distribution becomes an important management factor, a company typically anticipates early organizational changes, computerization and many systems revisions. Paper flow, in particular, seems to reflect the new concept's emergence.

At Hiram Walker-Gooderham & Warts Limited, emphasis moved initially in a different direction. A major shipper of large shipments, service and cost improvement opportunities showed up more clearly in operations than in administration.

Gross sales of almost $714 million in 1971, up from $450 million a decade before, reveal a pattern that demands continual expansion of capacity to fulfill market requirements. New manufacturing and distribution facilities, as well as continued expansion at the Walkerville, Ontario complex in Canada and at the large Peoria, Ill. distillery, add to the challenges facing the distribution department and others concerned with logistics functions of the company and its subsidiaries.

Planning for the future, the company increasingly systematizes its operations to maximize productivity from each added unit of capacity. Warehousing and handling automation, greater employment of bulk transport (both liquid and solid) and refinement as well as regrouping of traffic-distribution procedures play important roles. Some specific instances follow:

AN INDUSTRY FIRST: Hiram Walker's unique barrel drain-and-fill facility, created by Supervisor of Engineering Design George Thornton.

Bulk transportation—Sophisticated tank car and tank truck units for whiskies and spirits cut handling and shipping costs, as do hopper cars and hopper trucks for the company's substantial grain shipments.

Warehouse automation—A fully automated Western warehouse, and substantial mechanization of others, means greater capacity for existing facilities as well as any that may be added.

Integrated customer order processing—Regrouping and revision of manual procedures, increased traffic department order responsibilities, have improved paper flow and handling efficiency.

Distribution in general and traffic management in particular place heavy demands on professional capabilities here. **"Hiram Walker is a truly international company,"** notes **Distribution Manager Joseph M. Benson. "Our managers and their associates must maintain a three-way expertise embracing Canadian domestic, United States domestic and export-import traffic methodology."**

Hiram Walker exports to 170 countries, primarily via eastern Canadian ports for which documentation and booking are handled internally. On the 5 to 10% of such exports moving via the Port of New York, an outside forwarder is used. Most shipments destined to the United Kingdom and Europe move in 20-foot containers via the Canadian National Railway from Walkerville.

"Our outbound shipments consist 98% of full loads," states **Traffic Manager Robert J. LaVigne. "About 30% of these move rail carload, another 30% piggyback, some 35% common carrier truck and the remainder frequently in private carriage.** The latter includes distributor-owned trucks or, in the case of states with liquor control, state-owned ones, as in Alabama, for instance. Other than Pennsylvania, practically every liquor control state routes its shipments on the basis of Section 22 rates, the tariff regulation providing advantages for government shipments."

The heavy cross-border traffic keeps a special unit busy handling paperwork and taxes. **"We pay in excess of $100 million to U.S. customs and internal revenue (not including**

bonded shipments),'' observes Supervisor-Customs Section John P. Bedard. **"On imports, our duties and sales taxes to the Canadian government approach $1 million.**

Mr. Bedard and his five-man staff prepare customs papers for import-export between U.S.-Canada, at both the Port of Windsor and the Port of Detroit. In general, U.S. customs and internal revenue taxes are paid at Detroit, but shipments in bond are made to Peoria and to the rectifying plant at Burlingame, Calif. There are also approximately 50 bonded shipments each month to New York for movement to third countries.

Regular "two-way" movement involves bottles delivered from a Hillsboro, Ill. plant to Walkerville which subsequently return to the U.S market after filling. This requires the processing of drawbacks with the Canadian government, yielding a 99% refund of glass duty paid upon initial delivery. Similar arrangements apply to advertising matter.

The accompanying Customer's Order Flow Chart illustrates the relationship of traffic activities to the total order processing pattern. On

Canadian Club orders, for example, separate U.S. and Canadian sales units process orders received from district representatives and forward them to the order section of the distribution department. U.S. orders are consolidated to priority sheets which go to the bottling department and indicate shipping dates. On Canadian domestic orders, the priority sheet procedure is not necessary. A priority sheet copy is returned to the U.S. sales unit at Walkerville head-

DIRECT TELETYPE ACCESS to CP Rail's computer gives Operator Debbie Campbell instant tracer response for monitoring Hiram Walker car movements.

WORLD MAP behind Traffic Manager Robert J. LaVigne symbolizes company markets at a strategy session with (left to right) Supervisor-Rates and Tariffs George Musson, Senior Audit Clerk George Mosley and Foreign Export Clerk Wayne Davis.

quarters after processing. All orders are routed and rated.

Following the above action at the distribution department's main office, further processing prior to shipment is handled by a traffic unit located at the distillery offices convenient to the various other departments with which it interacts. Supervisor Traffic, Finished Goods Herbert J. Schofield and his associates handle the necessary paperwork and other arrangements for expeditious shipment of all orders.

A unique feature in the case of U.S.-bound truckloads is the necessity for "double billing." They are billed separately for the Windsor-Detroit move and for through movement beyond Detroit. Don's Cartage takes both bills with the trailer to Detroit, spotting the unit at its own lot just below the international bridge for pickup by the U.S. line haul carrier. Don's driver signs his bill and obtains the beyond carrier's signature as well at Detroit.

"This arrangement greatly simplifies handling for our U.S. motor carriers," notes Mr. Schofield. "Because their tractors need not enter Canada for the brief trip to our distillery, they are spared the expense and paperwork necessary to license vehicles for such deliveries. This way, any common carrier trucks licensed to operate into Detroit are at our service, giving the carriers and ourselves the advantages of greater flexibility."

Close liaison with the bottling department and the finished goods warehouse explains in part the successful shipment preplanning of the traffic staff. Equally important are the modern methods and facilities available for order assembly, preparation and shipping. In the pages following, many of these are explored.

AT WALKERVILLE finished goods warehouse, Supervisor-Traffic Herbert J. Schofield reviews scheduled intra-Canada shipments with Canadian Government Excise Officer Maurice Harbroe (left) and Senior Clerk-Traffic and Shipping Claude Lacombe.

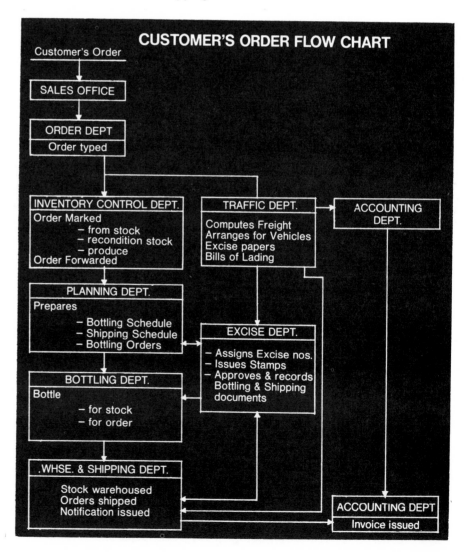

CUSTOMER'S ORDER FLOW CHART

Customer's Order

SALES OFFICE

ORDER DEPT
Order typed

INVENTORY CONTROL DEPT.
Order Marked
- from stock
- recondition stock
- produce
Order Forwarded

TRAFFIC DEPT.
Computes Freight
Arranges for Vehicles
Excise papers
Bills of Lading

ACCOUNTING DEPT.

PLANNING DEPT.
Prepares
- Bottling Schedule
- Shipping Schedule
- Bottling Orders

EXCISE DEPT.
- Assigns Excise nos.
- Issues Stamps
- Approves & records Bottling & Shipping documents

BOTTLING DEPT.
Bottle
- for stock
- for order

WHSE. & SHIPPING DEPT.
Stock warehoused
Orders shipped
Notification issued

ACCOUNTING DEPT
Invoice issued

A SMALL PORTION of the shipping area at Hiram Walker's immense Peoria facility—the world's largest beverage distillery—finds piggyback and over-the-road trailers taking on shipments preplanned by General Traffic Manager James G. Laffey and his staff.

A DISTRIBUTION DEPARTMENT policy review finds the management team assembled in the conference room. From left to right: Acting Supervisor-Order Processing John Ray, Supervisor-Customs John Bedard, Distribution Manager Joseph M. Benson, Traffic Manager Robert J. LaVigne and Assistant to Distribution Manager G. William Waldron.

HUGE GRAIN ELEVATOR at Walkerville can draw grain by suction from rail cars and barges alike at this convenient riverside location.

Bulk handling benefits two-way grain movements

GRAIN PRODUCTS loom large in Hiram Walker's processing and marketing activities. What remains of the major raw material after whisky distillation, "spent" grain, is in itself an important by-product, known as distillers dried grain with solubles. A medium high protein supplement for various animal feeds, it finds a particular market in dairy cattle areas.

President Robert I. Duddy of Hiram Walker & Sons Grain Corp., Ltd. and Riverside Elevator Co., wholly owned subsidiaries, sees to both raw material supply and subsequent distillers dried grain marketing. **"They are two quite different logistics activities,"** Mr. Duddy as-

serts. **"Our inbound raw materials represent several distinctly different grain products arriving at individual distilleries from numerous origins. Our outbound product is a single commodity sold to grain dealers throughout the continent."**

Standard boxcars handle much inbound grain, but jumbo hoppers assume a growing role. At Walkerville, Ontario, corn and some other grains arrive by truck as the distillery is in the heart of a corn-producing region and hauls are short. Boxcars and some hopper cars serve also, supplemented by occasional vessel shipments on the Great Lakes.

Peoria receives primarily boxcar and truck shipments inbound, augmented by barge movements. At this location, some grain also moves through the company elevators as a storage service for outside customers.

The Okanagan distillery in British

Columbia presents a significant contrast. Current inbound grain traffic is primarily by covered hopper cars, supplemented in a measure by truck shipments. In addition, a new intermodal program, combining rail and truck services, is currently under consideration. Newest of the company's distilleries, Okanagan includes a number of departures from prior conventional methods.

This newest operation also pioneers in bulk handling of outbound distillers dried grain. **"While we ship in bulk rather than sacks from all of our source points, Okanagan is the first where we have standardized hopper car outbound movements,"** notes Assistant to Distribution Manager G. William Waldron. **"We make good use of large hoppers both for receiving and shipping at this plant, creating substantial economies for both the railroads and ourselves."**

Mr. Waldron looks forward subsequently to further hopper shipments at Walkerville and Peoria, Ill. in lieu of a large proportion of the standard boxcar shipments. Satisfactory rates and adequate car supply are the necessary prerequisites.

An idea of the grain volume necessary to feed a major distillery can be gathered from Peoria's intake of corn alone. Observes General Traffic Manager Jerry G. Laffey: **"In a given year, our elevator absorbs some 20,000 truckloads plus 3,000 carloads of corn, supplemented by 300 barge loads as well."**

Adjacent to this world's largest beverage distillery, the Riverside Elevator (the only distiller-owned terminal elevator in the United States) handles a flow of more than 24 million bushels a year, with a storage capacity of 1¼ million bushels. Most of the corn flowing through here comes from farms lying within 40 miles of the Peoria location. Outbound shipments of distillers dried grain, however, represent longer movements, flowing in considerable measure to the Northeastern states as well as to Midwestern ones with large dairy cattle herds.

Somewhat similar conditions prevail at Walkerville, where distilling capacity is only a little less than at the giant Peoria facility. While Peoria is known for its bourbon, the Walkerville facility is home for Hiram Walker's best known product, the world-famous "Canadian Club" whisky.

The newest shipping system under development for company grain is a proposed intermodal movement, with 100-ton hopper cars drawing grain initially from the Minnesota region for movement to Oroville, Wash. via Burlington Northern Railroad. The grain will flow through a modern transfer facility at that point to hopper trailers supplied by Rice Truck Lines of Great Falls, Mont. for the 75-mile international run to Okanagan. Return traffic will be distillers dried grain moving either intermodally or, where destinations suggest otherwise, directly by truck. Such an operation, once proven out, is expected to yield substantial cost reductions on the affected portion of the tonnage. Nebraska and Iowa origins will also be included· subsequently.

PRESIDENT Robert I. Duddy (right) of Hiram Walker & Sons Grain Corp., Ltd. maintains a close liaison with Assistant to Distribution Manager G. William Waldron (left) in the foreward development of distribution systems. Their teamwork in the past accounts largely for company's successful bulk grain-handling systems.

PEORIA'S diversified bulk-handling facilities include this unique "tilting table" which lifts tractor and trailer as a unit to pour bulk grain through the truck tailgate.

SPECIALIZED barge-unloading facilities such as the above at the
Hiram Walker-owned Riverside Elevator augment rail and truck bulk
grain-handling terminal equipment. Below, a barge interior view shows
the same unloading operation from a different vantage point.

Giant whiskey tank cars speed Canadian Club shipments

BULK HANDLING has received growing acceptance at Hiram Walker in recent years. Not only grain moves in this fashion, but liquids also.

A more ambitious operation, breaking totally new ground in tank car usage, commenced in July, 1971. At Distribution Manager Joseph M. Benson's suggestion, six giant tank cars were leased from North American Car Corporation to fill a pressing need at the new Okanagan, British Columbia distillery. These stainless steel cars go west from Walkerville, Ontario with aged whiskies for bottling and distribution, returning with new whiskies from the western distillery. Each carries 20,000 imperial gallons, equivalent to 25,000 U.S. gallons.

These cars represent economies in transportation, handling effort and time for every shipment. Loading and unloading demands minimal labor, and exclusive use assures against contamination. They prove a ready answer to the problem of making six-or-eight-year-old whiskies readily available at a one-year-old distillery.

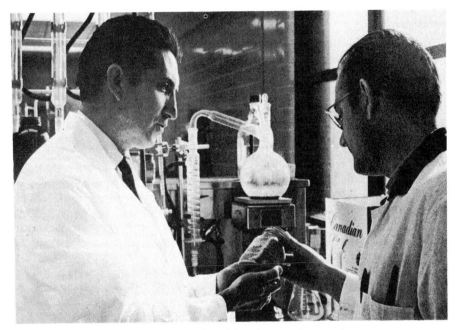

MURRAY SOBOLOV (left), superintendent-laboratory services, and a member of the professional staff check a grain sample to be analyzed.

Making this program work entailed more than selecting a car design and having it built, however. **"The problem is that at no point, either in plant or in transportation, will Hiram Walker tolerate more than $3/10$th parts per million of iron in its whisky,"** states Quality Control Supervisor Murray Sobolov. **"We prefer to shoot for even less, and in fact achieve less than $1/10$th part per million regularly."**

Meeting such standards calls for infinite care in manufacture followed by rigorous testing. Highly polished surfaces will generally not require a special acid treatment, but welds and complex passages in valves don't lend themselves to high polishing, thus making a nitric acid wash necessary to passivate the surfaces. If sand is believed to be present, a hydrofluoric acid treatment may be required as well. "Cast surfaces are particularly difficult to passivate," notes Mr. Sobolov.

ONE OF Hiram Walker's giant tank cars, spotted at Okanagan, British Columbia, is in process of exchanging a cargo of Canadian Club whisky from Walkerville for a load of grain neutral spirits to be taken east.

In the case of the six new tank cars, it was found necessary to sugar-sandblast the safety valves in order to pass the ferroxyl test—a procedure whereunder a sprayed-on solution instantly creates a blue spot if free iron is present, but which is readily removable.

As the cars were completed at North American's Texarkana plant, initial testing was done on site. Following their delivery to the company, a second series of tests were run by the quality control unit at Walkerville, with particular emphasis on certain of the valves, all of which proved satisfactory. The cars have developed no problems in operation from contaminants since initially entering service. Considering the value of six-to-eight-year-old whisky in 20,000 imperial gallon lots, the cost of even one failure would be significant.

Careful preplanning of operational as well as physical aspects paid off in the new tank car operation. Proper equipment and procedures kept loading and unloading operations functioning smoothly from the start. Bulk movement and bottling within the West Coast market area yield significant, continuing economies in contrast to what would have been the case if bottled goods had to move through from Walkerville.

Advanced barrel handling and transport system serves drain-and-fill facility

SEVERAL YEARS AGO Hiram Walker & Sons, Ltd. pioneered palletized handling, storage and maturing of whisky barrels at its Pike Creek maturing warehouse complex, 11 miles east of the Walkerville, Ontario distillery. A three-man crew at this location can handle 2,000 500-pound barrels a day in contrast to 16 men handling 600 to 1,000 barrels with conventional rack operation.

At this same time, the company installed a temporary facility to drain and fill whisky barrels at Walkerville, tying the locations with a fleet of 40-foot conveyor-bed trailers supplied by Don's Cartage that could load or unload in two minutes, forwarding new whisky to Pike Creek for maturing and bringing back aged whisky for bottling. Production schedules required a two-shift operation and relatively high manual labor content at the temporary location.

In the meantime, conceptual development proceeded on a radical new facility to increase productivity, improve methods and eliminate hazards in the manual handling of 500-pound barrels. After thoroughly investigating systems, concepts and costs proposed by outside consultants, management selected an original system (Fig. 1) proposed by Supervisor of Engineering Design George Thornton of the company's own staff.

Mr. Thornton assembled a special project force to produce layouts, equipment designs, shop details and complete manufacturing and material specifications. Company engineering personnel tested, developed and modified all finished equipment as necessary.

The building's three automated lines and one manual utility line (Fig. 2) were designed to meet projected production requirements, with stand-by capacity, for 15 to 20 years, and the complete system was integrated with a new barrel reconditioning facility. Provision was made also for servicing tank cars or trucks delivering or receiving whiskies in bulk.

Palletized barrels of matured whisky, ready for filtering, final blending and bottling, move from Pike Creek maturing warehouses in conveyor-bed trailers as before, each accepting 16 six-barrel pallets

CONVEYOR-BED TRAILERS maintain a day-long shuttle between Walkerville drain-and-fill location (below) and the whisky-aging warehouses, providing an effective link in an automated-mechanized handling system.

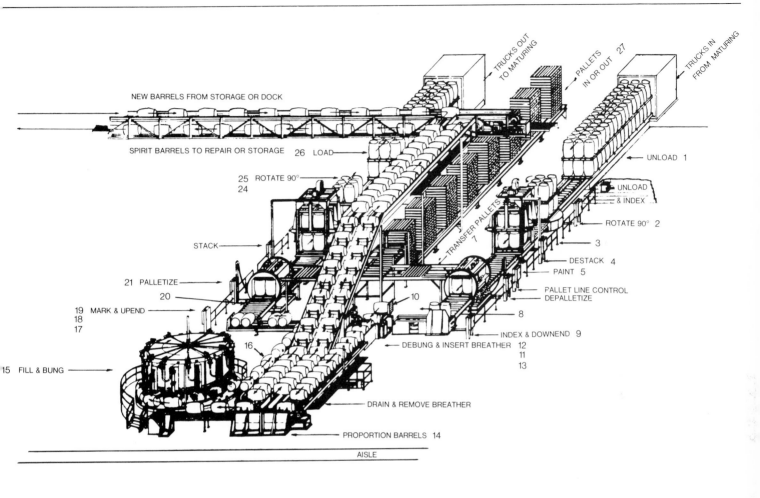

NEW BARRELS FROM STORAGE OR DOCK

TRUCKS OUT TO MATURING

PALLETS IN OR OUT 27

TRUCKS IN FROM MATURING

SPIRIT BARRELS TO REPAIR OR STORAGE 26 LOAD

UNLOAD 1

25 ROTATE 90°
24

UNLOAD & INDEX

TRANSFER PALLETS 7

ROTATE 90° 2

STACK

3

DESTACK 4
PAINT 5

21 PALLETIZE

PALLET LINE CONTROL
DEPALLETIZE

20

10

19 MARK & UPEND
18
17

8

INDEX & DOWNEND 9

16

11
13

12

15 FILL & BUNG

DRAIN & REMOVE BREATHER

PROPORTION BARRELS 14

AISLE

WALKERVILLE DRAIN-AND-FILL FACILITY: SCHEMATIC DIAGRAM OF OPERATION ON A SINGLE PROCESS LINE

(a total of 96 barrels or 48,000 pounds). The whisky is "in bond" en route, and truck drivers are in radio contact with the maturing warehouses, drain and fill supervision, and plant security forces at all times.

At the drain and fill dock, trailer doors are unlocked and seals removed. The trailer is backed onto lifting arms in line with the unloading conveyor [Fig. 1 (1)]; both conveyors are energized, and the complete two-tier load moves from trailer to unloading conveyor.

The leading two-pallet unit indexes automatically from the unloading conveyor to the turntable (2), which rotates 90 degrees and discharges the unit logitudinally via powered transfer conveyor (3) to the destacker (c).

The destacker lifts the top pallet unit and the lower unit proceeds to a transfer conveyor (f). The top unit is then lowered, following the previous one onto the transfer conveyor, where barrelhead identification marks are manually painted out.

The single pallet, six-barrel unit moves into the depalletizer (6), which clamps the barrels to the pallet and rotates 180 degrees. The barrels are released onto a powered roller conveyor, and the pallet is ejected to the pallet transfer conveyor (7).

The six-barrel block next moves onto a transfer conveyor (8) and is indexed in pairs at 90 degrees by a walking beam conveyor (9) to the barrel downender (10). Each barrel is rotated 90 degrees and ejected

onto a mechanism which lowers it to four rollers carried by the drain conveyor (11) chains. As the barrel approaches the debung machine (12), it contacts a rotating device controlled by the debung operator which stops the barrel "bung up" and extracts the bung.

A breather vent is inserted in the bung hole as the barrel moves onto the roll-over at the drain tank (13), where it rolls to "bung down" position and discharges whisky into the tank. When the barrel reaches the drain tank's end, it is empty. The operator removes the vent, placing it on the vent conveyor for return to the debung operator, and inspects the barrel. If it needs repairs or rejection, it is ejected to the overhead conveyor system from the car-

CENTRAL CONTROL LOCATION for all of the Walkerville drain-and-fill lines.

ousel feed conveyor (14) and a new barrel takes its place.

Empty barrels move to the carousel feed conveyor and are injected into a constantly rotating, 12-station carousel filler (15). Each barrel is filled automatically with new whisky, bunged and ejected, in three-quarters of a revolution, onto the carousel discharge conveyor (16), where it travels head first to the marking machine (17). New identification marks are stamped on the freshly painted heads, and the barrel is ejected at 90 degrees onto a trans-

fer conveyor (18) and into the dual upender (19), which upends two barrels onto the accumulating conveyor (20). The barrels move from the upender in pairs until a block of six is accumulated and moves into the palletizer (21).

Handling thereafter employs the same equipment as found handling inbound pallet loads, but operating in reverse mode to load trailers. The complete cycle repeats until eight blocks (96 barrels) have accumulated and are moved aboard a waiting trailer.

At 100% efficiency with seven operators per line, one complete load is discharged every 24 minutes. The trailer is locked and sealed, and the load proceeds to the maturing warehouses. The pallet stack line (27) will automatically feed or extract pallets into or from the system according to variances in the draining and filling schedules.

"All equipment is controlled automatically on a sequential, fail safe, logic basis employing 28 complex pneumatic logic systems per line," Mr. Thornton states. "Due to fire and explosion insurance ratings on

alcohol-handling facilities, pneumatics are used intensively, and all electric drives are thus controlled on a 'slave' basis."

Numatrol pneumatic logic control systems were selected for their reliability and repeatability after a thorough investigation of fluidic, electronic, electric and other pneumatic controls.

Two automated lines have operated since January, 1971 and currently exceed 90% efficiency. Productivity, in barrels per man hour, has increased over 300%. **"Strains, contusions and other injuries common to manual barrel handling have been virtually eliminated," observes Foreman-Drain and Fill Operations Charles Hesman.**

Main component suppliers were Martonair, Toronto; Link Belt, Toronto; Hamilton Gear, Toronto; Ladish Co., Brantford; Mathews Equipment, Port Hope.

Prime contractors were Valco Manufacturing Ltd., Windsor; R. J. Cyr Ltd., Windsor; McInnis Equipment, Windsor; Moncur Electric, Windsor; Numatics Inc., Detroit, Mich.

Automated warehouse yields major space savings

NEWEST and most modern of Hiram Walker's distillery operations, the Okanagan facility at Winfield, B.C. makes good use of bulk shipping techniques employing covered hoppers and the giant tank cars described earlier in this issue. **"We enjoy substantial cost advantages through our ability to use these tools as well as through unitization of our outbound finished product," asserts Traffic Manager Peter Koch.**

Effective unitization is but one of many benefits accruing from the distillery's automated case warehouse system. Built and installed by Matthews Conveyor of Port Hope, Ontario, it employs the Munck System—a patented design licensed by a Norwegian firm.

This storage system accommodates 3,100 pallets of cased product under one-man operation. Pallets can flow in and out of storage at a rate of one per minute. The warehouse comprises two double and two single racks divided by three aisles in which stacker cranes operate.

The 330-foot racking complex is 52 feet high with 74 horizontal storage bins on each side at seven vertical levels. The bins accept 48x40-inch pallets plus an overhang of $2^1/_2$ inches in any direction. About 200,000 cases store in an area of approximately 14,500 square feet, 60% less space than a conventional warehouse holding the same number of pallets three high requires.

The one-man control center is on the racking complex in-feed level. Pallets approach via palletizers from the bottling room on the floor above. They are turned 90 degrees and checked photoelectrically to ensure that the load is centered within bin clearance limits. The control operator identifies each pallet as it passes and addresses it to an empty bin by placing a punched card in the card-reader. Operation thereafter is fully automatic.

The pallet address is stored in a central memory unit, and the pallet proceeds by conveyor to the crane pick-up station, where its address is

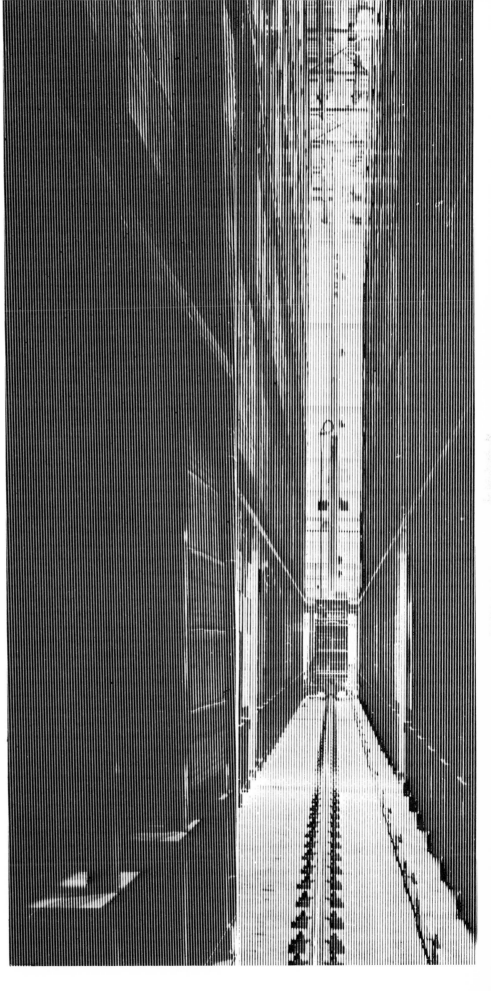

OKANAGAN'S fully automated warehouse includes a computer-controlled stacker crane picking operation (page 353) as well as automatic stockpiling (above). Superintendent-Finished Goods G. E. Hunt points out some of the features to Traffic Manager P. Koch.

OKANAGAN employs straddle carrier unit to move 48-barrel palletized lots between drain-and-fill facility and maturing warehouses.

transmitted from the memory unit to the crane itself. The crane lifts the pallet by forks and, after locating its address, deposits it in the bin.

The three floor-running cranes require aisles only six inches wider than an actual pallet. Photoelectric readers sense the horizontal and vertical positions of each crane's load and stop the unit only when its actual position agrees with the given pallet address. Once the pallet is placed and the forks return to their central position, the crane is ready to receive another instruction. The infeed cycle always takes precedence over the out-feed one, thus avoiding production delays. To remove pallets from storage, the operator places the identifying card into the out-feed card-reader, reversing the automatic process.

The punched cards simplify inventory control and the processing of shipping orders. Cards can be arranged into groups representing a full shipment and presented to the warehouse operator, along with instructions as to time and transport mode. The card-reader can accept up to 200 cards (pallets) at one time.

Each crane discharges outbound pallets onto a conveyor immediately below the infeed. The pallets then travel automatically to the end of one of three accumulating conveyors—two for truck shipments and one for railway. Each of these holds a full truckload or rail carload.

Since its installation, the automated warehouse system has worked out well. It functions in a fittingly complementary manner to the similarly modern, highly efficient drain-and-fill installation developed and tested initially at Walkerville, Ontario, then installed at the Okanagan distillery. Both systems lend themselves admirably to matching anticipated expansion of the total Okanagan operation in the years to come.

Pallet-oriented warehouse mechanization

HIRAM WALKER has continually maintained a facility at Walkerville, Ontario for 115 years, but everything about its present operation reflects the best current practices. This is particularly true of its finished goods division. Effective methods supported by high-capacity mechanized equipment speeds order fulfillment while minimizing inventory and processing cost.

The modern finished goods warehouse, completed about 10 years ago, houses substantial Alvey-installed conveyor lines and palletizers. **"They literally built a materials handling system and put a roof and walls around it,"** states Superintendent, Finished Goods Division Robert H. Brown.

Located adjacent to the huge distillery, the 200,000-case facility is as much a staging area as a stock warehouse. Orders for fast-moving items produced daily or almost daily by the distillery are drawn against production rather than against stock, and many items move directly from bottling and packaging operations to the shipping docks. Accordingly, out-bound shipments run considerably in excess of those normally anticipated from a 200,000-case distribution warehouse. It is largely the slow-moving items that are maintained in stock.

The finished goods division planning department determines whether each individual order will be filled **from stock, production or both. The planning unit develops initially a weekly bottling schedule and subsequently daily ones. At 10 a.m. each work day, Mr. Brown convenes a brief planning meeting with representatives of the planning, receiving, warehousing, shipping, inventory control and any other concerned divisional units which reviews any day-to-day changes in production plans. The planning division also issues daily loading schedules to the warehouse and others concerned summarizing shipments.**

Facility operations management lies within two departments:

Bottling—Under General Foreman C. T. Freeman, diversified equipment and necessary staff for bottling and packaging activities maintain all operations from the start of the bottling line to the release of completed cases into the warehouse conveyor system.

Materials Handling—General Foreman Robert C. Hunter's staff and equipment see to the supply of bottles and packaging materials to the bottling line, then assume responsibility for movement of packaged products following preparation by the bottling department.

While the product itself arrives at the bottling line via direct pipe system from the adjacent production facilities, the warehouse maintains an 80,000-case inbound capacity serviced by a six-car inside receiving siding and an inside dock accommodating six trucks. **"We receive our bottles in reshipper cartons,"** notes **Mr. Hunter. "These preprinted cartons protect the empties en route from the manufacturer, yet serve again for our outbound shipments of filled bottles."**

Receiving employs standard fork-lift trucks with side-shifters plus two Allis-Chalmers Pull-Pack lift trucks, also side-shifter equipped. Lift trucks throughout this warehouse are electric units.

The receiving department initially feeds cases upside down from its stock to an ABC packaging machine unloader. This machine drops the bottles out to the loading line, while cases are turned upright by a tilter and proceed by overhead conveyor to meet filled bottles at the other end.

At the bottling line's end, an automatic packer counts 12 bottles and places them back in the waiting empty cases. A case sealer then folds down the case top and seals it with glue. A Hiram Walker-designed case lift elevates cases from each line end to Alvey overhead conveyors. Counted on discharge from the lifts by Radex automatic counters, cases then move off for storage or shipping.

There are six automatic lines, each with case accumulating conveyors, feeding into Alvey automatic palletizers. In addition, three lines for lesser volume items feed hand-palletizing stations.

Each of the three automatic palletizers usually handle three lines, per-

FORKLIFT TRUCK draws palletized reshipper cases of empty bottles for bottling operation conveyor line feed.

WAREHOUSEMEN place inverted cases of bottles on line.

INVERTED cases and bottles, following separation (above), proceed via separate lines through the bottling area.

FOLLOWING BOTTLING OPERATIONS, six conveyor lines feed encased finished product to a battery of three automatic palletizers.

FROM THIS CONSOLE, an operator can direct flow of any conveyor line to any of the palletizers, determining as well the pallet patterns to be used.

AT OUTBOUND DOCK, truck-leveling devices simplify forklift-loading operations

EMPTY CASES are turned upright en route through bottling area for matching with filled bottles at line's end. Bottling operations are on the lower level.

ROBERT HUNTER (left), general foreman-material handling department, and Superintendent-Finished Goods Division Robert Brown inspect palletized stock awaiting shipment at the Walkerville finished goods warehouse.

mitting release of one unit for normal maintenance, but present heavy business finds two lines requiring the full capacity of a single palletizer. Any of the six automatic lines can be programmed to any of the palletizers. It is intended to add a fourth palletizer to this battery in the future.

Each pallet machine has its own console at an overhead control station, all operated by a single employee plus a spare. These units, installed in 1960, currently employ 10 different pallet patterns related to case size. Layers are stacked alternately for interlock on pallets, with height adjustment from one to seven tiers, suited to case sizes.

A pallet conveyor line to the west warehouse, which includes the shipping area, goes directly from one of the palletizers, while the others are served by forklift trucks, feeding either onto the west warehouse conveyor line or into east warehouse storage. A second pallet conveyor, adjacent to the line connecting one palletizer directly to the west warehouse, serves primarily as an empty pallet return, but can be reversed to feed the west warehouse as well. Both pallet conveyors cross over an enclosed automatic bridge to the west warehouse, with hydraulic elevators at each end. Electric eye units keep the pallets spread safely on the conveyor lines.

In addition to substantial storage capacity, the west warehouse includes the shipping accommodations. The two inside rail sidings can accommodate a total of seven standard cars, while there are nine truck locations at an inside dock, each with truck elevators to level loads.

Palletized loads require use of DFB (bulkhead) cars. Currently, 70% of production is shipped palletized, and the proportion grows steadily. The remainder is floor-loaded by multiple-tined fork trucks from take-it-or-leave-it pallets. Recently, Canada shipments reached the 100% palletized level. When possible, rail carload shipments are double-decked. Truckloads generally carry larger cases five tiers high, with more tiers added on smaller cases to make the maximum permissible weight.

Standard GMA (Grocery Manufacturers Association) 48x40-inch, four-way entry pallets are used for shipping. Some 40 truck lines lease Hiram Walker's pallets at 250 for $1 per year. This eliminates return charges because the truck line has title and can use them as it pleases, obviating the problem of any potential allegations of discrimination if carriers put in pallet return tariff provisions.

DAILY PLANNING MEETINGS, scheduled by Superintendent Robert H. Brown, keep operations smooth for the finished goods warehouse. Present on this occasion are (clockwise from left) Receiving Foreman William M. Cirker, Bottling General Foreman Clifford T. Freeman, Maintenance Foreman Alfred Handy, Production Records Clerk J. Paul Sylestre, Materials Handling General Foreman Robert G. Hunter, Production Analyst Edward Kaminski, Superintendent Brown, Bottling Scheduler Richard G. Taylor and Supervisor-Inventory Control Department Louis G. Rau.

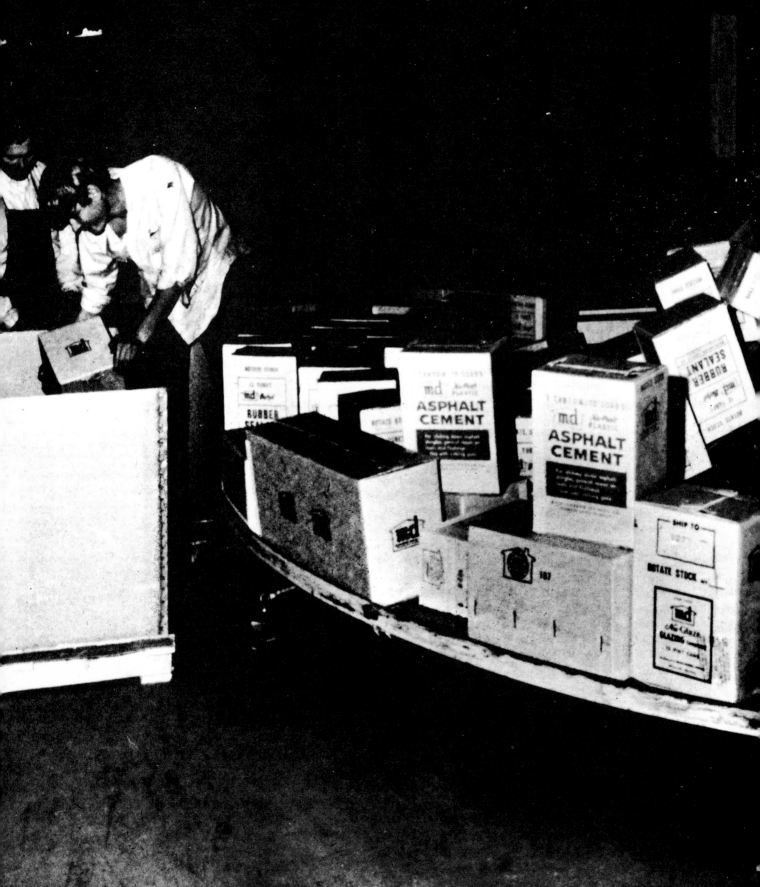

CHAPTER VII

Surmounting Small Shipment Problems

Ask any distribution manager where the greatest problems in current operations lie and he will probably answer "small shipments." Soaring costs accompany diminishing services, straining shipper resources and demanding new strategies during an era when the proportionate volume of small shipments increases steadily. Novel ideas to better small shipment services are coming to the fore in many companies, such as the three-phase consolidation system at Western Electric, described in Chapter II. Western Electric. however, encompasses a huge flow of larger shipments within its total volume. The firms surveyed within this chapter do not have this high proportion of larger movements to marry into their shipping schedules.

"Making big ones out of small ones" nonetheless remains the key strategy in bettering the small shipment situation. At Macklanburg-Duncan Co., centralized distribution nationwide from a single plant is a key element in just such an approach. Diversified consolidations moving over break-bulk points maximize large shipment mileage on fast schedules, with final individual shipment delivery turned over as much as possible to effective small shipment-oriented carriers. Solid loads move in company trucks to break bulk points for beyond movement by R E A Express to several regions, for example, while a diversity of comparable intermodal, intercarrier procedures function well in others.

Important, too, is proper marking and packaging, effective order processing and food field communications. These and other features of this company's operations, reviewed initially in the February, 1970 TRAFFIC MANAGEMENT, are described on the following pages:

Flexible Policies Benefit Growing Company's Traffic

OKLAHOMA CITY'S 50-year-old Macklanburg-Duncan Co., America's largest specialty hardware manufacturer, faces continual shipment volume increases in serving over 30,000 retailers and distributors. Its freight bill, climbing toward $1 million annually, includes a lot of small shipments, widely varied in sizes and shapes. Thus far, flexible policies and innovative shipping practices permit centralized distribution from the single Oklahoma City plant. "A little further expansion, however, and we start a new ball game," Vice President-Traffic C. D. Forbes comments.

Hardware store habitues know Macklanburg Duncan's products well. Their house-shaped yellow trademark with the black "M-D" monogram graces widely varied products, items that fulfill utilitarian roles in every part of the home. Calking compound, glazing compound, glue and sealants are part of a broad line of "expendables," supple-

menting such "hard" items as mail boxes, ladders, shelving, tools and miscellaneous goods for improvement or repair purposes. Weatherstripping, a major sales item, has a foot in both camps, varying from simple wool felt in rolls to metal or metal-and-plastic in a variety of configurations suited to differing conditions of application.

Traffic department responsibilities cover a broad range at "M-D." Keeping pace with company expansion, several functions get particular attention in this period of change, such as:

Flexible routing. Both common carriage and company vehicles link the plant with strategic break-bulk points. Some 50% of all traffic ultimately moves under R E A Express incentive rates.

Customized packaging. Produced-in-plant channel packaging cuts costs of packs and shipment weight; plastic containers conserve product and reduce claims formerly experienced with metal cans.

Communications betterments. Traffic department planning and control assure that the best-suited telecommunications equip-

Better freight handling and dock space utilization resulted from installation of a package carrousel designed and made in company plant.

U Sam Connor, vice president-cost control, and C. D. Forbes, vice president-traffic, review and adjust distribution cost breakdowns on the company's diversified individual products.

ment speeds order processing and other activities requiring such service.

Multiple travel services. While the traffic department handles most passenger bookings and reservations, substantial numbers employ the company plane. An outside agency is used for handling meetings.

Facility planning. Recognizing new logistics patterns as inevitable, alternative systems, equipment and facilities are under traffic department study.

In subsequent pages, we review the traffic department's approach to the aforementioned functions. There are, however, some additional or parallel activities worthy of note. Mr. Forbes, in addition to being vice president of traffic, is also vice president of new products, a vital post in an industry where growth and change are continuous. "If we can't gather raw materials and disperse new finished products profitably at competitive prices, we shouldn't handle them," states Mr. Forbes. "Distribution's costs represent the make-or-break factor in many cases."

Cost studies on proposed items, as well as continuing cost monitoring of the total logistics structure, find Mr. Forbes working in close and continuing liaison with Vice President-Cost Control U Sam Connor. They meet frequently to review and adjust cost breakdowns of all products, keeping abreast of experienced or anticipated cost changes.

They work together as well in preparing for rate negotiations and hearings. For this company, transportation costs alone represent a sizable portion of total product costs.

Diversified routing speeds small shipments

EVER-RISING small shipment costs make no exception of Macklanburg-Duncan. Only the constant review and effective employment of alternatives, many rather unusual, keep company traffic costs reasonably controlled. A decade ago, for example, the company pioneered air freight deliveries to distant post offices for beyond movement, with a volume approaching 50,000 pounds a month. This service halted when the Civil Aeronautics Board forced out the applicable rates, but, Mr. Forbes notes: "We would welcome the opportunity to resume air service when rate economics might permit it."

Biggest volume for today finds R E A Express and M-D trucks providing coordinated movements. Company truck operations started in 1958, running tri-weekly consolidated loads to Dallas and turning them over to common carrier trucks for beyond movement. Aluminum billets came back on these runs from Rockdale, Tex. This venture's success led to twice-weekly Dallas runs, augmented with a once-weekly Shreveport-New Orleans service and tri-weekly operations to Wichita and Kansas City.

During this same period, Vice President Forbes entered into studies with R E A Express, which led to the introduction of incentive rates on a wide scale. In 1959-60, most traffic shifted from motor carrier to the combined corporate truck-R E A operation, speeding service and reducing costs.

When R E A Express obtained broadened incentive rate coverage in 1960, therefore, the M-D trucks shifted to two triangular runs: Dallas-Memphis-Oklahoma City and St. Louis-Kansas City-Oklahoma City, running truckloads of small shipments to R E A terminals for fan-out.

This plan continued until R E A developed its "hub concept," under which shipments for various regions moved over "hub" terminals for final distribution, limiting the number of potential gateways through which traffic could reach any one region, with substantial running time increases on much M-D freight. Iowa traffic, for example, had to go east to Chicago, then return west to final destination with consequent delay.

Today's operation, therefore, makes all R E A deliveries at Kansas City and St. Louis, while freight for 11 states no longer routed via R E A moves largely direct from Oklahoma City by other carriers. A company truck leaves daily at 3:30 p.m. for the R E A Kansas City dock, where it halts for partial unloading around midnight. It makes the St. Louis R E A dock at about 5 a.m., completing unloading. Return loads are mostly generated in the St. Louis-East St. Louis area, but some freight may be picked up at Decatur, Ill. or as far east as Chicago.

Covering these runs are two air-conditioned White sleepercab tractors and four 40-foot American trailers. Back-up equipment is leased as necessary, but the base equipment is company-owned. A prior lease plan was discontinued in 1961.

Truck shipments employ a diversity of carriers out of M-D's Oklahoma City manufacturing center. Shown above are carriers' regional assignments.

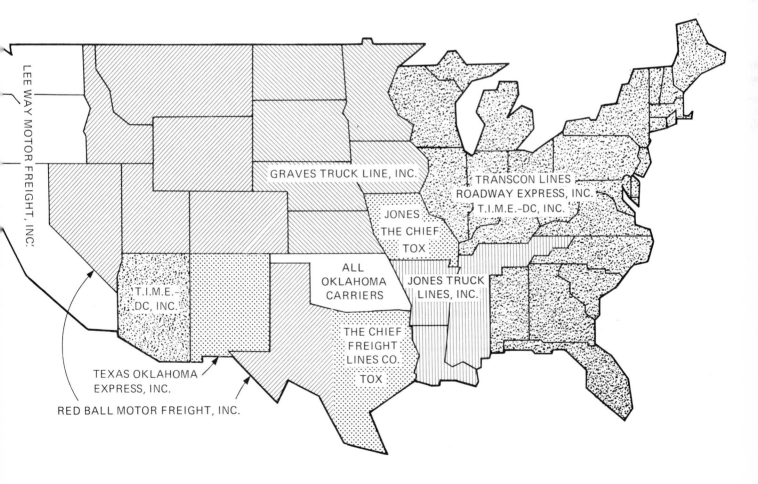

Benefiting company and carrier alike, computer prepares manifests for R E A Express shipments.

Additional equipment includes an International tractor for local operation and trailer shifting at the plant plus two Ford pickup trucks. The most unusual rolling stock, however, consists of two secondhand trailers that move and store ladders within the plant area. "Their $1,400 cost was far less than we would have paid for a small storage building," notes Mr. Forbes, "and their transferability yields a bonus in labor savings."

While approximately half of all shipments move via corporate truck-R E A Express, larger shipments flow to many other carriers, as indicated by the accompanying map of currently authorized motor truck carriers. "This map gets updated quite regularly," observes Jack D. Brooks, traffic and credit manager. "As carriers indicate greater or lesser service capability, we tend to become more selective."

Much motor freight to Dallas, Memphis, Kansas City and St. Louis moves on negotiated rates based on either a 10,000-pound minimum on the front 13 feet of trailer or 20,000 pounds on the front 26 feet. To Los Angeles, both minimum and maximum is 20,000 pounds for a 27-foot "pup" trailer. All of these rates are on a shipper-load, consignee-unload, single bill basis. Kansas City and St. Louis rates carry overflow freight from the private carriage operation. This group of rates was initiated at the behest of common carriers seeking to compete with the corporate fleet operation.

Computerized Shipment Preparation

M-D's IBM 360-30 computer plays a big part in order processing and shipment preparation. Tight order control prevails, with separate color-coded orders representing each work day, giving personnel a quick visual reminder of status and priority. Orders are acknowledged promptly on receipt, and if an order has not moved after three work days, a letter explaining the delay must be sent to the customer.

The computer supplies shipping tickets and packing lists, but the shipping department prepares bills of lading because mode must be determined at the weighing location, and routing varies day to day. Motor carriers alternate on a day basis for some destinations, while actual mode may shift depending upon total consolidated weight available for specific destinations.

The computer, however, prepares its out-

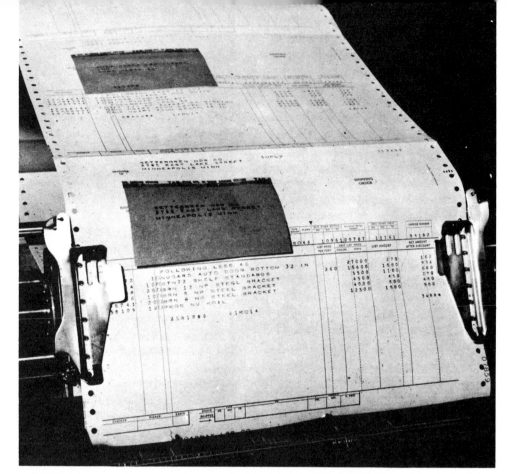

Computer-produced shipping tickets and packing lists include a computer-prepared stencil as well.

Common carrier and M-D trailers spotted for loading at the company's outbound platform.

put to fit whatever mode may apply. Shipping tickets, priced and unpriced packing lists, produced as a three-part form, have a computer-produced stencil attached as well. Print-out includes customer order and M-D sales territory number, postal zone from Oklahoma City and break point, if applicable, plus postal zone from break point, destination post office class, R E A scale to destination, applicable break point and R E A scale from the latter to destination. A typical form appears on page 35.

R E A Express shipments move on incentive rates published in R E A tariff No. 33-G based on 7,500-pound minimums applicable at Kansas City, St. Louis, Oklahoma City, Memphis and Dallas. Under present conditions, only the first two points normally handle M-D shipments. Manifesting for these is also handled by the company computer, as in illustration on page 35.

Computer output moves to the packing department for order assembly, the finished shipments flowing to the shipping department where bills are prepared and the goods sent by conveyor to the shipping platform.

Five boxcars (in background) wait to unload raw materials delivered by rail, while two trailers (right) wait to be placed for loading with goods slated for ultimate delivery via R E A Express.

Traffic and Credit Manager Jack D. Brooks (right) discusses private truck operating schedules with Traffic Assistant James C. Lucas in the Oklahoma City traffic department offices.

New Distribution Centers Foreseen

So far, M-D service fares well under centralized distribution. In Mr. Forbes' opinion, however, the time may not be too distant when both cost and service considerations will make multi-center distribution the better alternative. While a relatively significant number of "exceptions"—goods matched to specific customer requirements—can only reasonably be handled from one point, studies in progress suggest that substantial proportions of standard pack items can be advantageously stocked at regional locations. Should the company move in this direction, it is anticipated that a West Coast center would be the first added, possibly to be followed by an East Coast location and, finally, a distribution center in the eastern portion of the midwest.

Given such a system, the traffic department anticipates substantial changes in shipping procedures. A complete reorientation of carriers and modes would be necessary, with every effort made to develop efficient consolidation programs in both common and private carriage to the new centers, with appropriate distribution rates for beyond movement to individual customers.

Improved packaging, better handling, pay off

PACKAGING and material movement present diversified problems when products vary greatly in their nature and dimensions. At Macklanburg-Duncan, planning in these areas falls largely to the traffic department. In recent years, a number of innovations have sharply cut both labor and damage costs for moving and protecting goods varying from caulking compound to mail boxes.

A material-handling change that affected most goods leaving the plant is in prominent view on the freight dock's east end. A large

Cartons for product packaging are made in Macklanburg-Duncan's Oklahoma City plant to keep costs down. Address stamped on the top is made by a computer-produced stencil, which is part of the computerized order manifold. Many of the cartons are color-coded by products.

electric carrousel, similar to the type used for baggage sortation at some airports, provides five work stations for personnel packing final shipping containers.

Previously, goods arriving on the belt conveyor from the shipping room would enter a gravity conveyor extending the length of the dock, feeding adjacent shipping container-loading positions. If a 65-pound case of NuGlaze (an M-D product for installing glass panes) got past a busy packer, it would roll to the conveyor's end, forcing the man to carry it back as much as 75 feet to his work position. The carrousel, however, concentrates goods arriving from four scales and a prepack area at the east end. As it revolves, dockmen pick off items adjacent to spotted shipping containers, minimizing heavy hand lifts. The carrousel has five control switches located strategically so that platform men can start or stop its revolution to suit their convenience in loading.

As with other unique pieces of internal

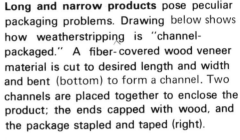

Long and narrow products pose peculiar packaging problems. Drawing below shows how weatherstripping is "channel-packaged." A fiber-covered wood veneer material is cut to desired length and width and bent (bottom) to form a channel. Two channels are placed together to enclose the product; the ends capped with wood, and the package stapled and taped (right).

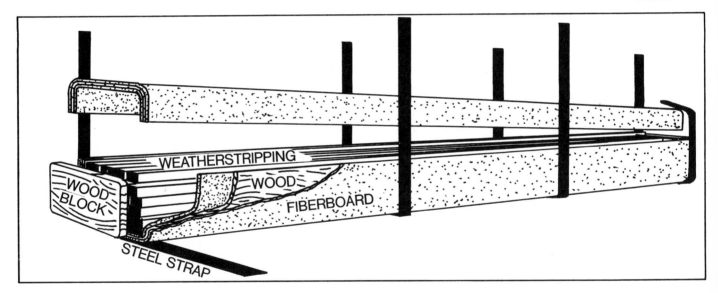

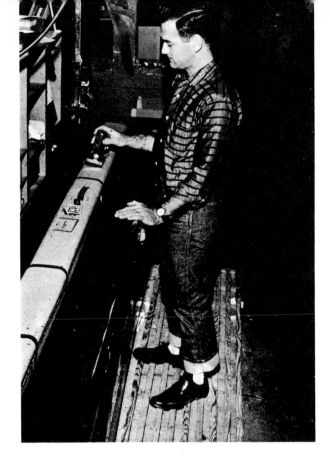

equipment, the carrousel is one-of-a-kind. Assuring this is the fact it was built directly on the premises in the company's very comprehensive shop facilities. While the normal shop function is product development and manufacture, an ability to develop specialized units for plant use frequently proves helpful in solving material control problems.

The shipping containers loaded from the carrousel also represent Macklanburg-Duncan development. Their bases are reusable skids made in the plant from hardwood and topped with Croveneer, a paper-covered wood veneer. Container sidewalls are sleeves of treble-wall corrugated board, 1,100-pound puncture test. The average loaded weight of the skid-and-sleeve unit is 1,200 pounds.

Skids and sleeves get up to 45 trips before wear necessitates discard. When moving common carriage, they are generally shipped back as regular freight. Those moving to R E A terminals in company units are picked up daily at the R E A Express terminals in Kansas City and St. Louis.

The company-owned containers are supplemented in some measure by carrier-provided cage containers as well. R E A is the principle furnisher of this equipment.

Long and narrow products pose peculiar problems for M-D packaging. Various forms of molding and weatherstripping, two typical products, need a different type of protection than conventional carton sizes afford. In the past, expensive boxing practices employed one by four-inch wood sides and ends with masonite tips and bottoms. The newer method, "channel packaging," cut package weight by two-thirds, reduced damage to products and shaved packing costs at the same time.

What is channel packaging? There are two classes of it at M-D. In one form, solid fiber material is cut to desired length and width, suited to the item being shipped, following which the material is bent to form a channel or half-tube. Matched with another piece for four-side protection, the resultant unit is capped with wood ends, stapled and taped.

Bending the solid fiber material is a simple process employing heat plus direct pressure through a device resembling a sheet metal bending brake. A second, somewhat stronger material, however, requires different handling. Where extra strength becomes necessary, the company employs a fiber-covered wood veneer material for channel assembly. Slower pressure bending, higher temperature steaming at properly controlled temperature is necessary to avoid splitting the wood and its losing its strength.

A packaging development offering wide-ranging benefits was the replacement of drive-in lid metal paint cans with plastic containers for spackling and glazing compounds. There were two initial reasons for the change:

• Drive-in cans have a lip which catches part of the material as a user removes it, dropping it back down into the can. This residue will dry out, causing the customer to think that what remains in the can is drying in its entirety.

• Frequent dropping during shipment caused much metal can damage. A 20-foot test drop of a one quart plastic container holding five pounds of NuGlaze onto a concrete floor caused no damage.

Subsequent experience confirmed test results. Damage to plastic containers has been insignificant.

Benefits extend beyond those sought initially. The new containers nest for economical storage and shipment. Coming in half-pint, pint and quart sizes, their tops are nonetheless the same diameter for easy storage and stacking. Color-coded lids simplify control for the retailer as well as for **M-D**—blue lids for spackle, yellow for glazing compound.

In the area of more conventional packaging, cartons are made at the Oklahoma City plant to keep costs down. The company buys 76 by 82-inch mill-run corrugated sheets as well as trimmed and scored one-way blanks. The mill-run sheets are printed and formed into cartons as needed for specific conditions. On high volume runs, the trimmed and scored blanks offer important time and labor-saving benefits. Many cartons are color-coded by products, eliminating shipping department errors, making stock control easier for dealers and helping company salesmen as well.

As with many other inbound products, the company trucks participate in delivering needed materials. Caulking and sealant tubes, purchased in St. Louis, are regularly delivered to the plant in company trucks returning from deliveries to the R E A Express St. Louis terminal.

Traffic-controlled telecommunications

AN UNCOMMON traffic responsibility, but one flowing to this department in an increasing number of firms under the logistics concept, is communication service. At Macklanburg-Duncan, it has been a long-standing departmental function. Policy points toward a continued expansion of telephone operations under present centralized activities,

with every likelihood of more varied telecommunications commitments in the event that additional distribution centers are placed in service.

Present equipment, though performing satisfactorily, faces the probability of considerable expansion. "The National Sales Executive Club," notes Mr. Forbes, "recently stated that the current cost of a business letter is $2.74. Forty letters a day would be $109.60. A full U.S.A. WATS line at current Bell System rates comes to about $100 a day. We feel this certainly gives us a reasonable yardstick for considering expansion of telephone order processing."

Set up in their own room, virtually as a "tactical control center," order handlers currently employ one telephone line through the main switchboard and one WATS line, which may be worked externally direct or alternately shunted through the board. The WATS line covers all of the United States except Oklahoma intrastate outbound calls. It is a 24-hour-a-day phone, basically for salesman contact.

Expansion under consideration includes an additional outbound WATS line as well as six additional inbound WATS lines. Of the latter, three would be on band 7 (Oklahoma intrastate) and three on band 3 (Tex., La., Ark., Mo., Kans., Neb., Colo. and N.M.). The added capacity would be used to encourage more direct dealer telephone orders, greatly speeding service while reducing costs now incurred in mail order processing. This broadened spectrum would also greatly facilitate the handling of salesmen's communications during peak periods, providing

M-D President W. W. Hulsey, center, and C. D. Forbes, traffic vice president, review telephone order processing system in modern telephone order center. Personnel at right, under time-zone wall clocks, speed order receipt via Bell System WATS lines at lower cost than under mail procedure.

TURE TE	DESTINATION	PASSENGERS	PURPOSE	RETURN DATE
'69	Houston, Texas Baton Rouge, La. Jackson, Miss.	K. Cook, V-P Sales C. Cox, Field Sales Mgr.	Contact dealers special problem: Camille	9/18/69
'69	Wichita, Ka.	John Beatty, Pilot	100 Hour Engine Check	9/24/69
69	New York, N.Y.	Dick Gaugler, Adm. V-P K. Cook, V-P, Sales P. Floyd, V-P, Sales Promotion (wives included)	National Hardware Show	10/4/69
'69	Chicago, Ill.	K. Cook, V-P, Sales Paul Floyd, V-P, Sales Promotion Ron Eitzen, Mgr. Advertising	Set up Cotter Show	10/16/69
/69	Chicago, Ill.	P. Floyd, V-P, Sales Promotion Lawrence Kosted, V-P, Sales Analysis C. Cox, Field Sales Manager	Cotter Show	10/16/69
/69	St. Louis, Mo. Ft. Wayne, Ind. Harrisburg, Pa.	Will Willis, Purchasing Herb Garvin, Engineering C. Cox, Field Sales Manager Troy Hill, Salesman	IBM School IBM School American Hardware Show	10/22/69
/69	Manhattan, Kansas	W. W. Hulsey, President	Meeting with Attorney	10/25/69
/69	Chicago, Illinois	Jim Owens, Extrusion Manager	American Council of Aluminum Extruders	10/30/69
	Detroit, Michigan	Bill Wells, Engineer Dick Gaugler, Administrative V-P Herb Garvin, Engineer Dick Warnke, Production Manager Charlie Faison, Engineer	National Packaging Show	

I request passenger space on the M-D company plane for myself and
_____ others.

Date of Departure_____

Destination_____

Date of Return_____

With additional stops at_____

_____

_____

Purpose of trip:_____

_____

Firms to be contacted:_____

_____

Address_____

_____

Telephone_____

Persons to be contacted_____

_____

Address_____

Telephone_____

Signature_____

Approved_____

Sample month schedule (left) of company plane shows diversity of services it offers, providing substantial time savings and greater reliability for executives in making and keeping appointments. Plant schedules derive from forms (right) filled out and submitted in advance of need.

more flexibility for the employment of additional order processing personnel and making service more conveniently available, as well, for other communication outside of the sales activity's province.

In the company's modern headquarters, operating under traffic department control, a 701-B dial system and a 608 switchboard are employed. Services available include 11 trunk and three direct lines. There are also four office lines through the switchboard. No immediate future changes are contemplated in the major equipment.

Looking ahead, numerous possibilities present themselves in connection with the contemplated addition of regional distribution centers. The possibilities for maintaining effective inventory control and order processing through such media as Bell dataphone or distribution center input devices with direct, on-line communication into the Oklahoma City computer are being held clearly in mind as plans develop to cope with an expanding business.

Transporting managers:
The methods

CORPORATE travel control is a three-way stretch at Macklanburg-Duncan. Straightforward reservations, both travel and lodgings, flow through the traffic department for any and all destinations. In addition, a corporate aircraft provides priority services nationwide as needed. A separate arrangement exists as well for the handling of meetings, conventions, group activities and such; a qualified, reliable travel agency handles these larger gatherings in complete detail.

The normal travel services supplied by the traffic department include more than just placing reservations, of course. Close contact is maintained with the airlines serving Oklahoma City, both to assure proper handling of individual flights and to keep things moving properly on a small but growing volume of air shipments. "Through good personal contacts, we can be assured of getting space when things are tight and, very importantly, of being properly cared for on connecting flight situations," Mr. Forbes observes. "Our direct air service, while generally good, is somewhat restricted in comparison with that available at some larger cities. Accordingly, the right connections and good beyond service mean a great deal."

Corporate Aircraft's Role

A great assist in effective management travel comes from the corporate aircraft. So often termed the "Sacred Cow" or "Queen Mary" in some companies, its schedule, accompanying this article, reveals it to be anything but what such terms imply at M-D. "We find it the perfect eliminator of 'off-line' points," states Miss Lynda Bagley, assistant to the president. Miss Bagley handles the scheduling of the aircraft, employing requests submitted on the illustrated forms to decide priorities and set up destinations. Although not a traffic department function, Miss Bagley works closely with Mr. Forbes on purely operational and equipment matters concerning the aircraft.

A Beech Queen-Aire, twin propellor craft with a capacity of seven passengers covers the service. The size has proven well suited to company needs.

At one time, the traffic department handled all common carrier passenger travel and related arrangements, but recently, it has turned over necessary preparations for sales meetings and other such large-scale gatherings to a reliable external travel service. The increasing size and complexity of these activities had started to place an undue burden on the traffic staff's time, creating the possibility of service problems in the movement of customer orders, as well as freight cost penalties.

Under present arrangements, the advantages of an agency's full-time commitment to this type of work, as well as its specialized contacts and experienced personnel, weighs heavily in its favor, particularly inasmuch as so much of the movement related to national meetings may, in fact, be concerned with trips whose origins and destinations are both distant points where the headquarters staff would not have the benefit of familiar personal contacts.

Multi-Phase Consolidations: Speed and Savings

CBS Records, like Macklanburg-Duncan and Western Electric, makes good use of multi-phase consolidations. Phonograph records require timely deliveries to mesh with advertising campaigns and because of the volatile changes in tastes among the record-buying public. Nationwide deliveries of small shipments at frequent intervals involves a number of unusual strategies.

The usual transportation theory is that the best carrier service derives from a single point-to-point movement in a single vehicle where this is possible—a luxury available to few small shipments. For CBS, transcontinental shipments move under a plan that seems deliberately aimed in the opposite direction, yet the results are the best that the distribution unit has found available short of using strictly premium transportation services. Records moving from New York city to Los Angeles distribution shift in rapid succession between up to five different vehicles en route, yet carefully programmed connections, systematized handling and efficient paperwork set origin-destination scheduled times comparable to the best available in truckload movements.

The CBS study initially published in the August, 1968 TRAFFIC MANAGEMENT follows:

FEW INDUSTRIES face more small shipment problems than phonograph record manufacturers. Fickle record buyers force stores to stock a wide variety, yet consumer tastes, changing virtually by the hour, readily convert today's "hit" to tomorrow's drug-on-the-market. Prudence demands, therefore, that retailers keep minimum stocks, placing small orders frequently. CBS Records, a division of Columbia Broadcasting System, Inc. knows the story well. The country's largest producer, most of their over 230 million annual record volume plus growing recorded tape production moves in small shipments.

With production growing some 10 to 15% per year after virtually doubling in the past five years, total distribution costs become increasingly significant. The CBS Records traffic department, however, by marrying existing private truck services to specialized common carrier consolidations, pulled savings in excess of $265,000 out of its hat in 1968. It intends to better this achievement in 1969. The complete integrated system is called "COLTRANS," an acronym for "Columbia Transportation."

On the surface, the system looks unpromising for service. A New York vendor shipment to the CBS Records Santa Maria, Calif. plant transfers five times before delivery; yet this LTL-sized shipment almost certainly will arrive on the fifth working day following pickup. "Despite all promises, guarantees or whatever, no one else yet can give us the consistent fifth working day West Coast de-

Traffic Manager J. V. Juliana (left) and H. A. Carr, director-distribution, review with satisfaction latest savings report on COLTRANS shipping program.

Series of five pictures, above, show how Pitman Driver Carl Drozdowski plays a key role in daily COLTRANS operation. (1) **Arriving at Elmhurst**, he prepares to open private trailer's tailgate before docking. (2) **Truck in place**, he employs warehouse electric lift truck to unload Pitman records for New York branch stock. (3) **Reviewing**

livery we get from COLTRANS," claims Traffic Manager John V. Juliana. "Many carriers solicit this buisness, but when we state our performance requirements, they throw up their hands and change the subject."

Further sweetening the service, air freight linked in at mid-continent yields a third-day West Coast delivery, equaling formerly available deferred air service at substantially lower costs.

In essence, COLTRANS is a nationwide material-handling structure whose building blocks are of three quite distinct varieties:

\#Long-haul common carriage. Eastern Express daily truckloads from east to Midwest and Pacific Intermountain Express consolidated LTL movements from Midwest to the West Coast, supplemented by Jet Air Freight service, develop the bulk of annual ton mileage.

\#Short-haul private carriage. CBS Records' own trucks based at Pitman, N.J., Terre Haute, Ind. and Santa Maria, Calif. gather small shipments, link the common carrier legs and effect many shipment deliveries.

\#Efficient transfer-consolidation operations. Scheduled, routinized shipment processing at both CBS Records freight docks and carrier terminals, on a daily basis,

make the most of the scheduled over-the-road movements.

"Our three existing private truck operations gave us a nucleus around which we built COLTRANS," observes Distribution Director Harold A. Carr. "Already existing to give our plants better ground service to airports, their return load and consolidation potential pointed the way toward substantial economies as well. Accordingly, we found it expedient three years ago to relate these capabilities to faster, more economical common carrier services than we enjoyed at that time."

Four-Phase System Expanded Truck's Run To Indiana Plant And Vendors

The traffic department's planning envisioned a four-phase system development. Phase I kicked off Oct. 9, 1967. This operation employed a CBS truck already in daily service between the Pitman record plant and three New York City area locations: Brooklyn (Columbia Record Club), New York (branch warehouse for New York region record distribution—now located in Elmhurst) and Hawthorne, N.J. (printing plant of CBS Records Division). Under the new scheme, this truck run's role, formerly limited to a Pitman plant service, expanded materially. Placed on a daily timetable, the

freight on hand for COLTRANS movement, he calls traffic department to check priorities before creating COLTRANS manifests. **(4) Cargo priorities established,** he loads westbound COLTRANS freight. **(5) Loaded** and ready to roll, private truck will shortly proceed to Hawthorne plant for final daily pickup.

truck now gathered freight from the above origins destined to both the Pitman, N.J. and Terre Haute, Ind. record plants plus vendors in the Terre Haute and Indianapolis areas.

Previously, freight destined to Terre Haute from the New York area achieved second-morning delivery only if the traffic department was specifically alerted to the need and could thus maintain close personal control with affected carriers. Phase I of COL-TRANS changed this markedly. The combined efforts of Eastern Express and the company's traffic department produced a scheduled daily service that assured regular second morning Terre Haute deliveries.

The key was a commodity rate which made consolidated truckloads possible. This rate applies to "Plastic Records and Related Articles," with large daily shipments of specially formulated plastic raw material, produced at Pitman, providing basic tonnage. While this commodity is the system's anchor, the critical elements are really the "related articles." These are the goods requiring timely delivery. There are, however, substantial savings on the whole mix. The new average rate yielded better than a 70% reduction compared to prior costs of moving separate LTL shipments, many of them at minimum charges. "Our saving on 'mins' borders on the astronomical," notes Distribution Director Carr.

New York And Pitman Westbound Freight Ready To Roll By 9 p.m.

The Phase I scheme found New York area and Pitman westbound freight assembled and ready to roll in an Eastern Express "Cargo Control"-type trailer by 9 p.m. each work day. Careful scheduling of the Pitman CBS truck and consistent on-time performance were the elements that made this possible.

As this new service improved running times sharply, the traffic department advised origins unable to assemble shipments in time for scheduled pickup to hold freight over for the following day. "A near-24 hour delay still provides earlier delivery via COL-TRANS than does LTL forwarding in common carriage," notes Traffic Supervisor Joseph Czechowski.

The new operation proved an immediate success, making its predicted schedules with impressive regularity. Each day, while the Eastern Express rigs tool westward, Pitman wires details of their loads to Terre Haute, expediting communication with area vendors as well. In this way, the latter can arrange prompt pickups when the trailers arrive, easing inventory demand pressures and minimizing storage and handling problems at the Terre Haute plant. "What really makes the whole thing tick is superb cooperation at Elmhurst, Brooklyn, Hawthorne, Pitman,

While one of daily Eastern Express trailers is unloading, dock personnel have already set up some of its cargo for pickup by Chicago truck at Terre Haute plant.

At Elmhurst warehouse, Kenneth Stack, assistant shipping supervisor (far right), examines one of many small but hot vendor shipments that arrive here daily for forwarding by COLAIR or COLTRANS.

Orders move via powered conveyor from picking area. Checkers confirm content, placing improper selections on the center pillars for return. In background, a Pitney-Bowes meter speeds preparation of U.P.S. shipments.

Gravity-feed conveyor feeds shipments to three packing stations for sealing and removal to shipping area.

Terre Haute and Santa Maria," states Mr. Carr. "Their enthusiastic support builds us a truly premium transportation service."

Phase II of COLTRANS went "on line" Jan. 15, 1968. This operation involved an existing run employing two straight trucks between Terre Haute and the Chicago area, primarily for freight to and from Chicago airports. Tying in the CBS Skokie branch warehouse as well, the expanded service developed a scheduled connection daily with Pacific Intermountain Express for Los An-

geles area LTL consolidated shipments. Now COLTRANS added several new "customers." Not only could New York area and Pitman CBS freight benefit from a coast-to-coast five-working-day schedule, but Terre Haute, formerly only a destination area, could share expanded service and cost benefits, building greater volume into consolidations to the advantage of all participants.

Following on the heels of Phase II, June 1, 1968 saw another option opened up for

COLTRANS partipants. Named "COL-AIR," it offered a high-speed alternative for shipments requiring better than COLTRANS five-day surface movement, yet less than first class air freight. Under this operation, shipments move surface to Chicago in standard COLTRANS fashion, but then go forward via Jet Air Freight, Inc. to far west destinations. Air shipments, although reduced in some measure by the fast surface operation, remain an important traffic factor. COLAIR, therefore, created an opportunity to further minimize high-cost, through-air movements. The third-morning West Coast service now regularly provided easily equals the old deferred-air cargo services.

Tie-In At Los Angeles
Provides Service To Santa Maria

Freight arriving at Los Angeles ties in with yet another CBS Records truck operation. Between there and Santa Maria, Calif., another CBS Records plant, regular daily truck operations add the final service touch for a basically "off-line" point. In this case, in addition to its other tasks, the private truck functions as a delivering carrier for COLTRANS and COLAIR, all movements being basically westbound at present.

The most recent COLTRANS extension, Phase IV, brought COLTRANS service to many of the company's eastern vendors. Thus, vendor freight shipped F.O.B. Hawthorne or Elmhurst, effective June 20, 1968, began to move to western CBS destinations in regular COLTRANS service, further widening consolidation speed and economy.

The multiple transfers involved in this operation could easily create a paperwork quagmire. Anticipating this, the traffic department, working closely with the company's systems group, sought a single-form system for internal control. They produced a "Progressive Manifest" which records the receipt of freight from numerous sources en route to common destinations. Separate manifests are prepared for each destination.

The complete seven-part sheaf is distributed to transfer points and terminal points, with further copies forwarded to the traffic department in addition. Each COLTRANS manifest's number is entered on related carrier bills and shipping labels. Common carrier bill of lading numbers are similarly cross-referenced in appropriate manifest spaces.

In the daily operation, the Pitman truck comes north each morning and deposits records and miscellaneous items at the Brooklyn and Elmhurst locations, picking up any COLTRANS freight dropped at these points by vendors. The driver manifests these shipments on acceptance, initiating a new form for each affected destination. While covering his circuit, he keeps the traffic department office informed by telephone as to his schedule and the nature of pickups. At his final pickup point, the Hawthorne printing plant, he checks freight priorities if the total tendered exceeds trailer capacity. Once loaded, the consist is telephoned to Pitman, enabling the plant to estimate the space needed on the westbound trailer that night. The driver's schedule calls for a 6 p.m. Pitman arrival, yielding ample time for freight transfers to the 9 p.m. Eastern Express trailer for shipments moving beyond Pitman.

Some of this truck's freight will go into the Pitman plant, but Pitman itself augments the westbound cargo with goods of its own. These are added to existing manifests or, if destined to points not already manifested, new forms are prepared. At Terre Haute, setouts and pickups will be processed in like manner.

CBS Records' traffic department, while performing several line functions at company headquarters, views its corporate role as primarily a staff function. COLTRANS and COLAIR, planned and controlled by the department, depend on men and equipment reporting to numerous company units to keep things rolling. So, too, the department functions in other distribution areas. "We're looking toward further improvements in the total material handling operation," comments Mr. Carr. "Our warehousing is under intensive review to assure that we are using the best methods and equipment. Continuing business growth indicates the need for further refinement and innovation in materials handling and warehouse mechanization. Studies are under way to these ends."

Mr. Carr's views on material handling are endorsed by CBS Records New York Branch Manager Michael A. Volkovitsch. "When the new tape cartridges and cassettes become a major factor, our warehouses may require different material handling procedures," he notes. "Tapes lend themselves to more varied handling techniques. This could lead to much greater warehousing automation in our business."

Small Shipments: Avon Calling

Avon Products, with its unique house-to-house merchandising system, necessarily creates a vast flow of small shipments nationwide on a steady basis. Here, too, consolidation is a principal element.

In Avon's case, overall volume to individual metropolitan areas can be fairly substantial, minimizing the problems of scheduling effective consolidations regularly into break bulk points. Greater effort must be concentrated, however, in developing effective, reliable delivery systems within the areas. The company employs two different approaches: Where effective local carriers are found that can provide service matching standards established by Avon, this mode is in use. In other localities, where traffic and regulatory conditions militate in its favor, the company operates its own leased vehicles under comparable service standards. In either mode, careful mapping and scheduling of delivery routes prior to installation is an important task performed by staff personnel.

Initially reported in the September, 1970 TRAFFIC MANAGEMENT, this case study follows:

IN AN ERA when "the small shipment problem" spells headaches for most shippers, fast-growing Avon Products, Inc. thrives in a market based upon a huge small shipment volume. With demand virtually doubling every five years 1969 sales approached $657 million. An army of representatives from coast to coast, selling company products door-to-door, generate this volume. Supplying these ladies keeps seven modern distribution centers busy moving shipments that average 40 pounds each on tight, biweekly schedules.

Rapid company growth reflects in the expanding transportation department work load. Each of the seven regional distribution centers has its own staff branch transportation departments.

"Our transportation function is highly decentralized," states Director of Transportation Wayne E. Hollowell. "We have our people where the action is. The home office sets policy and backs up the branches with staff support, but we encourage field responsibility and decision making. New procedures or developments invariably represent team action. Much of our central department development work arises from suggestions made by the branches."

During the past three years, under Mr. Hollowell's direction, functional and organizational changes took place designed to cope with rapid market growth. High service standards get first priority because Avon's field is intensely competitive. A leader in cosmetics and grooming aids, the company gears distribution to assure timely deliveries. Costs are important, but service must always come first.

Transportation department policy reflects clearly in the organization structure. Both the central and branch departments separate line-haul responsibilities for inbound distribution center movements from staff and operational duties that relate to direct representative service. In this way, two decidedly different functions get needed specialized attention.

Little is left to chance in branch transportation department day-to-day operations. Detailed procedures, spelled out in a large transportation department manual, cover duties, work schedules and a broad range of contingencies. An indication of its comprehensive nature may be gathered from the accompanying table of contents. (See page 37.)

"By spelling things out this way," notes Transportation Manager Lyman E. Waddill, "we free branch managerial time and talent to concentrate on the truly exceptional situations rather than routine conditions or anticipatable problems. Instead of constraining people, therefore, this manual serves to foster innovation."

Concentration on the exception typifies central department activities as well. Free to pursue staff programs, both long and short range, its response to the recent teamsters' work stoppage is a good short-term

DIRECT CUSTOMER DELIVERY is the Avon way. Sold exclusively through individual representatives, final delivery is a personalized

MODERN CONVEYOR SYSTEMS speed small shipment flow at Avon's branch distribution facility at Atlanta, Ga.

service. While motorcycle service is not necessarily standard, the attractive rider typifies the Avon representative.

case in point. The department, anticipating possible major disruptions, prepared detailed contingency plans well in advance. These went into action for several areas affected by walkouts.

In all, the plans covered several hundred vendors shipping to multiple destinations, with any plan involving questionable phases pretested in service to measure its value and its limitations. Going one step further, the department established a formula to develop acceptable rate adjustment levels based on whatever final contract terms the teamsters and carriers agreed upon.

The following pages review some of the distribution activities that the company employs in furthering service and cost goals while market growth surges ahead, including such topics as:

• The national transportation department's staff finds increasing opportunities in the refinement of vendor routings, more sophisticated consolidation plans and the possibilities offered by intermodal transport.

• Outbound operations at the distribution centers present an ever-changing picture, creating diversified challenges for branch transportation departments.

• In the larger communities, Avon's novel "in-house" consultant approach to solving local delivery problems reflects in tight coordination with common carriers and effective leased-fleet operations.

Continuous Surveillance Keeps Routing Efficiency High

Rapid company growth continually places new demands on Avon's total transportation system. Greater tonnage, changing route patterns and improving transportation technology make any set programs difficult to maintain for long periods. The central transportation department, therefore, is geared to continuing change, not only seeking better ways to do a total job, but constantly testing present procedures to ensure that they fulfill Avon's cost and service requirements.

Diversified vendors supply the four manufacturing laboratories at Suffern, N.Y.; Springdale, Ohio; Morton Grove, Ill., and Pasadena, Cal. With the exception of Suffern, each of these plants either shares its facility with or is adjacent to an Avon distribution center. Additionally, modern distribution centers at Rye, N.Y.; Newark, Del.; Atlanta, Ga., and Kansas City, Mo. draw stock from the four laboratories.

The transportation department's principle concerns lie with movement into the seven distribution centers. Outbound movements from these points occupy the attention of the branch transportation departments primarily, although the headquarters group offers them staff support as necessary.

The Avon logistics network, then, encompasses seven distinct territories related to the aforementioned branch centers, each in turn serviced by the laboratory complex and by outside vendors. Building volume movements for efficient flow between these points particularly concerns the transportation department—operationally at the branch level; from a systems and planning standpoint at the corporate level. Methods under current study or development by the latter group include advanced or expanded consolidation programs, further refinements of vendor routing procedures and the institution of piggyback operations in lieu of alternate modes as a potential tool for service betterments and cost improvement.

At the present time, a Hoboken, N.J. consolidation center regularly makes big shipments out of small ones for Avon. Numerous diversified vendors in the northeastern states move consignments to this point destined to Avon manufacturing laboratories or branch distribution centers. In addition, the Suffern laboratory funnels in a significant volume for beyond movement. Both the motor carriers and Avon enjoy substantial economies through the resultant truckload line hauls that replace a myriad flow of LTL shipments. More importantly, service speed and reliability gain from this arrangement.

Efficient vehicle movement arises from the regular use of an inbound, partially loaded trailer for some of the outbound movements. The Suffern laboratory frequently noseloads larger LTL shipments for long haul moves, the trailer then proceeding to the consolidation terminal, where miscellaneous vendor freight fills out the load for efficient beyond movement. An additional benefit accrues through reduced handling, thus diminishing potential damage exposure.

"What works well for the northeast looks good for other sections," notes Manager of Transportation Lyman E. Waddill. "We're studying similar developments currently for several other regions where vendor and laboratory tonnage might build economic volume loads. Such a consolidation network could greatly simplify our inbound movements, yielding better controllability, as well as improved cost-service patterns."

At the present time, Avon supplies its many vendors with routing letters stipulating modes of shipment to assigned Avon destinations. The department is looking to review and revamp this procedure, either through amplified and more detailed routing letters or through the development of a

routing guide. Among concepts under study is the possibility of assigning specific shipping days to individual vendors, smoothing the inbound goods flow and reducing individual vendor shipment frequency. This step would increase average inbound shipment weights and reduce confusion at Avon's inbound freight docks.

"If we build a routing guide," observes Supervisor-Transportation Analysts Anthony G. Matero, "it will give each individual vendor weight breaks for mode selection and proper Avon commodity descriptions to assure application of the best possible freight rates."

While line-haul movements are preponderantly by truck, a segment of this activity may shift to piggyback in the future. Study suggests that tri-weekly movements west from Hoboken may offer cost advantages. This operation would entail stop-offs en route to drop some units or to pick up trailers from other locations.

Regional Traffic Autonomy Builds Service

Avon's transportation department manual and related organization charts reflect a degree of uniformity in regional traffic administration. Branch transportation managers share similar responsibilities in carrying out corporate transportation policies and have supporting staffs matched in nature, contributing markedly to effective communication. To an extent, an Avon branch transportation manager can be transferred readily from one location to the other in the secure knowledge that familiar tools and procedures will make the transition smooth.

To an equal extent, however, a transferring manager expects to find substantial differences. "If there were no variances in regional conditions," Mr. Hollowell notes, "there would be little need for separate branch transportation departments." While Avon controls its "in-house" transportation procedures, no such uniformity can be anticipated from the multitude of common carriers serving the branch locations.

The company policy of working closely with carriers, both to assure

their understanding of Avon service requirements and to make certain that Avon itself makes things as convenient as possible for the carriers, clearly requires differing responses to local conditions. Branch Transportation Manager Charles B. Hertsenberg's Newark, Del. operation, which includes a somewhat specialized delivery service for the Philadelphia area, enjoys benefits and accepts problems largely foreign to those that Manager John F. Shannon at Pasadena, Cal. faces in feeding Avon leased-fleets at Los Angeles and San Francisco, as well as other far western areas.

Different, too, are the operations of Managers Bill A. Townsend at Morton Grove, Ill. and William F. Robinson at Atlanta, Ga. At the former's location, Avon laboratory facilities lie within a few hundred

ABOVE index shows the comprehensive nature of guidance materials in Avon's transportation manual.

TRANSPORTATION DIRECTOR Wayne E. Hollowell (right) discusses branch deliveries at company headquarters with Branch Transportation Manager William K. Walker (left) and Transportation Manager Lyman E. Waddill.

KICKING OFF delivery program in Detroit, Branch Transportation Manager William K. Walker talks to local representatives.

feet of the distribution center. Atlanta, however, draws its supplies from a nonadjacent laboratory and is concerned with a different set of inbound traffic conditions than apply at Morton Grove.

Continued company growth creates changing branch circumstances as well. At the newest distribution center in Springdale, Ohio, adjacent to Cincinnati, an Avon leased-fleet operation recently installed at Detroit meant changes in outbound procedures for Branch Manager Patrick J. Conlon and his staff. Rye, N.Y.'s manager, Urban S. Reininger, is now phasing in a number of outbound procedural changes as leased-fleet activity expands in the New York metropolitan area.

Of particularly local importance is the development of sales representative shipping schedules. If a large proportion of Avon representatives are working people, schedules may specify Saturday-Sunday deliveries for their convenience. In line with company policy regarding close cooperation with carriers, branch managers tie closely with local delivery carriers to determine when their peak traffic occurs, setting Avon deliveries for days that will cause them the least stress.

Branch order processing gets a boost from coded envelopes, with each representative sending orders using a code assigned by the traffic department. This simplifies schedule maintenance throughout the order processing operation. In turn, the order processing procedures develop labels that help expedite shipments. These labels, in addition to addresses, carry a routing symbol which suggests the preferred routing as well as feasible alternatives, if needed. Thus, if a prime carrier is unable to provide its normal service for any reason, people on the packing line are informed and they promptly shift shipment marking to the second choice routing.

Typifying company effort to make its freight desirable to the carrier, the Avon shipping label's back is a pre-printed delivery receipt. A carrier may present this for a representative's signature if it wishes, saving the necessity for cutting a carrier waybill.

Long-range planning of marketing campaigns materially assists the branch transportation management in securing service reliability. Local carriers get Avon shipping schedules far in advance. Branch transportation managers and carriers meet regularly to review shipping plans. At minimum, trailers are ordered not less than 48 hours in advance, greatly reducing carrier problems in providing equipment with consequent assurance of reliable pickup schedules.

How 'In-House' Expertise Upgrades Local Deliveries

Avon pays particular attention to delivery services rendered to its numerous individual representatives. Conducting 26 two-week sales campaigns each year, timely deliveries of merchandise to back up national sales promotions are a must. While Avon, like many other shippers, contends with cost and service problems that increasingly plague small shipment consignors, it has taken organizational measures to minimize their impact.

Working out of central headquarters, Manager-Branch Transportation Services William K. Walker's major responsibility is the upgrading of local delivery services. Mr. Walker takes a two-pronged approach to delivery betterments in metropolitan areas. It includes:

Consultation with local carriers: Working with delivery companies on a public carrier basis, he seeks to establish procedures that mutually benefit Avon, affected carriers and representatives alike.

Leased fleet development: Where traffic and regulatory circumstances favor such operation, he establishes leased fleet units that serve solely Avon representatives under company-established systems and procedures.

Both types of control benefit from the unique local delivery consultation service that Avon's central traffic unit provides. Mr. Walker, himself formerly an independent delivery service consultant, and his staff regularly work on site with carriers to review their handling methods and to make suggestions for effective development.

"In a typical case," states Mr. Walker, "a company serving our account will request our advice through the transportation manager at our branch with which his company deals. We will make studies with such a carrier, generally of about two weeks' duration, developing ideas on better package handling geared to his particular circumstances."

A basic ideal, in Mr. Walker's view, is getting a package from a trailer to its delivery vehicle in one physical move, which is accomplished regularly in the Avon leased fleet operations.

What does an Avon "consultant" do in an on-site survey of a delivery carrier? In addition to examining dock operations, he reviews the carrier's routing procedures and equipment, subsequently making recommendations as to both immediate and long-term objectives to optimize the carrier's costs and service capabilities. Immediate recommendations suggest improvements possible with existing equipment and facilities. Somewhat longer range suggestions may indicate a change in vehicle specifications for future replacements and consequent ultimate revisions of routes and schedules. Where fixed cost commitments in terminal facilities do not preclude it, physical facility revisions at terminals may also be advised. In all cases, these are strictly gratuitous suggestions with the dual objective of optimizing Avon representative service and improving the carrier's overall capability.

"Not all of our suggestions fall on fertile ground," Mr. Hollowell observes, "but a major portion of them have been adopted, and feedback from the carriers indicates they are well pleased with subsequent improvements in their internal cost picture."

Messrs. Hollowell and Walker agree that systems, however important, rank second to carrier attitude. In dealing with great numbers of independent local carriers, they find that a combination of energy, interest and client loyalty, summed up as dedication, means the most in maintaining consistently satisfactory service. While operation of fully controlled leased fleets provides ample experience to prove the worth of specific work methods, many carriers that work quite differently exceed Avon standards, while others that operate "by the book" fail to measure up.

"Attitudes are the answer," Mr.

Walker believes. "The firm that wants our business very much just naturally tends to work better at it. We want to help them where we can, but if a man is doing a good job for us in his own way, we recognize and respect the difference between being helpful to him and being an unwanted interference."

Population density largely determines choice of Avon delivery modes, with competitive service level requirements and cost factors as additional modifiers. As communities grow, local delivery carriers that are carefully selected and monitored take over. Where considerable numbers of Avon representatives reside in major metropolitan areas, the dedicated fleet operating vehicles solely in Avon service does the best job in Mr. Hollowell's opinion.

These leased fleets, or dedicated fleets, take several forms, as local regulatory and economic circumstances dictate. Each operation encompasses a specific group of vehicles and drivers assigned solely to serving Avon representatives in the prescribed manner.

Establishing a leased fleet operation entails substantial advance groundwork. Typically, Mr. Walker and his staff work with the affected branch manager to identify the number and timing of representatives' deliveries during the standard two-week selling campaign. Assisted by a computer printout of all deliveries for each day of a two-week cycle, the transportation department lays out routes on area maps, normally averaging 80 stops per day per truck.

"It took us 100 man-hours to completely map the Los Angeles area for

TRUCKS such as this, where leased fleets are used, supply Avon representatives.

one cycle," states Mr. Walker.

Setting up paper routes was only the opening move. Mr. Walker followed up the Los Angeles mapping project with a personal visit, renting a car and physically checking out all the routes. "Those ideal paper routes," he notes, "get some swift revisions when you encounter one-way streets, high-rise apartments and various physical circumstances that don't necessarily show up on a map." During this same period, a lessee was selected; drivers were hired, and equipment obtained.

One week from "D-day," in all new leased-operation cases, drivers are brought in for training and orientation. They learn proper handling

methods for Avon packages, the need for courtesy in dealing with Avon's lady representatives and how to get the best service out of the assigned vehicles.

Point-to-point movements benefit from controlled local delivery operations as well. At San Francisco, for example, shipments commonly moved to two separate carrier terminals, each billed as 20,000 pounds, but with an actual weight approximating 12,000 pounds per shipment. Under single terminal leased fleet operation, just one shipment moves forward, billed at actual weight, enjoying better service at lower cost from one carrier.

CHAPTER VIII

Modern Packaging: A Key to Distribution Reliability

The world's best transportation service is no guarantee against inadequate protective packaging. In the somewhat-less-than-perfect world of distribution, packaging's importance to delivery reliability grows steadily as product markets expand and increasing numbers of sensitive, complex or perishable items emerge from a growing technology.

The Micro-Switch division of Honeywell, Inc. typifies this trend. Distribution Manager Fredric L. Keefe, an authority on protective packaging, and his associates are charged with making reliable world-wide deliveries of delicate precision products. Their unique packaging philosophy envisions design as starting on the receipt of raw materials and serving every step of the way, not merely to the receiver's storage facility, but in some cases upon his production line as well. While the department exercises a comprehensive materials management-distribution responsibility, packaging is a particularly important concern in their logistics programs for Micro-Switch's high-value products.

A case study of Micro-Switch, prepared for the September, 1970 TRAFFIC MANAGEMENT, follows:

Packaging-Oriented Logistics

"GOOD packaging design considers more than getting a product from your shipping dock to your customer's door. Good packaging design considers every aspect of product environment from the initial gathering of raw materials through the customer's intended use. What matters really is the total cost-service environment that must be created for an item, both in itself and in relation to a complete product line. In effect, it is another approach to what we now call physical distribution, or logistics, or advanced traffic management." So states Distribution Manager Fredric L. Keefe of Honeywell's Micro Switch Division.

An enviable track record attests to the authority with which Mr. Keefe and his staff speak. Their national packaging awards and professional recognition in the past decade would reflect creditably on firms far larger than Micro Switch.

This major producer of sophisticated controls for the electronic age requires more than ordinary packaging expertise for its precision products, however. Delicate, costly switch mechanisms need careful handling from their initial manufacture stages through to ultimate installation in a customer product. Material handling, packaging and traffic functions joined in one management unit permit creation of coordinated systems that assure the development of total protection systems.

A good example of the Micro Switch coordinated approach lies in handling procedures for the "LF" type switch, produced in large quantities and moved regularly to Honeywell's Residential Division in Minneapolis, where they enter another production line for incorporation into electronic devices. Key element is a reusable vacuum-formed linear polyethylene tray, hardy enough to withstand repeated handlings, cleanings and reuse. The ensuing pictures and accompanying text illustrate the system in operation:

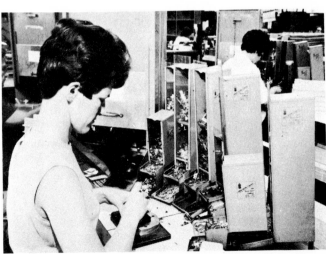

Picture 1 shows the start of assembly operations, with switches in the first phase of production being placed in waiting trays. Nested, empty trays, stocked at each work position, serve initially to hold work in progress, then move by cart to other operations.

Picture 2 finds trays, after passing through various manufacturing operations, holding switches ready for riveting of the halves in this final assembly phase.

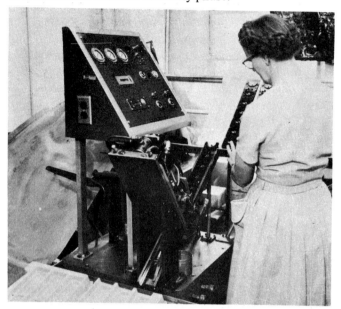

Picture 3 finds the same trays serving as both feeding and receiving units. The operator, by moving the tilted trays along the upper guide rail, successively feeds the switch rows to a branding machine. At this point, the catalog number and electrical rating are entered on each switch, which subsequently flows into an awaiting empty tray.

Picture 4 is the finale of the shipment packaging operation, in which five loaded trays, plus an empty unit for a dust cover, are placed on a die-cut corrugated pad, picked up and inserted in a corrugated container. With cartons containing 105 switches each, loading proceeds at 10,000 units per hour, yielding labor savings in this phase alone of almost 80% over prior methods.

Picture 5, some 400 miles away from the packing point, finds the vacuum-formed trays once again performing production service, but this time in the consignee's plant. The trays are subsequently unloaded, nested and shipped back to Micro Switch's Freeport, Ill. plant.

Picture 6 shows the returned trays being washed and dried at Freeport before entering the Switch Assembly Department to restart the cycle.

The trays have been in continual use for eight years, proving their worth as a rugged, returnable handling device. "With this switch type, as with many others," comments James R. Strong, supervisor-packaging design and material handling engineering, **"actual design commences with shipping requirements analysis, from which we back into the production process."** Messrs. Keefe and Strong note several benefits gained from this particular package and its related handling system, including:

• An efficient handling device in the switch assembly process.

• A similarly effective unit for incorporation in customer production line operations.

• A virtually dust-free shipping unit for precision switches.

• An aid to rapid counting of units, both in process and complete.

• A unit easily cleanable for reuse.

• Substantial savings in handling labor and package material costs.

In the 1961 Society of Packaging and Handling Engineers annual national competition, this package won "Best of Show" in Class 2 Material Handling. The subsequent performance amply vindicates this award. Similar tray-based systems, adapted to specific switch designs, now handle a number of other items as well.

What packaging materials do the job for Micro Switch? **"We'll use anything that gives our merchandise a proper protective environment at a suitable cost,"** claims Senior Packaging Designer John L. Ament. This includes such regularly used commodities as the following: Expandable polystyrene, high impact styrenes, oriented styrenes, urethane foam, Fibrecore, corrugated boxes, stock cartons, Polycell film, 40-pound bleached kraft film (nontransparent film) and propionate film for blister pack in various gauges.

Package testing plays an important role. A drop table in the package design department gets frequent use, while product laboratory equipment provides environmental testing and vibration table tests as well. Test shipments, both round-trip moves and direct customer moves for mutual evaluation, back up the plant tests. In some instances, Micro Switch has purchased tests from Package Testing Laboratories in Chicago.

Modern distribution practices are not limited solely to innovative packaging procedures. Traffic Manager Charles Franz and Superintendent-Materials Handling and Shipping Laurence D. Guile get a strong assist from computerized shipping papers. Prepared by a data processing unit including two Honeywell 2200 model computers plus a Model 800, employing both disk pack and tape equipment, the computer reduces traffic work by entering routing data, while reducing warehouse effort through a print-out of items in the most efficient picking sequence.

Shipping papers, termed "shippers," are spotted on receipt at the head of the bin row where the first line item to be picked is found. The computer location code entry shows both the location and type of bin. In the case of fast-moving items, flow racks hold the goods. By regularly measuring stock activity, the computer periodically prints out activity reports to assist in assigning locations for most efficient picking of specific goods. Normally, such reassignment is done twice yearly.

While diversified lift equipment, including side-loading trucks for long items, facilitates large piece movement, a Standard conveyor system speeds small-order assembly. At

PACKAGING-HANDLING SYSTEMS are reviewed at Micro Switch Division's Freeport plant by (l. to r.): Distribution Manager Fredric L. Keefe, TM Senior Editor Jack W. Farrell, Supervisor-Packaging Design and Material Handling Engineering James R. Strong and Assembly Foreman Donald L. Bingner.

EZ2C DISPOSABLE PALLETS, consisting of corrugated cap units supported by corrugated spiral-wound tubes, cut costs for moving packaged keyboard assemblies.

A RAYMOND 4-D TRUCK moves 12-foot rod stock through narrow aisles to the Screw Machine Department, its side-loading feature saving space.

MOLDED, expanded polystyrene handling-shipping trays simplify loading of keyboard buttons according to customer's keyboard specification sheet.

MICRO SWITCH packaging people win national recognition for their innovative designs and their fresh approach to shipment protection with impressive frequency in Society of Packaging and Handling Engineers' national contests.

PACKAGING DESIGNER J. L. Ament shows basic tray design that won second place in material handling at 1968 S.P.H.E. competition.

DATE	NAME	AWARD	LOCATION OF SPHE COMPETITION
November 1960	S. Schumacher	2nd place	Los Angeles
December 1961	S. Schumacher	"Best of Show" (1st place, Materials Handling)	Baltimore
December 1962	J. L. Ament	2nd place, Materials Handling --General 2nd place, Packaging --Class I Corrugated	St. Louis
December 1963	F. L. Keefe J. L. Ament J. D. Jacobs	"Man of the Year" 1st place, Materials Handling 3rd place, Pkg. - Class 4	Pittsburgh
November 1964	J. L. Ament J. D. Jacobs J. A. Olson J. L. Ament	1st place, Pkg. - Class 4 2nd place, Pkg. - Class 6 3rd place, Pkg. - Class 6 3rd place, Pkg. - Class 1	Dallas
December 1965	J. A. Olson J. D. Jacobs J. L. Ament	3rd place, Materials Handling 1st place, Materials Handling Hon. Mention - Plastics	Detroit
December 1967	J. L. Ament	3rd place	Dayton
December 1968	J. L. Ament	2nd place, Materials Handling	Hartford

packing stations, a double-deck operation finds goods arriving on the top level for packing, with the completed packages flowing from these stations to weighing locations on the lower level. Foreign and government shipments, each handled in separate areas, employ roller tables for order assembly.

Good handling and protection at minimum cost results, too, from larger shipments moving on EZ2C disposable pallets. Top and bottom corrugated cap units, strapped around shipping cases, stand on corrugated spiral-wound tubes affixed to the bottom cap.

While truckload shipments move regularly in both company truck and private carriage to Minneapolis and Toronto, most shipments move in the small shipment category. Weekly shipments of 5,000 to 10,000 pounds regularly merge with Honeywell Commercial Division material for ITOFCA piggyback movement to New York and export via Jet Air Freight.

In domestic movements, UPS, REA and Parcel Post, together with LTL shipments, account for the major traffic flow. While most freight is routed outbound FOB Freeport, more than half of customer shipments are routed by Mr. Franz and his staff. Claims are minor, posing no problems, in large measure due to the effective packaging systems employed.

Systemized Packaging Cuts Costs and Sharpens Service

Bay State Abrasives, like Micro Switch, faces packaging problems inherent in a fragile, diversified product line. Manufacturing grinding wheels in a myriad of patterns with diversified materials, extreme care in shipment preparation is essential to avoid breakage en route. The old-fashioned grinding wheel associated with the itinerant knife and scissor grinder is almost totally unlike the precision-engineered wheels required for modern machining techniques.

Bay State industrial engineers work closely with Traffic and Purchasing Manager Frank A. Rossi in designing new packages for specific wheel types, testing them before use and following up subsequently to be certain they are doing their job. The company enjoys a good record for timely deliveries in good condition, but it is only through such careful preparation that this is possible. The company furthers the cause of good packaging externally as well through committee activities in conjunction with the Grinding Wheel Institute and the Abrasive Grain Association.

Bay State Abrasives' logistics, a TRAFFIC MANAGEMENT case study in April 1969, follows:

IN THE TIME-HONORED CRAFT of grinding wheel manufacture, Avco Bay State Abrasives Division is a comparative newcomer with a strong track record. Started by three partners in 1922, Bay State became third largest in the industry when acquired by Avco in 1965. Each year, its share of the industry. market increases significantly. The division's annual freight bill runs currently at over $800,000.

To most people, grinding wheels are (a) something the boss wants them to keep their noses to, or (b) huge, indestructible discs that they would rather not drop on their feet. If the latter were ever true, it is no longer the case today. The tools of modern technology, engineered to microscopic tolerances, demand similar tolerances in their own production. Today's grinding wheels, in a myriad of sizes and shapes, must be delicately handled in many instances to avoid the slightest chipping or roughing of carefully made edges and surfaces.

Avco Bay State's plant in Westboro, Mass. keeps continuous surveillance over packaging performance, recognizing its major role in assuring delivery reliability. Under Senior Quality Control Engineer George Barnes' supervision, random samples of all shipments are regularly checked for package quality as well as product condition, with weekly reports prepared summarizing findings. Such control is essential to nip new problems in the bud when a production run designed to a particular customer's needs places unusual strains on standard packaging.

Such continuous checking keeps complaints down, but these, too, lead to improvements. "Our record of complaints has been less than one a week," noted Industrial Engineering Manager Raymond H. Tolman. "Analysis of this 'fan mail' helps us to spot weaknesses in one of our packages or to pinpoint a failure to live up to our standard practices. We learn by such complaints, but they are really few and far between."

Packaging Engineer John Vose corroborates this view. "In 1968." he states, "we received only 37 complaints on a total of 130.000 packages. This is a complaint rate of .0002%. Of these 37, only 21 related to broken wheels; 16 were miscellaneous other complaints such as requests for specific changes in a packaging method, requests for sawdust, etc."

Sawdust proves both blessing and curse in grinding wheel packaging. Heavy, prone to dampness problems, frequently difficult to handle, it remains a favored cushioning medium for many wheel types. Alternative modern materials encroach little by little on its role, but they can compete successfully only when they meet exacting test standards and prove themselves in use.

Packaging standards at Avco Bay State require all units to meet both National Safe Transit Committee and Grinding Wheel Institute Packaging Committee standards as well as more stringent requirements set by the company itself.

Drop testing and vibration testing are conducted regularly in the plant's own laboratory, in addition to revolving drum simulation of rough handling conditions, and incline plane tests.

A typical packaging problem arose when an upstate New York customer needed delicate 20-inch diameter thread grinding wheels delivered faster than by normal surface means. Diverted to air freight, one order moved in corrugated cartons containing six wheels each. The wheels showed up at the customer's plant broken. This led to package redesign as well as cooperative review by the National Safe Transit Committee, the Air Transport Association and McDonald Douglas Corp., in one of whose planes the initial shipment moved.

The new package developed employed extra cushioning in the form of polyurethane packing inserts, strategically placed. This material increasingly is replacing sawdust in certain types of Avco Bay State packaging. Field tests were made of the old and new packages, while Douglas Aircraft made simulation tests of cargo compartment vibration and the effect of temperature changes to see

Spot-checking packaging are Traffic and Purchasing Manager Frank A. Rossi, right, and Raymond H. Tolman, manager of industrial engineering, whose department, in its continuing program of packaging improvement, confers regularly with Traffic to ensure that new designs or modifications meet practical day-to-day requirements.

Edge of fragile, face-formed wheels shown here are only 3/16 inch thick. Shipped in special cartons fitted with circular pads which fit the wheel's inside diameter, the wheel edge rests about one inch from the box sides with a corrugated disc fitting the step on the wheel's side. Polystyrene foam pads are used as top cushioning.

Expanded polystyrene preforms to replace sawdust in packing 20-inch diameter vitrified bonded wheels, are being tested by Avco Bay State. The preforms protect both top and bottom at four points along wheel's periphery.

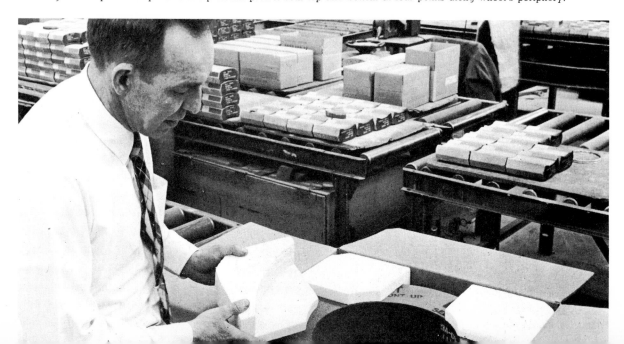

if these might account for wheel breakages.

The net results of these cooperative efforts proved that the new package gave assured protection, revealing that rough handling on the ground rather than aircraft environment caused the damage.

Like sawdust, wooden crating represents "old school" packaging that proves continually necessary and effective at Avco Bay State. While fiberboard packaging and other alternatives now share the burden, wooden crating proves intensely practical on certain heavy wheels and export shipments. The marriage of traditional wooden crating and modern plastic foam cushioning is proving a happy one for many applications.

Special Trailers Equipped For Pressure Loading Of Sawdust

Traffic Manager Frank Rossi works closely with Engineering in package use and development. At his suggestion, the company purchased four trailers in 1963 equipped with special reinforcement and sealed doors to permit pressure loading methods. Carrying 24,000-pound loads regularly, these units bring more than 1,500,000 pounds of sawdust annually from the Wilner Wood Products Co. plant in Norway, Maine. Wilner provides the tractors for the move, delivering in one day to the Westboro plant. Loading is by pressure system at the origin. About two years ago, Plant Engineering installed a vacuum-unloading system which sucks truck contents into internal storage and distribution lines, employing a vacuum hose handled by one man. Reduced unloading time yield $6,000 in annual savings.

This sawdust is not merely the by-product of other operations but a carefully processed, crushed wood material, prepared to exact specifications and sold to customers who manufacture various flooring materials, "wedgie" shoes and other unusual items. Avco Bay State's sawdust must have a maximum moisture content of 10% and a maximum "dust" content of 6%, the latter "dust" representing the finest particle sizes, which cause worker discomfort and tend to cause dirt accumulation in work areas. Moisture content not only adds unwanted weight to shipments but causes the packing material to stick excessively to different types of grinding wheels, creating a nuisance at the receiver locations. Because good quality sawdust comes out of Avco Bay State, many custom-

ers re-use it for different purposes, with the consequence that new packaging methods may cause customer dissatisfaction for reasons other than shipping performance.

Packaging and traffic meet for company benefit in another significant area as well—cutting costs on small shipments. Disposable containers, in conjunction with consolidations developed by Traffic Supervisor Frank Cianella, produce annual savings exceeding $25,000 each year. Consolidated truckloads move regularly to Cleveland distributors, while other points receive consolidations on an irregular basis as shipping conditions dictate, it being traffic department policy to move all LTL off the loading dock daily.

Once a consolidation has been set up on paper, physical preparation takes place at the traffic department end of the factory conveyor system. A 40 inch-by-40 inch corrugated cap is placed on a low-priced wooden pallet. A sleeve 40 inches high slips into this piece, forming a 40 inch-by-40 inch-by-40 inch corrugated container in which shipments of 50 pounds or less destined to the same break-bulk points are placed. After capping the unit, the packer steel-straps it together for forklifting into a waiting trailer.

Traffic Manager Also Wears Purchasing Manager's Hat

In addition to managing the traffic function, Mr. Rossi is also the company purchasing manager, thus eliminating a communication problem that frequently bedevils these functions elsewhere. Needless to say, Avco Bay State purchasing terms make certain that transportation costs are clearly identified, while the traffic function benefits as well from Mr. Rossi's employment of economic order quantity data to control inbound goods flow. "Ultimately," he observes, "I want to shift several traffic and purchasing functions into the computer. First priority for this will go to 'EOQ' (Economic Order Quantity). We've handled it successfully for several years manually, but the continued broadening of our production increases the job's size in geometric progression. With a new IBM 360 computer now on board, the time looks right to shift this work over to electronic data processing."

Heart of the physical operation in traffic is the terminal area of the division's large, unique conveyor system. From raw material assembly to checkout of the finished, pack-

Vitrified bonded cylinder wheel is packed into slotted corrugated carton with sawdust cushioning. Avco standard practice specifies one-inch layers of sawdust on both top and bottom. Overhead duct delivers sawdust as part of system which moves it by compressed air from central storage to packing locations.

In contrast to traditional sawdust-packing, the same wheel can, in many cases, move in a carton fitted with corrugated die-cut pads, eliminating some 26 pounds of sawdust from the package and reducing shipping costs.

Traffic Manager Frank Rossi, right, checks package markings with operator of transfer car, a movable segment of conveyor line that shifts products to conveyor spurs.

aged product, goods move on a series of conveyor lines, each tailored to its specific service. While most components are Lamson equipment, some home-engineered devices add to system capabilities. Typical are mechanical "jump-up" units which can change the direction of goods moving down a line, shunting one or more packages into holding spurs for various purposes. This equipment features a foot-pedal under the conveyor line which lifts small roller-bearing-equipped wheels in slim frames from slots between the conveyor system rollers over a distance of a typical standard carton length. When raised, the wheel-holding frames tilt at a slight angle, moving any carton or object resting upon them by gravity into the desired conveyor spur. The roller-bearing-equipped wheels are known to the layman as "roller skate wheels."

All goods leave Manufacturing on a single conveyor line which deposits them in the traffic area on a transfer car. This car, consisting of a short length of conveyor mounted upon a moving platform, travels on rails at right angles to the conveyor line. Its operator shifts goods to branch conveyors feeding any one of four warehouse locations, moving the car, when loaded, to whichever such branch conveyor suits his purposes. In the case of small packages, he lifts them directly off of the transfer car and sets them aside at the adjacent parcel post station for processing either as parcel post or United Parcel shipments. All other goods shift on the transfer car to one of the following conveyor lines:

Line 1—Pittsburgh, Chicago, Los Angeles area destinations

Line 2—Detroit, Cleveland, Houston area destinations

Line 3—Palletized goods, export goods, goods marked for customer hold and empty pallets

Line 4—Goods to be sent directly to the stock department

In addition to the parcel area adjacent to the transfer car, there is a traffic office in which shipping documentation is handled. As each shipment comes forward from manufacturing, the transfer car operator strips off a "manufacturing check" form detailing the size and content of each individual order. He gives these, with the packing slip, to a Flexowriter operator, who then makes a bill of lading, adding customer standard operation semi-automatically from Flexowriter cards kept on file by individual account adjacent to the machine. Upon completion, the papers are sent to accounting for invoice preparation.

Outbound Goods Accumulated In 13 Areas, Subsorted By Carrier

At lines' end for outbound goods, warehousemen spot shipments in 13 marked accumulation areas identified by overhead destination signs. Within these areas they subsort material by carrier. At present, 17 major carriers regularly move goods to the six principal warehouses as well as a number of distributors.

"We have guaranteed 48-hour delivery performance to the Midwest," states Traffic Supervisor Ciannella. "We regularly run truckloads via Spector to Chicago, P.I.E. to Cleveland and Middle Atlantic to Detroit. This way, the carriers enjoy enough of our business volume to value it while we cut the number of carriers and consequent confusion at our dock. As it is, with 17 carriers regularly serving us, it can still get pretty hectic."

The loading dock handles six trailers in a fully enclosed, heated area, protecting operations from the rigors of New England winters.

Inbound traffic poses no conflict. Clays from the south come in by rail, while phenolic resins from St. Louis, Mo. and Bound Brook, N.J. are trucked in, as are abrasive grains from various domestic sources. Six company trucks are available to bring in such material from a special warehouse three-quarters of a mile from the plant, as required by Manufacturing. These vehicles unload at a special inbound dock located in one end of the manufacturing facility.

From here, materials go to storage areas which feed various processes, including several storage units that directly feed an automated Hough Scale on the production floor. When this device is fed a group of computer cards representing the formula for producing a specific type of grinding wheel, it automat-

ically draws the exactly correct mix of abrasive grain and the proper bonding agent from overhead sources by gravity into mixing containers, preparatory to moulding and burning of ceramic bonded grinding wheels.

It is these vitrified wheels, in particular, which pose the greatest problems in package

Regular shipments of sawdust in substantial quantities warrant specialized equipment for unloading the company's private trailers. Two unloading positions, equipped with powerful suction apparatus, automate transfer of sawdust from trailers directly into the plant's air-operated sawdust handling system.

Rate data in Flexowriter cards is checked out by rate clerk and Flexowriter operator. Repetitive information for shipments to regular accounts, stored in cards, speeds preparation of bills of lading and other documentation.

design and handling. Machinable to fine tolerances, many of them are necessarily quite delicate. The resinoid wheels, made with resins, are particularly tough and can withstand more stress in both handling and operation than vitrified wheels.

While Avco Bay State Abrasives has been a part of the Avco Corporation since 1965, physical distribution operations continue to function independently, much as they did in the prior era of local ownership. Instead of superimposing a corporate structure atop its subsidiaries, Avco has instead seen fit to develop a different type of relationship. "Working within Avco made available a whole pool of traffic brainpower," Traffic Manager Rossi observes. "The company has instituted meetings among subsidiary traffic managers where we gather as equals and discuss our activities much as we would in a trade association, but with the advantage, of course, that we are free to examine more confidential problems than would be the case in an external meeting. There is no question but that we all bring home new approaches from these get-togethers that lead to subsequent improvements in our own bailiwicks. More than that, it establishes good, informal personal relationships that assure us of good counsel or direct assistance when we individually need it that is no further away than the telephones on our desks."

An industry tackles packaging problems

Packaging of abrasives has been long recognized as a vital problem in the abrasives industry. In 1952, the Grinding Wheel Institute and the Abrasive Grain Association established a joint packaging committee which worked with various government agencies to develop equitable packaging requirements for the industry's products. The committee's initial efforts clearly demonstrated the need for continued broad research in this area, and in 1957, an enlarged committee tackled its first assignment: developing a recommendation for minimum packaging quantities for small wheels. The recommendation was issued March 25, 1968.

In the late fifties, packaging, transportation and materials handling were all in a state of ferment. New methods and materials were surfacing rapidly, while older materials and systems were going into decline or discard. Packaging committee assignments deemed advisable or necessary were increasing in size, scope and number at such a rate that the two trade associations saw fit to establish separate packaging committees in the interest of accomplishing more faster.

Although operating separately on two distinct packaging programs, the packaging committees of the Grinding Wheel Institute and the Abrasive Grain Association continue to share in some projects as well, including the issuance of a packaging manual. Jointly developed, it offers a quick reference to all material at present issued, or to be issued, concerning abrasive packaging.

In issuing their manual, the two committees have not presumed to set arbitrary standards or issue authoritarian edicts as to packaging practices. Rather, they offer their findings as suggested approaches which have proven their worth in tests or in the service of specific producers. They wisely recognize that plant location and facilities, distribution methods and availability of materials can substantially alter the values associated with specific methods or materials.

Avco Bay State Abrasives Division, an active member of the Grinding Wheel Institute, employs these packaging manual standards and recommendations in large measure. GWI's Packaging Committee is, in fact, currently chaired by Avco Bay State's Manager of Industrial Engineering Raymond H. Tolman. A committee member for the past decade, he has made it possible for the industry to enjoy the fruits of Avco Bay State research just as his company has benefited from the activities of the industry's two active packaging committees.

Container-Based Shipping Speeds Delivery

The John Deere Company services much of the Northeast through a major parts depot at Syracuse, New York. A large proportion of its outbound shipments is necessarily in small packages moving to dealers and individual purchasers. In the past, the depot sought to attain some efficiency through the use of collapsible wooden containers which went forward to dealers and had to be shipped back after unloading.

Cumbersome and costly, they have been replaced by fibreboard units that reduce shipping weight, eliminate the need for return and save both in transportation and packaging costs. Additionally, their handling convenience proves a material asset within the depot as well as in transit. Such innovation is just one phase of a modern distribution system embracing an effective consolidation program and a multi-purpose computerized stock control system. Marriage of these elements into a smooth-flowing system meant significant dealer service benefits.

Initially reviewed in the April 1968 TRAFFIC MANAGEMENT, the John Deere Syracuse Parts Depot study follows:

IMPROVING TECHNOLOGY and severe labor shortages on the farm spell stronger demand for the newest and best in agricultural equipment. Deere & Company, long a major supplier, has grown into a billion-dollar corporation without mergers or acquisitions outside its own fields. Increased use of its equipment inevitably expands markets for its parts and supplies. At Syracuse, N.Y., where the company maintains a parts depot and sales branch, parts alone account for more than $8 million in annual sales in a nine-state area.

Agricultural and industrial parts service must be fast and reliable. Downtime on a farmer's tractor means more than inconvenience. It is dollar-time irrevocably lost. In such markets as farming, lumbering, and heavy construction, Deere's ability to keep its products productive creates an important competitive advantage.

"We put service to customers and dealers ahead of cost," says Parts Depot Manager Richard J. Boyle. "Service builds sales. We watch costs, too, but we know that cost savings at the expense of service end up costing us more in unrealized sales dollars."

Steady, rapid growth, already straining the capacity of the present 100,000-square foot parts storage warehouse with its inventory of 58,000 line items, provides a constant challenge to management. Continuing refinements, however, have culminated in a three-element system that flows goods smoothly, holding the cost line in some areas while developing decided economies in others. These elements include:

• Containerized parts delivery. Disposable fiberboard containers and bases reduce ship-ping costs, eliminate container return and maintenance.

• Computerized stock control. Order processing and picking, stock control and invoicing benefit from a coordinated program employing an IBM 360 computer with its foundation in EOQ. (Economic Order Quantity) statistical procedures.

• Pool truck operations. Full truckloads scheduled regularly to three strategic New England points assure faster and more reliable deliveries, while reducing LTL costs through effective consolidation.

Containerized parts shipments, in themselves, represent no novelty at Syracuse. Wirebound wooden box pallets move regularly between company plants, warehouses and dealers. On the latter shipments, Traffic Manager Loren D. Bailey and Parts Depot Manager Boyle felt that shipping costs and related paperwork, all of which required empty container returns, might be eliminatable headaches.

The cure they chose was a disposable container made of Dinacor, Container Corp. of America's specially-formulated double-wall corrugated board. These 1,000-pound test cartons, though loaded on the average to a 500- to 600-pound level, consistently handle loads in the 1,800- to 2,000-pound range with no failures. Any loads previously shipped out in company standard wooden box pallets, therefore, move with equal facility in the new disposables.

More than just container return faded from the picture when Dinacor entered the scene. The disposables entered stock folded flat, 1,000 of them storable in space once filled fully by just 72 of the banded wooden

A New England pool truck is shown in the process of being loaded. The Dinacor containers will constitute a major part of the load, but they will share space with outsize pieces such as lubricating oil drums, wheel rims and spare tracks for wheel-tracked farm and industrial machinery.

box pallets. Labor for container maintenance was completely wiped out as was the insurance complication posed in storing great numbers of dried-out wooden containers that posed a warehouse fire hazard. Company containers still come in from other Deere locations, but they are collapsed and banded for return when emptied and few remain long on the Syracuse premises.

On the traffic side, the most obvious saving remains in the return elimination, a $5 pallet returning from northern Maine at a cost of $4.50, for example. There are also substantial savings on the outbound hauls, however. Straight truckloads to New England normally include 30 to 32 pallets. Because the Dinacor units weigh only 35 pounds, they move dunnage free under the 1,000-pound allowance. The company pool pallets, by comparison, weigh 62 pounds apiece, so the same truckload would create charges for at least an additional 860 pounds. Outbound freight savings on such movements are substantial, therefore.

The pallet return procedures meant effort and expense for dealers and company alike. Some pallets were lost, many were damaged

and all created paperwork costs in addition to the expense of return transportation. No less than three memo-billings became unnecessary with empty pallet return discontinued. On an annual volume approaching 10,000 such bills, accounting savings are appreciable.

Dealer reaction was swift and positive. Overshadowing their pleasure in eliminating pallet-return efforts was their satisfaction at the condition of the shipments themselves. Past problems of occasional small parts loss through the wooden box pallet's slats disappeared, while many dealers commented that the general condition of parts packages received in the new containers was decidedly better than in the past.

Within the Syracuse warehouse the new containers proved beneficial as well. Their 30 inch-by-30 inch-by-30 inch size, comparable to the company box pallet design, permitted continued use of small four-wheeled trucks for movement during order assembly operations. Pickers soon noted that reduced weight meant less effort in moving around the warehouse. They appreciated as well the elimination of splinter-and-snagging irrita-

Picking parts for a dealer order based on picking cards supplied by computer, order preparation is speeded by placing goods directly in the ultimate shipping container. These 30 inch-by-30 inch-by-30 inch Dinacor units, initiated as air freight containers, now find increasing use in surface applications as well.

tions formerly incurred when working with the wirebound wooden box pallets. Where forklift operators could move only three of the old units at a time, even when empty, 60 Dinacor containers can be forklifted as one load. Setting up the individual container from the collapsed form in which it is stored takes but a few moments and needs only to be done on the site where it will be filled.

In addition to the Dinacor units, other container types are under test for shipments weighing 500 pounds or less. Management opinion, while influenced by somewhat lower prices of certain competitive fiberboard units, recognizes as well the existing cost trade-offs that a single standard unit affords. The single unit minimizes safety stock requirements, eliminates error possibilities, such as fracturing a 500-pound box with a 1,000-pound load, and minimizes costs and problems arising when multiple vendors supply materials. The lighter, more flexible Dinacor boxes readily handle most loads within the normal Deere & Co. density range.

Container flats come in from New Brunswick, N.J. on a 15-day cycle from order to delivery. Container bases, manufactured in Bridgeport, N.Y. eight miles from the warehouse, arrive in one day.

A few wirebound wooden pallet boxes still reach the dealers, but their impact on warehouse operation is slight. When dealers require a large enough stock of a single item to equal or exceed a palletload, the warehouse will forward intact one or more company pool pallets as received from the plant. In several cases, parts will be ordered shipped direct from plant to dealer by pool pallet, circumventing any warehouse handling. In practice, however, 95% of all parts shipments move through the parts depot. These parts mean big business to the dealers, accounting for 30% of their total sales.

In-house operations find the containers playing an important part. They serve as picking cart-bodies for setting up orders prior to shipment, minimizing packing labor and reducing warehouse equipment requirements. They are a significant element in a total order-handling system wherein order processing, inventory control and order assembly are coordinated through computer programming.

At Syracuse, a stock exceeding 58,000 individual parts meets the continuing needs of dealers in nine Northeastern states. Aisles carefully laid out to permit easy movement of 40 inch-by-40 inch containers on four-wheeled trucks help picking personnel speedily assemble orders which go directly into shipping containers.

The parts depot employs telephone recording service (Code-A-Phone) offering seven-day, 24-hour access to dealers, who are assured that the records are checked each morning at 8 a.m. and at regular intervals throughout the day. Direct telephone service during working hours, in-person calls and mail also bring orders, this flexibility being essential in a business where ultimate customers' needs can often mean serious losses if not fulfilled promptly.

"Machine-down" orders, those stipulating parts for machines actually disabled at order time, get rush treatment. Any found on hand at 8 a.m. go immediately to data processing. They are often picked, packed and out the door by 11 a.m.

More routine orders go through an "interpreter," who checks order accuracy, sorts by type and assigns a transaction number to each individual order. This number subsequently goes on all related picking tickets, invoices, back orders or other related paper, assuring ready identification of all related elements in the data flow.

The set-up orders proceed to the keypunch unit preparatory to computer processing. Once punched and fed to the IBM 360 unit, they are augmented by computer-stored data relating to the specific dealer, his location, and the standard shipment routing to service his location.

As orders pass through the computer, it stores some information for control purposes, including development of monthly stock control reports based on Economic Order Quantity statistical procedures. Its immediate output is an invoice deck, including the invoice itself, picking tickets and a packing slip. Subsequently, bills of lading and tally sheets are expected to be included, but these are as yet manually prepared.

The printed-out invoice accounts for each part number ordered by the customer, either by ordering the part shipped, back ordering against the parts depot, back ordering to a Deere plant, order transfer to the complete goods department, cancellation of the request or notification of additional processing. For every line item ordered by the customer, therefore, a specific action must be stipulated by the computer.

Because warehouse location information is also computer-stored, the picking tickets can be sorted to location, after which they move with the invoices to the scheduler in

Computer-produced cards representing individual line items in each order are reviewed and assigned for item picking by the warehouse scheduler. Reviewing the day's assignments are, from left, Richard A. Olszewski, ware-.house supervisor; Edward C. McConnell, parts depot supervisor and Arthur Kimball, scheduler.

the warehouse itself. Based on this information, he determines the time when picked goods must be ready and the packing station where they should be placed, assigning personnel as needed to maintain schedule demands. If necessary, he can shuffle men between the parts depot and the finished goods warehouse to cover peaks.

Bills Of Lading, Invoices Forwarded Manually By Shipping Clerk

From the scheduler, the invoice passes to the shipping clerk, who enters the date, total weight and bill of lading references. The shipping clerk manually generates bills of lading and forwards invoices to the parts office for final check and completion prior to submission to the accounting section, where control tapes are run and statements are key-punched.

It is after the scheduler gets the picking tickets that Dinacor units come into play. After the scheduler assigns a picker an order, the latter assembles necessary containers from flats in stock, placing these and their associated wooden pallet bases on special four-wheeled carts used in the picking operation, as well as for moving stock about the warehouse.

These carts, custom-designed at the parts depot, have special coupling hooks and eyes,

so that they may move in trains, either hand-propelled or behind forklifts or towmotors. They make possible the complete unloading of over-the-road trucks and rail cars with only one opening of the unloading dock doors—an important consideration in the snow-belt city of Syracuse.

After setting up containers, the picker walks his one- or two-car "train" through the picking regions. These are laid out so that the 25% of line items that constitute "fast-moving" stock are concentrated to minimize waste time and motion. All bins are labelled with Dymo tapes for easy identification, with the most-active small parts bins and drawers set at eye level. On fast-moving items that move in large individual order quantities, bulk-tickets fastened to the wood bin fronts show whether further stock is available in pallets in the rear at manually controlled locations. If a picker finds that his order demands more of such an item than is at hand in the fast-moving goods picking area, he can call for more stock to be brought forward to fill his needs.

Facilitating the picking process is a small, divided wooden box that hangs from metal hooks on the container lip. These can hold pencils, labels, stamps, tape, shipping papers, picking tickets, and whatever other "tools" a picker needs for a specific type of

Old and new at the Syracuse parts depot. In the background, several wirebound wooden containers offer a sharp contrast to the new Dinacor units at left. While the latter handle the great majority of dealer deliveries, wirebound units account for much inbound volume from various Deere sources.

order.

Upon completing selection, the picker moves his containers forward to packing positions, in the case of small bin items. Any necessary packaging of loose items is completed here and the containers are then readied for closure and sealing to their pallets with steel tape for shipment. At the same time, containers holding bulk items are similarly closed and made ready to leave.

The containers go next to a 10,000-pound scale. After weighing, lift trucks move them to the loading dock or carrier trucks. The Syracuse depot is currently studying a built-in scale attachment for forklifts to speed this step. The attachment will weigh containers or any other freight while it is being transported, reducing forklift and loading time with consequent labor cost savings.

In the case of numerous smaller shipments, of course, the Dinacor containers are not required; these flow from the packers on a seven-station conveyor line, powered at the stations and gravity-operated between them. Freight routed R E A, UPS, or parcel post moves forward to an on-line scale and shipping personnel in this fashion.

Efficiency Of Warehousing Based On Two Freight Classification Items

Basic to the flexible, efficient warehouse operation are two freight classification items in whose creation Deere's General Traffic Manager Paul E. Gans was largely instrumental. Together, Consolidated Motor Freight Classification items 133450 and 133452 effectively make Column 85 rates

apply to all parts items moving from the depot in mixed lots. As a result, random warehousing, without regard to beyond shipping requirements, became feasible, simplifying warehouse location selection and eliminating any problems in mixing goods to fill orders.

Inbound freight arrives almost entirely in straight car or truckloads for the parts depot. The mix is somewhat different for the sales branch, reflecting the fact that 95% of complete merchandise sold, such as tractors and cultivators, move directly from affected plants to dealers, whereas in parts the opposite is true, with only 5% of dealer parts orders routed from plant to dealer.

Outbound is quite another matter. Traffic Manager Bailey lives largely with small shipments. During peak periods some dealers order truckload quantities, and a few larger receivers draw occasional full loads throughout the year, but LTL is far more the rule than the exception.

Under these circumstances, pool trucks proved an important economy. Making use of Inland Express through distribution tariffs on commodity rates, pools move regularly to Portland, Me., West Springfield, Mass. and Boston. At least equal to savings in importance, the pool trucks sharply improved delivery times. The most distant run, the Portland pool, makes it overnight from Syracuse. While the latter serves a fixed northeastern New England territory, the West Springfield and Boston pools vary their delivery boundaries between them. These runs tend to somewhat lower weights than Portland, so juggling destinations assigned helps to assure optimum loading of both runs for service and cost benefits. "The major cost saving in any pool distribution," observes Traffic Manager

Bailey, "is the ability to load goods direct from back-area into conveyance, thus decreasing labor costs."

Consolidation economies apply inbound as well. While several plants in the Illinois-Iowa area ship direct on more sizable orders, a central warehouse at Moline, Ill. consolidates freight from several of these sources to create a Syracuse pool truck about once weekly, handling smaller, non-rush items.

In the case of the New England pools, Messrs. Boyle and Bailey are convinced that more than operating economies have been gained. Through this means, a faster, cheaper dealer service results. They feel this is clearly recognized by dealers as a competitive advantage, and therefore modern traffic management practices come to mean more sales dollars captured in addition to saving previously existing sales dollars from transportation cost erosion. The computer-container-consolidation triple-threat pays off where it really counts, therefore—in the never-ending battle for a better spot in the market.

Controlling stock by computer

Increasing prices compel management to hold down inventories. Competitive service pressures make stockouts an increasingly serious problem. Caught between the two, suppliers devote increasing attention to the problem of accurately matching stock on hand to market demand in any given season or circumstance.

A key to successful control lies in application of appropriate statistics to develop economic order quantities for each item stocked, together with safety stock standards based on normal customer demand and the level of service the company wishes to provide. Measured for each individual item stocked, such procedures result in far lower inventory investment than does the setting of a single time-standard for inventory or the

Checking out computerized monthly stock status report are (from left) Parts Depot Manager Richard J. Boyle, Stock Analyst Herman J. Snavely, and Traffic Manager Loren A. Bailey.

use of arbitrary, subjective judgments for individual items to avoid stockouts.

At Deere's Syracuse parts depot, such EOQ data, applied to over 58,000 items, comes forth regularly from the computer, guiding order decisions continually on the basis of both past performance and sales forecasts. While EOQ analysis is quite practical in application as a clerical tool if stock variety is not too great, the myriad calculations necessary on Deere's volume makes computer control mandatory.

The monthly stock status report comes forth from the computer showing each individual item by part number and name. If recent orders brought stock on any items below safety levels, the report reflects the number of times when "critical item" cards were produced on such parts. Subsequent columns show stock on hand and stock backordered. A "To Be Ordered" column details both quantities on order and the number of orders placed within the preceding quarter year. The "Reorder Point" column, determined by safety stock levels deemed necessary in relation to time needed to obtain replacements and economic size of shipment, gives a clear performance check of preceding data. If things are going right, stock on hand and stock on order should exceed this figure.

An EOQ column shows for each part the number determined as the most economical quantity for a single shipment. When stock reaches the reorder point, therefore, replenishment orders should be no smaller than the EOQ figure shown. Depending upon whether it is a fast or slow-moving item being measured, EOQ may sometimes appear unusually large considering the need existing to hold inventories down. On slow-moving items, however, paperwork and shipping costs may far exceed inventory holding costs. The Deere stock status report shows whether an item is a fast or slow mover and in the case of the latter, it is not unusual for the EOQ to represent 20 times the reorder point quantity. Obviously, while one small bolt or bracket may prove to be an adequate safety stock, delivering 20 at once means savings in order processing, paperwork, handling and transportation exceeding the minute cost of storage space at the warehouse as well as the insignificant investment.

The stock status report shows also the sales forecast for the next four quarters and number of sales and unit sales for the year to date of the report, as well as similar data for the latest quarter. This data, when related to performance indicated in the preceding columns, gives both management and the computer a check of their performance, indicating where future adjustments in safety stock levels or EOQ might be adjusted in recognition of changing demand patterns.

CHAPTER IX

Logistics and Foreign Trade

Export-Import transportation-distribution operations have a character of their own. Customs requirements, other paperwork essentials, packaging, handling, modes and customer relations create a climate totally unlike that found in domestic logistics. Where operations are limited in overseas markets, distribution managers must either wear two hats or place their reliance upon outside agents. Given more appreciable volume, a separate departmental activity attuned to overseas market service needs can prove the more effective approach.

Such is the case at Ford Motors. Domestic transportation is controlled through corporate headquarters, but prime responsibility for export-import operations lies with an export traffic department located in Newark, New Jersey, in close communication with carriers and facilities at the Port of New York. Charged with handling movements that roll up an annual freight bill exceeding $12.5 million, it ties together both marketing and manufacturing facilities wherever Ford sells or manufactures throughout the world.

TRAFFIC MANAGEMENT's October, 1970 review of Ford export department operations follows:

Ford's World Traffic Gets Specialist Attention

THERE'S a lot more to Ford manufacture and distribution than serving the U.S. market. The giant firm today builds and sells diversified vehicles and equipment through a multination facility complex covering the free world. While many large producers expand export markets and supply foreign nations through "offshore" plants, Ford carries international trade one step further: its modern American operations find both imports and exports in large volume supplying world markets, assuring competitive diversification everywhere at maximum advantage.

The challenging job of moving hundreds of millions of pounds of freight annually belongs to the overseas distribution operations department. As Newark Export Supply Manager Michael Colletti notes, "We exercise a fully integrated worldwide distribution activity, encompassing every management function necessary to provide reliable, competitive service from the production line's end to the overseas dealer's door."

Mr. Colletti's organization enjoys the highly specialized services of a 52-man export traffic department that ships parts and accessories as well as completely knocked-down, semi-knocked-down and built-up vehicles from company and vendor service locations to worldwide markets. Traffic Manager Norman E. Beatty and his staff coordinate with Ford locations overseas, along with the firm's central staff, in processing company material imports from outside-U.S. sources. In excess of 100 steamship companies and 70 airlines participate in department-controlled traffic, with the department's annual freight bill exceeding $12.5 million.

Because the export traffic department is a complete, self-contained group, rather than an arm of a conventional domestic traffic department, its activity scope is quite broad. With a shipping section covering operating responsibilities and a documentation section handling overseas shipping's complex paper work, it enjoys the benefits, in addition, of an analysis section which fulfills heavy staff responsibilities. Keeping an eye on current services and costs, this section concurrently provides strong support for long-range planning and development of the department's role.

"The complete independence of the overseas distribution operation finds our department engrossed in domestic activities as well as export-import functions," states Mr. Beatty. While Ford plants in the United States will cut bills of lading on port-bound freight, the department handles expediting and handling beyond these locations. It is concerned as well with the proper inland movement of Ford's growing import traffic and, in turn, with the coordination of traffic where imported and domestic materials combine for third-nation deliveries. As Ford's world trade expands, the department's significance grows along with that of the total overseas distribution operation.

What it takes to cope with this trade and its growth from a traffic standpoint is examined in the following pages, which review the unique specialized activities that keep overseas company service competitive and assure that export materials arrive in first-class condition.

CONTAINERIZED Ford parts serve overseas markets with speed, economy.

Improving world distribution for today and tomorrow

AN ANALYSIS SECTION fulfills the traffic department's major staff responsibilities. No mere ivory tower research group looking solely towards a distant future, it fulfills a continuing watchdog role with respect to daily operations unparalleled in the normal domestic traffic operation.

"There is a certain pleasant security in studying U.S. domestic traffic," comments Analysis Section Supervisor Paul A. Romberg. "Rates may change and competitive positions shift from time to time, but there is a degree of logic and consistency that the rest of the world by no means duplicates. If one would consider, for instance, the fact that a difference of perhaps 80% may be found between eastbound and westbound rates on a commodity moving in the same vessel operated by the same steamship company."

Mr. Romberg's staff must keep close tabs not only on rates, but also upon the changing regulations of myriad foreign countries relative to taxes, commodity restrictions, duties, port regulations and other matters. These watchdog operations, designed to maintain favorable costs while scrupulously following trade and other regulations, require an endless vigil.

The analysis section's staff, therefore, must be highly versatile. Fully familiar with the technical aspects of both domestic and international traffic, they must keep similarly acquainted with the worldwide vehicle-producing and marketing facilities of the Ford Motor Company. A firm grasp of economics and a clear understanding of international traffic's legal aspects, backed up by ample statistical know-how, creates a productive punch that spots latent problems early and makes possible medium-to-long-range forecasting that permits rational traffic planning despite international shipping's typical cost and service uncertainties.

Because Ford's international trade operations span the globe, virtually every transportation medium gets departmental attention. In addition to overseas concerns, the analysis section watches the domestic aspects of import-export movements. The department assumes responsibility for service on international shipments immediately upon departure from source points, so that choice of route and mode in reaching ports from U.S. sources, as well as port choice itself, has considerable bearing on systems development and evaluation.

A typical analysis section study involved movement of vehicles from various source plants to overseas locations through U.S. and Canadian ports to achieve least total cost for movements to Japan, including not only the best C.I.F. (cost, insurance and freight) costs, but the best mix of these elements with related tax and duty costs.

The study determined that Ford Galaxie automobiles sourced at Los Angeles and delivered to buyers at West Coast ports for movement to Japan via roll on/roll off service moved at a considerable savings per vehicle as compared to conventional sourcing at the Mahwah, N.J. plant for movement via East Coast ports, despite ostensibly favorable ocean freight rates from the latter location.

Negotiation as well as study resulted in a contract with a local cartage company that resulted in a substantial savings annually in the movement of parts and accessories from Ford's Delaware Valley Parts Depot at Pennsauken, N.J. to Philadelphia. Differing from the prior example in scale of study and cost impact, it illustrates the analysis section's broad range of activities. Typically, 15 to 20 such analyses are under way at any given time.

On a totally different front, a 1969 analysis section study compared export packaging costs at Detroit and vendor plants with the cost of New

EXPORT SHIPMENTS are discussed by (l. to r.): P. E. Romberg, supervisor-analysis section; A. S. Cincotta, supervisor-shipping section; N. E. Beatty, manager-traffic department; M. C. Colletti, manager-Newark Export Supply; J. B. Gannon, supervisor-documentation section, at the Newark, N.J. headquarters of Ford's Overseas Distribution Operations.

WHILE OPEN HOLD STOWAGE prevails for most vehicles, containerization grows in importance on many overseas routes. Johnson Line shipment is shown above.

CHECKING CAR TIE-DOWNS before sailing. Proper tie-down tension is essential so that vehicles do not shift, as well as so that parts will not be damaged by the tie-downs themselves, thus assuring damage-free deliveries.

York port area export packaging. In some cases, New York was found to have a decided cost advantage. Another alternative, however, beat out both choices in the cases where it is available—containerization.

As yet, the computer impacts the traffic department in only a peripheral fashion, essentially with respect to various accounting functions. An analysis section task force, however, working closely with computer personnel, is reviewing the entire document processing activity of the traffic department. Despite the complexities and diversity of paper work required to reach all the world's markets, early results suggest that computerized documentation may well prove feasible, reliable and lower in total cost.

The container captures research attention currently in another area— movement of completely knocked-down shipments. Some trial shipments already made show promise. There are problems unrelated to containers themselves, nonetheless, which must be surmounted before such operation becomes practical. Present export crates, on overseas arrival, are regularly stored out of doors. Storing in containers would be clearly inexpedient, whether from the standpoint of high demurrage charges or the effect of exposure on the stored units. Thus, such a modal shift would require warehousing where today there is none, plus changed handling equipment and techniques.

How a shipping section maintains worldwide delivery reliability

PHYSICAL MOVEMENT of Ford export-import shipments holds the shipping section's continuing attention. Ford's domestic traffic activities originate export shipment movements from inland plants, but the export traffic department's shipping section takes over responsibility as soon as freight clears a plant's outbound dock. From that point forward, the section expedites inland transportation, checks the condition of goods at port of exit, arranges beyond transportation and ascertains that proper precautions are taken in placing and protecting goods aboard vessels.

Through the section's port movement and control unit, close coordination to assure timely sailings of ocean freight is maintained. In addition to overseeing the combining of freight from inland sources and its handling through warehousing and cartage to final ship stowage, this unit inspects all vehicles shipped and, where repair work is found necessary, checks to make certain it is properly performed. It makes absolutely certain that all vehicles placed aboard ship are in perfect condition.

In ocean shipping, even more than in land movement, this unit finds it necessary to supervise "hot" cargo to make certain it is loaded aboard its scheduled steamer and properly stowed. Comments Shipping Supervisor Andy S. Cincotta, "Our port movement personnel work closely with pier and steamship management to make certain that special shipments receive priority handling and proper stowage." While it would be impossible to coordinate fully every ocean shipment, concentration on "hot" movements keeps the department record for making scheduled sailings quite high.

Because the closest quality control at the plant loses its value when damage occurs in transit, traffic personnel make a point of "on the scene" inspections, particularly in the loading and stowage of vehicles moving in conventional lift on/lift off vessel movement. Uncrated cars are highly vulnerable to damage if not properly chained down for ocean movement and if lifting operations are not performed with care. Not only body finish, but suspension parts and other elements may be readily damaged if not lifted properly or if improper lashdown permits movement when a vessel encounters rough seas.

The foregoing problems cause the traffic department to look with growing favor on the use of roll on/roll off vessels as well as container handling for vehicles that move intact. "We find the roll on/roll off ships superior in ease of loading, safety of handling and damage prevention," Mr. Cincotta claims, "with some steamship lines, practice of containerizing automobiles similarly effective in improving vehicle protection."

In the highly competitive automobile market, service gets considerable emphasis. The department's expediting, claims and airfreight unit sees to it that shipments get where they are needed on time and, when damage does occur, that claims get prompt handling.

Not only is the department concerned with keeping things moving on the inland portion of the haul, but it makes certain also that vessel space is available well before many shipments reach port. By the time a Mahwah, N.J., Metuchen, N.J., or Detroit plant shipment reaches Newark, the department's planning and paper work is well in order. On occasion, given such necessary data as motor numbers, the department will even book space for a car that the Mahwah plant, for example, has not yet assembled, knowing that rigid scheduling and controlled transportation will assure the vehicle's arrival dockside at loading time.

Actual vessel loading varies considerably in numbers of vehicles. From one to 200 vehicles may be found aboard in a given moment, while solid blocs of 400 units regularly move to Puerto Rico under department supervision.

Not only completed units, but partially knocked-down and completely knocked-down vehicles, flow through the overseas distribution operation channels. The shipping section's completely knocked-down unit handles the latter category, which consists of the total parts necessary to assemble complete vehicles in export pack, moving from the packing plant in

UPON ARRIVAL at Puerto Rico, cars may be loaded aboard trailers for road carriage or driven off on their own wheels.

Tillsonburg, Canada to assembly plants at numerous free world locations. Included in this group are complex operations involving three-nation assemblies for final shipment.

Approximately six weeks prior to the scheduled pack date, steamer space is booked and the overseas location is advised that completely knocked-down material by lot identification number will depart the U.S. on a specific sail date and arrive at overseas destination on a given date. The overseas assembly plant production schedules are based on this timing commitment being adhered to. When the material is packed at Tillsonburg, it is loaded in gondola rail cars to the port of Philadelphia to be loaded on a ship that was booked approximately six weeks ahead of the shipment date.

In the reverse direction, similar multinational production reflects in the import of motors from Ford's European operation to be incorporated in U.S.-produced Pinto automobiles, some of which, in turn, will move through export channels when the model is placed on sale.

While completely knocked-down vehicles feed assembly plants overseas, the partially knocked-down units move as they do for shipping economy. Truck shapes being what they are, the department learned that shipping two chassis in a pack, with the two cab units moved separately in another pack, resulted in substantial reduction of cubic shipment measurement. Since density is all important in determining ocean shipping costs, partially knocked-down shipping in these instances yields savings far exceeding the trade-off costs of packing and reassembly.

Airfreight shipments average some 20 per day. During a year, over one million pounds of parts, machines and accessories leave the country as air cargo. Thus far, these represent essentially emergency movements.

"We watch the changing air vs. ocean freight rate pattern closely, however," states Traffic Manager Beatty. "The gap is thinning between them, and the day may not be far distant when regularized air movement for higher value components will be standard routing."

To date, the ports of New York and Philadelphia handle the major share of Ford exports. A broadening span of locations participates in company traffic, nonetheless, with vehicles regularly moving through the Port of Miami and Port Everglades, Fla., while San Francisco handles not only vehicles in volume but parts and accessories as well. Philadelphia and New York also share heavily in the latter traffic. On the Canadian side of the border, completely knocked-down shipments move in volume through the ports of Montreal, St. John and Halifax.

Export-import paper work: A critical, complex responsibility

IN NO OTHER ASPECT does international shipping differ from domestic more than in its paper work. Individual foreign shipments vary widely in documentation requirements, both as to the forms necessary and the manner and timing of their processing. By the time the United States government, overseas carriers, foreign government consulates, collection institutions, foreign consignees and others concerned have their requirements fulfilled, some 18 separate documents may be required for a shipment to reach one of the hundred countries and their possessions that the Newark export supply staff serves.

In addition to a 1969 ocean freight bill approximating $12,500,000, the traffic department paid over $369,000 covering consul fees imposed by various overseas governments. Port and other costs unique to international shipping also represented substantial amounts, requiring close vigilance by the documentation section to avoid waste through error or inadequate communication.

While domestic company operations benefit from stipulated regulations and guidelines, export traffic's unique nature precludes guidance from established company procedures in reaching decisions and implementing systems affecting material shipments. Exceptions, special requests and rule changes issued by domestic and foreign governments are regular and frequent occurrences. All too often, sudden developments take place which are not under the Newark overseas distribution officer's control. Only personnel highly knowledgeable in foreign trade operations can react with the necessary speed and responsibility in these cases.

SOME 2,000 CONTAINERS of this type, shown at Ford Motor Co. Ltd. in London, speed parts movements as well as knocked-down cars between eight European cities.

Working closely with the shipping section, the documentation section itself encompasses two units: a bill of lading and consular invoice unit and a final documents unit.

The bill of lading and consular invoice unit prepares ocean bills of lading affecting more than 100 different U.S. and foreign flag steamship lines in accordance with letter of credit or financial commitment instructions. It also prepares export declarations and advance notification of shipment information for overseas locations to assure customs clearance and to inform certain affected dealers so that they may arrange foreign insurance coverage.

Consular documents are issued in the required languages of foreign countries, as well as certificates of origin and summary invoices, while the unit also executes consular invoices and import licenses required by recipient countries. Where special documentation is necessary for certain destinations, such papers as boycott certifications, port-of-call certifications, legalization of price lists for foreign government import controls and letters of correction are prepared.

In fulfilling these duties, the unit delivers and, where required, follows for legalization documents going to 43 foreign consulates in New York, New Jersey, Pennsylvania and California. Similar tasks concerning U.S. bodies involve the New York Commerce and Industry Association, chambers of commerce and county clerks of New York, New Jersey and Pennsylvania, the New Jersey Secretary of State and the U.S. Secretary of State. All of these steps are necessary to comply with credit instrument requirements, as well as the regulations of various countries.

The final documents unit works with the more directly traffic-oriented paper work, although here, too, the differences from typical domestic operation far outweigh the similarities. Speed as well as accuracy is important, because overseas Ford activities and other consignees need prompt documentation to clear their material through customs when vessels arrive, avoiding cost penalties or delayed deliveries and assuring prompt fund collections for Ford Motor Co. against covering credit instruments. A wide range of payment terms, including those of Ford Motor Credit Co., come into play because of the variety of overseas distribution operations' customers throughout the world.

Ocean freight charges are a principal concern, taking into account as well such factors as heavy lift charges, extra length charges, port charges, surcharges and others. The unit also applies and calculates worldwide insurance and war risk costs. It computes and prepares shipping expense costs. Other documents in its charge include collection documents, insurance certificates (or advices of insurance), special certification letters, collection drafts, transmittal letters, A.I.D. certificates and related documentary requirements. In the case of short shipments, it arranges redocumentation. It ascertains sufficient financial coverage of all shipments.

Not only is paper preparation important here, but paper flow as well because of lengthy distances and related scheduling factors. Timely mailing of foreign consignee documents to effect material clearance at destination is vital, for instance, as is also the processing of collection documents to financial institutions.

Where paper work delays or errors on domestic shipments more commonly create cost headaches by causing more work or by delaying transactions, the element of expensive penalties enters the scene on foreign shipments. "Strict adherence to U.S. and foreign government regulations must be maintained on all overseas movements," states Documentation Supervisor Joseph G. Gannon. "Failure to meet documentation and presentation standards can result in penalties imposed by U.S. customs, heavy fines from foreign governments, confiscation of material, shipside clearance delay and other penalties that mean severe financial loss both to the company and the foreign purchaser."

Backing the paper complex is a major liaison function that is essential to keeping documentation practices in line with changing conditions and regulations. In addition to close contact with the U.S. customs, foreign embassies and consuls general, changing world conditions make it necessary at times to confer with the U.S. State Department and U.S. Commerce Department, as well as foreign embassies, with regard to rules and regulations introduced by foreign countries that effect shipments and their documentation.

The financial aspect of export-import operations demands close daily contact with the management personnel of approximately 35 large collection institutions and associated companies. Operationally, there must be similarly constant contact with the various freight forwarders under contract, assuring performance of their services in accordance with Federal Maritime Commission regulations.

An International Distribution Powerhouse

Westinghouse Electric International Company, the overseas arm of Westinghouse, operates an independent logistics function somewhat parallel in nature to the previously described Ford unit. Like the Ford department a long-standing independent activity, it is also an expanding activity within the parent organization's total trade pattern.

With a department organized to assure specialist attention to individual trade areas, good overseas liaison is assured. In addition, it includes specialists prepared to cope with unusual handling problems necessitated by oversized, high value, frequently one-of-a kind products whose delivery to ultimate destinations may demand the literal invention of transport tools and techniques. Large pieces destined for atomic power plants, hydroelectric plants and comparably sized installations are included among these.

Presented to TRAFFIC MANAGEMENT readers in October, 1968, the Westinghouse Electric International Co. survey follows:

OVERSEAS CUSTOMERS can buy everything from a light bulb to a complete atomic power plant through the Westinghouse Electric International Company (WEICO). A virtual export funnel for its huge parent, 8,000 commodities are its normal stock, but an almost infinite custom variety of goods and services spews forth as well. These range up to and include the construction and installation of huge desalinization plants, power complexes and comparable major projects employing both vendor products and the parent company's own. Westinghouse overseas customers enjoy one-stop shopping on a large scale.

A highly specialized traffic department supports this international marketing arm of Westinghouse Electric Corp. "WEICO poses unusual traffic requirements," notes Traffic Manager Carl G. Moberg. "We've organized a seasoned, capable group of people, insuring that the right skills and knowledge continually service the situations needing them most."

What are some of these specialties that make this department a little bit different? Consider the following:

—Project Traffic. Major jobs such as complete plant installations flow through a group long experienced in moving huge yet delicate equipment to places where it has never gone before.

—Heavy air shipping. Over 10,000 shipments annually flow worldwide to customers demanding speed or to destinations where Westinghouse volume makes air economical.

—Area Export Control. Major trade areas are individually serviced by teams well versed in conditions unique to the countries of their assigned regions.

—Domestic Export Control. A domestic traffic group conversant with the special problems of brokers, agents and others who assemble such shipments for beyond movements controls shipments turned over to receivers in the United States but destined overseas.

The function of WEICO's project traffic unit is best illustrated by a recent example. Spain's first nuclear power plant, largely a WEICO venture, commenced operation in July. The project traffic staff, however, started solving related traffic problems in 1962. Key elements were three mammoth units manufactured in the United States, including a reactor, an electric generator and, largest of all, a steam generator. These and other material had to be moved from many sources to the Zorita plant site.

Advance planning reviewed several alternatives for final delivery. The only ship in the world capable of unloading such heavy pieces onto a dock was considered as an alternative to a large floating crane, built for salvage operations, in conjunction with a conventional vessel. Ultimately, the latter mode was chosen. Once ashore, greater problems were faced. Transportes Modernos SA of Spain built a special trailer with 56 articulated wheels to effect final delivery, but bridges, culverts and drains required reinforcement for a highway delivery. Innumerable power lines would have to be cut and many existing curves widened. Five provinces with individual traffic codes and many governing bodies with whom arrangements would have to be made complicated things further. At best, highway movement meant speeds of less than three kilometers per hour restricted to daylight hours.

By contrast, developing a second specialized vehicle for rail haulage over the major inland trip portion appeared more economical. A pair of special 10-axle units, each of which would fasten to an end of a major unit such as the steam generator, making it in effect a vehicle frame member, provided the

The **Yugoslavian crane** "Veli Jose" shifts the steam generator from the transporting vessel to the dock at Cartagena.

The **railway-highway transition** at Taracon required three days' work. The Transportes Modernos SA crew is shown making ready for final placement and connection of the reactor vessel on the highway equipment, which was specially built for these tasks.

answer. This held down shipment height substantially. Coupling provisions between shipment and vehicle components, moreover, permitted sideways motion of 30 centimeters as well as up-and-down movement of 24 centimeters. This flexibility paid off in passing countless trackside obstacles, tunnel walls, etc.

Too much was at stake to move solely on theory. Before the car was ordered, a mock-up was prepared employing standard equipment. Run over the rail line from the port of Cartagena to the highway transfer point at Taracon, it proved that the shipments could clear safely, assuming correct manipulation of the horizontal and vertical displacement devices. Tolerances were critical at several points, but it could be done.

In addition to building the special car, the inland haul required other physical arrangements. A special unloading siding was installed at Taracon plus equipment to facilitate transfer between road and rail carriers. The highway from Taracon to Zorita was straightened and widened, its surface contours being concurrently reshaped to withstand the unusual stresses anticipated.

As "D-Day" approached, it became apparent that unloading would have to be by crane as the heavy-lift vessel initially considered could not be chartered at the needed time. A floating, sheer leg derrick, brought by sea from Yugoslavia, was leased for a period coinciding with scheduled arrivals of the three major components. This unit not only could unload the vessel, but would also hold each piece in position for hookup to the rail car, eliminating costly extra rigging and materially speeding the operation.

Came June 19, 1966 and planning shifted to action. "The reactor vessel and I left Chattanooga together on a barge bound for New Orleans," Supervisor, Project Traffic Leslie J. Leigh noted. "We pressurized the unit with nitrogen, preventing entry of moisture laden air. Happily, the run was smooth. Just an occasional added shot of nitrogen was the only en route service necessary. The reactor vessel went aboard the *S.S. Steel Scientist* at New Orleans and sailed for Cartagena on July 15."

While this operation progressed, the sheer leg derrick was towed across the Mediterranean with a 50-man crew. On August 11, she unloaded the reactor and a careful three-day rail run brought it to Taracon. Three more days saw the huge cargo shifted to the special highway equipment, but the tow assembly, hauled by four tractors, completed the Zorita site run in a day and a half.

Rail Unit Converted And Returned As Highway Movement Begins

While the highway movement was under way, the rail unit was compressed to normal dimensions and returned to Cartagena. Its successful first delivery simplified the next and most critical operation—delivering the heat exchanger, which arrived on the *S.S. Oceanjet* at Cartagena August 25 along with the electric generator. The heat exchanger moved inland with no difficulty, while the

Rolling through Spain, the rail equip-

generator remained at the dock until the special rail equipment returned from the heat exchanger delivery. The generator then moved off smoothly, with this final special run performing yet another foresighted role: Feeler mechanisms were installed on this shipment, simulating the dimensions of still larger units that will ultimately follow the

The Last Leg. On the high road to the

ment, fastened directly to opposite ends of the heat exchanger, creates one huge, 20 axle unit.

same route when a second Zorita nuclear power plant is built. This proposed plant will couple to the existing operation, providing three times the initial plant's power capacity.

"Project Traffic doesn't pick up assignments of this magnitude every day," comments Traffic Manager Moberg, "but their number amply justifies a staff group devoted

exclusively to detailing and executing the complicated logistic programs they require. When every shipment is unique, dependence upon disinterested outsiders to foresee problems and handle scheduling would be a costly mistake."

Air freight moves a growing international volume for Westinghouse. "We handled 3,-

Zorita plant site, four road tractors carefully ease the steam generator toward its destination.

000 air shipments in 1957. This figure will break over 10,000 for 1968," comments Raymond G. Dawson, supervisor, distribution and warehousing. "About 15% of our freight payments are for air shipments." Heavy appliance movement takes place from Miami, with air shipments throughout the Caribbean area. Virtually all "advanced technology" items and other small, valuable materials move in significant volumes to many countries. In addition, a considerable number of air charter flights handle nuclear fuel each year.

The major part of the international air movement is through New York, both forwarders and direct carriers sharing in the traffic. Air Traffic Coordinator Irwin Schubert chooses the mode for individual shipments. Located in rented space at a large forwarding company facility adjacent to JFK International Airport, he makes on-the-spot decisions as to whether any shipments should enter specific consolidations the forwarder may have available on a given date. As circumstances dictate, he routes either forwarder or direct airline to achieve maximum advantage for WEICO and its customers.

Assistance From Forwarder's Staff Members, Internal Air Traffic Group

Mr. Schubert has two members of the forwarder's staff working with him full time, while internal support comes from an air traffic group under his control at WEICO headquarters. The latter staff provides liaison with sales and other company groups and customers as well as handling necessary paper work to back up the activities at JFK. The close control that this setup provides keeps costs in line without sacrificing the inherent speed advantages of air cargo.

Sea shipments at present move through virtually all major U.S. ports. Public warehousing, because of its flexibility, handles back-up stocks as well as providing for shipment assemblies of non-stock or custom items delivered from Westinghouse sources. Warehouse Coordinator Vincent S. Leshine keeps close watch on these operations, making certain that Westinghouse standards and procedures apply at all of these locations.

The huge and varied volume handled by WEICO means more than average problems in serving widely differing overseas markets.

While much of the routine export documentation goes through international forwarders at the affected ports, a great deal of planning and paperwork remains to be done by company personnel. "Our staff must know not only our products, but the regulations, requirements, transportation facilities and climatic conditions of every free-world country as well," states Supervisor, Export Traffic Stanley Lopienski. "By processing specific areas through assigned groups, better handling is assured because specialist rather than generalist knowledge governs our actions and decisions." European shipments flow through a three-man sub-section, and a two-man unit handles exclusively African traffic. Middle and Far Eastern shipments require a three-man unit. A team of three also controls most South American traffic

Giant heat exchanger unit travels through Spain on special rail cars equipped with side devices which permit side-to-side and up-and-down adjustments, simplifying passage through tight trackside clearances. In this scene, clearance adjustment devices on the rail vehicle prove their worth as the train inches its way through one of serveral narrow cuts and tunnels along the way.

and a separate, two-man unit covers the Central American-Caribbean area. One man from the South American group divides his time as needed with the Central American-Caribbean group. Shipments to territories not indicated in basic assignments are made on the basis of geographic rationale.

Domestic Traffic Section Maintained For Customers Doing Own Forwarding

Why does a clearly export-oriented department maintain a domestic traffic section? Although all WEICO traffic ultimately moves overseas, much of it is, in fact, sold to on-shore customers who arrange for their own forwarding to ultimate foreign destina-

tions. "In these instances," notes Supervisor, Domestic Traffic Thomas F. Driscoll, "our traffic and distribution service is essentially and typically domestic in nature." The department also handles shipments to Canada and Mexico which, while actually export in point of fact, have many characteristics typical of domestic shipments in routing and handling.

The domestic traffic unit works very closely with distribution and warehousing. In the area of warehousing, for instance, while operation is essentially under the latter group's control, packaging standards for warehouses are suggested by the domestic traffic unit. "Tom Driscoll and I work so close we can anticipate the tempo of each

Discussing staff activities in office of Traffic Manager Carl Moberg (far right) are, from left, Stanley Lopienski, supervisor, export traffic; L. J. Leigh, supervisor, project traffic and Thomas Driscoll, supervisor, domestic traffic.

other's breathing," comments Supervisor, Distribution and Warehousing Dawson.

As with most major export shippers, Westinghouse moves increasing quantities of material in containers. "Containerization is not an unmixed blessing, however," observes Traffic Manager Moberg. "The expansion of container service is so rapid that in many trades it is drying up available open-hold tonnage. The result is an increasing service problem in moving large and heavy materials that do not lend themselves to container movement."

Old-Timer In Export-Import Field Dates Back To 1916

While many other companies are only now starting to give their international trade

Reviewing activities at J. F. Kennedy Airport, are, left to right, Irwin Schubert, air traffic coordinator, Westinghouse; R. O. Bell, TWA's manager-domestic cargo terminal services, at JFK; M. N. Lovio, general manager-air export, Penson Forwarding Co.

potential the attention it merits, WEICO is already an old timer in this particular area. Functioning exclusively in the export-import field since 1916, its traffic department is seasoned by long experience, handling huge volumes under the most diversified of circumstances. In a market where growing competition from both domestic and foreign producers is a fact of business life, the cost-and-service benefits such a department affords its employer provide a significant competitive edge in an area where it counts.

Physical Distribution: Exporting the New Look

Another major firm with large and expanding overseas activities is the Cabot Corporation. A major manufacturer of carbon black, the company has steadily expanded its overseas production and markets in recent years.

Because of added volume moving between the United States and Europe, Cabot's distribution management sought means of systematizing the flow using techniques similar to those that have aided stateside shipping efficiency in recent years. Establishing a distribution center at Rotterdam in the Netherlands, serviced by large shipments on frequent schedules, it was believed that improved customer service and more efficient inventory control would be made possible.

Just how effective the company found the new arrangements was the subject of a TRAFFIC MANAGEMENT review in October, 1971, as reported on the following pages:

CABOT CORPORATION's overseas business is expanding steadily. Servicing European and other markets from regional plants, it nonetheless exports considerable volumes of specialized carbon blacks and other products from United States sources.

In recent years, orthodox export market service methods have proven increasingly unsatisfactory in maintaining customer service levels, however. Accordingly, the corporate distribution department, working closely with Cabot Europa and other European subsidiaries, has developed an overseas distribution concept that reduces order cycle times from the 10 to 12-week range down to typically seven days.

"What we did was move the order fulfillment source on U.S.-produced products up to the European shore," states Corporate Distribution Director Charles Sell. "In the process, we not only achieved our initial objective, but tied in other subsystems for additional European customer service benefits as well." Among the elements building Cabot's new look in European distribution are these:

Continental distribution center: Situated at Rotterdam, this facility brings to export distribution the same benefits that comparable regional, semiautonomous order-inventory processing centers provide in domestic distribution.

Superconsolidation programs:

Again borrowing a leaf from proven domestic methods, large shipments moving on schedule into distribution center stock enjoy speed and reliability unavailable to long-haul small shipments going directly from U.S. plants to European customers.

Coordinated European truck deliveries: Necessary routing changes incident to the distribution center program led to betterment of inland shipping arrangements for European production, as well as materials exported from the United States.

Corporate overseas distribution performance audit: Regular quarterly meetings between Corporate Distribution Director Sell and members of Cabot overseas management units

A GANTRY CRANE at Cabot N.V.'s modern Rotterdam pier-warehouse keeps costs down in the handling of containers and unitized loads, which are the company's standard shipping methods for both inbound and outbound freight.

CHARLES L. SELL (center), director of physical distribution, reviews charter vessel schedule with Manager-Distribution Logistics Robert W. McClelland (left) and Manager-International Transportation Donald F. McDonald.

AT THE ROTTERDAM OFFICE of Cabot N.V., Assistant Manager Bernard de Neef (left), Inventory Control Supervisor Jan van't Veer (center) and Manager Henry Glerum discuss adjustments proposed in present inventory levels.

HENRY GLERUM (left), Cabot N.V. manager, meets with European Distribution Manager Derek Ryan on one of the latter's regular visits to Rotterdam.

aid the continuing development of both intra-European and interregional physical distribution programs.

The new distribution center went into Rotterdam for a number of reasons. A particularly significant factor was the wealth of recognized expertise in the Netherlands in European physical distribution. Important, too, was Rotterdam's status as both a seaport and an inland transportation hub. Finally, the availability of both physical facilities and port services well suited to the job at hand made this location particularly advantageous. Hamburg, Bremen and Antwerp were also considered, but the total mix of assets clearly weighed in Rotterdam's favor.

Distribution Manager Henry Glerum and his staff of four constitute the working force of a Netherlands subsidiary, Cabot NV, which operates the Rotterdam distribution centers. Orders formerly flowing through from customers via Cabot's Boston headquarters to U.S. plants now get a quick turnaround by this group. Incoming orders must still be approved at Boston headquarters, which is now done by direct wire. Following Boston's clearance, remaining paper work, as well as order fulfillment, takes place at Rotterdam. All but the most distant continental points may regularly anticipate fulfillment of orders within seven days of placement.

More than a time advantage is gained through the reoriented procedures. Under the old arrangements, paper moving by mail could readily get out of phase with actual shipping schedules, in some cases actually reaching the customer more slowly than the order itself, with resultant time losses and confusion at ports and occasional penalty charges as well.

The new system, in effect, puts the ocean leg behind the warehouse. Instead of filling orders directly, with every shipment therefore having direct marketing performance requirements placed upon it, the company now ships only to replenish individual commodity stocks, with reasonable safety margins assuring no customer service problems in the event of delayed shipment.

Opened initially in 1970, the 63,-000-square foot warehouse and adjacent office are on a pier in the Lek-haven district of downtown Rotterdam. Leased from the William H. Muller Co., Cabot also employs the landlord firm to perform stevedoring and other labor functions as required.

Stock for the center off-loads from vessels directly onto the pier, then moves to storage using forklift trucks and other modern procedures for material handling. At the start, there were 76 varieties of carbon black stocked plus various other Cabot products. Continuing changes in the line reflect in Rotterdam inventories as well, which have been refined to a total of approximately 50 product lines at the present.

The Cabot NV staff handles more paper than order processing alone. Documentation, invoicing, shipping arrangements and the securing of transportation equipment for inland movement are included among their activities. Their ready availability to answer queries by telephone and to work closely with continental customers on specific problems or special requirements add to the values the center creates for Cabot in maintaining a competitive customer service edge.

Chartered Vessels

The Rotterdam facility now receives its carbon black supplies via charter vessel from Galveston, Tex. It also receives shipments of Cab-O-Sil, a very finely divided silica the company manufactures, but this material comes into the Rotterdam stock from Boston via containers moving in conventional shipping. In the past, Cab-O-Sil, like carbon black, moved directly from U.S. source to customer, but the new distribution center arrangement means both faster customer order response and more effective use of containers than was previously the case.

In the fall of 1969, Corporate Distribution Director Sell and Manager International Transportation Donald McDonald entered into discussions with knowledgeable people in the ship-chartering field to determine the feasibility of handling carbon black under a charter arrangement.

Detailed studies ensued and an initial operation under charter com-

OFF-LOADING charter vessel cargo on its scheduled arrival from the United States. Unit loads and containers make handling fast and efficient.

OUTBOUND CONTAINERS and unit loads move via barge to many inland European river ports, taking full advantage of Rotterdam's strategic location.

THE "TIR" PLATE on the tractor's front indicates a properly sealed load that may move freely across many European borders without halting for customs.

menced, initially running a full ship every second month between the port of Galveston and Rotterdam. These vessels handled seven million to eight million pounds per voyage. After initial testing, it was decided to run smaller tonnages more frequently. The Galveston-Rotterdam operation now consists of smaller shipments per vessel running on a monthly schedule operated by the Swedish-American-Wilhelm line.

Cabot's charter arrangement gets rid of a wide variety of headaches, particularly in its close coordination with the distribution center operation. Under former procedures, plants in Louisiana would export through New Orleans, and the Texas plants would feed their export orders through Houston. Small lots required consolidation of perhaps eight shipping units to build a truckload, with the further complication of multiple pier deliveries.

There were problems with occasional vessels that would leave ahead of time, or other instances where, for one reason or another, orders would be shut out at the piers and piled up at the docks for costly delays. Distance factors coupled with inadequate communication added to the problems frequently encountered.

Cabot employs a space charter set up on an F.I.O. basis in this operation, and is responsible for the stevedoring at both ends of the vessel movement. With its regularly scheduled movements and its on-the-pier distribution center at the Rotterdam end of the voyage, this works out well. "The important consideration is the schedule regularity," asserts Mr. Sell. "With this assurance, we can maintain a lower stock level than would ever be possible employing conventional vessel services. Without this 'custom' transportation, the Rotterdam distribution center would be impossible to justify."

In the course of studies leading to and following development of the Rotterdam distribution center and the ship charter "superconsolidation" operation, the corporate distribution department, as well as the European units of Cabot, had an opportunity to examine regional distribution as a total unit. With separate plants and managements in several countries, individual distribution

A LUMIPRINT COPYING MACHINE is employed by Cabot N.V. Secretary Riek van Leeuwen to produce file copies of shipment documentation.

networks developed through the years.

What came to light, among other things, was the fact that individual divisions were supplying other divisions with specialized products by truck without the benefit of planned backhauls, which can be an important factor under the more flexible manner of rate negotiation common to Europe. Clearly, this represented an opportunity to develop arrangements more advantageous to the carriers in terms of their costs and to Cabot in terms of service improvements, as well as cost factors.

Conditions such as this led to the establishment of a new approach to continental distribution. Cabot Europa now employs a European traffic manager, stationed in Paris, who works with the various continental facilities to optimize goods flow while seeking to better customer service. European Traffic Manager Steve Thomas has inaugurated this activity following his service in charge of this function at Stanlow, England, Cabot's largest European area plant. Reporting on a line basis to Derek Ryan in Cabot Europa, Mr. Thomas maintains a close, continuous liaison with Mr. Sell and his associates in the corporate distribution department at Cabot's Boston headquarters.

In fostering this activity, the corporate department's role is basically a combination of auditor and adviser. Mr. Sell or Mr. McDonald, sometimes both, meet at regular, three-

month intervals with Mr. Thomas and other distribution personnel, shifting the scheduled locations among European cities to ease and to multiply on-the-site contacts. Present performance and specific problems receive attention on these occasions, but forward planning is of primary importance at this relatively early stage of development.

In Mr. Sell's opinion, the meetings in themselves, as well as the total distribution systems approach, are doing a great deal to develop a unified viewpoint on Cabot management questions. Each of the European plants is increasingly aware that what their distribution units do independently or in tandem have important effects on the total corporate distribution picture.

As for the corporate distribution department, Mr. Sell and his associates feel that their recent experience has taught them one signal point above all others in their international operations: the crucial importance of direct personal communication. "There is no substitute for it," Mr. Sell claims. "Virtually all of our European management people speak English, but the same words mean different things to different people, even within the United States.

"When you find people having to translate into seven different languages, the potential variants in shades of meaning become astronomical. Letters aren't the answer; we found that out early. Telephone calls don't help that much either.

"There is a subjective aspect to understanding one another, and it only surfaces when you are physically together, able to sense a mood or read a gesture. We tell each other things in several different ways until we can see the light dawning in each other's eyes, and then we "spell it back" between ourselves to be certain of it.

"Oddly enough, once a good personal rapport develops, there seems to be something in individual communication that leaps the language barriers. The best advice we can give to others setting up overseas distribution is that they get together early and often with their management in the countries they serve. Both sides profit immeasurably from the clearer understandings this develops."

Toyomenka Trades up to
Total Distribution

Toyomenka Trading Co., recently renamed Toyomenka(America), Inc., is the United States arm of the Toyomenka Co. of Osaka, Japan. Its most visible purpose is the movement of Japanese goods into the United States, but company operations are considerably more complex than that. Part of a world-wide trading network, its export-import operations may involve the movement of goods and/or purchase money between two, three and more countries in activities adding dimensions to distribution economics that call for the utmost finesse in cost control. Effective communication with customers and between company units is absolutely essential as is scrupulous, timely handling of paperwork and movement of proffered goods.

TRAFFIC MANAGEMENT examined Toyomenka's U.S. operations in October, 1967 in the following study:

TOYOMENKA, INC. HAS no distribution department. Why not? "For the same reason that Campbell's has no soup department," states President Toshio Takeuchi. "Toyomenka is synonymous with distribution. It is our principal service and the core of our expanding trade."

Strong winds of change are blowing at Toyomenka. Both the U. S. company and its parent, Toyo Menka Kaisha of Japan, seek to become more than "go-betweens" relating Japan to other countries. Such a

role lacks the broad scope sought by an internationally-minded management. Accordingly, traditional Japanese business methods are being augmented or revised to meet this challenge. These changes are comparable to those taking place similarly in large U. S. organizations today:

—Decentralizing management of national or regional units as "profit centers." A U.S.-incorporated subsidiary provides U.S. services.

—Centralizing traffic and related functions

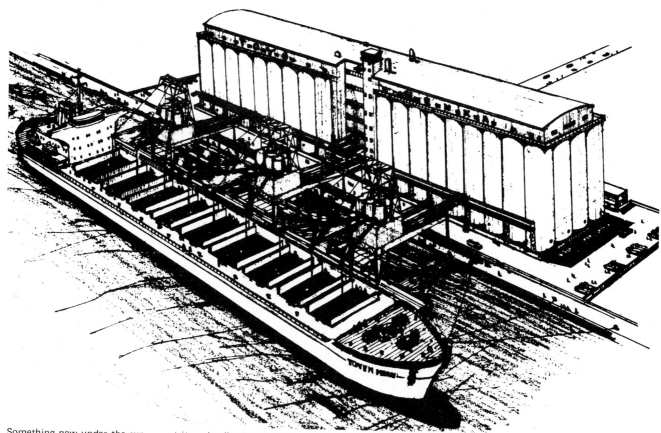

Something new under the sun . . . at its unloading berth outboard of Japan's newest and largest grain elevator is the soon-to-sail Tomen Maru, 46,000-ton grain carrier specially designed to service this automated facility with grain from United States Gulf ports. The elevator is property of Toyo Menka Kaisha.

to maximize shipment sizes, upgrade customer service and gain rate advantages. Improvements under way were impractical or overlooked under divided operation.

—Vesting managerial responsibility in local personnel. Home office people serving short terms "in the field" rotated too frequently to adapt to regional business methods.

—Working with carriers and customers to develop distribution systems custom-tailored to specific commodity movements. Greater emphasis on service to long-term, high-volume, repeat customers is leading to new cost reduction ideas.

—Modernizing communication and data-processing systems. Early computer installation is expected.

Greater authority is vested in Toyomenka's U. S. management than has been characteristic of resident Japanese trading company operations. As the organization chart indicates, management control is exercised by President Takeuchi and his staff, who operate U.S. activities from their New York office. While responsible to the Japanese parent company, policy is largely of local origin, speeding the decision process for dealing with U.S. clients and customers.

The staff group, whom Mr. Takeuchi dedescribes as "finders, minders and drivers." have developed a gross sales volume currently running at $275 million annually. Of this sum, from 10% to 20% derives from a growing "third country" business between the U.S. and nations other than Japan. The reminder splits roughly between U.S. imports from Japan and exports to Japan from the U.S.

Imports run 80% in finished goods. The remainder consists of such semi-finished items as electronic components and sewing machine heads. Exports are 90% raw materials, with consumer goods constituting most of the other 10%.

The company's U.S. growth was swift. Operations as a full-scale trader commenced 15 years ago with a starting capital of only $10,000 and a New York office. Today's company is a high-volume, financially potent organization with regional offices in ten cities.

The new traffic and billing department typifies changes under way. Formerly, each specialized trading section performed its

President Toshio Takeuchi

own distribution functions or was represented by a separate delivery department unit handling this service or commodity in complete isolation. The present approach centralizes these activities, eliminating much duplication and confusion in shipment scheduling and handling.

Traffic Manager Thomas J. Howard, whose prior experience combined domestic and import traffic activity, represents the total operation in making carrier arrangements, seeking needed services and negotiating rates. In turn, carriers and others find it easier and cheaper to handle Toyomenka's varied traffic through contact with a single, fully responsible department.

What is this department's policy in seeking traffic efficiency? Several areas are checked continuously. Carrier routing and selection, warehousing, rates (general and commodity) and port selection are prominent among these.

Because much traffic moves through the Port of New York, a Toyomenka routing guide now covers domestic freight between New York and inland points. Shipments vary widely, ranging from 100 pounds to a high of about 300,000. Commodities cover a broad spectrum. Chemicals, heavy and light machinery, metals and minerals figure prominently among them. Important, too, are radios, sewing machines, toys, cameras, optical goods, textiles, jute and canned foods. Such bulk commodities as coal, ore and grain contribute heavy tonnage. Toyo-

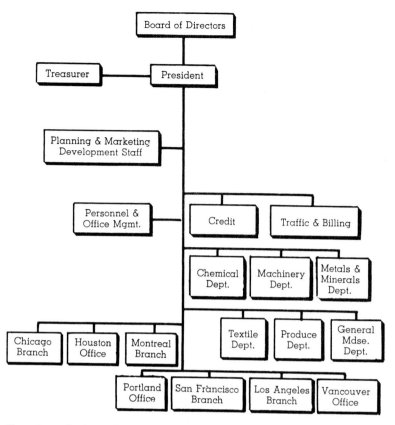

Chart shows distribution's functional role in the overall organization of Toyomenka.

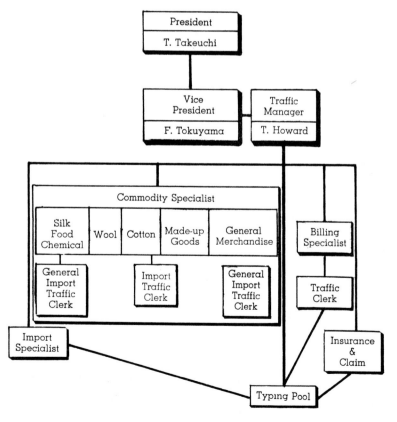

Centralized distribution department specialists fulfill unique requirements.

menka's carriers can anticipate considerable diversity in their freight.

Recognizing the cost and service values of fewer carriers handling maximum tonnage, the guide breaks service points by states and individual metropolitan areas, generally suggesting two alternative surface carriers to or from these points. Where possible, carriers selected serve numerous points within a specified region, maximizing consolidation possibilities. This proves particularly advantageous in pier pick-ups, where a carrier knows that it will load 3,000 to 4,000 pounds at a time instead of tying up equipment separately for myriad small shipments. Late pier pick-ups are becoming a thing of the past, therefore.

The many commodities suggest a diversity of carriers, which is indeed the case. Rail, truck and piggyback are used extensively. Both surface and air forwarders are employed. Air freight is a growing factor, while at the other end of the spectrum, barge lines move substantial bulk shipments for the company

What about U.S. ports other than New York? The Chicago cover photo of the Gloria Maru speaks graphically of heavy shipments that never see New York. Ports on the Lakes, the Gulf and the West Coast share Toyomenka's tonnage increasingly. Determination is based on comparative transit times, relative port congestion, feasibility of inland distribution and rates.

OCP (Overland Common Point) rates from Japan via West Coast ports for goods bound inland are attracting shipments. Many Toyomenka products enjoy rates 10% to 18% below prevailing ocean levels on shipments destined to specified points west of the Mississippi River. This is one of several categories in which the traffic and billing department seeks further commodity rate development and refinement.

Premium transportation is used readily where the gain is worth the price. Sea-air movement is growing. Some shipments which move Japan-New York in 30 days via ocean are now diverted to West Coast ports, taking 8-12 days for the voyage, proceeding via Flying Tiger Line to the East for normal total transit times of 10 to 14 days. Freight costs are somewhat higher, but the trade-off against interest savings through faster capital investment turnover is an important potential offset. "There are cases where air vs. truck rate contrast is $10.65 versus $9.64 per 100 pounds," states Traffic Manager Howard. "This is a relatively small differential. It is being watched closely." Some high value merchandise also moves Japan-U.S. via United Air Consolidators or Tokyo Air Consolidators as well as standard air freight.

Local warehousing and trucking practices have changed drastically. Both were formerly on a piece basis. Cartage is handled currently on tariff rates set per hundred pounds, to both carrier and Toyomenka advantage. Warehousing tariffs are now based on cubic feet or 100 pound rates. These steps have greatly assisted development of uniform cost and accounting procedures.

Inventory control uses a card system broken to lot number, pieces, in and out control data and current dollar inventory. Traffic and billing personnel have individual commodity assignments and are keenly aware that transit costs alone may determine the loss or profit in this high-volume, low-margin company's sales.

Marriage of billing activities to the traffic function is in keeping with growing trends in American distribution departments. It is particularly logical for this company as virtually every bill results from a shipment and related traffic activity. Here, too, functional consolidation makes feasible the use of modern, high-volume Burroughs billing equipment.

Directly related to the consolidation function, a growing proportion of trans-ocean freight is containerized, speeding shipments, minimizing handlings, reducing losses and damage to goods in transit. Test operations started earlier this year are now becoming routine. Greater container acitivity will commence as more equipment and wider service diversity become available.

How did the new look come to Toyomenka's transportation-distribution activities? Early in 1966, President Takeuchi became concerned with a traditional management structure's inability to cope with growth. One of his particular interests was customer service improvement in order processing and delivery. He reasoned that a modern, centralized department, pooling work from many units, could effectively employ specialized equipment and personnel. The decision made, a new traffic and billing department became operative in the fall of 1966.

Such changes require strong top-management support. Fortunately, Traffic Manager Howard reports to Vice President Fred M. Tokuyama, a University of Chicago alumnus who did graduate work in transportation-distribution and is an ICC Practitioner. Through his efforts, transition to modern methods has been smooth and swift.

World traffic patterns of both U.S. Toyomenka and the Japanese parent company benefit markedly from a single U.S. traffic control. Toyo Menka Kaisha's centralized traffic department in Tokyo, under Manager Ichiro Oyamada, maintains a continuing liaison with Mr. Howard to ensure maximum utilization of charter vessels and proper fulfillment of contractual obligations where two or more separate affiliates are tied in complex trades. The Tokyo department's responsibilities are largely concerned with trans-ocean movements, including control of charter vessels, rate and service negotiations with shipping lines, arrangements for specialized or major volume movements, return load development to avoid lengthy movement of vessels in ballast, and staff support to all units in planning and developing multilateral trades.

The parent company, Toyo Menka Kaisha, has prospered for many years as a Japanese international trading operation, but its role broadens steadily. While not yet a major manufacturer in its own right, it is increasingly willing to invest in facilities as well as inventory for delivery and sale. Where ownership and operation of functions will open new markets or make existing ones more competitive, Toyo Menka Kaisha participates with sellers, servicers and buyers alike to create effective distribution systems.

Typical of this approach is Toyo Menka Kaisha's huge new grain handling complex at Kobe, Japan. The country's largest grain elevator, it is Japan's first private automated distribution project. Principal products stored will include soybeans and corn. Five grain-processing plants are adjacent to the elevator, directly served by conveyor lines. With storage capacity exceeding 67,000 tons, it can handle vessels up to 55,000 tons dead weight by pneumatic suction type unloading equipment, designed to serve lighters for harbor and coastwise transfer as

Toyomenka's first container ship, the Montana Maru, is shown being loaded at Yokahama for voyage to the U.S.

well. Channel limitations, however, will not permit vessels much in excess of 45,000 tons to use the facility at present.

A new vessel, the 46,000-ton Tomen Maru, is now under construction, designed specifically to feed the elevator with grain from U.S. Gulf ports. To be operated by "K" Line, she will make five voyages a year at rates substantially below those prevailing on smaller vessels in this trade. Previous experience with increased ship capacities indicates just how substantial this reduction can be: grain carried in 36,000-ton vessels enjoys savings approximating $2 per ton versus costs when moved in 18,000-ton ships.

In effect, the elevator, its related plants and the Tomen Maru are an integral, total distribution system, each a component geared to yield maximum advantage in conjunction with the related units. The Tomen Maru, for example, could be used in other services, but its carefully tailored size and equipment will yield their greatest cost benefits in this specific operation. She will be supplemented by standard high-tonnage vessels to stock the elevator, but another similar vessel may be constructed in the near

future to attain optimum utilization of the large elevator's capacity. Even bigger vessels are contemplated if channel conditions are further improved at the port of Kobe.

Brazil offers a good example of Toyo Menka Kaisha's growing external diversification as well as cooperative effort among its units. The parent company, Japan's largest cotton importer, regularly purchases large amounts of the Brazilian product. Cotton activity has also been extended to include a cottonseed oil plant producing for local consumption, plus the manufacture of cotton yarns. Concurrently, U.S. Toyomenka ships insecticides to Brazil, while importing Brazilian yarns. In the future, the U.S. company intends to build an insecticide plant of its own in Brazil, to be supplied with chemicals from the U.S. As the insecticides are used by cotton growers, these separate activities of U.S. Toyomenka and Toyo Menka Kaisha are complementary.

Like other worldwide companies, Toyo Menka Kaisha faces problems of absentee ownership. Control was formerly highly centralized. Policy was a home-office responsibility and field managers were Japanese

Seamen secure containers in the hold of the Montana Maru.

nationals who worked brief periods in foreign locations and were then rotated to headquarters. Today, many managers are citizens of the countries where they are employed, enjoying substantially more responsibility than was once typical of trading company operations. Several benefits accrue from this change:

—Improved morale for both field and home office managers. Home office personnel are not uprooted and thrust into strange environments for extended periods with resultant disruptions of family life and cultural ties. Local managers can do a better job because they are in their home environment, staying in positions long enough to develop their skills fully and enjoying a greater assurance of promotion because headquarters personnel are not being continually thrust above them.

—Improved customer relations. The local Toyomenka men, in addition to having ample familiarity with regional business customs and conditions, offer the further benefit of continuity in positions over longer periods. Previously, dealings with a manager over periods beyond six months or a year almost assuredly meant changes

At Portland Ore. docks, the Toyo Maru, only three weeks old and on its maiden voyage, loaded 4,500,000 board feet of lumber and logs aboard for the return trip.

Discussing distribution plans at Toyomenka's New York offices are (from left) Vice President Fred M. Tokuyama, President Toshio Takeuchi and Traffic Manager Thomas J. Howard.

in the specific individuals assigned, with resultant inefficiencies because new people had to learn specific customer problems. By having managers "on post" for longer periods, more satisfactory personal relations with customers are now assured.
—More efficient liaison activities. Greater field responsibility reduces need for home office communication, cutting costs and reducing the work load of home-office executives. Conversely, greater responsibility poses a challenge to local management to reach goals exceeding prior attainments and to maintain a high competitive standing in relation to attainments of other local sectors of Toyomenka.

The company's worldwide commitments make communications of more than usual significance to operations. Leased teletype lines serve Japan-London, Japan-New York and New York-London. All other offices outside Japan feed either New York or London via Telex. Normal data flow is London-New York-Japan for inbound information and Japan-London-New York for communications from the world headquarters offices. In this way, both London and New York are able to see at least one side of all such activity, alerting them to changing circumstances.

Related to the communications operation is the expansion of electronic data-processing facilities at the Osaka headquarters. Replacement of the present computer opera-

tion with an IBM 360 installation is a first step toward marrying the worldwide information system to computerization. U.S. Toyomenka already employs some EDP through external service bureaus in New York. Here, too, a 360 installation is comtemplated. "When the two computers start talking to each other, communication and paper flow will be greatly simplified," states Vice President Tokuyama. "In addition, it is anticipated that faster, more comprehensive market analysis will result, further aiding the company's continuing growth."

Like many other traders, Toyomenka's U.S. role was once merely that of gateway to a foreign market. Relatively uncomplicated buying and selling operations on U.S. shores were but a frontier of the large marketing and distribution entity in Japan. Today it is more complex. A U.S. company grossing close to $300 million annually, with offices and services nationwide, is no simple buying and selling operation. Organized along U.S. lines to take advantage of the newest distribution techniques, it is enriching the field with precepts of its own. The Japanese concept of trading companies as specialized marketing-distribution organizations fits in well with the evolving electronic communication and data processing techniques now revolutionizing American business practices. U.S. Toyomenka trades in more than commodities and money—it trades in ideas.

Total Logistics Control Aids
Precision Equipment Exporter

Gerber Scientific Instruments Co. is a young firm producing highly specialized automated electronic machinery that has been exporting since its inception. Its shipments are uniformly high value items and premium transportation is a not uncommon requirement. Packaging is an important factor, notably for such pieces as flat-bed table units for electronic pattern cutting that measure some 20-feet long with a near-zero surface tolerance.

As a smaller company, Gerber necessarily maintains a simpler distribution organization than is the case at Ford or Westinghouse. Nevertheless, it must cover the same bases and maintain a proper level of efficiency to keep it competitive in overseas markets. That it does so is clearly evident in TRAFFIC MANAGEMENT's account of their operations, initially published in October, 1970, as follows:

CHANGING company size inevitably demands new ways of doing business. For The Gerber Scientific Instrument Company, overall rapid growth makes methods review and revision a continuing necessity. Grossing just above $2 million in 1964, fiscal 1970 sales ran above $11 million, with the present growth rate running approximately 25%.

Far exceeding the total company's healthy rate of expansion is one particular Gerber activity. "Since 1967," Vice President-Marketing L. C. Arnett states, "company exports have more than tripled." In addition, during this period, the company acquired a subsidiary manufacturing operation in Israel, as well as establishing marketing and servicing subsidiaries in Brussels and London.

TYPICAL OF Gerber custom production, this 28-foot automated drafting table will readily convert digital information supplied by a computer source to line drawings, speeding the processes of design and refinement.

MRS. ELIZABETH GORDON, executive secretary, reviews travel arrangements for a visiting customer group with International Contract Administrator Matthew S. Gut (left) and International Traffic Manager Frank Cyrkiewicz.

THOROUGH PRETEST OPERATION of a custom-engineered automated drafting system finds test unit personnel feeding program cards into the computer unit.

MARK P. BEAULIEU (left), contracts manager, discusses Gerber's fast-growing overseas business with International Traffic Manager Frank Cyrkiewicz.

Export practices suited to 1967 clearly needed checking by 1970. Accordingly, management undertook a study which suggested shifting from external agents to in-house operation, employing outside services where justified, but coordinated by a company manager with the experience and capability to expand his functions to match anticipated export volume increases. Top management concurred and established the new function.

This decision had an immediate salutary effect. International Traffic Manager Frank Cyrkiewicz' prior experience in export and transportation systems development at Combustion Engineering, Inc. (see "Killing a Paper Tiger Pays Off," TM, Feb., 1968) suggested early and beneficial changes. "In the period following his appointment, 'annualized' export expenditures well above the six-figure mark were chopped 75% despite continued, even expanded, premium service employment," notes Contracts Manager Mark P. Beaulieu, to whom the international traffic activity reports.

Gerber equipment places heavy demands on the transportation function. A typical automated drafting system can be huge and heavy, with a table bed as much as 28 feet long, yet so precisely manufactured that bed flatness is within a tolerance of nine-thousandths of an inch.

Mated to intricate electronic controls, with price tags that reflect the custom nature of each order, it is clear that moving this company's production requires close supervision. From initial receipt of a customer inquiry through system delivery and ultimate forwarding of auxiliaries and warranty parts, the international traffic manager maintains continuous liaison with Gerber engineering, production and marketing personnel, the customer's staff, carriers, customs people, foreign freight forwarders and representatives of foreign governments concerned.

Parallels between export and domestic shipping plus opportunities to keep costs down through pooled activities find Mr. Cyrkiewicz working closely with Manager-Materials Control Charles W. Estelle. Shared contacts and knowledge benefit both portions of the traffic picture in a company where no two significant shipments are ever alike.

The primarily "to order" nature of Gerber business virtually forces a total logistics orientation upon management. A typical export customer puts Mr. Cyrkiewicz in action even before his order is placed. In soliciting an order following initial inquiry, design and production elements join forces with accounting and other affected company functions to establish design requirements, costs and feasible delivery schedules. The international traffic unit participates actively in this work, working in close tandem with International Systems Contract Administrator Matthew S. Gut. Throughout the development and fulfillment of any systems contract, Messrs. Gut and Cyrkiewicz maintain a running review so that developments affecting costs or schedules may be coped with promptly.

Once the client places an order, Mr. Cyrkiewicz establishes early contact to determine not only the nature of final delivery modes available at the client's facility, but location installation circumstances as well. A first floor delivery creates less packaging concern than a sixth floor installation involving rigging arrangements. Whether or not aisle space within a building suits itself to moving packages of varied bulk must also be determined.

During the three-to-nine-month manufacturing cycle, varied components must be scheduled into stock for assembly, while arrangements must be made for assured, safe movement from Gerber's South Windsor, Conn. plant to the air or seaport of embarkation, subsequent movement by overseas carrier, inland movement to consignee and final placement at the latter's premises with the necessary Gerber specialists at hand to ensure fault-free installation.

"These units must not only move safely," claims Mr. Cyrkiewicz, "they must also move fast. A day's production time lost to a customer on a six-figure hardware system represents substantial expense."

Time pressures find airfreight sharing significantly in Gerber's shipping pattern. Export operations typically entail a 40% air volume, with a somewhat greater proportion in European shipping where air-water differentials

HEAVILY CRATED, delicate electronic equipment gets added moisture protection from the application of polypropylene sheeting.

CUSTOMIZED, HIGH-PRECISION TABLES make every packaging operation a new challenge. The wooden bed with foam inserts in the foreground will be a perfect fit for the new table in the left rear awaiting shipment.

CHARLES W. ESTELLE (left), manager-materials control, and International Traffic Manager Frank Cyrkiewicz check out a ready-to-go drafting unit protected by foam inserts, fitted plywood top, fiberboard over cover and polypropylene sheeting.

create a lesser premium in contrast to trans-Pacific service. There is also substantial airfreight movement, both domestic and export, of emergency shipments, largely parts or components.

On the domestic side, Mr. Estelle finds that in many cases, it is cheaper to ship by air than it is to maintain stock. "On one high-cost commodity that our plant uses in some volume," he observes, "the trade-off nets a 20% saving for us."

While airfreight's role is significant, the sheer size of many Gerber units precludes their loading aboard conventional jets. "When all-cargo 747s become available that will accept our longer and wider system components, our air-shipping volume will increase substantially," Mr. Cyrkiewicz claims.

Similar constraints apply at sea, with hold stowage essential for many huge packs. Where service is available and pack sizes permit, however, containerization is employed increasingly. Substantial savings accrue through the reduced packaging and lowered cubic measurements for shipping charge assessment that the steel cocoons make possible. Messrs. Cyrkiewicz and Estelle determined through testing that sensitive table components, carefully prepared, could be "double-decked" safely within standard containers without full export packaging, making good use of the space available.

It is at this point that outside services perform a major role. Under Mr. Cyrkiewicz' control, Foreign Shipping Service Co. of New York performs the normal paper work functions of the overseas freight forwarder and, in addition, provides export packaging for hold stowage or air movement. It also supervises container loading for the routes and shipments where it is required. Continuous close liaison between this company and Mr. Cyrkiewicz on all shipments assures that the odd and the unusual items get needed attention. For Gerber, this includes virtually every shipment.

Somewhat more conventional shipments flow regularly to the overseas subsidiaries, whose transportation policies are also guided by Mr. Cyrkiewicz. Overseas visitations from time to time for consultation and re-

view assure that efficient transportation employment prevails at Beta Engineering and Development, Ltd. (Beer-Sheva, Israel), Gerber Scientific-Europe, S.A. (Brussels) and Gerber Scientific-U.K. Limited (London). External agents such as Distributors Corporation Pty., Ltd. of Australia and Marubeni-Iida Co., Ltd. of Japan maintain continued contact with the Gerber traffic unit as well.

Products leaving the South Windsor plant, other than occasional small parts flowing through U.P.S., almost invariably occupy air ride electronic vans. North American Van Lines handles the preponderance of this traffic. "They give us consistently good service despite frequent short notice movements and odd-hour requirements," notes Mr. Estelle. "Our North American agent, Russ Schofield, really does an outstanding job for us. He has the equipment, and he never fails to keep it available."

Passenger traffic plays a bigger-than-normal part in Gerber operations. Mrs. Elizabeth Gordon, secretary to the vice president-marketing, finds an increasing portion of her time devoted to this activity. In addition to writing her own air tickets, she fully controls all hotel reservations, car rentals, miscellaneous transportation orders and other travel-related matters for both Gerber marketing personnel and the numerous customer visitors from both domestic and overseas areas.

Why such heavy personal travel? It starts with the customer order. At least one customer visit to South Windsor is essential both to confirm design specifications and to witness highly critical tests, as well as to obtain necessary advanced operational training. These steps generally require a trip to South Windsor for a number of individuals and, not infrequently, several such visits. Equally important is the work of Gerber engineers in preparing for and accomplishing actual installation of the finished systems, wherever in the world this may take them. So complex and delicate are various elements that only men closely familiar with both the specific system and its intended task are qualified to do this work.

No less than one visit by a Gerber party to the client is essential, therefore, and multiple visits are more the

rule than the exception. "Our guest roster has not quite blanketed the world," Mrs. Gordon observes, "but the list of countries that have yet to send visitors to our plant is rapidly shrinking."

Although final export packing continues under outside management, all domestic packaging and preliminary export shipment preparation takes place in the South Windsor plant. Every step is taken to assure that delicate items get the respect that is their due. The plant itself is fully air-conditioned with controlled humidity for this reason, and blast heaters on the freight dock protect winter movements from thermal shock, even though goods moving aboard vans are already well protected by packaging.

Basic boxes provide a measure of standardization on some shipments, but packing within is unique to each order. Because a pack must reflect both delivery conditions and the nature of the contents, close coordination between the contract group, the shipping department and the customer prevails at this stage, as at every other on the path from getting an initial order to fulfilling warranty requirements.

Mr. Estelle's staff experiments continually with new packaging techniques and materials, and a number of current materials meet their particular favor. The shipping unit employs loose fill, such as Pellaspan or Altapack, on many table parts. Individual parts themselves are wrapped in four-mil poly plastic sheeting.

"We use a lot of this," states Mr. Estelle. "It keeps dust off and moisture out. We also use CRC spray a great deal on parts subject to oxidation."

Another current practice that appears to be paying off is the employment of clear plastic wrap in lieu of crating. With the clear plastic, handlers can see where switches and other delicate parts are located, actually making it easier for them to place handling gear for damage-free maneuvering. In Mr. Estelle's view, truckers and airfreight forwarders have been more careful with these shipments, a fact clearly reflected in the past year with improved handling on several million dollars' worth of goods. Bright red-orange, press-apply labels, made in the plant, simplify

GERBER SYSTEMS AND PARTS destined overseas move largely by air cargo. High per-pound value places a premium on time.

marking the transparent-pack pieces.

A typical major item, one of the finely machined table tops, gets packaging protection that is highly substantial. With 2x4-inch lumber along its edges, the entire table space within receives a foam skin filler. Over the filler goes plywood. Corrugated board is then taped in place, and a heavy poly sheeting covers the complete unit.

Up to this point, plant packing requires little differentiation between domestic and export shipments. At this phase, procedures differ somewhat, with domestic control consoles mounted on wheels, while skids are fitted to the export equipment, creating unit-packs in both cases.

The foam skins that protect table surfaces are a highly economical filler material. These are actually the outer layers of baked styrene foam sheets

peeled off in manufacture to keep the basic product at a uniform thickness. The relatively minor thickness variation in these outer portions creates no problem for filler use. For sheets running roughly 4 by 8 feet or 5 by 7 feet, costs are as low as $3 apiece.

Package avoidance also plays a part. As Contract Manager Beaulieu notes, when a typical Gerber Garment Cloth Cutter, with a cube running around 6,500 cubic feet, moves overseas, packaging charges will easily run $9,000. "What we are considering at this time," he notes, "is the possibility of either redesigning to reduce shipping cube or building uncritical table parts overseas, thus reducing both packaging costs and, through cube reduction, total transportation costs."

Vice President-Operations Robert J. Maerz, to whom Mr. Estelle re-

ports, sees also the possibility for further sophistication in packaging as some of Gerber's new, smaller systems enter the market. "Our system 40, for example, doesn't fill a whole van," states Mr. Maerz, "so the emphasis for these units may well shift from shock-absorbing vehicles to creation of shock-absorbing packs." Under such a development, regular common carrier trucks, in place of air-ride electronic vans, would perform suitably. The decision, then, would lie in the trade-off of premium cost packaging against premium-cost transportation, with selection varying to match the cost ratio.

Gerber equipment's unique ability to draw or to cut according to computerized or taped instructions, translated electronically, has an important obverse capacity as well. Properly equipped, the same systems "read"

CONTAINERIZED MOVEMENTS capture an increasing proportion of Gerber export traffic. This initial test shipment clearly demonstrated the practicality of such operations for service to Japan and other areas of the Orient.

an existing pattern or drawing. In garment technology, this can mean that an artist's initial design for, say, a jacket can be "read" while lying on the table, the resultant mathematical data flowing to computer storage. With the system shifted from reading to cutting mode, it may then be programed, not merely to duplicate the initial pattern, but to cut additional related patterns in every variety of size that the garment manufacturer may require. More than that, multiple layers of material may be so cut.

New applications for such technology grow daily. With many of the world's leading automotive and airframe manufacturers as steady customers, in addition to major electronics and electrical equipment producers, the increasingly important garment area means still greater total tonnage, as well as diversity in shipping. As Mr. Beaulieu observes, "We've gone through three generations of equipment in four years' time. This rapid technical evolution coupled with sheer growth alone will keep department roles ever-changing."

With this picture in mind, Messrs. Cyrkiewicz and Estelle, though solving day-to-day problems in unending flow, are already laying the groundwork for added departmental assignments to match whatever changes lie ahead. Both men agree that today finds them at a turning point: the vital necessity of continued effective interdepartmental communications demands an increasing vigilance in a necessarily specialized production and marketing concern.

Small Shipper Solves Mystery of Exporting to Out-of-the-Way Places

Warner Press is a unique business in many ways. Owned by the Church of God, it supplies religious literature and related materials to over 85 countries from a single plant in Anderson, Ind. Though not a large business within the family of American corporations, it nonetheless performs import-export functions internally that firms many times its size "farm out" to other agencies. Careful paperwork, maintenance of an up-to-date reference file and good communication with the consular offices of destination countries underlie Warner's success. Important, too, is effective, standardized packaging that holds down claims and aids timely deliveries.

What TRAFFIC MANAGEMENT learned at Warner Press, initially reviewed in May, 1967, is on the following pages:

THE U.S. DEPARTMENT of Commerce contends that a less-than-giant business can successfully penetrate export markets. Warner Press, owned by the Church of God, offers clear confirmation of this. From a single plant at Anderson, Indiana, it ships religious literature in growing quantities to any and every country seeking its goods.

Such commodities as bibles, religious texts, church bulletins, pamphlets, greeting cards, artworks and notions are produced and stocked at this single inland location. This traffic is moving in ever-increasing volume to religious specialty stores, churches, missionaries, publishers, book stores, door-to door sales people and individual mail order purchasers throughout the world. Sales exceeded $5,000,000 in 1966, doubling the 1946 volume. Since 1962 alone growth has approached 20%, much of it in international trade.

Recognizing their potential and the need for more effective control of physical distribution, management appointed Allen S. Hart to the position of materials handling and traffic manager in 1946. Coincidental with his appointment, the Press observed a modest increase in international sales. While no specific effort has ever been made to develop this field, its volume has improved steadily ever since. Indications are that international volume will continue to expand at a greater rate than domestic business, in itself notable for a continuing, long-term upward trend.

The marked growth of international traffic has resulted in development of an expertise in import-export shipment processing not commonly found at mid-continent points such as Anderson. Warner Press is its own importing agent, clearing all such shipments. Full documentation, including

Conferring with Material Handling and Traffic Manager Allen S. Hart about a shipping program in Africa are (left to right) Shipping Administrator Frances Ballard and Traffic Administrator Ruth Leedom.

Incoming materials received by truck and rail are unloaded at Warner's receiving dock in Anderson, Ind. Inbound rail freight is picked up by three plant trucks.

consular invoicing, is performed on export shipments, many of which are destined to countries having unique and complex trade regulations as well as limited accessibility. Africa, with its multitude of new and emerging nations, is the largest export area in shipment volume, although Australia is the greater in value of shipments. Because of its diversified experience, the traffic department is frequently called upon by other Anderson firms for assistance in the handling of overseas shipments.

"International shipping is too often depicted as some sort of complex mystery," states Mr. Hart. "Our experience proves that if you go to people who are thoroughly familiar with it and confess your ignorance, they will teach you much of what you need to know rather quickly. In addition, familiarizing youself with the standard reference works and maintaining them close at hand can keep you clear of most of the traps. Our working library includes some of the basic yet important tools in handling foreign traffic. They are the International Mail Section of the Postal Guide, Leonard's Guide, the International Trade Reporter and Schedule II—Statistical Classification of Domestic and Foreign Commodities Exported from the United States. With these, kept properly up to date, we can answer most of our own questions. On the few occasions when doubts remain, a quick call to an affected nation's consular office normally yields a prompt solution. We are in full agreement with the Department of Commerce's contention that more U.S. firms can and should enter the export market for profit as well as to aid the balance of trade."

Loss and damage problems were largely resolved by the complete redesign of packaging in 1946. Picture frames, long a principal source of claim problems, were shifted to a new, dual-sleeve pack that is largely responsible for a better-than 99% drop in shipment damages. This pack contains a roll-in sleeve for initial insertion of the frame, the ends being tucked or rolled back into the sleeve body for end and corner protection. This sleeve is, in turn, inserted into a second corrugated sleeve with the corrugations running in the opposite direction from those of the inner sleeve for greater support, the whole being protected by the outer carton, also of fibreboard. All freight now moves in domestic pack, including overseas shipments. Thus, while containerization has been considered for service benefits, there is no indication that it would affect the already satisfactory claim experience.

Inbound freight is received by rail and truck. Paper shipments are generally delivered at the Central Indiana Railroad's team track for pickup by one of the three plant trucks. Outbound shipments of finished merchandise move regularly to Chicago via Daum's Overnight Express or McLain Dray Line, to Grand Rapids via Interstate or Holland Motor Express, Detroit via Ellis Trucking and Cleveland via Allstate or Transport Motor. Direct truck shipments are also made with some frequency to numerous other points. A typical day will find 30 to 40 consignments forwarded via truck, varying in size from 50 pounds to solid truckload.

A substantial volume also is given to U.P.S. and Parcel Post. During the September-December peak period when 60% of

Reviewing shipping plans are Allen S. Hart (left) and Executive Vice President T. F. Miller, to become Warner's president in July.

Parcel post and U.P.S. shipments, following assembly and packing, are shown as they move down the Blackstone conveyor to metering stations.

annual sales are handled, combined U.P.S.-Parcel Post billing averages $6,000 weekly, with the heaviest weeks reaching $12,000. Outbound daily truck tonnage at this time will run to two or three solid trailer loads plus heavy LTL.

Working with an inventory of 6,000 items, the material handling and traffic department is responsible for assembly and preparation of shipments in addition to arranging deliveries. Subsequent to billing and editing, orders are forwarded in batches to material handling, where they are sorted for processing on either the mail side or the freight side of the assembly area. Mail items are placed in baskets shelved in control rack locations marked to show day and time of receipt. A supervisor can check this rack at a glance to determine the current level of mail order on-time performance. Unfilled orders are taken in groups from these baskets for assembly.

Freight orders are similarly controlled, but on a daily rather than hourly basis.

Mail orders are assembled by pickers from the stock shelves using 4-wheel carts and specially designed tote boxes for delivery to the packers. Upon completion of assembly and packing, the shipments move down a Blackstone conveyor to metering stations where postage or U.P.S charges are applied. Parcel Post items are loaded in wheeled tubs which are rolled directly into plant trucks for delivery to the Post Office. Experience with the tubs has shown a saving of two-thirds in the time formerly required for these deliveries using mail sacks. The Post Office has also benefited from the easier unloading that tubs afford. As compared to the original practice of loose-loading the mail truck, tubs offer the further advantage of a substantial increase in vehicle capacity.

Depending upon the size of individual

Skidded cartons of "Sunshine Line" greeting cards are a major element in Warner's warehousing. Future plans call for the addition of two more warehouses.

Loaded trucks prepare to leave Warner's shipping dock. On a typical day, 30 to 40 consignments, varying in size from 50 pounds to a truckload, are forwarded.

orders, freight shipments are assembled by pickers on skids or 4-wheeled flat hand carts. These are delivered to packers who load cartons back on the skids or trucks for movement to outbound shipping area.

Plans developed by Mr. Hart call for construction of two warehouses plus a new shipping area and additional related production space. When completed, shipping will be linked to production by an elevator handling 6 skids and a power truck in comparison to the present elevator which handles 3 skids plus power truck. Overhead conveyors are to be installed to handle stock from shipping shelves to the packing line. Packers will be provided with a separate conveyor system in lieu of carts or skids for moving shipments to the outbound freight area. The existing Blackstone conveyor will be reinstalled as the meter feed in the mail packing line.

The business climate is a bit different at Warner Press. In part, the not-for-profit corporation status has a bearing on this. Perhaps more significant is the allegiance staff members hold toward the Church of God, sole owner of Warner Press. "I came here in 1946 to do something for my church," states Allen S. Hart. "Some of us can be clergymen, some may achieve fulfillment in charitable activity or missionary work, but I feel that keeping things rolling efficiently here is a service to my church in which I can offer the most."

CHAPTER X

Specialist Answers to Exceptional Distribution Demands

In logistics as in every phase of business management, there are firms that don't fit the usual rules. Sometimes it is the nature of the product that makes the difference. Sometimes it is the service requirements or the unusual character of the market. Sometimes it is all of these, none of these, or more.

Such a firm is Kaiser Engineers. Building plants, developing ports, erecting bridges or buildings—all these and many other projects demanding the utmost in engineering and construction capabilities mean a never-ending succession of non-repetitive logistics programs. For Kaiser Engineers' Procurement Division, there is a continual redevelopment and redeployment of managers to control logistics operations at locations requiring such services for an average of about eighteen months, after which those concerned with an operation must make ready to set up and operate the needed transport and storage functions at other, newer project sites.

A highly unusual transportation-distribution activity, reported by TRAFFIC MANAGEMENT in December, 1971, is presented on the following pages:

Controlling a Worldwide Logistics System

KAISER ENGINEERS, largest operating division of Kaiser Industries Corp., faces logistics problems quite different from those experienced by a typical manufacturing and marketing firm. Performing $500 million worth of work for somewhat more than 100 clients in 1970, at year's end a backlog existed of $1.6 billion.

Complex engineering projects, large and small, are this company's stock-in-trade. At any given time, Kaiser Engineers will be progressing 10 to 12 projects representing $80 million to $100 million or more each, with perhaps twice as many smaller projects concurrently under way. With the world as its marketplace, some two-thirds of its current activities lie overseas.

"Kaiser is profit-centered both by industry and by geographical area," asserts Vice President for Administration Charles O. Parker. In accordance with this philosophy, Kaiser Engineers' organization is divided into three functional categories: industry, geography and support.

Under Vice President Parker in the support group, among other administrative functions, is the procurement division. What would be "physical distribution," "logistics" or "materials management" in a more conventional industrial organization carries a name here that is appropriate to the necessarily differing emphasis among the skills employed in this sector. Kaiser Engineers' logistics role is that of a buyer, shipper and receiver at worldwide origins and destinations, each with its own special requirements, and each project an active assignment for typically 18 months to two years.

Not only are the firm's destinations lacking in long-term uniformity, but the "products" themselves represent an unusual diversity. All sorts of engineered equipment (conveyors, furnaces or other technical units specially built to Kaiser specifications), parts and construction materials, moving from innumerable vendors, must reach project destinations on precise schedules to fulfill commitments to clients.

Director of Procurement Harold B. Andresen's department necessarily operates along somewhat different organizational lines than its counterparts elsewhere. As indicated by the accompanying organization chart, there are several distinctly different types of management within this group.

Procurement's responsibilities

At the Oakland, Cal. headquarters, under Procurement Services Manager George V. Leonard, traffic, expediting and administration units are grouped, performing in large measure staff-oriented functions. Project operations, reporting to Procurement Manager V.L. Frankson, supported by a purchasing manager and a materials manager at Oakland, concerns itself directly with specific major projects in the field. Some of these have supporting procurement staff reporting directly to the Oakland organization, while on many larger projects, department-supplied procurement specialists report on-site to the project managers, but maintain functional contact with Oakland.

"Successful management of design and construction projects demands that purchasing, subcontracting and materials logistics be closely coordinated with the engineering and construction operations for the best scheduling of work and control of costs," notes Mr. Andresen. **"The procurement department of Kaiser Engineers judges its performances in terms of the money and time it is able to save for each project."** These savings include items like the following:

- Cost minimization through skillful evaluation of bids.
- Savings through astute negotiation of purchases and contracts.
- Economies derived through expert negotiation for transportation services and effective rate analysis.
- Cost benefits of efficient and economical procurement operations.
- Time savings through vigilant and skillful expediting of suppliers and transportation services, in turn creating cost benefits for both Kaiser Engineers and its clients.

Company projects are essentially of two different types: Those in which Kaiser Engineers performs the total engineering and construction assignment with its own personnel and equipment, and construction management projects, particularly overseas. These latter entail the use of subcontractors in large measure, which can prove particularly advantageous in distant countries where local expertise adapted to a specific environment can save much time and money.

Working under the construction management approach, the firm finds substantially heavier demands placed upon the procurement department. Not only are more detailed engineering specifications necessary, but more precise scheduling becomes essential to interface the many subcontractors.

To note but one instance among many, a site clearing and grading contractor must complete his work on schedule before a foundation contractor is due to start his assignment. A delay by the former can trigger a chain reaction requiring substantial effort and expense if the time loss is to be recaptured before the planned project completion date. **"In our opinion,"** states Mr. Andresen, **"construction management requires a particularly high caliber of people."**

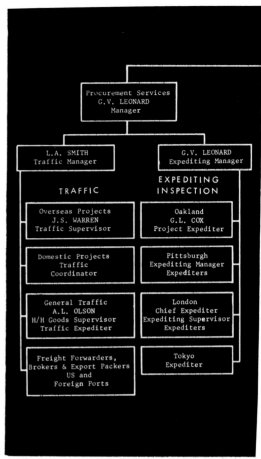

ORGANIZATION CHART in motion.

Organizing logistics

The procurement department's permanent organization essentially matches that of engineering. Working together closely, they build a team for each major project, carefully fitted to the type of assignment and recognizing the geographic factors.

Reporting directly to the project manager on any large operation is a project procurement manager provided by the procurement department. While fulfilling line reporting responsibility to the project manager on the site, he maintains a continuing staff relationship with the procurement department. His responsibilities on a specific project embrace purchasing, subcontracting, expediting, traffic and material control. A sizable assignment will find him with a supporting staff, including a resident traffic manager in many cases, as well as an expediter, a purchasing and subcontracts man, a warehouse supervisor and others.

In fulfilling these project obligations, the procurement department becomes, in part, a professional labor pool. It selects and trains managers not only in general professional skill areas, but in specific requirements of individual project assignments as well, establishing procedures to fit each situation and subsequently auditing performance. In addition, the central staff may perform some portions of the actual line work prior to the arrival of the on-site procurement staff. Where items to be purchased have a high engineering content and a long delivery date, the department will handle their purchase, rather than the project procurement manager.

The many major projects continually under way necessarily involve a substantial number of procurement department specialists, and as a result, a major department burden is the scheduling and maintenance of its

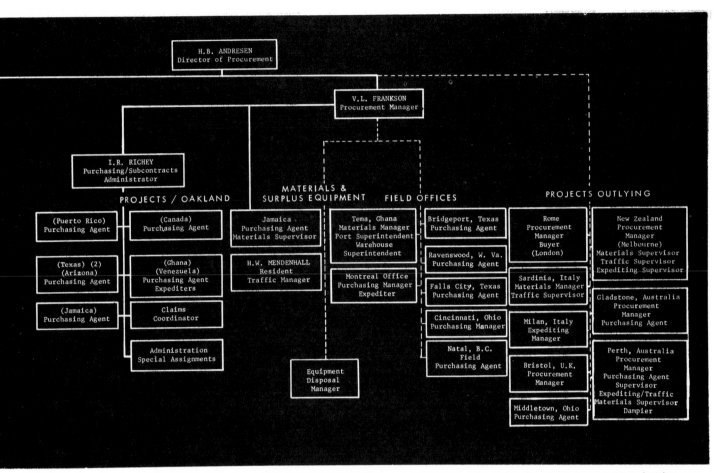

```
                    H.B. ANDRESEN
                    Director of Procurement

                                        V.L. FRANKSON
                                        Procurement Manager

        I.R. RICHEY
        Purchasing/Subcontracts
        Administrator
                                    MATERIALS &
                                    SURPLUS EQUIPMENT    FIELD OFFICES              PROJECTS OUTLYING
          PROJECTS / OAKLAND
```

(Puerto Rico) Purchasing Agent	(Canada) Purchasing Agent	Jamaica Purchasing Agent Materials Supervisor	Tema, Ghana Materials Manager Port Superintendent Warehouse Superintendent	Bridgeport, Texas Purchasing Agent	Rome Procurement Manager Buyer (London)	New Zealand Procurement Manager (Melbourne) Materials Supervisor Traffic Supervisor Expediting Supervisor
(Texas) (2) (Arizona) Purchasing Agent	(Ghana) (Venezuela) Purchasing Agent Expediters	H.W. MENDENHALL Resident Traffic Manager	Montreal Office Purchasing Manager Expediter	Ravenswood, W. Va. Purchasing Agent	Sardinia, Italy Materials Manager Traffic Supervisor	
(Jamaica) Purchasing Agent	Claims Coordinator			Falls City, Texas Purchasing Agent		Gladstone, Australia Procurement Manager Purchasing Agent
	Administration Special Assignments			Cincinnati, Ohio Purchasing Manager	Milan, Italy Expediting Manager	
			Equipment Disposal Manager	Natal, B.C. Field Purchasing Agent	Bristol, U.K. Procurement Manager	Perth, Australia Procurement Manager Purchasing Agent Supervisor Expediting/Traffic Materials Supervisor Dampier
				Middletown, Ohio Purchasing Agent		

Continual, planned change characterizes the procurement department, reflecting new projects and others reaching fruition.

managerial work force. Fortunately, careful planning minimizes actual turnover of total personnel, but the department's top management must constantly plan for the inevitable transfers, rotations and reassignments of its professional personnel as projects mobilize and phase out.

Though a substantial task, this constant personnel scheduling gives the department some significant benefits. Not the least of these is the opportunity, through preplanned assignments, to enhance an individual manager's training and experience, adding greatly to his productivity and, from the individual's own viewpoint, enhancing his earning power.

Observes Project Operations Procurement Manager V. L. Frankson: **"The transfer of managers between staff posts at headquarters and major field project assignments yields a dual advantage. Men who have worked in both types of environment respect and understand the capabilities as well as the limitations that others must acknowledge in these positions, thus**

STARTING THE GROUNDWORK for a major project. Kaiser Engineers Director of Procurement Harold B. Andresen (second from left) reviews progress in developing a facility logistics program with Project Manager V.L. Frankson (left), Traffic Supervisor Joseph S. Warren and Traffic Manager Lawrence A. Smith.

building an effective team approach. At the same time, we benefit from an ability to switch people between these differing work situations when sudden needs arise."

Modern operations research techniques play a substantial part in Kaiser Engineers activities, with the procurement department significantly involved. The critical path method (CPM), a mathematical charting procedure well suited to computer development, schedules work and equipment for individual projects. The traffic unit, as well as other department activities, contributes substantial data for the establishment of individual project CPM schedules.

Augmenting the CPM schedules are specialized procurement scheduling and status reports (PSSR). Under this program, it becomes easily possible to set specific milestones to the CPM schedules developed for an individual project. Given a desired completion date plus a class schedule (category of time required for a type of job

and equipment), the computer literally backs into the individual step completion dates necessary to reach the overall objective.

Working off a programed timetable, the computer can, for example, print a final shipping date for a specific major engineered item, the release-to-manufacturer date, award date, bid receipt date, date to go out for bid, and date to start preparing specifications within the Kaiser Engineers organization. This detailed, specific timetable can be produced in a matter of minutes.

A procurement scheduling and status report serves both project management and the client, giving a systems method to control the scheduling while constantly monitoring the progress of engineering, procurement, manufacturing and shipping against the construction schedule's specific demands for equipment and materials.

Another significant computer application is the departmental source

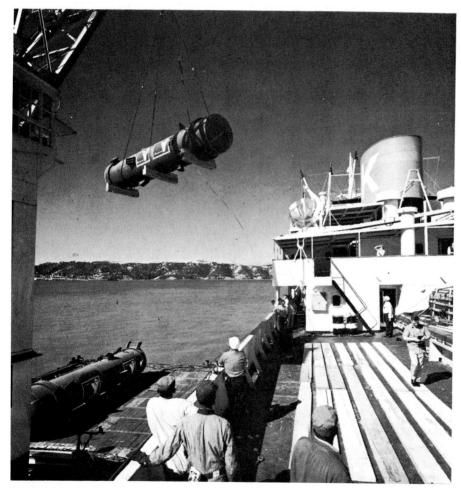

THIS 28-FOOT-LONG HEATER, containing more than 1,000 tubes, is en route to Jamaica from Yuba Industries, Inc. of Benicia, Cal.

BENICIA, CAL., JULY 15, 1971: High-pressure heat exchangers, each weighing 63 tons, are loaded aboard the K-Line freighter "Tasmania," bound for the ALPART alumina plant in Jamaica. Twelve of these units and 16 low-pressure heaters plus bauxite slurry digesters will form the heart of a 950,000-ton-per-year plant being built by Kaiser Engineers, constituting largest facility of its type in the Caribbean.

records system, which contains comprehensive information on innumerable qualified suppliers of equipment and materials, as well as qualified contractors for construction work. This system allows prompt retrieval of information for preparation of bid lists covering engineered equipment, building materials and construction work. Purchasing agents get bid lists on request and vendor updates as regular reports.

Direct access to stored computer data is provided by an Administrative Terminal System (ATS), a softwear terminal package utilizing a specially equipped IBM Selectric typewriter as a terminal. These ATS terminals are at seven locations, and can exchange information with each other as well as with the computer. Through this arrangement, the procurement department can query the technical reports department for data on earlier projects, while they, in turn, can get an immediate response from the procurement department on vendor data needed, thereby speeding information flow and reducing paper work.

Vendors are cross-referenced by product, based upon Kaiser Engineers nomenclature. On the product list, each item is followed by applicable vendor codes. After each vendor code is a code letter indicating if a previous bidder has actually provided an item, or is listed purely because he is considered qualified to bid. Products are also coded by the type of project for which previously required.

An important advantage of the computer-ATS setup is the ease of changing vendor listings. A vendor may now be changed or eliminated in a single step instead of requiring manual changes up to 20 in number with a risk of clerical error. Daily updating of these listings is now a simple matter.

Though the organization chart, like most, indicates the segregation of specialties within the department, procurement activities are characterized by a particularly high degree of unified, team effort. Interdependency among the specialties is high, and a substantial, natural degree of overlap, in contrast to other industries, is characteristic.

In the following pages, two important department activities, traffic and expediting, both of which necessarily interface heavily with other department functions, are reviewed. The manner in which these two department segments must continually adjust to the constantly changing nature of Kaiser Engineers business necessitates a flexible, innovative outlook worthy of note by other traffic and distribution managers.

Managing traffic in an ever-changing market

TRAFFIC at Kaiser Engineers is a planning and control activity, rather than an orthodox freight transportation function. Outside help is used in large measure as a matter of policy in lieu of full-time rate clerks and other specialized technicians performing routine functions.

"We're still traffic specialists," observes Traffic Manager Lawrence A. Smith, "but we must become increasingly management generalists to do an effective logistics job under Kaiser Engineers' circumstances."

These circumstances include in particular the necessity to continually develop new traffic managerial talent to operate what might be termed "mini-traffic departments" for major projects, as well as the specialized systems their support requires. With typically a dozen current projects in the $80 million to $100 million range demanding worldwide traffic support plus a score or more of smaller but by no means minor projects also demanding attention, personnel and procedures developments are continuous tasks.

Materials for these projects are purchased and shipped from a considerable diversity of origins, with destinations potentially anywhere in the world. The largest part of traffic activity at present, in fact, concerns the servicing of construction activities outside of the United States.

A typical project was the Volta Aluminum Company reduction plant in Tema, Ghana. Completed in 1967, a second project is now under way at the same location, providing the client with a fourth pot line.

The initial project represented a $110 million assignment for Kaiser engineers. Material delivered during

EMERGING from Ordway Bldg. at Kaiser Center in downtown Oakland are (left to right): Traffic Manager Lawrence A. Smith, Project Expediter George L. Cox and Traffic Supervisor Joseph S. Warren, after an overseas project control session.

construction had a value of $57 million, involving 100,000 long tons of freight. It encompassed over 10,000 individual shipments, including 1,000 by air. Ocean freight costs alone amounted to almost $5 million.

On such projects as the above, freight forwarder assignments are made through competitive bidding on a bid list. Miscellaneous and fringe-type shipping out of Oakland, Cal., however, is regularly handled by a major forwarder that has long served Kaiser Engineers.

In an accompanying chart showing a shipping program for a project is illustrated the sequence of activities in such a program's development. This procedure in general applies to both domestic and overseas projects, the latter currently representing the major segment of company business.

Because timing of a complex series of interrelated events is critical on virtually all of these projects, the shipping program for an overseas project in particular must be carefully planned to assure uniform, controlled flow of scheduled goods to the job, employing a centralized document distribution and processing plan for formal clearance through customs, import licensing and entry, marine insurance, freight payments, shipment posting, job site port clearance, warehouse receiving and information reporting. Initial information required to develop an overseas project shipping program includes the following:

—Scope and location of project.
—Type of contract (turnkey, lump sum, cost-plus).
—Services to be performed by Kaiser Engineers, including some or all of the following: engineering, procurement, expediting, shipping, construction, con-management.
—Type of financing for project.
—Restrictions either in the prime contract or the financing vehicle with respect to shipping (flag participation, etc.).
—Purchasing of engineered equipment.
—Purchasing of construction equipment.
—Closest deepwater port or ports and facilities available, including heavy lift equipment.
—Stevedoring and master porterage and the related prevailing terms.
—Public or private wharves available.
—Discharge to be made with shallow draft vessels and facilities for same, if required.
—Potential necessity to improve existing facilities.
—Location of construction site from port of entry.
—Inland transportation facilities and equipment.
—Maximum load (dimension and weight) that can be physically handled by each inland transport mode.

KAISER ENGINEERS OVERSEAS SHIPMENTS alone number in excess of 1,000 annually, including a substantial use of charter services.

AT A GIFFORD-HILL CO. cement plant site, Kaiser Project Engineer Hal Meyers (right) supervises the unloading of heavy engineered equipment, as looking on is Gifford-Hill Production Manager Buck Rush.

—Permits required for oversize weight loads.

—Carriers' rates and shipping documents.

—Customs regulations and duty rates.

—Steamship lines serving the port of entry and applicable originating ports on the East, Gulf, and West coasts of the United States or relevant originating ports in other countries.

—Conference lines and applicable tariffs.

—Project freight agreements in effect to general area.

—Frequency of vessel sailings, average transit time and ports of call prior to port of entry.

—Heavy lift capability of steamers serving the trade.

—Air cargo service available—airline, cargo capacities, schedules, costs and related information.

—Name of corporate entity under which the company will operate.

—Name of party in whose name goods are to be consigned both to and from the port of origin. On many overseas projects, it is required that goods be consigned at all times in the name of the ultimate owner who is incorporated and doing business only in the overseas country.

Once such preliminary information is assembled, the traffic unit's next step is the development of freight costs, including ocean freight as well as inland haul to site. In doing this, traffic personnel develop major tonnages by commodity to be shipped from all sources, applying anticipated ocean shipping costs by conference and/or charter vessels.

The resultant data forms the basis for an economic study from which a shipping program is developed to be presented for project management approval. With such data at hand, a basis exists for negotiating favorable project freighting agreements or seeking adjustments in existing tariff rate structures.

In some cases, chartering may offer an economical alternative to scheduled conference lines, while in others, it may be the only means of reaching a designated port of entry. Where charter is considered, a program for staging and chartering of cargo must have sufficient time built into the schedule to permit accumulation of cargo for chartering quantities.

PURCHASING MANAGER Irv R. Richie (right), conferring here with Lawrence A. Smith, traffic manager, plays a major role in procurement department projects through his staff located at project sites, as well as in the Oakland headquarters.

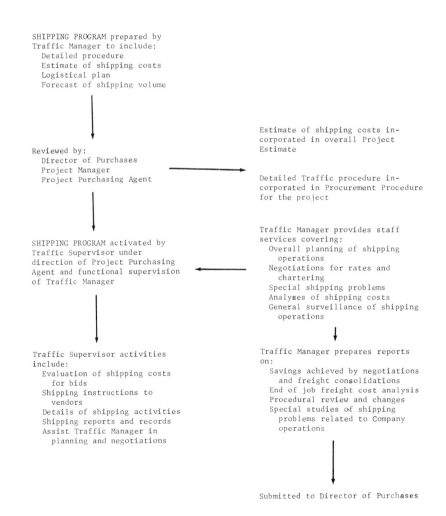

FLOW CHART pictured above demonstrates a typical Kaiser Engineers traffic unit approach to project shipping program development.

If the overall schedule cannot accept delays for staging cargo, the economic benefits of chartering may be overruled by the primary demands of construction scheduling. Even in these instances, however, situations will sometimes arise permitting arrangements for a single voyage or space charter, and when they do, the traffic unit makes good use of them. When chartering is approved, the traffic staff makes certain that vessel capabilities are adequate to the task and checks out any needed arrnagements for stevedoring as well.

Although the traffic organization plans, organizes, directs, controls and coordinates the overall shipping program for each project, it "buys" its freight forwarding and import brokerage service at each port. With the multiplicity of ports employed and the constantly changing spectrum of projects and products, it would be totally unfeasible to provide these services "in-house."

On any given project, the traffic organization will normally solicit at least three formal bids from its list of major, reputable and financially sound FMC-certified forwarders who have; either through a direct or knowledgable relationship with Kaiser Engineers, established their competence to successfully perform freight forwarding for major projects. These bids may also require approval of the client. The request for quotation describes the project's scope and longevity, tonnages anticipated and as precise as possible outline of required services. Award will be to the lowest bidder capable of performing the service, subject where necessary to client review and approval.

Prior to making such an award, however, Traffic Manager Smith visits the successful bidder's office to review and inspect his facilities, capabilities, personnel and related matters. Assuming his satisfaction with the conditions, he will then meet with the forwarder staff members who would be assigned to the project and review the specific requirements step by step. Assuming full agreement at this point, the necessary business relationship is established.

Traffic works closely with the project purchasing agent, both in the preliminary stages and throughout the project development. Initially, the unit supplies traffic cost factors and carrier service evaluations to facilitate com-

MRS. ANNEVA OLSON (right), assistant to the traffic manager, handles more than 500 household moves for Kaiser Engineers staff members each year.

parison among bidders. Subsequently, traffic supplies shipping, documentation, marking and packing instructions in conjunction with the affected buyers.

As with the purchasing function, close and continuing ties exist between traffic and expediting on any given project. Expediting keeps traffic currently informed of progress toward and details of final order shipments from factories. Additionally, sellers must furnish the traffic organization with document copies verifying shipping, while freight forwarders and export packers are required to verify receipt at ports; steamship lines must furnish on-board bills of lading, and air freight forwarders are instructed to telephone details of all air cargo forwardings.

This information flow feeds a shipping log and an interim shipping file system, giving the traffic staff sufficient timely data to monitor shipment progress, assuring that all possible shipments board the vessel on schedule. Those that are delayed, in turn, are pinpointed and receive the necessary traffic expediting attention.

In the case of the St. Elizabeth alumina plant in Jamaica, a special private port facility had to be set up for handling of inbound materials. Harold Mendenhall of the traffic staff was assigned to this activity as port captain, not only managing this specific physical facility but covering many other aspects of cargo importation and movement as well.

A major problem during the final construction phase in 1968–69 was the large U.S. port strike just when the shipping schedule turned critical. "We had to air freight much of the material," states Traffic Supervisor Joseph S. Warren. "In all, there were 43 charters. Most originated at Miami, but others came from Boston, Mobile, Japan and West Coast. Before, we staged at Mobile and chartered vessels twice monthly."

With the constant reorientation of projects and people, household moves loom large among traffic activities. Under the control of Mrs. Anneva Olson, assistant to the traffic manager, these can amount to over 500 per year worldwide, accounting for a major portion of Mrs. Olson's activities.

Air freight, notably air charter, plays an important part in keeping project schedules on time. "We're seeking lowest total cost consistent with service requirements," notes Mr. Smith. "If we need air charter, we use it, but even here we can realize economies. In a recent instance, we needed, and we got, a charter flight to Australia, but we succeeded in finding another firm with a similar need, so our cost was only $30,000 instead of $70,000. In other instances, we have often filled in with additional Kaiser freight to attain maximum charter craft utilization."

Though travel is a big item for Kaiser Engineers, it is the only traffic function maintained for Kaiser Engineers by a central organization, Kaiser Services. Handled by Manager Travel Services Matthew M. Connors and staff, Kaiser Engineers is second only to Kaiser Aluminum as their major customer. Employing an American Express Space Bank and Holiday Inn Holidex terminals, speedy booking of hotel reservations is assured. The department has 10 employees. All domestic air flights are ticketed "in-house."

Expediting key to scheduled performance

EXPEDITING, for the average industry, is an infrequent necessity that may arise due to breakdown in a normal supply channel or because of a sudden material demand. For Kaiser Engineers, it is a daily business activity of substantial proportion. So much of the firm's work involves custom-manufactured, specially engineered materials to be installed at individual installations that close schedule control is mandatory.

Company policy is to use the preventive form of expediting: stopping delays wherever possible before they start, keeping continual watch over essentially three principle factors—materials, engineering and production. To accomplish this mission, expediters work as two coordinated groups: project and regional. Each individual project is assigned an expediter, who may work on one or more such projects at a time as dictated by the level of expediting required. These men coordinate in turn with regional expediters who have territorial rather than project responsibility.

When purchase orders are released on a given project, the project expediter forwards them to affected regional expediters with an indication of the degree of expediting he deems necessary, based upon his knowledge of vendor performance, the type of equipment, the date required and information obtained at monthly reviews with the project engineering manager.

A project expediter is assigned basic responsibility for expediting a project, acting as coordinator and liaison between the regional expediters and other project personnel. His functional responsibilities include:

—Selecting and assigning to the regional expediters purchase orders to be followed and expedited (generally about 35% of all orders will require expediting). Other orders are monitored at frequent intervals by telephone or wire contact with suppliers.

—Reviewing expediting reports from regional expediters and disseminating information to affected project personnel.

—Continuously reviewing status of all orders against project requirements and initiating corrective action with regional expediters and project personnel on matters adversely affecting delivery schedules.

—Maintaining liaison with project engineering and construction personnel to keep current on schedule requirements and relative importance of purchase orders and contracts.

—Informing regional expediters of delivery requirements for all equipment and materials, providing direction on expediting of critical orders or problems to overcome actual or potential delays.

—Coordinating between project drawing control and regional expediters for the submission and approval of vendor drawings.

—Reviewing status and delivery requirements of all orders periodically with the project manager (or engineer) to identify orders that require expediting and instructing regional expediters accordingly.

—Issuing periodic procurement status reports for the individual project.

The regional expediters with whom project expediters maintain continuing liaison are at seven different locations. Oakland handles the United States west of the Mississippi River, while a Pittsburgh expediting office handles the territory to the east. The latter office carries a substantial burden, as roughly 75% of orders expedited originate in the East.

Most of Europe is expedited from a London office, supplemented by a Milan office, which is responsible primarily for Italy. Other locations include Tokyo for Japanese sources, while Montreal covers Canada, and Sydney is responsible for the Australian area.

Regional expediters establish and maintain contacts with vendors and subcontractors to develop information concerning the status and scheduling of their work, initiating action wherever necessary to assure materials and equipment deliveries that satisfy construction schedule requirements. In pursuing this objective, the regional expediters perform the following functions:

—Develop information concerning drawings being prepared and vendor's anticipated completion dates for drawings to be submitted for project engineers' approval. If scheduled completion is unsatisfactory, the district expediter seeks to have the vendor accelerate the work.

—Develop information concerning vendor's ordering and receiving of materials and components for equipment manufacture.

—Review shop schedules and observe work progress to determine if performance by the manufacturer matches the overall order delivery schedule.

—Continually evaluate the vendor's work progress to discover potential problem areas and initiate action to prevent or mitigate conditions which may cause delays.

—Apply intensive expediting effort on critical problems affecting the vendor's schedule.

—Prepare reports following each vendor contract informing project engineering, procurement and con-

EXPEDITING MANAGER George V. Leonard (right) reviews scheduled deliveries of engineered equipment for a current project with Expediter John Lambert (left) and Project Expediter George L. Cox.

struction personnel of the delivery schedule, the vendor's progress and all problems requiring special attention. These expediting reports go to interested project personnel and are the basis of information for status reports prepared by project expediters.

The necessarily close liaison between expediting and transportation finds the two functions work closely together. Procurement Services Manager George V. Leonard, in fact, had been Kaiser Engineers' traffic manager earlier. Traffic's role in assuring scheduled delivery performance is a major one, the department's staff including a full-time traffic coordinator and expediter, thus assuring an effective liaison in the operation of this vital activity.

How Air Containers
Speed Information Flow

Readers Digest is another organization with logistics operations like no other. An unusual company in many ways, its products as well as its resources stand apart from those of almost any other company.

At its Pleasantville, New York headquarters there is a computer complex that would make almost any operation short of the Pentagon seem small. Its nightly output of printed material is immense, including a mountain of material destined for Indianapolis on a daily basis. Instead of employing data transmission lines for information not required until the following morning, the company wisely forwards the actual printout paper itself in fibreboard containers via air freight, making it available for use at the start of the following work day. This is but one of several unique transportation-distribution operations. Perhaps not everyone shares Readers Digest's logistics needs, but their operations prove a spur to the imagination of every creative distribution manager.

TRAFFIC MANAGEMENT's Readers Digest study, appearing initially in the June, 1968 issue, follows:

MENTION *Reader's Digest* and most people think of a magazine with a large country-wide circulation. To a traffic manager, this suggests a complex and unusual transportation pattern, requiring close control. Traffic Manager Henry C. Povall's department unquestionably qualifies as unusual. It does indeed operate closely controlled, tightly scheduled service, but only a minor part of this activity directly involves magazines or other retail merchandise.

By far the majority of *Reader's Digest*-controlled traffic pours forth from a mammoth computer center at the company's Pleasantville, N. Y. headquarters, augmented by printed matter, documents and advertising inserts. The latter move forward for ultimate consolidation with other litera-

Development of outbound shipping plans for growing computer output is a result of efforts of *Reader's Digest* Traffic Manager Henry C. Povall, at right, and Rudolph E. Weiss, the firm's manager, computer operations.

Nightly outbound shipment of computer output being placed aboard aircraft for Indianapolis, one of many points receiving frequent *Reader's Digest* container shipments.

ture or company products. Destinations include book publishers, phonograph record producers and printing plants manufacturing *Reader's Digest* products as well as direct mail advertising firms assembling mailing pieces slated for computer-selected sales prospects.

This traffic department moves information rather than goods. To the company, it is high value freight, yet it has little or no worth to anyone else. Product labels, coded and sequenced, not only save shipping and packing labor at manufacturing points, but provide a control as well for scheduled release of commodity orders and personalized advertising matter. Speed is all important—deliveries must be made overnight nationwide. Fully two-thirds of the volume moves air freight, while the remainder is trucked to points within a 250- to 300-mile radius where overnight schedules by surface are normal.

Air containerization and related density rates made this program possible. With such a speed requirement, many firms forward data by direct wire from computer centers or by teletype. Overnight air deliveries of 18-20,000 pounds nightly at attractive rates,

however, plus another 10,000 pounds by truck, yield the needed service level without tying up valuable space and expensive equipment at company headquarters and the several regular destination points.

"We prefer the Type 'D' container because it gives us maximum flexibility and a smooth flow," notes Traffic Manager Povall. "It is ideally suited to normal batch sizes coming from our computer operation, which simplifies control. If we tried using a large container, we'd have all our eggs in one basket and a single stray would be a king-sized headache. The Type 'D' measures 57x42x45 inches, readily carrying 1,200 pounds of our computer print-out. This is a substantial amount of material, yet limited enough for quick and easy replacement in the rare event of a stray or damage."

Type "D" Dynacor containers, supplied by T. R. Levine & Sons, Paterson, N. J., make two or three outbound air trips loaded with computer output or other printed matter, returning as flats by truck. When deteriorated beyond acceptability for air movement, they are given a final loading of shredded waste paper by a compressed air piping system and move off by truck to New Jersey

In sequence; Preparation of "D" container shipment;
1. Flat-packed container is opened.

2. Assembling styrene pallet rails and container base.

3. Loading starts before sidewall assembly complete.

4. Fourth sidewall is installed.

5. Container is capped on completion of loading.

6. Strapping completed container for shipment.

7. At air terminal, container is picked up for placement on aircraft loading pallet.

8. Complete multiple-container *Reader's Digest* shipment on aircraft pallet.

9. Lifting shipment pallet to aircraft's loading hatch.

10. Pallet is locked in position, ready for beyond movement to Indianapolis.

where they are burned. Thus even their disposal gives a service instead of a dead loss as refuse.

What manner of computer operation churns out such a huge volume of material? *Reader's Digest's* installation must be one of the largest commercial concentrations found anywhere. Under Manager, Computer Operations Rudolph E. Weiss are three separate sections operating nine separate medium-to-large computer systems plus substantial auxiliary equipment. An input section reads specially prepared forms with optical scanning equipment, while other information is key punched to cards for conversion to computer tape. Scannable document data, read by an IBM 1428 optical scanner, is fed to an IBM 1401 computer in the central processing section, while punched cards move to the third section, electronic printing, where one of the three IBM 360-40 systems converts cards to tape. The tape, in turn, moves to the central processing unit.

This section operates a 360-65 computer and two older IBM 7074 systems, but is phasing out the latter units. Replacing them is a second 360-65 system, equipped with a Hypervisor, with double the storage capacity of the currently installed 360-65 system. The Hypervisor can literally split the new 360-65 complex in half and run it as two separate computers. This yields the near equivalent of three 360-65 large-scale computers in the central processing section. An RCA Spectra 70-45 medium-capacity rounds out this impressive roster.

The typical commercial computer installation finds a computer absorbing information, performing required computations or analysis and, finally, activating a printer to yield intelligible results. This doesn't hold true at *Reader's Digest*, however. So great is the data volume and program variety that central processing produces only taped output, which then moves either to the electronic printing section for high-speed reproduction or to the 24,000 reel tape library for storage.

Electronic printing keeps three 360-40 systems and one 360-30 busy feeding 13 high-speed electronic printers and a Videograph which prints Dick Strip labels for use on magazines. Readily transferrable between the available computer systems, as many as five high-speed printers may be coupled into a single computer system at one time. It is here that information converts from an electric phenomenon to measurable, shippable paper tonnage.

Traffic and computer functions harmonize following printing. A special program determines label batch sizes, varying from 800 to 1,200 labels per carton. The batch size is set to maximize loading density for "D" containers, assuring most economical employment of the air density rates. Study is under way to develop still tighter density control, although the existing program yields significant savings.

Computer-traffic cooperation shows up in another parallel program. The batched labels, separated in groups by zip code order, are accompanied by three punched cards which are computer-produced. These cards show a count of labels in the batch, batch control number and destination code number as well as the beginning and final zip code numbers of addresses included in the batch.

One of these cards goes forward with the batch, informing the recipient of the content and providing a control for releasing merchandise to which the labels will be affixed in predetermined sequence. The label shipment card thus becomes an order activator, eliminating the need for any additional separate communication and consequent delay or confusion in matching.

A second card is removed from each batch for the traffic control section. Daily accumulation of these cards provides a means for determining container requirements as well as guidance for billing and routing. Similar control applies to the separate Dick Strip cartons which move independently in air freight.

The final card goes to output control. Should anything go wrong with a container or a carton, resulting in its loss or damage, the output control card becomes the reference for immediate label replacement by the electronic printing section.

While computer output moves forward on a 24-hour basis, close-out time for the day's shipments is about 4:00 p.m. Freight cleared through traffic control is then made ready for movement, either in "D" containers or in other standard packs and relevant data is teletyped to the affected destinations, advising of total containers or pieces, identifying marks and contents. At 5:00 p.m. Atlantic Air Freight picks up freight for all airlines, trucking it to Kennedy airport for beyond movement, while other carriers, notably Quinn Trucking and Mt. Kisco-New York Motor Express, pick up shipments for points within overnight reach of Pleasant-ville.

Materials handling, expedited considerably through the internal conveyor system, is augmented by container palletization and, in the case of single cartons, by skids. Domestic containers are mounted on styrene rails with corrugated caps which serve as pallets and permit ready fork lift movement at a minimum cost. Skids have also proven their merit in handling miscellaneous outbound freight between the staging area and outbound trucks at the seven truck loading positions, all equipped with self-leveling loading platforms.

Ultimate distribution of *Reader's Digest* end products is generally accomplished by other contractors, but there are several areas remaining under the headquarters traffic department's control, notably import-export freight. With affiliates and subsidiaries in most free countries, the company generates numerous, varied shipments in and out of the U.S. In the past, various company units habitually shipped individually with results not always meeting expectations. Too often shipments went astray or met with varied misfortunes, at which point Traffic Manager Povall was called in to pull other people's chestnuts out of unexpected fires. Steady internal education by the traffic department, however, changed this pattern. Today virtually all import or export shipments clear through the traffic department, with resultant economies in routine shipping costs and the avoidance of numerous minor crises. Company units now prepare a simple, clear instruction form covering each such shipment and submit it to the traffic group. Mr. Povall's staff handles necessary documentation and provides full shipment protection, filing the company's own closing advices on marine insurance.

As in the import-export aspect, air freight similarly benefits from internal documentation. "We find no occasion to use air forwarders," comments Mr. Povall. "With our volume, it is more economical to handle our own air line relations."

What of the future? Conceivably, further advances in computer communications could make wire service preferable to physical movement of computer output. At the same time, air freight technology also anticipates dramatic improvements ahead. The effect of either or both on this unique operation is not readily predictable. The department has already proven its adaptability to an unorthodox shipping situation. It looks forward confidently and expectantly to continuing challenges and adjustments in a growing business embracing the latest techniques.

Computer Distribution — Premium Service Cuts Costs

Electronic Associates Inc. of Long Branch, New Jersey is a computer manufacturer with a difference—most firms produce digital computers whereas EAI is the principal manufacturer of analog computers and hybrid analog-digital units. Digital equipment is the more common in business usage, whereas analog units are essentially of value in engineering and related applications, although particularly suited to simulation studies.

All of EAI's equipment is delicate and costly. Logistics management here looks for transport speed and security first, with only a secondary thought to expense. A computer designed for a specific use at a multi-million-dollar cost cannot sit idle for a moment beyond final testing. Every hour that it is not operational represents a substantial amortization cost either to EAI or to the customer. Timely and secure delivery means everything, therefore, to ensure prompt transfer of title and immediate usability.

The way that EAI's distribution function meets this challenge was reviewed in TRAFFIC MANAGEMENT's May 1969 issue as follows:

DISTRIBUTION MANAGERS generally choose services that land their shipments in reasonable time consistent with favorable total costs. It works out differently at Electronic Associates Inc. This large manufacturer of analog computers and hybrid (analog-digital) equipment brooks no delays in delivering its products. Hold back an astronaut-training space vehicle simulator for several days and a space program will be held up for a like time. It is as clear and direct as that.

What are these analog computers? The typical business digital computer shares some of its features, but produces different end results. It acts essentially as a high-speed calculator, solving repetitive mathematical problems. Analog equipment, in contrast, employs given data to simulate total systems, comparing design or material change effects on such operations as a complete oil refinery, an airplane, an electric power system or other complex entities. In briefly describing a voluptuous girl, the digital computer prints out a report form reading "36-22-36"; the analog computer flashes a color-video image that causes every male viewer to bang his head against the nearest wall.

Started in 1945, this rapidly expanding company's annual sales volume today ranges over $40 million worldwide. A substantial part of these sales are overseas, creating healthy demands on EAI's West Long Branch, N.J. plant. While certain numbered "models" or "lines" imply some product standardization, each computer shipped represents custom specifications jointly developed by EAI engineers and the purchaser.

"We rarely ever do the same thing twice," notes Manager-Traffic and Supply Joseph H. Schachter. "While such customers as NASA, for example, buy from us regularly, their purchases generally serve to do a single job and the next time they call on us, they're up to something new, facing us with entirely different shipping circumstances."

Reliable, timely delivery of customer orders guides every job in EAI's traffic and supply group. In purchase price alone, EAI computers typically represent over $5 a pound. Their vital roles in both major planning and operations of vast customer enterprises place far higher indirect values upon them as well. Traffic's role, therefore, puts heavy emphasis on three elements:

—Premium transportation. Delaying a million-dollar computer en route means a day's interest cost to someone for every excess 24 hours from shipment date until the unit enters service.

—Careful packaging. There is no such thing as "minor" damage on equipment where a single part failure among thousands of components kills the complete operational capability.

—Coordinated material handling. In-plant movement as well as shipment comes under traffic scrutiny, assuring that goods released from production can be promptly packed and shipped following final tests.

Air transportation figures heavily in Traffic Administrator Raymond F. Martineau's shipping scheme. "We fly a lot of our domestic orders," he notes, "but fully 95% of our overseas volume moves by air. The schedule reliability means as much to us as the speed. It means great savings in packag-

Because shipment planning commences before manufacture is completed, Traffic keeps close watch on manufacturing progress of individual orders. Traffic Administrator Raymond F. Martineau, left, discusses status of an order with Contract Administrator Edwin Heinemeyer in EAI's West Long Branch plant.

ing and far less risk of costly damage to products where 99% perfection is considered a total failure."

Mr. Martineau recently shipped a 39-unit system to England's Central Electric Generating Board. This EAI 8900 integrated system, a large but not untypical order, weighed 48,045 pounds and was worth $2,580,000. On delivery, the consignee's plans called for the equipment to simulate the operations of complete atomic power stations in studying economic distribution of nuclear reactor-created electricity. The carefully packed and assembled system left West Long Branch in three padded vans supplied by North American Van Lines for delivery to Circle Airfreight at Kennedy airport. Processed by this forwarder, the shipment departed early on a Sunday via BOAC for a carefully timed delivery in England, allowing the new equipment to be put "on-line" with a minimum of expensive delay.

While international shipments move largely by air, domestic movements split between air and LTL with a sprinkling of smaller units and parts moving through parcel post, United Parcel Service and REA. Domestic represents 70% of sales, but Traffic's work load runs 50% export-import due to the greater complexity of its paperwork. While forwarders are employed at airports, piers and overseas locations, the traffic group develops its own export licenses, export declarations, supporting documents and related papers. No international shipments leave the West Long Branch plant until fully invoiced, including freight and insurance.

Because every computer purchase represents a scheduled production delivery, shipments for individual customers can be pre-planned. The traffic staff employs a monthly shipping schedule which can be modified as EAI sales engineers or customers may require. Customer requests generally funnel through a specific contract administrator who works with the account, but in some cases such changes develop through direct telephone contact between customer and the traffic staff.

Timely shipment forwarding concerns an-

Reviewing proposed material for a comprehensive traffic manual with Traffic Administrator Raymond F. Martineau, left, is Manager-Traffic and Supply Joseph H. Schachter. On the walls behind them, detailed flow charts describe the operations and procedures that the manual will cover.

other management group within EAI as well —the accountants. When single shipments mean the transfer of sums in the six- and seven-figure brackets, the exact date of title transfer takes on considerable significance. Inventory carrying costs run up disturbingly when such shipments face any delay, so careful scheduling with reliable carriers means a great deal.

Inbound shipping control, while directly exercised by buyers under purchasing manager supervision, remains indirectly under the traffic group's watchful eye. Each buyer routes freight according to specific procedures supplied in a traffic department manual. If buyers make exceptions, the traffic group spots them on the bills and informs the purchasing manager, indicating any cost differentials so that he may solicit explanations from the responsible buyers. Naturally, routing exceptions become necessary in a time-priority business, so buyers with good cause for individual routing shifts make them without hesitation, while the audit procedure discourages others from making arbitrary changes for inadequate reasons.

A three-truck fleet augments common carrier services on movements up to 400 miles from West Long Branch. Faster deliveries and reduced packaging frequently become possible through this means, with pickups from suppliers creating a satisfactory number of return loads, thus holding down costs. In emergencies, the 400-mile maximum haul rule occasionally gets overlooked. A

high-value shipment to South America, for instance, unable to make a specific New York connection, faced a delay that would be extremely costly to the client. The shipment configuration permitted it to fit through

A roll of Air Pac, a dual-plastic sheeting containing air bubbles for protective cushioning, is readily available above bench.

Surface shipments move in closed crates or cartons, but many air shipments are protected only by outer wraps of various kinds of plastic.

the hatch of only a limited few cargo planes, none of which were due to leave New York in reasonable time. The solution proved to be a flight scheduled from New Orleans in two days with an EAI truck loading promptly and taking off on a 1,000 mile-plus run to the airport, eliminating the anticipated damaging delay.

While traffic department responsibility in day-to-day operation nominally commences following product tests, Traffic Administrator Martineau works closely with EAI engineers on material handling procedures. All product movements are wheeled. The largest computer units, for example, start through manufacture as raw frames received from the metal shop. Special dollies for moving heavy units, designed by Mr. Martineau and the staff engineers, go under these frames

immediately. The frames move from receiving through a lengthy group of specialized manufacturing stations, each of which adds components—and weight—according to contractual specifications until ready for test.

Claims cause virtually no headaches for EAI. "At most, we get one loss claim a year," observes Mr. Martineau. "We may submit four or five for damage annually, but no more than that. As a policy, we prefer to spend money on truly effective packaging."

Packages, like EAI products, get careful testing. In the dual product testing that checks actual specifications (quality control) and performance under customer program operation (quality assurance), every component receives vibration testing. Such tests, therefore, become unnecessary for the final package. All package designs, however, are

Plywood crating is built up around an individual computer section. Compressed air staple guns make a fast and simple job of assembling side panels, building the crate up from the plywood base.

Starting a long journey. EAI shipping personnel load the first of 38 units aboard padded vans for the first leg of a journey to Britain. Valued at $2,500,000, the EAI 8900 integrated system can simulate complete atomic power station operations as well as the distribution of the power they produce.

Loaded and ready to go. A late winter Saturday evening finds three vans ready to move out for the airport with their Britain-bound shipment. Nestled between them is a unit from EAI's private fleet.

Sunday morning at Kennedy airport, the EAI 8900 series equipment goes aboard a cargo flight, ready for set-up in England on Monday morning. All 38 units moved forward as a single air shipment.

drop-tested. Sample shipments to carefully selected points are also used, the packing components thus being checked under actual shipping conditions.

As new developments appear in the rapidly changing packaging field, EAI tests all that show promise. There is no rigid policy concerning materials employed. Rubberized hair sheets, corrugated sheets, Air Cap and plastic spaghetti each provide cushioning on shipments where one or the other appears most appropriate. Other new lightweight plastic filler materials are also being considered and tested.

In addition to the rubberized hair sheets, some units in larger sizes have employed large rubberized hair molds fitted to protect unit tops and bottoms. Recently, tri-wall polyurethane molds have been substituted, lowering the cost for a top-and-bottom set from $47 to $24.

Air Cap provides effective protection on numerous shipments. A layer of air bubbles between two coated plastic sheets, it comes in large rolls of convenient working width for mounting above a wrapping bench much like kraft paper. Easily trimmed to odd-sized pack requirements, it is none the less tough enough to control substantial shocks in movement.

When delivery conditions permit, air shipments frequently move as open shipments.

These may be given a plastic outer wrapper or other minimal protection, relying upon the unit's own nature and the satisfactory environment of the aircraft to avoid damages.

Truck shipments generally move closed, either in fiberboard cartons or plywood crates. A recent small table model line, however, employs a $27-pack consisting of a sleeve, cap, cushioning and base. While a simple box would cost less, it would create damage potential on delivery because the 300-pound computer must be lifted from a box, while the new unit can be simply unsleeved on receipt.

Packages weighing less than 100 pounds in fiberboard cartons are banded with plastic tape having a tensile strength of 300 pounds per square inch. Wood packs and any packs weighing 100 pounds or over receive metal banding. Wooden packaging on larger units is built up right around the product itself, with plywood sheets cut to fit and fastened together with compressed air staple gun.

Heavier units, based on steel "I" beams, are mounted on pallets for easier handling in shipment. Shipping personnel bolt a plywood base to the bottom, which in turn bolts to a pallet, with a polystyrene sheet interposed between plywood base and pallet. This construction creates a vibration-damping "sandwich" that protects against road shock.

In a company grossing sales in the $40 million range which, only ten years ago, grossed $14 million, growth responsibilities weigh heavily. Today's EAI traffic department operates with an office staff of six and a shipping group of four. In 1962, a three-man staff was ample. Messrs. Schachter and Martineau, therefore, keep their sights set on larger demands that loom clearly on the horizon. That is why a major project now under way is a new and very thorough manual of traffic systems and procedures. Additional volume and new markets will require more traffic personnel and the development of additional techniques to serve increasingly diversified customer requirements. By carefully spelling out job requirements and analyzing both existing and proposed methods, they hope to assist newcomers and veterans alike in assuming increasing burdens as sales continue to rise.

Cold Country Gets Hot Service

Grocers Wholesale of Anchorage, Alaska, would seem a proper subject for Chapter VIII's examination of food industries. It is such a unique operation, however, that it merits review as one differing markedly from the conventional.

Alaska's separation from the "lower 48" states means inbound freight normally must move partially by sea. Though no customs or other international paperwork is involved, Grocers Wholesale's supplies flow in somewhat the manner of imports, therefore. Moreover, the company maintains a buying unit in Seattle that must be coordinated with management activity at Anchorage and a significant part of company inventory at any given time is actually in transit between Seattle and Anchorage, taking many more days en route from vendor to company warehouse than is the usual case for "lower 48" firms. Couple these conditions with the need to make deliveries over an area that could comfortably absorb Texas a couple of times over in a particularly tough climate and you have a distribution network with few parallels.

The company thrives and prospers in its unusual market, as the following report, initially published in the July, 1968 TRAFFIC MANAGEMENT, indicates:

PENETRATING ALASKA'S MARKETS presents serious challenges to manufacturers in the "lower 48." Transportation is scarce, expensive, unusual and sensitive to the widely varied climatic conditions. It is a growing market, however. A 1958 population of 213,000 jumped past the 275,000 mark in 1967 while personal income rates increased even more rapidly. Major oil and mineral strikes promise faster expansion ahead. Foresighted firms increasingly seek access to this prosperous economy and its assured rich tomorrow.

Grocers Wholesale, Inc., of Anchorage, Alaska, long a major factor in the state's distribution, sees and understands the picture better than many. The disastrous 1964 earthquake virtually wiped out its physical assets, but with typical frontier fortitude, the firm quickly bounced back, ending that fiscal year with $5,600,000 sales. The current year should level well in excess of $10,000,-000. President Edwin M. Suddock and his management intend to hit the $20,000,000 mark by 1973.

Growing sales can mean growing profits. To realize them, proprietary skills and managerial foresight must maintain a heady pace. In the high-volume, low-profit-margin grocery business, physical distribution is a critical factor. At G.W.I., its advancement holds a strong and continuing priority. Rising from the quake's rubble with renewed determination, the company moved forward aggressively, penetrating ever-larger segments of Alaska's vast territory while whittling costs which, in the past, seriously deterred Alaska's economic growth. Several continuing programs make G.W.I. distribution sharply competitive:

—Modern Facilities. Built rapidly after the earthquake, the warehouse and headquarters were none the less carefully conceived and designed. Strategically located astride main transportation arteries, with generous allowance for expansion, they take advantage of modern storage and handling methods.

—Flexible Transportation. Sea-Land and other container services inbound feed an outbound net encompassing rail, air, piggyback, barge and truck. Private carriage supplements all these, cutting costs and creating a competitive service edge in numerous previously "difficult" areas. A unique air distribution program is revolutionizing merchandising in sub-arctic regions.

—Modern Management. Determined to build needed staff matched to its mushrooming business, G.W.I. blends skilled specialists from other states with the innovative generalists characteristic of its own region. Backed up by effective computer procedures and growing operations research applications, the "one-man-band" attitude of pre-World War II Alaska is just ancient history to these people.

While the disastrous 1964 earthquake destroyed the company's physical property, it also freed management to assess the future without concern for a current investment's fate. Within a month of the quake, a replacement site was chosen, contractors broke ground and a new departure in Alaskan warehousing got under way. The Butler Manufacturing Co.'s Illinois plant closed its doors to other customers and prepared the necessary prefabricated building sections, finishing their work in just three weeks. In October, just six months after "wipe-out," G.W.I.'s Anchorage facility was ready with a

Loading at Anchorage, cargo plane prepares to deliver G.W.I. shipments through Alaska's sub-artic region.

Remains of G.W.I.'s downtown warehouse adjacent to Anchorage rail yards after disastrous 1964 earthquake.

greater service and capacity potential than ever before.

The new building's enclosed truck loading dock handles 14 vehicles indoors, secure from the weather. A rail siding extends down one side with six weather-protected loading doors. In the rear, a garage services the company's truck fleet. The warehouse building houses company headquarters as well, including computer facilities. Ample land is available for expansion.

The existing unit runs at 70% of capacity currently, but rapidly increasing sales lift this figure almost daily despite careful inventory control. "We're very comfortable here today," notes Operations Manager Norman L. Henderson, "but population growth, expanding accessible area and improving company services mean more volume. We keep one eye on the future continually, so that whenever volume makes another breakthrough, we're ready and waiting for it."

Thus far, 12-foot aisles make stock movement simple, but continuing growth will soon demand a drop to a seven-foot standard, yielding a 40% space gain. The operation is fully palletized with 32-inch by 40-inch pal-

The new facility, strategically located at Anchorage's edge, climatized to shrug off Alaskan winters, with built-in capacity to cope with anticipated rapid expansion. The truck bays in the foreground are complemented by a rail siding in the rear accommodating three cars.

lets, a size increasingly standard in the west and, in Mr. Henderson's opinion, a sharp competitor of the older 48-inch by 40-inch standard. Fork lift trucks, including several Rider Walkie units, are mostly electric. Plans are also under way for a conveyor line which will expedite broken-lot picking.

The 100,000-foot warehouse enjoys a 21-foot stacking height. In addition to its main storage area, there are two large cooling areas for cheese and for eggs, fully palletized. A separate large palletized freezer section's temperature is kept at 10 degrees. Normal warehouse stock is at a $1 million level, covering 6,551 line items, in contrast to only 1,500 in 1953.

Alaskan labor is expensive and building costs are high. Both factors make maximum utilization mandatory to justify costs. To increase productivity, the warehouse now operates on a three-shift basis. By the end of the first month's operation, warehousemen were averaging 170 pieces per hour compared to the old standard of 85 pieces per hour. Giving the shifts specialized functions, yet retaining adequate flexibility, improved equipment utilization greatly while

cushioning the effects of sharp deviations in tonnage flow.

How do the shifts function? Essentially, the cycle commences on the second shift, which reports to work at 3:30 p.m. During their work period, the assigned crew receives and stocks freight, concerning itself almost entirely with inbound operations. Though this shift is nominally relieved at midnight, an additional two hours overlap is common, permitting a double-shift to "hit" any oversized or delayed arrivals, leaving the house in good order for third shift specialties. Shift Three goes on duty at midnight. These men pick orders, check and load the merchandise. By 4 a.m., the first outbound private trucks start rolling and by the shift's end, major work activity has moved from within the warehouse to the outbound loading platforms. As with the second shift, two hours overtime into the following shift is common.

The normal first shift, or day shift, then, tends to be the clean-up shift at G.W.I. It gets out the long-haul vehicles by 10 a.m. and takes care of distribution to supermarkets in the Anchorage area. It is also particularly concerned with the assembly and dis-

Discussing major corporate developments that followed the 1964 earthquake are (center) President Edwin M. Suddock and (right) Operations Manager Norman L. Henderson, with TM's Executive editor, Jack W. Farrell.

patch of air parcel post and air freight orders. These normally run 40,000 pounds in a 40-foot van for daily delivery to the Post Office and the air lines. Starting work at 7 a.m., Shift One usually cleans the docks by 3:30 p.m., but often overlaps the second shift for two hours to assure prompt inbound goods handling.

Inbound freight poses peculiarly Alaskan problems. Virtually all stock comes by water from Seattle. If it moves by Sea-Land, vans arrive at Anchorage every five days in their vessels. Other containers may be delivered at Whittier or Seward on similar headways by Puget Sound—Alaska Van Lines or the Alaska Steamship Co. and moved forward by the Alaska Railroad for Anchorage delivery. In any case, none of these ocean services are on a uniform daily basis and running times can be affected by weather conditions considerably less than ideal through much of the year. Therefore, while an average day will see seven or eight Sea-Land vans arrive at G.W.I., a not-so-average day may see none at all or it may see 15 of them looking for a berth and unloading help. This by-no-means minor problem is never far from a distribution man's mind when he's pumping goods into Alaska.

The region's still-low population density prevents any carrier from maintaining very frequent services. Competition is restricted, too, by limited physical facilities. Rail, water, and highway services exist, but many places enjoy only one of these modes, and in the case of several river communities, this means just three services per year by barge,

requiring huge inventories and grossly excessive warehousing to support even limited retailing.

Modern distribution methods and steadily improving air freight services, fortunately, are bringing a new day to merchants in the sub-arctic regions and other similarly isolated sectors. Conventional air services bring in some goods from the lower 48 states, including such carriers as Alaska Air Lines, Northwest Airlines, Western and Pan American, while beyond service to foreign points is offered by these as well as SAS, KLM and Lufthansa. It is the unique intra-Alaskan carriers, however, whose role grows steadily greater in today's circumstances. These companies are old hands at their business. They provided scheduled, dependable service to isolated Eskimo communities and lonely Aleutian hamlets before World War II, when comparable towns elsewhere rarely saw a commercial aircraft. G.W.I. makes substantial use of local services provided throughout mainland and southeastern Alaska by Alaska Airlines, Western Air Lines and Wien Consolidated Airways. Reeve Aleutian Airways shares traffic destined westward to such points as Cold Bay and the various hamlets and military bases in the Aleutian Islands. Better service with newer and larger planes plus improved rates assure continued growth of this activity.

In particular, G.W.I. and Alaska Airlines have jointly sought to convince outlying merchants that weekly air shipments of relatively valuable goods are cheaper than thrice yearly water shipments supporting huge, ob-

Fully enclosed dock and loading space at G.W.I.'s new Anchorage location protect men and equipment from potentially fierce weather conditions. Alaska Railroad and Sea-Land trailers are among those loading for movement by piggyback or over-the-road to interior points.

solete warehouses. Fire and weather damages cost these merchants even more than the capital burden of holding such large inventories. At a typical far northern point, ocean charges are $4.36 per cwt. from Seattle by water. G.W.I., however, receives goods at Anchorage from Seattle in containers at about $1.36 per cwt., then moves them via Alaska Airlines at $4 per cwt. on a deferred air rate with a 20,000-pound minimum. This represents an additional dollar over vessel direct but is traded off against warehousing costs, insurance, inventory financing, ocean packing and the cost of local handling between warehouses and stores. Because weekly or better air service eliminates any need for a local warehouse at each store, there is a capital saving on facilities and a variable cost saving on warehouse labor as well.

With new oil and mineral finds occurring regularly in the far north, more people are going there, while the long time residents are steadily raising their living standards. The competitive edge given by its modern Anchorage warehouse and correlated air services assures G.W.I. an important part in this developing market.

While air is a key to Alaska's outposts, effective and surprisingly modern surface transport makes the difference in the more populous territories. Conventional sea movement still applies in reaching some ports, but rail cars and containers are the major elements today. Modern ferry and barge operations all but eliminate the old port handling chores, speeding and cheapening intermodal transfers, greatly increasing reliability and virtually curing staggering loss and damage problems of the past.

Containers and rail cars of all types now move uninhibited from all points into and out of Anchorage. Both the Alaska Railroad itself and Sea-Land provide container services not only from the States below, but to a great many inland points. Beyond movement

A fast freight returns containers and auto-rack cars from Fairbanks to Anchorage via Alaska Railroad.

is frequently intermodal rail-truck, with rail schedules set to give passenger-train speed on the nearly 400-mile run to Fairbanks. Sea-Land itself now owns and operates a trucking network which assures prompt beyond movement of containers from Fairbanks to many destinations, plus various points served directly from Anchorage. Conventional common carrier truck services are also used to points south to supplement G.W.I.'s private fleet, Arctic Motor Freight, Peninsula Fast Freight and Weaver Brothers performing much of this work.

The company's private trucking grew out of its local delivery operation in the Anchorage area. Study showed that running their own fleet direct from Anchorage on carefully selected and scheduled long-haul runs would be faster and cheaper than fighting the traditional battle of small shipments via common carrier. Long-haul service employs three heavy-duty Kenworth tractors and six 40-foot high-cube vans, augmented by seven 2½-ton straight jobs devoted primarily to Anchorage area services.

Each Monday and Thursday a tractor and trailer depart Anchorage on G.W.I.'s "North Run." This circuit covers a 1,000-mile trip to Palmer, Glenallen, Copper Center, Tok Junction, Big Delta and Fort Greely, dropping shipments at numerous stores. It is a three-day trip during which the truck engine is never shut off through colder periods. Temperatures can drop to 62 degrees below zero in this region when winter strikes.

A 500-mile "South Run" feeds Soldotna, Kenai and Seward, departing each Wednesday for two days. A second "South Run" rolls on Thursdays, taking two days and 800 miles in stride reaching Soldotna, Anchor Point and Homer. Remaining available time on the heavier equipment is employed making larger deliveries in the Anchorage area, supplementing the smaller straight trucks. G.W.I. owns all the vehicles, maintaining them in their own shop facility adjacent to the Anchorage warehouse.

All truck runs face peculiarly Alaskan problems from time to time, particularly during the "break-up" period each spring. Melting ground frost creates serious road hazards at this time. Each week the State Highway Department reduces permissible truck loads by a percentage factor until the problem ceases. Load limits are frequently set at 75% of standard load, but not uncommonly will be dropped to only 50% during some weeks. It can be extremely dangerous to exceed these limitations. The effect on truck economics becomes little short of disastrous when these conditions arise.

Rail service figures importantly in G.W.I. distribution both directly and indirectly. Box car freight moves north via the Alaska Railroad to Tenana for barge movements to several points during the navigation season, but the major rail participation is through containerization and piggyback movements. In addition to Sea-Land containers that traverse this route, the railroad itself picks up a van each Tuesday which it loads at G.W.I.'s dock carrying drop shipments for points north. This van is picked up by the Alaska Railroad's own tractor.

Where does distribution "head in" organizationally at G.W.I.? Essentially, the whole company is a distribution activity. Conventional job designations are scarce, however, because responsibilities follow function and constant growth forces steady changes. Added to this are circumstances uniquely Alaskan that require special management attention. The specific traffic activities, in particular, while largely controlled by Operations Manager Norman Henderson are of no less concern to Mrs. Joanne Mardock, controller. Reporting to Mrs. Mardock is Mrs. Jennine Clement, manager, traffic control, whose staff watches over inbound freight and coordinates traffic functions between the Controller's Department and Operations.

Why this controller concern with day-to-day traffic flow? The key lies in a formula worked out by management during the four years following the earthquake. While most Alaskan firms turn their inventory over four times each year, the company regularly holds to a 12-time annual turn. Closely controlled inventory and purchasing make this possible despite an eight-week buying cycle caused by lengthy shipping times. A further complication is the unpredictability of military demand, a highly volatile situation involving a very major customer.

The company's objective is maintenance of what they term "The Perfect Blend." Under proper conditions, value of inventory on hand at month's end, accounts receivable and month's sales should be equal. Any deviation acts as an advanced warning signal to management, particularly to Purchas-

ing Manager Samuel Vasconi, who promptly adjusts his purchasing pattern to match conditions. The three "Perfect Blend" elements are checked daily by computer.

What is "The Perfect Blend's" value to corporate management? It assures a turnover rate that will maintain a fast-growing company's financial equilibrium without requiring external working capital, which is available only at 8% interest locally. Good communications, effective traffic control and computerized management information are putting capital to work that is wasted and neglected in firms less watchful of these elements. "This approach would be as beneficial in Brooklyn as it is in Anchorage," comments Controller Mardock. *"Too often firms blindly follow conventional accounting practices and settle for a passive recording of things past, generally when it is already too late to correct problems in progress. We want to make history—not record it."*

The computer is a vital factor in this activity. Its story here is the reverse of the usual. Where many other firms started by computerizing accounting and then gradually expanding to other functions, G.W.I.'s 1440 kicked off on inventory control. Its role then expanded to other management controls and only now is it commencing to absorb routine accounting operations. "We now have about 40 programs on disc-pack," notes Electronic Data Processing Manager John W. Todd. "This yields far faster program input than conventional tape or card program input. Our needs are outgrowing our equipment. We're switching our computer language from Autocoder to Cobol right now to facilitate a future conversion to an IBM 360 computer and to make future programs readily comprehensible to people other than computer specialists. With Cobol's words replacing Autocoder's numbers, program content becomes more directly intelligible."

Mr. Todd's short term planning includes continued inventory data expansion and refinement preparatory to adopting IBM's "IMPACT" program package when the 360 computer becomes operative. "IMPACT" is a group of management information report programs related to standardized data inputs which IBM makes available in packages separately planned for retailers and wholesalers. With the wholesale-model "IMPACT," G.W.I. will easily and speedily obtain comprehensive sales forecasts, economic order quantity studies, turnover re-

Reviewing proposed program modifications, Norman L. Henderson, operations manager, and John W. Todd, electronic data processing manager, discuss methods of speeding up inventory control for the benefit of purchasing and accounting and assuring maintenance of a 12-time annual inventory turnover.

EDP report of container and van shipments received from Seattle is examined by Operations Manager Norman L. Henderson and Joanne Mardock, controller.

ports, sales reports and other vital current data for close financial control.

The computerized inventory procedure supports, in turn, a computer purchasing operation. Running analysis of inventory yields regular reports of line items by vendors, the print-out showing items on order, in transit, balance on hand, recent sales history, statistically derived sales trend data, invoice cost, landed cost and selling price, among other items. The buyer reaches decisions on his purchases from this material and sets up his orders on these forms. They are key punched and orders are run on the computer for necessary distribution. Three copies go to the G.W.I. Seattle office, which places actual vendor orders and sets up consolidated van shipments to Anchorage. One set of these computer orders precedes the relevant shipments back by air mail. Because voyage time is five days compared to two-day air mail service, Traffic Control enjoys a 3-day information lead. This data is promptly fed into the computer, up-dating "in transit" stock status and assuring that Purchasing, Operations, the controller's department and other staff units know exactly what is in the pipeline at any given time. When the goods actually arrive, bills of lading immediately come through Traffic Control, which again updates computer data, transferring "in transit" goods to "in stock" status, concurrently informing other affected units.

The close surveillance this system offers, providing a more rapid information entry into accounts, builds an accuracy into monthly level financial statements previously only attainable quarterly. It is one of the factors contributing to a computerized running inventory control assuring that a spot inventory drawn at any specific moment from the computer will be accurate within a tolerance of one-half of 1% on an inventory in the million dollar range.

Effective though the company's computer operations have been, still greater benefits lie ahead. They aid development of a management sophistication level still uncommon in Alaska, yet one which management considers only a jumping-off point for greater future development. Parallel with learning to live with the computer, staff members are working with Controller Mardock toward effective employment of budgets and forecasts in preparing for continued rapid expansion. William D. Gibson, a newly-appointed assistant general manager with strong corporate planning and development experience, anticipates carrying forward this type of development in all management areas. As President Suddock sums it up, "The native Alaskan's pioneering drive, augmented by growing business professionalism, is creating a new management breed, ideally suited to the goals of growth-oriented companies such as G.W.I."

Conclusion

Total materials control from farm or mine pit to ultimate consumer remains a largely unrealized objective for the physical distribution profession. This goal may, in fact, prove neither necessary nor desirable when related to an individual company's cost, market and financial patterns. The real value is best measured within the microeconomy of the individual firm, therefore, rather than across the total field. Effective physical distribution applications are necessarily diversified to match varying total management concepts and industrial-commercial requirements.

Since its inception, *Traffic Management* magazine has monitored the profession's expansion through "on-site" studies of carefully selected case organizations. Wherever innovative management makes logistics improvements of proven value, *Traffic Management* believes there are lessons to benefit others—managers, vendors and academicians alike. In a companion volume, *Physical Distribution Forum*, the views of successful professionals illustrate the philosophies governing physical distribution management today. This present work, however, reviews the actual practices of just such managers within their own organizations, providing a background for their viewpoints and a measure of their realization.

From over 100 leading companies thus far studied by *Traffic Management*, 42 of those visited by the author within the past few years have been portrayed here. Many provide food for thought in remarkably diversified logistics areas. While grouped in chapters based upon parallels or contrasts that illustrate specific concepts and trends, a comprehensive index at the end of this volume simplifies comparison among all companies by topics, regardless of the chapter groupings.

Jack W. Farrell
Executive Editor
Traffic Management

Index